Death, Society, and Human Experience

seventh edition

DEATH, SOCIETY, and HUMAN EXPERIENCE

Robert J. Kastenbaum

Arizona State University

Allyn and Bacon

Boston   London   Toronto   Sydney   Tokyo   Singapore

Series Editor: Sarah L. Kelbaugh
Editor-in-Chief, Social Sciences: Karen Hanson
Production Administrator: Susan Brown
Editorial Assistant: Lori Flickinger
Editorial-Production Service: Matrix Productions Inc.
Cover Administrator: Linda Knowles
Composition Buyer: Linda Cox
Manufacturing Buyer: Megan Cochran
Composition: Omegatype Typography, Inc.

Copyright 2001, 1998, 1995, 1991, 1986, 1981, 1977, by Allyn & Bacon
A Pearson Education Company
160 Gould Street
Needham Heights, Mass. 02494

Internet: www.abacon.com

Library of Congress Cataloging-in-Publication Data

Kastenbaum, Robert.
    Death, society, and human experience / Robert Kastenbaum. — 7th ed.
        p.   cm.
    Includes bibliographical references and index.
    ISBN 0-205-31936-X
    1. Death—Psychological aspects.   2. Death—social aspects.   I. Title.

BF789.D4 K36   2000
306.9—dc21   00-028860

Photo Credits:
Frontispiece: Everett Collection. 1: Corbis/Bettmann. 18: Spencer Grant/Photo Edit. 22: AFP/Corbis. 28: Billy E. Barnes/Stock Boston. 33: The Kobal Collection. 35: Giraudon/Art Resource. 47: North Wind Picture Archives. 60: Dreyfuss/Monkmeyer. 69: Keith Dannemiller/Saba. 75: John Nordell/The Image Works. 85: Scott Stewart/AP/Wide World Photos. 90: Hulton-Deutsch Collection/Corbis. 105: Gary A Conner/Photo Edit. 126: History & Special Collections Division; John C. Liebeskind History of Pain Collection; Louise M. Darling Biomedical Library, UCLA. 134: Frank Siteman/Stock Boston. 154: Richard Hutchings/Photo Edit. 164: Dick Blume/The Image Works. 171: Stock Montage. 174: Corbis-Bettmann. 181: T. Arruza/The Image Works. 188: Bonnie Kamin/Photo Edit. 189: John Maier, Jr./The Image Works. 190: B. Daemmrich/The Image Works. 191: AP/Wide World Photos. 210: George Kochaniec/Rocky Mountain NewsSygma. 226: Peter Kemp/AP/Wide World Photos. 230: Hulton Getty Picture Library/Liaison Agency. 234: North Wind Pictures. 235: Greg Smith/Saba. 244: Martin S. Pernick, The Black Stork (Oxford University Press, 1996), fig. 5; Motography April 14, 1917. 249: H. Armstrong Roberts. 253: Sygma. 261: AP/Wide World Photos. 269: AP/Wide World Photos. 274: Laura Dwight/Corbis. 277: Gale Zucker/Photo Edit. 282: Teri Stratford. 295: Paoni/Contrasto/Saba. 312: Simon/Saba. 314: Frank Siteman/Stock Boston. 315: Will Hart. 321: Kevin Capon/Pool/AP/Wide World Photos. 336: H. Armstrong Roberts. 343: AP/Wide World Photos. 348: Stuart Cohen/The Image Works. 356: FSP/Liaison Agency. 359: Buddy Mays/Corbis. 366: Scala/Art Resource. 374: Hulton Deutsch Collection/Corbis. 376: Agence N7/Sygma. 379: David Simson/Stock Boston. 386: J. Scott Applewhite/AP/Wide World Photos. 396: Giraudon/Art Resource. 413: NASA. 414: Hulton-Deutsch Collection/Corbis. 416: Superstock. 420: Corbis. 432: Chris Hondros/AP/Wide World Photos. 435: Superstock. 440: Michael McGovern/Index Stock Photography. 446: Robert Harbison. 450: E. Crews/The Image Works. 459: Filip Horvat/Saba. Endpiece: B. Daemmrich/The Image Works

Printed in the United States of America

10   9   8   7   6   5   4   3   04   03   02

For Cynthia

and for those

you have loved…

CONTENTS

3   THE DEATH SYSTEM   *61*

4   DYING   *91*
Transition from life

5   THE HOSPICE APPROACH TO TERMINAL CARE   *127*

6   END-OF-LIFE ISSUES AND DECISIONS   *155*

10 DEATH IN THE WORLD OF CHILDHOOD *275*

11 BEREAVEMENT, GRIEF, AND MOURNING *313*

12   THE FUNERAL PROCESS   *357*

13   DO WE SURVIVE DEATH?   *397*

14 HOW CAN WE HELP? *433*

The promise of death education and counseling

15 GOOD LIFE, GOOD DEATH? *451*

Trying to make sense of it all

INDEX *476*

PREFACE

The first business of life is to stay alive. With the gift of life comes the opportunity for love, friendship, skill, achievement, creativity, adventure, and perhaps even understanding. There is no guarantee, however, that life will be ours as long as we might desire. Furthermore, we know that the people dearest to us are also vulnerable. Yesterday's and today's companions may not be with us tomorrow. And then there is that stubborn fact that refuses to go away no matter how we choose to regard (or ignore) it: all lives, even our very own, end with death.

Life can and often does succeed with its first business. Ask the blades of grass that struggle up to the sunlight through the hard surfaces of a city street. Ask our resourceful adversaries, the virus and the microorganism, which continue to reinvent themselves whenever we launch a new pharmacological assault. Ask the child of a devastated homeland who has already experienced massive loss, stress, and deprivation but has determined to survive it all, and does. Ask nurses, paramedics, and physicians, and perhaps they will share with you some of their experiences in which people made remarkable recoveries, seemingly because they had such a strong will to live. Ask firefighters why they risk their own lives, and perhaps they will feel comfortable enough to admit that there is no joy to compare with saving a life—even those of a cat and her frightened kittens.

Even at its most resourceful and most fortunate, though, life does not succeed indefinitely in its first business of staying alive. That's a pretty good reason for having this book and for courses focused on dying, death, and grief. For many years, society's strategy was to ignore death and practically everything connected with it—including the dying and the grieving person. Unfortunately, the rule of silence created more problems than it solved. It was not polite to talk about... (well, you know what), and it was wrong even to think much about... (that same thing). There was little comfort for the dying or grieving person, little counseling for the troubled mind of the suicidal person. Inadequate communication contributed to tense and conflictful relationships. Health care professionals had their own share of misery: responsible for care of the "incurable" (as dying people often were known) yet not prepared to deal with mortality in their own thoughts and feelings.

So what were the choices? Many people participated in the systematic avoidance of death and paid the price in anxiety, burdensome defenses, and hard knocks from a reality that would not let itself be ignored when the defenses failed. Others trembled or brooded alone, haunted by death-related anxieties that isolated them, because these feelings scared off friends, families, and colleagues. Still others tried to challenge death by engaging in risky actions. These episodes had the advantage of turning passive anxiety into active thrills but too often the disadvantage of bringing about serious injury or death. Few had the opportunity to reflect on dying and death with the help of a sensitive instructor and knowledge-based writings.

Today there may still be moments when we ignore, brood, tremble, or challenge death to a showdown—but there is also more opportunity to apply our minds to the study of death as we are accustomed to do with so many other subjects. There was at first considerable resistance to what has now become known as death education. By now, however, many people recognize that *thanatology*—the study of life, with death left in—can be one of the most valuable projects for a student of any age. There is a growing awareness that understanding our relationship to death can be of great value not only in facing our own mortal moves, but also in progressing through life with zest, wisdom, and compassion. Death education, grief counseling, hospice care, and suicide prevention agencies are among the positive responses in a society that is starting to come to terms with the realities of death.

This book is intended to contribute to your understanding of your relationship with death, both as an individual and as a member of society. For example, you will learn—

- How our thoughts and feelings about death develop from childhood's hour and how we struggle with anxiety and denial toward a more mature and effective view of death.
- What very different ideas and meanings have been associated with death throughout the centuries.
- How and why the ideas of "death" and "dead" have become unsettled in our own time.
- How dying people are perceived and treated in our society, and what can be done to provide the best possible care.
- What choices and decisions we have about the way we are treated at the end of our lives.
- How people respond to the loss of bereavement, the sorrow and anxiety of grief, and the challenge of moving on with their lives.
- Why the funeral and memorialization process is still with us today after so many centuries.
- Who is most at risk for suicide and who is most likely to become either a killer or a victim of homicide.
- What is happening in the continuing controversy over physician-assisted death—especially the facts that are now coming to light.
- What the evidence tells us and what is left to our own judgment and intuition about near-death experiences and reincarnation as proof of survival of death.
- How we can help others cope with their death encounters.

These and many other topics are presented as interactions between the individual and society. It is true that we live and die as individuals. However, it is also true that we live and die within a particular society during a particular time in world history. Preoccupation with our thoughts and feelings as individuals could lead us to lose sight of the larger picture in which social dynam-

ics so often influence the timing, mode, and experience of dying as well as our basic interpretations of life and death.

We draw upon the best available scholarship and research, as well as upon the words of people who have found themselves in the middle of death-related situations. Often we will note the limitations of present knowledge and offer alternative interpretations. It is our intention to present information clearly, but without undue simplification.

I would like to welcome you personally to this book and to the course to which this book may contribute. When I taught a course on death more than thirty years ago—one of the first to have been offered—there were few death educators, counselors, and researchers, and we had to go mainly by what we had been able to learn through our own experiences. Today both the cadre of death educators and their knowledge base have expanded considerably. Take advantage of your instructor's expertise: do not hesitate to ask your questions and share your experiences. Explore the ever-growing literature on the human encounter with mortality; discover what observers from many different perspectives can offer to us. Now join us in one of humankind's oldest—and newest—voyages of discovery.

NEW FOR THE SEVENTH EDITION

Several important changes have been made for this edition of *Death, Society, and Human Experience.*

A. Changes in Substance

1. Sudden and unexpected deaths have continued to violate society's sense of security and order, as well as to arouse grief for the lost lives. These episodes—the school shootings; the deaths of John Kennedy, Jr., his wife, and sister-in-law; and Princess Diana—have required us to think again about how we respond to "special" deaths as a society.
2. New theoretical approaches have been needed to improve our understanding of the dying process. We present some of the newer approaches here.
3. Care providers have come to realize that there is a large category of people who are not dy-

ing or terminally ill but who live each day at particular risk. We consider hemophilia as one important example.

4. Our understanding of suicide risk is expanded when we consider the population theory of suicide increase, "suicide by cop," AIDS-related suicide, and the sometimes lethal effects of bullying and harassment, especially in childhood and adolescence.

5. In addition to the alarming school shootings, we also give attention to children who kill parents, adults who kill infants, and men who kill women.

6. We deepen our understanding of the assisted-death controversy by acquainting ourselves with the "black stork" movement that made its appearance in the United States earlier in this century.

7. Our knowledge of funeral and memorialization practices is expanded with consideration of the Vietnam Memorial wall and its significance; the process of mummy making both in dynastic Egypt and in the (late) Soviet Union upon the death of its founder, Lenin; the history of cemeteries in the United States, and insights into how changes in American life have affected the funeral process and our relationship to death.

8. To the ancient mystery of survival of death, we have added consideration of the Native American Ghost Dance, ghosts as possible proof of survival, the status of near-death experiences as private experience and as possible G-LOC (gravity force) phenomena, and Ian Stevenson's mammoth collection of cases "suggestive of reincarnation."

9. The challenging concepts of "the good death" and "virtual death" are given attention.

Other new information is presented throughout the book, and previous information is updated where possible.

B. Changes in Structure

1. Some instructors have requested chapter summaries, and I was pleased to add them. (The chapter-end glossaries added for the sixth edition are also included.)

2. Information on causes and rates of death has been tucked into Chapter 3 instead of standing as an independent chapter.

3. Information on HIV/AIDS has been redistributed to chapters in which specific problems are addressed, e.g., dying, grief, and suicide.

4. A new chapter (6) is devoted to end-of-life issues and decisions. Some of this material was previously included in our examination of assisted death and the right to die. New developments and the increasing saliency of end-of-life issues have warranted a full chapter's coverage.

5. A new chapter (15) offers the opportunity to reflect on some of the major findings, questions, and concerns encountered throughout the book. "Good Life, Good Death? Trying to Make Sense of It All" is not a mechanical summary of the book, but rather an encouragement to further reflection on the part of the reader.

6. The appendix has been updated and substantially expanded.

I thank the reviewers for their useful suggestions: Andrew M. Barclay, Michigan State University; Daniel J. Klenow, North Dakota State University; Patrick Mazzeo, SUNY-Canton; and Wulian Serdahely, University of Wisconsin, Oshkosh. I hope this book will play a useful role in your learning experiences.

John F. Kennedy, Jr. salutes the casket of his assassinated father as his mother, sister, and other members of the family stand by him (November 25, 1963)

chapter 1

AS WE THINK ABOUT DEATH

John F. Kennedy, Jr. may have lost control of his plane in the final moments before its terrifying plunge into the sea. National Transportation Safety Board officials said Kennedy's plane made a series of rapid turns and changes in altitude during its final moments on approach to Martha's Vineyard airport, which aviation experts said clearly indicated he lost control of the aircraft. "We call that a graveyard spiral," said Erin Carnahan, a flight instructor of 18 years experience.
—Tony Munroe, July 21, 1999

Three days before he was to receive the Oklahoma City Police Department's Medal of Valor, Sgt. Terrance Yeakey tried to slit his wrists, then shot himself to death. He had rushed to the scene of the bombing that killed 168 people at the Alfred P. Murrah Federal Building and rescued four people before he injured his back when the floor collapsed beneath him.
—Associated Press report, May 11, 1996

I never try to reason, to bargain, or to make sense of the why. I have no arguments with men or gods. I take the children on as they are from the time of the first connection and work on ways to make living a little better. It continues to amaze me that a "little" better can make such a huge difference. Reflections of the dying are etched in one's memory like on stone. Parents remember the way in which their child died throughout their entire lifetime.
—Pediatrician Gerri Frager, R.N., M.D., 1996, p. 41

Far fewer people die of a wrong diagnosis than did in an earlier era—the enormous majority succumb because of our inability to change the course of an accurate pinpointed disease.
—Sherwin B. Nuland, M.D., 1993, p. 78

Life is supposed to go on. And on. Yes, there is death, but not here, not now. We wake to a familiar world each day. We splash water on the same face we rinsed yesterday. We go through our familiar routines. We talk with people whose faces are familiar to us. We see the streets and buildings we have seen many times before. It is so comforting…this ongoingness of daily life. Why disturb this pattern? Why think of death?

- The Kennedy's have often been described as the United States' closest equivalent to a royal family. John F. Kennedy, Jr. had a special place in the nation's memory since the moment little John-John saluted the passing funeral cortege for his assassinated father. The sudden and unexpected deaths of John F. Kennedy, Jr., his wife, Carolyn Bessette Kennedy, and her sister, Lauren Bessette, was more than front page news around the world. It resonated with other sudden deaths by violence that had struck the family over the years: Joseph P. Kennedy, Jr., killed when his bomber exploded over the English Channel on a secret World War II mission, and the murders of first John, then Robert Kennedy. One death can bring back intense feelings associated with previous deaths, but the responses to the fatal plane crash were even more diverse and complicated. We will explore some of these responses later. The point for now is that events do not allow us to ignore death even if we have become very good at this trick.
- The Alfred P. Murrah Federal Building was not only a familiar landmark in Oklahoma City, but also the workplace of many people and the destination of many others who had business there. This scene of active life blew apart on April 19, 1995. Police and firefighters rushed into the building. Sergeant Yeakey and his fellow officer Jim Ramsey were among the first to enter the ruins. Both put their own lives at risk in searching for victims in the smoldering, collapsing structure. Both would later be praised for their heroism. Sergeant Yeakey did not feel much like a hero, however. He was despondent because he had not saved even more victims of the bombing—although it was physically impossible for him to do so after suffering the back injury. Like the firefighers and

other emergency response personnel, Sergeant Yeakey was part of the community's first line of defense against catastrophe, a defense that in this instance could not protect all of his neighbors from violent death. The disaster was unthinkable—but it had happened, and now in Sergeant Yeakey it claimed another victim.

- Perhaps there is no more stressful and painful situation than being with a dying child. There is added stress for physicians and nurses when they find that none of their skills can save the child's life. Gerri Frager was a nurse before she became a doctor. She calls upon both perspectives as well as her own sense of values as she tries to comfort dying children and their families. There is no way that people such as Dr. Frager can hold fast to the illusion that anybody, even the youngest child, is safe from the threat of death.
- Physicians were not always held in high repute, nor did people feel confident when they entered a hospital for treatment. Attitudes toward health care have changed markedly since those bad old days. Medical advances have contributed to higher expectations on the part of the public. Physicians have so many ways to diagnose and treat our ailments; hospitals are "pit stops" where we are given effective care and put back on the road again. However, as Nuland observes, there is a large disparity between the ability of health care professionals to diagnose our ills and their ability to cure them. More and more people are finding themselves in a situation that was uncommon in the past: expectations for a long life, protected by medical science, versus the hard reality that often death still has the upper hand.
- Many families today have fading photographs of relatives who died years ago of pneumonia, tuberculosis, cholera, typhoid, scarlet fever, infantile paralysis and other widespread diseases. These people wanted to live. One hoped to survive the diseases that threatened children and young adults. One hoped for the chance to realize personal dreams for a good life. Again, however, expectations have changed. There are now increasing demands for release from life when the quality of that life has been reduced by painful or incapacitating illness. Death, once

the problem, is being regarded as the answer by a growing number of people.

Catastrophic accidents, increased acts of terrorism and violence, the vulnerability of children, the failure of medical advances to meet ever-heightening expectations, and the feeling that life can be too burdensome to continue are among the current circumstances that make it difficult to persist in avoiding thoughts of death. The question is changing from: "*Should* I think of death?" to "*What* should I think of death?"

In this chapter, we begin our exploration of thoughts, knowledge, attitudes, and feelings about death with particular emphasis on the current situation. Although our focus is on the United States, we will also consider dying, death, grief, and suicide in other societies. It is not enough, though, to attend only to the way other people think about death. Therefore this chapter also provides the opportunity to take stock of our own thoughts, knowledge, attitudes, and feelings.

NOT THINKING ABOUT DEATH: A FAILED EXPERIMENT

We have tried not thinking about death. The educational system cooperated. Millions of us completed our school days without being exposed to substantial readings and discussions about dying, death, grief, and suicide. Who would have taught us, anyway? Our teachers were products of the same "never say die" society. Making it through college did not add anything to our store of knowledge or our ability to cope with death-related circumstances. Death did surface occasionally as a number or event remote from our own experiences. X number of gunmen popped each other off in a famous shoot-out. Some king or other died and somebody else grabbed the throne on a date we might need to remember for the exam.

Those who persevered until they had a graduate degree in hand received only further lessons in death avoidance. Nurses, physicians, psychologists, social workers, and others who would be relied on to provide human services were not expected to understand their own death-related feelings and attitudes, let alone anybody else's. During these long years, even clergy often felt unprepared to cope with the death-related situations they would face. Few of their instructors had themselves mastered the art of ministering to the dying.

The media also cooperated. Nobody died. Nobody had cancer. Instead, people "passed away" after a "long illness." Deaths associated with crime and violence received lavish attention, then as now, but silence had settled over the everyday death of everyday people. When a movie script called for a deathbed scene, Hollywood offered a sentimental and sanitized version. A typical example occurs in *Till the Clouds Go By* (1946), a film that purported to be the biography of song writer Jerome Kern. The dying friend tries to communicate his realization that this will be the last time they see each other, but Kern steadfastly rejects these efforts. In doing so, Kern's character was obeying the Hollywood dictum that deception is the best policy: even mature adults cannot face the reality of death, so it is best to play "let's pretend." As a result, the friends never actually "connect," never offer significant words of parting to each other. A physician then enters the room and nods gravely to Kern, who immediately departs. Another mortal lesson from Hollywood: the moment of death obviously belongs to the authority of the doctor, not to the dying person and the bereaved. Audiences today see this scene as shallow and deceptive. One student spoke for many others in complaining, "It was as phony as can be—what a terrible way to end a relationship!"

Not thinking about death proved to be an ineffective maneuver. People continued to die, and how they died became an increasing source of concern. Survivors continued to grieve, often feeling a lack of understanding and support from others. Suicide rates doubled, then tripled among the young, and remained exceptionally high among older adults. And there was more. Scattered voices had been warning us that in attempting to evade the reality of death, we were falsifying the totality of our lives. Who were we kidding? Neither an individual nor a society could face its challenges wisely without coming to terms with mortality.

It is still difficult to think about death, especially when our own lives and relationships are involved. Nevertheless, the days of enforced silence and frantic evasion seem to be over. There is an increasing readiness to listen and communicate.

Listening and Communicating

"Doctor, I want to die. Will you help me?" This question is the title of an influential article by Timothy E. Quill, M.D. He advised that:

dying patients need more than prescriptions for narcotics or referrals to hospice programs from their physicians. They need a personal guide and counselor through the dying process—someone who will unflinchingly help them face both the medical and the personal aspects of dying, whether it goes smoothly or it takes the physician into unfamiliar, untested ground. Dying patients do not have the luxury of choosing not to undertake the journey, or of separating their person from their disease. Physicians' commitment not to abandon their patients is of paramount importance. (1993, p. 872)

Statements of this kind are becoming increasingly common. What is most remarkable is the simple fact that more physicians are now listening and communicating. Unlike in years past, there is now the expectation of dialogue between patient and physician. Patients and family members feel more empowered to express their concerns, needs, and wishes. Physicians feel more compelled to take these concerns, needs, and wishes into account.

"Do you believe in reincarnation—that is, the rebirth of the soul in a new body after death—or not?" This is one of the questions that the Gallup organization has added to its surveys in recent years. The pollsters observed a revival of interest in the question of life after death and, in particular, to the possibility of reincarnation (Gallup, 1991). You can verify this interest for yourself by checking out book stores, radio and television talk shows, and holistic or "New Age" seminars and fairs. Life and death are viewed as having an integral relationship with each other. Believers in reincarnation tend to take their beliefs seriously, that is, it influences their everyday attitudes, decisions, and interpersonal relationships. Because these believers are usually interested in sharing their views with others, there is more discussion

and stimulation among the public at large. Those who are critical of the reincarnation concept may nevertheless be challenged to examine and defend their own beliefs.

"I don't believe in reincarnation, and I never will!"

"That's what you told me in our last life!"

"There's nothing to think about. When you're number's up, it's up."

This idea goes back a long way. It is part of that general view of life known as *fatalism.* Outcomes are determined in advance. There's really nothing we can do to affect the outcomes so, to quote a well-known philosopher: *"What—me worry?"* Fatalism is a way of excusing ourselves for our perceived lack of ability to predict and control events. There is something to be said for respecting the limits of human knowledge and efficacy, but there is also something to be said for doing what we can to reduce suffering and risk within our limits. The person who is quick to introduce a fatalistic statement often is attempting to end the discussion before it really begins. It is what communication experts call a "silencer."

Fatalistic attitudes in today's world are perhaps more dangerous than ever. As we will see, many deaths in the United States can be attributed to lifestyle. Our attitudes, choices, and actions contribute to many other deaths across the entire lifespan. Ironically, it is the belief that there is no use in thinking about death and taking life-protective measures that increases the probability of an avoidable death.

YOUR SELF-INVENTORY OF ATTITUDES, BELIEFS, AND FEELINGS

We have touched briefly on a few of the death-related questions and beliefs that are current in our society. Perhaps some of your own thoughts and feelings have come to mind. One of the most beneficial things you can do for yourself at this point is to take stock of your present experiences, attitudes, beliefs, and feelings. This will not only give you a personal data baseline but will also contribute further to your appreciation of the ways in which other people view death. After exploring your own configuration of experiences, attitudes, beliefs, and feelings, you will also be in a better position to understand the general relationships that have been observed between what we think and what we do in death-related situations.

Before reading further, please begin sampling your personal experiences with death by completing Self-Inventories 1, 2, 3, and 4. It is in your own interest to complete these exercises in a frank and serious manner. As a personal bonus, try to notice the thoughts and feelings that come to mind as you answer these questions. Which questions make you angry? Which questions would you prefer not to answer? Which questions seem foolish or make you want to laugh? Observing your own responses is part of the self-monitoring process that has been found invaluable by many of the people who work systematically with death-related issues.

As you begin these exercises, please note that each of the inventories takes a distinctive perspective. We begin with your knowledge base, sampling the information you have acquired regarding various facets of death. This is followed by exploring your attitudes and beliefs. We then move on to your personal experiences with death. Finally, we look at the feelings that are stirred in you by dying, death, and grief. As you go along, you will see with increasing clarity that our total view of death comprises knowledge, attitudes, experiences, and feelings—and that is it useful to identify each of these components accurately. For example, if I fail to distinguish between my personal feelings and my actual knowledge of a death-related topic, I thereby reduce my ability to make wise decisions and take effective actions.

Please complete the Self-Inventories now.

INVENTORY #1:
MY KNOWLEDGE BASE

Fill in the blanks or select alternative answers as accurately as you can. If you are not sure of the answer, offer your best guess.

1. What is the leading cause of death among children in the United States?

   _____

2. What is the leading cause of death among teens and young adults in the United States?

   _____

3. What is the leading cause of death among adults between the ages of 35 and 64 in the United States?

   _____

4. What is the leading cause of death among people 65 and older in the United States?

   _____

5. What is the leading cause of workplace death among women in the United States?

   _____

6. What are the odds that a death certificate will state the specific cause of death?

   _____

7. What percentage of all deaths in the United States are subject to investigation by a medical examiner or coroner because they are violent, suspicious, unexpected, or not attended by a physician?

   _____

8. How does the lung cancer risk for food service workers compare with that for the general population?

   _____

9. A has health insurance. B does not. Which of these people is more likely to be alive ten years from now?

   _____

10. Each year, about _____ Americans die.

11. In third world nations, which of the following is the leading cause of death?

    AIDS _____   Cancer_____

    Heart disease _____   Measles_____

12. Serum total cholesterol levels have been studied in adults of all ages for more than thirty years. What is the main finding?

    _____

    What does this finding suggest?_____

    _____

13. In the United States, one child in _____ dies before age 1.

14. In the United States, one person in _____ is killed by gunfire before age 20.

15. Capital punishment (the death penalty) is:

    legal throughout the United States _____;

    legal in some, but not all states _____;

    not legal in the United States _____.

16. Cryonic suspension is a technique intended to preserve a body in a hypothermic (low temperature) state until a cure is discovered for the condition from which that person suffered.

    How many people have actually been placed in cryonic suspension? _____

    Efforts have been made to revive how many of these people? _____

    With what results? _____

17. The Living Will is an early example of an

    _____ .

18. _____ is the first state to have enacted legislation that legalizes physician-assisted death under specified conditions.

19. Cremation is more likely to be the preferred means of body disposal for:

    (a) elderly men _____; (b) elderly women _____; (c) young men _____; (d) young women _____; (e) no age or sex differences in preference _____.

20. There are about _____ hospice organizations in the United States.

    All _____ Some _____ None _____ provide 24-hour service and are accredited under the National Hospice Reimbursement Act.

21. There are approximately _____ suicide prevention centers in the United States.

    All _____ Some _____ None _____ are certified by the American Association of Suicidology.

22. In the United States, the highest suicide rate occurs among:

    African Americans _____; Asian Americans _____; Hispanic Americans _____; Native Americans _____.

23. How much money does an organ donor's family receive for this "anatomical gift?"

    _____

24. A Gallup poll finds that about _____ percent of the American population believes in reincarnation.

25. People with the hereditary condition known as _____ became at much higher risk for death during the early years of the AIDS epidemic.

Answers to self-inventory questions are found later in this chapter. Please don't peek!

INVENTORY #2:
MY ATTITUDES AND BELIEFS

Select the answer that most accurately represents your belief.

1. I believe in some form of life after death:

   Yes, definitely ____
   Yes, but not quite sure ____
   No, but not quite sure ____
   No, definitely ____

2. I believe that you die when your number comes up: it's in the hands of fate:

   Yes, definitely ____
   Yes, but not quite sure ____
   No, but not quite sure ____
   No, definitely ____

3. I believe that taking one's own life is:

   Never justified ____
   Justified when terminally ill ____
   Justified whenever life no longer seems worth living ____

4. I believe that taking another person's life is:

   Never justified ____
   Justified in defense of your own life ____
   Justified when that person has committed a terrible crime ____

5. I believe that dying people should be:

   Told the truth about their condition ____
   Kept hopeful by sparing them the facts ____
   Depends upon the person and the circumstances ____

6. In thinking about my own old age, I would prefer:

   To die before I grow old ____
   To live as long as I can ____
   To discover what challenges and opportunities old age will bring ____

7. The possibility of nuclear weapon warfare or accidents that might destroy much of life on earth has been of:

   no concern ____ little concern ____ some concern ____ major concern ____ to me.

8. The possibility of environmental catastrophes that might destroy much of life on earth has been of:

   no concern ____ little concern ____ some concern ____ major concern ____ to me.

9. Drivers and passengers should be required to wear seat belts.

   Yes, agree ____ Tend to agree ____
   Tend to disagree ____ No, disagree ____

10. The availability of handguns should be more tightly controlled to reduce accidental and impulsive shootings.

    Yes, agree ____ Tend to agree ____
    Tend to disagree ____ No, disagree ____

11. A person has been taken to the emergency room with internal bleeding that is likely to prove fatal. This person is 82 years of age and has an Alzheimer-type dementia. What type of response would you recommend from the ER staff?

    Comfort-only ____ Limited attempt at rescue ____ All-out attempt at rescue ____

12. You have been taken to the emergency room with internal bleeding that is likely to prove fatal. You are now 82 years of age and have an Alzheimer-type dementia. What type of response would you hope to receive from the ER staff?

    Comfort-only ____ Limited attempt at rescue ____ All-out attempt at rescue ____

13. Another round of chemotherapy has failed for a woman with advanced breast cancer. The doctor suggests a new round of experimental therapy. She replies, "I wish I were dead." What do you think should be done—and why?

    _____

    _____

    _____

INVENTORY #3:
MY EXPERIENCES WITH DEATH

Fill in the blanks or select the most accurate alternative answers.

1. A. I have had an animal companion who died. Yes _____ No _____

   B. My feelings when my pet died can be described by words such as:

   _____, _____, and _____.

2. The following people in my life have died:

   Person   *How Long Ago?*

   A._____

   B._____

   C._____

   D._____

   E._____

3. The death that affected me the most at the time was _____ .

4. My feelings when this person died can be described by words such as: _____, _____, and _____.

5. This death was especially significant to me because_____

   _____

6. In all the circumstances surrounding this person's death, including what happened afterward, my most positive memory is of:

   _____

   _____

7. My most disturbing memory is of: _____

   _____

   _____

8. I have conversed with dying people.

   Never _____ One person _____
   Several people _____ Many people _____

9. I have provided care for a dying person.

   Never _____ One person _____
   Several people _____ Many people _____

10. I have known a person who attempted suicide.

    Not to my knowledge _____
    One person _____ Several people _____

11. I have known a person who committed suicide.

    Not to my knowledge _____
    One person _____ Several people _____

12. I have known a person who died in an accident.

    Not to my knowledge _____
    One person _____ Several people _____

13. I have known a person who was murdered.

    Not to my knowledge _____
    One person _____ Several people _____

14. I have known a person who died of AIDS-related disease.

    Not to my knowledge _____
    One person _____ Several people _____

15. I know a person who has tested positive for the AIDS virus.

    Not to my knowledge _____
    One person _____ Several people _____

SELF-INVENTORY #4:
MY FEELINGS

Select the answer that most closely represents your feelings.

1. I would feel comfortable in developing an intimate conversation with a dying person.

   Yes, agree _____ Tend to agree _____
   Tend to disagree _____ No, disagree _____

2. I would hesitate to touch someone who was dying.

   Yes, agree _____ Tend to agree _____
   Tend to disagree _____ No, disagree _____

3. My hands would tremble if I were talking to a dying person.

   Yes, agree _____ Tend to agree _____
   Tend to disagree _____ No, disagree _____

4. I would have more difficulty in talking if the dying person were about my age.

   Yes, agree _____ Tend to agree _____
   Tend to disagree _____ No, disagree _____

5. I would avoid talking about death and dying with a person who was terminally ill.

   Yes, agree _____ Tend to agree _____
   Tend to disagree _____ No, disagree _____

6. I would avoid talking with a dying person if possible.

   Yes, agree _____ Tend to agree _____
   Tend to disagree _____ No, disagree _____

7. I have had moments of anxiety in which I think of my own death.

   Never _____ Once _____
   Several times _____ Often _____

8. I fear that I will die too soon.

   Yes, agree _____ Tend to agree _____
   Tend to disagree _____ No, disagree _____

9. I have no fear of death as such.

   Yes, agree _____ Tend to agree _____
   Tend to disagree _____ No, disagree _____

10. I have no fears associated with dying.

    Yes, agree _____ Tend to agree _____
    Tend to disagree _____ No, disagree _____

11. I feel good when I think about life after death.

    Yes, agree _____ Tend to agree _____
    Tend to disagree _____ No, disagree _____

12. I am anxious about the possible death of somebody I love.

    Yes, definitely _____ Tend to agree _____
    Tend to disagree _____ No, disagree _____

13. I am grieving over somebody who has already died.

    Yes, definitely _____ Tend to agree _____
    Tend to disagree _____ No, disagree _____

14. I have a hard time taking death seriously: it feels remote to me, not really connected to my own life.

    Yes, definitely _____ Tend to agree _____
    Tend to disagree _____ No, disagree _____

15. I have some strong, even urgent feelings regarding death these days.

    Yes, definitely _____ Tend to agree _____
    Tend to disagree _____ No, disagree _____

Note: Questions 1–6 are part of a scale introduced by Hayslip (1986–1987).

SOME ANSWERS—AND THE QUESTIONS THEY RAISE

Knowledge Base

Here are the answers to Self-Inventory #1:

1. The leading cause of death among children (age 1 and older) in the United States is accidents. Further information about causes of death is provided in Chapter 3.

2. The leading cause of death among teens and young adults in the United States is accidents. Homicide and suicide are the next most common causes of death for those in the 15–24 age range.

3. The leading cause of death among adults between the ages of 35 and 64 in the United States is "malignant neoplasms," more commonly known as cancer.

4. The leading cause of death among people 65 and older in the United States is heart disease.

5. Homicide is the leading cause of workplace death among women in the United States (McClain, 1993). Men are far more at risk for workplace death in general (93 percent), but homicide is the greater specific risk for women (40 percent to 15 percent). What are the patterns of sex differences in homicide, and how are these to be understood? *See Chapter 9.*

6. A recent study of death certificates has found that the specific cause of death was given in only about a third of the certificates studied (Hanzlick, 1993). Why is this basic information so often missing, and how might these omissions affect our decision-making as a society? *See Chapter 9 and 12.*

7. About 20 percent of all deaths are subject to investigation by coroners or medical examiners (all states have one or both of these medical officers). These include cases in which homicide or murder is suspected, and also those in which the person may have had a disease or suffered an accident with the potential for public hazard (e.g., plague or radiational injury). Many cases are not "suspicious," but involve people who were living alone at the time of their death. Why

does society consider it important to establish a cause for all deaths? *See Chapter 3.*

8. Food service workers (i.e., restaurant employees) have about twice the lung cancer risk of the population at large (Siegel, 1993). This finding is directly attributable to the higher levels of environmental tobacco smoke in restaurants than in office workplaces of other businesses and even in residences with at least one smoker. What should the student of death-related behavior know about smoking in light of recent and emerging developments? *See Chapter 3.*

9. B has only half the chance of survival (Franks et al., 1993). This assumes that A and B are similar in age, gender, and health status at Time 1, differing only in health insurance coverage. This finding of differential mortality is evident in all sociodemographic groups for which data were available. What's going on? *See Chapter 3.*

10. Each year, about 2 million Americans die. The most recent data (National Health Statistics Center 1999) show 2,314,738 deaths. (During the same year there were 3,894,494 births.) This means that we lose the distinctive knowledge, experience, and socioemotional support that was provided by a great many people. It also introduces many people to the role of the bereaved survivor and adds to the burden of grief for those who have previously lost other significant people in their lives. What do we really know about bereavement, grief, and mourning—and what can we do to help? *See Chapters 11 and 12.*

11. In third-world nations, measles kills more people than AIDS, cancer, or heart disease (World Health Organization, 1990). An effective inoculation against measles has been available for years, but it is not administered universally, and each year many thousands of children die from this preventable disease. Why is there such a deadly gap between knowledge and action? *See Chapters 3 and 14.*

12. The serum total cholesterol level of adults in the United States has been declining significantly over the past three decades (Johnson et al., 1993). This finding suggests that public health programs are proving successful in

protecting against the life-threatening effects of high cholesterol. Does this mean that public programs will be successful in reducing other risks to life? *See Chapter 14.*

13. In the United States, 1 child in 132 dies before the age of 1. Infant mortality varies widely throughout the world and even within the country. *See Chapter 3.*

14. In the United States, 1 person in 680 is killed by gunfire before age 20. Opinions differ about the advisability of increased gun control, but the basic facts about gun-related murder in the United States are clear. *See Chapter 8.*

15. Capital punishment is legal in some, but not all states. The death penalty is not on the books in thirteen states, as well as Puerto Rico, the Virgin Islands, and the District of Columbia (Kastenbaum, 1993c). What is the place of capital punishment in our society's overall death system? *See Chapters 3 and 8.*

16. At last count there were twenty-six persons in cryonic suspension in the United States; make that thirteen complete bodies and thirteen heads (no headless bodies!). Are these people alive or dead? How should we interpret and respond to this invitation to "freeze-wait-reanimate!"? *See Chapter 6*

17. The Living Will was an early example of an *advance directive* to guide end-of-life decisions. What has happened since? *See Chapters 6 and 9.*

18. Oregon is first state to have enacted legislation that legalizes physician-assisted death under specified conditions. What are the issues involved? *See Chapter 9.*

19. There are no systematic age or sex preferences with respect to cremation (Kastenbaum, 1993b). Usually the deceased person's expressed preference has guided the choice of cremation. What are some considerations when deciding on the method of body disposal? *See Chapter 12.*

20. There are about 1,700 hospice organizations in the United States; no precise number is available (Kastenbaum, 1993a). Are these hospice organizations living up to our hopes and expectations? *See Chapter 5.*

21. There are approximately 170 suicide prevention centers in the United States, of which 37 have been certified by the American Association of Suicidology (Farberow, 1993). Like hospices, suicide prevention centers differ significantly in their operations, but all emphasize the value of opening lines of communication and sharing one's concerns with caring and responsible listeners. What are some of the most pressing challenges that face those who would understand and prevent suicide? *See Chapter 7.*

22. Among ethnic and racial subpopulations of the United States, the highest suicide rate appears among Native Americans (McIntosh, 1993). Young male Native Americans are at especially high risk for suicide. Significant differences exist in suicide rates among various tribes. Why is suicide so prevalent in this group? What might be done to reduce suicide and other self-destructive actions? *See Chapter 7.*

23. No payment is made to the donor or donor's family for the right to use organs following an individual's death. It would be a violation of the National Organ Transplant Act to purchase human organs (Evans, 1993). *See Chapter 3.*

24. The most recent Gallup poll (1991) finds that, excluding those with no opinion, one person in four in the United States now expresses a belief in reincarnation. This seems to be an increase, although comparable data are not available for the past. Two out of three people hold an overall belief in some form of life after death. What observations and arguments are now being advanced in favor of—and in opposition to—belief in an afterlife? *See Chapter 13.*

25. People with the hereditary condition known as *hemophilia* became at increased risk for death when the nation's blood supply became contaminated with HIV. *See Chapter 3.*

Attitudes, Experiences, Beliefs, Feelings

Perhaps you now have a clearer picture of the assumptions and facts that you have picked up about death-related topics over the years. You may also have noticed that facts about death are subject to change, even if death itself is notoriously as certain as taxes. We do not live by facts alone, however. It is time now to explore the attitudes, experiences, beliefs, and feelings that we bring to our encounters with death.

Attitudes refer to our action tendencies: I am ready to act or I am not ready to act. I am ready to approach or to avoid this situation. *Beliefs* refer to our relatively stable and broad interpretations of the world and our place in it. Fatalism, already mentioned, is one type of belief. *Feelings* provide us with qualitative information on our total sense of being, a "status report." I feel safe or endangered. I feel happy or sorrowful. I feel aroused or lethargic. Two people may hold identical beliefs and attitudes, but differ greatly in their feelings. On Inventory #2, question 10, for example, these two people may answer, "Yes, agree: the availability of handguns should be more tightly controlled to reduce accidental and impulsive shootings." However, one of these people may have relatively little feeling attached to this view. Perhaps he or she thinks that it is risky to have a lot of handguns around on general principles. The other person might be the widow of a physician who was shot to death by an emotionally disturbed person who did not even know him. Her feelings could hardly be more intense. (This is a real person, the former owner of a home my wife and I purchased. Incredible as it may seem, the young widow herself became the recipient of death threats because she spoke up in favor of gun control.)

Personal *experience* influences our attitudes, beliefs, and feelings. For example, people who have had near-death experiences while in a life-threatening situation often develop a different perspective on both life and death (*Chapter 13*). A paramedic who has responded to a thousand motor vehicle accidents is likely to have a stronger attitude and more intense feelings when he or she notices children without seat belts in a car. A person who has never suffered the death of a loved one may be more impatient with a bereaved colleague who does not seem to "snap back" right away.

The most significant experiential difference is between people have who had a personally significant death and those for whom death has remained a distant topic, or even just a word. Death stopped being just a word for a graduate student of social work when both her parents were killed in an automobile accident. She could not go on with her own life until she fully *realized* their deaths as well as her own mortality. "Before all this happened, it was just a word to me, death. I could hear death. I could say death. Really, though, it was just a word. Now it's like something under my own skin, if you know what I mean." Simply knowing intellectually that people die was not enough; she now had to connect death with life in a very personal way.

This challenge is ours as well. If we have experienced a death that "got" to us—whether the death of a person or an animal companion—we are also more likely to realize what other people have been going through. This is one of the most powerful dynamics at work in community support groups. Organizations such as Compassionate Friends (Klass, 1988), and Widow-to-Widow (Silverman, 1994) provide understanding and emotional support for bereaved persons from those who have already experienced the sorrow and stress of loss. New support groups continue to be formed to help people with specific types of death-related stress, for example, for parents whose children have been killed by a drunk driver or for persons with AIDS.

And yet there are limits to the value of experience. Just because a person has had a particular kind of loss experience does not necessarily mean that this person also has the ability to support others. Furthermore, some people have proven helpful to the dying, the grieving, and the suicidal even if they have not had very similar experiences in their lives. The basic point to consider is whether at this point in your life you are "part of the club" that has experienced death in an undeniably personal and significant way, or whether you still have something of an outsider's perspective.

Some people have an inner relationship with death that goes beyond basic realization. A person's thoughts, attitudes, and feelings may be *dominated* by death-related experiences. The sense of being dominated, controlled, or haunted by death can emerge from one critical experience or from a cluster of experiences. Perhaps you have mourned the deaths of so many people that you could not even list them in the space provided. Perhaps several people died unexpectedly at the same time. Or perhaps you are still responding strongly to the death of one person who had been at the center of your life. The question of whether or not your life is being highly influenced, even dominated, by death-related experiences cannot be answered by examining a simple list. We would have to appreciate what these people meant to you, and what lingers in your mind regarding the deaths themselves…the funeral…the memorialization process. Furthermore, we would have to examine your own involvement in the situation. For example, people who have provided direct personal care for a dying friend or relative have a different set of experiences than those who have not. Perhaps you have a clear and powerful memory of your last visits with a person who was a very important part of your life. On the other hand, perhaps you were thousands of miles away when this person died and had no opportunity to be with your loved one. We may be much influenced by *how* a person has died as well as by the fact of death itself. A death by suicide, for example, has often been considered tainted, resulting in additional stress and social isolation for the family survivors.

These are but a few of the ways in which our past experiences with death are likely to influence us in the future. It is helpful to keep in mind that people differ markedly in the kinds of experiences they have had with death. Paramedics who have rushed to more accident scenes and other emergencies than they would care to remember are likely to respond differently to the next death-related situation they encounter than are people who have never been with a dying person or a corpse. Therefore, if we behave differently when we encounter a situation, the answer may be found in the fact that it is not really the "same" situation for each of us.

How Does State of Mind Affect Death-Related Behavior?

Much remains to be learned about the link between what goes on in our minds and how we actually behave in death-related situations. Following are a few studies that have addressed specific aspects of this question.

- *The living will: why most of the living won't.*
  The document known as the *living will* has

been available since 1968 for people who want to limit the type of medical interventions that would be carried out if they were close to death and at that point unable to express their wishes (*see also Chapter 6*). Although this document was designed to meet the growing public expression of interest in controlling end-of-life decisions, most people have not yet completed the form. Why? VandeCreek and Frankowski (1996) found that most people had not thought much about their own death and also considered that their last days were a long way off. The authors conclude that "completing living wills connotes personal death, and this appears to be a substantial barrier to completing the document" (1996, p. 80). Avoidance of death thoughts was therefore closely associated with letting a significant opportunity go by to influence their situation when the last days do come.

- *Should I sign an organ donation card?*
  A set of studies (reviewed by Robbins, 1990) has inquired into the attitudes of organ donors and nondonors. All of the states, as well as the District of Columbia, have enacted some version of the Uniform Anatomical Gift Act. Despite the widespread availability of this option (in association with the driver's license), relatively few people sign and carry organ donor cards. Personal attitudes play a major role in this decision. The studies show that nondonors tend to be more anxious about death. Furthermore, there was a specific fear among the donors—of being declared dead prematurely. In her own investigation, Robbins found that nondonors were also more uneasy about their physical condition in general. Additionally, there was a relationship between willingness to donate organs and the sense of self-efficacy: people who think of themselves as effective and self-reliant are more likely to sign the donation cards. Whether or not a person is willing to donate organs to save another person's life seems closely related to the individual's general attitude and personal fears and anxieties.

- *Stepping off the curb*
  Is there a relationship between state of mind and risk-taking behavior in everyday life? Laura Briscoe and I (1975) observed 125 people as

they crossed a busy street between the Detroit Art Institute and Wayne State University. There were equal numbers of street-crossers in five risk categories. People classified as Type A, the safest pedestrians, stood at the curb until the light changed in their favor, scanned traffic in both directions, entered the crosswalk, moved briskly across the street, and checked out traffic from the opposite direction lanes before reaching the halfway point. At the opposite extreme were Type E pedestrians, who crossed in the middle of the block, stepping out from between parked cars with the traffic lights against them, and did not look at traffic in either direction (miraculously, all twenty-five in this study did survive their crossings!). All street-crossers were interviewed when they reached the other side. The observed street-crossing behavior was closely related to the individual's general attitudes toward risk-taking. For example, the high-risk pedestrians also classified themselves as high-risk drivers and judged that they put their lives in jeopardy about 16 percent of the time in an average week, as compared with only 2 percent for Type A crossers. The Type E crossers were four times more likely than the Type A crossers to have contemplated or attempted suicide. They also reported a higher level of frustration with life. Within the limits of this study, it was clear that a person's general attitudes and feelings can be expressed in behavior choices that either increase or decrease the probability of death.

HUMANS ARE MORTAL: BUT WHAT DOES THAT HAVE TO DO WITH ME?

Our attitudes toward life and death are challenged when a person close to us dies. In *The Death of Ivan Ilych*, Leo Tolstoy provides an insightful portrait of the complexities, confusions, and urgencies that may afflict a survivor, as well as the dying person. Consider just one passage from a novel that has lost none of its pertinence and power over the past century:

The thought of the sufferings of the man he had known so intimately, first as a schoolmate, and later as a grown-up colleague, suddenly struck Peter Ivanovich with horror.... "Three days of frightful suffering, then death! Why, that might suddenly, at any moment, happen to me," he thought, and for a moment felt terrified. But—he himself did not know how—the customary reflection at once occurred to him, that this *had* happened to Ivan Ilych and not to him.... After which reflection Peter Ivanovich felt reassured, and began to ask with interest about the details of Ivan Ilych's death, as though death were an accident natural to Ivan Ilych, but certainly not to himself. (pp. 101–102)

Peter Ivanovich is a responsible adult who presumably knows that death is both inevitable and universal, sparing nobody. Yet we catch him, with Tolstoy's help, playing a desperate game of evasion. Consider some of the elements in Peter Ivanovich's response:

1. He already knows of Ivan Ilych's death; otherwise he would not have been participating in an obligatory paying of respects. But it is only on viewing the corpse that the realization of death strikes him. There is a powerful difference between intellectual knowledge and emotional impact or realization. For one alarming moment, Peter feels that he himself is vulnerable.

2. Peter Ivanovich immediately becomes concerned for Peter Ivanovich. His feelings do not center on the man who has lost his life or the woman who has lost her husband.

3. Yet he cannot admit that his outer line of defenses has been penetrated, that his personal anxieties have been triggered. He is supposed to show concern for others, not let them see his own distress. Furthermore, he hopes to leave this house of death with the confidence that death has, in fact, been left behind.

4. Peter Ivanovich's basic evasive technique here is the effort to *differentiate* himself from Ivan Ilych. Yes, some people really do die, but not people like him. The proof was in the fact that Peter was the vertical and mobile man while Ivan (that luckless, inferior specimen) was horizontal and immobile. We witness Peter Ivanovich, then, stretching and tormenting his logic in the hope of arriving at an anxiety-reducing conclusion.

5. Once Peter Ivanovich has quelled his momentary panic, he is able to discuss Ivan Ilych's death. Even so, he is more interested in factual details than in feelings and meanings. He has started to rebuild the barriers between himself and death. Whatever he learns about how his friend died will strengthen this barrier: all that was true of Ivan obviously is not applicable to him.

ANXIETY, DENIAL, AND ACCEPTANCE: THREE CORE CONCEPTS

Three concepts that are central to understanding death attitudes are interwoven through this excerpt from Tolstoy's masterpiece. Peter Ivanovich felt tense, distressed, and apprehensive. *Death anxiety* is the term most often applied to such responses. Anxiety is a condition that seeks its own relief. To reduce the painful tension, a person might try many different actions—taking drugs or alcohol, for example, or fleeing from the situation. One form of avoiding death anxiety has received most of the attention: *denial.* This is a response that rejects certain key features of reality in the attempt to avoid or reduce anxiety. "If I acknowledge X I will feel devastated—so X is not there." To distance himself from the death, Peter Ivanovich denies the basic fact that he is as mortal as Ivan Ilych.

Many writers have urged that we should *accept* death. This advice sounds positive and appealing. However, people are not always clear about what they mean by acceptance: for example, how does it differ from resignation or depression? Precisely what should we accept—and on whose authority? And what is it that makes acceptance the most desirable response? In Tolstoy's novel, Ivan Ilych eventually achieves a sense of acceptance, but Peter Ivanovich seems to be as self-deceived and befuddled as ever.

Anxiety, denial, and acceptance are not the only death attitudes that we encounter, although most research has concentrated on these concepts. Depression and a sense of loss are often experienced by people when death is in prospect. Although sorrow and anxiety have much in common, neither can be reduced to the other. Sorrow is oriented toward the past, anxiety toward the future. As an example of a more neglected phenomenon, some people attempt to reduce their own death anxieties by killing others, whether in reality or in games and fantasies. Perhaps researchers will give more attention to a wider spectrum of death attitudes in the future.

THEORIES AND STUDIES OF DEATH ANXIETY

Death anxiety is the most frequently studied topic by academic researchers. To develop a perspective on their findings it will be useful first to give some attention to theory and method.

How Is Death Anxiety Studied?

Most studies of death anxiety use self-report questionnaires. The most popular instrument is Donald Templer's *Death Anxiety Scale (DAS)* which consists of fifteen true/false items such as the following:

"I am very much afraid to die."
"The sight of a dead body is horrifying to me."
(Templer, 1970)

Respondents receive a total score based on the number of answers keyed in the direction of anxiety. Another often used instrument is the Collett-Lester scale (Lester, 1994) which has the advantage of providing separate scores for "death of self," "death of others," "dying of self," and "'dying of others." Self-report instruments such as these have the advantage of brevity, convenience, and simple quantitative results. What we actually learn from them, however, is limited by a number of problems, as I have addressed in more detail elsewhere (Kastenbaum, 2000). The most significant difficulties with death anxiety scales are as follows:

1. Little is learned about the respondent's overall attitude structure or belief system. Therefore death anxiety is taken out of context and difficult to interpret.
2. Low scores on death anxiety scales are especially difficult to interpret. Do they mean low anxiety or high denial? The scales themselves provide no way to make the distinction.
3. How high is high anxiety, and what is a "normal" level? The fact that an individual's score

is higher than that of most others does not by itself demonstrate that it is "too high"—too high for what? Little has been learned about the level of death anxiety that is most useful and adaptive in various situations.

4. Respondents too often are selected opportunistically. College students continue to be overrepresented (are you pleased to be so popular?), and members of ethnic and racial minorities continue to be underrepresented.

5. The typical study is a one-shot affair. How the same respondents might express their attitude at another time or in another situation is seldom explored.

6. No link is established between attitude and behavior. The findings do not tell us how people with low, average, or high scores will cope with real-life situations that involve dying, death, or grief.

Some useful innovations in self-report methodology (e.g., Neimeyer and Moore, 1994; Meshot & Leitner, 1994) are starting to yield valuable data. And, despite the limitations of most death anxiety studies, some findings are worth attention, especially when they have been obtained repeatedly. For more detail, see "Death in the Midst of Life," (Kastenbaum, 2000) and *Death Anxiety Handbook* (Neimeyer, 1994).

How Does Death Anxiety Influence Our Lives? Theoretical Perspectives

There are two classic theories of death anxiety, and they could hardly be more opposed to each other.

Sigmund Freud reasoned that we could not really be anxious about death:

> Our own death is indeed quite unimaginable, and whenever we make the attempt to imagine it we can perceive that we really survive as spectators... at bottom nobody believes in his own death, or to put the same thing in a different way, in the unconscious everyone of us is convinced of his own immortality. (1913/1953, p. 304)

Our "unconscious system" does not respond to the passage of time, so the end of personal time through death has no deep meaning. On the unconscious level, we do not have the concept of negation, so there is no death that can erase life. Furthermore, we have not actually experienced death, so what is there to fear?

The practical implication of Freud's view is that when we express "death anxiety," we are really experiencing some other kind of fear. For many years psychoanalysts spoke of *thanatophobia,* an expressed fear of death that serves as a disguise for some other source of discomfort. (Freud's view of death anxiety became more complex as he moved through life, but it is this "no death–no fear" concept that has been most influential.)

The *existential* position takes just the opposite approach. Awareness of our mortality is *the* basic source of anxiety. Our fears take many specific forms but can be traced back to our sense of vulnerability to death. A leading advocate of this view was Ernest Becker (1973). He argues that death anxiety is at the root of severe psychopathology, such as *schizophrenia.* The schizophrenic person suffers because he or she does not have enough insulation from the fear of death. If we are not devastated by death anxiety, it is because society works so hard to protect us from the realization of personal mortality.

One might say that a primary responsibility of society is to help us all pretend that life will continue to go on and on. Becker's writings have stimulated the development of *terror management theory* (Rosenblatt, Greenberg, Solomon, Pyszczynski, & Lyton. 1989), which suggests that we try to control our death anxiety by socially sanctioned evasions and fantasies. To put it crudely, society's job is to help each of us to pretend that we are safe, that death really doesn't have much to do with us. We agree to believe that we are protected by both our own self-esteem and our sense of belonging to a powerful entity greater than ourselves. A recent study found support for the proposition that people with higher self-esteem had less need to protect themselves against the breakthrough of death anxiety by relying on a culturally endorsed belief system (Harmon-Jones et al., 1997). There may be potential in the idea that we can find protection against death anxiety either by increasing our self-esteem or by investing heavily in reassuring sociocultural constructions of life and death. The other side also deserves consideration: we might become much more vulnerable to a death anxiety breakthrough if our society fails to offer reassuring beliefs.

A new theoretical approach has been offered recently by Tomer and Eliason (1996), who emphasize the regrets that people may have about what they have accomplished in life and what yet remains to them. According to this view, we are more likely to experience a high level of death anxiety if we perceive ourselves as not having made good use of the years through which we have already traveled. This anxiety is intensified when we also judge that we will not live long enough to accomplish our goals in the future. Death anxiety is therefore a function of past and future regrets. Is this death anxiety, or anxiety about having an incomplete life? Either way, the effect is the same. We are not as likely to stew about the quality of our lives if we see death as still being a safe distance away. When the prospect of personal death comes into sharp focus, however, we may become acutely concerned about all that we have not accomplished and all that we will not accomplish. Additionally, anxiety may be either increased or decreased by our interpretation of the meaning of death. As we will see in the next chapter, many interpretations of death exist, and each of these may have distinctive implications for anxiety arousal or reduction. The new "regrets" theory of death anxiety perhaps places too much emphasis on "accomplishments," as distinguished from relationships and other sources of strength and satisfaction. Nevertheless, one can only welcome a new approach that might lead to new understanding.

Along with these identifiable theoretical positions is the general belief among many counselors and educators that most people are afflicted with too high a level of death anxiety. As individuals and as a society we should learn to accept death as part of life and also acquire improved coping skills that will reduce our fears.

We will return briefly to these theoretical positions after a review of the research on death anxiety.

How Much Do We Fear Death?

Self-report studies consistently find a low to moderate level of death anxiety. This is consistent with responses to a Gallup Poll (1991) in which

three out of four adults declared that they did not fear death. Should we take these results at face value? Or should we suspect that most people are in the habit of suppressing their anxieties, trying to convince themselves and others that death holds no terror? The self-report studies themselves do not provide information that would enable us to decide between these competing answers. However we interpret the results, we find relatively little support for the proposition that most people consider themselves to be very anxious about death as they go about their everyday lives.

I am inclined to believe that the self-report instruments measure death anxiety only when the scores are very high—when the respondent is in a genuine state of alarm. If we really want to identify death anxiety, we may have to do what we should have been doing all along: make direct observations of emotional response and behavior in death-related situations.

Are There Gender Differences in Death Anxiety?

Women tend to have higher death anxiety scores on self-report scales. This finding has come out of many studies. Does this mean that women tend to be "too" anxious? Probably not. There is some evidence that women are more comfortable than men in dealing openly with their thoughts and feelings on many emotionally intense subjects.

Over the years, I have observed that women almost always outnumber men decisively in seminars and workshops that deal with dying, death, and grief. I have met many more women than men in hospice and other caregiving situations as well. If this is anxiety, perhaps we should be grateful for it, given that relatively few "low death anxiety" men have responded to these challenges. In any event, research findings reveal a gender difference but do not demonstrate that women are "too" anxious.

Are There Age Differences in Death Anxiety?

It is often assumed that anxiety increases as the distance between ourselves and death decreases. If this assumption is correct, elderly adults might

A typical scene in a death education course. Why are women more likely to enroll, or why are men less likely?

be expected to express a higher level of death anxiety. Not so. Self-report studies show either no age differences or somewhat lower death anxiety for elders. Again, this type of study does not tell us whether the lower scores represent greater acceptance or more effective denial.

Death anxiety tends to be relatively high in adolescence and early adulthood, decreasing as life becomes more settled and predictable. Death anxiety is likely to rise again in later middle age, perhaps occasioned by the death of friends and family and signs of one's own aging. After this rise, there is a decline to a new low in death anxiety for people in their seventies. This lifecourse pattern of death anxiety must be confirmed by studies that follow the same people throughout their lives. Almost all available studies are cross-sectional: different people at different ages. More information is also needed regarding the particu-

lar sources of death anxiety at various points in the lifecourse. An adolescent may fear sudden violent death, for example, while parents might fear primarily for their children's welfare if they should die. Thorson and Powell (1994) have found that adolescents tend to have strong death-related fears of decomposition, immobility, uncertainty, pain, helplessness, and isolation. By contrast, elderly adults are more likely to be concerned about loss of control, dependency, and the prospect of an afterlife.

Is Death Anxiety Related to Mental Health and Illness?

Death anxiety that is high enough to be disabling is a problem at any age and may warrant the attention of professional caregivers. Generally, self-reported death anxiety is somewhat higher in people with diagnosed psychiatric conditions. Furthermore, it is not uncommon for mental health workers to observe panic reactions centering around death fears on the part of their clients. The usual interpretation is that death anxiety rushes to the surface when a person's "ego defenses" are weakened and can no longer inhibit the impulses, fears, and fantasies that are ordinarily suppressed.

We should bear in mind, however, that death concern is not limited to people who are emotionally disturbed, nor to any one particular "type" of person. For example, it is not unusual for people to experience an upsurge of death anxiety when they realize how close they have come to being killed in a motor vehicle accident. The sudden, unexpected death of another person can also heighten one's own concern. Situations in which people feel alone and unprotected can also arouse a passing sense of separation anxiety, which for most purposes is indistinguishable from death anxiety.

There are both reasons to be anxious about death and reasons to keep our anxiety within bounds. People with a sound mental health status have learned to avoid the extremes of too much anxiety and too heavy a reliance on defenses against anxiety.

Does Religious Belief Lower or Raise Death Anxiety?

The influence of religion in death anxiety has been a subject of controversy for many years. Bronislaw Malinowski (1948), a notable anthropologist, interpreted his observations as demonstrating that religion has the basic function of reducing an individual's intense fear of death. That is really what religion is all about. A fellow anthropologist, A. R. Radcliffe-Brown (1952) came to just the opposite conclusion: religion gives rise to fear of evil spirits, punishment, torment, and hell. Both sets of observations are most directly based on preliterate societies and therefore do not answer the question of whether or not religion serves the same function in societies at a higher level of general development. Although there have been many studies on this topic, the results have not added up to a clear and coherent picture.

James M. Donovan (in press) has made an interesting attempt to combine these two proposi-

tions that seem so much at odds. He reminds us of the marked differences in the substance of religious belief from one society to another. In many tribal societies, death is believed to be followed by a life very similar to the one that has already been lived (this is the continuity model discussed in *Chapter 2*). There is little to fear from death, then; it is neither annihilation nor some frightening new state of being. By contrast, spirit possession is a major component in some religions, so interactions between the living and the dead are vital concerns. Some religious belief systems may therefore mitigate death anxiety and others heighten it. Donovan's field research in Brazil and his analysis of the literature leads him to the suggestion that it is the certitude of one's belief that may be most decisive:

> Yet all that really matters for the mitigation of death anxiety is that the individual have a firm commitment to some solution to the existential problems raised. Any solution, even one deemed awful or unattractive, is preferable to unresolvable incertitude. (Donovan, in press)

People who believe strongly in something that is not called "religion" may therefore be able to maintain a low level of death anxiety, while those who are weak or vacillating in their religious beliefs may experience sharper twinges of mortal fear.

Back to Death Anxiety Theory

Neither the Freudian nor the existential position on death anxiety has been validated by the available research. Both theories make assumptions that are difficult to subject to empirical investigation. How can we know with any degree of certainty what the "unconscious system" knows or does not know (even if we accept the reality of unconscious processes)? How can we prove that all anxieties have their roots in the fear of nonbeing? There are many useful observations in the writings of insightful psychoanalysts and existentialists (including existential psychoanalysts). We will probably have to devise theories that are closer to testable propositions if we wish to have a well-supported model of death anxiety. The "regrets" theory is untested but is starting to receive some research attention. There is room for other theories as well. I have proposed an *edge theory* that distinguishes between our everyday low level of death anxiety and the markedly different state aroused when we encounter danger (Kastenbaum, 2000). The experience of death anxiety is the self-awareness side of a complex organismic response to danger, to feeling ourselves to be at the very edge of the safe and known, perhaps just one step away from disaster. Edge theory emphasizes our survival and adaptation functions—the ability to detect sources of potential harm both through built-in biomechanisms and through the development of cognitive and social skills. There is no need to be anxious all the time, but it can be life-saving to move to an emergency footing when called for by the situation.

ACCEPTING AND DENYING DEATH

We now focus on death-related feelings, attitudes, and actions within our everyday lives.

Sitting in his favorite chair after dinner, the man suddenly went pale. He felt severe pain in his chest and had to gasp for breath. His wife was by his side in a moment. "What's wrong? Oh! I'll get the doctor, the hospital…" The man struggled for control and waved his hand feebly in a dismissive gesture. "It's nothing—really…I'll just lie down til it goes away."

This scene, with variations, has been repeated often enough to become well recognized by professional caregivers. The concept of denial may come to mind when a person has delayed seeking diagnosis and treatment for a life-threatening condition. Accepting the reality of serious illness might help to extend that person's life. Both denial and acceptance show their true power in real-life situations such as the one just sketched rather than in self-report questionnaires.

Types and Contexts of Acceptance and Denial

"Acceptance" and "denial" are used in a variety of ways, and sometimes their meanings become so blurred that they mislead more than they help. From a psychiatric standpoint, *denial* is regarded as a primitive defense, perhaps the most primitive of all. Denial rejects the existence of threat. This kind of defense is available to infants and children long before they develop more adequate ways to cope with stress and threat. Basic denial is a strategy that may be effective for a short period of time, and for situations in which there is one particular overwhelming threats. This strategy becomes increasingly ineffective when prolonged or used repeatedly: we do not survive long in this world when we ignore crucial aspects of reality. Denial is most often found among people who are suffering from a psychotic reaction, or as any person's first response to crisis and catastrophe.

Denial in this basic sense is not usually part of our everyday repertoire of coping strategies, but we do engage in a number of behaviors that look more or less like denial. There has been a widespread tendency to speak of all forms of resistance or evasive action as though they were denial. "Oh, she's just in denial!" By using this term as a buzzword, we often come to glib and premature conclusions. Usually, the person is not "denying" in the psychiatric sense of the term: a primitive and ineffective mechanism. Rather, the person is more likely to be coping with a difficult situation in the most resourceful way he or she can discover at the moment. This will become clearer as we distinguish among several process, all of which can be mistaken for denial (*see Box 1-1*)

1. *Selective attention.* Imagine a situation in which many stimuli and events are competing for our attention. We cannot give equal attention to everything that is going on. A person who has never been in a hospital before, for example, might find many new, interesting, and challenging things to observe. These may seem more vivid and perceptually real than something as abstract as the diagnosis and prognosis that eventually will be made. This often happens with children. The individual is not "in denial," but simply directing his or her attention to whatever seems most salient in the immediate situation.

2. *Selective response.* Persons exhibiting this behavior may have significant thoughts and feelings about death, but they have judged that this is not the time or place to express them. "I'm not going to open up to this young doctor who looks more scared than I am," the person may think. Or, "There is nothing effec-

---

> **BOX 1-1**
> **DENIAL AND DENIAL-LIKE RESPONSES TO DEATH**
>
> - Selective attention   "I will feel less anxious if I don't allow myself to notice some things."
>
> - Selective response   "It would be better if I did not let others know how I feel right now."
>
> - Compartmentalizing   "One subtracted from one will not be zero as long as I keep these two numbers separate from each other."
>
> - Deception   "I will deliberately mislead you in order to reduce your anxiety and mine."
>
> - Resistance   "Of course I know that my life is in danger—but I'm not going to give in to it in any way."
>
> - Denial   "A touch of indigestion, that's all."

---

tive I can do about the situation at this moment, so I will talk about something else or just keep quiet." The person may also decide that "There is something very important I must accomplish while I still have the opportunity, and it must take priority over dealing with my death." Therefore, people who may seem to be denying their death might actually be working very hard at completing tasks, in full awareness that time is running out.

3. *Compartmentalizing.* The individual is aware of being in a life-threatening situation and responds to some aspects of this situation. However, something is missing: the connection between one aspect of the situation and another. For example, the person may know that the prognosis is poor. This is an accurate perception; no denial is involved. The person may also be cooperating with treatment and discussing the situation rationally (adaptive response and still no denial). Yet the same person may be making future plans that involve travel and vigorous exercise, as if expecting to be around and in good health for years to come. In compartmentalizing, much of the dying and death reality is acknowledged, but the person stops just short of *realizing* the situation. All of the pieces are there,

but the individual resists putting them together to complete the picture.

4. *Deception.* People sometimes deliberately give false information to others, and this can happen in dying and death situations. When people are telling each other lies (for whatever purpose), it makes sense to acknowledge this deceptive action for what it is and not confuse the issue with the buzzword "denial."

5. *Resistance.* People who are in stressful situations may recognize their danger but decide not to "give in" to it. Some people in war-torn Bosnia, for example, decided to go about their daily rounds of shopping and visiting although these activities increased their vulnerability to snipers. These people were not denying the death risk. Rather, they had resolved to defy the war and keep their spirits up by not becoming prisoners of fear. A person who has been diagnosed with an incurable medical condition might become angry instead of anxious. "I'll show them!" And sometimes, as we all know, a person with an apparently terminal condition does recover. There is a significant difference between a person who cannot accept the reality of his or her jeopardy and one who comprehends the reality but decides to fight for life as long as possible.

Is it really life as usual in Pristina, Kosovo after the guns have fallen silent? Trying to get on with life is one of the most adaptive responses to bereavement and trauma even though people are intensely aware of both their losses and the continuing threat. A British member of the NATO force stands guard.

6. *Denial* (the real thing). This is the basic defensive process defined earlier. The individual is not just selecting among possible perceptions and responses, limiting the logical connections between one phenomenon and the other or engaging in conscious deception. Rather, the self appears to be totally organized against recognizing death-laden reality. Such an orientation can be bizarre and may accompany a psychotic reaction. It does not have to be that extreme, however. We can sometimes detect the existence of a true denial process that weaves in and out of other, more sophisticated ways of coping.

Temporary denial responses can be experienced by anybody who is under extreme stress. Denial responses are often seen in the wake of overwhelming catastrophes. For example, a woman was discovered intently sweeping the floor of her home after a tornado had passed through the city; the floor was practically all that was left of her home. Another woman was so debilitated by her long illness that she could no longer take nourishment by mouth or carry out other basic activities of everyday life. She had participated actively in decisions about her impending death: cremation, a simple memorial service, gifts to her church's youth program in lieu of flowers, and so forth. One morning, though, she astonished her visitors by showing them a set of travel brochures and her new sunglasses. She spoke of feeling so much better and being very eager to take a long-delayed vacation. Two days later she was dead.

The Interpersonal Side of Acceptance and Denial

Each person in a dying and death situation influences and is influenced by others. The process of acceptance and denial therefore is both interpersonal and *intrapsychic*. Change the interpersonal dynamics, and the dynamics of acceptance and denial are also likely to change. Furthermore, both the immediate situation and the historical background must be considered. One man may come from an ethnic background that treats dying and death in a straightforward manner: the Amish, for example. But suppose that person finds himself dealing with a medical establishment in which death is still a high-anxiety, taboo topic: here is a potential death accepter trapped among the deniers. The reverse also happens. Consider a woman who grew up learning how to deny death, especially the deeper emotions associated with it. Suppose that she becomes a patient in a more liberated health care establishment in which the staff is relentless in practicing its belief that we must be open and sharing with each other. Here, then, is the denier confronted by the accepters. To understand what is taking place between the dying person and the caregiver, we must be aware of the forces operating in the present situation and the individual's previous life pattern.

Weisman (1972) has observed that a person does not usually deny everything about death to everybody. More often, a selective process is involved. We must go beyond the question, "Is this person denying death?" It is more useful to ask instead, "What aspects of dying or death are being shared with what other people, under what circumstances and why?" The same questions could be asked about acceptance. A person might "deny" with one friend and "accept" with another. Apparent denial on the part of a patient may derive from a lack of responsive people in the environment.

A related point has to do with the *function* of so-called denial. "The purpose of denial," writes Weisman, "is not simply to avoid a danger, but to prevent loss of a significant relationship." All of the adaptive processes that have been described here might be used, then, to help the other person feel comfortable enough to maintain a vitally needed relationship. An individual faced with death may have to struggle as much with another person's anxiety as with his or her own. Instead of placing the negative label of denial upon these adaptive efforts, we might instead appreciate the care and sensitivity with which they are carried out.

Anxiety, Denial, and Acceptance: How Should We Respond?

Anxiety is an uncomfortable, at times almost unbearable condition. It would be a mistake, however, to consider anxiety as either completely negative or completely useful. Small doses of anxiety can alert us to danger: "Something's wrong here—what?" It can also prepare us for action: "I've been on stage a thousand times, and been a bundle of nerves a thousand times—but that's just how I want to feel before the curtain goes up!"

The response strategies of acceptance and denial likewise are not necessarily good or bad in themselves. We must examine the contexts in which these processes are used and the purposes they seem to be serving. If what we are calling denial really *is* denial, we may be dealing with a person who is making a desperate stand against catastrophe. He or she has been forced to fall back on a primitive defense process that rejects important aspects of reality. This person needs psychological help and, quite possibly, other types of help as well.

On the other hand, the person may not be denying so much as selectively perceiving, linking, and responding to what is taking place. This pattern of coping with difficult reality may have its evasive aspects at certain times with certain people, but there is method, judgment, and purpose at work. Even flashes of pure denial may contribute to overall adaptation, such as when challenges come too swiftly, last too long, or are too overwhelming to meet in other ways. A little later, the individual may find another way to deal with the same challenge, once the first impact has been partially deflected and partially absorbed.

I suggest that we proceed with the following set of premises:

1. Most of us have both acceptance and denial strategies available for coping with stressful situations. These strategies may operate within or outside our clear awareness, and one strategy or the other may dominate at various times.
2. States of total acceptance and total denial of death do occur, but they usually occur in extreme circumstances: when the individual is letting go of life after achieving a sense of completion and having struggled as long as

struggling seemed worthwhile, or when the individual is resisting the first onslaught of catastrophic reality.

3. Much of what is loosely spoken of as denial can be understood more adequately as adaptive processes through which the person responds selectively to various aspects of a difficult situation.

4. The individual's pattern of adaptation should be considered within the context of the acceptance and denial that characterize the larger interpersonal network of which he or she is a part.

5. Acceptance and denial can be evaluated only when we are in a position to understand what the person is trying to accomplish and what he or she is up against.

Another Kennedy Died: How Did We Respond?

The plane crash that ended the lives of John F. Kennedy, Jr.; his wife, Carolyn; and her sister, Lauren Bessette, on July 16, 1999, aroused some of the same feelings of shock and sadness that occur whenever people die so suddenly and unexpectedly. These deaths, like many others, had both a personal and a public side. Those who were very close to the deceased had to deal with the intense grief that followed the loss of people who had been a significant part of their own lives. In this case, though, the public response was not only on a much larger scale but also more complex than usual. How did the family and the public respond to these deaths? Following are some points to consider.

• People differed in their readiness to believe that Kennedy and his two passengers had died in the crash. Aviation and rescue experts almost immediately concluded that there could be no survivors, given the circumstances. Some people who felt emotionally attached to the Kennedy family, even if they had little or no personal contact with them, continued to believe in the possibility of their survival until the bodies were actually found. The core family, however, recognized the facts as soon as they became evident. There was little evasion and no denial.

Much has been written about our inclination to avoid facing up to death, but not

enough has been learned about the ability of some individuals and families to accept even the most traumatic news. The Kennedy family had suffered a series of tragic deaths throughout the years and had somehow learned to face and cope with these realities.

• Rescue efforts continued despite the general belief that there were no survivors. Even a very small chance of possible survival was enough to motivate continued efforts. The government, with public support, invested resources, and rescue experts risked their own lives. Note that it is possible to hold one proposition ("They are almost certainly dead,") while at the same time acting upon another ("We must do everything we can, no matter what the effort, risk, and expense"). Just a flickering of hope can be enough to continue efforts intended to preserve life, as we see in many other situations.

Yet sometimes cost effectiveness considerations outweigh attempts to preserve or protect life. Health organizations, for example, have been criticized for denying the most effective treatments to some of their clients because of the expense involved, and a major automobile manufacturer has been charged with manufacturing vehicles with unsafe fuel tanks because it would have cost another eight dollars per car to make them safe. Choices are made every day: should we do all that we can to protect and preserve life or do only what is "cost effective"? In the very special case of the Kennedy party, the decision was not difficult to make, but what happens to people who are not perceived as "very special"?

• Recovery operations continued until the bodies were found. Why was it thought necessary to invest this additional effort and expense when it was already clear that there were no survivors? We often find it difficult to comprehend emotionally that somebody close to us has died if the death occurred someplace else and the body is not available for viewing. Many experts believe that the grieving process cannot really begin until we have the emotional realization that the person really is dead. Furthermore, the family and community often feel that they must respect and honor the deceased person by conducting the funeral and memorialization rituals called for by their belief system. A family that does not have the opportunity to do what it considers right and proper for the deceased may be haunted by this failure throughout their lives.

Against this background, the response of the Kennedy family was extraordinary: they accepted the deaths and started to deal with the loss soon after it occurred, not having to wait until the bodies were recovered. Like any other family, the Kennedys were comforted to have the bodies returned for proper burial, but their previous history of repeated tragedies had prepared them to absorb the trauma of another sudden death through an all-too-experienced family support network.

- The media's quest for meaning and explanation was intense. How did this terrible thing happen? What does it mean? Who was to blame? Sudden, unexpected death frequently produces anxious questions of this kind. The underlying reason may be our tendency to believe that death should occur only to certain people (not like us) in certain ways (not like that), and in other places (not here). The sudden, unexpected death of vibrant young people punctures for a moment our illusions that death follows our rules and preferences. One seldom hears the same questions being raised when an aged person dies after a long illness. It is not just the death—it is the threat to our own sense of safety and control that stimulates the uneasy questioning.

Furthermore, it does not seem "fair" that people so full of life should die before they have had the opportunity to experience and achieve all that is within them. This is another understandable source of distress, but it is also another clue to our tendency to construct death according to our own needs and rules. In this case, many efforts were made to attribute blame for the deaths: perhaps inadequate information from the weather service, perhaps inadequate maintenance of the plan, perhaps John F. Kennedy's inexperience as a pilot, and so on. Death becomes somewhat less disturbing if we have or believe we have a solid explanation.

- There was also a quest for a "silver lining," that is, something positive that might come from the tragedy. It may be just too painful to accept that such a devastating loss could have happened by

accident, therefore be seen as "meaningless," and also have no redeeming qualities. We have a strong tendency to discover or invent some compensating feature, something that allows us to "reframe" the deaths in a more positive way. The intense quest for such a silver lining was not successful in this case, and the effort was soon abandoned.

- Significant generational differences were observed in the responses to these deaths. People who remembered John F. Kennedy and Robert Kennedy felt more involved with the recent deaths than did many younger people, who lacked this emotional connection and historical perspective. The "same" death is not perceived by everybody in the same way, because each of us brings our own background and needs to that perception.
- A death is not only the end of a life, but it may also have powerful consequences for the future. In this case, a lingering fantasy was destroyed. Some people hoped that another Kennedy might some day be in the White House, with "John-John" being the most likely prospect. This future scenario died on July 16, 1999.
- For about a week, the media inundated us with images and words about John F. Kennedy, Jr. and the fatal crash. It was THE story. It was the only important thing. A few days later, however, the media were off to newer disasters and scandals. The high-powered, short attention span of the media in our society differs greatly from the enduring griefs with which many of us live.

These brief comments about one episode will perhaps serve to prepare us for our consideration of the variety of thoughts, feelings, and actions that we engage in as individuals and as a society when a mortal twinge comes our way.

SUMMARY

Life is supposed to go on. Why pause to think of death? It is useful to remind ourselves of some the ways in which death breaks into our awareness: catastrophic accidents, acts of terrorism and violence, the vulnerability of children, and the limitations of even our state-of-the-art health care system. Not thinking about death has been a failed experiment. Listening and communicating are far more helpful approaches. You monitored your own knowledge, attitudes, beliefs, and feelings about death in a series of self-inventories. These exercises provided you with a stronger base for looking at the way other people think about death and at how state of mind can affect death-related behavior.

We explored the dynamics of accepting and denying death with the help of characters in Leo Tolstoy's probing novel, *The Death of Ivan Ilych*, and then looked carefully at the core concepts of anxiety, denial, and acceptance. Freudian and existential theory offer competing ideas about death anxiety and its place in our lives. More recent theoretical approaches and empirical studies provide further information but also raise some questions that have not yet been answered adequately. One of the most consistent findings is that people generally report themselves to have a low to moderate level of death anxiety, with women having somewhat higher scores. We also saw that "denial" of death is a term often used too loosely. Some responses that are misinterpreted as denial are better understood as selective attention, selective response, compartmentalizing, deception, or resistance. Attention was also given to the kinds of interactions we have with each other in death-related situations, and some suggestions were offered. We concluded by identifying some of the complex thoughts, feelings, and attitudes that emerged after the deaths of John F. Kennedy, Jr., his wife, and his sister-in-law in a recent plane crash. Although this was a unique tragic event, the responses can help prepare us to understand the many other ways in which individuals and society attempt to cope with death.

REFERENCES

Associated Press (1996: May 11). Oklahoma City rescuer kills self.

Becker, E. (1973). *The denial of death*. New York: Free Press.

Doka, K. J. (1993). *Grief*. In R. Kastenbaum & B. K. Kastenbaum (Eds.), *Encyclopedia of death* (pp. 127–131). New York: Avon.

Donovan, J. M. (in press). Reevaluating the curvilinear relationship between religion and death anxiety. *Omega, Journal of Death and Dying*.

Evans, R. W. (1993). Organ procurement expenditures and the role of financial incentives. *Journal of the American Medical Association, 269:* 3113–3118.

Farberow, N. L. (1993). Suicide. In R. Kastenbaum & B. K. Kastenbaum (Eds.), *Encyclopedia of death* (pp. 227–230). New York: Avon.

Frager, G. (1996). Bearing witness. In C. K. Cassel (Ed.), *Caring for the dying: Identification and promotion of physician competency* (p. 41). Washington, DC: American Board of Internal Medicine.

Franks, P., Clancy, C. M., & Gold, M. R. (1993). Health insurance and mortality. *Journal of the American Medical Association, 270,* 737–741.

Freud, S. (1913/1953). Thoughts for the times on war and death. In *Collected Works* (Vol. IV, pp. 288–317). London: Hogarth Press.

Gallup Poll. *Fear of Dying* (1991).

Hanzlick, R. (1993). Improving accuracy of death certificates. *Journal of the American Medical Association, 269,* 2850.

Harmon-Jones, E., Simon, L., Greenberg, J., Pyszczynski, T., Solomon, S., & McGregor, H. (1997). Terror management theory and self-esteem: Evidence that increased self-esteem reduces mortality salience effects. *Journal of Personality and Social Psychology, 73,* 24–31.

Hayslip, B. (1986–1987). The measurement of communication apprehension regarding the terminally ill. *Omega, Journal of Death and Dying, 17,* 251–261.

Johnson, C. L. et al. (1993). Declining serum total cholesterol levels among US adults, *Journal of the American Medical Association, 269:* 3002–3008.

Kastenbaum, R. (1993a). Hospice: Philosophy and practice. In R. Kastenbaum & B. K. Kastenbaum (Eds.), *Encyclopedia of death* (pp. 143–147). New York: Avon.

Kastenbaum, R. (1993b). Cremation. In R. Kastenbaum & B. K. Kastenbaum (Eds.), *Encyclopedia of death* (pp. 57–60). New York: Avon.

Kastenbaum, R. (1993c). Death penalty. In R. Kastenbaum & B. K. Kastenbaum (Eds.), *Encyclopedia of death* (pp. 57–60). New York: Avon.

Kastenbaum, R. (1993d). Cryonic suspension. In R. Kastenbaum & B. K. Kastenbaum (Eds.), *Encyclopedia of death* (pp. 61–66). New York: Avon.

Kastenbaum, R., & Briscoe, L. (1975). The street corner: A laboratory for the study of life-threatening behavior. *Omega, Journal of Death and Dying, 7:* 351–359.

Kastenbaum, R. (2000). *The Psychology of Death*. (3rd ed.). New York: Springer.

Klass, D. (1988). *Parental grief*. New York: Springer.

Lester, D. (1994). The Collett-Lester fear of death scale. In R. A. Neimeyer (Ed.), *Death anxiety handbook* (pp. 45–60). Washington, DC: Francis & Taylor.

McClain, J. D. (1993, Oct. 2). How Americans die on the job. Washington, DC: *Associated Press* news release.

McIntosh, J. (1993). Suicide: Native Americans. In R. Kastenbaum & B. K. Kastenbaum (Eds.), *Encyclopedia of death* (pp. 238–239). New York: Avon.

Meshot, C. M., & Leitner, L. M. (1994). Death threat, parental loss, and interpersonal style: A personal construct investigation. In R. A. Neimeyer (Ed.), *Death anxiety handbook* (pp. 181–192). Washington, DC, Taylor & Francis.

Munroe, T. (1999: July 21). Kennedy likely lost control in final moments. Reuters report.

National Center for Health Statistics (1999). Washington, DC: United States Public Health Service.

Neimeyer, R. A. & Moore, M. K. (1994). Validity and reliability of the Multidimensional Fear of Death Scale. In R. A. Neimeyer (Ed.), *Death anxiety handbook*, pp. 103–120. Washington, DC. Taylor & Francis.

Neimeyer, R. A. (Ed.) (1994). *Death anxiety handbook.* Washington, DC: Taylor & Francis.

Nuland, S. B. (1993). *How We Die.* New York: Alfred A. Knopf.

Quill, T. E. (1993). *Death and dignity.* New York: Free Press.

Radcliffe-Brown, A. R. (1952). *Structure and function in primitive society.* New York: Free Press.

Robbins, R. A. (1990). Signing an organ donor card: Psychological factors. *Death Studies, 14,* 219–230.

Rosenblatt, A., Greenberg, J., Solomon, S., Pyszczynski, T., & Lyton, D. (1989). Evidence for terror management theory: I. The effects of mortality salience on reactions to those who violate or uphold cultural values. *Journal of Personality and Social Psychology, 57,* 681–690.

Siegel, M. (1993). Involuntary smoking in the restaurant workplace. *Journal of the American Medical Association, 270,* 490–493.

Silverman, P. L. (1994). Philips L. Silverman: An Omega interview. *Omega, Journal of Death and Dying, 28,* 251–260.

Tomer, A., & Eliason, G. (1996). Toward a comprehensive model of death anxiety. *Death Studies, 20,* 343–366.

Templer, D. I. (1970). The construction and validation of a death anxiety scale. *Journal of General Psychology, 82,* 165–177.

Thurson, J. S., & Powell, F. C. (1994). A revised death anxiety scale. In R. A. Neimeyer (Ed.) *Death anxiety handbook* (pp. 31–44). Washington, DC: Taylor & Francis.

Tolstoy, L. (1960). *The death of Ivan Ilych.* New York: The New American Library. (Original work, 1886).

VandeCreek, L., & Frankowski, D. (1996). Barriers that predict resistance to completing a living will. *Death Studies, 20,* 73–82.

Weisman, A. D. (1972). *On dying and denying.* New York: Behavioral Publications, Inc.

World Health Organization (1990). Statistical report.

Yip, R., & Sharp, T. W. (1993). Acute malnutrition and high childhood mortality related to diarrhea. *Journal of the American Medical Association, 270,* 587–590.

GLOSSARY

Anatomical Gift Act: A law that permits people to designate their body organs for transplantation to another person upon their own death.

Coroner: A physician who functions on behalf of a governmental agency to regulate and, when necessary, investigate the condition of human corpses. The same functions may be carried out by a physician with the title of medical examiner.

Death Anxiety: Emotional distress and insecurity aroused by encounters with dead bodies, grieving people, or other reminders of mortality, including one's own thoughts.

Denial: An extreme response in which one attempts to cope with danger or loss by ignoring important features of reality.

Existentialism: A philosophical position that emphasizes people's responsibilities for their own lives and deaths.

Fatalism: The belief that future events have already been determined; therefore, one is powerless to affect the future.

Hospice: (1) A program of care devoted to providing comfort to terminally ill people through a team approach, with participation by family members. (2) A facility in which such care is provided.

Intrapsychic: Events that occur within a person's mind, for example, thoughts, images, feelings, memories, and dreams.

Living Will: A document that specifies for medical personnel an individual's wishes in case a situation arises in which that person cannot communicate directly. Almost always involves a request to limit the type of medical interventions. The living will is one of a class of documents known as *advance directives.*

Patient Self Determination Act: A federal law requiring that health care organizations ask patients whether they have a living will or other instructions for their care in the event of a life-threatening situation.

Schizophrenia: A form of mental and perhaps biomedical illness in which a person is out of contact with reality and emotionally alienated from others.

Self-Efficacy: The ability of a person to act competently in meeting needs and pursuing goals.

Thanatophobia: Fear of death.

Terror Management Theory: A theory based on the proposition that many of our sociocultural beliefs, symbols, and practices are intended to reduce our sense of vulnerability and helplessness.

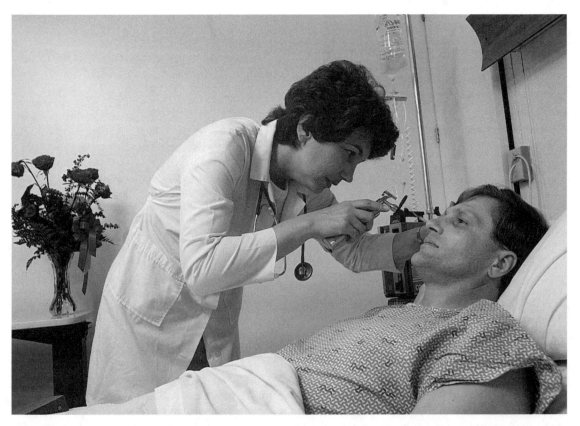

Ophthalamoscopes are used routinely to evaluate the health of our eyes, but also may be called on to determine signs of death.

chapter 2

WHAT IS DEATH?

What does death mean?

Scenes related to death crowd the movies of our culture. Sensational and violent death, actually presented or hinted at via threat or risk, dominates all other presentations of death.... This distortion of death is compounded by sensationalized reactions to death, primarily aggression, fear, shock, injury and escape.... These films rarely show parallels to the reality of death experiences faced by average Americans.
—Ned W. Schultz & Lisa M. Huet, in press

None of the commonly accepted signs of death can be fully relied upon to answer the question, "Is this person really dead?"
—Jack Kevorkian, M.D. 1961, p. 54

Even though a person may be "dead" because his heart stops working, some muscle, skin and bone cells may live on for many days. So, while the entire person as a functioning organism is dead, parts of the biologic organism live on for varying periods of time. The amount of time these cells and tissues live depends on their ability to survive without oxygen and other nutrients, and with an increasing amount of metabolic waste products building up within them...Then when is a person dead?
—Kenneth V. Iserson, M.D., 1994, p. 3

The EEG is flat and there is a complete absence of spontaneous respiration.
—From the Harvard Criteria, 1968

Then, when lust hath conceived, it bringeth forth sin; and Sin, when it is finished, bringeth forth death."
—New Testament, James: 1:15

So death, the most terrifying of ills, is nothing to us, since so long as we exist, death is not with us, but when death comes, then we do not exist. It does not then concern either the living or the dead, since for the former it is not and the latter are no more.
—Epicurus, 3rd century B.C.

"Death? It's a change of clothes. That's all!"
—Interview respondent

COMPETING IDEAS ABOUT THE NATURE AND MEANING OF DEATH

Were all these people talking about the same thing? Clearly, they were not talking about death in the same way. It is risky to assume that everybody has the same idea about what death is and what death should mean to us. Some of these alternative and contradictory views may even exist side by side in our own minds, acquired in different circumstances in our lives and never really examined for consistency. We begin, then, by looking at some competing ideas about the nature and meaning of death.

We ask: what is this *death* that one person "accepts" and another "denies?" That one person seeks and another avoids? That one person cannot stop thinking about and another believes is hardly worth thinking about?

Not only do individuals differ in their attitudes and feelings, but the same person may differ from situation to situation—as when I noticed that the starboard engine of the ancient DC-3 had burst into flame. "Death" was no longer a word for scholarly contemplation, but the vivid prospect of a rapid plunge into the green hills of West Virginia. Many survivors of near-death experiences have reported an enduring change in their conceptions of death and life alike (*see Chapter 13*). There are practical consequences to the fact that death can mean different things to different people, or to the same person at different times. If you and I hold varying assumptions about the nature of death, we may also take different courses of action at decisive moments.

"When," "What," and "Why" Questions about Death

Most questions about death center around the "when," the "what," or the "why." In the health care system today many people seem concerned most about the "when" of death. Is this *body* still alive? Is this *person* still alive? There are compelling reasons for this focus on the moment in which death intersects life. Medical, administrative, and legal processes will go into different modes of operation, depending upon the way that Dr. Iserson's question is answered. Many stressful family–physician situations and many cases brought into the judicial system are concerned with the "when" question. Advances in biomedical technology have created new possibilities and new dilemmas. It is for this reason that we will be examining biomedical perspectives on the definition of death, including the influential Harvard Criteria excerpted above.

It is rather new in history for the "when" question to receive so much attention. Through the centuries, there has been more interest in the "what" and "why" of death, and these questions remain with us, along with the competing answers. The traditional "what" and "why" issues have not been resolved by the biomedical specialists. It is up to us to come to our own conclusions.

In the third century B.C., *Epicurus* offered a philosophy that has continued to influence many people from ancient times to the present. (An attractive way to become familiar with this view is to read *On the Nature of Things,* the narrative poem in which Lucretius articulates many of Epicurus' ideas.) Epicurus did not traffic in gods and mysteries. Instead, he argued that the universe comprises atoms in motion, and that our own actions—indeed, our innermost thoughts and feelings—are determined by the pattern of past events. We live and die in a materialistic universe. What, then, is death? It's really not much of anything—simply one more event in a long sequence of events that have no intrinsic meaning or value. We never actually experience death, and the fact of death does not violate any contract we might imagine that the gods have cosigned with us.

How, then, should one live? A wise person appreciates life and maintains a sense of balance and proportion. We are not major players in a great cosmic drama. We just happen to be here for a while and then become again part of the vapor from which we arose. A depressing view? Not for Epicurus, at least. He formed a community known as The Garden, in which like-minded people—women as well as men, poor as well as rich, slaves as well as free citizens—lived in equality and friendship (this community endured for about 500 years). He offered a model for harmonious living within a universe that does not seem to care about either our lives or our deaths, but most people prefer a version in which the universe is rule-abiding and purposeful and in which human lives and deaths do count for something. The Christian version has met this need for many people over many years.

The *New Testament* is a collection of selected writings that tell the story of Christ's life and teachings. The story is told somewhat differently from one gospel to the next, and a bewildering variety of interpretations has been offered by preachers and Biblical scholars. It is not surprising that the Christian message regarding death can be read as simple or complex, depending much on the reader's preference. The quotation from James delivers one facet of this message. Lust—sexual feeling, thought, and activity—is associated with death. Before the emergence of Christianity, other religions in the ancient world had emphasized a connection between withering

away and fertility. Life was regenerated through death. Careful observance of rituals might persuade the gods to allow crops to succeed and babies to thrive. Sacrifices (human or animal) could also help matters along—a little death here and there to facilitate life.

The Christian version was different, however: it specified that sexuality itself is sinful and carries the death penalty. A person responsive to this facet of the Christian message may find it difficult to think about sexuality without also thinking about death. Within this frame of reference, virginity and abstinence have theological resonances. Suicide and martyrdom, especially in earlier eras, were seen by some Christians as an appropriate alternative to or consequence of sexual activity other than that necessary for procreation within the bounds of marriage. Not only the "deathification of sex," but also the "sexualization of death" have been consequences of the concept put forth in the gospel of James and other passages in the New Testament. A passionate and mystical union with God became an increasingly dominant theme in the version of Christianity that became known to the world through the interpretations of *Paul the Convert* (Segal, 1990). At the same time, sexual union between two humans and their bonds of attachment were seen as less spiritual and worthy. Long before celibacy became a requirement for priests, there was a strong advocacy for choosing religious devotion over sexual relationships. Not all Christians favor this intertwining view of death and sexuality, but it is undeniably an influential part of the tradition.

The man who said death is "a change of clothes. That's all!" identifies himself with a current social movement in the United States that is often called "New Age" (although the individuals themselves sometimes reject this term). In this view, life is a journey through multiple lives. Death is not an ending; it is a transition, a doorway through which one passes on the way to the next life. This conception clearly differs from the others. Unlike Epicurus and other atomists, life and death are purposeful—there is a point to it all, and a progression. Unlike the New Testament view, death is not a punishment for sexuality or for anything else. A flat EEG is not impressive, because the life and death of the spirit are not seen as byproducts of brain activity. By whatever name we might choose to describe this approach, New Age bookshelves offer many treatises about a life of the spirit that is not stilled by death. We will look again at this approach when we consider reincarnation as an answer to the question of survival of death (*see Chapter 13*).

Some contemporary scholars see death as a *symbolic construction.* What is death? An idea, a concept. Something our minds have constructed from our experiences, our guesswork, our needs, and our ignorance. Death is therefore subject to the same rules and limitations as any other concept. This does not mean that death is unreal or fictitious. Death is a concept we need because it has so many important referents, associations, and consequences. Note, for example, that water is also a concept. We look at ice, snow, mist, rain, standing pools, and flowing streams and write the formula H_2O on the board, calling them all "water," even though the forms seem so different. Water is not simply something that presents itself to our eyes, but also a useful concept. When we try to determine the difference between "alive" and "dead" and to define death itself, we are dealing with symbolic constructions. We are working with the words, concepts, and ways of thinking available to us in a particular society at a particular time.

Pernick (1988) describes the changing ways in which experts have attempted to define death. Medical discoveries have been challenging our conceptions of death for centuries, present-day uncertainties and controversies are not as new as they might seem. For example, a century ago some doctors had observed that vegetative life could continue for extended periods of time in people who had permanently lost consciousness. These and other observations have raised questions not only about the nature of "dead" and "death," but also about what is means to be a person.

What are the moral and practical implications of the symbolic construction view of death? We are left with the feeling that "dead" and "death" are concepts still under construction, still subject to question, challenge, and revision. For example, I have often had to sort out my own observations and feelings at the bedside of an unresponsive person who has been given little or no hope of recovery. If I judge that this person is dead (as a person), I do not have much reason to attempt to communicate with him or her. If I judge, how-

ever, that I cannot really know this person's state of being with any assurance, I might well choose to attempt to communicate as best I can. Symbolic constructions of death may lead us to either increased or reduced interactions.

Some of the most influential constructions of death in our society come from movies and television productions. The average person today is less likely to have direct, unfiltered encounters with dying and death than in the past. At the same time, we are frequently exposed to depictions of dying and death in the movies. A recent study by Schultz and Huet (in press) examined twenty-five popular films, sixteen popular/award films, and twenty-four award films. Trained observers categorized the number and type of death events, including the responses of others to the deaths. As reported in the opening quotation, most deaths were presented in a sensational and violent manner. Seldom were we shown anything resembling the actual course of dying and death experienced by most people in our society. Encouragingly, perhaps, films that had received awards for special merit were much more likely to include expressions of sorrow and sadness. Gender differences were striking: male characters were six times more likely to instigate death, and female characters were twice as likely to be the victims. The authors conclude that "In American film, death is distorted into a sensational stream of violent attacks by males, with fear, injury, further aggression and the absence of normal grief reactions as the most common response."

What, then, would a person think who knew death only from the movies? Death must be the result of anger and brutal assault by men, mostly against women. Furthermore, people usually don't spend a lot of time feeling sad—they're too busy getting ready to get even. We will see (*Chapter 10*) that it takes a while for children to understand that death is not always intentional or accidental, but something that will befall everybody in one way or another. A child's attempt to understand the nature and meaning of death is certainly not assisted by the aggressive and violent constructions of death in popular movies.

The ideas about death that we have sampled have recently taken on a more urgent aspect. "Right to die" and "death with dignity" had already become familiar rallying cries, gaining re-

In pop culture men are most often the killers and women the victims. In reality, men are most often the killers and the victims.

newed national attention when Dr. Jack Kevorkian and organizations such as Compassion in Dying (Mero & Kastenbaum, 1994) began actively lending a hand to suffering people who wished to end their lives (*see Chapter 9*). The ancient question, *What is death?* has been joined by an even more pressing concern: *When is dead?* We turn now to biomedical approaches to answering these related questions.

BIOMEDICAL APPROACHES TO THE DEFINITION OF DEATH

Death is "certified" thousands of times every day by physicians. The physician meets society's need for verifying that one of its members has been lost. This verification is a signal to the survivors that they have to begin the process of reorganizing their lives around the fact of this loss. It is also a signal to society that many arrangements are to be altered. For example, insurance benefits are to be paid, the deceased will not be expected to vote at the next election, this individual death will become part of mortality statistics, and so on. To perform these functions for society in a consistent and rational way, physicians must have an answer to the *"when* is dead?" question, which takes the practical form, "Under what conditions should a person be considered dead?"

Traditional Determination of Death

The most common signs of death have been lack of respiration, pulse, and heartbeat as well as failure to respond to stimuli such as light, movement, and pain. Lowered body temperature and stiffness are expected to appear, followed later by bloating and signs of decomposition. In the past, a competent physician usually had no need for the equipment available today. Simple tests, carefully performed, made clear whether or not life had fled. In many instances, the physician and family could also take some time before making burial arrangements, thereby allowing more opportunity for a possible spontaneous revival of function.

Nevertheless, life-threatening errors could be made on occasion. Victims of drowning and lightning, for example, were sometimes taken for dead, when in fact their vital functions had only been suspended. Those who suffered a stroke, epileptic seizure, or diabetic coma might also be pronounced dead instead of receiving treatment. The same fate could befall a person gifted in the once popular art of hysterical fainting. The possibility that people might be pronounced dead while still alive was an unsettling one, and Edgar Allan Poe seized upon this fear for some of his most popular writings. One of my favorite articles from the past was published in the land where, popular mythology has it, the undead have been most active. Writing in the *Transylvanian Journal of Medicine* (1835), Dr. Nathan Shrock reports that his own uncle had almost been buried alive until, at the last minute, he showed faint signs of life. Shrock then led the reader through all of the traditional signs of death and showed how almost all of them, even the lack of moist breath on a mirror held in front of the nose and mouth, can be misleading.

Mark Twain later gave his own version of the possibility of unexpected resuscitation, calculated to horrify or amuse, depending on the reader's mindset. He claimed to have visited a municipal "dead house" in Munich:

> Around a finger of each of these fifty still forms, both great and small, was a ring; and from the ring a wire led to the ceiling, and thence to a bell in a watch-room yonder, where, day and night, a watchman sits always alert and ready to spring to the aid of any of that pallid company who, waking out of death, shall make a movement—for any, even the slightest movement will twitch the wire and rings that fearful bell. I imagined myself a death-sentinel, drowsing there alone, far into the dragging watches of some wailing, gusty night, and having in a twinkling all my body stricken to quivering jelly by the sudden clamor of that awful summons! (Twain, 1883/1972, p. 189).

A very different kind of observer devoted himself to exploring the what and when of death some years later (Kastenbaum, in press). A pathologist working in a Detroit hospital instructed nurses to call him when a patient's death was imminent. He wanted to be there at the moment of death or as close to that time as possible. The physician's name did not become well known for some time yet, but Jack Kevorkian, M.D., was already drawn to the mysterious transition between life and death. Kevorkian was one of the few physicians in our own time who wrote about the status of the eye at death. He believed that the condition of the eye provided the most reliable basis for determining whether or not the person was dead (and, if dead, for how long). He reported his observations with fifty-one consecutive cases (1957), and discussed his method and overall findings in a later paper (1961). Specifically, he found that the status of the eye at death included (a) segmentation and interruption of blood circulation, (b) a haziness of the cornea, and (c) the appearance of homogeneity and paleness.

Kevorkian urged other physicians to do as he had been doing: examining the patient's eyes with the use of an ophthalmoscope. Few took up his suggestion. Neither health care providers nor the general public was ready to look death in the face. Kevorkian was considered by some to be a morbid and creepy person, even though his deathbed observations were in the service of im-

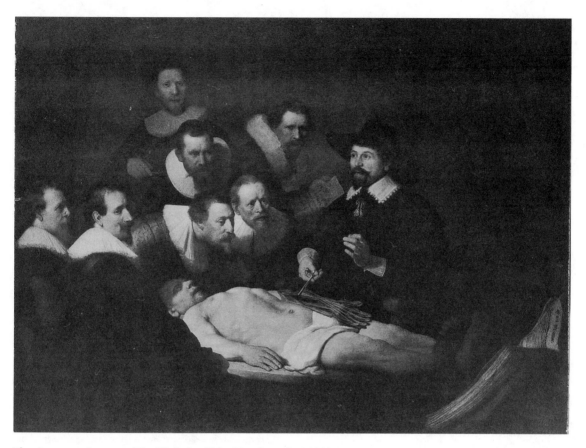

The Anatomy Lesson of Dr. Nicholus Tulp (Rembrandt, 1632)

proved medical practice. Here he was, standing as close as possible to the very people other physicians were trying to avoid, and staring at death through the ophthalmoscopic lens. Most people, even now, prefer to construct death from a safer, less harrowing distance.

Medical advances and a growing set of rules and regulations have now transformed the realm that only Kevorkian and a few others dared explore in the past. There may not be just one way of "being dead" anymore.

Ways of "Being Dead"

Medical advances have made it possible to maintain the body of a nonresponsive individual in a vegetative state for an indefinite period of time—a matter of months or sometimes years.

The heart continues to beat, the respiratory system continues to exchange its gases, and reflex responses may also be elicited. The person, however, no longer seems to be "at home." Under such circumstances we may hesitate to evoke either category, *alive* or *dead*. Sooner or later, though, somebody may have to make a decision, and this decision will require a definition of "deadness," if not of death. Consider the following brief examples, each dependent on a firm definition of death:

1. Family members and the attending physician agree that the life support system should be withdrawn because the patient is unresponsive and has no apparent chance to recover. Would "pulling the plug" constitute murder? Or is the *person* already dead? And, if we cannot murder the dead, is it nevertheless a crime

of some sort because vegetative functions could have continued indefinitely?

2. Another patient is also comatose and unresponsive, but vegetative processes continue even in the absence of an elaborate life support system. (Intravenous fluids are being given, but there is no ventilator to maintain respiration.) Elsewhere in the hospital an organ transplant team is urgently seeking a kidney that might keep somebody else alive for many years. The needed kidney could be obtained by a ruling that the comatose patient is dead. The organ must be removed while the host body is still relatively intact if it is to have its best chance to function in the other patient. Removal of the kidney is a procedure that will probably be fatal for the comatose patient. Would this operation be an act of murder or some other crime for which we do not yet have a name? Or is it a desirable procedure because it might help one person and cannot harm another because he or she is actually dead?

3. The vegetative functioning of a comatose, nonresponsive woman is being maintained by elaborate life-prolonging procedures. If a person in such a condition should be considered dead, this is a dead woman. However, there is a living fetus within. The fetus will not survive unless society decides to keep the woman's vegetative processes intact until it has become more viable. Does this mean that society is keeping a dead person alive? And does it mean that society knowingly kills that dead person in order to deliver a baby who has a fighting chance to survive?

Either the similarities or the differences among these conditions could be emphasized. How vital is the distinction between cessation of bodily processes and loss of the person as a person? What difference, if any, is there between the "deadness" of a body that continues to function on a vegetative level, with or without an elaborate life support system? Who or what is it that no longer lives—perhaps still a person but not the *same* person?

Brain Death and the Harvard Criteria

In trying to cope with questions such as these, physicians and others now give considerable at-

tention to the concept of brain death. By the 1950's, it was known that some unresponsive patients were "beyond coma," that is, no electrophysiological activities could be detected from the brain. Postmortem examinations revealed extensive destruction of brain tissue consistent with the premortem evaluation of electrophysiological activity. This condition came to be known as *respirator brain*. The implication was clear: at least some patients who were connected to ventilators had lost their brain function—irreversibly—and therefore should be considered dead.

At first the concept of brain death served mainly to help physicians decide that additional medical procedures would be of no benefit to the patient. Soon, however, the new concept was being used in a new and controversial way:

> As the original intention of recognizing brain death was to spare patients from treatment that was likely to be futile and burdensome, it appears paradoxical that a diagnosis of brain death has, more recently, become a guarantee that a full range of such treatment will be imposed, provided the individual is suitable as an organ source and accessible to facilities for transportation.... there have been some radical modifications of previous practice. Undoubtedly, the most striking of these has been the adoption of the practice of undertaking organ removal from beating-heart donors rather than waiting upon the cessation of effective pumping of blood by the heart.... (McCullagh, 1993, p. 9)

Here was certainly a remarkable change in the construction of deadness. The heart was still beating—in fact, physicians made sure the heart was still beating—but the patient was dead, or dead enough to be classified as an appropriate organ donor. And here biomedical advances led us into a twilight zone in which ethical standards and value priorities seem elusive and ambiguous.

One consequence of making the diagnosis of brain death was increasing pressure on those faced with this responsibility. Both the health care and the justice systems felt the need for guidance. About a decade later, a committee of Harvard Medical School faculty issued its opinion (Ad Hoc Committee, 1968). Since that time, the Harvard Criteria for determination of brain death have served as the primary guide. The first three criteria (given below) would have come as no surprise to

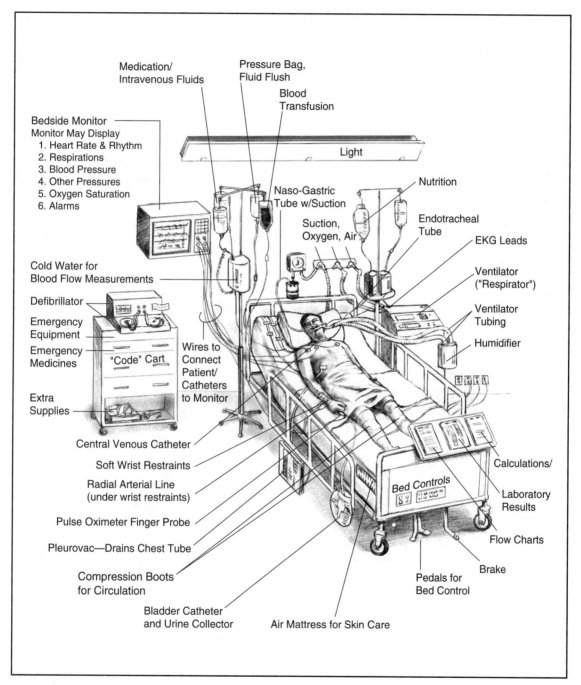

FIGURE 2.1

A comotose patient lies in a critical care unit room. The diagram represents the types of equipment that may be seen there. While equipment may vary in appearance at different hospitals, its function to monitor and support remains the same.

physicians of an earlier generation. It is the last two criteria, dependent on twentieth-century technology, that introduce a new consideration.

The Harvard Criteria

1. *Unreceptive and unresponsive.* No awareness is shown for external stimuli or inner need. The unresponsiveness is complete even when ordinarily painful stimuli are applied.
2. *No movements and no breathing.* There is a complete absence of spontaneous respiration and all other spontaneous muscular movement.
3. *No reflexes.* The usual reflexes that can be elicited in a neurophysiological examination are absent (e.g., when a light is shined in the eye, the pupil does not constrict).
4. *A flat EEG.* Electrodes attached to the scalp elicit a printout of electrical activity from the living brain. These are popularly known as brain waves. The respirator brain does not provide the usual pattern of peaks and valleys. Instead the moving stylus records essentially a flat line. This is taken to demonstrate the lack of electrophysiological activity.
5. *No circulation to or within the brain.* Without the oxygen and nutrition provided through blood circulation, brain functioning will soon terminate.

The first three criteria—the traditional ones—usually serve the purpose. The Harvard report was not intended to require the use of the EEG in all cases, only those in which a question remains and the traditional criteria may not be sufficiently reliable. It was recommended that in such situations, the tests of brain functioning should be repeated about 24 hours later.

The Harvard report provides useful guidelines and has found widespread application. However, the definition of death and its ramifications were for some time a continuing source of concern. The situation was considered urgent enough to require attention from a presidential commission concerned with ethical problems in medicine and biomedical research. This group produced its own monograph, *Defining Death.* The commission concluded:

> The "Harvard criteria" have been found to be quite reliable. Indeed, no case has yet been found that met these criteria and regained any brain

functions despite continuation of respirator support. Criticisms of the criteria have been of five kinds. First, the phrase, "irreversible coma" is misleading as applied to the cases at hand. "Coma" is a condition of a living person, and a body without any brain function is dead, and thus *beyond* any coma. Second, the writers of these criteria did not realize that the spinal cord reflexes actually persist or return quite commonly after the brain has completely and permanently ceased functioning. Third, "unreceptivity" is not amenable to testing in an unresponsive body without consciousness. Next, the need adequately to test brainstem reflexes, especially apnea, and to exclude drug and metabolic intoxication as possible causes of the coma, are not made sufficiently explicit and precise. Finally, although all individuals that meet "Harvard criteria" are dead (irreversible cessation of all functions of the entire brain), there are many other individuals who are dead but do not maintain circulation long enough to have a 24-hour observation period. (1981, p. 25)

Perhaps you have noticed something odd in this otherwise straightforward passage. It speaks of individuals who are "dead but do not maintain circulation long enough to have a 24-hour observation period." This quirky turn of thought alerts us again to the contemporary breakdown of the old, comfortably secure concept of *dead.* A presidential commission here seems to be rebuking some dead individuals for not maintaining their circulation. It may not yet have become a patriotic duty for the dead to make themselves available for all possible testing. Nevertheless, the message conveyed here is that there are echelons among the dead—some appear to be "deader" than others. This is surely a departure from the usual conceptions of *dead* and *death* in Western society, although it would not have raised eyebrows in some other cultures.

Whole-Brain or Neocortical Death?

Controversy still exists about what constitutes brain death. The term can refer to any of the following conditions:

- *Whole-brain death* is the irreversible destruction of all neural structures within the intracranial cavity. This includes both hemispheres and all

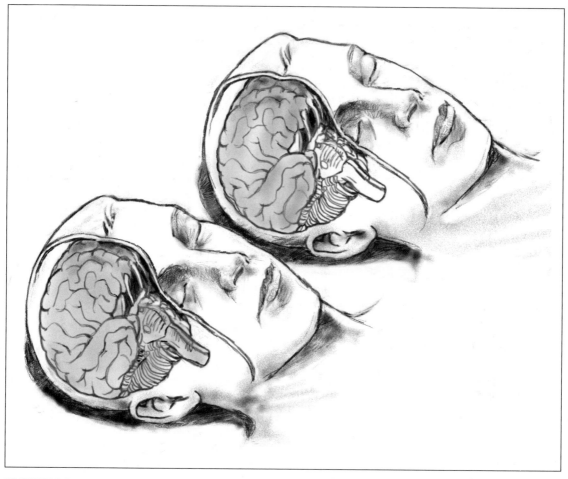

FIGURE 2.2
Neocortical death (top) involves loss of the higher brain functions. Whole-brain death (bottom) includes also the loss of function in subcortical structures that are vital for survival.

tissue from the top (cerebral cortex) through the bottom (cerebellum and brainstem).

- *Cerebral death* is the irreversible destruction of both cerebral hemispheres, excluding the lower centers in the cerebellum and brainstem.
- *Neocortical death* is the irreversible destruction of neural tissue in the cerebral cortex—the most highly differentiated brain cells, considered to be of critical importance for intellectual functioning.

Whole-brain death is the most frequently used biomedical definition today and the one that ap-

pears most often in regulatory documents. It is a conservative definition; the certification of death is delayed as long as there is observable functioning in any subsystem of the brain. Some advocates of this view suggest that the lack of neocortical functioning might be caused by dysfunction in lower centers such as the reticular formation in the medulla and midbrain. If this is true in some cases, absence of consciousness and electrical activity of the neocortex could represent a potentially reversible situation.

What is the situation today? Possibilities of error have been sharply reduced by the health care system's use of the more conservative, whole-brain definition of death. McCullagh (1993) concludes that "There do not appear to have been any adequately authenticated incidents in which subjects meeting all the criteria of brain death have been recovered." Unfortunately, though, there is a tendency to blur the distinction between "cannot recover" and "already dead." A nonresponsive person whose minimal brain activity and overall physical status indicates "cannot recover" may nevertheless still be alive. A great many people have physical problems that cannot be reversed, but they are still among the living and deserve to be so recognized.

Another question is still in the air: how long can a person remain in the brain-dead state? A few years ago, it seemed to many physicians and researchers that brain death could not continue beyond two weeks or so because general collapse of body systems would soon occur. In fact, many articles and books insisted on this brief duration as an established fact. Practical necessity and value priorities have led to a revision of this view. The most striking instances have involved pregnant women who suffered traumas that resulted in brain death. The women would not recover, but the unborn infants might still have a chance for life. Placed on a life support system, some pregnant women have been maintained for more than two months after suffering brain death, thereby providing crucial time for development and survival of their infants.

Brain death therefore might be considered a symbolic construction in which certain features of an individual's medical condition have been combined into a significant and useful concept—but still a concept subject to various interpretations and modifications.

Choice of definitions—even the choice of particular words—can have important practical consequences. For example, philosopher Josef Seifert (1993) points out that some definitions of brain death actually do not refer to the state of the brain at all. Instead these definitions focus on the presence or absence of "consciousness" or of "mental activity"—concepts that are themselves subject to controversy and varying definitions. Seifert is among a number of contemporary thinkers who believe that we still do not have a firm and clear definition of either *death* or *dead*.

Event Versus State

We create some of our own difficulties by using the same word for two different, though related, ideas. Death is sometimes treated as though it were an event—that is, something that occurs in a specific way and at a specific time and place. When death as an event concerns us, it is often possible for us to be factual and precise. ("This is the room where the victim was found. There is the blunt instrument. The clock was toppled over and still shows the exact moment that this dastardly act was committed!")

Quite different is our use of the same word in referring to the *state* that *follows* the event. Life has ceased (death as event). What happens from now on? The answer to this question is much less accessible to ordinary sources of information. Some interpretations of death as state follow, including a challenging new construction that is, well, still under construction.

WHAT DOES DEATH MEAN?

Let's take an example before looking systematically at the meanings summarized in Table 2-1.

The soloist in Bach's haunting "Cantata No. 53" sings:

Schlage doch, gewunschte Stunde,
brich doch an gewunschter Tag!
Strike, oh strike, awaited hour,
approach thou happy day!

The hour that is awaited eventually will be displayed upon the face of an ordinary clock. It belongs to public, shared, or mortal time. The hour and day of death will be entered into the community's vital statistics. What the devout singer an-

TABLE 2-1

Meanings That Have Been Given to Death

- Death is an enfeebled form of life.
- Death is a continuation of life.
- Death is perpetual development.
- Death is waiting.
- Death is cycling and recycling.
- Death is nothing.
- Death is virtual and therefore not really death after all.

ticipates, however, is entry into a new realm of being in which the time changes of terrestrial life no longer apply. The survivors will continue to measure their own lives by clock and calendar. They may remember that the deceased has been dead for six months, five years, and so on, but this conventional manner of marking time has no bearing upon the deceased. She will have entered heaven. The death event will have cleaved her from the community's shared time framework at the same instant that it transports her to eternity. The hour that strikes refers to death as an event; the heavenly blessing that follows refers to death as state.

This, however, is only one interpretation of death as a state. Let us now consider other meanings that have been attributed to death.

INTERPRETATIONS OF THE DEATH STATE

Following are competing interpretations of the death state that have long been influential, plus a new interpretation that is emerging in our society and deserves consideration.

Enfeebled Life

Young children often think of death as a less vigorous form of life. The people who "live" in the cemetery don't get hungry, except once in a while. The dead are tired, sad, bored, and don't have much to do. A 3-year-old girl was saving her comic books for grandmother but was worried that she might have forgotten to take her bifocals with her to the grave.

A little child of today who offers this interpretation is in a sense carrying forward the belief system common in Mesopotamia thousands of years ago. The deceased person is gradually submerged into the underworld, where he or she is transformed into a repulsive and pitiable creature one might expect to find today in a horror movie. The mightiest ruler and the fairest maiden lose all power, all beauty. The dead become equal in their abysmally low estate.

The decremental model of the death state ruled throughout much of the ancient world. Abandonment, depletion, and endless misery were the lot of all mortals—with the possible exception of mighty rulers and those of very special

merit. The idea that the death state can be influenced by pious belief or moral conduct had not yet taken firm hold.

Continuation

Passage from life on earth has sometimes been interpreted as a transition to more of the same. This notion might seem odd today. We are accustomed to concepts of the afterlife that involve a profound change, a transformation. Because death seems to extraordinary, it must also lead to something extraordinary. Yet a number of tribal societies have pictured the death state as one that has much in common with life as usual. One hunts, fishes, plays, makes love, becomes involved in jealousies and conflicts, and so forth. Life remains a hazardous journey, even after death. In fact, life after death even includes the risk of death! The individual faces challenges and crises just as before, including the possibility of a final annihilation. For example, the Dayak of Borneo believe that the soul returns to earth after its seventh death and there enters a mushroom or fruit near the village. This returned soul invades the body of a woman who chances to eat the morsel, and one is therefore reborn. One may be less fortunate, however. A buffalo, deer, or monkey might find this delicacy first, and the soul will then be reborn as an animal, losing its human identity in the process.

Perpetual Development

Suppose that the universe itself is not completely determined, that all of existence is en route to making something else of itself. Suppose further that what we make of our lives is part of this universal process. What might be the death state in such a flowing, changing universe?

The answers to this question do not come from the ancient people of Mesopotamia or tribespeople maintaining their traditional customs against the encroachment of technology. Instead the answers come from the prophets and philosophers of evolution, individual thinkers who either anticipated or built upon Darwin's discoveries in fashioning a radically different view of life and its place in the universe. For example, Philosophers Samuel Alexander (1920) and Lloyd Morgan (1923) went beyond Darwin with their suggestions that evolution applied not only to species but to the universe as a whole. Life itself, in this view, is an emergent quality from a universe that continues to transform itself. Mind is a further quality that has emerged from life. In Alexander's words, the universe itself is in the process of "flowering into deity": God is still being created. In this view, the relationship between life and death also continues to evolve. The basic law is continuing development for both individual minds and the universe at large.

One of the most striking conceptions was offered by a man who also made enduring contributions to scientific methodology. Back in 1836, Gustav Theodor Fechner proposed a model of the death state itself as perpetual development. Death is a kind of birth into a freer mode of existence in which continued spiritual growth may occur. Precisely what the death state *is* or *means* to the individual depends on the stage of spiritual development attained by the person up to the moment of the death event: In Fechner's view, not only does the death state vary among different people, but the state itself is subject to change as the entire universe continues to evolve. In a sense, then, the death state provides everyone with at least the opportunity to become more alive than ever.

Do these ideas seem merely quaint? Current work in evolutionary biology (Kauffman, 1993) and chaos theory (Hall, 1991; Ruelle, 1991) focuses on the premise that one cannot predict the future state of a system from knowledge of its starting point. In other words: change is real (or reality is change). Biological systems are subject to change within the larger system we call the universe, which is itself subject to change. Why should what we call "life" and "death" be the exceptions to the apparent "changingness" of the universe at large?

Waiting

What happens after the death event? We wait!

In Western society, this waiting period is often regarded as having three phases. It begins with a period of suspended animation period in which the person is presumed to exist in a sleeplike state. This is followed by a dramatic Day of Judgment. Finally, the soul proceeds to its ultimate destination or condition. "The sleeper awakens," receives judgment, and takes his or her place either for "eternity" or "for all times" (concepts that often are treated as though functionally equivalent, although philosophers hold them to be sharply different).

These three phases may be given different priorities by particular individuals and societies. Some Christians, for example, emphasize the taking-a-good-long-rest phase. Others focus attention upon the critical moment of judgment. Still others contemplate that ultimate phase when sorrows and anxieties will have passed away, when the just are rewarded and everlasting radiance and peace prevail. Some believers have embellished this phase by predicting that their own redemption will be accompanied by the punishment of unbelievers and other enemies. In ancient Egypt, by contrast, the act of judgment was thought to occur rather promptly after the death event. More emphasis was placed on the phases of judgment and final disposition than on the preceding sleeplike state of suspended animation.

I have characterized this general conception of the death state as *waiting* in order to emphasize its implications for time, tension, and striving. A tension exists between the death event itself and the end state. The dead may seem to be at rest—but it is actually a time for watchful waiting. Judgment and final disposition are still to come.

Furthermore, the sense of waiting cannot be contained on just one side of the grave. The aged and the critically ill are sometimes regarded as waiting for death. In this view, death is not simply the cessation of life, but a kind of force, perhaps a kind of deliverance as well. From a broader perspective, all of the living, regardless of health status, are only "putting in time" until they, too, move through the event into the state of death. The waiting is not over until all souls have perished and then awakened for judgment and final disposition. Not everybody shares this view of death. However, it has been common enough in Western society for long enough to influence almost everybody. Perhaps some of our daily tension derives from this apprehension that our success, failure, or fate will not be determined until the end of the end...beyond death.

For thoughtful Christians, the situation is even more complex and perhaps ambiguous. In examining *Life and Death in the New Testament,* Leon-Dufour (1986) notes that the man who most forcefully interpreted Jesus' message himself wavered between radically different alternatives. Paul at first conceived that the Kingdom of Heaven would not open its gates until the end of time, that is, when the last generation of life on earth had perished. Later he expressed the belief that one would experience the gratifications of eternal life immediately after death. Moreover, according to the scholar's analysis, Paul conceived of death itself as both a welcome release and a catastrophic event. However one chooses to interpret the interpretations, the concept of waiting both for death and for the final outcome of death may have more influence on us than we usually realize.

Cycling and Recycling

One of the most traditional and popular conceptions of the death state is also one of the most radical. It is simply this: death comes and goes, winding in and out of life. This view is often expressed by children. After a person has been dead for a while, he or she will probably get up again and go home. Sure, the bird was dead Friday, but maybe it's been dead long enough.

Some adults also have regarded death as a temporary condition that alternates with life and that represents a stage of transition between one form of life and another. Death has been seen, for example, as just one position on a constantly revolving wheel, the great wheel of life and death. (We may forgive ourselves if the "Bankrupt" place on "The Wheel of Fortune" television program comes to mind—it's not a bad analogy at all!)

In his classic *The Wheel of Death* (1971), Philip Kapleau points out that the wheel itself is one of the core symbols of Buddhism. Another important symbol is a flame passing from lamp to candle. This indicates a rebirth that continues an ongoing process, not the simple transference of a substance. Kapleau also reminds us of the *phoenix,* "a mythical bird of great beauty who lived for five hundred years in the desert. It immolated itself on a funeral pyre and then rose from its own ashes in the freshness of youth, living another cycle of years" (1971, p. viii). The phoenix represents both death and regeneration. As discussed in *Chapter 12,* the funeral process can also be re-

garded as a way of encouraging the regeneration or recycling of life through death.

Kapleau argues that the cyclical view of life and death is more rational than many people in Western society are willing to grant:

> The assertion that nothing precedes birth or follows death is largely taken for granted in the West, but however widely believed, it is still absurd from a Buddhist viewpoint. Such an assertion rests on the blind assumption—in its own way an act of faith—that life, of all things in the universe, operates in a vacuum. (1971, p. xvii)

Kapleau's comparison between the states of prebirth and postdeath also makes me think of the all-too-bright 10 year old who attended one of my classes with his mother. At the end of the class, I asked him if there were anything he would like to say. He replied, "Just a little question. I mean, what are we *before* life and where are we or is it only nothing and would that be the same nothing we are after life or a different kind of nothing and..." As you will not be surprised to learn, I have since grown more cautious in asking 10 year olds for their questions!

The recycling of life through the death state was an article of faith for many peoples in the past. This idea has regained popularity in recent years in the United States as one of the core beliefs of the Aquarian or "New Age" movement (Ferguson, 1987). A typical statement: "Death is simply a transition from one life to another. We all live many lives."

Nothing

Perhaps we are deceiving ourselves when we imagine death to be any kind of state at all. This self-deception can be encouraged by the failure to distinguish between dying and death. Dying *is* something. However we define the term *dying,* significant bodily changes occur, with consequences for thought, feeling, and social interaction. The *death event* is also something: the final cessation of life processes. But is death a *state?* One might think instead of death as total absence: absence of life, absence of process, absence of qualities. The more we say about death, the more we deceive ourselves and use language to falsify. Even when I say, "This person is dead," I may be slyly contradicting

FIGURE 2.3
After consuming itself in fire, the mythical phoenix rises from the ashes to a new life.

myself. This person *is?* No, the whole point is that this person *isn't.* Our language forms lead us repeatedly into subtle affirmations of being even when we are trying to acknowledge nonbeing.

The concept of death as *nothing* is repugnant to many people—much too barren and devoid of hope. Furthermore, it is difficult to cope with the concept of *nothing.* And calling it *nothingness* is a useless exercise that essentially reifies a reification, making a bigger *something* out of *nothing.* We know little if anything about *nothing.* Our minds do not know what to do with themselves unless there *is a little something* to work with. Yet the difference between even *a little something* and the concept of *nothing* is enormous. Furthermore, we tend to become anxious when faced with formlessness and with experiences that do not fit into our usual fixed categories of thought.

Sometimes people attempt to deal with this anxiety by calling death a *void* or a *great emptiness.* It seems reassuring to give things a name: perhaps giving *nothing* a name can be helpful, too. Unfortunately, even terms such as *void* tend to obscure the recognition of death as a nonstate. We have to watch ourselves carefully: how resourcefully we construct images that are intended to conceal the possibility of *nothing.*

Few people seem to care for the definition of *death* as *nonstate,* and fewer still exercise the mental rigor it would require to adhere consistently to this view. But as much as we ignore or reject *nothing,* it refuses to vanish into, well, nothingness.

Virtual, Therefore Not Death

Very quickly, indeed, many of us have become involved with people who are not exactly either here or there. We also see, hear, and interact with beings, scenes, and events that never were nor will be. *Virtual reality* first came to general attention through audio-video devices that delivered impressions so vivid and lifelike that our brains are tempted to suppose them real. An abundance of applications exists in design and education. With a menu and a virtual hand, one can design a safer highway or an earthquake-resistant building. We can also teach and learn scientific concepts in "immersive virtual worlds" such as NewtonWorld, MaxwellWorld, and Pauling World (http://www.virtual.gmu.edu). There is no doubt that virtual reality is opening new opportunities for learning, experiencing, and achieving.

So what does all this have to do with death? And what, if anything, is the problem? It is already a cliché to intermix living people with the deceased in movies or television commercials. And we already have "virtual cemeteries" on the internet, where not the bodies and not exactly the souls, but something of the deceased reside. No, not where they reside—*where the dead can be accessed.* The more we become accustomed to remote interactions, the less our senses and feelings are guided by the breath and presence of real

people who really live and can really die. The more we become engrossed in virtual reality, the greater may be the temptation to see death as something without dimension and place. Virtual reality has the compelling characteristic of being everywhere and nowhere at the same time. It can also be shuttled back and forth between existence and nonexistence at our pleasure. The virtual universe can go dark at our command and return in all its glory whenever we choose to access it again. The engrossing, but distant and sanitary world of virtual reality is not as messy as real life and death. It offers the illusion of control without asking very much of us in return. And perhaps, ever increasingly, it will become an alternative for spiritual approaches to life and death. How freely these images float; how they move and morph and sport! What a model for out-of-body experiences and for all of our attempts to transcend the limits of our physical being! Virtual death is perhaps the natural accompaniment to the virtual life that has so rapidly entered our culture—a life that cannot truly die because it was never truly alive. Here, then, is a new modality to accommodate our desires to transform death into something safer, less disturbing, less consequential, less personal. People sometimes regard the images on television and movie screens as more real than the people and events in their own lives. Virtual reality may result in a quantum leap in the tendency to see both life and death as being somewhere else.

Implications of the Ways in Which We Interpret Death

The way we interpret the state of death can influence our thoughts, feelings, and actions. A person may refuse to touch or approach a corpse, even though it is that of a much-beloved individual. The ancient Babylonians, Egyptians, and Hebrews revered and attempted to comfort their aged. But who among them would want to be contaminated by a body that was beyond the pale of life? In fact, elaborate decontamination rituals were prescribed for those who inadvertently or by necessity had touched a corpse:

Whoever touches the dead body of anyone will be unclean for seven days. He must purify himself with water on the third day and on the seventh day…Whoever touches the dead body of anyone and fails to purify himself…must be cut off from Israel….(Old Testament: Num. 19)

The people of ancient times and distant lands were not alone in shunning the dead, fearing great harm to themselves. Religious rituals and individual behavior patterns prevalent today also have as their purpose the avoidance of contact with what is thought to be the alien and contaminating aura of the human corpse.

By contrast, if death is waiting, and waiting is mostly a restful sleep, death may be regarded as a tranquil state. The emphasis might be on the first phase of death after life: a serene period of restful repose. Yet the prospect of waiting would be anything but tranquil for a person attuned to the moment of judgment instead of to the interlude between death event and final state. Two terminally ill people who are equally firm in their religious convictions might differ in their specific anticipations of death and therefore in their mood and behavior. A terminally ill person who believes that death is simply a passage to his or her next reincarnation may be less concerned about the moment of judgment than either of the foregoing people, and more interested in what is to come than the life that one is leaving.

These are but a few implications of the ways in which we interpret death as a state. Because of the difficulties encountered in trying to interpret death as any kind of state, humankind has often used a supplementary approach—comparing death to conditions with which we have more direct knowledge.

CONDITIONS THAT RESEMBLE DEATH

We can liken death to something else, or we can liken something else to death. Exploring death analogies will not only help as we continue the task of defining death, but it will also lead us into several problem areas that deserve further attention.

Inorganic and Unresponsive

Fire, lightning, whirlpools, floods, earthquakes, and other natural phenomena have always impressed humankind. But we can also be impressed by an apparent *lack* of activity in the world. This perception may contribute to a sense of comforting stability. Look at those everlasting mountains! They were here in the days of our ancestors and will continue to tower above our children's children! At other times, however, the inert, unresponsive character of a particular environment may elicit a sense of deadness. "Stone cold dead in the marketplace" goes one old phrase. The parallel with the stiff form of a cadaver is obvious; "stone cold" reinforces the deadness of the dead.

The hard, unyielding surface of a rock contrasts with our vulnerable flesh and sensitive feelings that can be wounded so easily. A person exposed to stress and danger may envy the durability of the rock. When we hear that somebody has "stonewalled it" in a difficult situation, we understand that he or she attempted self-protection through a shield of unresponsiveness, emulating the lifeless character of rock. Stone as a representation of death is also familiar to us through a succession of mythological unfortunates who were transformed from flesh and blood into insensate rock by incident or unwise action—a glimpse of Medusa's terrifying visage on one of her "bad hair days," or that fatal backward glance made by Orpheus upon leaving Hades.

We live in an invented as well as a natural world. The motor has died. Perhaps a "dead" battery is at fault. We age, and our machines wear out. Ancestors who lived close to the rhythms of earth had fire and stone to inspire their representations of life and death. We have added the mechanical and electronic apparatus, from windmill to computer and beyond. For example, stand at the bedside of a critically ill person who is connected to an external support system with multiple lifelines. Interpret the situation. Is this a living person, or is it a set of machines functioning? Or can the situation best be understood as an integrated *psychobioelectromechanical* process in which the human and nonhuman components have merged to form a special system of their own? While you are considering this situation, it ends. The monitor reveals a flat line: life activity has ceased. But *what* has ended? Do we say that the machines failed or the body, or—?

Today the machine is more than a casual analogy to human life. Many have come to look upon the termination of human life as a mechanical failure. And perhaps this is more than an analogy. When we liken death to the hard, cold unresponsiveness of a stone, we usually recognize that we are dealing in an evocative figure of speech. But the distinction between analogy and fact is easy to blur. Failure of the machine can be seen as the failure of the machine that is the person as well. "Pulling the plug" is a revealing phrase that bridges analogy and fact. The mechanical model may come to dominate our conceptions of a person's last phase of life without our ever being quite aware that we have given precedence to this model.

Sleep and Altered States of Consciousness

Sleep has long served as another natural analogy to death. The ancient Greeks pictured sleep (*Hypnos*) as twin brother to death (*Thanatos*). Sleep and death remain entwined in cultural traditions. Orthodox Jews, for example, thank God for restoring them to life again on arising from sleep in the morning.

Some people today still replace the word *death* or *dead* with *sleep* when they want to speak in a less threatening way, such as to children. However, when children are told that a deceased person is "only sleeping," we may question what message is intended and what message is coming across. Does the parent intend only to soften the impact of death somewhat, or actually to lie to the child and deny that a death has occurred? The young child is not likely to have a firm grasp on the distinction between sleep and death. The analogy, therefore, may register as reality. Late in the evening, the child is told," Go to sleep!" Earlier the same day, this child may have been told by the same parent that Grandmother is asleep, or that death is a long sleep. It should not be a surprise if the child has difficulty falling asleep that night. Children do have nightmares in which death-related themes are prominent.

Adults as well as children may experience insomnia when death has intruded in their lives. While working in a geriatric hospital, for example, experience taught me to expect insomnia and other nocturnal disturbances on any ward where a patient had died unexpectedly. An aged man or woman might speak matter-of-factly about the death and seem not to have been personally affected but then awaken in terror and confusion that night, seeking a living face and a comforting word.

Whether used wisely or foolishly, however, sleep remains one of the most universal and easily communicated analogies to death. Myth and fairytale abound in characters who, believed dead, are actually in a deep, enchanted sleep. Snow White and Sleeping Beauty are perhaps the examples best known to our children.

Altered states of consciousness occurring in sleep or resembling sleep have also been used as analogies to death. People dream that they are dead and feel frozen, immobilized, powerless to act. Drug- and alcohol-induced states of mind sometimes are likened to death, whether as a joyful or

Briar Rose and Sleeping Beauty are among the classic folk tales in which a woman remains in a prolonged slumber resembling death until rescued by a handsome young man.

a terrifying "trip." The now rarely employed technique of insulin coma therapy was known to generate terrifying deathlike experiences.

Normal sleep differs from the altered states of consciousness that can result from disease, trauma, drugs, alcohol, or other special circumstances. The coma of a seriously ill person, for example, is not likely to represent the same psychobiological state as normal sleep. The temporary loss of consciousness in some epileptic seizures has at times been interpreted as a deathlike state, but again, the status of the brain during these episodes differs markedly from that of both normal sleep and cerebral death.

Beings Who Resemble or Represent Death

In Homer's epic, Ulysses ties himself to the mast of his ship to protect himself from an unusual peril. Enormous birdlike creatures with the heads of women menace him and his crew. Some are perched on a rock, trying to lure them with sweet song; others are circling near the vessel. The hybrid bird-person has been a compelling figure in art and mythology for many centuries. Not all winged creatures are associated with death, but such imagery is very common. In post-Homeric Greek times, *sirens* were distinguished from *harpies*. Both were rather nasty creatures. Sirens brought death, and harpies had the special knack of obliterating memory. Death, then, might come with or without loss of memory, as represented by two different fabulous beings.

The winged hybrid at other times was depicted as a soul bird. This represented the spirit leaving the body at the time of death, suggesting resurrection. Later the bird-people were joined by a variety of fish-people many of whom are also associated with death. The hybrid death-beings usually are portrayed as females. Some historians hold that among ancient peoples, there was a tendency for peaceful death to be represented in masculine terms, whereas painful and violent death came through female agents. This characterization hardly seems fair: consider how many people have died violently in man-made wars and how many have been comforted in their last days by woman. The *Muses*, arriving a bit later in history than the sirens and harpies, were females who were depicted in a more kindly light. They sing at funerals and guided departed souls on their journeys through the underworld. (Some also devoted themselves to inspiring artists, writers, and musicians in their creative ventures.)

Orpheus was a being fabulous for his powers rather than his appearance. A master musician, Orpheus represented power over death. He could not only liberate his beloved Eurydice from Hades through his song, but also bring rocks and trees to life. Orpheus is one of many personified symbols of resurrection that the human mind has created through the centuries.

The *skeleton* has also enjoyed a long career as a deathly being. Examples can be found from many scattered sources in the ancient world. Artifacts from the buried city of Pompeii include a rather modern-looking depiction of a skeleton boxed inside a black border, suggesting a symbolic depiction of death. The skeleton flourished particularly in medieval Europe, appearing in numerous works of art from approximately the thirteenth through the fifteenth centuries. We see the skeleton, for example, bearing a scythe on its shoulder and confronting young men with the world behind them and hell gaping open underneath. This depiction appears on the title page of one of many books of the time called *Ars Moriendi* (The Art of Dying). The skeleton is also a prominent figure in van Eyck's rendering of *The Last Judgment*.

The animate skeleton did not simply pose for pictures. It danced. One whirl with this dancer was enough for any mortal. Images of The Dance of Death flourished during the fourteenth and fifteenth centuries, when the effects of the bubonic plague ("The Black Death") were keenly felt. Skeletal death was a quiet, almost sedate dancer; such was its power that extreme movements were not required.

We have not entirely forgotten this representation of death even today. The skeleton still dangles from many a door on Halloween, and the image of skull and crossbones appears on bottles containing poisonous substances, on highway safety brochures, and on old Erroll Flynn pirate films. The skeleton is especially conspicuous on the Day of the Dead, celebrated in Mexico and in Mexican American communities in the United

States. The living and the dead greet each other and renew old acquaintances on this day. Special religious services are held in private homes, churches, and graveyards, and skull-shaped candies are among the delicacies of the day (perhaps not what the pious quite had in mind when singing "Come sweet death").

These are but a few of the shapes resembling and representing death that have formed themselves in the human mind. The next shape to consider is the human form itself.

DEATH AS A PERSON

The field glitters in the intense sunlight. In the field, a solitary worker is attempting to harvest the crop with his scythe. This worker is:

…a vague figure fighting like a devil in the midst of the heat to get to the end of his task—I see in him the image of death, in the sense that humanity might be the wheat he is reaping.

So it is—if you like—the opposite to that sower I tried to do before. But there's nothing sad in this death; it goes its way in broad daylight with a sun flooding everything with a light of pure gold. (Gottlieb, 1959, p. 161)

This was Vincent Van Gogh's own interpretation of his painting. Many other artists have also chosen to present death in the form of a person or personlike figure. Death has also had starring roles in movies. In two of death's most notable film appearances, we find him as a somber man in a monk's robe in Ingmar Bergman's *The Seventh Seal* and as Mr. Brink in Paul Osborne's *On Borrowed Time*. A determined knight delays the death-monk's victory in a chess match, and an elderly man captures Mr. Brink in a tree. Nobody can be taken by death while these serious games are in progress.

It is not only the artist and the filmmaker who have created compelling images of personified death. Personifications of death take many forms and can be found throughout the spectrum of human expressive activity from ancient times to the present (Aries, 1981; Tamm, 1996). For example, children's games through the centuries often have involved the participation of a character who represents death. Hide-and-seek is a game that has thrilled children the world over, possibly because the child who is "It" can be understood as a stand-in for Death who will catch the unwary. The child who is tagged can later enjoy taking a turn as impersonator of Death (Opie & Opie, 1969).

Personifications can help individuals and societies to cope with death by (1) objectifying an abstract concept that is difficult to grasp with the mind alone; (2) expressing feelings that are difficult to put into words; (3) serving as a coin of communication among people who otherwise would hesitate to share their death-related thoughts and feelings; (4) absorbing some of the shock, pain, anger, and fear experienced as a result of traumatic events; and (5) providing symbols that can be reshaped over and over again to stimulate emotional healing and cognitive integration.

How We Personified Death: 1971

Studies of death personification can tell us something useful about the ways in which both the individual and society are interpreting death. We are now in a position to compare young adults' personifications of death at two times: 1971 and 1996.

Four types of personification were offered most frequently by participants in the first (1971) study. The *macabre* personification vividly depicted ugly, menacing, vicious, and repulsive characters. One undergraduate replied:

I see Death as something I don't want to see at all. He or she—I guess it's a he, but I'm not sure—has jagged, sharp features. Everything about how he looks is sharp and threatening, his bony fingers with something like claws on the end of all of them, even a sharp nose, long, sharp teeth, and eyes that seem as though they can tear and penetrate right into you. Yet all this sharpness is almost covered over by…hair, bloody, matted hair.

A young nurse had difficulty in personifying death at first and then said:

I can imagine him, Death, being nearby. It makes me feel trembly and weak, so I don't want to take a good look at him. No look at him could be good, anyhow, if you know what I mean. I feel his presence more than actually see him. I think he would be strong, unbelievably strong, and powerful. It could make your heart sink if you really had to look at him. But if he wanted you, there wouldn't be anything you could do about it.

Macabre personifications sometimes included outright physical deterioration. It was common for the respondents to express emotional reactions to their own images—for example, "When I look at this person—don't think it isn't possible— a shivering and nausea overwhelms me." The macabre personification often was seen as an old person and almost always as a terrifying being who is the sworn enemy of life. The relationship between age and personification is not so simple, however, as the next image reveals.

The *gentle comforter* could hardly be more different. Although usually pictured as an aged person, there was little physical and no psychological resemblance to Mr. Macabre. The gentle comforter was the personification of serenity and welcome. People who described this kind of personification generally were those who also found the task easiest and least threatening to do. The following typical example is from a registered nurse:

A fairly old man with long white hair and a long beard. A man who would resemble a biblical figure with a long robe which is clean but shabby. He would have very strong features and despite his age would appear to have strength. His eyes would be very penetrating and his hands would be large.

Death would be calm, soothing, and comforting. His voice would be of an alluring nature and, although kind, would hold the tone of the mysterious. Therefore, in general, he would be kind and understanding and yet be very firm and sure of his actions and attitudes.

Although often seen as an aged person, the gentle comforter could also be seen as a younger individual, most often a male. Respondents were not always clear as to whether this was a male or female being. In general this personification seems to represent a powerful force quietly employed in a kindly way.

The *gay deceiver* is an image of death that is usually seen as a young and appealing or fascinating individual. (The term does not refer to a homosexual orientation: "gay deceiver" was applied to this form of death personification before *gay* became widely used as a synonym for male homosexuality.) The personification can be either male or female, often with sexual allure. The gay deceiver tends to be an elegant, knowing, worldly person who can guide one into a tempting adventure. But "one could not trust him. He would be elusive in his manners, hypocritical, a liar, persuasive. Death would first gain your confidence. Then you would learn who he really is, and it would be too late."

One young woman described death in the following manner:

She is beautiful, but in a strange way. Dark eyes and long dark hair, but her skin is pale. She is slender and she is sophisticated looking.... I imagine her beckoning me to come with her. She will take me to a new circle of people and places, a lot fancier, more exotic than what I have in my own life. I feel sort of flattered that she would want my company, and I sort of want to go with her, to discover what I may have been missing.... But I am scared, too. How will this evening end?

The gay deceiver is unique for its mixture of allure, excitement, and danger. Death remains the outcome, but at least the getting there is interesting.

The *automaton* does not look like anything special. He is undistinguished in appearance. One might pass him on the street and not really notice him. The automation tends to be dressed conservatively. There are no striking mannerisms. If there is any distinctive quality at all, it is a sort of matter-of-fact blandness, a blank expression. This "ordinariness" is an important facet of his personality and meaning. One woman, for example, characterized him as:

...Having no feeling of emotion about his job— either positive or negative. He simply does his job. He doesn't think about what he is doing, and there is no way to reason with him. There is no way to stop him or change his mind. When you look into his eyes you do not see a person. You see only death.

The automaton, then, appears in human guise but lacks human qualities. He does not lure, comfort, or terrify; he just goes about his business as might any bored but competent functionary. It has always seemed to me that there is something rather modern about this depersonalized personification—does he represent a quality of alienation in mass society?

Respondents were most likely to see death as "a gentle, well-meaning sort of person." The "grim, terrifying" image was the least frequently selected. Death usually was personified as a relatively old person. Masculine personifications were given much more frequently than feminine. In more recent samples, the percentage of feminine personifications has increased across all categories. Masculine representations continue to remain most common, however.

How We Personify Death Today

Much has changed in our society since the first study. For example, there are now many death education courses, grief counselors, peer support groups, and hospice care programs—as well as a raging controversy over physician-assisted death. There are also larger societal changes, such as the reduction of nuclear war menace, the increase in terrorism, transformations in electronic communication, and continued progress in the empowerment of women. Have our personifications of death also changed?

What was learned from the more recent study (Kastenbaum & Herman, 1997)?

- Death is still represented predominately as a male—but there is a sharp increase in female personifications from female respondents.
- Men and women now differ more in the type of personality they attribute to death. Women continue to favor the image of death as the gentle comforter. Men, however, now most often describe death as a "cold and remote" person. The men were also more likely than the women to see death as "grim and terrifying." More than three-fourths of the men but a little less than half the women saw death as either cold or grim.
- The relationship between advanced age and death personification is somewhat weaker.

This finding holds for both female and male respondents. There is still a tendency for the gentle comforter to be viewed as an elderly person, but this is no longer true of the other personifications.

An additional finding is not easily explained—perhaps you would like to help us with it.

Has Dr. Kevorkian Become a Death Icon?

After completing the death personification items, respondents were asked to identify Jack Kevorkian. Most correctly reported that he is the physician who "puts people out of their misery" and who always seems to be in court defending his right to do so. They had seen him on television and magazine covers. The respondents were divided in their attitude toward Kevorkian's philosophy and practice, although the majority were favorably inclined.

We had wondered whether Dr. Kevorkian's central role in the public controversy on physician-assisted death—so actively covered by the media—might have produced a new or modified personification, one that might be modeled after him. The answer was clear. Nobody mentioned Dr. Kevorkian as a person who comes to mind when they think about their death personifications. Some respondents named people in their own lives (e.g., a kind but stern grandfather), and some named other public figures, usually actors or actresses. Despite his name and face recognition and his media image as "Doctor Death," Kevorkian has not influenced death personifications. Perhaps our personifications come from deeper levels of the mind, as discussed by Jung (1959) and Neumann (1971), and therefore cannot easily be moved aside by passing faces and events. Perhaps the respondents were resistant to Kevorkian and the physician-assisted death controversy. Perhaps there are other reasons. What do you think? And why are today's young men more likely to have negative images of personfied death than were those a quarter of a century ago—while young women continue to feel that death is gentle and comforting?

CONDITIONS THAT DEATH RESEMBLES

People sometimes enjoy spirited interactions. They are having a "lively" time together. We observe the other extreme as well: people sharing time and space, but little else. "That was an awfully dead party," we might say, just as actors might remark when the final curtain drops, "Whew! What a dead house tonight!" Or we say about a particular individual: "He has no life in him, just going through the motions." "Look how tired she is—she's dead on her feet!"

These are examples of using *death* or *dead* as metaphors to describe other things. Following are some other ways in which deadness serves as an instructive way of acknowledging certain aspects of life.

Social Death

You are with other people, but nobody is paying attention to you. You might as well not be there at all.

Social death must be defined situationally. In particular, it is a situation in which there is an absence of those behaviors we would expect to be directed toward a living person, and the presence of behaviors we would expect when dealing with a deceased or nonexistent person. Social death is read by observing how a person is treated by others. The individuals themselves may be animated enough. They may even be desperately seeking interaction. Despite their readiness for recognition and contact, however, they are being disconfirmed and excluded. The concept of social death recognizes that when we die in the eyes of others, we may become somewhat less a person.

Social death can be seen in some of these ways:

- A person has violated one of the taboos of the group. As a result he or she is "cut dead." This could be the West Point cadet who is given the silent treatment or the child who married somebody of the "wrong" religion, race, or socioeconomic echelon.
- A taboo violation is considered to be so serious that the offending individual is ritualistically expelled, the equivalent (and, in some circumstances, the alternative) to being killed. The law may strip a person of the privileges of citizenship; the church may excommunicate. A more striking example is a bone-pointing ceremony. The tribal community certifies one of its errant members as dead. This public ritual does not harm a hair on the offender's head but has the effect of terminating his or her life as a group member. Property that once belonged to this person may be redistributed and the name itself discarded or assigned to somebody else after it has become decontaminated. When an agency supervisor was dismissed on the basis of sexual harassment charges, a corporate official issued a command to all agency employees: this man's name was never to be mentioned again. Here was bone-pointing, minus the bone.
- An intrinsic change in an individual results in the loss of "live person status." I have observed this phenomenon all too often in facilities for the impaired and vulnerable aged. The social transformation of a living person into a custodial object can occur in modern facilities with cheerful decor as well as in grim and physically deteriorating institutions. Even an old person who lives independently in the community can be the victim of the "socially dead" treatment (e.g., being passed over while trying to get the attention of a store clerk or being placed at the bottom of medical or educational priorities).

Exclusionary actions may also operate against people who have developed feared diseases such as AIDS or who make others uncomfortable because of scars or physical infirmities. A person whose face has been severely burned in an accident, for example, may discover that others avert their eyes and keep a greater distance.

- A dying person may be treated as though already dead. An elaborate pattern of aversive and person-denying behavior may be generated around a living person whose demise is anticipated. This pattern is likely to include little or no eye contact, reluctance to touch, and talking to others in the presence of the person as though he or she were not there. What makes this kind of situation even more unfortunate is that the person taken for dead may still be very much alive, alert, and capable of meaningful interaction.

Phenomenological Death

Concentrate now on what is taking place *inside* a person. Regardless of society's attitudes and actions, is the individual alive to himself or herself?

There are two types of *phenomenological death*. First, *part of the person may die in the mind of the surviving self*. Partial death can range in personal significance from the trivial to the profound. Two examples follow:

- A young man undergoes surgery that saves his life but results in the loss of the capacity to father children. In his own mind, one part of his total self has died. He will never be a parent. Although much else about his own self remains alive to me, there is now the mental and emotional challenge of working through the loss of one of his most valued potential roles and sources of satisfaction.
- A young athlete is physically fit by most standards. But she has suffered an injury in athletic competition that is just disabling enough to end her career. She is a runner with bad knees. She was an accomplished athlete both in her mind and in the minds of others. Now she has to remake her identity while still mourning privately for the athlete who has perished.

The essence of phenomenological death in this first sense is that there is a surviving self who recognizes the loss of one or more components of the total self. "I am still here, but I am not the person I once was or might have become." There is an element of mourning for the lost aspect of the self.

The other type of phenomenological death is quite different. Here, *the total self takes on a deadened tone*. The person does not experience life as freshly or intensely as in the past. Pleasures do not really please. Even pain may fail to break through the feeling of dulled indifference.

Feeling dead to yourself is a quality of experience that can shade into depersonalization: "I have no body," or "This body is not mine." Some psychotic people present themselves as though they were dead. This can be either in the sense that they have actually died or through the impression that they do not relate to their own bodies and biographies as though they belong to living persons. This may be accompanied by a depersonalized attitude toward other people as well. The person may be mute, slow moving, and given to maintaining a rigid posture for protracted periods (as in the catatonic form of schizophrenia). The self we expect to be associated with this body seems to be receiving and transmitting few messages.

The sense of inner deadness or fading out sometimes is experienced with the use of alcohol or other drugs. It can also accompany other alterations in bodily state. Whatever the cause, the circumstances, or the outcome, we must recognize a state of mind in which the person becomes as though dead to himself.

Strange though it may seem, a person might choose pain over relief—but this choice becomes less enigmatic when we understand the relationship with the sense of aliveness:

> Mrs. A. was a 62-two-year-old Puerto Rican who constantly refused to take any medicine, even when in great pain. Her rationale was similar to other Puerto Rican patients (with far advanced cancer) I met. Doctors don't know as much as they think they do about the person's body. Each body has a soul, and if the doctor cannot see the soul, then he cannot see the body. "I know, I know that my family does not want that I suffer …but suffering is part of life…and without it you are not a man. No medicine can help with any pain…or, sometimes it could help putting all your body asleep…like a baby…*and then it takes away my pain…but it also takes away all that I feel and see. If I could feel the pain I can also feel my body…and then I know I am still alive.* (Baider, 1975 p. 378)

One person, perhaps in good physical health, reduces his or her sense of aliveness in an effort to avoid emotional pain. Another person, perhaps in extremely poor health, accepts intense physical pain as a link to life itself. These differences in our relationship to phenomenological aliveness and deadness are but two of the variations that must be acknowledged as we continue our exploration into the human encounter with death.

DEATH AS AN AGENT OF PERSONAL, POLITICAL, AND SOCIAL CHANGE

The meanings of death often can be encountered in public as well as in personal life. The way we interpret death can serve either to support the *status quo* or to hasten political and social change. Following are a few examples.

The Great Leveler

Since ancient times, the people of the world have been sorting each other out by class, by caste, by sex, by race, by geography—by just about any imaginable criterion. This process of setting some people above others on some basis other than ability and achievement occurs within as well as between groups. For example, the latest wave of immigrants from "the old country" often were looked down upon by those who had made the same transition a little earlier. Those who have themselves been victims of discrimination on the basis of religious or racial identities have sometimes discriminated against people within their own groups (e.g., as "too orthodox," or "too liberal," or looking too much like or too much different from those in the mainstream). Where does this all end?

On the eve of his execution in 1672, Peter Patrix wrote these lines in his dungeon cell:

> I dreamt that, buried in my fellow clay,
> Close by a common beggar's side I lay.
> And, as so mean a neighbor shock'd my pride,
> Thus, like a corpse of quality, I cried,
> "Away, thou scoundrel! Henceforth touch me not;
> More manners learn, and at a distance rot!"
> "Thou scoundrel!" in a louder tone, cried he,
> "Proud lump of dirt! I scorn thy word and thee.
> We're equal now, I'll not an inch resign;
> This is my dunghill, as the next is thine." (1910,
> p. 292)

Yes, death has often been used in an ironic and forceful manner to support the cause of equal worth and rights during life. If death has equal power over the mighty and the lowly—but we have Shakespeare to say this for us in a speech he gives to *King Richard II:*

> Within the hollow crown
> That rounds the mortal temples of a king
> Keeps Death his court; and there the antick sits,
> Mocking his state, and grinning at his pomp;
> Allows him a breath, a little scene,
> To monarchize, be fear'd, and kill with looks;
> Infusing him with self and vain conceit—
> As if this flesh, which walls about his life,

> Were brass impregnable; and humor'd thus,
> Comes at the last, and with a little pin
> Bores through his castle wall, and—
> farewell king! (III:2)

This speech probably did not increase the comfort level of crowned heads the world over. With no weapon other than his pen, Shakespeare had advanced the cause of a society in which the living as well as the dead might regard each other as people with certain inalienable rights.

Works of art commissioned during medieval times often displayed the theme of death as the great leveler. Gallant knights and beauteous maidens are interrupted on their journeys by death, often in the form of a skeleton. Skulls stare sightlessly from tables, shelves, and nearly hidden corners of the room as scholars ponder their books or marriage rites are performed. In such ways did the elite remind themselves that pride and triumph are fragile commodities.

The enormous toll of lives taken by the bubonic plague during its several major visitations temporarily unseated both the aristocracy and the church. Death did not seem impressed with the powers-that-be on earth. Peasants observed how royalty and church officials either fell prey to the disease or scurried away, unable to exercise any control. The first clumsy revolutions were attempted, and a few reforms were achieved (only to be lost when the power establishment had recovered itself). Many years later, a new and more equitable social order would take hold. As the winds of social change swept through Europe, death the leveler had a distinctive role, embolding the common person to resist the established system. Peter Patrix would have liked that.

The Great Validator

Society can also use death to measure the value of its deceased members. Funereal splendor is perhaps the most obvious and traditional way of using death to demonstrate the worth of the individual—and his or her survivors. A Midwestern funeral director expressed the situation as he sees it:

> I do what you want me to do. You come in here and say you want simple arrangements, and that is exactly what I will provide. You know what

you want, and I am here to meet your needs…But let me tell you why I sell some of the more expensive items—it's because the people themselves want it that way!…They are not satisfied until they feel they are getting the best funeral for their loved one that they can afford. …If everybody wanted bare-minimum funerals, that is what we would be providing. When you see a big, a magnificent funeral, you are seeing what the family felt it truly must have.

Interestingly, the tradition of a "big funeral" in which no expense is spared has its roots in early American tradition. In colonial days, families sometimes spent themselves to the verge of poverty to publicly validate both their worth and that of the deceased. Religious leaders such as Cotton Mather decried the lavish funerals much as critics do today, but many of his brethren remained intent on proving their piety and worth by funereal displays.

The opportunity for survivors to affirm their own worth through the funeral process (*see Chapter 12*) has been seized upon throughout the centuries. The heroine in a Greek tragedy risks her own life by arranging for the proper burial of her outcast brother. Committees meet in closed session to decide whether a deceased person is distinguished enough to deserve burial in sacred soil. And the legendary cowboy simply implores, "Bury me not on the lone prairie."

We have found that obituary notices in Boston and New York newspapers give more space and more often use photographs in reporting the deaths of men as compared with women (Kastenbaum, Peyton, & Kastenbaum, 1977). Studies by other researchers in regions of the United States confirmed this finding, and now the same pattern has been discovered in the United Kingdom. Bytheway and Johnson (1996) found that most of the obituaries were written by men. It will be difficult to convince anybody that both sexes are equally valued by society as long as their deaths are treated in such a differential manner.

Death Unites/Separates

Death radically alters our relationships with others. It can be seen either as the opportunity to rejoin others who have gone before us or as an act of separation from all hope of companionship.

Occasionally death has even been seen as a way of bringing friends and foes together. Alexander Pope wrote in the eighteenth century:

> The grave united, where even the great find rest
> And blended lie the oppressor and oppressed.

Two centuries later, a British soldier and poet imagined his own death in battle—an event that soon thereafter actually happened as World War I neared its end. Wilfred Owen (1918) conveyed a fervent antiwar sentiment as he wrote of unity through death. The poem concludes with this poignant stanza:

> I am the enemy you killed, my friend.
> I knew you in this dark, for so you frowned
> Yesterday through me as you jabbed and killed.
> I parried; but my hands were loath and cold.
> Let us sleep now.

Death may be seen as uniting the individual with God. A despairing or dying person may yearn for this opportunity. The unity-with-God sentiment has been expressed in many hymns and carols. Typical is this brief piece included in a popular collection of 1844, *The Original Sacred Heart*:

Northfield

How long, dear Savior, O how long
Shall this bright hour delay?
Fly swift around, ye wheels of time,
And bring the promised day.

Mortal life on earth merely delays the promised hour. This promise, however, was not without its threatening aspect. The gravestone marker for Miss Polly Coombes of Bellingham, Massachusetts (dated 1785) takes a somber and challenging tone:

READER ATTEND: THIS STATE
   WILL SOON BE THINE
BE THOU IN YOUTHFUL HEALTH
   OR IN DECLINE
PREPARE TO MEET THY GOD

The prospect of arriving at a secure, homelike heaven could be tempered, then, by doubts as to whether one was prepared for the judgment of God. Some people have lived in terror of that moment.

Perhaps the most common form of the union-through-death theme is the wish to be with loved ones who are "on the other side." An old woman dreams that she has become a little girl once again and is being welcomed by her father. A boy wrestles privately with thoughts of suicide so that he can join the big brother he misses so much. The survivor of a random, drive-by shooting consoles herself with the expectation of being reunited some day with her friends.

Although some of us may find comfort in the prospect of reunion with loved ones through death, the more obvious consequence is separation. The familiar face of someone who has died is not to be seen again. One has lost a treasured companion, and the pain of separation can be overwhelming.

"I felt like part of me had been pulled apart. Like I wasn't a whole person anymore. And then I went numb. Like I was in shock, with loss of blood, just like I had lost an arm or a leg or worse." This is the way a young woman felt when she learned that her husband had been killed in Vietnam. He had been alive to his loved ones until the message came, although in objective fact he had been dead for an indeterminate time. The moment that his wife learned of their final separation is the moment when the death event occurred for her. The moment we as survivors feel the shock and anguish of separation may be the most significant moment of death.

This sense of separation can occur in advance of the actual death and can also linger long afterward. Some families undergo the extreme stress of facing the probable death of their living children while still suffering from the loss of one or more who have already died.

> The family were still grieving Ann's death when Roy began to exhibit symptoms of the same disease…The doctor confirmed her worst fears. Having lost one child the parents faced the situation once more…. Adam has a similar form of the same illness…. "We know it all now—we shall be left with nothing—no children—nothing." (Atkin, 1974, p. 66)

Children also experience the sorrow of separation from each other even if they do not fully understand the concept of death.

> He had lost one sibling and was facing the experience a second time. His sister, in the latter stages of her illness, seemed unaware and unrespon-

sive. Yet her little brother seemed to evoke some faint recognition. She appeared to smile with her eyes—a last window into the darkness. He said: "I don't mind if you don't talk to me. It's lonely without you. I can talk to you." He prattled on about his rabbit, his cars, and his wish to have a party on his birthday. (Atkin, 1974, p. 69)

The difficulty in understanding death, coupled with the strong need to continue the relationship, can lead both children and adults to behave at times as though final separation had not really taken place (*See also Chapters 7 and 10*). The deceased person may still be spoken of in the present tense ("Jimmy only likes smooth peanut butter"), and interaction patterns may seem to include the expectation that he or she has only been temporarily detained.

The Ultimate Problem or the Ultimate Solution?

Death is sometimes regarded as either the ultimate problem or the ultimate solution. As individuals or as a society, we may even hold both views at the same time.

A dark jest made the rounds in the aftermath of the French Revolution. "Come and see the wonderful new machine—a miracle! One treatment by the good Dr. Guillotine and—phoof!—never again a headache!" The Guillotine brothers were actually appalled by public executions and suggested the device as a replacement for slower and more painful methods. But why have public executions in the first place! Are there no other ways to resolve conflicts and protect the legitimate interests of society?

Death as ultimate solution has been applied on a mass level as well. History reveals many examples of one group of people slaughtering another to achieve what at the moment seemed to be an important objective (*see Chapter 8*). Hitler's "final solution of the Jewish problem" translated into the genocidal murder of more than 6 million men, women, and children. Unfortunately, the attempt to solve a problem by killing others neither started nor ended with the Holocaust. People who were once fellow citizens of Yugoslavia or the Soviet Union are not yet through with shedding each other's blood and engaging in atrocities Angola…Burundi…Haiti…Somalia…

The Sudan…these names only start the list of nations from which reports of mass violence continue to reach us. Never mind history: we need read only today's news.

Students of death, society, and human experience tend to focus on the death of individuals and the grief of their survivors. It is important, however, to look beyond our personal lives and sorrows from time to time and recognize the large-scale destructive forces through which people bring threat, disruption, and death to each other. We will consider what Daniel Levitan (1991) calls "horrendous death"—genocide, environment degradation, man-made starvation—in Chapter 15.

Poised against this theme is the conviction that death, far from being the final solution, is humankind's worst enemy and most profound problem. Death may be seen as the ultimate problem because it ends our opportunity to achieve. This is certainly a threat in a society in which the need to achieve has been a dominant motive: "I can't die just yet—I have so much to do!"

Death may also be seen as the ultimate problem because it closes down the theater of inner experience. We will have no more thoughts, no more feelings. Consciousness, awareness, will be extinguished. Still again, death may be seen as the ultimate problem because it defies understanding. Faith takes the place of understanding for some people, but others are anxious and frustrated because so significant an aspect of their existence—the prospect of nonexistence—seems to be beyond the penetrating powers of human intellect. "Last words" are sometimes given special attention in the hope that those who are closest to the mystery might also be closer to the answer and somehow able to impart this answer to us. Unfortunately, this logic is questionable (Kastenbaum, 1993). We can learn much from the strength and resourcefulness of many people as they cope with the dying process, but they do not necessarily understand death any better than the rest of us.

The Ultimate Meaningless Event

Random, senseless death might be regarded as the ultimate meaningless event. In recent years, the news has been filled with incidents of people being killed by others for no apparent reason. A young man fires an automatic weapon into a group of people working out in a health and fitness facility. A pregnant woman is fatally wounded by a gunman in a passing car. A person later described as a "disgruntled former employee" returns to the workplace and fires at everybody who happens to be there. And on it goes.

The family, friends, and colleagues of these victims suffer not only the grief of loss, but also the shock and confusion that accompany an event that is outside one's normal frame of reference. We can understand why violent death might occur in the course of some activities, including crimes of passion. Some deaths, however, appear to make no sense at all, especially those in which the killer did not know the victim or have anything palpable to gain from the act of murder.

Fatal accidents can also raise the question of meaninglessness. A man survives many hazardous battle situations but is killed by a neighbor backing her car out of the driveway. An infant is left unattended for a few minutes and drowns in a bathtub that contained only a few inches of water. Two children are playing quietly on a sidewalk near the school when a van swerves over the curb, strikes them dead, and then plows into another group of people. In tragedies of this kind, the family survivors and society in general can understand the specific reasons for the accident (e.g., it is learned that the driver of the van had been impaired by the prescription drugs he had taken, ignoring cautions against operating a motor vehicle). But the "why" of the deaths is not as easily answered. The consequences of a few minutes of inattention or a disregard for safety precautions seem so tremendously out of proportion to the "little" error that was involved. Like random killings, accidental deaths seem to violate our basic expectations about life. This is not the way things are supposed to happen, not the way that lives are supposed to end.

Most people are reluctant to conclude that there is no answer, or to set aside the relentless question: "*Why?*" It is difficult to accept the proposition that a death could be meaningless, because this implies that life, too, might not be part of a rational and coherent universal pattern. A philosopher of our own times, Odo Marquard (1991) reminds us that Georg W. F. Hegel, a great thinker of an earlier period, had argued that "philosophical reflection has no other object than to get rid of what is accidental." Marquard offers the alternative view that we can develop a sense of the meaningfulness of life only by acknowledging the reality of the accidental—of things that did not have to happen, but did. So far, however, this challenge does not seem to have attracted many advocates: we tend to feel more comforted when there is a persuasive reason for "why" a death occurred and occurred in a particular way (*See also the functions of the* death system, *Chapter 3*).

Perhaps we are misled at times by faith in rationality. There has to be a good explanation for everything—even death. Everything has to make sense; everything (even *nothing*) has to be logical.

But maybe not.

SUMMARY

There are many competing answers to these related questions: What is death? What does death mean? Epicurus (third century B.C.) held that the universe consisted fundamentally of atoms in motion without any guiding principle or purpose. In this indifferent universe, neither life nor death had any special meaning. Christianity entered with a powerful message of hope—a sanctified life after death—but also with the complications of death itself as punishment for sin. For people who are often described as "New Agers," death is not meaningless, punishment, or salvation. It is simply one of the way stations in a long, perhaps infinite spiritual journey across many lives. These and other competing ideas about death are symbolic constructions, drawn from our experiences, needs, and guesswork. It would be difficult to do without a concept of death, but it seems almost as difficult to agree on the specifics.

In our society at present are two very different sources of death constructions: the visual media (films, television) and biomedical practice and research. In movies, death is chiefly the result of male violence. The biomedical approach is more complex and tends to focus on the question of when (under what conditions) a person is dead. The traditional methods for determining death have occasionally proven unreliable. The development of life support systems and organ transplant procedure has created more situations in which questions can arise. The Harvard Criteria for determining brain death were introduced as guidelines, but some questions still remain.

Several interpretations of the death state were examined in detail. The traditional interpretations are death (1) an enfeebled state, (2) a continuation of life, (3) perpetual development, (4) waiting, (5) cycling and recycling, and (6) nothing. We also considered an emerging new interpretation: death as virtual and, therefore, not really death at all. We also explored conditions that resemble death. These include inorganic and unresponsive objects, sleep and altered states of consciousness, and the condition of beings who resemble or seem to personify death. The most commonly given death personifications were identified and discussed, social and phenomenological death.

Death has often served as an agent of personal, political, and social change. It has taken the form of The Great Validator who measures the social value of deceased people. However, death has also been seen as either uniting or separating people, and as representing the ultimate problem, the ultimate solution, or the ultimate meaningless event.

REFERENCES

Ad Hoc Committee of the Harvard Medical School to Examine the Definition of Brain Death (1968). A definition of irreversible coma. *Journal of the American Medical Association, 205*, 337–340.

Alexander, S. (1920). *Space, time, and deity.* (Vols. 1–2). London: Macmillan.

Aries, P. (1981). *The hour of our death.* New York: Alfred A. Knopf.

Atkin, M. (1974). The "doomed family": Observations on the lives of parents and children facing repeated child mortality. In L. Burton (Ed.), *Care of the child facing death.* London & Boston: Routledge & Kegan Paul.

Baider, L. (1975). Private experience and public expectations on the cancer ward. *Omega, Journal of Death and Dying, 6*, 373–382.

Bytheway, B., & Johnson, J. (1996). Valuing lives? Obituaries and the life course. *Mortality, 1*, 219–234.

Fechner, G. T. (1836/1977). *The little book of life after death.* New York: Arno Press.

Ferguson, M. (1987). *The Aquarian conspiracy: Personal and social transformation in the 1980s* (Rev. ed.) Los Angeles: J. P. Tarcher.

Gottlieb, C. (1959). Modern art and death. In H. Feifel (Ed.), *The meaning of death.* New York: McGraw-Hill, pp. 157–188.

Hall, N. (Ed.) (1991). *Exploring chaos: A guide to the new science of disorder.* New York and London: W. W. Norton

Iverson, K. V. (1994). *Death to dust.* Tucson, AZ: Galen Press.

Jung, C. G. (1959). *Four archetypes.* Princeton, NJ: Princeton University Press.

Kapleau, P. (1971). *The wheel of death*. New York: Harper & Row.

Kastenbaum, R. (In press). Looking death in the eye: Another challenge from Doctor Kevorkian. *Omega, Journal of Death and Dying*.

Kastenbaum, R. (2000). *The psychology of death*. (3rd ed.) New York: Springer.

Kastenbaum, R. (1993). Last words. *The Monist, An International Journal of General Philosophical Inquiry, 76*, 270–290.

Kastenbaum, R., & Herman, C. (1997). Death personification in the Kevorkian era. *Death Studies, 21*, 115–130.

Kastenbaum, R., Peyton, S., & Kastenbaum, B. (1977). Sex discrimination after death. *Omega, Journal of Death and Dying, 6*, 33–44.

Kaufmann, S. A. (1993). *The origins of order: Self-organization and selection in evolution*. New York & Oxford: Oxford University Press.

Kevorkian, J. (1957). Rapid and accurate opthalmoscopic determination of circulatory arrest. *Journal of the American Medical Association, 164*, 1660–1662.

Kevorkian, J. (1961). The eye in death. *CIBA Clinical Symposia, 13*, 51–62.

Leon-Dufour, X. (1986). *Life and death in the New Testament*. New York: Harper & Row.

Levitan, D. (Ed.) (1991). *Horrendous death, health, and well-being*. New York: Hemisphere.

Marquard, O. (1991). *In defense of the accidental: Philosophical studies*. New York: Odeon.

McCullagh, P. (1993). *Brain dead, brain absent, brain donors*. New York: Wiley.

Mero, R., & Kastenbaum, R. (1994). Ralph Mero: An Omega interview. *Omega, Journal of Death and Dying*.

Morgan, L. (1923). *Emergent evolution*. London: Williams & Norgate.

Neumann, E. (1971). *The origins and history of consciousness*. Princeton, NJ: Princeton University Press.

Opie, I., & Opie, P. (1969). *Children's games in street and playground*. London: Oxford University Press.

Owen, W. (1959). Strange meeting. In E. Blunden (Ed.), *The Poems of Wilfred Owen*. New York: New Directions.

Patrix, P. (1910). In F. P. Weber (Ed.), *Aspects of Death and Correlated Aspects of Life in Art, Epigram, and Poetry*. London: H. K. Lewis & Co.

Pernick, M. S. (1988). Back from the grave: Recurring controversies over defining and diagnosing death in history. In R. M. Zaner (Ed.). *Death: beyond whole-brain criteria*. Dordrecht and Boston: Kluwer, (pp. 17–74).

President's Commission for the Study of Ethical Problems in Medicine and Biomedical and Behavioral Research (1981). *Defining death: Medical, legal and ethical issues in the determination of death*. Washington, DC: U.S. Government Printing Office.

Ruelle, D. (1991). *Change and chaos*. Princeton, NJ: Princeton University Press.

Schultz, N. W. & Huet, L. M. (In press). Sensational! violent! popular! death in American movies. *Omega, Journal of Death and Dying*.

ScienceSpace (no date). vrinfo@gmu.edu

Segall, A. (1990). *Paul the Convert*. New Haven: Yale University Press.

Seifert, J. (1993). Is "brain death" actually death? *The Monist, An International Journal of General Philosophical Inquiry, 76*, 175–202.

Shrock, N. M. (1835). On the signs that distinguish real from apparent death. *Transylvanian Journal of Medicine, 13*, 210–220.

Tamm, M. E. (1996). Personification of life and death among Swedish health care professionals. *Death Studies, 20*, 1–22.

Twain, M. (1972). *Life on the Mississippi*. Norwalk, CT: Heritage Press. (Original work published 1883)

GLOSSARY

Brain Death: A condition in which vegetative processes of the body may continue, although the capacity for thought, experience, and behavior has been destroyed.

Coma, Comatose: A state of nonresponsiveness to the environment, which is associated with impairment to brain functioning but is not identical to brain death and is sometimes reversible.

EEG: The electroencephalogram (EEG) is a sequence of ink tracings on paper that record the electrical activity of the brain in several of its regions.

Intravenous Fluids: Liquids that are introduced directly into the veins to restore metabolic balance and provide nutrition, avoid dehydration, or serve other medical goals.

Martydom: The heroic sacrifice of one's life for a cause or a faith.

Respirator Brain: Physical destruction of the brain as observed in postmortem (after-death) examinations.

Vegetative State: The persistence of vital body functions over a period of weeks, months, or even years despite the individual's lack of responsiveness (often maintained through the use of a ventilator and/or other life support devices, but may also exist spontaneously).

Virtual Reality: Computer-generated scenes, beings, and events that simulate actual or possible versions of the world.

Amish communities, unlike mainstream American culture, have traditionally regarded and accepted death as a natural part of their lives.

chapter 3

THE DEATH SYSTEM

As more people move to more hazard-prone areas, "catastrophes, the really big ones, are getting larger", said Dennis Meleti, director of the National Hazards Research and Applications Information in Boulder, Colorado. Disasters are a growing problem. Seven of the nation's 10 costliest have struck in the last decade.
—Seth Borenstein, May 11, 1999

A 344-pound killer nicknamed "Tiny" bled all over himself as he was put to death in Florida's new electric chair Thursday, prompting demands that all executions be suspended.
—Ron Ward, July 9, 1999

Seven newborn boys, six of whom were black, were injected with radioactive iodide in the early 1950's at a hospital in Memphis, Tenn., as part of a study funded by the federal government…it was one of at least five done around the country on a total of 235 newborns and older infants.
—Scripps Howard, December 22, 1993

It's a private memorial fireworks show. The ashes of the deceased are dispersed amid the booming flashes of color and light of a professional pyrotechnic display…The ashes of an average-size person fill the special compartments of about seven shells.
—Chris Smith, August 8, 1999

Simon was the family angel. He was handsome. He was perfect. Everybody loved him. Of course, he got more attention than I did, but you couldn't get angry at him. Then he died. It was diphtheria. Most people today don't even know that word. Diphtheria was just terrible. My mother's sister died about the same time after delivering her second baby. That baby died, too, or was

born dead, I don't know which. Ellie came down with rheumatic fever. She made it to her 15th birthday, and couldn't even blow out the candle; that's a fact. The graveyard kept filling up with family. When I was about 10 or so, I remember coming back from the graveyard and thinking: "Why, there are as many of us here as home." Maybe that's why I've always felt at home at graveyards.
—A man of 93, reflecting on his childhood

Each of these statements reveals something about our *death system*. The death system might be pictured as the negative or shadow-image of our society. Everything that makes a collection of individuals into a society and keeps that society going has implications for our relationship to death. We will be looking systematically at the death system in this chapter. First, however, we will take these examples as our introduction.

- Where we choose to live may seem to have little relationship to the prospect of death. We make our decision based on the attractiveness of the region, career opportunities, proximity of friends and family, and other reasons that have a lot to do with how we prefer to live and not much to do with thoughts of death. Specialists in disaster and catastrophe, however, continue to compile facts that demonstrate an increased risk to life as more and more of us move into hazardous environments. Earthquakes, the most lethal type of natural disaster *(Chapter 8)*, can take a much greater toll as larger numbers of people crowd into a hazardous area.

  Life decisions have had major consequences for death in the past as well. For example, conditions for the spread of contagious disease were markedly increased as people started to crowd into cities. The point here is not that we should stay away from attractive places, but simply that many of the decisions we make as part of our lives affect our chances for death whether or not we happen to be aware of the connections. Our society's pattern of beliefs and practices has much to do with the choices

we make and, therefore, with the ever-shifting potentials for risk.

- Capital punishment—the death penalty—has long been a controversial subject in many countries, including the United States. The execution of Allen Lee "Tiny" Davis brought another, more personal issue to the surface. Davis had murdered a pregnant woman and her two daughters during a robbery. The appeal process had given him another seventeen years of life before his execution was finally scheduled. His lawyer and the American Civil Liberties Union of Florida had tried to delay the execution on the grounds that "the voltage wouldn't be enough to kill a man as fat as Davis quickly and painlessly" (Ward, 1999, p. A10).

  During the execution, blood stained his collar and shirt. Officials said it was from a nosebleed and defended the effectiveness of the new chair that had replaced "Old Sparky," which had executed more than 200 people. Critics maintained that the execution had been cruel and inhumane. Is any execution humane? Is society at ease with capital punishment but only if the end is sanitized and the viewer shielded from an unpleasant sight? Do we have different attitudes toward death at a remove—death as an abstraction—as compared with the actual death of an actual person with all of the disturbing events that might take place? The vegetarians and the carnivores among us might answer these questions differently.

- The act of injecting newborn infants with radioactive iodide as part of a government-funded study met with severe criticism by physicians and ethicists as soon as the facts came out (after nearly forty years of silence). John Gofman, a leading expert on the dangers of low-level radiation, stated that this experiment increased the risk of cancer for these children: "It's like saying, 'We're going to visit cancer on some of you—not necessarily all of you—but we have increased the risk individually and some of you will get it.' It's not a nice thing to do with children" (Scripps Howard, 1993).

The fact that this was an official government project exposes still another type of conflict within our society's death system. The government is supposed to be a mechanism through which we can protect ourselves against threats to life and security, but here was the government playing an active role in increasing the probability of illness and death—and for newborns! The study was further disturbing in its revelation that "liberty and justice for all" may not have been applied to infants of color. Racism in life prepares for racism in death.

- Another traditional value is the serious tone considered appropriate when we are parted by death. The idea of turning a funeral or memorial service into a display of fireworks would outrage many people. Others, though, might find it both exciting and appropriate ("That's just the way he would want to go!). The Vikings and some other past societies who believed the dead should travel to the next world through a heroic and purifying firestorm might have been delighted. Most of us, however, are aware of the more conservative and somber tone that traditionally is expected when commemorating a death. For example, only a limited number of things is considered appropriate

to say or to inscribe on a gravestone. Every time one of these stereotyped inscriptions is carved into a stone, the tradition is affirmed and the surface of society is kept smooth and placid. In Sapinta, Romania, however, there is a "merry cemetery" in which the dead often speak their mind in ironic and humorous ways. Do we dare break the code of propriety? Or can we be ourselves, as was the village bartender whose marker tells us:

During my life I had two wives. One was my lover, the other my maid. As a bartender, I always served big glasses filled to the top. I leave you with a mug of beer and say goodbye. (Thurow, 1994)

These are but a few of the conflicts and complications that are found in any society's death system. Perhaps we should make things simpler for ourselves—why don't we just get rid of death?

A WORLD WITHOUT DEATH

Suppose that the world is just as we know it, with one exception: Death is no longer inevitable. Disease and aging have been conquered. Let us also suppose that air and water pollution have been much reduced through new technologies.

Take a few minutes to consider the implications and consequences. What will happen? How will people respond to this situation, individually and as a society? How will the quality of life change?

Think first of the effects of the "no death" scenario on the world at large. In the left side of Box 3-1, write down the changes you think would be likely to happen.

BOX 3-1
GENERAL AND PERSONAL CONSEQUENCES OF A WORLD WITHOUT DEATH

Consequences for the World	*Consequences for Me*
_____	_____
_____	_____
_____	_____
_____	_____
_____	_____

Think next of how the "no death" scenario would influence *your own* thoughts, feelings, wishes, needs, beliefs, and actions. In the right side of the box, describe some of the major ways the "no death" situation would be likely to influence you. After you have completed this thought exercise, please continue and see how your prophecies compare with those most often made by other students in classes such as this one.

None of us can know for sure what would actually happen if this hypothetical situation became reality. Nevertheless, many plausible and interesting predictions can be offered. Compare your ideas with those that follow, as given by other students who have completed this exercise.

General Consequences

- Overcrowding would lead to infringements on privacy, mobility, and other individual liberties. "Space would be incredibly precious." "People would develop new mental and physical habits to keep others at an emotional distance." "Turf mentality would be all-powerful." "After a while, nobody would feel comfortable being alone even if you could be." "I don't see how people could still be individuals."
- Stringent birth control would be enforced. This control would be highly selective, representing the power establishment and societal values. "It will all depend on what the elite want people bred for." "If basketball coaches get control, they'd want to breed for 7-foot centers." "Every group of crackpots and bigots would try to use selective birth control to exterminate the kind of people they don't happen to like."
- New laws would be needed because relationships between people would have changed so much. "Inheritance might not mean anything anymore. The younger generation couldn't expect anything from the older generation unless we cooked up new laws." "I think that babies with genetic or with birth defects might not be allowed to survive because there would be room for so few babies when adults are not dying off."
- Society would become very conservative and slow to change its ways. "Old people would outnumber young people so much that anything new would hardly have a chance." "The

world wouldn't really have a future. There'd only be a terrific bias to keep things as they are or even to roll things back to the past."
- The economic structure of society would change greatly, but in ways that are difficult to predict. "Life insurance—who would need it? And then, what would happen to not only life insurance salesmen but to that whole industry that handles so much money now?" "People wouldn't have to put money away for their funerals. In fact, there would be hardly any money to be made on the dead." "Doctors might not make as much money because there wouldn't be all this fear of death. But maybe they'd make even more money with plastic surgery and fancy ways to try to keep people looking young. Who knows?"
- Moral beliefs and priorities might change in many ways. "That would be just about the end of marriage, and maybe of divorce, too, as we know it. People would think, hey, what's the point of being married to just one person forever and ever. Everybody'd either screw around a lot with everybody else or maybe just get tired of it after a couple of thousand years and play video games instead."
- Death will take on a different aspect. "Religion is mostly getting people to shape up or go to Hell. If we're not going to die, then who's going to listen and what's going to happen to religion?" "Death has always been the enemy. Now it might be the biggest friend ever. If there's no natural death, we might hire people to kill us in some really decisive way, like blowing us to pieces. I think I would buy shares in the Mafia. Or maybe governments would arrange special wars only for the purpose of getting a lot of people killed." "I really don't think we can do without death psychologically. Society would find some way to make death possible, and this would be considered the right thing, not an evil thing."

Personal Consequences

- We would plan and organize our lives differently. "I don't know if I would have the same ambitions and make any progress on them. As it is now, about the only way I get anything done is when a deadline is staring me in the face, which happens all the time in my classes. If there's all the time in the world, there wouldn't be any pressure, and I might not ever get anything done." "I would just give up trying to plan ahead. There would be just too much ahead, so much that it would be very hard to comprehend." "I'd be really afraid of making some terrible mistake in what I do, because the consequences could follow me I guess forever, for centuries anyhow."

- We would be free from the fear of death. "I've always been afraid of death, really afraid. I don't know why. If I found out that there really and truly wasn't going to be any more death, I would feel light and free for the first time and I could really enjoy life. I hope I'm not kidding myself either, but even the thought of a no-death world makes me feel wonderfully free." "My brother's got himself almost killed at least three times. He's into being a macho risk-taker. I'm a lot more careful. I think I would probably take more chances with my life, and do some more exciting things, because it really wouldn't be taking such a chance, would it? I wonder what my brother would do?"

- Our personal relationships would extend indefinitely, creating new opportunities and new challenges. "It's a crazy idea, but I like it and wish it would be true. Then the people I care about would always be with me." "I find it hard to think of becoming an old person and being an old person right along with my parents and grandparents. Would I still feel like a child? What would become of generations if we all spent most of our lives being old together?"

- Our ideas about the purpose and meaning of life might change. "It would be a hard idea to get used to, especially with all that I have always believed as a Christian. I would want to keep my beliefs—I would have to—but it might make some difference, there not being natural death and therefore not being eternity and heaven. Or would there still be? It could be confusing." "I have to wonder what value anything would have any more. Maybe the only thing I would value is how to fill all that time, how to fill all that time."

A world without death would differ in many ways from the world we know today. You may have thought of some consequences that go beyond those presented here, and the list certainly could be extended. The main point is that many of our individual and societal patterns of functioning are connected with death in one way or another. Death is never the only factor involved. Life insurance, for example, depends also on the profit motive, and the profit motive in turn arises from complex ideological and social conditions. Yet, as respondents have often observed, no death means no life insurance. Take as another example the relationship some respondents have predicted between the elimination of death and the establishment of stringent birth control measures. "If nobody dies, then nobody can get born."

Individual implications of our relationship to death cannot easily be separated from the general consequences. Consider, for example, those who fear they would lose their drive for accomplishment if time were endless. This is certainly a personal matter. However, it is also connected with a cultural ethos in which the achievement motive is highly valued. Social philosophers have argued that one of the most powerful driving forces in Western society is the need to achieve a kind of salvation through achievement. We accumulate material goods and acquire status to demonstrate to ourselves and others that we are splendid souls who should be among the blessed. Perhaps you have seen the wry bumper-sticker that comments on this theme: "The winner is the one who dies with the most toys."

Lessen the need to achieve and acquire, and we begin to have a different relationship to time and death. The work-and-achievement-oriented lifestyle is being increasingly challenged by enthusiasm for a leisure lifestyle. Being a very diligent worker now may earn a person the sobriquet of "workaholic." Notice, though, that many devotees of the leisure lifestyle actually "work religiously" on their hobbies. Members of the baby boom generation, now babies no longer, sometimes work very hard at play as the early signs of aging and the shadow of mortality arise. A colleague of the baby boom generation may have spoken for many others when he confided to me, "If I work any harder at playing and staying young, I'll be old before my time and kill myself for sure." And then he was off jogging again under simmering Arizona skies.

Whatever our individual lifestyle might be, however, each implies a relationship between what we do now and what will become of us in the future. And the future is shaped in part by the expectations and realities of death. Whatever alters our expectations of death, then, is likely to alter also our sense of self and future.

This no-death thought experiment raises many questions that require us to think of society as well as the individual. The *death system* concept, touched on earlier, provides a way of doing so. We will now start thinking more systematically about the death system.

BASIC CHARACTERISTICS OF THE DEATH SYSTEM

Understandably, we often focus on our own personal situations when they cross paths with death. How serious is *my* health problem? What should *I* say to *my* neighbor whose child was killed in an automobile accident yesterday? Would *I* be better off dead than old? These individual confrontations, however, take place within a dynamic society. It is true that we live and die as individuals, but it is also true that we are linked with each other by language, expectations, customs, and needs. In this section, we shift our focus to the ways in which our confrontations with death are systematically influenced by our participation in society.

A Working Definition

The concept of the death system invites our attention to interconnections, to the subtle network of relationships and meanings through which one sphere of action influences another. We cannot fully comprehend our relationship to death by treating specific phenomena as though they exist in separate compartments.

These compartments are given many different labels, such as "recovery from grief," "adolescent suicide," and "management of pain during the final illness." We will miss some of their most important determinants, correlates, and consequences, however, unless we recognize how artificial it is to keep them in those separate compartments. We will remain unaware, for example, of the way in which management of pain during a final illness may depend on the physician's own value judgments, which he or she has never stopped to examine and which, in turn, may be closely related to experiences with death during childhood. Concentrating exclusively on the suicide attempt of a particular adolescent may keep us from learning about widespread trends in society that might be producing a greater vulnerability to suicide in an entire generation. Examining recovery from grief as a phenomenon in and of itself may lead us to neglect lifelong patterns of coping with stress and conflict that contribute much to the nature and severity of the grief reaction. Furthermore, we may fail to observe clues that relate an adolescent suicide attempt to difficulty in recovering from a never-shared grief for the pain suffered by a dying parent. Phenomena such as these require connections, not compartments. And so, strange as it may sound at first, it is useful to think of death as operating through a network of relationships among diverse phenomena. Furthermore, this network behaves in a more or less systematic manner.

For a working definition, then, *we may think of the death system as the interpersonal, sociophysical and symbolic network through which an individual's relationship to mortality is mediated by his or her society.* We face death alone in one sense, but in another and equally valid sense, we face death as part of a society whose expectations, rules, motives, and symbols influence our individual encounters. This will become clearer as we turn our attention now to the components and functions of the death system—in other words, what the system if made of and what purposes it serves. Examples are drawn from the past and the present and from a variety of cultures because all societies have developed systematic relationships to mortality.

Components of the Death System

People

All people are potential components of the death system. Tomorrow I might be called on suddenly to use the techniques I learned in a cardiopulmonary resuscitation course—or somebody else may be called on to use his or her skills on me. (I hope we've both learned well!) Most of us phase in and out of the death system as circumstances and our own actions dictate. Others have a more continuous role, whether or not they think of themselves as regular components of the death system. A smaller number serve as core participants, people whose social roles and personal identities cannot easily be separated from their functions in the death system.

Funeral directors are an obvious example of permanent and conspicuous participants in the U.S. death system. One funeral director described the typical situation members of this trade must contend with: "When I walk into a room, Death walks in with me. That is how people react to me." The fact that many of us find it difficult to think of a funeral director as a normal and distinct individual testifies to his or her embeddedness in the death system.

Agents who sells life insurance are also very much part of the death system. The same may be said for all of the clerks, adjusters, marketing people, and executives. The members of the custodial staff who clean up the high-rise offices of MegaMoolah Insurance Company late in the evening are unlikely to reflect on their role in the death system, but their paychecks have their origin in somebody's decision to make a financial investment in anticipation of death. The premiums we pay to guarantee death benefits are part of a complex network of investments. The death money may be used to create new jobs or abolish old ones, support a local business or challenge it with a competitor, and so on. People associated with the insurance industry have a major role in the nation's economy—and it is our reaction to the prospect of death that keeps much of this enterprise in motion.

Florists are also part of the death system. "Floral tributes" help flower growers and merchants stay in business. Lawyers are also likely to be associated with the death system on a regular basis. Take for just one example their role in drawing up wills and living trusts. This is one of the few situations in which a healthy adult is likely to sit down and discuss personal death-related issues. Even so, many lawyers report that their clients usually prefer to delay making a will or living trust as long as possible because of the obvious connection with death. A lawyer is frequently called on after a death as well, helping to interpret and implement the provisions that have been made for distribution of the deceased's estate.

People working in a variety of occupations earn their livelihoods, in whole or in part, from services they perform in connection with death. Although these people influence our lives, we also affect them by our own attitudes and actions. A consumer movement that encourages less elaborate and costly funerals affects funeral directors, florists, cemetery associations, and so on. A trend toward multiple marriage with "his, her, and our" children might complicate the inheritance process. The growing popularity of life care retirement communities might reduce the amount of money that can be passed along to children, and therefore also reduce somewhat the importance of will making. (Life care retirement communities provide housing and a variety of personal services; senior adults who choose to enroll in such a plan usually are required to sign over most of their financial resources to the management of the facility.) A change in one facet of our social or economic life, then, can show up as pressure or opportunity elsewhere. More often than we realize, our relationship to death has us caught up in these changes.

Other people associated with the death system may not come to mind so readily. Think, for example, of the big truck you saw pull up behind a supermarket the other day. It was filled with pet food, case after case. Every can in every case depicts a contented dog or cat, while the inside contains some type of meat product. All of that meat, of course, came from what once were living creatures. The truck driver, the person who shelves the cans, the assistant store manager who makes sure they are priced correctly, and the clerk at the checkout register are but a few of the people who participate in the death system through their processing of pet food. Those who raise, those who slaughter, and those who process a variety of living animals to become food for pets also should be included. The people in the canning factory should be included, as should the accountants, the executives, and the advertising agency. The cat who meows so convincingly for its favorite brand on television is also part of the death system—as is the cat at home who, unimpressed by the advertising programs, sniffs disdainfully at the food dish, turns up his or her tail, and walks away with an offended air. As purchasers of this product, are we not all part of this complex network as well, a network that requires the death of animals to feed other animals?

The people in the death system represent a greater variety of lifestyles than we might have thought at first. Still unmentioned are the health professionals and the clergy, all of whom have important roles in the death system. It would not do to leave out the scientists who are spending tax dollars to design lethal weapons, the legislators who vote budget appropriations for the weapons' production, and the armed services personnel who take the new devices into custody. The people who run the National Rifle Association and those who are involved, pro or con, in the gun control controversy are also among those who are deeply involved in the death system. What other jobs have an important bearing on death and might not even exist otherwise? This open list is in your hands to extend as you like.

At any moment, you or I might become drawn actively into the death system, and through a variety of paths. A friend unexpectedly reveals to us that she has a fatal illness. We are in an automobile accident in which somebody dies. A funeral procession interrupts our cruise down the street. Or perhaps it is the insurance agent, gently inquiring whether we have made adequate provisions for the education of our children. The points of entry are numerous, and of course when we exit, we are all part of the death system.

Places

Certain places have become identified with death. The cemetery and the funeral home are obvious examples. There are other places whose associations with death are more variable, subtle, or dependent on the particular ideas and experiences we carry around with us. Consider the hospital, for example. Today people come and go from the hospital all the time. We have many different associations with the hospital: it is the place where babies are born, routine surgical procedures are performed, accident victims are treated, clinics are available for outpatient care, and so on. It is also the place where people die sometimes, but this is only one facet of a modern medical center. People with long memories,

however, give a different perspective. A spry woman of 93 explained:

> The doctors would say, "We're taking you to the hospital, Mike." And Mike, he would directly close his eyes and turn his face to the wall. Then the doctor would say, "Now, now Mike. Don't take on like that. We're going to make you well at the hospital." And Mike, he wouldn't say a word. But when the doctor walked out of the room, Mike, he would say, "I'm a dead man." Everybody knew it. You went to the hospital to die.... And even to walk by the hospital, you would shudder right down to your shoes. And you'd walk a little faster.

Within the corridors of a modern hospital we find that death is often given its small, isolated territory in return for promising to stay within those bounds. What makes a particular ward a death place is usually the fact that this is where the most seriously ill patients are housed. But any ward can become a death place after an unexpected demise. I have seen how staff members and surviving patients respond to a raid by death on a ward that was thought to be safe. It can take months before the ward feels safe again. In the meantime, you can see a variety of decontamination rituals as those associated with the ward attempt to rid the environment of its newly acquired "deathness."

Similar measures have been taken in private homes as well: a bed may be given away because it is the one in which Uncle Otto "expired," and its continued presence somehow keeps the unwelcome aura of "deathness" in the household atmosphere.

Historic battlefields may be thought of as death places for decades or even centuries. The royal murders said to have occurred in the Tower of London have added to the fame of this grim edifice by the bank of the Thames. The Ford Theater in Washington D.C. is remembered mostly as the place where Lincoln was assassinated. A pathway in the woods may be spoken of in hushed tones by the schoolchildren who discovered a human corpse while on a nature walk. Even an ordinary and familiar house across the street can be a death place in the minds of neighbors who now feel uncomfortable as they pass by. Whether famous historically or locally, once a place has become associated with death we no longer think and feel

Once family, always family. The Mexican Day of the Dead affirms respect and affection for those who have departed.

the same way about it. The people of Oklahoma City may never forget how a major downtown building suddenly became a place of death.

Times

Death also has its times or occasions. Memorial Day, for example, is a regularly occurring time set aside in the United States to honor those who have fallen in defense of the nation. Both the original purpose of Memorial Day and the way its meaning has changed through the years raise questions about American society's strategies for coping with death. In some tribal societies, one or more days are devoted to communal mourning that honors all who have died during the preceding year. (Simpler burial rituals are held immediately after the deaths.) The Day of the Dead in Mexico can startle unprepared visitors who expect death observances to be somber and restrained. The carnival atmosphere that prevails is not as odd as it might seem, and one might not be aware of the more reflective and somber rituals conducted at the family level. Many societies have established periodic occasions when death is granted dominance over everybody's thoughts and feelings. Just as we might grant death its own space in return for its not invading our space, so we might set aside special times for death, hoping that it will not steal the time of our lives. (Answer that doorbell now. It's Halloween, and mini-ghouls are inviting us to bribe them with sweets in order to save our flesh and bones for another year.)

Times devoted to death in the United States do not begin and end with Memorial Day. Prayers for the dead are offered on regular occasions—for example, by Jewish and Japanese Americans who are keeping the faith—while Catholics celebrate Mass. December 29 is a date observed by some Native Americans in honor of the Sioux annihilated by the Seventh Cavalry at Wounded Knee, South Dakota, in 1890. Anniversaries of the disasters in Waco, Texas, and Oklahoma City *(see Chapter 8)* have been observed by many of those who were affected. Some of us acknowledge a death time that has deep personal significance, even if it is not shared by others. This can take the form of what psychiatrists call an "anniversary reaction" in which the survivor may fall ill, behave erratically, or suffer an "accident."

The clock and the calendar treat each passing moment, each passing day with equal disinterest. For individuals and for society, however, certain times seem to fall under the particular auspices of death, and we tend to treat these times in a special manner.

Objects

Death has its objects and things as well as its people, places, and times. Hearses and death certificates are among the conspicuous objects in the American death system. Death notices have their own separate section in the daily newspaper. The noose, the gallows, and the electric chair are also among our more obvious images of death, as are tombstones, shrouds, and skull-and-crossbones labels on bottles. An unexpected telegram often arouses concern. The little spraying device that "kills bugs dead" is an object in our society's death system; the same may be said of the nuclear devices that we aimed at potential enemies for years while they aimed their nuclear devices back at us.

Objects whose intended uses have little to do with death may produce lethal effects through accidents or misuse. The continuing difficulties with the safety of nuclear plants and the disposal of radioactive and other toxic waste illustrate how objects intended for constructive purposes can come to arouse death-related thoughts and feelings. Both automobiles and cigarettes have been spoken of as instruments of death, although both were conceived as positive additions to the quality of life. Alcoholic beverages and other pharmacological substances have also been viewed as instruments of death, although they are neither intended nor marketed for such a purpose.

Things, like people, places, and times, can be recruited into the death system, and when this happens their meanings are transformed, even though the objects themselves remain the same.

Symbols

Language and other symbols play a major role in Western culture's death system. The black armband tells a story. Funeral directors generally provide black or other dark-hued limousines for the funeral procession and garb themselves in similar colors. Not all societies symbolize death with dark colors, but we soon learn to recognize those particular colors and other symbols meant to convey death-related messages in a given society or subculture. In some neighborhoods, closing all the shutters has been a traditional signal of a death within, although this practice is fading. Administration of the priestly ritual for the sick often is related to the prospect of death (although technically it is not regarded by the Catholic Church as "last rites," despite this common attribution given to the ceremony).

Death symbols tell us something about a culture's attitudes toward death. The choice of music is one example. Slow, solemn music intoned on an organ suggests an orientation different from that of simple folk song with guitar accompaniment and is different again from a brass band strutting down the street playing "When the Saints Go Marching In." When gang members decided to organize the funeral for a slain member, they included a rap song written in his memory (Holveck, 1991). It is probable that conceptions of the type of music appropriate in the presence of death will continue to change along with changes in cultural needs and values.

The words we use and those we refrain from using also reveal much about the nature of our culture's death system. For many years in our society, people "passed on," "expired," or "went to their reward." I have noticed a decrease in euphemisms and an increase in antisentimental expressions in recent years, such as, "She OD'd" (overdosed), and "He croaked." Both the euphemistic and the dysphemistic approach serve to keep a distance between the speaker and the raw reality of death. Currently, health care professionals prefer "terminally ill" to the still uncomfortably emotional, "dying."

Although today more people discuss death openly than was the case some years ago, we still tend to code the topic with indirect, symbolic, and sometimes downright evasive language. I know of one major hospital system, for example, in which a deceased patient is still spoken of as having been transferred to "Tower Nine." There are eight towers, or units, in this hospital, the ninth is not of this world. Notice with what linguistic garments people clothe their communications about dying and death, and you will also be observing something important about their underlying attitudes.

Functions of the Death System

We have now completed an introductory survey of the components of the death system. Next we will become acquainted with seven of its major functions.

Warnings and Predictions

A core function of society is to protect its members. All societies issue warnings and predictions intended to stave off threats to life. These warnings and predictions can be based on folk customs, science, pseudoscience, organized religion, or individual revelation. The threats that are forecast may be accurate, exaggerated, or completely imaginary. And society may choose either to respond to or ignore the alarms. Cassandra's plea to destroy the horse that the Greeks left as a gift at the gates of Troy is a classic example of a warning unheeded and its disastrous consequences.

Often it is difficult to determine which warnings should be taken seriously. Although all cultures have had their share of warnings and predictions of danger, perhaps none have had such a profusion of alarms sounded as has Western society. A central problem for our times, then, is how to navigate successfully between the extremes of constant hypervigilance and smug neglect. How much of our attention should be devoted to the threats posed by air and water pollution? To the possible effects of overhead high voltage wires? To radon, asbestos, and lead in our homes and workplaces? Is air travel safe? Are we tempting death if we dine in a shushi bar? Or if we drive across one of the nation's many bridges that are considered to be hazardous?

Both federal and local agencies provide predictions and warnings of storms that could threaten life. "Small-craft warning" and "tornado watch" are familiar phrases in some parts of the United States. In Arizona we hear occasional "flash flood" warnings, although it is not easy to imagine that a dry ravine might suddenly resound to the roar of a deep and vigorous current of water. We expect to be advised of impending floods, blizzards, dust storms, avalanche conditions, and so on. More controversial are warnings about hazards that may be associated with consumer goods and services. The complexity and power of the death system is demonstrated every time a government agency attempts to toughen the cautionary language on cigarette packages or take a drug off the market. Business and industry must also respond when death-related warnings and predictions are hoisted. In recent years the corporate world has increased its efforts to assure the public that its products are safe.

The death system provides warnings and predictions to specific individuals as well as to larger units of society. The physician is an obvious example. "Tell me, Doc, what do these laboratory reports mean? How serious is my condition? Anything to worry about?" Many others can also warn us of impending dangers, for example, the mechanic who declares that your car is an accident waiting to happen. Repair those brakes. Replace those worn tires.

Receiving the communication that there is a threat to our well-being does not end the story. We must still decide what we are going to do about it. Mr. Macho Guy and Ms. Lucky Goose might well ignore the warnings, as might those who live life by the numbers and figure that there is nothing they can do about when their own number comes up.

Preventing Death

All death systems have techniques and strategies intended to prevent death. In Western society, we tend to think first of physicians, allied health professionals, and scientists. One of the great accomplishments of the past few generations has been the control of contagious diseases that once took a high toll, especially among the very young and the very old. Efforts are still being made to prevent other causes of death, such as cancer and heart disease.

The treatment of acute and emergent conditions has attracted the most interest. Specialists and advanced equipment are rushed to the bedside of a person suffering from a condition that almost surely would have been fatal in the past. Surgery has become increasingly sophisticated and successful. The number of pharmacological treatments also continues to expand.

Hard-won medical victories create rising expectations. As one physician with more than forty years of experience explained:

> People don't want much these days. All they expect is to live forever and, well, maybe to be young forever, too.... I guess it's our fault for knocking off typhoid, scarlet fever, diphtheria, tuberculosis, and whatever. They expect us to cure everything now. I guess we almost expect it, too.

We seem to enjoy the idea of "making war" on death and disease. Perhaps this image suits us because it is active and easy to grasp. There are some problems with this conception, however, two of which deserve immediate attention here:

- The "war against death" often is conducted in a selective manner: more vigorously on behalf of certain favored subpopulations, and less vigorously on behalf of others. This selectivity follows society's general paths of discrimination and unequal opportunity. Whatever makes some people appear to have high social value in general makes them more favored candidates for death-prevention efforts. "If you are going to have a heart attack, make sure you are wearing a good suit and are in the right part of town—also, try to be young and white!" Cynical comments of this type unfortunately retain a core of truth even today, as disclosure of the radioactive iodide studies has reminded us.

Another source of selective prevention has recently been verified (Franks et al., 1993). The study involved about 5,000 people for whom information was collection over a sixteen-year time period. The sample was divided into two categories: those with and those without health insurance. The groups were comparable with respect to age, gender, health status at the beginning of the study, and several other variables. The uninsured group showed a death rate that was almost double that of the insured group. The excessive death rate among those without health insurance was not caused by any conspiracy against them, but by a system that responds differentially to individuals with medical problems, based on considerations other than their medical status. People without health insurance were less likely to survive throughout the study period, no matter what their socioeconomic class. The investigators concluded that "a lack of health insurance is causally related to a higher mortality rate, because of decreased access and lower quality of care" (1993, p. 740). It appears that the "war on death and disease" follows along the same lines that have been carved out through years of differential access and opportunity in society in general.

- The "enemy" in this war is to some extent the face that stares back at us from the mirror. Many studies have examined the causes of death in the United States. McGinnis and Foege (1993) analyzed the studies. They found a very high preponderance of what might be called "lifestyle deaths." Take a moment to inspect Table 3-1, which I have prepared from data presented by McGinnis and Foege. The estimated numbers of deaths from nine major causes are given in this table, not included are deaths that can be attributed to genetic causes. Altogether, the causes included encompass about half of all deaths in the United States in 1990.

I have italicized *microbial agents* (the source of infections, other than the human immunodeficiency virus, HIV) because it is the only cause on this list that is not clearly a function of lifestyle. Subtract the microbial deaths from the total and we still have nearly a million deaths—in one year—that medical researchers view as primarily related to

TABLE 3-1

Nongenetically Related Causes of Death
in the United States, 1990

Cause	Estimated Number of Deaths	Percentage of Total Deaths
Tobacco	400,000	19
Diet/activity patterns	300,000	14
Alcohol	100,000	5
Microbial agents	*90,000*	*4*
Toxic agents	60,000	3
Firearms	35,000	2
Sexual behavior	30,000	1
Motor vehicles	25,000	1
Illicit use of drugs	20,000	<1
Total:	1,060,000	

how we live. The "war on death," then, seems to include us against ourselves. We would be naive to muster all of our resources to defeat death as an external enemy when so many lives end in deaths that derive from our own choices and habits.

Caring for the Dying

A staff member in one of the world's most sophisticated medical research centers was describing her work to me in a completely professional manner. Suddenly tears of sorrow and frustration intruded as she tried to explain what happens when the decision is made to shift from "cure" to "comfort care":

Sometimes the point comes when the doctors decide that's it. There's nothing we can do—or should do—all the cards have been played, and there's just no way we can really hope to arrest the illness. The brakes screech! We all have to come to a full and sudden stop. We may have been doing everything in the world to keep this person alive for months and now we have to stop all that and change what we do, but it is a lot harder to change how we feel about the patient and ourselves, about what we're doing. I don't think human thoughts and feelings were made for such sudden stops and starts!

Fortunately, the transition between trying to prevent death and providing care to a dying person is not always this drastic. Prevention and

comforting can be encompassed within the same philosophy and carried out by the same people in many situations. Patients and their families may play an active part in the decision making, and health care providers may function as a team (e.g., hospice care, *see Chapter 5*).

How can the various health professionals (each with distinctive skills, points of view, and needs), the family, and the life-threatened person work together harmoniously if some of them persist in the objective of prevention while others believe that comfort and relief should take precedence? Should the prevention of death continue to be the overriding goal until the very end, or are there circumstances in which the emphasis should shift to comfort?

Advocates of both positions can be found in the ranks of those associated with terminal care. Some physicians take quite literally the never-say-die orientation: so long as life has any chance, it is the physician's responsibility to do all within his or her power to support this chance. Other physicians more readily accommodate their efforts to the signs of impending and inexorable death. This attitude seems to be more in keeping with earlier medical practices, when physicians had fewer options to work with and were inclined to see themselves as Nature's assistants. There is reason to believe that the United States is working seriously toward a revision of its philosophy and practice for caring for the dying (*see Chapters 5 and 6*).

Disposing of the Dead

"Disposing of the dead" is a heartless-sounding phrase, but it refers to a task that all societies must perform. At the very minimum, there is a need to dispose of the physical remains. Seldom, however, is a society content with the minimum. The funeral and memorialization process (*see Chapter 12*) tells much about the overall stability and cohesiveness of a culture as well as what that society makes of death.

Following are a few examples from American society:

- A minister dies unexpectedly. His wife and children are stunned, then griefstricken. Forced to think of funeral arrangements, they find themselves in perfect agreement. He had been a family-oriented person who preferred the simple, the intimate, the natural. The funeral, then, should be without ostentation. Only the family and a few special friends should be involved. But this plan offends the congregation. A small, simple, private commemoration would fail to symbolize the deceased's significant place in the community. It would, in effect, diminish the status of the congregation itself. The congregation would also be deprived of this opportunity to express its respect for the departed spiritual leader. No, it just wouldn't be right to let this death pass without a conspicuous public ceremony.

This might appear to be an unfortunate time for conflict between family and congregation, but that is precisely what happened. The power of the many prevailed in this instance. The disposal of this man's body and the accompanying ritual became a public event. It was a "beautiful" funeral, with participation from community leaders as well as the congregation.

How did the family feel? They reacted as though not only their husband and father had been taken away from them but so had his death. What they experienced deeply as private loss and grief had become a public exhibit. And yet the community felt that it, too, had strong rights and needs. Just as much of this man's life had been devoted to the public sphere, so his death should be shared. This is one of many examples that could be given of the contest between private and public "ownership" of the deceased. Some death systems emphasize one side, some the other, but the private-versus-public dialectic seems to be present in all of them.

- Two young men are pushing a stretcher through the corridors of a large, modern hospital. This action has been planned to take as little time as possible and to attract little or no attention from others. Soon they have reached the service elevator, and the door closes behind them.

A casual observer will have noticed only an empty stretcher. A more sophisticated observer will know or guess that this is a false-bottomed device designed expressly for the disguised transportation of the dead. A society whose health care establishment goes out of its way to wrap a cloak of invisibility around the dead is telling us something about its fundamental attitudes toward the meaning of life. Do we think of the dead as fear-

ful, disgusting, or dirty? Are we as afraid of being "contaminated" as were members of any preliterate society? Such questions arise when we observe avoidance-of-the-corpse rituals, even within the corridors of a modern hospital system.

- The old man has died. Family members converge from everywhere. There is a problem, however. The oldest generation, including the widow, expects a strictly traditional observation of the death. All of the time-honored rituals must be observed. The younger generations are more Americanized and consider the old way too formal, too consuming of time and money, and generally not to their liking. The funeral director is caught squarely in the middle. The death of a respected family patriarch, then, threatens to bring a bitter intergenerational conflict to the surface.

This example clearly illustrates the fact that our death system undergoes change with every new generation. And, because three- and four-generation families are becoming increasingly common in the United States, we face the challenge of understanding each other's viewpoints when dealing with body disposal and other death-related decisions. Whatever improves intergenerational communication and understanding will help our death system to function in a more harmonious and effective manner.

- The rain and floods that devastated large sections of the United States in the summer of 1993 created problems for the dead as well as the living. In Hardin, Mississippi, flood waters churned through the local cemetery. This burial ground had been used for about 200 years and was a core of the community's history. Hundreds of bodies were unearthed from their graves. Despite the pressing need to deal with flood recovery, the community showed no less concern for making things right with the dead. They did all they could to identify the corpses and return them to their designated burial places. Anthropologists, pathologists, and other outside experts offered their assistance. Eventually, about a hundred bodies were identified; the others, still anonymous, were provided with caskets and given a mass burial. As shown on a television report, members of the community, still very much emotionally involved with

The home can also be a church where a family can cherish and pray for those who have died, whether as infants or elders, as in this home altar.

this process, spoke of their relief in helping their loved ones "rest in peace."

Our diverse American society includes subgroups whose lifestyles are rather distinctive. Kathleen Bryer's (1977) observations of the Amish way of death provide an instructive example of alternative approaches. There are approximately 80,000 Amish people in the United States and Canada, descendants of Swiss Anabaptists who were persecuted for their beliefs until granted refuge and religious liberty by William Penn in 1727. The Amish maintain a family-oriented society that emphasizes religious values, a simple agrarian lifestyle, separation from the non-Amish world, and a strong doctrine of mutual assistance. Marital separation and divorce are not sanctioned. The infirm and the mentally ill are looked after in the community rather than in institutions. The Amish people function "at the same unhurried pace as...their forefathers, using horses instead of automobiles, windmills instead of electricity, and facing death with the same religious tenets and steadfast faith of their fathers" (1977, p. 256).

The Amish way of life and death is clearly expressed in behavior associated with body disposal. The deceased is dressed in white garments by family members.

It is only at her death that an Amish woman wears a white dress with the cape and apron which were put away by her for the occasion of her death. This is an example of the lifelong preparation for the facing of death, as sanctioned by Amish society. The wearing of all white clothes signifies the high ceremonial emphasis on the death event as the final rite of passage into a new and better life. (1977, p. 254)

The funeral is very much a home-oriented event. A large room is cleared for the simple wooden coffin and the hundreds of friends, neighbors, and relatives who will soon fill it. The funeral service is held in the house or barn, a practice of the Amish for many generations. The grave itself is dug by neighbors on the preceding day, and all watch in silent prayer as the coffin is lowered and the grave filled with earth. Other families see to it that the mourners are fed. The coffin is in the center of the room; there are no adornments or distractions from the basic fact of death.

The Amish have avoided the problems and conflicts involved in body-disposal practices for American society at large. Their different way of life seems to involve a different way of death as well. This is expressed all through life, for example, by an old woman who carefully washes, starches, and irons her own funeral clothing so it will be ready when the time comes. A death may occasion grief and lead to hardships for an Amish family as it does for any other, but many of the doubts, tensions, and conflicts that have become commonplace in the larger death system seem to be absent for these people, who have developed and perpetuated a distinctive lifestyle of their own.

Social Consolidation after Death

Death does not merely subtract an individual from society. It can also challenge society's ability to hold itself together, to assert its vitality and viability after death's raid. In relatively small societies, the impact of every death challenges the integrity of the entire group. In a mass society, this challenge usually becomes obvious only when death unexpectedly strikes down a powerful leader.

The assassinations of John F. Kennedy, Martin Luther King, Jr., and Robert Kennedy exemplify the types of death that shake even the largest and most powerful nations. Each of these men was highly visible, a part of the national consciousness. Each man also represented political power as well as something on a more personal and emotional level to millions of others. The manner of their deaths intensified the impact. The sudden, unexpected death of a significant person makes ordinary people feel vulnerable. The series of assassinations came too quickly to allow for repairing the psychological shield that usually protects our feelings. Our defenses could not remain securely in place as they sometimes do for lesser or passing threats.

Furthermore, each of these deaths was not only sudden, but also violent. The impact of sudden violence and its resulting social disorganization added to the force with which each death struck society. And this was not all. Each death was intentional. The chain reaction of fears and alarms that followed has not entirely dissipated with the passing years. Both then and now, people have wondered how even the most powerful among us could be so vulnerable. What protection do any of us have? How safe are we as a nation when the life of a powerful leader can be so quickly destroyed? Conspiracy theories remain popular, perhaps still fueled by the anxieties aroused when a powerful person dies suddenly.

One major function of the death system, then, is to meet the challenges posed to the individual and the group by the loss of a member. This challenge may be of broad scope, as in the violent death of a powerful leader, or it can be as silent and personal as a death in the family.

The realtor's illness didn't appear serious, but he died a day after entering the hospital, even before testing could be completed. From that point on, the family hardly seemed to be a family any more. They went their own ways, found things to do that kept them from being home at the same time, and seldom took a meal together. At first the 16-year-old son appeared to be the least affected. He continued his usual routines, although he did spend even more time behind the closed door of his room. Within a few months, though, it was obvious that the young man was really not doing so well after all. Most of the time he barely spoke, but then he would explode in anger without known reason and stalk away. An observant teacher noticed that the only time he mentioned his father, he used the present tense, as though he were still alive.

This is an example of the temporary failure of social consolidation after a death. The family had fragmented, and relatives, friends, and neighbors had also failed to provide useful support. For contrast, consider again the Amish. Consistent with their general orientations toward life and death, the Amish provide direct and long-term support to those whose lives have been disrupted by the death of a loved one. It is not a case of many people coming by to express sympathy for a short period and subsequently disappearing; instead, vital functions in the home may be taken over for months by relatives or friends until the family can get back on its feet.

Social consolidation after death is vital if the survivors are to continue as confident and competent members of the culture. Therese Rando (1993), a specialist in grief therapy, observes that a lack of social support can undermine mourners in all areas of readjustment. Most obviously, survivors need emotional support in the form of consolation, encouragement, and empathy. But support is also needed in the form of practical assistance and information. "If others do not support reality testing and provide feedback, it will be difficult for the mourner to alter emotions, cognitions, expectations, and behaviors. Similarly, problems may arise from a lack of instrumental or practical assistance to manage tasks necessary for daily living or for readjusting to the death" (1993, p. 432). Coping with the loss and getting on with life is facilitated when the death system proves willing and able to lend its support to the bereaved. The failure of social consolidation after death can contribute to many years of sorrow and stress on the part of the survivors.

Making Sense of Death

Our efforts to explain death to each other represent another important function of the death system. Some explanations are handed down from generation to generation in the form of philosophical statements, poetry, and commentaries on holy scriptures. There are also famous last words and scenes that have been attributed (often misattributed) to heroes, leaders, and other celebrated people of the past.

Still other explanations are passed along informally within a particular subculture or family, or through successive cohorts in the military service or schools of nursing or medicine. "This is what *we* say and this is what *we* think and this is what *we* do." Nurses, physicians, clergy, funeral directors, insurance agents, and terrorists are socialized to express the attitudes and explanations of death that come with the trade.

Laconic statements such as "Nobody lives forever!" hardly qualify as explanations. Yet much of our discourse on the subject of death is on this superficial level. Such statements might reduce the anxiety of the people who make them through bridging what might otherwise be a tense and awkward silence. Perhaps hearing any words at all on the subject has some value to the recipient.

I spent several days in a hospital waiting area unobtrusively listening to conversations among visitors to terminally ill friends and relatives. The conversation was usually on other matters, and most of the death-oriented talk was limited to clichés. The visitors seldom, if ever, seemed to say anything new or thought provoking to each other. Nevertheless, there was some comfort taken and some comfort given in exchanging words.

Consider the alternative. Not to have words spoken might confirm the fear that death is unspeakable and therefore perhaps unthinkable as well. We might feel more helpless and alienated than ever. When we can at least go through the motions of exchanging words in this difficult situation, we are showing the ability to function under stress. We are trying to make sense of death, and this mental and emotional activity helps keep us going.

At other times, however, we are not searching for just any words about death. We are looking for the most cogent and powerful understanding possible. The kind of explanation we seek cannot be separated, of course, from the particular questions we have in mind. These may be personal and highly specific, or they may relate to the meaning of life and the universe on the broadest level we can conceive. A child, a young adult, and an aged adult might have different questions in mind as well as different ways of evaluating possible answers. So, too, a person deeply rooted in Asian tradition and one with equally strong roots in the Western world are likely to differ in their approaches. Individual differences are also important. For example, many people are mostly concerned with the "purpose" served by death. In other words, death would make sense only if we could understand what it accomplishes. Other people consider this to be a misleading, perhaps nonsensical question. Why should we assume that death has a purpose or is intended to accomplish anything? In this view, death makes sense to us when we understand its place in the general biological or cosmic scheme of things, without any particular reference to our hopes and fears.

Making sense of death becomes an especially high-priority activity for us when our security is shattered by a death that comes to us in a circumstance (e.g., murder, accident, suicide) or time of life (e.g., a child) that undermines the way in which we interpret the world. Most of us can easily call upon the range of explanations available to us within our particular death system. It is more challenging, however, to examine the credentials of these various explanations and more challenging still to work toward our own explanations.

Killing

All death systems have another major function: killing. This function is carried out in many ways. Capital punishment is an obvious example. It is practiced by some, but not all, cultures, with widely varying criteria for the conditions under which a person should be put to death. Ordinarily only a few people have their lives ended by this mode, although there have been times and circumstances in which execution became a salient mode of death (e.g., the procession to the guillotine in the aftermath of the French Revolution). English criminal law, upon which much of our own legal system is founded, made death the punishment for an astonishing array of offenses, but in practice, relatively few people were actually executed. Capital punishment conveys a mighty theme even when it is responsible for few deaths: the same society that on many occasions functions to protect and prolong life on certain occasions acts on behalf of death. Capital punishment is as susceptible to local circumstances and general social forces as any other function of the death system. For example, in recent years there has been an international trend toward the abolishment of the death penalty. In the United States, support for capital punishment has gone through cycles of support and criticism.

Today, individual states continue to differ somewhat in the crimes considered punishable by death and the methods of execution. Hanging, once a common form of execution, is legal now as an option only in Montana and Washington. The firing squad, a dramatic remnant from the past, is still on the books in Idaho and Utah. There is no capital punishment at all in District of Columbia, American Samoa, Guam, Puerto Rico, and the Virgin Islands, nor in the states of Alaska, Hawaii, Iowa, Maine, Massachusetts, Michigan, Minnesota, North Dakota, Rhode Island, Vermont, West Virginia, and Wyoming. Some states have abolished capital punishment while their neighboring state has not (e.g., North Dakota and South Dakota).

Additionally, there are differences in the types of crime that are punishable by death. In Missouri, for example, capital punishment applies to those who commit murder in the hijacking of public conveyances or who murder employees of correctional facilities. Maryland has a concise rule: subject to the death penalty are those who commit "first degree murder, either premeditated or during the commission of a felony." By contrast, Alabama lists "murder during kidnapping, robbery, rape, sodomy, burglary, sexual assault or arson; murder of peace officer, correctional officers, or public official; murder while under a life sentence; contract murder; murder by a defendant with a previous murder conviction; murder of a witness to a crime."

Public opinion and local tradition are powerful influences on the way in which a state exercises the option of capital punishment. There is now pressure to reinstate the death penalty or use it more frequently as a consequence of drive-by shootings and other homicides in which killing seems to be a kind of sport. Advocates and opponents of the death penalty continue to present opposing sets of arguments and data. The average murder rate in non–death penalty states in 1997 was lower (3.6) than in states with the death penalty (6.6), and states with a death penalty usually have a higher murder rate than their neighboring non–death penalty states. Nevertheless, the effectiveness of the death penalty is only one part of a larger set of issues related to society's basic sense of the value of life and the meaning of justice.

The death penalty is only the most obvious example of the death system's exercising the function of a killer. Reference has already been made to the people who participate in the pet food industry. This component of the death system broadens even further when those who raise, slaughter, process, and consume meat-bearing animals are included. Even the casual fisherperson kills ("drowning worms," as they say), whether or not a fish is landed for the family table. Any culture that is not thoroughly vegetarian is involved to some extent in killing for food. (And isn't pulling a turnip up by its roots also a form of killing?)

Living creatures may be killed for other reasons as well. The quest for fur and feathers has brought several species to the edge of extinction. The belief that the horn of the rhinoceros can bestow sexual powers has led to the profitable slaughter of many a beast. Hunting may be pursued as an exercise in skill, proof of manhood, or just an excuse to be outdoors. There are also consequences when hunting is restricted or banned. Canada is still trying to cope with the social disorganization and loss of morale that developed when Inuits, with a long tradition of seal hunting, were forced to abandon this activity (even though they have received some benefits in return). It is probable that all societies have many adjustments to make when they decide to reduce the killing function in their death systems.

Warfare has brought death to millions through the centuries, our own not excluded. Our propensity for slaughtering each other raises fundamental questions about human nature. Are we killers at heart? Is there a deep-rooted aggressive instinct that must find expression in bloody triumphs? Or does war arise from situational pressures that could be reduced by improved knowledge, skills, and social organization? Does the commandment "Thou shalt not kill" express our real moral position, or is it undermined by a more basic conviction that we have the right to take the lives of others?

War has often been considered the natural state of affairs. Every tribe, every city–state, and every dynasty expected armed conflict. It was taken for granted that one group would raid another's lands to steal cattle and other valuables, and that the other group would retaliate as opportunities arose. Much of the routine fighting took the form of raids and skirmishes. Killing and being killed were possible outcomes, but not necessarily the main objectives. It was so much easier if we could surprise and scatter the enemy in order to loot at our leisure and return unharmed. However, there would also be raids of reprisal in which a previous death on one side would have to be avenged by killing somebody on the other side.

War held true as a normal fact of life for the most sophisticated civilizations of the time. The ancient Greek city–states were following the examples of their own gods when they took the field to sack and subdue another people. Had not their own deities triumphed over the Titans after the most awesome battles? In its days of greatness, Rome sent its legions on missions of conquest, and its successors, the Holy Roman and Byzantine Empires, both excelled in the military arts. Their holy men generally affirmed that deadly force was a right, indeed a responsibility, of the state. When the devout Thomas More created the concept of Utopia (1516) many centuries later, he also affirmed the legitimacy of war and its attendant taking of life: the Utopian must simply go about the business of killing in a thoughtful and cost-effective manner.

By the eighteenth century, a great philosopher, Immanuel Kant, had become convinced that Perpetual Peace (1795) was an absolute necessity and could be achieved by international organization and cooperation. Years later, however, Karl von Clausewitz (1832) could still persuade many that the capacity to make war is vital to the success of any nation. The psychological dimensions of war were examined in a memorable exchange of correspondence between Albert Einstein and Sigmund Freud (1933). The physicist believed that the most critical problem facing humanity was not the nature of the physical universe but human nature itself—especially our so-often demonstrated propensity for violence. The psychoanalyst agreed that an aggressive instinct did exist and was not likely to be rooted out of our nature. We might, however, learn to love the other in ourselves and ourselves in the other person—in other words, to experience and respect our common humanity. Having survived "the war to end all wars," Freud believed that civilization had at least one chance left to channel its aggressive tendencies to more constructive use. Alas, a few years later he was an old man dying in a foreign land (England) because the unthinkable second war had already flamed out from his own country to engulf the world. The physicist who had feared so deeply for our ability to survive our own warlike nature would soon be known as godfather of the nuclear bomb.

We can find examples that seem to prove almost any theory of war and human violence. Religious faith, for example, can be seen to provide visions of universal human kinship and perpetual harmony—or incitement to the most relentless and pitiless slaughter. War has taken the aspect of a rational instrument of state policy, but also of a catastrophe we blunder into from time to time for any number of trivial reasons. Human nature itself has a warlike component at its core that at best can be diverted from its most destructive aims only by ceaseless effort and a bit of good luck, or human nature becomes warlike only when so shaped by circumstances. No simple answer encompasses all the themes, motives, and events that have issued from warfare.

We have become ever more a deadly species as we have become more "civilized." The invention of the standing army, for example, made it possible to wage war in any season and extend the duration of the hostilities. The application of assembly-line tactics for raising livestock ensures that astounding numbers of chickens are hatched each day (17 million is one estimate) and rapidly moved along from egg to fast-food sandwich without ever having seen a barnyard. Improved technology has made it possible for military units to conduct night warfare against each other and, as a spinoff, increase the hunter's advantage over his prey. Killing on behalf of society or one of its special interest groups is a function of the death system that thrives on organizational expertise.

The systematization of killing by the state can be seen in the careful specification of precisely how executions are to be conducted in relationship to the crime. Consider the following verdict passed on a thirteenth-century Englishman (Jankofsky, 1979):

> Hugh Dispenser the Younger...you are found as a thief, and therefore shall be hanged; and are found as a traitor, and therefore shall be drawn and quartered; and for that you have been outlawed by the king, and...returned to the court without warrant, you shall be beheaded and for that you abetted and procured discord between the king and queen, and others of the realm, you shall be embowelled, and your bowels burnt. Withdraw traitor, tyrant and so go take your judgment, attainted wicked traitor.

This example of "overkill" was not a random emotional outburst but a deliberate attempt to strengthen those in power. A respected individual who had taken the wrong (losing) side in a conflict or who was a member of the aristocracy might simply have his head severed. As a special privilege, the head of the executed might not be placed on a spike of the city gates. Capital punishment, then, could either inflict agony and heap disgrace on the condemned, or be content with taking life but not reputation.

Killing by the death system—or, to put it another way, society turned killer—can take more subtle forms, and it is these forms that actually result in more deaths than capital punishment. Infant mortality in the United States, for example, has consistently been higher in families who live below the poverty level. Nonwhite subpopulations have an exceptionally high risk, with respiratory illnesses being the most frequent specific cause of death. Excessive risk of death follows impoverished and socially disadvantaged people throughout their lives. One emerging risk, for example, is the tendency to locate toxic waste dumps in areas whose residents are already at greater than average risk for death because of poverty and discrimination. Whether or not the term *kill* is used, the outcome of systematic deprivation may be premature death. There is often controversy on the particulars, but it is difficult to avoid the conclusion that the premature death of its own citizens is often the outcome of a society's policies and practices.

The United States is a society in which acts of lethal violence occur with remarkable frequency in entertainment such as films and television programs. It is also a society whose homicide rates are remarkably high when compared with those of other nations (*see Chapter 8*). And yet it is also a society that has been remarkably generous to individuals and nations in their times of crisis and which includes a strong antiviolence tradition. For example, intensified efforts are now being made to reduce the frequency and intensity of violence on television, in hopes of also reducing lethal violence in our communities. Perhaps systematic action can restrain the killing function that currently seems to be all too prominent in our death system.

HOW OUR DEATH SYSTEM HAS BEEN CHANGING—AND THE "DEATHNIKS" WHO ARE MAKING A DIFFERENCE

We have completed an overview of the death system, with particular attention to the United States. Now we can go just a little further. We can ask where this system has been and where it is going. And we can try to identify the kinds of people who have emerged as counselors, educators, researchers, and change agents in the death system.

Changing Ways of Life, Changing Ways of Death

A thorough analysis of changes in death systems through the centuries would require an intensive re-reading of world history. We would find a strong connection between ways of life and ways of death in every culture in every epoch. (For useful examples, see Ariès, 1981; Eire, 1995; Huizinga, 1926/1996; Laungani, 1996.) Here we use a more narrow focus. First we identify one of the main influences on death systems throughout history—the ways in which people died. In the next section, we see how the "deathniks" and *thanatology* (the study of death) have emerged and contributed to the current death system.

Many societies have been dominated by a particular image of death. Their systems for interpreting and coping with death have centered around these images. But where do the images come from? One very important source is of interest to us here: images of death are strongly influenced by the ways in which people die. More specifically, dominant sociocultural images of death are likely to be shaped by the types of catastrophic dying with which a society has become intimately familiar. Table 3-2 presents some of the major forms of catastrophic dying known to human societies through the centuries, along with the markers and signifiers associated with each (Kastenbaum, 1993).

It becomes easier to understand why people thought of death in a particular way when we understand the types of dying that were salient in their experiences. For example, tuberculosis was a real and present source of anxiety from the nineteenth century through the early part of the twentieth century. People who felt helpless as loved ones lost their vitality, suffered, became emaciated, and died also had reason to fear that they might have the same fate as a result of a disease that is more readily contagious than AIDS. The avoidance of death that became so entrenched in our culture was certainly influenced by experiences with people who died the harrowing death of tuberculosis victims.

We have already touched on one of the forms of dying that is making an impact on our current death system—the persistent vegetative state (*see Chapter 2*). Our feelings and ideas about death often are influenced by what we know or think we know about how people die. As one or another

mode of dying becomes more prominent in society, the death system is likely to change in response. Similarly, as sociocultural conditions change, the types of death that are most prominent are also likely to change. There may be no logical connection between how people die and what death means. Nevertheless, we are all likely to be influenced by the circumstances that surround death. Yesterday the death systems of most societies were organized around the prospect of death at an early age as a result of contagious diseases and infections. Today deaths related to lifestyle have become salient. Tomorrow?

The Beginnings of Death Education, Research, and Counseling

As we noted in the first chapter of this book, the death system in the United States (and many other nations) was once devoted to avoiding even the thought of death. This situation started to change after the end of World War II. The reality of violent death could not easily be denied, nor could the loss and grief experienced by survivors. Reflective people also wondered anew about this strange and frightening race known as Homo sapiens, which periodically expends its resources and passions in killing each other. People of religious

TABLE 3-2

Modes of Dying and the Images of Death They Have Encouraged

Condition	Markers and Signifiers
The Black Death	Agony, disfiguration, partial decomposition while still alive, putrefaction >*human vanity and pride, punished and abandoned by God*
Syphilis	Facial disfiguration, dementia, moral degradation >*wages of sin*
Tuberculosis	Breath stolen by death; blood flowing from our bodies, which increasingly become skeletonized >*curse of the cities and factories, but also romantic exit for beautiful, brilliant, doomed youth*
Live Burial	Imagined and occasionally actual fate of some who fainted, seized, or otherwise lost consciousness >*terror of life in death*
Cancer	Pain, anxiety, body damage and distortion >*insidious attack by an enemy from within*
Persistent Vegetative State	Profound helplessness, inability to think or act on one's own behalf >*terror of death in life*
AIDS	Symptoms and stigma of many of the earlier forms of catastrophic dying—blood and body fluids affected, disfiguration, dementia, skeletonization, respiratory distress, plus linkage with taboo sexuality >*death embraces the most frightening experiences and outcomes that have ever haunted the imagination*

Source: Kastenbaum (1993, pp. 84–85).

faith were hard-pressed to discover purpose, re-deeming value, and God's love and mercy in a slaughterhouse world. From the devastating experience of war and its lingering aftereffects, there arose insistent questions about the meaning of life, death, and personal responsibility. More and more thinkers came to the conclusion that one had to come to terms with death in order to live a coherent and positive life.

There was also an increasing awareness of the private sorrows experienced by many people. These people included not only those who had lost loved ones in the war, but also a great many others who had to remain silent about their griefs because there were so few who were willing and able to listen. Mental health specialists started to recognize that unresolved grief was a major factor in some of the behavioral and emotional problems that came to their attention.

Meanwhile, another massive problem was also working its way to the surface. Biomedical advances had led to some effective measures for reducing the risk of death. Many people who would have died quickly of virulent diseases and uncontrolled infections made prompt recoveries with the newly developed antibiotics and other "wonder drugs." But these biomedical advances had achieved only limited results with other life-threatening conditions, such as many types of cancer and progressive neurological disorders. More and more people were therefore being maintained in the borderlands between life and death. These people often suffered physical pain, social isolation, and despair. The state of the art in medicine could not restore health but could keep people alive in stressful circumstances. Some health care professionals and some members of the general public became distressed and outraged by this situation. Why should people be made to suffer in this way—especially in a society that considers itself humane and technologically competent?

These were some of the issues that forced themselves into public and professional awareness. Instrumental in this movement were people from various backgrounds who broke through the taboo against acknowledging death. There were few if any "experts" in death half a century ago (although there were funeral directors with skills in specific areas). The people who taught the first classes on death and dying had never taken such courses themselves. The people who provided counseling to dying or grieving people had never received professional training for these services. The people who designed and conducted the first research projects likewise had to develop their own methods, theories, and databases. Included among these people were anthropologists, clergy, nurses, physicians, psychologists, sociologists, and social workers. Many had to overcome deeply entrenched resistances before they could offer educational or therapeutic services, or gain entry for research. These pioneers of thanatology were hardy people, however, and soon made themselves understood and welcome in many quarters. Some described themselves as *thanatologists* (from the Greek, *thanatos*, for death); some smiled and accepted the appellation, "deathnik." Generally, they were not concerned about titles, nor did they believe that a whole new profession had to be created. Instead, the mission was—and still is—to bring concern for the human encounter with mortality into the awareness of caregivers, educators, and researchers within existing disciplines. The "nurse-thanatologist," for example, must first be a knowledgeable and skillful nurse.

Few workers in this field would claim that the mission has been fully accomplished, but there is a growing cadre of people with expertise to give a hand. We will catch up again with death educators and counselors in later chapters and will continue to share useful contributions from researchers throughout the book.

Causes of Death: Yesterday, Today, and Tomorrow

A child born in 1900 had a life expectancy of about 47 years, a little more if female, but considerably less (about 33 years) if "Black and other." By the middle of the twentieth century, life expectancy had increased by about another 20 years for people of all racial backgrounds. Children born in 1997 (the most recent data) have an average life expectancy of 76.5 years—again, a little more for females but this time only a little less for "Black and other." Life expectancy at birth has also increased in many other nations. Furthermore, this trend applies as well to people at age 50, 60, 70, 80, or 90. In general, the graveyards are not filling up so quickly with family, especially with the young.

Obviously, conditions of life have much to do with length of life. Changes in life expectancy and population structure have resulted from and have also affected the nature of society. Nevertheless, death is still with us. In succeeding chapters, we will be considering the dying process in general, and some of the specific ways in which death occurs, including suicide, accidents, disaster, murder, war, and terrorism. This section provides a brief overview of causes of death.

BASIC TERMS AND CONCEPTS

Several terms and concepts are used frequently in presenting mortality data. *Mortality* refers to death, as distinguished from *morbidity*, which refers to illness. Following are several other key terms and concepts:

Life Expectancy: The estimated number of years remaining in a person's life at a particular time (e.g., birth). This is an average for the population under consideration (e.g., both sexes, females only, Native Americans only, etc.). It is useful to keep in mind that half of this population is expected to live longer and half is expected to live shorter lives than the mythical "average person."

Longevity: The average number of years between birth and death for a particular population. This statistic is based on lives that have ended, as distinguished from life expectancy, an estimate of years yet to be lived. There is another meaning of this term for geneticists and other people concerned with the maximum possible lifespan: longevity as the upper limit of survival for a particular species.

Cause of Death: This determination is made by a physician and recorded on the death certificate. The three general categories are degenerative biological conditions, disease, and socioenvironmental causes (such as accident, suicide, murder). In practice, these categories may overlap, and the completeness and accuracy of the information is subject to question.

Mortality Rate (also known as *Death Rate*): This is a measure of the proportion of people have died within a particular time period compared with the number of people in the population. The mortality rate is calculated on the basis of number of deaths either per 1,000 individuals or per 100,000 individuals within a one-year period unless otherwise specified. (Unfortunately, both 1,000 and 100,000 are used in various statistical reports, we must be careful!). It is important not to confuse the mortality *rate* with a percentage.

For example, in 1997, the mortality rate for motor vehicle accidents was 16.1. This does *not* mean that 16.1 percent of the population died in motor vehicle accidents in that year—that would be death on a catastrophic scale. It means, instead, that in a population of about 250 million, there were 43,200 deaths from this cause. Still alarming, but very different from the toll that would have been exacted from a percentage of 16.1.

Crude Death Rate (CDR): This measure does not control for age. It is simply the total number of deaths divided by the number of people in a population. Much of the data about deaths that comes our way is in the form of CDR—the easiest and least expensive kind of information to obtain. It is also the easiest kind of information to misinterpret. The number of deaths in a population is affected by the age structure. The United States today, for example, has a much higher proportion of elderly—that is, long-lived—people than it had at the turn of the century.

Age-Standardized Mortality Rate (ASMR): This measure does make adjustments for age. When data are presented in this form, we can make more reliable comparisons between the death rates of various populations. As Gee (1993) notes: "It is a hypothetical rate, based on the assumption that age composition has remained constant over time in one population or is constant across populations. By convention, the U.S. population in 1940 is the standard used (1993, p. 183).

For the United States, census data provide the most comprehensive and accurate information on causes and rates of death. These data themselves age somewhat in the ten years between census reports; therefore various techniques have been devised to provide useful estimates for the intervening years. These reports take some time to compile, so the most recent data available often go back about two years.

With this background information in mind, we can now look at changing patterns of mortality.

Death Learns to Wait: The Increase in Life Expectancy and Longevity

It has become easier to keep thoughts of death out of conscious awareness as death itself has loosened its grip on the young. By contrast, the aged man quoted at the beginning of this chapter had death etched in his mind in childhood as he lamented the all-too-short life of his brother, Simon. In his generation, people who reached the middle and late adult years were the survivors; most carried with them the memories of people they had loved and lost. Statistics are only statistics; nevertheless, they help us to understand the conditions of life and how these conditions have influenced our thoughts, feelings, and behaviors regarding death.

The general mortality rate (CDR) in the United States has been declining throughout the century. In 1900 the CDR was 17.2 per 1,000. By 1920 it had fallen to 13.0. The first single-digit rate occurred in 1948, although just barely: 9.9. From that point forward, the general death rate in the United States has always been in single digits. This was a remarkable pattern of decline— or, to put it more positively—a remarkable pattern of reducing the risk of death. In the past half century the decline has been much smaller and, most recently, it has stabilized (*see Table 3-3*).

Infants and children were at much greater risk for death in the past. Childbearing also brought to mothers a serious risk that had to be measured by deaths related not only directly to pregnancy and delivery, but also to lingering health problems that foreshortened their lives. Unlike the general mortality rate, the infant mortality rate in the United States has continued to decline markedly in the past half century (*see Table 3-4*).

How does the current infant mortality rate in the United States compare with that of other nations? As might be expected, the United States is at about the same level as a number of other nations that have advanced educational, public health, and medical care systems in place. The most recent data (again for 1997) reveal the lowest infant mortality rate in U.S. history: 7.1 Nations that are still struggling to establish effective human service programs for their citizens and/or that have been ravaged by famine, political unrest, or internal violence have much higher infant mortality rates. Infants are most at risk in the following nations (compare with the U.S. rate of 7.1): Bangladesh (107), Pakistan (102), India (78), Egypt (76), and Kenya (74). Infant mortality rates are lowest in Japan (4), Finland (5), Netherlands (6), Norway (6), and Sweden (6).

What does death mean to people who live in nations that still have very high infant mortality rates and very high rates of mortality and morbidity among childbearing women? In understanding how various nations and cultures deal with death, we must surely take into account both their past and their current patterns of mortality.

Leading Causes of Death in the United States Today

Changes have occurred not only in the death rate, but also in the most common causes of

TABLE 3.3

Decline and Stabilization of the United States Mortality Rate: Selected Years

Year	Death Rate per 1,000
1900	17.2
1910	14.7
1920	13.0
1930	11.3
1940	10.8
1948	9.9
1950	9.6
1960	9.5
1970	8.6
1980	8.7
1990	8.6
1992	8.5*
1994	8.8
1997	8.6

Source: National Center for Health Statistics.

*The, first and so far only, time in which the mortality rate has been less than half that of 1900.

TABLE 3.4

Infant Mortality Rate, United States, 1940–1997

Year	Death Rate per 1,000 Live Births
1940	47.0
1950	29.2
1960	26.0
1970	20.0
1980	12.6
1990	8.5
1994	8.0
1997	7.1

Sources: National Center for Health Statistics; U.S. Bureau of the Census.

Thousands have created and millions have viewed quilts to honor the memory of those who died of AIDS.

death. Pneumonia and influenza (considered together) and tuberculosis are important examples of this pattern of change. In 1900, these were the two leading causes of death, almost equal in their toll. The third most common cause at that time was a set of intestinal illnesses in which diarrhea and enteritis were frequent symptoms. Twenty years later, these intestinal maladies had vanished from the list of major causes of death and have never returned. Pneumonia/influenza still topped the list—in fact, the nation and much of the world were still trying to recover from a devastating epidemic of influenza. Tuberculosis was still a major threat to life, but its death toll had declined markedly (from 194.4 to 113.1 per 100,000 between 1900 and 1920). By 1920, another condition had risen almost to the top of the list: heart disease.

By 1940, heart disease had become the leading cause of death in the United States, and so it has remained. Why? Fewer people are dying young of infectious diseases. This means that more people are living long enough to develop physical problems in various organ systems, many of these problems having an impact on the functioning of the heart and of the entire cardiovascular system. Additionally, changes in diet, activity, and stress patterns may be putting many people at risk for heart problems.

Cancer is another condition to which people become more vulnerable with increasing adult age. By 1940, cancer had become the second most common cause of death in the United States, and this also remains true today. The increase in cancer rates cannot be attributed entirely to the "graying" of the population, however. The use of tobacco products is linked to lung cancer as well as a variety of other life-threatening conditions. The American Cancer Society estimated that more than half a million Americans would die of cancer in 1995, about 1,500 a day. Lung cancer is the most common cause of cancer deaths. Nearly 100,000 men and more than 60,000 women die of lung cancer each year. Cancer death rates for children have been reduced by an estimated 60 percent for children since 1950, with smaller declines for young and middle-aged adults. The death rates have increased somewhat for older adults and are increasing markedly for African American males, for reasons not yet determined.

As more people survive into the later adult years, the risks to life shift from acute infections and contagious diseases to chronic and progressive conditions. In past generations, fewer people lived long enough to die of heart disease, cancer, or stroke (the most common cardiovascular risk to life). They were more likely to have been carried away by epidemic diseases such as tuberculosis or by opportunistic infections prior to the development of effective antibiotics.

In general, the pathway from health to death has lengthened for many people. Biographies, memoirs, and novels written a hundred or more years ago often depict people going through intense life-or-death crises. The person either died or pulled through within a matter of days, and there was not much the physician could do in most cases, except to join in the prayers. In our own times, people often live for years with a life-threatening condition (see "lingering trajectory," *Chapter 4*). The protracted and uncertain courses of heart disease and cancer have unsettled even the way in which we speak of the at-risk person. Is this woman "dying" if, in fact, she operates a business from her home and continues to do much of the child care? Is this man "terminally ill" if he gets by with just a little assistance here and there and still enjoys a rewarding family life? Both people are afflicted with the condition that will probably be cited eventually as the cause of their death. Although it is likely that their lives are being foreshortened, they do not function from day to day as "terminally ill" or "dying" people. Essentially they are people who are trying to make the best of their lives under difficult circumstances.

We may also think of people in their late eighties or nineties who are alert and active, yet rather frail. These people also are not terminally ill or dying, and it would be inappropriate to apply these terms to them. They, too, are trying to make the best of each day for as long as they can. We must develop a new vocabulary and new concepts for describing the slow procession from vigorous life to death. A simple "dying/not dying" distinction is not very useful in a society in which so many people move through life resourcefully despite a variety of stresses and constraints.

Changes in causes of death and mortality rates have many implications for the way we interpret and respond to people who are at particular risk for their lives. With these considerations in mind, we now look at the most recent data on major causes of death in the United States (*Table 3-5*).

TABLE 3-5

Leading Causes of Death: 1997

Cause	Rate	Deaths
1. Heart Disease	271.2	725,790
2. Cancer	200.8	537,390
3. Cerebrovascular*	59.7	159,877
4. COPD**	41.3	110,637
5. Accidents	34.4	92,191
6. Pneumonia, Flu	33.0	88,363
7. Diabetes mellitus	23.3	62,332
8. Suicide	11.1	29,725
9. Kidney disease	9.6	25,570
10. Liver disease, & cirrhosis	9.3	24,765
ALL CAUSES	864.9	2,314,729

Source: National Center for Health Statistics.

*"Stroke" and related conditions.

*Chronic Obstructive Pulmonary Disease.

Several points stand out when these statistics are compared with those presented in the most recent previous edition of this book, in which 1990 data were the latest available:

- The death rate for heart disease has dropped steadily through the 1990s, probably as a result of increased public interest in exercise and "heart-friendly" foods. Nevertheless, the actual number of people dying of heart disease increased by about 15,000, reflecting the growth and aging of the general population.
- The cancer death rate has continued to creep upward, as it has for many years—but this overall trend masks the fact that some types of cancer are responding to treatment, while lung cancer continues to take a high toll. Deaths from chronic obstructive pulmonary disease (COPD), also related to use of tobacco products, increased both in rate and absolute number— for the first time, more than 100,000 people died of this cause in a single year. As part of our general population aging, people who have smoked heavily through the years become increasingly vulnerable to COPD and other life-threatening tobacco-related conditions.
- AIDS has quickly become one of the leading causes of death in the United States. There was an alarming jump from 1985 to 1990 and continuing large increases through the mid-90s. By 1994, AIDS was eighth on the list of major causes of death. As we can see in Table 3-6, however, more recently there has been a sharp reduction in AIDS-related deaths. It is unusual to have a cause of death come out of nowhere and then subside this quickly. Nevertheless, it is too soon to become complacent. There are still thousands of new cases each year, many among heterosexual people who mistakenly believe themselves to be in no danger and therefore do not take precautions.

Causes of Death in the Future?

As always, the future is uncertain. Nevertheless, the following possibilities are among those worth considering.

In the United States, there may be an increasing risk of death from infectious and contagious diseases. The trend has been toward decreased risks of death from these sources throughout much of the world. To some extent, the health care establishment and the public have relaxed (e.g., fewer parents have been making sure that their children receive innoculations against contagious diseases). Tuberculosis, however, is showing signs of making a comeback, often in association with AIDS among people with weakened immune systems. It may be time now to "unrelax."

Even the most effective public health systems are being stressed by many factors, including problems with funding, service delivery to some populations, and a sector of the public that ignores or resists basic preventive health measures. Furthermore, some nations have been devastated by internal conflicts and natural disasters that

TABLE 3.6

AIDS Deaths in the United States, 1985–1997

Deaths	1985	1990	1992	1994	1995	1996	1997
	6,854	31,145	40,674	48,110	47,858	34,557	14.185

Source: National Center for Health Statistics.

have weakened both individuals and the health care system, leaving the way open to a variety of opportunistic diseases. The many people who have been uprooted from their homelands often live in substandard circumstances and are especially vulnerable to contagions and infections.

Additionally, diseases can now spread rapidly through the world so that an illness once restricted to a small and isolated area can enter the mainstream. Some public health authorities believe that the organism responsible for AIDS has had this kind of history. An alarming example of another possible epidemic has been receiving close scrutiny by physicians and researchers around the world. The Ebola virus, spread by blood, saliva, and feces, was first discovered in 1976, when it had a lethal outbreak in a small community in Zaire. This virus is fast-working, deadly, and at present without a definitive form of treatment. It reappeared in Zaire in 1995 in another brief and contained episode—but there are fears that there might be a "next time" in which the virus spreads to large population centers. Health authorities recognize that they do not yet understand much about this condition, nor do they have any way of knowing what other lethal contagious conditions might exist in various parts of the world and emerge at any time as major threats. A new scientific journal (*Emerging Infectious Diseases*) has been established to share information on this topic.

Still another problem that has public health authorities very much concerned is that the antibiotics that have been so valuable in subduing infections are starting to lose their effectiveness. Some viruses and other microorganisms have developed resistance to the most frequently used antibiotics. The unwise use of antibiotics for minor ailments and the public's more than occasional failure to use them as directed may also be responsible for the loss of effectiveness. Perhaps we will be lucky. But perhaps the *Evolution of Infectious Disease* (Ewald, 1994), and *Emerging Viruses* (Morse, 1993) will result in a catastrophic increase in death rates. Should we urge more support for the public health system and medical research, and more attention to disease prevention in our school curricula? Now would be a good time to take the prevention function of the death system quite seriously.

We will have other glimpses into possible scenarios of the "future of death" as we continue through this book. Indeed, whatever we can learn about the past and present of our relationship with death may serve us well as we try to make wise choices in our lives that could affect the future.

SUMMARY

Everything that makes a collection of individuals into a society and keeps that society going has implications for our relationship to death, as we have seen through many examples. At first we tried to imagine a world without death. This helped us to freshen our perspective on the world in which we live as mortals and on the death system in which we participate. We may think of the death system as the interpersonal, sociophysical, and symbolic network through which an individual's relationship to mortality is mediated by his or her society. The death system of any society can be analyzed in terms of its components and functions. The *components* include *people, places, times, objects,* and *symbols* (including language) that have special death-related meanings. The *functions* include *warnings and predictions, preventing death, caring for the dying, disposing of the dead, social consolidation after death, making sense of death,* and *killing.* Each of these functions was illustrated with key examples that often revealed conflicts, biases, and strains in society (e.g. unequal protection from life-threatening conditions, the influence of lifestyle on vulnerability to death, the capital punishment controversy, and war. A brief historical review showed how various modes of dying (e.g., Black Death, syphilis, and tuberculosis) have influenced society's images of death itself. We also became familiar with the beginnings of death education, research, and counseling.

Leading causes of death were examined after we solidified our knowledge of terms such as *mortality, morbidity,* and the various ways in which mortality (death) rates are reported. We saw that the general mortality rate in the United States decreased throughout the twentieth century, accompanied, as we would expect, by increases in longevity. Infant mortality rate is now at its lowest level in U.S. history, although not the lowest in the world. The ten leading causes of death were identified—heart disease is still number 1—and current trends were noted, such as the sharp decline in AIDS-related deaths in the past few years. New risks to life may be on the horizon, however, as several examples indicated.

REFERENCES

Ariès, P. (1981). *The hour of our death.* New York: Alfred A. Knopf.

Borenstein, S. (1999: May 11). Study urges disaster management. *Arizona Republic,* p. 10A.

Bryer, K. B. (1977). The Amish way of death. *American Psychologist, 12,* 167–174.

Clausewitz, K. V. (1984). *On War.* Princeton, NJ: Princeton University Press. (Original work published 1832)

Einstein, A., & Freud, S. (1933). Why war? In C. James & S. Grachen (Eds.), *Collected papers of Sigmund Freud* (vol. 4, pp. 273–287). London: Hogarth.

Ewald, P. W. (1994). *Evolution of infectious disease.* Oxford, New York: Oxford University Press.

Franks, P., Clancy, C. M., & Gold, M. R. (1993). Health insurance and mortality. *Journal of the American Medical Association, 270,* 737–741.

Gee, E. (1993). Causes of death. In R. Kastenbaum & B. Kastenbaum (Eds.), *The encyclopedia of death* (pp. 38–41) New York: Avon.

Holveck, J. (1991). Grief reactions within the adolescent gang system. Tempe, AZ: Arizona State University: Department of Communication, project paper.

Jankofsky, K. (1979). Public execution in England in the late middle ages: The indignity and dignity of death. *Omega, Journal of Death and Dying, 10:* 433–458.

Kant, I. (1932). *Perpetual Peace.* Los Angeles: U.S. Library Associates. (orginal work published 1795)

Kastenbaum, R. (1993). Reconstructing death in postmodern society. *Omega, Journal of Death and Dying, 27,* 75–89.

Laungani, P. (1996). Death and bereavement in India and England: A comparative analysis. *Mortality, 1,* 191–212.

McGinnis, J. M., & Foege, W. H. (1993). Actual causes of death in the United States. *Journal of the American Medical Association, 270,* 2207–2212.

More, T. (1516). *Utopia.*

Morse, S. S. (Ed.) (1993). *Emerging viruses.* Oxford, New York: Oxford University Press.

Rando, T. A. (1993). *Treatment of complicated mourning.* Champaign, IL: Research Press.

Scripps Howard (1993, December 22) Babies in U.S. study got radioactive shots.

Smith, C. (1999: August 8). Now you can go out with bang. Ashes in fireworks give bright send-off. *Santa Rosa Press Democrat,* p. 26A.

Thurow, R. (1994: June 28). "Merry cemetery" of Romania is proud of its epitaphs. *Wall Street Journal.*

Ward, R. (1999: July 9). 344-pound killer bleeds during electrocution. *Associated Press Dispatch.*

GLOSSARY

Age-Standardized Death Rate: A *mortality rate* in which age is statistically removed as a source of possible misinterpretation.

Capital Punishment: Execution carried out by the legal system in accordance with the death penalty.

Cardiovascular Resuscitation (CPR): The process of re-establishing respiration and heart action by opening the airway, performing rescue breathing, and compressing the chest, as required by the circumstances.

Cerebrovascular Accidents (CVA): Commonly known as *stroke.* Primary effects are on speech and voluntary movement. Can be fatal.

Cohort: The name given to a set of people who were born at the same time (birth cohort) or who entered a particular situation at the same time (e.g., students entering college in the year 2000).

COPD: Chronic obstructive pulmonary disease. Includes *emphysema* and *chronic bronchitis,* both of which progressively create "air hunger" (*dypsnea*).

Crude Death Rate: Not corrected for age (see *Mortality Rate*)

Life Expectancy: Estimated length of time between a specified point (e.g., birth) and death.

Death System: The interpersonal, sociophysical, and symbolic network through which society mediates an individual's relationship to mortality.

Excessive Death Rate: A measure of the extent to which the death rate of a particular population is higher than the rate that would have been expected for the population as a whole.

Longevity: The number of years between birth and death.

Microbial Agents: Bacteria and viruses.

Morbidity: Illness.

Mortality: Death. Also, the condition of being vulnerable to death.

Mortality Rate: The proportion of people in a particular population who die within one year, based on the number of deaths per 1,000 or 100,000. Also known as *death rate.*

Pathologists: Physicians who specialize in examination and study of corpses (cadavers).

Radioactive Iodide: A substance used in diagnosing and treating disorders of the thyroid gland.

Thanatology: The study of death and death-related phenomena.

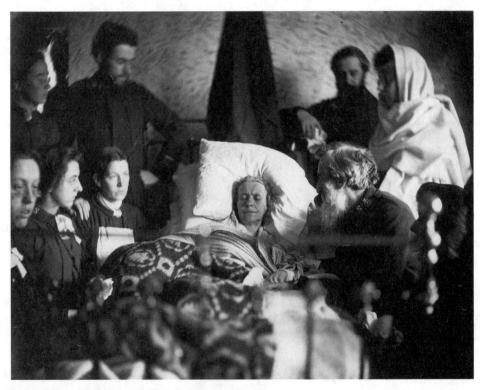

For centuries, many people have hoped for a peaceful deathbed scene in the company of their loved ones. Here William Booth, founder of the Salvation Army, kneels at the bedside of his dying wife, Catherine.

DYING

transition from life

You looked full of life, full of mischief, of energy, of playfulness, and laughter that Easter weekend during which your parents had to make the excruciating decision of whether to attempt another treatment or to attend as best as possible to your comfort. They opted for the former. From the admission to the hospital and the development, that very same day, of a benign infection following the introduction of the catheter to start yet another bout of chemotherapy, you were never well again. You died five weeks later.
—Dembour, 1998–1999, p. 194

My father died in his ninety third year. He was alert, comfortable, and still very much himself. What he said most often to everybody was, "Thank you, thank you, thank you."
—Yohei Sasakawa, 1996

Patients in the study experienced considerable pain during most of their final 3 days of life. Communication between physicians and patients was poor.... Physicians misunderstood patients' preferences regarding cardiopulmonary resuscitation (CPR) in 80% of the cases. Furthermore, physicians did not implement patients' refusals of interventions.
—Editorial, *Journal of the American Medical Association*, 1995, p. 1635

Whatever we do—people still die.
—Shigeaki Hinohara, M.D., Ph.D., 1996

All of these observations have to do with what most physicians call "terminal illness" and what the rest of us call "dying." Hinohara, at age 87 one of the world's most distinguished physicians, has a wealth of personal and professional experiences to draw upon. He quietly reminds us that it may not be wise to overestimate what can be accomplished in preventing death—especially if this leads to the neglect of humane care for dying people.

The editorial in the *Journal of the American Medical Association* was commenting on a study published in the same issue, a study that found that there are still substantial shortcomings in the care of seriously ill hospitalized patients, including those with a terminal illness (SUPPORT, 1995). The study and its accompanying editorial represent the continuing efforts of the medical establishment to improve the quality of life for seriously ill and dying patients. Should we be surprised that the medical profession is still struggling with the issue of providing compassionate care to dying people a century after this need was clearly identified by Sir William Osler, one of the most respected practitioners of his time? (Golden, 1997–1998).

Sasakawa is the executive director of a major philanthropic organization that has a special interest in quality-of-life issues. His late father, founder of the organization, lived and died peacefully after a life of significant achievement and service. Such examples demonstrate that death does not have to be regarded as failure on part of either physician or patient.

By contrast, Isaline, the child in the first example, was a 2 year old whose life ended all too soon. Neither her parents nor the medical team could bring themselves to regard her as terminally ill. The health care system did everything it could to keep her alive and therefore did little to provide comfort in her last days. Isaline is one of many people, young and old, who cannot easily be classified as terminally ill and who yet face significant threats to their lives.

In this chapter, we consider dying not as an abstraction, but as an experience that takes many forms, depending on the nature and management of the illness, the social support system available, and the unique person whose life is in jeopardy.

Dying as Transition

Dying is one of many transitions that we experience in our lives. This means that we can call upon what we already know from other new experiences and transitional situations. For example, most of us have already experienced our first day of school...our first date...our first solo ride behind the wheel of a car...our first day on the job.

Many of us have moved on to such other memorable transitions as the first time we held our baby or the time we discovered our first gray hair.

We all experience transitions in our lives. Some may have been long awaited ("At last, I'm old enough for a driver's license!"). Some may have been dreaded ("Do I actually have to support myself now?"). Many transitions are tinged with ambivalence ("I'm kinda ready to get married, sort of, but sort of not"). The transition from life itself is unique because the separation is so complete and so final. However, the dying process does have points in common with other types of transition: there are *interactions* that can either be upsetting or comforting, *communications* that can either inform or confuse, and *self-evaluations* that can either undermine or strengthen one's sense of identity. Perhaps most significantly, what the dying process *means* depends much upon the way that everybody involved thinks, feels, and behaves. It follows that the transition from life is unique for every individual. No two people bring the same thoughts, feelings, accomplishments, and illness-related experiences. Furthermore, no two people have the same set of human relationships. The quality of life during a final illness depends much on the quality of the individual's relationships with others and the availability of those who are most capable of providing comfort and support.

As we develop an overview of the dying process, we look first to the basic question of what dying is and when it begins. Next we look at some of the different "trajectories" or forms the dying process can take. The sometimes difficult question of distinguishing between terminal illness and an "at risk" condition is considered, with particular attention to hemophilia. The challenge of communicating well throughout the dying process is then explored, including attention to the problems reported in the *JAMA* study. The influences of age, gender, interpersonal relationships, disease, treatment, management, and environment are considered. This is followed by an exploration of several models of the dying process: stage theories, developmental task theory, and a new multiple perspective approach, and the implications of each for guiding our interactions.

This is a good time to pause and consider dying from a very personal perspective. I suggest that you give your attention now to the thought exercise outlined in Box 4-1. Why not try this exercise right now? It has proven helpful to other people who were beginning the study of dying and terminal care. The questions raised in this exercise are taken up later in the text, and your instructor will have other observations to add.

WHAT IS DYING AND WHEN DOES IT BEGIN?

Individual and Interpersonal Responses

"What is dying?" and "When does it begin?" The knowledge that "I am dying" introduces many changes in an individual's view of self and world.

A New England artist (Lesses, 1982–1983) who was terminally ill described the comfortable familiarity of her home:

I live with an oak coffee table
beside my bed where
my silver-framed clock ticks hard
through the night
like my cat when she purrs.

But this sense of comfort could not disguise the fact that her life had changed decisively:

I hate every morning
hating it
with my stomach jumping
before I've had a chance to think
of anything I awake non-thinking and I am
like a small animal backed into the corner
of a cage to escape from the hand clutching,

reaching through the wire door
I feel the power of the hand's grasp
and fear it
without knowing what the power is.

Other terminally ill people have different experiences to report, but the feeling that "How I live now is not as I lived before" is hard to escape. The lives of close friends and relatives also change. Structured interviews were conducted with the significant others of cancer patients receiving chemotherapy in an ambulatory care setting (Hart, 1986–1987). Friends experienced a total stress level just as high as that of family members and responded to the stress in a similar manner.

Family and friends of the chemotherapy patients had to contend with uncertainty. Was their friend or relation *really* dying? Some of the patients would recover, others would live for several years, and still others would die within a short period. The *possibility* and the *certainty* of dying both generate stress, but they tend to produce somewhat different responses. A pair of case examples further illustrates this difficulty.

Greg was a college student who lived more than two years with the knowledge that he would probably die in the near future. He suffered from a form of leukemia that was unusually puzzling to his physicians. Greg recognized that the disease itself was his central problem, but often he was more concerned about the ways in which other people related to him:

I have had to develop almost a whole new set of friends. My good old buddies just felt awfully uncomfortable around me. They couldn't be

---

BOX 4-1
YOUR DEATHBED SCENE

A Thought Exercise
They are planning a movie about your life. This film is intended to be as faithful as possible to the facts. Help them plan the deathbed scene. Describe the ending of your life in as much detail as you can, based upon what you expect is most likely to happen. It would be best if this description were complete enough to help locate

the setting, the time, who else might be on the scene, and anything else that is needed. (Yes, of course—they're giving you lots of money for your cooperation, but you are in control of planning this scene according to your best guess at what the future will bring.)

Please use a separate sheet of paper for this exercise.

themselves anymore. I realized they'd be relieved if I would just sort of drift away from them.

What seemed to disturb Greg's friends most was the discrepancy and ambiguity. Greg was a powerfully built young man who had been healthy and vigorous for most of his life. His sturdy appearance made it difficult to accept that he was in the grip of a life-threatening disease. None of the "good old buddies" could relate to *both* facts: that Greg looked healthy and functioned well, and that he was also terminally ill. Most of his friends and family chose to relate only to the healthy Greg.

> I guess it was my own fault. If I wanted to make things easier for everybody, I could have just shut up about my condition. But I didn't think I had to. I mean, you talk about important things with your best friends, don't you? I didn't go on and on about it. When something new happened, or I started feeling shaky about it, I would say something. Oh, man—they just couldn't handle it!

Greg posed a problem for his friends as well as his physicians. He touched on his illness often enough to make it hard for his friends to ignore it, but often he looked well enough. When he had an acute episode, he was in the hospital. Afterward he kept to himself for a while. "I didn't like to show my face around when I felt rotten," he said. This pattern crossed his friends' expectations. Everybody knew that a dying person looks different, so Greg *should* have looked different. Similarly, it was assumed that dying was the last thing a dying person would want to talk about. A young man might be expected to be especially keen to preserve his "macho" image by concealing any signs of pain, weakness, or fear. Greg was a deviant, then, in behaving as a dying young man should not.

By contrast, Matilda D. was depleted by many years of illness and seemed too frail to survive much longer (Kastenbaum, Barber, Wilson, Ryder, & Hathaway, 1981). She was admitted to a geriatric hospital at age 86, suffering from a painfully advanced rheumatoid arthritis condition, anemia, and difficulty in taking and utilizing nutrition. Attentive nursing care enabled her to remain relatively stable for several months, but Matilda's condition gradually worsened. She spent most of her time sleeping or lying on her bed in considerable discomfort. At this point, she was regarded as "failing" but not dying. This distinction was meaningful to staff members because it indicated to them what pattern of care would be most appropriate. They did not face the ambiguity that Greg's friends and the significant others in the chemotherapy study had to contend with. Furthermore, the staff (and Matilda's daughter, her only visitor from the community) also expected that dying and death would soon follow. This again contrasts with Greg and the chemotherapy patients for whom there was some hope of recovery or remission.

Matilda was officially considered a dying person when her lungs started to fill with fluid and her general condition weakened. The next "proper" action was to relocate Matilda to the intensive care unit (ICU). Although some patients were treated successfully for a medical crisis on the ICU, it also served as the tacitly approved exit ward. Matilda's status change to that of a dying person meant that she would be moved to a death place. (When a facility has an agreed-upon "death place," it is possible to maintain the illusion that death will not visit elsewhere.) Her new status could also be seen in an altered pattern of staff interactions. Basic care was still provided in a conscientious, professional manner, but the contacts were now briefer and more mechanical. The subtle change from a living to a dying person had taken place in the perceptions and actions of staff members. The certainty of her death made it easier for staff to shift their patterns.

Fortunately, Matilda's life did not end with the isolation and dehumanization that might be suggested by this description. A therapeutic companion had formed a close relationship with Matilda just before the failing and dying sequences. There was time to discover some of Matilda's distinctive personal qualities and values. Her therapeutic companion (Andrea George) and her daughter continued to relate to Matilda as a distinctive human being even when the old woman could no longer respond in words. Matilda's favorite music was sung and played to her, and she died literally in touch with two people for whom she remained a distinctive and valued person.

We treat people differently when they are perceived as dying. When Lester (1992–1993) replicated a study conducted in the mid 1960s, he found that undergraduates still prefer to keep a large social distance between themselves and people who are dying of cancer, are in pain, or are suicidal. People dying of AIDS-related complications were subject to exclusionary attitudes even more strongly than were terminally ill people in general. Personal background and education can affect our perception of dying people as well. Although most registered nurses have accepting attitudes toward people with AIDS, negative attitudes were found among nursing assistants and licensed practical nurses who had less education and less preparation for working with terminally ill people (Demmer, 1999).

Both the classification of a person as "dying" and the particular modality of death influence our willingness to associate with that person. For example, it has been observed that nurses took a significantly longer time before going to the bedside of a dying patient as compared with other patients. The nurses were surprised and upset when they learned of their differential pattern of response and decided to make a special effort to respond promptly to terminally ill patients. After a few weeks, however, the original pattern reinstated itself (LeShan, 1982). As much as they wanted to treat all patients equally, the nurses could not avoid being influenced by the attitude they share with the rest of society: dying people are different, and contacts should be kept to a minimum. (There is no reason to believe that nurses engage in more avoidant behavior than do other health care professionals; indeed, they spend more time with them with terminally ill patients than do any other professional caregivers.)

Onset of the Dying Process: Alternative Perspectives

When dying begins depends on our frame of reference. Perhaps the most abstract perspective is the one proposing that we die from the moment we are born. This view can be useful as we develop a personal philosophy of life. It does, however, encourage evasion. "We die from the moment we are born" accepts the general but trivializes the specific. "There is nothing really special here. Maybe you *are* dying, but *everybody*

is dying, and isn't it a lovely day?" Often this "We are always dying" perspective is simply a way of reducing our own discomfort and anxiety.

The concept is also questionable as a direct statement of fact. It is true that there is a continual sequence of death among the cells that constitute our bodies. The outer layer of the skin, for example, is composed of dead cells that are replaced in turn by other dead cells. Certain forms of tissue death are programmed to occur at particular times in psychobiological development. The loss of the umbilical cord after birth is one of the clearest examples of a biological structure phasing itself out after its function has been served. Nevertheless, it would be misleading to insist that the normal turnover of cells and the atrophy of unnecessary structures constitute a process of dying for the organism as a whole. Should the term *dying* be used so loosely, we would simply have to find a new term to represent the very different processes observed when life actually is in jeopardy.

A more challenging concept has been with us for many years. Three centuries ago, Jeremy Taylor, chaplain to King Charles I of England, likened aging to a form of terminal illness (Taylor, 1651/1977). The concept of aging as dying has more impact than the proposition that dying begins with life. It is also interesting to consider Taylor's suggestion that aging might be regarded as slow dying and dying as fast aging. However, elderly people cannot be described as dying without ignoring the vigor and vitality that many continue to express at an advanced age. It is also difficult to equate dying with aging when we look at the details. For example, a young person may die because of a specific bodily failure (e.g., an unexpected drug reaction or heart failure) although he or she is otherwise in good health and does not resemble an aged person at all.

Dying usually begins as a psychosocial event. Organ systems fail, but it is in the realm of personal and social life that dying occurs. To put this a little differently: we construct the idea of "dying" from many experiences, communications, and related concepts. Let us now consider some of the contexts in which the onset of dying is discovered or certified. The process of constructing "dying" is often complex, so we cannot give ourselves the luxury of making it seem simple.

1. *Dying begins when the facts are recognized.* Physicians' offices are visited by people with varying types of concern for their health. Included are essentially healthy people who have been convinced for years that they are dying and people who have just come in for a routine checkup (yet the latter may be the ones who actually have a life-threatening illness that is about to be discovered. Perhaps, then, the dying process begins when a physician observes it. However, the physician in turn is likely to rely on clinical and laboratory diagnostic procedures. *From this perspective, the dying process begins when a physician has obtained and analyzed enough information to make such a judgment.* The physician might suspect that the patient has been on a "terminal trajectory" (see the next section) for some time before the diagnostic evaluation was established. But this had not been "official" dying; it is only now that the person is considered a dying patient.

2. *Dying begins when the facts are communicated.* There is a big difference between the physician's prognosis and the patient's awareness. Perhaps, then, it would make more sense to date the onset of the dying process *from the moment at which the physician informs the patient.* This would give *two* possible beginning points of the dying process: physician awareness and physician-patient communication. Patients and physicians operate within different frameworks for interpreting the terminal process, and it is useful to respect both perspectives. When we ask, "Is this person dying?" it is important to bear in mind where the answer is coming from.

   The actual situation is even more complicated. There is likely to be an interval between the physician's determination of the prognosis and the time when it is shared with the patient. Physicians seldom break the news at the same instant they reach their conclusions. There may be a delay of days, weeks, or even months before the physician tells the patient what has been found. Furthermore, *sometimes the physician never does tell the patient,* so we cannot depend entirely on the physician's communication as the definitive starting point of the process from the patient's standpoint. But even when the physician does share the findings with the patient, can

this be taken firmly as the onset of the dying process? Not necessarily. The patient must be ready and able to understand the prognosis.

3. *Dying begins when the patient realizes or accept the facts.* More than one nurse has returned from the bedside of a patient almost bursting with anger at the physician. "Why hasn't he leveled with this patient? This man is dying, and nobody has told him what's going on!" At times this concern is well justified. The physician has not provided the terminally ill patient with a clear statement of the condition. But at other times, the patient's apparent lack of knowledge cannot be laid at the physician's doorstep. The patient was told, but he or she "didn't stay told." Somehow the patient was able to forget or misinterpret the central facts. Or perhaps the physician said one thing with words and something else with facial expression and tone of voice.

   Note also that the physician's communication can be subtle or direct, couched in clear language or technical jargon. After an interaction with the physician, the patient may either have a clear understanding or be left in a state of uncertainty and confusion. There can be another time lag, then, between communication and realization of terminal illness, depending on the physician's communication skills. For examples of poor and competent physician-patient communication, see Box 4-2.

Communication may fail because the patient has lost the ability to process information and understand concepts adequately. In many situations, it is not easy to determine how much the patient does understand. My colleagues and I found that many aged patients who appeared to be completely unresponsive were capable of responding when approached with patience and touch-enhanced communication (Kastenbaum *et al.,* 1981). Jansson et al. (1992–1993) have made use of videotapes to demonstrate that communication is possible with terminally ill people even when they are suffering from Alzheimer's disease, if caregivers are attentive to nonverbal as well as verbal responses. These patients may not be able to understand that they are dying but may be appreciative of compassionate human contact.

BOX 4-2
"BREAKING THE BAD NEWS": PHYSICIAN-PATIENT COMMUNICATION

How Not To	*A Better Way*
Give the bad news right away and get it over with.	√ Take the time to establish a relationship with patient and family.
Give all of the facts at one time.	√ Share a fact…see how the patient responds…wait until one fact has been "digested" before going on.
Impress patient and family with your medical knowledge.	√ Keep it simple. Don't "snow" them with details unless they ask for more details.
Tell the diagnosis, then move on.	√ Take the time to discover what this diagnosis means to the patient; explain and educate.
End the session after you have told all.	√ Allow pauses, breathing spaces so patient/family can ask questions.
Make sure that you have broken through denial.	√ Respect what may seem like denial; the message will be heard when the patient is ready.
Stretch the truth if necessary to cheer up the patient.	√ Do not say anything that is not true; this destroys trust and sets up later anger and sorrow.
Make it clear that nothing more can be done for the patient.	√ Make it clear that you will be with the patient all the way and respond to his or her needs and desires.

A person is not dying to himself or herself until the situation has been realized and personalized. In this sense, the dying process cannot be dated from the medical prognosis nor from the act of official communication, if there is one. We must be aware of the individual's thoughts and feelings. This often leads to disagreement as to whether or not a person knows. Disagreements arise because some of us are better observers than others, and some of us are looking for clues to support a particular opinion. For example, a terminally ill person may talk about a relatively minor symptom. This may lead me to assume that the patient is not aware of the more critical situation that threatens life. But someone else may notice that this patient slips into the past tense when talking about family and occupational life, suggesting that she does not project herself far into the future. We come to different

conclusions, then, based on different observations. Perhaps I did not make that additional observation because I wanted to believe that the patient was unaware of her terminal prognosis.

Disagreements may also arise because the terminally ill person, like anybody else, behaves differently depending on the situation. A different attitude toward the illness may be expressed to a member of the immediate family than to a physician, a colleague, or a stranger. Most of the health care staff may be under the impression that the patient does not know, but one nurse may realize that he is keenly aware of the situation because he has selected that nurse as the person with whom to share his innermost thoughts and feelings.

Additionally, the person's own estimation of his or her condition may shift from time to time. "Middle knowledge" (Weisman, 1993) is an awareness that floats from one level of consciousness to another. The individual suspects or senses what is taking place but is hesitant to put these thoughts into clear focus. Depending on our relationship with the person and the situation in which we are interacting together, we might come away either with or without the impression that the patient sees himself or herself as dying.

4. *Dying begins when nothing more can be done to preserve life.* This is a pragmatic definition that has important consequences for the care of very ill people. The physician may not have classified the person as dying, despite the diagnostic signs, because avenues of treatment remain open. "I haven't tried all possible combinations of drugs," the physician may reason, or "Building the patient up with transfusions might make her a better candidate for another surgical procedure." The physician is also likely to know that individuals with this particular condition have a certain probability of survival (e.g., 5% survive more than a year). Perhaps this patient could be one of the survivors. Furthermore, the probabilities might shift when a new treatment regime is introduced. The physician might, then, be able to appreciate the seriousness of a patient's condition without having to classify her as dying, at least not until all treatment possibilities have been exhausted. This often happens when the patient is a person the medical and nursing staff has exceptionally strong motivation to keep alive, for example, a child or a person of their own age and background. (It is this ability to hold off defining a patient as "dying" that often stands in the way of discussing the possibility of hospice care; *see Chapter 5.*) Furthermore, the family physician may have a different opinion from that of the specialist— and one specialist from that of another. As long as there is one more procedure that might be tried to halt or reverse the pathological process, some members of the medical team may decline to think of the patient as terminally ill.

The judgment that a person is dying could be considered premature if it discourages actions that might lead to recovery. As late as the eighteenth century in a city as sophisticated as London, special efforts had to be made to persuade the establishment that victims of drowning could be restored by prompt treatment. By contrast, we might conclude that the classification of a person as dying has been delayed too long if painful and socially isolating treatments are continued beyond reasonable hope of success and therefore prevent the person from living his or her final days as he or she might have chosen. When to shift from "prevention of death" to "care of the dying" and how to accomplish this shift in an effective and humane manner are questions that hinge in part upon our definition of dying.

And what of euthanasia or physician-assisted death? Those who favor the legalization of "death by request" have been most effective when they focus on the person who is dying, and dying in great pain (e.g., Gomez, 1991). The strongest resistance has been encountered when the list of "eligibles" is increased to include people with chronic impairments who express the wish to die before their condition deteriorates beyond an endurable level. Kevorkian's willingness to make his "suicide machine" available to people who are not dying has outraged some people who are sympathetic to the more restrictive application of "mercy killing." The larger issue will be considered in more detail in *Chapter 9.* The point to bear in mind here is that attitudes toward termination of life are influenced by how we define "dying" in general and how we apply this definition to particular individuals in particular situations.

TRAJECTORIES OF DYING: FROM BEGINNING TO END

We have been exploring the *onset* of the dying process as interpreted by the various people involved. The end usually takes place in a hospital or nursing home, but with the advent of hospice care (*see Chapter 5*) more people have been spending their final days at home. The next chapter examines in detail the hospice approach, with its emphasis on the home and family. Here the emphasis is on what are still the most common pathways to death—those that conclude in a health care facility.

A series of pioneering studies by Barney Glaser, Anselm Strauss, & Jean Quint Benoleil (1966, 1968), identified a variety of sequences and their distinctive characteristics. The research team observed interactions with dying people in six medical facilities in the San Francisco area. Keep in mind that field researchers do not have the responsibility for patient care that occupies so much of the energies of the hospital staff. Furthermore, the researchers are not the husbands, wives, or children of a dying patient, nor are they terminally ill themselves. This emotional distance gives field researchers a unique perspective.

The San Francisco research team organized many of their observations according to the concept of *trajectories of dying*. All dying processes take time; all have a certain shape through time. The combination of duration and shape can be seen and even graphed as a trajectory. For one person, the trajectory might best be represented as a straight downward line. For somebody else, it might be represented more accurately as slowly fluctuating, going down, leveling off, declining again, climbing a little, and so on.

Certainty and Time

Staff members must answer two questions about every patient whose life is in jeopardy: "Will this patient die?" and "If so, when?" These are the questions of *certainty* and *time*. The questions are important because the attitudes and actions of the health care staff are based largely on what they take to be the answers. It is easier for the staff to organize itself around the patients when the answers are clear. Like other bureaucratic organizations, hospitals rely heavily on standard operating procedures. It is uncomfortable and disrupting when a patient's condition does not lend itself to straightforward expectations such as "This man will recover," or "This woman will die, but not for some time."

The time framework can vary a great deal, depending on circumstances. In the emergency room, the staff's initial uncertainty can change to certainty in just a few minutes. The fate of a premature baby may be determined in a few hours or a few days, but the outlook for a cancer patient may remain indeterminate for months.

Together, certainty and time yield four types of death expectation:

1. Certain death at a known time.
2. Certain death at an unknown time.
3. Uncertain death but a known time when certainty will be established.
4. Uncertain death and an unknown time when the question will be resolved.

The Glaser-Strauss research team found that staff interaction with patients is closely related to the expectations they have formed about time and certainty of death. These expectations are important even when they do not prove to have been correct, because they form the basis for interactions among staff members as well as with patients and their families. Especially important are situations in which staff expectations change. One example given is that of a physician's decision to discontinue blood transfusions. The nurses may reject this hint and continue to do everything in their power to give the patient still another chance. This sequence has significant implications no matter who (physician or nurse) has made the more accurate assessment of the patient's condition in this instance. The subtle pattern of communication among staff in such a case affects everybody:

> Since the doctor had said nothing official, even nurses who believe the patient is dying can still give him an outside chance and stand ready to save him. They remain constantly alert to counterclues. "Everybody is simply waiting," said one nurse. If the doctor had indicated that the patient would die within the day, nurses would have ceased their efforts to save him, concentrating instead on giving comfort to the last, with no undue prolonging of life. (1968, p. 11)

It is possible, then, for one member of the treatment team to come to a conclusion but still leave room for others to follow an alternative course. In the instance cited, the physician did not carelessly forget to instruct the nurses to alter their approach. By putting nothing into words, the physician allowed a little leeway for others to continue their efforts to maintain life against the odds. The physician, then, had decided that the *prevention* function of the death system could not be achieved, but he offered the nurses some maneuvering room to maintain the possibility of a reprieve while devoting most of their efforts to the *caring and comforting* function.

We can increase our awareness of the differential patterns of communication likely to accompany the dying process by considering three of the dying trajectories identified by the Glaser-Strauss research team: *lingering trajectory, expected quick trajectory,* and *unexpected quick trajectory.*

The Lingering Trajectory

The caregivers display a characteristic tempo and service pattern when a patient's life is fading slowly and gradually. Seldom is there a dramatic rescue scene. The staff tries to keep the patient comfortable and viable on a day-to-day basis. But when the patient is clearly failing, staff members are inclined to believe that they have already done "all that we can," and that the patient has "earned" death after a long downhill process. In the geriatric ward, for example, it would be unusual to find a team of specialists racing to apply a battery of heroic measures. A quiet fading away seems to be both expected and accepted by the staff as a fit conclusion to the lingering trajectory.

Perhaps the death that terminates a lingering trajectory is more acceptable because the person may have been considered *socially dead* for some time (Sweeting & Gilhooly, 1991–1992). Even within the institution itself, some patients may be considered more alive than others. Staff members become attached to some patients more than others as they interact with them through the months. Yet, although the staff is likely to feel sorrow when these patients die, this reaction is moderated by the belief that their lives no longer had much value to either themselves or society. For every patient who has somehow attracted the special attention and sympathy of staff members, however, there are others whose distinctive human qualities have not been perceived by staff or reinforced by friends and relatives.

Patients on a lingering trajectory seldom have much control over the management of their condition. Family members also seem to leave everything to the staff, especially as time goes by. The frequency and duration of visits from family members characteristically fall off when the lingering nature of the trajectory has become established. Furthermore, the slowly dying person usually does not speak of final things to family and friends. (As already noted, however, there is often more awareness and communication than one might think.)

In summary, the lingering trajectory most often does not produce obvious disruptions in the environment. Staff members tend to assume that the patient also moves rather gently toward death:

> These patients drift out of the world, sometimes almost like imperceptibly melting snowflakes. The organization of work emphasizes comfort care and custodial routine, and is complemented by a sentimental order emphasizing patience and inevitability (Glaser & Strauss, 1968, p. 64).

But the picture is not always so tranquil and orderly. Occasionally there is a patient, family member, or staff member who does not accept the impending death. Glaser and Strauss also noticed incidents in which a next of kin would upset the staff by showing "too much emotion" after the patient died. Perhaps strong reactions to a patient's death challenged the staff's assumption that the social loss of a "lingerer" did not amount to much.

By contrast, the patience of family and/or staff may be strained when a patient fails to die on schedule. My first experience with this phenomenon occurred many years ago when the daughter of an aged patient strode angrily back from his ward and complained, "They said he was on the Death List, so I came here as soon as I could. And there he was—you can see for yourself! Sitting up in bed and playing cards. And winning!" There had been a misunderstanding. A member of the hospice staff had informed the daughter that her father was on the "D.L.," a term that actually means "Danger List." Nevertheless, the main problem was that the daughter did have reason to believe that her father was close to death and had organized her emotions accordingly. After a few minutes of cooling off, she made it clear that she did not really want her father dead, but that it was difficult to keep thinking of him as all but dead and waiting "for the other shoe to drop."

The lingering trajectory has the advantage of giving both the patient and the family *time*—time to grow accustomed to the idea of dying, to make plans, to work through old conflicts and misunderstandings, to review the kind of life that has been lived, and so on. But this trajectory also can have the disadvantage of attenuating relationships and creating situations in which the person is perceived as not quite alive and yet not securely dead. The lingering trajectory is not the image of dying that usually seizes the imagination of the media and the public; however, it is becoming the most typical pattern in Western society, especially in nursing care facilities.

The Expected Quick Trajectory

Time is truly of the essence when a patient is perceived as being on an expected quick trajectory. The staff organizes itself to make the most effective use of the time that remains on the side of life. This contrasts vividly with the more leisurely pattern of care and staff organization that surrounds a patient on a lingering trajectory. As staff devote themselves to the patient's urgent needs, there may be a series of implicit redefinitions in their minds—for example, "He is out of immediate danger but probably will not survive very long" changes to "I think he has passed the crisis point and has a real chance of pulling through."

Several types of expected quick trajectories were observed. Each involved a different pattern of interaction with the staff. In a *pointed trajectory*, the patient is exposed to a very risky procedure, one that might either save his or her life or result in death. In this situation, the staff often has enough time in advance to organize itself properly. The patient may also have the opportunity to exercise some control and options (e.g., share precious minutes with a loved one, see that certain personal matters are acted upon). By contrast, the *danger-period trajectory* requires more watching and waiting. The question is whether or not the patient will be able to survive a stressful experience such as high-risk surgery or a major heart attack. The patient may be unconscious or only partially aware of the surroundings as compared with the alert state of a patient with a pointed trajectory. The danger period can vary from hours to days. This is the type of situation in which the family may remain at bedside or in the corridor, with doctors, nurses, and monitoring devices maintaining their vigilance.

The *crisis trajectory* imposes still another condition on both the patient and everybody else. The patient is not in acute danger at the moment, but

his or her life might suddenly be threatened at any time. Obviously, this creates a tense situation. The tension will persist until the patient's condition improves enough so that he or she is out of danger or until the crisis actually arrives and rescue efforts can be made.

Different from all of these is the *will-probably-die trajectory*. The staff believes that nothing effective can be done. The aim is to keep the patient as comfortable as possible and wait for the end to come, usually within hours or days. In more recent years, there has been an increase in administrative pressure to move will-probably-die patients to units or facilities that require less expensive resources: "Open this bed for somebody who really needs it!" Concerns about health care cost containment are increasing bureaucratic impatience with people who, through no fault of their own, are not quite ready to die but are seen as expensive or inconvenient to serve in a cure-oriented medical center.

Some common problems that arise in connection with the expected quick trajectory. For example, family members are likely to be close by the patient and their presence confronts the staff with increased demands for interaction and communication. What should those people in the waiting room be told? Who should tell them? Is this the time to prepare them for the bad news, or can it be postponed a little longer? Should the whole family be told at once, or is there one person who should be relied on to grasp the situation first? The staff must somehow come to terms with the needs of the family while still carrying out treatment. This situation challenges the staff's stamina, judgment, and communication skills. In my experience, however, the presence of the family can also be helpful to the staff and, more importantly, to the patient as well. The presence of a familiar and supportive person can make a powerful difference to a person for whom death seems to be in near prospect.

The most salient features of the expected quick trajectory are time urgency; intense organization of treatment efforts, rapidly shifting expectations, and volatile, sensitive staff-family interactions. In the midst of this pressure, errors can be made. For example, as Glaser and Strauss observed, there may be attempts to save a patient from a disease he or she does not have. A person may arrive at the hospital in critical condition, with no medical history available to guide the staff. The pressure of time may then force medical personnel to proceed on the basis of an educated guess rather than secure knowledge.

Whether or not there is a chance to save the patient's life sometimes depends on the resources of a particular hospital or even a particular ward at a particular time. The lack of an oxygen tank or a kidney machine can make the difference between the will-probably-die trajectory and one with more hope. The *perceived social value* of the endangered person can spell the difference between an all-out rescue attempt and a do-nothing orientation. This is especially likely to happen when the medical team has pressing decisions to make about who will receive emergency treatment first or be given the benefit of life-support apparatus that is in short supply. "When a patient is not 'worth' having a chance," say Glaser and Strauss, "he may in effect be given none" (1968, p. 72).

The definition of dying that we construct, then, is no less critical at the end than it is at the beginning. This is also a reminder that social stereotypes holding that one person is more important than another (whether on the basis of age, sex, race, occupation, economic status, or whatever) can play a decisive role in the death system when quick decisions must be made about the priority and extent of life-sustaining effort.

The Unexpected Quick Trajectory

The significance of the interpersonal setting in which dying takes place is emphasized again by the unexpected quick trajectory. Personnel in the emergency room, for example, expect to be called on for immediate life-or-death measures. The experienced ER team adjusts quickly to situations that might immobilize most other people. But the appearance of an unexpected quick trajectory in other areas of the same hospital constitutes a crisis. On these wards, there is less preparation for emergency, and personnel may experience a "blow up" (Glaser & Strauss, 1968, p. 121).

Perhaps Weisman's concept of "middle knowledge" should be applied to personnel as well as to terminally ill patients. The staff in nonemergency areas *know* but do not *believe* that a life-or-death situation might arise at any moment. It would be too stressful for them to function every day with that expectation in mind, an expectation that is also at variance with the kind of care they are called upon to deliver on a routine basis. In this sense, something really does blow up when a patient unexpectedly enters a crisis phase on the "wrong" ward: the staff's security-giving myth of an orderly and manageable universe.

Some unexpected deaths prove more disturbing than others to the staff. The "medically interesting case" is one of the most common examples. The staff is more likely to be taken aback and regret the death of a patient who presented unusual features to them. Personnel also tend to be affected more by the death of a patient whose life they had tried especially hard to save. They see their heavy investment in time and energy as having been wasted. This is not the same as mourning the loss of a patient as a person. Instead it is the loss of the staff's effort that is felt as a blow. Glaser and Strauss report that it is the "poor physician who tried so hard," not the patient, who receives the sympathy of other staff members. The patient may have never seemed like an individual human being to the staff during their intensive lifesaving efforts.

A patient who dies for the wrong reasons also dismays and alarms the staff. Treatment may have been focused on one critical aspect of the patient's condition, while death was approaching by a different route.

The staff's need to shield itself against surprise is a major theme that runs through observations of the unexpected quick trajectory. Everybody in a life-threatening situation has a need to exercise control—professional staff as well as patient and family. This need often leads both to an *illusion of control* and to persistent efforts to maintain the illusion (Kastenbaum, 1978). The well-practiced and institutionally supported defenses of the physician or nurse may become dangerously exaggerated or suddenly give way when reality punctures the illusion.

Unfortunately, the hospital itself at times precipitates an unexpected quick trajectory. Glaser and Strauss observed confusion in the mobilization of treatment resources, the turning of attention away from other patients to concentrate on an urgent case, accidents attributable to carelessness or poor safety practices, and a variety of problems that can arise when a hospital is understaffed.

The combination of time pressure and surprise can lead to what Glaser and Strauss term *institutional evasions*. There is not enough time and opportunity to make the moves officially required in the situation, so available staff members must improvise a response or use an alternative approach that could expose them to reprimand or even to legal action. There may not be time to bring a physician to the scene, for example. If nurses carry out the potentially lifesaving procedures without direct medical supervision, they have exposed themselves to the possibility of criticism and liability action—but if they do not act promptly, the patient may die before the physician arrives. Evasions of institutional rules may be minor or substantial. The institution itself may choose either to notice or to carefully ignore the infractions. One extra source of tension within the unexpected quick trajectory, then, is the conflict between doing what seems to be best for the patient without delay and abiding strictly by the regulations.

Life-or-Death Emergencies

Another type of "quick trajectory" can occur at any time, at any place. A person in good health may suddenly become the victim of an automobile accident, a small child may fall into a swimming pool, an "unloaded gun" may discharge, a restaurant patron may choke, a person with a history of heart disease may suffer another attack. These are just a few of the emergency situations that can result in death.

Several types of problems are more likely to arise when there is a life-or-death emergency in a community setting as compared with a health care facility:

- *Panic:* "What's happening? What should we do?"
- *Inappropriate action:* "Let's get him on his feet."
- *Misinterpreting the situation:* "Stop whining and go back to bed!"
- *Minimizing the danger:* "I don't need a doctor. It's just a little indigestion."
- *Preoccupation with own concerns:* "I'd better clean this place up before I call anybody."

Fortunately there have been many examples of prompt and competent response from family members, neighbors, colleagues, and passersby. For example, a man in his eighties had the presence of mind and the skill to perform cardiac pulmonary resuscitation (CPR) on a toddler who had fallen into a pool—an all too frequent occurrence in Arizona. This child recovered, but many have died or suffered permanent injury. Errors and poor decisions can be made within health care settings also, but the risk is greater in most community settings. A camper's friends, for example, may think they are doing the right thing by carrying out a snake bite remedy that has been passed along for generations—but they would be doing more to save this person's life by rushing him to a poison control center.

Emergency medical technicians and paramedics are often called upon when life-endangering situations arise in the community. Trained to provide society's front line response to emergent health crises, these men and women may have more encounters with disaster in two or three days than most people do in a lifetime. Relatively little attention has been given to their experiences by researchers and educators. Dale Gladden recalls one of his first experiences as a paramedic:

> It was at a (community fraternal club). There was a dance going on—lots of loud music, dim lights. No one dancing. Everyone was just standing around. An elderly man had collapsed. Communication was bad. We would give medicine, then call a physician on the phone and tell him the situation and what we had done. The man had gone into ventricular fibrillation. I intubated him, and the RN with me tried to get an IV in him—it was hard for her because of the bad lighting. He was a diabetic. IV (intravenous) was hooked up and we started defibrillation. There was that smell of burning hair associated with defib machines. We got a pulse and blood pressure back. Got an ambulance. The man was breathing fine so I took the tube out and we transported him to the hospital. He survived and was very thankful to me. (Kastenbaum, 1993–1994, pp. 6–7)

This man almost certainly would have died without the prompt and skilled intervention. Sometimes, however, no amount of skill and effort can prevent death, and it is not unusual for a paramedic to discover that there are one or more people already dead on the scene. Even though the paramedic knows that a person is beyond resuscitation, it may be necessary to carry out CPR and other procedures in order to conform with regulations. At such times, the paramedic is likely to feel—as Gladden did after responding to another call—that it is wrong "to go through all this trouble for a dead person, why not let her be at peace? I had lots of questions why we went through the whole routine when she was already dead."

Another odd situation can arise when a person dies suddenly in a community setting. Although paramedics or nurses on the scene may know that the person is dead, the legal declaration of death may not be made until the body has been transported to a medical facility. This means that some of the deaths reported as having occurred in a hospital actually occurred elsewhere. Hospital physicians simply confirmed the ER team's assessment that the patient was beyond resuscitation.

An important change is taking place throughout the nation with respect to the options available to paramedics and emergency technicians (EMTs). In some communities, emergency response personnel are now following "Field Termination of Resuscitation Guidelines" that enable them to forego useless procedures when it is obvious that the person has no chance of survival. This revised set of guidelines has recently been approved for Mesa, Arizona, one of the author's neighboring communities. One example has already been reported. A chronically ill 90-year-old woman refused breakfast one morning, sat in her favorite chair, and stopped breathing. Her son later commented that "We didn't know what to do. She wanted to die at home. We wanted to handle it as quietly as we could." The paramedics who came to the home honored the family's wishes. Instead of performing unwanted and ineffective resuscitation procedures, they stayed to talk with the family and help them deal with their first wave of grief and the arrangements for disposition of the body. The Mesa paramedics receive training in the basics of grief support—certainly a good idea for police officers as well and for all people who may be called upon when a death occurs.

At the present time, there are local differences in the rules that govern the responses of emergency medical personnel. In some jurisdictions, it is possible for people to complete a medical care directive that forbids resuscitation measures (this is sometimes known as "the orange card"). Where this law applies, paramedics and EMTs can refrain from performing resuscitation procedures without exposing themselves to legal risk. What is the law in your state and community? Your local department of health, hospital, or medical association can answer this question for you.

Research into Trajectories of Dying

Unfortunately, there have been few research follow-ups to the pioneering studies of Glaser and Strauss. A recent study of terminally ill cancer patients in Sweden, however, may stimulate additional research. Most of these patients had quick trajectories after they entered the hospital. This was especially true of those who received treatment in a surgical unit as compared with those who were receiving care in an inpatient hospice ward. Family members of patients in a hospice ward felt that they had received more timely and accurate information from the staff than did those whose relatives had been on the surgical unit. Medical evidence indicates that the people who received treatment on the surgical unit entered with more complications and were in poorer condition than those in the hospice unit. Was hospice care more effective in reducing pain and other symptoms? Or were people with more complicated medical conditions better served on a traditional medical or surgical unit? Questions such as these remain to be answered.

HEALTHY PEOPLE WHO ARE AT RISK: HEMOPHILIA

The familiar categories for health status do not serve us very well when we consider people who are not terminally ill—in fact not ill at all in the usual sense of the term—but who nevertheless are at a consistently high risk for death throughout their lives. It is helpful to distinguish the situation of consistently at-risk people from the more traditional concern with people who have other kinds of life-threatening conditions. Hemophilia is the example we will take here.

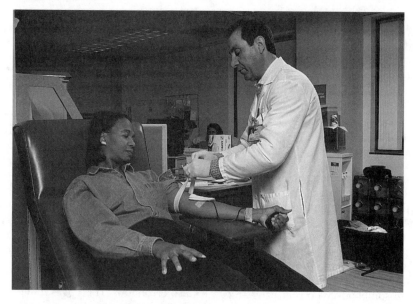

Giving blood is a way of helping to save the lives of people with hemophilia, accident victims and surgical patients.

Hemophilia is a condition that arises from a defect in the blood coagulation process. The person may be otherwise healthy and vigorous but is in danger when bleeding occurs, whether through an external wound or internal dysfunction. The bleeding can continue until death without medical intervention. As you can well imagine, a person with hemophilia has to be especially careful to avoid situations in which there is a heightened risk of bleeding. Not all such situations can be predicted and avoided, however, so there is always the possibility of a bleeding incident.

More than 15,000 people in the United States have hemophilia, and additional people have other types of bleeding disorders. Two types of hemophilia are known, both inherited as X-linked recessive disorders. Jonathan C. Goldsmith, M.D. explains:

This generally means that women carry the trait and men have the clinical disorder. The most famous carrier of hemophilia was Queen Victoria of Great Britain whose carrier daughters spread the disorder to royal families in Germany, Spain, and Russia.... All daughters of affected men will be carriers of the gene for hemophilia. (Goldsmith, 1994, p. 2)

The risk of serious or fatal complications of hemophilia can be much reduced through early diagnosis, precautions (such as soft, cushioned helmets for preschool children), drug therapy, and the use of safe plasma transfusions. People with hemophilia become at exceptional risk when available blood products are contaminated. The nation's public health establishment (including the Red Cross) was slow to respond to the dangers of HIV contamination, leading to AIDS infections among people with hemophilia, who depend on blood product transfusions. Any pathological agent that contaminates the blood supply places people with hemophilia at a special risk for their lives. The warning and prevention functions of our society's death system must be ever alert to prevent catastrophes of this kind.

It is also clear that health care professionals, teachers, counselors, and others who serve the public should make themselves aware of the special challenges faced by people with hemophilia. And all of us who are concerned about the fragility of life and the ever-present risk of death will want to learn more about the perspectives of individuals and families who must cope with hemophilia and other bleeding disorders. A logical place to start is The National Hemophilia Foundation: (800) 42-HANDI. The foundation's website is http://www.hemophilia.org.

GUARDED FEELINGS, SUBTLE COMMUNICATIONS

Most of us exercise discretion in the way we communicate our thoughts and feelings. We do not say everything on our minds to whomever we happen to be with in every situation. Generally we speak more openly with those we have learned to trust and who demonstrate understanding and good will. Furthermore, we take the other person's state of mind into account—should we alarm somebody who is already anxious or who has a difficult task that requires complete concentration? And precisely how should we get a message across? Should we be as quick and direct about it as possible? Or should we work our way up, starting with something relatively neutral and gradually getting to the point? Must we lay out thoughts and feelings as though making a formal presentation? How we communicate with another person depends on our own personality style, who that other person is, and the nature of the immediate situation.

Difficulties in Communication

We should not be surprised to find feelings guarded and communications subtle among people faced with the prospect of death. One might conclude—erroneously—that the dying person either does not know what is happening or is unwilling to discuss it. Often clear communication has been made very difficult. For example, while working in a geriatric hospital I found that hospital personnel usually responded to patients' direct communications about death in a manner that quickly ended the interaction. The odds were about three to one that the staff member would not be willing to listen to what the patient had to say. Giving false reassurance ("Oh, you'll outlive me, Charlie!"), changing the subject, and

a variety of other evasive responses were more common than an openness to what the dying person really wanted to communicate.

This attitude is still prevalent in many places. Aged patients on a lingering trajectory frequently are treated as though socially dead and are therefore denied even the opportunity to die as a person. I have heard staff members make remarks such as the following in the presence of the patients:

"This one, she can't talk. She doesn't know what you are saying."

"You should have seen her when she first came here, but look at her now!"

"The poor thing would be better off going in her sleep." (Kastenbaum, 1984 p. 6)

These remarks were not only degrading, but also erroneous. There was independent evidence that these patients, although vulnerable and failing, could hear and understood what was being said over their (socially dead) bodies. One example that I will always remember occurred during an inspection of an extended care facility. This facility (operated by a state agency) had been under court orders to improve both its physical plant and its treatment program. The whistle had already been blown, time had been provided to improve care, and my visit as a consultant for the federal government was expected. However, there was no evidence of improvement. Part of the explanation was "These people [the patients] don't understand anything anyhow."

I asked the staff to show me the most impaired, uncomprehending patient on the ward. This request seemed to throw them into confusion, so I walked to the furthest corner of this large, dark, and filthy ward. An old, pale, scrunched-up woman was lying in bed, her hair tangled and untended, her body smelling of neglect. The charge nurse assured me that their patients were beyond being worth the effort. I asked for the patient's name and some information about her background. Did she have a husband, children, visitors? What had been her interests, activities, and achievements before she came here? and so on. All the staff knew was her name, the fact that her husband visited once in a great while, that she could not speak or understand anything, and that she probably did not have long to live.

I then tried to engage the woman in some form of interaction, simply taking her hand and talking to her, and using the small bits of information I had been given. In less than a minute, she had painfully faced around and squeezed my hand in return. In another few minutes, she was speaking and moaning. I could not make out all the words, but there was no mistaking that she knew somebody was trying to communicate with her and that she had the need and the ability (although limited) to respond. The staff noted this interaction and retreated from it. But at the end of the inspection visit, the charge nurse turned to me and muttered, "If you're going to write anything about this, I'd better tell you that this is not the patient I told you it was. I mixed the patients up somehow. That was Mrs. ___, not Mrs. ___."

This story is not told to criticize nurses or geriatric facilities in general. The situation on this particular unit was the outcome of systematic neglect of the frail elderly and of those who try to provide care for them. Having their own sense of horror to contend with, the staff responded by psychologically depriving the patients of individuality and humanity. In the extreme circumstances I have mentioned, this woman had almost no opportunity to communicate to anybody about anything. Whatever she might be feeling about life and death would remain unknown. It is not simply that we often have difficulty communicating about "mortal matters." There are many people close to death who are deprived of the opportunity for normal social interaction of any kind. And how unnecessary!

Doctor-Patient Communication: The SUPPORT Study

Effective physicians must do more than diagnose, prescribe, and treat: they must also create a bond of trust with patients. A recent study has demonstrated that problems in the communication process contribute greatly to shortcomings in the treatment of seriously and terminally ill hospitalized patients. This major project is known by the acronym SUPPORT: Study to Understand Prognoses and Preferences for Outcomes and Risks of Treatment (SUPPORT, 1995).

The SUPPORT researchers acknowledged the need to improve the total care of seriously and terminally ill people:

> Many Americans today fear they will lose control over their lives if they become critically ill, and their dying will be prolonged and impersonal. This has led to an increasingly visible right-to-die movement.... Physicians and ethicists have debated when to use cardiac resuscitation and other aggressive treatments for patients with advanced illnesses. Many worry about the economic and human cost of providing life-sustaining treatment near the end of life. (1995, p. 1591)

The SUPPORT project was intended to help physicians make better decisions about end-of-life issues, and to prevent "a mechanically supported, painful, and prolonged process of dying." A major research effort was mounted, consisting of the following pedantic:

- More than 9000 adult patients with life-threatening diseases in five teaching hospitals
- A two-year observational study for about half of the patients
- A two-year intervention phase for the other patients, in which attempts were made to improve communication and care

The observational phase examined the process of decision making and patient outcomes through extensive review of case records and interviews with patients and their surrogates, as well as the senior physicians involved. Major shortcomings were documented (*See Box 4-3*).

The observation study found that physician-patient communication was unreliable and ineffective. The blunt truth was that physicians often showed little interest in the patients' own preferences and little inclination to honor them. This nonresponsiveness to the wishes of seriously and terminally ill patients worked almost exclusively in one direction. If the patient did not want to have CPR used, physicians often continued the plan to use this procedure despite the patients' stated preference. However, if the patient did want to have CPR used, physicians did not counter this preference by excluding CPR. Pain control was

---

BOX 4-3

THE SUPPORT STUDY OF SERIOUSLY AND TERMINALLY ILL HOSPITALIZED PATIENTS: MAJOR FINDINGS

I. The Observation Study

1. Half of the patients who died during the course of the study had moderate or severe pain during their final three days of life.

2. Physicians often used jargon that the patient did not understand when talking about cardiopulmonary resuscitation (CPR)—and often (41%) never even discussed this subject with their patients.

3. In 80% of the cases, physicians misunderstood what the patients wanted with respect to the use of CPR.

4. Physicians often did not follow the patients' stated preference to avoid the use of CPR: in about 50% of the cases, the physician did not write a do-not-resuscitate (DNR) order.

II. The Intervention Study

1. There was no increase in discussions between physicians and patients.

2. Physicians often continued to disregard patients' preferences to have CPR withheld, even when these preferences were known to them.

3. There was no improvement in pain control.

4. Computer projections of the patients' prognoses were no more accurate than those made by the attending physicians.

5. Much of the patient information generated during the intervention phase failed to reach the physicians because of various communication problems.

---

also ineffective. The outcome was that many patients were exposed to unrelieved pain and aggressive treatment—and many also spent at least ten days on life support equipment in the intensive care unit. *This is an alarmingly poor showing for hospitals and physicians two decades after the hospice movement, with its palliative care approach, started to prove its worth in the United States. (See next chapter.)*

The intervention phase of the study attempted to improve this situation by providing the physicians with more information about their patients' preferences as well as their physical status. Nurses with special training were an important part of this phase, making multiple contacts with patient, family, physician, and hospital staff. These nurses encouraged attention to pain control and to better physician-patient communication, with the aim of contributing to better decisions in planning the course of treatment. Unfortunately, these interventions did not work. Communication remained flawed; physicians' preferences for aggressive treatment were not modified in light of patients' preferences; and pain control was as poor as before.

The SUPPORT project was a major study with laudable goals. The findings were disturbing enough to prompt an editorial response from the *Journal of the American Medical Association*, which acknowledged that much stronger and more systematic efforts must be made to improve communication between physicians and patients with life-threatening conditions. Value issues were also recognized. The anonymous editorial writer urged other physicians:

> Don't project our concept of a good death onto patients.... Respect for patient autonomy means that physicians must allow informed patients to determine what value they place on such a chance of survival and what risks they are willing to undergo. (Editorial, 1995, p. 1635)

Improving Communication

Communication is everybody's responsibility, whether physician, nurse, patient, family member, or friend. Whatever improves self-respect, reduces fear, and encourages open communication in general is likely to have a positive impact on death-related communication as well. Following are a few suggestions:

First, *be alert to symbolic and indirect communications,* as illustrated by the following examples:

1. *Sharing dreams.* People may prepare themselves for their final separation through dreamwork before conscious thoughts and direct interpersonal communications occur. Dreams reported by terminally ill cancer patients have been found to differ from those of healthy older people (Coolidge & Fish, 1983–1984). Among the differences was a greater frequency of death content in dreams, but it was usually somebody else who was seen as dead. The dreamer often attempted to discover the identity of this person.

> I dreamt of a funeral and in the funeral was a little girl going to be buried. In her coffin I couldn't get to her so I tried to open it to see who it was and it was one of my daughters. Little Antonette. She was lying on her side and the lid was falling in the coffin…. I went to fix the lid…. I kept on doing things that would upset the coffin. I felt like a criminal that didn't belong there. (1983–1984, p. 3)

Listening to each other's dreams can be a valuable way to supplement and enrich interpersonal communication for people who are comfortable with their own dream lives. It is not essential that a patient or listener come up with the "right" interpretation of these dreams. Simply being able to share these inner experiences with another person can provide an additional supportive line of communication.

2. *Symbolic language.* Although dreams provide a treasury of symbolic language and actions, such characteristics can also appear in everyday speech. Following is an example that came to our attention during a research project in a geriatric hospital:

> The 75-year-old former stonemason had lost some of the vigor he had shown earlier in his hospital stay, but otherwise appeared to be in stable condition and doing well. One morning he asked for directions to a cemetery near his former home. Although he made the direct statement that he was expecting the undertaker, this was not taken up by the staff as a clue to impending death. It was just a statement that didn't make much sense. The next day, he told several people that his boss (going back many years, in reality) had called for him: he was supposed to help dig graves for eight people. The delusion now became persistent. He insisted on staying around the ward so he could be available to the people who would come to take him back to the cemetery.
>
> Two days before he died, the patient had several teeth extracted (a procedure that was seen as having little risk because of his good condition). He then told staff that it was time to call his sisters—about whom he had never before said a word. His death came as a surprise to the staff although, apparently, not to himself. Cause of death was determined to be cerebral thrombosis. Despite all the clues this man had given, no notice had been taken. His "crazy talk" seemed even less crazy when a subsequent review indicated that the old stonemason had outlived seven siblings—his reference to digging a grave for eight people no longer seemed so arbitrary. (Weisman & Kastenbaum, 1968)

After a number of experiences such as this one, both our clinical and research staffs markedly improved their ability to identify patients whose death was more imminent than might have been expected and learned to pay close attention to what was said, whether in direct or symbolic language.

3. *Leave-taking actions.* Deeds as well as words can help to express the needs and intentions of people who are close to the end of their lives. My colleagues and I in both institutional and community settings have observed such behaviors as sorting through possessions and giving some away; creating the occasion for one last interaction of a familiar kind, such as playing checkers or going fishing together; and terminating mutual obligations and expectations (e.g., "Thanks for the loan of the bowling ball. I won't be needing it anymore").

Most people who are aware of their terminal illness do hope to have the opportunity to bid farewell to the important people in their lives—but not necessarily all in the same way (Kelleher, 1990). It is wise to take our cues from the dying person rather than impose a particular kind of farewell scene than happens to appeal to us.

As shown in the three examples, increasing our awareness of dreams, symbolic language, and leave-taking actions can make it easier for a dying person to convey messages that might not lend themselves as well to direct verbal expression. It also gives us more opportunity to express our own thoughts and feelings in return.

Second, we must *help to make competent and effective behavior possible*. Illness, fatigue, and reduced mobility make it difficult to continue functioning as a competent person. This is true whether or not the individual is suffering from a terminal condition. The progressive nature of terminal illness, however, tends to increase the individual's dependency on others and limits the range of spontaneous action. A person attempting to cope with terminal illness often retains a strong need to be competent, effective, and useful to others. Family, friends, and other caregivers can not only improve communication but also help to support the dying person's sense of self-esteem by striking a balance between meeting the realistic needs associated with dependency and creating an environment in which the person can continue to exercise some initiative and control.

Timely and appropriate support is needed, not a total takeover of the dying person's life. Attentive listening and observing are required to match the style, level, and intensity of care with the individual's physical condition and psychosocial needs. By accomplishing one side of the communication process—listening and observing—others can make it more probable that the patient can maintain a core of competent and effective behavior and continue to communicate needs and attentions.

Doka (1993) makes the following useful point:

Dying persons and their families sometimes need to be told that they are misinterpreting signals. In one case a middle-aged man dying of cancer complained to me that his wife was withholding information about the school and behavioral problems of their teenaged son. I discovered that she was reluctant to "dump" more problems on her dying husband, particularly because in the recent past he seemed to balk when these topics came up in conversations. With my assistance they were able to understand their past communication difficulties. The husband recognized his own ambivalence: on the one hand he was the boy's father, but on the other hand there were days when he just couldn't cope with another problem. Husband and wife were able to develop a code that could communicate their intentions.... Moreover, both husband and wife were able to identify alternate sources of support to assist the wife and son. (1993)

Third, *recognize that the dying person sets the pace and the agenda*. There is no schedule that has to be met, no set of tasks that the dying person must accomplish—unless the dying person has a schedule and a set of tasks of his or her own. This is no time for the listener to impose his or her own set of needs or to expect the dying person to behave in accordance with any preconceived idea of just what it is that a dying person is supposed to do. Although the patient will usually introduce thoughts concerned with dying and death, there are individual differences regarding when and how this topic is brought up. For example, during a particular interaction the patient may choose to say nothing about death. This does not necessarily mean that the patient is "denying" or is "behind schedule." It may be that the patient is hoping for a little "vacation" from this overwhelming topic, or that other matters require attention. Furthermore, on close listening and reflection, it may become evident that the conversation has a lot to do with how the person feels in prospect of death without having ever to mention death per se. One terminally ill person might choose to discuss specific death-related issues (e.g., reviewing funeral plans or the distribution of property), while another might choose to discuss feelings and relationships. I have known many dying people who had not much left to say about death because they had already had all the time they needed to settle their thoughts and communicate their concerns and desires. These people still had need for supportive everyday communication, but they did not need to be reminded that they were dying!

Fourth, *do not confuse the dying person's values and goals with our own*. Communication can be distorted or broken off when others project their own needs on the dying person. We have already seen that substituting our needs and values for the patients' is a major problem in medical care of dying people. Requiring that the dying person move along from one "stage" to another also imposes an unnecessary and unrealistic burden on everybody in the situation. A similar—or greater—stress may be introduced if we insist that the patient give up "denial." As noted earlier (*see Chapter 1*), "denial" has become an overused and often misused term. There are many reasons that a person might not acknowledge his or her terminal condition at a particular time and to a particular individual. Furthermore, denial-like behaviors may be useful strategies. Connor (1992) has provided research confirmation for this observation. He was able to classify terminally ill cancer patients into those who did and those who did not engage frequently in denial-related behaviors. It turned out that the "deniers" were downplaying the seriousness of their illness because this strategy was helping them to maintain their most significant interpersonal relationships. Connor makes the important point that some people have had a dysfunctional lifestyle for many years and continue to make excessive use of denial-like behaviors in their terminal illness. Others have functioned well until confronted with the loss, stress, and uncertainties associated with a life-threatening illness. Our response to the "denying" terminally ill person, then, might depend on the place of denial-like behavior in that person's total life history and on the values supported by denial-like behavior in the immediate situation.

INDIVIDUALITY AND UNIVERSALITY IN THE EXPERIENCE OF DYING

Does everybody die in the same way? If so, it should be possible to discover general laws or regularities upon which care and management can be based. Or does everybody die in a unique way, depending on many different factors? We are more likely to be good observers and useful caregivers if we understand the specifics of each situation. This can be exemplified by a survey of some of the factors that influence the nature and experience of dying. The discussion begins with respect for both universal factors and individual dimensions of dying.

Factors That Influence the Experience of Dying

The following factors are discussed in the next sections: age, gender, interpersonal relationships, and disease, treatment, and environmental context.

Age

Age by itself is an empty variable that exercises no direct influence. Nevertheless, chronological age serves as an index for a variety of factors that can make a significant difference throughout life, including the process of dying.

- *Comprehension of dying and death.* Our intellectual grasp of death is related both to the level of development we have achieved and to our life experiences (*see Chapter 10*). At one extreme is the young child who is keenly sensitive to separation but who may not yet comprehend the finality and irreversibility of death. At the other extreme is an aged adult who not only recognizes the central facts of death but has seen many close friends and relations die through the years. The "same" experience will be different for people with varying life histories and cognitive structures.
- *Opportunity to exercise control over the situation.* Children have fewer enfranchised rites than do adults. Even the latest "natural death" acts passed by state legislatures do not strengthen a child's position as a decision maker, nor have the advocates of these bills taken up the cause for children's rights. In coping with the many life changes associated with serious illness, children and adults differ in the amount of control that is theirs to exercise, a difference in "social instrumentality" that affects personal experience in many ways (see the experiences of Marie in *Chapter 5*).
- *Perception and treatment by others.* Perceived social value differs with age. In practice this can influence not only the quality of the dying process but even the possibility of recovering from life-threatening illness. Elderly patients often are victimized by the assumptions that (1) they are ready to die and (2) nobody would miss them much. Both professional caregivers and the general public tend to act upon these

assumptions without first inquiring into their accuracy. For example, doctors are much more likely to withhold resuscitation efforts in patients over the age of 75, even though they are likely to force CPR on younger patients who would prefer not to have CPR (SUPPORT, 1995).

It is all too easy to mistake a depressive reaction for a terminal course. Many circumstances can lead to depression among elderly adults, including the fatigue and depletion associated with medical conditions that have not been effectively treated. Expertise in assessing and treating depression (e.g., Gilbert, 1992) is required, along with the independence of mind to break free of the "ready to die" stereotype and look carefully at each individual's situation. Unfortunately, there are depressed elderly men and women whose chances for survival as well as a renewed quality of life are diminished by society's inclination to see older adults as ready for the grave.

Misperceptions often occur at the other extreme of the age range as well. For example, there remains a stubborn belief among some physicians that infants do not experience pain to any appreciable extent. Bone marrow samples are taken, needles are inserted into the spine, and burn dressings are changed without adequate analgesia. A life-threatened infant may undergo very painful procedures repeatedly. Although this attitude is gradually changing, it may be difficult to eliminate because the belief that infants do not experience pain serves anxiety-reduction purposes for the physicians and nurses responsible for their treatment. It is painful to think that one is causing pain to a baby, so let's persuade ourselves that no pain is experienced.

Gender

A man with cancer of the prostate may be concerned with the threat of becoming impotent as well as with the risk to his life (although in practice, timely diagnosis and treatment can sharply reduce both risks). Cervical cancer may disturb a woman not only because of the life risk but also because one of the treatment possibilities—hysterectomy—would leave her unable to become pregnant. Both the man and the woman described above may be troubled about the future of their intimate relationships even if the threat to their lives is lifted.

Some people interpret physical trauma affecting their sexual organs as punishment for real or imagined transgressions. Others become preoccupied with their physical condition in a way that interferes with affectionate and sexual relationships. "I'm no good any more" may be a self-tormenting thought for either the man or the woman, each experiencing this in his or her own way. Even if the treatment is completely successful, there will have been a period during which concern about death was intensified by doubts as to the individual's intactness as a sexual being. These are not the only types of reactions that people express regarding cancer of the reproductive system; they simply illustrate some of the many possible interactions between sex role and disease.

When a woman is faced with a life-threatening illness, she is likely to have concerns about the integrity and well-being of her family. Will the children eat well? Can her husband manage the household? What most troubles the woman-wife-mother may be the fate of her family as much as or even more than her own.

The man-husband-father in the traditional family is likely to have distinctive concerns of his own. Has the illness destroyed his career prospects? Will he lose his job or his chance for advancement even if he makes a good recovery? Has he provided well enough for his family in case he doesn't pull through? Is he, in effect, a "good man" and a "real man" if he cannot continue to work and bring in the money? There may be a crisis in self-esteem if he is confined to hospital or home for a protracted time, away from the work situations that support his sense of identity.

Gender differences are important from the standpoint of professional caregivers as well as patients. Direct care to a dying person is usually provided by women—often nurses, licensed practical nurses, or aides. Responsibility for the total care plan, however, is often in the hands of a male physician. The physician may be more time conscious and achievement oriented, characteristics that favor survival of the rigors of medical training. He may therefore be more persistent in cure-oriented treatments but also quicker to withdraw when death is in prospect. The nurse may be more sensitive to the patient's relationship with significant people in his or her life and less apt to regard impending death as a failure.

Changing patterns of sex roles in Western society can show up in adaptation to terminal illness. When one marital partner is disabled, the other may have more experience in the ailing one's sphere of responsibility, and be better able to maintain the integrity of the family. It is more likely now than in past years, for example, that the wife is also a wage earner and familiar with financial management. Similarly, the husband of today may have had more time with the children and more responsibility for running the household than in the past. Furthermore, the healthy one may be more attuned to the needs and concerns of the sick partner because there has been more commonality in their experiences.

It is likely that there will be many other effects of changing sex-roles on the management of terminal illness. For example:

- As more women enter or reenter the work force, the number of people available to serve as volunteers and informal helpers is declining. It remains to be seen whether the small but perceptible increase in male volunteers will compensate for the reduction in female volunteers. In addition to career-oriented interests, economic pressures for two paychecks in the family have prevented some women from giving time as volunteers in hospice (*see Chapter 5*).
- The traditional emphasis on home and family is being replaced for some women by career-related interests. Career-dominated single adults of either gender might have different concerns when facing death without spouse or child to worry about—and also without spouse or child to provide support and comfort to them.
- Changing lifestyles may be resulting in changing probabilities of death by various modalities. One of the clearest examples is the increased cigarette smoking by American women throughout this century, with a resultant rise in mortality from this cause. Certain pathways to death may become more frequent and others less frequent as both women and men move beyond traditional gender-linked lifestyles.

Interpersonal Relationships

It is difficult to overestimate the importance of interpersonal relationships in the terminal phase of life. Among hospitalized patients who were likely to die within a few months, those who maintained active and mutually responsive relationships were found to survive longer than those with poor social relationships (Weisman & Worden, 1975). The patients who died rapidly also tended to have fewer friends, more distant relationships with their families, and more ambivalent relationships with colleagues and associates. They became more depressed as treatment failed. The investigators noted that the patients with poor relationships often expressed the wish to die, but that this did not represent an actual acceptance of death: it was a product of their frustration and disappointment with life. The same investigators (Weisman & Worden, 1976) later found that the terminally ill patients who were experiencing the most distress also were those with the most interpersonal difficulties. Not only the length of survival, then, but also the quality of life was associated with the kind of interpersonal relationship enjoyed or suffered by the patient.

In some situations, it is the family more than the dying person who needs the most support. For example, an elderly man going through a lingering trajectory toward death was at home, under the care of his wife, with assistance from other family members. Mr. Tchinsky himself was in a semicomatose state and, by all observations, not suffering either physical or emotional distress. His wife, however, was struggling with anxiety about her perceived inability to care for her husband. In actuality, Mrs. Tchinsky was a loving and attentive caregiver, but she had difficulty in controlling the leakage from his colostomy bag. This relatively small problem was the source of great distress because to Mrs. Tchinsky it meant that she was failing her husband in his time of need. A visiting nurse identified and responded tactfully and effectively to this problem. Within a short time, Mrs. Tchinsky was again secure in her role as loving wife and caregiver, and the rest of the family was also relieved. This intervention did not involve the application of either high technology or counseling. A caring family just needed a little timely help to fulfill its obligations toward the dying man (Kastenbaum & Thuell, 1995). Elliott J. Rosen's *Families Facing Death* (1998) is a useful source for further reading on the role of home and family.

Disease, Treatment, and Environment

Disease, treatment, and environment together constitute another set of critical influences on the experience of dying. A person does not *just* die. A person dies of *something*—or of many things. And he or she dies in a particular place whose characteristics contribute to comfort, to misery, or to both. Similarly, the nature of the treatment also deserves consideration. Discussions of the dying process sometimes become so abstract and generalized that we neglect the specific medical problems involved. Think, for example, of the difference between a person whose likely cause of death will be kidney failure and its complications and a person suffering the impairment of respiratory function (perhaps a coal or uranium miner). The person with kidney failure may fade away as waste products accumulate in the body. Over time, he or she may become more lethargic and less able to sustain attention and intention. There may be intermittent periods of better functioning when the patient seems more like his or her old self. The final hours or days may be spent in a comatose condition.

By contrast, a degenerative respiratory condition is likely to produce more alarming symptoms and experiences. Perhaps you have seen a person with advanced emphysema struggle for breath. An episode of acute respiratory failure is frightening to that individual and likely to arouse the anxiety of those who observe it. After a person has experienced this kind of distress, it is difficult to avoid apprehension about future episodes.

Some conditions are accompanied by persistent pain and discomfort unless very carefully managed. Other conditions can reach peaks of agony that test the limits of both the individual and the state of medical comfort giving. Nausea, weakness, and a generalized sense of ill-being may be more dominant than pain for some terminally ill people. It is difficult to be serene when wracked by vomiting or diarrhea. All possible symptoms of all possible pathways of ter-

minal decline need not be catalogued here. But friends, relatives, caregivers, and researchers should appreciate that the person is not dying in an abstract sense: there is a unique set of conditions, which continue to change over time. Furthermore, different types of treatment may be carried out for the same condition, depending on characteristics of the patient and the hospital.

THEORETICAL MODELS OF THE DYING PROCESS

People have hesitated to interact with dying people for many reasons. One of these reasons has been the lack of a coherent and useful perspective. Theoretical models of the dying process have not yet been well developed and tested, but some of the approaches are worth our attention here. We begin with stage theory, the most popular approach, and then turn to more recent efforts.

Do We Die in Stages?

Two stage models of the dying process have been especially influential—although seldom to the same people. There is a basic similarity between these theories: both regard dying as a sequence of psychological or spiritual stages. The differences are also substantial, however, as we will see.

A Buddhist Perspective

The dying process has been given particularly close attention in the Buddhist tradition. Buddhists have long been aware of individual differences in the way people die. A person might be killed instantly in an accident or might have outlived his or her mental powers through a lengthy period of decline. In such situations, there is no opportunity to progress through the stages. Furthermore, some people are anxious and beset by emotional conflict as death nears. For these people also, the transition from life to death is not likely to proceed through the stages of spiritual enlightenment. His Holiness, Tenzin Gyatso, the fourteenth Dalai Lama, states that Buddhism does not assert that all people move through the stages as they die (Gyatso, 1985). One must have some time and be in a state of mind that is con-

FIGURE 4.1
Through the ages, Buddhists have studied the stages of dying, culminating in the clear light of death.

ducive to spiritual development. Those who have developed spiritual discipline throughout their lives are more likely to experience the entire cycle of stages.

For Buddhists, the relationship between mind and body is quite complex, involving "coarse," "subtle," and "very subtle" connections. At death, the coarse connections between mind and body are severed—but the very subtle connections continue. A broad philosophical conception characteristic of Buddhism becomes especially significant when death approaches. As the Dalai Lama expresses it, "…when you are able to keep impermanence in mind—seeing that the very nature of things is that they disintegrate—most likely you will not be greatly shocked by death when it actually comes" (1985, p. 170).

There are eight stages in the Buddhist journey toward death. Perhaps our first surprise is that these stages occur in ordinary life as well. "In more subtle form, the eight transpire each time one goes in or out of sleep or dream, sneezes, faints, or has an orgasm" (Gyatso, 1985, p. 98). Only a sensitive and disciplined person is aware of these subtle forms of dying that occur in everyday life.

The fundamental changes that occur as one moves from the first to the final stage of dying are as follows:

Stage 1. Eyesight dims, but one begins to have miragelike visions.

Stage 2. Hearing diminishes. There is a new internal vision: of smoke.

Stage 3. The sense of smell disappears, and there is now an internal vision that is "likened to fireflies in smoke." The dying person is no longer mindful of other people.

Stage 4. Sensation is lost from the tongue and the body. The dying person is no longer mindful of his or her own concerns. Breathing ceases. (At this point the person would be considered dead by a Western physician, but not so to a Buddhist.)

Stage 5. This is the first of the pure visionary stages. White moonlight is perceived.

Stage 6. The person experiences visions of red sunlight.

Stage 7. The person experiences visions of darkness, faints, and then awakens into the final stage.

Stage 8. The clear light of death appears. This unique state of consciousness persists until death.

The Buddhist stages, then, all focus on the experiential state or phenomenology of the dying person and are divided equally into those that occur while the person is still alive by ordinary standards and those that occur when the person to most observers appears to be dead.

This model of dying served as a guide to Buddhists for many centuries before the current death-awareness movement arose in Western society. (There is also a somewhat less elaborate stage theory of dying within the Islamic tradition [Kramer, 1988].) We turn now to the stage theory that has become most familiar to readers in the Americas and Western Europe.

Kübler-Ross: The Five Stages

Five stages of dying were introduced by Elizabeth Kübler-Ross in her book *On Death and Dying* (1969). These stages are said to begin when an individual becomes aware of his or her terminal condition. The stages are presented as normal, or nonpathological, ways of responding to the prospect of death and the miseries of dying. The patient begins with a stage known as *denial* and moves through the remaining stages of *anger, bargaining, depression,* and *acceptance*. Some people do not make it all the way to acceptance. Progress may become arrested at any stage along the way; furthermore, there can be some slipping back and forth between stages, and each individual has a distinctive tempo of movement through the stages. This conceptualization, then, emphasizes a universal process that allows for a certain amount of individual variation.

Stage 1. Denial is the first response to the bad news. "No, not me, it can't be true!" is the typical feeling communicated. The denial stage is fueled by anxiety and usually runs its course in a short time. It could also be described as a "state of shock from which he recuperates gradually" (1969, p. 37).

Stage 2. Anger wells up and may boil over after the initial shock and denial response have passed. "Why me?" is the characteristic feeling at this time. Rage and resentment can be expressed in many directions—God not excluded. The patient is likely to become more difficult to relate to at this time because of the struggle with frustration and fury.

Stage 3. Bargaining is said to be the middle stage. The dying person attempts to make some kind of deal with fate. He or she may ask for an extension of life, just long enough, say, to see a child graduate from high school or get married. The bargaining process may go on between the patient and caregivers, friends, or family, or God.

Stage 4. Depression eventually follows as the person experiences increasing weakness, discomfort, and physical deterioration. The person can see that he or she is not getting better. The symptoms are too obvious to ignore. Along with stress, strain, and feelings of guilt and unworthiness, there may be explicit fear of dying. The person becomes less responsive, and his or her thoughts and feelings are pervaded by a sense of great loss.

Stage 5. Acceptance, the final stage, represents the end of the struggle. The patient is letting go. Despite the name, it is not necessarily a happy or blissful state. "It is almost void of feelings. It is as if the pain had gone, the struggle is over, and there comes a time for 'the final rest before the long journey' as one patient phrased it" (1969, p. 100).

Interwoven through all five stages is the strand of *hope*. Realistic acknowledgment of impending death may suddenly give way to hope for a miraculous recovery. Subtle though its expression may be, hope flickers back now and then throughout the entire sequence.

In addition to describing these stages Kübler-Ross indicates some of the typical problems that arise at each point and suggests ways of approaching them. She emphasizes, for example, the need to understand and tolerate the patient's anger during the second stage rather than to retaliate and punish him or her for it.

Evaluating the Stage Theory

The first set of points presented here concentrates on shortcomings of the stage theory. This is followed by observations that are more supportive of the theory.

First, *the existence of the stages as such has not been demonstrated*. There is no clear evidence for the establishment of stages in general, for their being five in number, for their being those specified, or for their alignment in the sequence specified. Dying people sometimes do use denial, become angry, try to bargain with fate, or lapse into depression or a depleted, beyond-the-struggle way of being. However, the reality of these moods or response sets has nothing necessarily to do with stages. Dying people have many other moods and responses as well. These include expressions of the *need to control* what is happening and to *preserve a continuity* between themselves and those who survive them. For a particular person at a particular moment, any of these needs may take highest priority.

These are just two of the many other dynamics that can be observed among dying people. Which dynamics are powerful and universal enough to be fixed as stages? What criteria and evidence should be used? Neither Kübler-Ross nor any subsequent observer has provided operational definitions of the stages and carried out competent research to test the theory. Results from the

few studies that have examined facets of stage theory have not supported this model.

Second, *no evidence has been presented that people actually do move from stage 1 through stage 5*. Brief clinical descriptions of various patients are given in the Kübler-Ross book as examples of the stages, but evidence that the same person passed through all stages was not offered then and still has not been offered three decades later. One might as well offer snapshots of five different people in five different moods as proof that these moods occur in a particular sequence. The theory won acceptance and continues to have its adherents despite the lack of data. This casual attitude regarding the factual basis of a theory suggests that it meets social or emotional needs rather than scientific criteria.

Third, *the limitations of the method have not been acknowledged*. The conclusion that there are five stages in the terminal process was based on psychiatric-type interviews conducted by one person and interpreted by the same person. This is a reasonable way to gather information, gain insights, and develop hypotheses to be tested within the structure of a formal research project, a potentially useful beginning. However, the research effort never moved past this beginning, and the inherent flaws and limitations of such an approach were never transcended. The interview method necessarily relies much on the particular experience, personality, and purpose of the interviewer and the type of relationship formed with the interviewee. The step from observation to interpretation is a critical one, but neither the basic observations nor the process of interpretation has been checked against the judgment of other qualified people. Furthermore, what a dying person says and does in the presence of a psychiatrist is only a small and highly selective sample of his or her behavior. The nurse who cares regularly for the patient's physical functioning often sees important aspects of the personality that do not show up in an interview, and the same may be said of the physician in charge and of family members and friends. Behavioral studies might reveal a different perspective, as might a diary kept by the patient.

In other words, one valuable but limited source of information about the experiences and needs of dying patients has taken the place of extensive, multilevel, cross-validated approaches. Conclusions have been widely accepted without concern for the obvious limitations of the methodology used for obtaining and analyzing the data. This would not be an acceptable practice in any other area of research, and it is not sound practice here.

Fourth, *the line is blurred between description and prescription.* Stage theories in general often fail to distinguish clearly between what happens and what should happen. After a stage framework has been established, it is typical for people to attach positive values to prompt movement from one stage to the next. Kübler-Ross has cautioned against trying to rush a person through the stages, but the impulse often can be observed among caregivers or family who are acquainted with the basic idea of the stages. People may draw the implication that the patient should be moving "on schedule" from denial right through to acceptance and that it is a mark of failure for everyone concerned if the timing is off. This expectation adds unnecessary pressure to the situation and enshrines the image of acceptance as the universally desired outcome of the dying person's ordeal. The concept of universal stages lends itself to misuse by those who find their tasks simplified and anxieties reduced through a standardized approach to the dying person. An examination of the case descriptions of Kübler-Ross (1969) has lead Moller (1996) to conclude that she has presented her own preferences for an ideal death as though she were reporting validated facts: "Kübler-Ross and those practitioners who accept her ideal of 'the good death,' have become travel agents for the dying, offering therapeutic intervention to a singular destination: tranquil, peaceful death" (1996, p. 51). Moller is also critical of Kübler-Ross's insistence that people should make themselves ready for death, rather than resisting or bargaining.

Fifth, *the totality of the person's life is neglected in favor of the supposed stages of dying.* The stage theory has tended to make dying people seem very special. The supposed universality of the stages sometimes leads to a dying person's being treated as a kind of specimen moving along predetermined paths, rather than as a complete human being with a distinctive identity. But each dying person is male or female, of one ethnic background or another, and at a particular point in his or her life. The nature of the disease, its symptoms, and its treatment can all have a profound effect on what the dying person experiences. Perhaps most important of all, *who the person is* deserves prime consideration in this situation as in any other.

Even if the stage theory were clarified and proved, it is unlikely that it would account for nearly as much of a dying person's experience as has been widely assumed. We take the entire course of our lives with us into the final months and weeks. Emphasis on the still hypothetical stages of reaction to terminal illness tends to drain away individuality, or at least our perception of it.

Finally, the resources, pressures, and characteristics of the immediate environment can also make a tremendous difference. There are still medical environments in which almost everybody denies death almost all of the time. When a terminally ill person denies, it may be primarily an act of conformity to the implicit social rules of the situation rather than a manifestation of either individual personality or the hypothetical sequence of stages. The same terminally ill person might respond quite differently in a community hospital, a major medical center, an Amish community, or a hospice program. Too much has been learned about environmental dynamics for us to treat these in a simple or neglectful manner when considering the experiences of a terminally ill person.

Nevertheless, several valuable contributions of Kübler-Ross's approach, including the stage theory, should be kept in mind. The value of her work in awakening society's sensitivity to the needs of dying people has not been called into question. Accepting the stage theory is not essential for appreciation of her many useful observations and insights. Some of the practical problems that have arisen in the wake of Kübler-Ross' presentations should be attributed to their hasty and uncritical application by others.

There is also a facet of her original presentation (1969) that deserves more attention by theorists and practitioners. Her book and some of her subsequent writings and lectures might be of more value for their report of *communicational interac-*

tions than as evidence for a fixed set of stages. When Kübler-Ross and other observers report what terminally ill people have said and how they have responded in personal interactions, they are providing what could be very useful information to guide our own communications. Problems arise when these communications are taken as evidence for an assumed intrinsic state of an individual. The communications are more convincing as communications *between* people rather than as proof of stages *within* a person with a life-threatening condition.

In summary, the need for a guide to the plight of dying people—and the need to keep our own anxieties under control—led to a premature acceptance of the Kübler-Ross conceptualization as well as to simplistic and overly rigid uses of her observations. These range from the dismissal of a patient's legitimate complaints about poor treatment as "Just what you would expect in stage 2" to the assumption that further research is not really important because the stages tell it all. At the very least, however, the timely and charismatic presentations of Kübler-Ross have done much to heighten awareness of dying people and their needs, making it possible for the dialogue to begin.

A Developmental Coping Model of the Dying Process

Charles A. Corr (1993) has recently taken all these factors into consideration with the intention of helping caregivers, researchers, and educators move beyond the flaws and limitations of the stage theory. He believes that "An adequate model for coping with dying will need to be as agile, malleable, and dynamic as is the behavior of each individual" (1993, p. 77). The model must encompass the fact that people may try out certain coping strategies only to reject them firmly, or may pursue several strategies at the same time, even if they are not compatible. Furthermore, people differ in the tasks and needs that are important to them, as well as in their methods of coping. The model must respect individuality as well as universality, and it must offer practical guidelines for caregivers. It is not enough just to identify a coping process and give it a name.

Corr identifies four challenges that dying people encounter: the physical (satisfying body needs and reducing stress); the psychological (feeling secure, in control, and still having a life to live); the social (keeping valued attachments to other individuals and to groups and causes); and the spiritual (finding or affirming meaning, having a sense of connectedness, transcendence, and hope). We face challenges throughout the course of our lives, so when we must cope with the challenges of the dying process, we can draw upon what we have already learned and achieved.

Above all, Corr advocates greater empowerment for dying people and for those who are intimately involved in caregiving. With open communication and trusting relationships, we might feel less need for simple theories of a dying process. It is also a useful approach for recognizing that the dying person remains a living person who is attempting to cope as resourcefully as possible with challenges and stresses, and useful for including the full range of factors that influence the experience and course of the dying process. This approach has not yet been documented in action or research, but it could prove useful in the future.

The Dying Person's Own Reality As the Model

Another emerging approach focuses on the patient's own reality. The emphasis here shifts from the observer's frame of reference—away from stages or developmental tasks that an outsider might find useful to make sense of the dying process. Instead, the challenge is to learn how a dying person interprets his or her own situation. In this view, there may be as many theoretical models of dying as there are dying people. Debbie Messer Zlatin (1995) found that terminally ill people had a variety of different life themes to share. She also observed that there are important differences between people who do and who do not have integrated life themes to call upon as they face the stress of the dying process.

An example has been provided through the journal kept by a distinguished researcher during the last weeks of his life (Kastenbaum, 1995–1996). William McDougall was a British-born physician who became one of the most eminent researchers of the early twentieth century. He was a founder of the field of social psychology and an influential thinker in several other areas of scholarly activity. His terminal illness was a painful ordeal, occurring in 1938, years before palliative care techniques became widely available. The last weeks of his life centered on a confrontation between the relief of pain and his determination to exercise his will power as long as possible. The essence of McDougall's own theoretical model of dying can be drawn from the pages of his journal. When his pain was at its most intense, the exercise of his intellect was also at its most inspired. As long as he could maintain his intellectual effort against pain, he could avoid becoming what he perceived as a passive and defeated victim.

McDougall's intellectual approach to the dying process is quite at odds with the current emphasis on emotions, relationships, and peaceful acceptance, and it does not follow any standard list of "developmental tasks" that might be assigned to a dying person. Instead, McDougall continued to be McDougall—even more so—as he called upon all his knowledge and skills to integrate dying and death into his overall view of self and world. A person who decided to treat McDougall from an outsider's perspective would very likely fail to understand and, therefore respond usefully, to this man's distinctive interpretation of the dying process.

This individual-centered approach by no means takes attention away from all of the contextual influences on the dying process (e.g., how the symptoms are being managed, the kind of interpersonal support available). It does remind us, however, that each person is a unique center of value and reality.

A Multiple Perspective Approach

Is it possible that we might focus so much on what is unique about dying that we do not give enough attention to what dying shares with many other human experiences? Upon reflection we begin to see that much of what a dying person experiences has its counterpart in other situations. This suggests that the more clearly we recognize the similarities, the more we can draw upon our knowledge of these other phenomena to help us understand and support dying people. A new multiple perspective approach asks us first to identify these other processes one at a time and then to gradually put them together to form both a more comprehensive and a more detailed understanding of a dying person's situation. The central fact that the person is terminally ill is then added to complete the picture (Kastenbaum, 2000).

Here we will very briefly describe five of the seventeen partial models, selected for their diversity.

1. *The restricted activity model.* We are likely to become frustrated, angry, and depressed when circumstances prevent us from doing what we usually do and from what we strongly feel needs doing. Some people become tense and agitated when confined to bed for just a few days. Some people in perfect physical health either stew or feel helpless when their activities are restricted by external circumstances (such as bad weather, bureaucratic delay, or insufficient funds). Part of the tension and frustration experienced by dying people can be attributed to restricted activity. Everything we know and everything we can devise to help people deal with a restricted activity situation could relieve some of the stress of dying people.

2. *The distorted or altered body image model.* You have never been upset because the mirror suggests you might be too thin or too heavy. You have never had a bad hair day. You will certainly not be concerned when your hair begins to silver and wrinkles and age spots appear. And certainly you felt just as good about yourself as ever when you had that runny nose or outbreak of zits. Many of the rest of us, though, do respond with concern when our bodies no longer look the same. Our anxiety tends to increase further when our bodies no longer perform the same way. We may experience anything from mild to severe distress as we experience both visual and biological feedback suggesting that we are not now as we were. A dying person is subject to prolonged and ever-intensifying feedback that is hurtful to self-image and confidence. What do

we know about coping with distorted and altered body image? What can we do to help? These are among the constructive questions we can ponder when we want to be helpful to a dying person.

3. *The disempowerment model.* Other people are now making all of the decisions. You are pretty much out of the loop. Life is going along without you. Once you were at the center of things; now you are a disenfranchised outsider, not really abused but not really taken seriously as a real player, either. People experience disempowerment in many situations: the one-hit pop singer, the executive whose leverage disappeared during the latest corporate reorganization, the wife who has become a widow and lost much of her social status along with her husband. Some people are relieved to relinquish positions of power in the family, community, and workplace, but others feel rejected, abandoned, and bitter. There is often a period of doubt and seeking regarding one's own identity: "Who am I now, and am I worth anything?" Many dying people experience disempowerment in various forms. If we can heighten our awareness of this phenomenon, we can put ourselves in a better position to be helpful.

4. *The time anxiety model.* Will you ever get it done in time? How can you write all of those term papers, and prepare for all of those exams with so little time left? Schedules and deadlines are ever present in the lives of many people. It is not unusual to face several sets of schedules and deadlines at the same time as personal, family, social, and work demands converge on us. Everything seems to be moving too fast, and we feel tense and irritable as we look for some way out of the dilemma. The situation is intensified when we have too little time to accomplish something that is of great importance to us.

Dying people sometimes find themselves in precisely that situation. They may have such crucial end-of-life issues as making financial arrangements to benefit the family or rescuing an intimate relationship that had come apart. We might be more helpful if we recognized that a dying person might be struggling with a foreshortened future and pressing needs to accomplish some things.

5. *The journey model.* The idea of journey is embedded in most if not all world cultures (Cole, 1992). Galen, Aristotle, and other voices from ancient times described the life course as a journey from one age or stage to the next. Christian theologians spoke of "spiritual ages," and in our own time Erik H. Erikson's (1950) "Eight Ages of Man" is among the more influential updatings of the journey idea. Rituals have long been closely associated with journeys. Anybody who has ever moved into a new relationship, new job, or new community has probably experienced something of the anxiety that can be associated with even a positive change. Ritual protects. Dying people are in transition from the world they have known; some of their thoughts and feelings might well be understood in these terms. Are there forms of ritual that would be meaningful and supportive to dying people?

This converging multiple perspective approach is intended to help us draw upon much that is known and knowable about human experience in order to be more helpful to those who are living at the very edge.

Your Deathbed Scene

Perhaps you took a crack at the deathbed scene exercise suggested in Box 4-4. Following is some information on the way that other people enrolled in death-related classes have depicted their own deaths (Kastenbaum and Normand, 1990). The typical respondent:

- Expected to die in old age
- At home
- Quickly
- With the companionship of loved ones
- While remaining alert
- Not experiencing pain or any other symptoms

What was the most common alternative response? Those who did not expect to die in the manner summarized above instead saw themselves as perishing in an accident, usually on the highway and while they were still young. In fact,

---

---

those who thought their lives would end in a fatal accident tended to expect these accidents to occur in the near future. Almost all thought they would be alert and experience no pain or other symptoms as they neared death, whether death happened at home in old age or on the road in youth.

These deathbed scene expectations by mostly young college students will take on more meaning when we continue our exploration of the dying process in the next chapter, with the focus on hospice care. You can enhance the personal meaning of the next chapter, by pausing to answer the questions raised in Box 4-3.

SUMMARY

Dying, the transition from life, is unique because the separation is so complete and so final. However, the dying process has points in common with other types of transition with which we are all familiar: interactions that can be either disturbing of comforting, communications that can either inform or confuse, and self-evaluations that can either undermine or strengthen one's sense of identity and value. This chapter has considered dying as part of the total life experience while at the same time attending to what is distinctive about living with terminal illness.

You were given the opportunity to imagine your own deathbed scene before we turned to the fundamental questions: What is dying? and When does it begin? Our answers are consequential because a person is often treated very differently by others when defined as dying or terminally ill. Several competing alternatives were identified. Dying might be said to begin when (1) the physician draws this conclusion; (2) the physician informs the patient; (3) the patient accepts this conclusion; or (4); nothing more can be done to preserve life.

The transition from life to death can take one of several different trajectories, as described by Glaser and Strauss. We gave particular attention to the lingering trajectory, the expected quick trajectory, and the unexpected quick trajectory. The life-or-death emergency, a special case of the unexpected quick trajectory, was also given special attention. It was clear that medical and nursing staff usually feel and respond differently to people who are on different trajectories. Awareness of these differences can help us to provide more effective support to patients, family, and staff.

Familiar terms such as "healthy," "dying," and "terminally ill" do not apply to all individuals. We looked at hemophilia as an example of a life-threatening condition in people who are healthy and vigorous yet go through their lives with greater risk.

Some people end their lives in social isolation because of inadequate communication with others. We identified some of the problems involved, including the special issues that arise in doctor-patient communication. A major hospital-based study (SUPPORT) has documented continuing gaps in communication between many physicians and their terminally ill patients. A physician's inability or unwillingness to listen to a patient's statements all too often leaves the patient with uncontrolled pain and violates the patient's preferences for end-of-life management. Suggestions were made for improving communication with dying family members and friends.

We reminded ourselves that dying is both a universal and an individual experience. Age, gender, interpersonal relationships, and the nature of the disease, its treatment, and the environmental setting were considered as influences on an individual's experience of dying.

Theoretical models of the dying process include two stage theories that have originated in markedly different contexts: the ancient Buddhist conception, and the clinical observations made by Kübler-Ross. The eight-stage Buddhist model is intimately related to that religion's view of the ever-changing and disintegrating process we call everyday life. The last four of these stages are said to occur past the point at which a physician would have certified death. The well-known Kübler-Ross model consists of a sequence of responses that moves through denial, anger, bargaining, depression, and acceptance. Individuals do not always proceed through all stages in either of these models. The Kübler-Ross stage theory was carefully evaluated. Attention was also given to three more recent theoretical approaches: a developmental coping model, accepting the dying person's own reality as the model, and a multiple perspective model in which many different physical, personal, and interpersonal processes are considered separately and then brought together. We concluded by revisiting the deathbed scene you created and by inviting you to consider some further questions about how you might feel in the last days of your life.

REFERENCES

Andershed, B., & Ternestedt, B-M. (1998). The illness trajectory—for patients with cancer who died in two different cultures of care. *Omega, Journal of Death and Dying, 37*, 251–272.

Cole, T. R. (1992). *The journey of life.* Cambridge: Cambridge University Press.

Connor, S. R. (1992). Denial in terminal illness: To intervene or not to intervene. *The Hospice Journal, 8*, 1–15.

Coolidge, F. L., & Fish, C. E. (1983–1984). Dreams of the dying. *Omega, Journal of Death and Dying, 14*, 1–8.

Corr, C. A. (1993). Coping with dying: Lessons that we should and should not learn from the work of Elisabeth Kübler-Ross. *Death Studies, 17*, 69–84.

Dembour, M-B. (1998–1999). The conscious death of a two-year-old: Beautiful and unbearable. *Omega, Journal of Death and Dying, 38*, 187–200.

Demmer, C. (1999). AIDS attitudes and attitudes toward caring for dying patients. *Death Studies, 23*, 433–442.

Doka, J. K. (1993). *Living with Life-Threatening Illness.* New York: Lexington.

(Editorial) (1995). Improving care near the end of life: Why is it so hard? *Journal of the American Medical Association, 274*, 1634–1636.

Erikson, E. H. (1950). *Childhood and society.* New York: Norton.

Gilbert, P. (1992). *Depression: The evolution of powerlessness.* New York: Guilford.

Glaser, B. G., & Strauss, A. (1966). *Awareness of dying.* Chicago: Aldine.

Glaser, B. G., & Strauss, A. (1968) *Time for dying.* Chicago: Aldine.

Golden, R. L. (1997–1998). Sir William Osler: Humanistic thanatologist. *Omega, Journal of Death and Dying, 36*, 241–258.

Goldman, J. C. (1994). *Hemophilia: Current medical management.* New York: National Hemophilia Foundation.

Goldsmith, J. C. (1994) *About hemophilia.* New York: The Hemophilia Foundation.

Gomez, C. F. (1991). *Regulating death.* New York: Free Press.

Gyatos, Tenzin, the 14th Dalai Lama (1985). *Kindness, clarity, and insight.* Trans. J. Hopkins, Ithaca: Snow Lions Publications.

Hart, K. (1986–1987). Stress encountered by significant others of cancer patients receiving chemotherapy. *Omega, Journal of Death and Dying, 17*, 151–168.

Hinohara, S. (1996). Comments. QOL in medicine and nursing international conference. Tokyo: The Life Planning Center.

Jansson, L., Norberg, A., Sandman, P. O., Athlin, E., & Asplund, K. (1992–1993). Interpreting facial expressions in patients in the terminal stage of Alzheimer's Disease. *Omega, Journal of Death and Dying, 26*, 309–324.

Kastenbaum, R. (1978). In control. In C. A. Garfield (Ed.) *Psychosocial care of the dying patient.* New York: McGraw-Hill, (pp. 227–244).

Kastenbaum, R. (1984). The changing role of the physician with the terminally ill elderly. In I. Rossman (Ed.) *Clinical geriatrics* (3rd ed., pp. 618–620). New York: Lippincott.

Kastenbaum, R. (1993). Gender as a shaping force in adult development and aging. In R. Kastenbaum (Ed.) *The encyclopedia of adult development.* Phoenix: Oryx, pp. 165–170.

Kastenbaum, R. (1995–1996). "How far can an intellectual effort diminish pain?" William McDougall's journal as a model for facing death. *Omega, Journal of Death and Dying, 32,* 123–164.

Kastenbaum, R. (2000). *The psychology of death.* (3rd ed.). New York: Springer.

Kastenbaum, R., Barber, T., Wilson, S., Ryder, B., & Hathaway, L. (1981). *Old, sick, and helpless.* Cambridge, MA: Ballinger.

Kastenbaum, R., & Normand, C. (1990). Deathbed scenes as expected by the young and experienced by the old. *Death Studies, 14,* 201–218.

Kastenbaum, R., & Thuell, S. (1995). Cookies baking, coffee brewing: Toward a contextual theory of dying. *Omega, Journal of Death and Dying, 31,* 175–188.

Kelleher, A. (1990). *Dying of cancer. The final year of life.* London: Harwood.

Kramer, K. (1988). *The sacred art of dying.* New York: Paulist Press.

Kübler-Ross, E. (1969). *On death and dying.* New York: Macmillan.

Lesses, K. (1982–1983). How I live now. *Omega, Journal of Death and Dying, 13,* 75–78.

LeShan, L. (1982). In Bowers, M. N., Jackson, E. N., Knight, J. A. & LeShan, L. *Counseling the dying* (pp. 6–7). New York: Nelson.

Lester, D. (1988). Prejudice towards AIDS versus other terminally ill patients. *American Journal of Public Health, 78,* 854.

Lester, D. (1992–1993). The stigma against dying and suicidal patients: A replication of Richard Kalish's study twenty-five years later. *Omega, Journal of Death and Dying, 26,* 71–76.

Moller, D. W. (1996). *Confronting death. Values, institutions, & human mortality.* Oxford, New York: Oxford University Press.

Rosen, E. J. (1998). *Families facing death.* San Francisco: Jossey-Bass.

SUPPORT (1995). A controlled trial to improve care for seriously ill hospitalized patients. *Journal of the American Medical Association, 274,* 1591–1599.

Sweeting, H. N., & Gilhooly, M. L. M. (1991–1992). Doctor, am I dead? A review of social death in modern societies. *Omega, Journal of Death and Dying, 24,* 251–270.

Szsakawa, Y. (1988). Introductory Remarks. QOL in Medicine and Nursing International Conference. Tokyo: The Life Planning Center.

Taylor, J. (1977). *Holy dying.* New York: Arno Press. (Original work published in 1651.)

Villa, J. (1996: February 2). New rule widens role of EMTs. *The Arizona Republic.*

Weisman, A. D. (1993). Avery D. Weisman: An Omega interview. *Omega, Journal of Death and Dying, 27,* 97–104.

Weisman, A. D., & Kastenbaum, R. (1968). *The psychological autopsy: A study of the terminal phase of life.* New York: Behavioral Publications.

Weisman, A. D., & Worden, J. W. (1975). Psychosocial analysis of cancer deaths. *Omega, Journal of Death and Dying, 6,* 61–65.

Weisman, A. D., & Worden, J. W. (1976). The existential plight in cancer. Significance of the first 100 days. *International Journal of Psychiatry in Medicine, 7,* 1–16.

Zlatin, D. M. (1995). Life themes: A method to understand terminal illness. *Omega, Journal of Death and Dying, 31,* 189–206.

GLOSSARY

Cardiopulmonary Resuscitation (CPR): Massage, injection, or electrical stimulation intended to restore heart and breath.

Colostomy Bag: A container for the collection of feces, attached to an abdominal opening following a surgical procedure on the bowel.

Danger List (D.L.): A classification used by some health care systems to indicate that a patient is at risk for death.

Euthanasia: Originally: painless and peaceful dying. Currently: ending a person's life to avoid continued or increased suffering.

Hemophilia: A genetically linked defect that interferes with the coagulation of blood and therefore can result in excessive bleeding.

Institutional Evasions: Techniques used by staff members to bypass the rules in order to get through a difficult situation.

Middle Knowledge: A state of mind in which a person has some awareness of death but shifts from time to time in acknowledging and expressing this awareness.

"Orange Card": A legal document in which a person renounces the use of CPR and other emergency procedures.

Stage Theory: Holds that the phenomena in question occur in a fixed sequence of qualitatively different forms.

Surrogate: A person who acts in the place of another person who is not available or unable to respond.

Trajectories of Dying: The distinctive patterns through time that can be taken by the dying process, e.g., long fading away (lingering trajectory) or unexpected (quick trajectory).

Dame Cicely Saunders, nurse and physician, is the founder of the international hospice movement.

chapter 5

THE HOSPICE APPROACH TO TERMINAL CARE

I told her gently that it was part of the disease progress, and that all she could do was to keep her mum comfortable. She burst into tears and ran into the kitchen. I followed her but when I put my arms around her, she pushed me angrily away. I stood back helpless, as she shed her silent tears. When she stopped crying, I asked her if she would like to talk about it, but she just shrugged her shoulders. "It's all so hopeless," was all she said, and then she changed the subject.
—McGrath, Yates, Clinton, & Hart, 1999, p. 25

Louise was seventy-seven at the time she died. She was tiny, no more than 5 feet tall.... She had a cart in which during the day she kept four suitcases. Every night she brought the cart with her and took the cases one by one up a series of steps to the shelter. She would set up a foldout chair and table that served as her "dining room," and open her can of tuna, or maybe sardines...whatever little snack she had, as she waited for the shelter to open. Every morning she would pack the four bags down to her cart and spend her day walking the streets of the city.
—Wright, Jones & Wright, 1999, p. 240

Desperate refugees flooded the nation by the hundreds of thousands. Hospitals and rehabilitation centers were overwhelmed by the number of wounded people. The mass media was filled with reports of killing, torture, revenge, and extreme suffering physically, emotionally, socially, and spiritually. The question was raised: does it make any sense to speak about 'dying with dignity' amid so many terrible and extremely humiliating deaths? Is it realistic to speak about dying decently in a country where so many persons now cannot live decently"
—Anica Jusic, M. D., 1997, p. 126 founder of the first palliative care unit in Croatia just before her country was invaded by the Serbian/ Yugoslav army

The hospice approach has become an international model and beacon of hope for terminally ill people and their families. A snapshot of hospice care in action would show us an intact and loving family that is providing support for a terminally ill person, with guidance and assistance from nursing and medical personnel and community volunteers. The scene is probably the dying person's own home, although it might also take place in a residential setting. We assume that the patient is be a well-integrated, mentally competent person and, of course, that the community itself is peaceful, orderly, and well functioning.

We have started this chapter, however, by reminding ourselves that this idyllic picture does not always hold true. Many kinds of people die under many kinds of conditions. The nurse who was rebuffed by the angry and resistant daughter had come up against the fact that family members are not always ready to deal with the loss and do not always have the ability to communicate openly on emotional issues. More challenging yet was Louise's situation. She was a mentally ill widow who had suffered years of abuse from her husband and had little or no contact with her other family members. The staff members of the shelter for the homeless had few resources and little or no legal standing as they tried to care for her during her final illness and try to arrange a dignified funeral and memorial service. And even more challenging was the situation confronting the new Croatian Society for Hospice/Palliative Care in the midst of the deprivations and devastations of war. Nevertheless, the caregivers did help some people to die "decently" and are continuing its work today. The world is not perfect, not for the living, not for the dying, and not for those who provide care. The hospice approach itself was created by imperfect people within this imperfect world

In this chapter, we describe the origins and nature of hospice care for terminally ill people. We also consider both the still unfulfilled potential of the hospice movement and the difficulties that limit and threaten its distinctive role in society. It is important to understand not only the workings of hospice programs but also the ways in which they are affected by their host communities and national cultures.

We begin where hospice began: in the compassionate vision of those who were moved by the suffering and despair of dying people long before the advent of the modern health care system. This historical background provides the foundation for understanding hospice today and tomorrow.

HOSPICE: A NEW FLOWERING FROM ANCIENT ROOTS

Temples of healing ministered to the psychological and physical ailments of the Greeks. The priests and other healers recognized that health and illness involved more than physical condition: one must consider the whole person. The temples of healing were designed to please, soothe, and encourage the anxious and ailing people who journeyed to them. Music as well as medicine was part of the healing program. Every effort was made to restore the patients through an appealing physical environment, therapeutic conversation, positive imagery, bathing, massage, and walks in the countryside.

Imperial Rome established hospitals for military personnel. You would probably recognize something of the modern bureaucratic style of organization in these early hospitals, just as you would recognize the resonance between the holistic approach offered in the temples and the approach taken by modern hospice programs. However, neither the temple nor the hospital was designed for the care of dying people. Health care providers, then as now, were more interested in working with people who were thought to have a chance of recovery.

And yet there is no reason to doubt that some compassionate people did provide comfort to the dying as best they could. It is likely that the earliest examples of hospice-type care did not leave documentary traces for the historian. Perhaps in the *har-em* of a Byzantine ruler there were women with special skill and sensitivity in caring for the dying. Perhaps some wealthy families in Syria or Athens saw to it that the poor were treated well in their last days of life. The documentary trail becomes clearer with the advent of the Christian era. Public infirmaries (*nosocomeia*) were established in Greek-speaking areas of Christianity during the fourth century. These facilities provided care for people dying of epidemics as well as patients who were likely to recover. Roman emperor Julian, an opponent of the upstart Christian movement, acknowledged that these hospices had made a very favorable impression on everybody, "owing to the humanity evinced by Christians toward outsiders" (Phipps, 1988). Julian resolved to establish his own hospice in every city, but his own death aborted this plan.

The hospice movement spread to western Europe near the end of the fourth century through the influence of Fabiola, a wealthy Roman widow who had been inspired by the care for the sick that she had witnessed in monasteries in the Holy Land (Phipps, 1988). Fabiola brought this concept back with her to Italy, not only supporting hospices financially but also serving as a nurse herself. St. Jerome knew Fabiola and honored her contributions, writing that "often too she washed away the matter discharged from wounds which others, even though men, could not bear to behold.... She gave food with her own hand and even when a patient was but a breathing corpse she would moisten his lips with liquid" (Phipps, 1988, p. 93). And so Fabiola, this woman who lived and died about 1,600 years ago, may have given an enduring gift to humankind that in our own time has been renewed as the modern hospice program.

The hospice became well established in the fifth century. The term itself derives from *hospitium*, a Latin term that has also given us such words as *host* and *hostess*. The medieval hospice was usually a house in which people in need could find food, shelter, and other comforts under Christian auspices. Those undertaking the arduous pilgrimage to the Holy Land and other travelers who were fatigued, ill, or dying found welcome there. Certain religious orders became especially known for their hospice care. Established by Benedictine monks in the sixth century, the Monte Cassino monastery was one of the most noted hospices; unfortunately this historic shelter was destroyed during World War II in a misguided military operation. Throughout the medieval period, the hospice functioned as one of the purest expressions of Christian piety: here the hungry were fed, the thirsty given water, the naked clothed, the homeless sheltered, and the sick provided care and comfort. Medical treatment was minimal—probably just as well, considering how ineffective or even dangerous most "remedies" were at that time.

Unfortunately, something went very much wrong between the time that the early hospices flourished and the beginning of the modern hospice movement. During the intervening centuries, the original hospice tradition clung to life in only a few scattered facilities. Phipps (1988) suggests that hospices became an innocent casualty of the Protestant Reformation and then were replaced by state-run institutions with different types of personnel and philosophies. Whatever the reasons, the religiously oriented hospice and its mission of mercy for the dying faded away, although the spark was kept alive in a few places. Bureaucracy and technology-oriented medicine took over the scene. The newly emerging systems of health care evaded dying people who were now seen as disquieting reminders that "to all things there is a season."

The renewed hospice approach made its appearance in 1879 with the opening of Our Lady's Hospice in Dublin (Gilmore, 1989). Again it was a woman who led the way: Sister Mary Aitkinhead. By 1905 a similar facility had been established in London, St. Joseph's Hospice. The hospice movement took its next major step forward when a medical officer at St. Joseph's Hospice introduced improvements in pain control for dying people. Dr. Cicely Saunders subsequently founded St. Christopher's Hospice in London, which has served as an inspiration and model for many others. Starting out as a student of philosophy, politics, and economics, Saunders enrolled in a nurse training program during World War II. A back injury made it difficult for her to continue as a nurse, so she became a social worker, and then a physician. This triple perspective on caregiving liberated Saunders from seeing dying people from the limitations of any one health provider's standpoint. Her vision of hospice care has always emphasized contributions and interactions from people of diverse backgrounds.

Emphasis upon expertise has also been associated with Saunders and hospice from the beginning. As noted in the opening quotation, she followed the advice given to her many years ago: "You will only be frustrated if you don't do it properly, and they won't listen to you." Hospice would not have succeeded if it had only sensitivity and good intentions to offer.

I asked Dame Saunders about the circumstances that led to her introduction of modern hospice care. The inspiration provided by two people was especially important. Lillian Pipkin, a Salvation Army matron, had taught her the basics of pain management for terminally ill patients, which she was then able to apply for the first time herself at St. Joseph's and, subsequently, St. Christopher's. Pipkin was also a role model for Saunders in understanding and communicating with dying patients. The other person was David Tasma, a dying man who

> ...needed not only symptom relief, but also the time, space, and atmosphere in which to come to his own terms with his life. At this point, David was feeling that his life had been unfulfilled and perhaps meaningless. Something emerged during our long conversations that not only sparked the inspiration for hospice but also made possible his own quiet peace.... David had made a personal peace with the God of his forefathers before he died, and he left me with the assurance that he had found his answers—and with the belief that all our caring must give total freedom to others to make their own way into meaning." (Saunders, 1993, p. 264)

Tasma also contributed his small legacy to Saunders for what would become the hospice project.

And what was the first response of physicians and nurses to her innovations? Would they be dubious and resistant?

> I was therefore soon able to demonstrate to an increasing number of visitors that dying patients could be alert, as well as free from pain, and very able to do the teaching themselves. Without this opportunity, I do not think the modern hospice movement would have been established and I am everlastingly grateful to the patients and Sisters of St. Josephs who, together with David Tasma and the patients of St. Luke's, I see as the true founders. (Saunders, 1993)

These personal reflections are valuable for what they tell us about the spirit in which the hospice movement was conceived:

- From Fabiola onward, women have been the prime movers in attempting to improve the care of dying people.

- Unique personal interactions and relationships have been crucial to the development of hospice. Both in its origins with Dame Cicely Saunders and with its later introductions to other nations, hospice has grown from the efforts of a few highly motivated individuals, rather than as part of a formal plan hatched by bureaucratic committees.
- The stereotype that doctors "know better" than their patients has been reversed in hospice philosophy. All care providers are invited to learn from the people who really know what it feels like to cope with the physical and psychological stresses of dying: the patients themselves.
- Although hospice leaders often are people with strong religious beliefs, the emphasis is on giving "total freedom to others to make their own way into meaning." This was evident at the start in the interaction between a Christian physician (Saunders) and her Jewish patient (Tasma).

By the early 1970s it was clear that hospice care was a promising alternative to the "never-say-die," high-tech, impersonal approach increasingly dominant in Western medicine. Many questions and problems remained, however, including the establishment of standards of care and the challenge of establishing hospices in other nations, including the United States.

STANDARDS OF CARE FOR THE TERMINALLY ILL

An International Work Group on Death and Dying (IWG), including Dr. Saunders and other pioneers, saw the need to develop guidelines that could help to stimulate the further development of hospice care. The task force decided first to give expression to the *implicit* assumptions that governed the care of the terminally ill. As you read this list, please remember that these were not the standards that the task force intended to recommend—rather, it was a way of identifying the *hidden standards*, the preferences and biases that influenced the way in which terminally ill people were treated.

The items on the following list were seen as the typical pattern of a "good or "successful" death from the perspective of the facility in which a terminally ill person spent his or her final days of life.

Hidden or Implicit Standards of Care

1. A successful death is quiet and uneventful. The death slips by with as little notice as possible; nobody is disturbed.
2. Few people are on the scene. There is, in effect, no scene. Staff is spared the discomfort of interacting with family and other visitors whose needs might upset the well-routined equilibrium.
3. Leave-taking behavior is at a minimum: no awkward, painful, or emotional good-byes to raise the staff's anxiety level.
4. The physician does not have to involve himself or herself intimately in terminal care, especially as the end approaches.
5. The staff makes few technical errors throughout the terminal care process and few mistakes in medical etiquette.
6. Attention is focused on the body during the caregiving process. Little effort is wasted on the unique personality of the terminally ill individual.
7. The patient expresses gratitude for the excellent care received.
8. The person dies at the right time, that is, after the full range of medical interventions has been tried out and before the onset of a long period of lingering.
9. After the patient's death, the family expresses gratitude for the excellent care received.
10. The staff is able to conclude that "we did everything we could for this patient."
11. Physical remains of the patient are made available to the hospital for clinical, research, or administrative purposes (via autopsy permission or organ donations).
12. A memorial (financial) gift is made to the hospital in the name of the deceased.
13. The cost of the terminal care process is determined to have been low or moderate, that is, money was not wasted on a person whose life was beyond saving or, more important, the hospital came out ahead after expenses were compared with reimbursements.

The task force itself proposed a very different set of standards!

Proposed Standards Recommended by the International Task Force

- *Patients, family, and staff all have legitimate needs and interests.*
- *The terminally ill person's own preferences and lifestyle must be taken into account in all decision making.*

These were the basic guidelines from which the others were generated. The first proposition was intended to promote honest interactions and reduce conflicts. Recognition that everybody in the situation is human and has legitimate needs and interests provides a realistic starting point for care. The second proposition suggests that treatment should not be overly standardized. The specific standards follow.

Patient-Oriented Standards

1. *Remission of symptoms is a treatment goal.* Even if it is expected that the person will die within hours or days, efforts should be continued to maintain functional capacity and relieve pain and anguish. A dying person should not be made to endure thirst, for example, or gasp for breath when a change of position might afford relief.
2. *Pain control is a treatment goal.* Uncontrolled pain not only intensifies the anguish of dying but also disturbs interpersonal relationships and can lead to demoralization. The patient's ability to maintain psychological equilibrium is severely tested by pain.
3. *The patient's intentions will be respected as one of the main determinants of the total pattern of care.* This does not mean that every expressed wish of the patient will automatically be granted. The rights and responsibilities of family, staff, and society as represented by the legal system must also be taken into account. The point is the willingness of family and health care providers to take seriously any document through which patients express their own wishes. (*See Chapter 6 for a discussion of advance directives.*)
4. *The patient should have a sense of basic security and protection in his or her environment.* This

standard is met when dying people feel that they can depend on the caregivers to perform their functions and maintain effective communication. Patients should feel safe. They should not have to live in apprehension of unexpected diagnostic or treatment procedures, brusque interactions, or breakdown in medication and meal routines.

5. *Opportunities should be provided for leavetakings with the people most important to the patient.* This requires flexibility in visiting hours and rules for admitting visitors (for example, children were often excluded). There should be a good place to sit, privacy, and freedom from interruption. The patient should also have the opportunity to take leave of other patients and staff members if desired.

6. *Opportunities should be provided for experiencing the final moments in a way that is meaningful to the patient.* For example, patients should be afforded the opportunity to listen to music or poetry of their own choice. Physical contact should be made possible if desired, unless there is some major contraindication (e.g., a highly contagious disease). This certainly includes a dying person's being held in the arms of a loved one if this is what they both want.

Family-Oriented Standards

1. *Families should have the opportunity to discuss dying, death, and related emotional needs with the staff.* It is not acceptable for the staff to disregard requests for information or expressions of the need to share feelings. Although this increases the time demands on the staff, it helps the family to maintain its own integration and thus to be of greater comfort to the patient.

2. *Families should have the opportunity for privacy with the dying person, both while living and while newly dead.* This might include the participation of close kin and friends in dressing the corpse and accompanying it to the funeral home. Or it might include simply being alone with the dead spouse, sibling, or parent for an hour or so without interruption by staff members.

Staff-Oriented Standards

1. *Caregivers should have adequate time to form and maintain personal relationships with the patient.*

This is not a priority in most medical facilities, so it would require developing a new attitude toward the needs and utilization of personnel. Hospital scheduling practices seldom make it possible for a nurse or other staff member to maintain a steady relationship with a patient. There is still a pressing need for hospitals to schedule around the needs of the patients, especially those who are most vulnerable.

2. *A mutual support network should exist among the staff.* Care for the terminally ill can become an emotionally depleting experience, especially in high death rate situations. A medical facility in which staff are given little opportunity to discuss experiences and share feelings about their work with the terminally ill would be seen as deficient, regardless of the facility's competence in other respects.

ESTABLISHMENT OF HOSPICE PROGRAMS IN THE UNITED STATES

From Guidelines to Operational Programs

The standards proposed by the international task force have become well established in the hospice movement. The philosophy and practice of hospice care is further elaborated by the National Hospice and Palliative Care Organization (1994) in making a set of comparisons with traditional medical care:

- *Hospice offers palliative, rather than curative, treatment.* Under the direction of a physician, hospice uses sophisticated methods of pain and symptom control that enable the patient to live as fully and comfortably as possible.

- *Hospice treats the person, not the disease.* The interdisciplinary team is made up of professionals who address the medical, emotional, psychological, and spiritual needs of the patient and family.

- *Hospice emphasizes quality, rather than length of life.* Hospice neither hastens nor postpones death: it affirms life and regards dying as a normal process. The hospice movement stresses human values that go beyond the physical needs of the patient.

- *Hospice considers the entire family, not just the patient, as the "unit of care."* Patients and families are included in the decision-making process, and bereavement counseling is provided to the family after the death of their loved one.
- *Hospice offers help and support to the patient and family on a 24-hours-a-day, seven-days-a-week basis.* For hospice patients and their families, help is just a phone call away. Patients routinely receive periodic in-home services of a nurse, home health aide, social worker, volunteer, and other members of the hospice interdisciplinary team.

The hospice movement, though, did not simply materialize from definitions. Although hospice principles had found their way into several existing health care systems, it was the establishment of the Connecticut Hospice in New Haven in 1974 that marked the first full-service program of its type in the United States. Like St. Christopher's, the Connecticut Hospice provides both inpatient and homecare services. Unlike St. Christopher's, however, the New Haven program started with home care and later added an inpatient facility when the National Cancer Institute agreed to provide start-up support.

The founders of the Connecticut Hospice had to solve many organizational and financial problems that have also confronted most of the other programs that followed. The goals and methods of hospice care were often misunderstood, many physicians were reluctant to participate in the new approach, and reliable sources of funding were difficult to find. It is a tribute to hospice leaders throughout the United States and to the flexibility of healthcare agencies that significant progress has been made despite all of the obstacles.

Today the Connecticut Hospice is far from alone. You will probably find one or more hospice programs in your vicinity. Hospice organizations take several forms in North America and may even use different titles (e.g., *palliative care unit* is the term more frequently used in Canada). Some hospices are hospital based; others are free standing. St. Christopher's, the model for most hospice programs worldwide, was created as an independent organization, and this has set the pattern for most other hospices in Britain. In the United States, economic considerations have favored the hospital-based approach, perhaps because surplus hospital beds existed at the time that hospice care was introduced here. Either type of hospice can provide sensitive and high-quality service.

Full-Service and Partial-Service Hospices

Important differences exist in the spectrum of services offered by particular hospice organizations. At one extreme are the programs that limit themselves primarily to home visits, in which a variety of personal services are performed. A volunteer may provide companionship to the at-home patient for a few hours so that the patient's family can attend to other needs and responsibilities. The hospice may also provide welcome assistance in a variety of ways, such as helping to obtain health-related supplies and equipment.

It is the more comprehensive, professional, and systematic type of hospice service that has won the support of the federal government. The National Hospice Reimbursement Act of 1983 established a Medicare Hospice Benefit that provides support for the full-service and fully accountable hospice. In return for financial support, a hospice must agree to:

- Ensure continuity of care and professional management at all times, whether the patient is at home, in a hospital, or a respite care setting.
- Establish and maintain a detailed plan of care for each patient.
- Evaluate quality of care and correct any problems that are identified.
- Provide an interdisciplinary team that includes a physician, registered nurse, social worker, and pastor or counselor.
- Comply with licensing regulations in its state and locality.
- Maintain clinical records for each individual receiving hospice care.
- Provide all core services required by the individual, and any additional services that might be needed, (physical therapy, speech-language rehabilitation, and so on).
- Guarantee that essential services are available around the clock every day.
- Operate an in-service training program to maintain and improve the skills of staff and volunteers.

Hospice care offers a more personal and comforting approach to helping terminally ill people.

The Medicare Hospice Benefit applies only when all three of the following conditions are met (Miller & Mike, 1995):

1. The patient's physician and the hospice medical director certify that a patient has a life expectancy of six months or less.
2. The patient chooses to receive care from a hospice as an alternative to basic Medicare coverage.
3. Care is provided by a hospice program certified by Medicare.

A hospice can be of high quality and in compliance with the most essential features of the legislation and yet not be a participant in the current reimbursement program. Some hospice organizations that offer the full range of services have decided not to apply for federal reimbursement.

This nonparticipation is based primarily on concern that the reimbursement plan is not sufficient for the financial survival of the hospice. All hospices have expenses that are not reimbursed by the federal program. It is for good reason that they conduct fund-raising programs and events and depend on community generosity to maintain their services.

For patient, family, and physician alike, it is important to become well acquainted with the local hospice services available. All should at least know whether partial or full services are offered. Many other questions can arise in the decision as to whether or not to select hospice care for a terminally ill person. Because of local differences in the nature and scope of hospice organizations and the possibility of continuing changes in national legislation and policy, it is advisable to discuss the current situation with representatives of the hospice organization(s) in your own area. You are almost certain to receive an attentive, frank, and useful response. Information can also be obtained from NHPC's Hospice Helpline at (800)658-8898 or its website, http//www.nho.org/

THE HOSPICE IN ACTION

"Should we choose hospice or traditional care?" is an important question. We will be in a better position to consider this question after exploring just what it is that hospice does. The following are a few examples of how a hospice actually works.

Entering St. Christopher's

The first example is an observation I had the opportunity to make during a visit to St. Christopher's. Word was received that a person was arriving for admission. A station wagon had just pulled up to an entrance facing the hospice's attractive garden plaza. The patient-to-be was a frail, emaciated woman who looked to be in her sixties. She was accompanied by a younger man. Dr. Saunders and the woman greeted each other as sunlight propitiously broke through the cloudy London skies. The woman smiled and said, "Well, I finally made it!" On her face there was the mark of physical ordeal, but no indication of anxiety, anger, depression, or confusion.

The patient was immediately introduced to the nurse who would be responsible for much of her care and then assisted her to what would be her own bed (which had been transported by elevator to the ground-floor entrance). Just a few minutes later while touring the hospice we came upon this woman again. She was already settled into her own place, sipping tea with the man who had driven her to the hospice. As it turned out, he was her husband. Because of the debilitating effects of advanced cancer, the woman was appreciably younger than her physical appearance had indicated.

This simple incident tells much about the aims and techniques of the hospice. The patient and her family were already well acquainted with the hospice before admission. Consequently, she had

a sense of having made the next logical stop on her journey through life rather than a jarring transition from home to an impersonal institution. Much of St. Christopher's effort is devoted to its home care program, and this has become true of other hospices as well. With the guidance of hospice personnel, some families are able to provide high-quality care to their terminally ill members throughout the course of the illness. Patient and family know that the inpatient facility is there when and if they need it.

A hospice can be thought of more aptly as a process and as a spirit of mutual concern rather than as a place. The sociophysical environment of a hospice or palliative care facility is designed for life as well as death. In the incident just described, for example, the staff recognized the importance of the first few minutes of the admission process. Efficiency was improved by the appropriate use of technology (such as having the patient's own bed ready to meet her). Many other up-to-date techniques are used throughout St. Christopher's when these are seen as beneficial to patient care. But perhaps more important was the affirmation of human contact by both the medical director and the nurse. The prompt welcoming of the husband through the tea service further signified the hospice's interest in encouraging the maintenance of interpersonal relationships and comforting habits. These are small details, but Saunders and her staff recognize the significance of details such as these as well as the more obviously important aspects of patient care.

The family of a terminally ill person is not merely tolerated at a hospice such as St. Christopher's. Instead the family is both a provider and a recipient of care—the philosophy of care encompasses the entire family unit. Many family members not only visit with their own kin but also befriend other patients. This permeability of the hospice much reduces the likelihood of social isolation for the patient and the sense of helplessness for the family. It does raise the possibility, however, that the family might spend so much time and effort at the inpatient facility that they do not look after their own needs adequately. To place a friendly limit on family involvement, St. Christopher's established a weekly "family's day off." This allows the family a brief vacation without any sense of guilt attached.

Mother's Last Moments: A Daughter's Experience

Another example comes from an American hospice and expresses the viewpoint of a family member: the young adult daughter of a woman who had been terminally ill for several months after a lifetime of good health. The woman was being cared for at home during what proved to be the final phase of her illness.

The next day I woke up and went in to see my mother. I noticed the difference immediately. She had this rattle in her throat. She kept trying to talk, but all her words were garbled by the mucus in her throat.... And I called the doctor and he gave me a good idea of what was happening. It was very hard for me to believe that she was so close ["to death" were the words implied but not spoken by the daughter]. She looked so calm and serene. In her room and among all her things. She looked really okay. She didn't look like she was in distress. She looked like she was just glowing. And my sister came over. She brought over a tape made by a priest on death and dying. We put it on and we let my mother listen to it; isn't that awful? And it was talking about acceptance of death and it seemed to be quite appropriate at the time. And then my sister went to the movies and I stayed around with Emma [a housekeeper with some experience in caring for invalids, employed by the family to help out at this time]. And my sister had left a picture of her little boy so my mother could see him. And it was just as if everything was in preparation.

I got out her make-up and lotion and started to make her up. Put lotion all over her skin. She knew what I was doing, because she held out her arm like this, and moved a little here and there to make it easier to make her up. But I was afraid in touching her body. She was so *frail*, I was afraid her skin might break if I touched her too hard to hug her. Before this time, she hadn't wanted to be touched, because it hurt. But now it didn't seem to hurt her at all; her pain had diminished. I put blush on her face...and lipstick on...and I brushed her hair.

And then I explained to her that I was going out for a cup of tea, because Emma said, "Why don't you go out—you deserve a break. It's good for you to go out." Okay, after I finished making

her up, I told her I was going out for a cup of tea and I would be right back.

As I bent down to hug her, she—her body—I don't know how to describe it: she opened her mouth as I was holding her, and blood came out. And I thought at first, "What's wrong, what's happening?" And Emma said, "It's okay, It's nothing. She's fine. She'll be okay." But it was hard for me to let go of her. A part of me felt like "that was *it*," but, oh, no, it couldn't have happened. When I looked at her again, she looked—beautiful. She was glowing. She looked so smooth. She was just—beautiful. It was the only time I saw her look so beautiful during her whole illness.

And when I came back the hearse was in front of our house. And I said, "Oh, no! You're not going to take my mother away!" And my father was there. The people he had listed in his preparation. The people who were supposed to be there; the things that were supposed to happen...I resented it all. "They're not going to go into the room. I'm going into the room first!" I wanted to touch her. I wanted to be alone with her. I went in and closed the door. And I touched her all over, and took her all in. And then I realized, I realized... she had gone without a struggle. It was really right, it was all right, you know? She looked very good. She looked as if it was right. It wasn't painful It was the right time, and she was ready to go.

This is part of just one person's experience with death. The other family members responded in their own distinctive ways to the situation. The father, for example, did much planning and managing—his way of coping with the impending loss. The other daughters had their own ways of relating to their mother and her illness. The daughter quoted here had a very close relationship with her mother and was able to continue this relationship on an intimate basis, not only up to but also through the moment of death. It would have been much more difficult for all the family members, as well as the terminally ill woman, to respond like the distinctive people they were had they been constricted by a traditional hospital situation.

There were other positive features as well. This woman died free of pain and suffering. She felt safe. The final impression that "it was right" could well be a valuable core around which the daughter integrates her mother's death into her own ongoing life. The daughter also took full advantage of the opportunity to relate with her dying mother. She will not have to live with regret, self-recrimination, or anger about her own actions. Would she have felt comfortable applying lotion and make-up to her mother if they had been in a hospital? Would this even have been permitted? Would she have been allowed to stay to the very end or been shooed away by hospital staff? And would she have been allowed to return for a few minutes of privacy with her mother after death?

The hospice (in this instance, Hospice of Miami) was one important source of support for this family. Hospice may have made the difference, but the strength obviously was in the family itself, the feelings that members of an intact and affectionate family had for each other. Perhaps the hospice offered just enough to help the family be itself through the entire period of crisis. This does not mean, however, that the relationship between hospice and family was smooth at all times. The family at first had some resistance to the hospice's approach because it confronted them with the realization that they would soon lose the mother/wife to death.

The experience reported here was not "successful" if the aim of terminal care is to keep everybody's feelings under control and maneuver through the death event with minimal impact. The daughter's life had changed at the moment she first learned of her mother's terminal illness some months before. The circumstances of her mother's death and dying influenced her so much that she is now pursuing a career that involves providing care and comfort to others. It is not "life as usual" for this woman; she regards both the fact of her mother's death and the particular circumstances under which it occurred as strong motivation for her own continued growth as a person. And it is very clear that she would not have wanted to be deprived of the opportunity to be with her mother to the end, within the freedom and familiarity of their own house.

Adult Respite Care

Hospice programs usually provide care at the patient's home and in medical care facilities, as needed. A third alternative, however, is becoming increasingly important. *Adult respite care* offers an intermediate placement. At some point in the course of a terminal illness, the patient may feel more comfortable in a respite care setting than either at home or in a hospital. For example, Walter, a robust businessman with "never a sick day in his life," had to admit that he could not shake off an uncharacteristic feeling of fatigue and discomfort. When finally persuaded by his family to see a doctor, he learned that he had an advanced and incurable cancer.

The family already knew something of hospice through a friend's experience. When it was clear that there was no realistic hope for recovery, the family agreed to select the hospice alternative. His condition was stabilized for several weeks, during which Walter worked out a satisfactory business deal with his partner, said his good-byes to old friends, and immersed himself in the daily life of his very supportive family. As his functional capacity declined sharply, he noticed that his family was becoming increasingly concerned, stressed, and overtaxed in trying to care for him, even though they also had access to hospice services. With great tact, Walter suggested that he be given "a few days off" until he recovered his strength. In retrospect, the family and the hospice nurse realized that he had wanted to relieve the unremitting pressure on his family—and that he sensed his death was imminent.

At his suggestion, Walter was taken to a respite care center, housed in a comfortable homelike setting that had indeed once served as a family dwelling. He thanked his wife and son and gently ordered them to take good care of each other and the rest of the family until he perked up a little and could come home. About an hour later, the hospice nurse came by to see how he was doing. "I can go now," he smiled, "and so can you." He died peacefully within a few minutes.

In this instance, the respite care center did not have to offer any special services. What Walter needed was a way of establishing a little distance between himself and his loving family at the very end of his life. It is not unusual for a dying person to feel that he or she has accomplished everything possible in "taking care of business" and expressing feelings to the people who matter most. The availability of an adult respite care center can give family members a valuable relief from constant responsibility, even though this may be for only a few days. These brief "vacations" can be useful to the terminally ill person as well as the family. As one woman confided within a week of her death, "I try my best to keep their spirits up, but it's getting harder and harder. I don't like to be alone either, but at least when I'm alone I don't have to perform." A few days with considerate and expert caregivers who are not part of one's interpersonal network can liberate the dying person from investing limited available energy in meeting the needs and expectations of others.

Corr and Corr (1992a) believe that even shorter periods of respite can be valuable. They suggest that more attention be given to *hospice day care* programs. Instead of being moved from their homes to an inpatient facility for several days, people with a terminal (or a chronic) illness spend much of the day in an interesting and active environment and then come back home for the evening.

Adult day care centers of many types already exist. Few of these centers, however, were developed with the needs of terminally ill people foremost in mind. Perhaps one of the next major steps in the hospice movement will be to follow up on the suggestions of Corr and Corr that appropriate and high-quality day care centers be established as an alternative to home and hospital settings. Adult day care centers will not replace either of these settings. In many situations, either full-time home care or hospital care provides the best alternative. Furthermore, respite services seldom are appropriate when enrollment in a hospice program is delayed until death is close at hand. Nevertheless, both day care and inpatient respite care services may become of increasing importance for patients and families who are coping with the stresses of terminal illness over an extended period of time.

HOSPICE-INSPIRED CARE FOR A VARIETY OF PEOPLE

Most hospice patients are adults with end-stage cancer or progressive neurological conditions, most often amyotrophic lateral sclerosis (known in the United States as "Lou Gehrig's dis-

ease"). From the start of the modern hospice movement, there has been interest in providing care for other people as well. Here we consider the limited but promising work that has been done to achieve this goal.

Hospice-Inspired Care for Children

Consider this description of an episode in the life of Marie, "a ghostlike seven year old" who had already undergone three unsuccessful kidney transplants from cadavers and was being kept on dialysis treatment until a fourth transplantable organ could be located:

As Marie sat on the child-life worker's lap, she ground her teeth with great intensity and anxiously shifted the position of her blood-pressure cuff. She incessantly scratched and picked at the gauze pads which guarded her old abdominal wounds. 'My tummy hurts! My tummy hurts!' she announced, in hope that she would be permitted a day off. After Marie's blood pressure was read, she reenacted the procedure, detail by detail, with the child-life worker. Marie methodically placed the cuff on the child-worker's arm, pumped forcefully, and, stethoscope in hand, engagingly admonished her to be still and not to cry. Satisfied with her work, Marie carefully folded the cuff and put it away. She took the child-life worker's hand and hesitantly hobbled toward the scale where she was weighed....

When the preparations for dialysis were over, reality robbed Marie of her tenuous control over her experience. Her dialysis rituals could no longer protect her, and her fear was apparent in her eyes. As the staff placed Marie's papoose, or restraint, under her back, she frantically pleaded, 'Have to make pee-pee...Mommy coming?... Bleeding! Give me something to put me to sleep!' Three adults...wrestled with Marie as in panic she squirmed and fought to release herself from the papoose. Marie's right hand, the only part of her body free of restraint, blindly gripped the child-life worker's fingers.... Marie's mother would not be waiting for her after the ordeal had ended. Sedatives would not be used to ease the passage of time. (Meagher & Leff, 1989–1990)

This was a typical experience in Marie's life. She suffered physical and emotional pain throughout her final hospital stay—during which she was, to all purposes, abandoned by her family because they could no longer tolerate the stress themselves. Astoundingly, the medical staff systematically denied Marie the partial relief she might have experienced from pain-killing medication. Instead they attempted to deceive her by pretending to inject medications into her tubing. Why? So that she would not become a drug addict!

Marie experienced the torment of pain and abandonment in addition to the ravages of her disease. Her caregivers were not evil or unfeeling people, but they were working within the framework of aggressive, cure-oriented medicine. This "pull out all the stops" approach often reaches its peak of intensity when the patient is a child. The death of a child is an exceptionally powerful blow and violates our expectations in a society where so many people survive into advanced adult years. Sometimes this approach is successful; more often the child dies anyway but experiences more suffering and less comfort than would have been provided if a hospice-inspired program of care had been selected.

It is very difficult in the case of a child to say, "Let her go with love and comfort" as long as there seems to be any chance at all to prolong her life. This is probably the main reason that hospice care for dying children has not become more common. The decision to select hospice care involves the recognition of impending death, a recognition that is usually avoided by family and caregivers as long as possible (and even a little longer).

Ida Martinson, a nurse who has played a significant role in the development of palliative care programs for children, observes that:

> ...there is a greater sense of urgency for the health care professional to respond quicker when it is a child that is dying. Perhaps parents believe they are managing, and then suddenly panic and need advice or help quicker than, say, the wife or husband who is caring for a dying spouse. Symptom control is the basic need for both groups. Explaining the signs and symptoms and how dying occurs are essential for both groups as well. I still find nurses who do not believe they could work as well with families who have a dying child in

contrast to a dying adult. I really believe they *can* function as well. (Kastenbaum, 1995, p. 257)

Child's Hospice International estimates that about 100,000 children die each year in the United States, and ten times as many are seriously or chronically ill. Education and confidence building for health care professionals as well as for parents can be helpful in avoiding the panic-generated decision to rush a dying child to a hospital or to engage in additional treatment procedures that are distressing to the child without offering realistic hope for success.

Corr and Corr (1992b) point out that it is possible to provide home care for many terminally ill children if adequate preparations are made. The opportunity to stay at home may be even more important for children than for adults because it avoids the pangs, even the terrors, of separation. Parents can continue to be parents to their ailing child. To carry out their demanding responsibilities, however, parents will need assistance from knowledgeable health care providers who also have the communication skills to deal resourcefully with this difficult situation. The program of care might be furnished either by a hospice organization or by other agencies and individuals whose approach might be called "hospice-inspired." Careful decisions must be made, based upon the unique realities of each situation. For guidance on these matters, see Ida Martinson's (1989) valuable book, *Pediatric Hospice Care: What Helps?* and/or contact Children's Hospice International, 901 N. Washington Street, Suite 700, Alexandria, VA 22314, (800)24-CHILD.

Hospice Care for People with AIDS

A person whose HIV infection has converted to an active case of AIDS encounters many of the same sources of stress as does any person afflicted with any terminal illness. These include (1) the progressive loss of functions; (2) pain, fatigue, and other symptoms; (3) disruption and potential loss of interpersonal relationships; and (4) a future in which hopes, plans, and ambitions become replaced by the prospect of death. Hospice care is as applicable to people terminally ill with AIDS as it is to people with other life-threatening conditions. Palliative care and effective management often reduce the stress level and maintain a higher degree of comfort and individual lifestyle for patients during the final phase of the illness.

There have been barriers, however, to hospice care for people with AIDS, including the following:

- Willingness of the community to support hospice operations through volunteer services and fundraising if hospice programs accept AIDS patients.
- Willingness of hospice staff and administrators to provide services to AIDS patients.
- Willingness of AIDS patients to select the hospice option and willingness of their families to serve as participating caregivers.
- Willingness of the health care system to make whatever adjustments might be necessary in admission and management of AIDS patients.

Hospice programs are called upon to make an extra effort and take on extra risk when they make themselves available to AIDS patients. It would be understandable, then, if a hospice organization hesitated before accepting AIDS patients on the grounds that it could not place further burdens on its human resources or face the possible loss of volunteers and other forms of community support. Furthermore, AIDS is a complex condition from the medical and nursing standpoint. There are many symptoms to treat and many difficult decisions to make about balancing the advantages and disadvantages of the available treatments. Furthermore, more people with HIV/AIDS have been living longer in recent years—certainly a very positive development, but also one that can make it difficult to decide whether and when a person is terminally ill as defined by current regulations (usually six months or fewer to live). Some people with HIV/AIDS are themselves reluctant to enter hospice care because they either hold out hope for remission or deny the severity of their illness. Individual prognosis for people with HIV/AIDS is uncertain, so people may differ in the way they evaluate the situations, as well as change their outlooks from time to time.

Despite these and other difficulties, there is evidence that hospice programs are responding to the needs of terminally ill AIDS patients. Nearly a thousand hospice programs responded to a recent survey (Cox, 1998) whose results indicate that people with AIDS are receiving the full range

of palliative care and social support services. Along with anecdotal information from patients and caregivers, it appears that hospice programs in general are not exhibiting a bias against AIDS patients. For the most part, volunteers have continued to volunteer, and overall quality of care is comparable to that of hospice services for people with other types of terminal conditions. Specific findings from the survey are both positive and negative. The positive is that terminally ill young women with AIDS are turning to hospice care in increasing numbers. This is especially important because women of childbearing age are the fastest growing group of people likely to contract AIDS, and some already have children. Hospice care often can manage their complex physical and emotional needs more adequately than can traditional medical practice, and it can do more for the children as well. The negative is that Hispanics and African Americans with AIDS seldom make use of hospice programs. This is troubling because it is unlikely that they are receiving the full range of palliative care and support services elsewhere.

Hospice Care for Nursing Home Residents

Dame Cicely Saunders has long been concerned with the welfare of frail and vulnerable elderly people. She and her colleagues have provided residential care to elders on the St. Christopher's Hospice campus for many years. It is clear that hospice-inspired dedication to the physical, social, and spiritual well-being of terminally ill people would be beneficial to residents of geriatric facilities as well, but it is not clear how such programs could be established and maintained, given the limitations in funding and human resources. Over the past half century, there has been heightened concern for institutionalized elders. Conditions have improved overall, and in some facilities the staff's skill and devotion are at the highest level. There is still a conspicuous gap, however, between the multiple resources that converge to help dying people over a relatively short period of time and the resources available to help institutionalized elders who may still have years to live.

However, indications show that hospice-inspired care is becoming more available to institutionalized elders during the final phases of their lives. More skilled-care facilities are now providing adequate pain relief to their terminally ill residents (Castle, 1997–1998). More elderly people are ending their lives in a nursing home or private residence instead of a hospital. Recent studies (Brock & Foley, 1998) confirm earlier findings (Weisman and Kastenbaum, 1968) that many institutionalized elders have a higher degree of cognitive functioning in their last year of life than had been generally assumed.

The growing number of elders ending their lives in a nursing facility and the fact that many are alert and capable of expressing their needs and desires makes it ever more pressing to offer a full range of palliative care. Furthermore, our society has higher expectations for the care of dying people since the introduction of hospice programs, and families, the community, and regulatory agencies will continue to expect more from nursing care facilities. Some nursing homes are already responding by developing special care hospice units (Castle, Mor, & Banaszak-Holl, 1997).

Hospice-Inspired Care for Prisoners, the Homeless, and the Impoverished?

Timely and quality health care is not equally available to all people. The United States and many other nations are still struggling with the challenge of providing health care to all who are in need while constrained by financial and other considerations. Hospice leaders strongly advocate helping terminally ill people no matter what their social or financial status. Only slowly and gradually is society starting to respond to this challenge. Canadian bioethicist David J. Roy (1999) places the problem before us:

How do the poorest of the poor die? Do we really want to know? That knowledge could be very disturbing, loaded as it might well be with imperatives for action. It could also be accusatory knowledge if those of us "in the know" do nothing to mobilize lethargic ministries, governments, health care institutions, and professional schools to develop and organize the services the poorest of the poor need, to have a chance of dying well. But the imperatives cannot stop there. It would

be humanly and socially grotesque if our passion for the poor stopped at helping them to die well. If the end of this century is question period time, the question of how the poor both *live* and *die* has to be raised clearly, loudly, and persistently. (1999, p. 3)

A recent study has confirmed the impression that terminally ill people who live in extreme poverty also die with more pain and suffering (Daneault & Labadie, 1999). People who have not become or remained securely integrated in society are likely not only to die at an earlier age, but also with less medical and social support. This group includes individuals who have ethnic and language backgrounds that are not part of the mainstream, as well as those who have become isolated and nearly invisible because of their poverty. The researchers call for a greater awareness by the health care system of the needs of impoverished terminally ill people.

Prisoners are also at excess risk for inadequate palliative care during a terminal illness. More than 1.5 million people are imprisoned in the United States, and more deaths are occurring in prison than ever before because of longer sentences, the general aging of the population, and the high rate of HIV infection among inmates. More than 3,000 prison inmates died in 1994, the last year for which definitive data are available (Maull, 1998). About three of every ten deaths were HIV related. This means that a terminally ill person experiences a fairly long period of decline and is vulnerable to pain, nausea, delirium and respiratory problems. Hospice-inspired care would be very much welcome in these circumstances.

Fortunately, the American Correctional Association and many prison systems are working to improve the situation. The prison setting is not what the founders of hospice care envisioned; it is certainly not a warm, open, and family-oriented environment. Nevertheless, a variety of efforts are being made to bring hospice-type palliative care into the institution or to provide compassionate release into hospice programs in the community.

We have already touched on the plight of people who depend on shelters for the homeless. Life is hard enough for them, and facing death is often harder than it has to be. Up to this point, few communities have given attention to providing end-of-life comfort and care to homeless people.

Hospice Care on the International Scene

Humane and effective care for dying people is a universal challenge. This challenge has been met to some extent by the development of palliative care programs in the United Kingdom that served as the model for hospice programs in the United States, Canada, and several European nations. The future of hospice care, however, is taking shape in many other nations whose culture and living conditions differ markedly from those in which hospice first took root. For the broader view of hospice care and a useful perspective on our own situation, it is useful to examine the international scene. The information presented here comes from an international survey of hospice programs (Wilson & Kastenbaum, 1997) and from a few of the many reports received from individual hospices.

We find that:

- Hospice programs are growing rapidly throughout much of the world. Almost all of reporting hospice or palliative care programs outside the United Kingdom and the United States have been established since the mid-1980s, and many came into existence in the 1990s. These programs are therefore on a rapid learning curve and dealing with many issues crucial to their fulfillment of the hospice mission and their own survival.
- The programs vary greatly in the size and characteristics of their cachement areas. In Australia, for example, one hospice reports a cachement population of about 20 million, while another serves about 50,000. Some hospices serve small populations in a sprawling rural area with difficult road access, few telephones, and limited health care facilities. Others serve large but compact populations in technologically developed urban areas. Clearly, what works well for one hospice organization may not be feasible for another.
- Throughout the world and in every geographical region, the largest number of hospice patients fall within the 60–79 age group, with only about one patient in nine being under the age of 40. One of the reasons: accidents, homicide, suicide, and warfare have been taking a high toll of young adults in some parts of the world, with cancer ranking low on the list of major causes of death. Men and women are using hospice services more or less equally, with some local variations.
- Home care is the type of service most often received by hospice clients in every world region—even in nations or areas in which there had been no previous home care services of any type.
- All world cultures are proving to have traditional strengths that can contribute to the success of palliative care programs. "Family values" are salient among these strengths. Traditional cultures may at first resist hospice services, but reports from around the world indicate that love and concern for dying members of the family eventually brings forth a warm and caring response.
- The early phases of hospice development invariably encounter resistance from some medical practitioners and governmental officials. The public often misinterprets and fears the effort to discuss dying and terminal care openly—avoidance of this "taboo" topic is not a special characteristic of the United States, but has been reported by hospice pioneers in Africa, Asia, the Near and Middle East, and South America.
- Pain relief remains the central objective of palliative care, no matter how the program is structured or what cultural group it serves. Most hospice programs around the world have had to work strenuously to persuade physicians and lawmakers that it is possible to relieve the suffering of terminally ill people without creating drug addicts or causing premature death.
- Education of the general public, human service professionals, and governmental decision makers has been recognized as a high priority by hospice programs around the world. Palliative care requires a host society that is able to integrate dying and death into its conception of the life course.

Additionally, it has become clear that hospice programs can be developed even within societies that are experiencing severe stress and deprivation. Croatia and Zimbabwe, for example, were subjected to widespread violence and social disorganization, and Poland was still under an oppressive Communist regime, but effective hospice programs emerged in those countries nevertheless.

DOES HOSPICE CARE PREVENT AND RELIEVE SUFFERING?

The alleviation of pain is the primary goal of palliative care programs. Although there is consensus on this goal, it remains difficult to assess the level of pain—and, therefore, the level of relief from pain, because the experience is private or subjective. We can observe a person's body language and often we can ask a person about his or her experience of pain, but the "measurement" of pain remains one of the most elusive problems for all health care providers and researchers. Measuring pain or pain relief is not an exact science, and this limitation should be kept in mind as we attempt to evaluate the control of pain.

Why Pain Must Be Controlled

Why is pain control so important? The reasons are not difficult to identify:

- Pain is, by definition, a stressful experience.
- Pain reduces the ability to give attention to other matters, thereby isolating the sufferer and reducing his or her opportunity to reflect, interact, and accomplish.
- Pain can intensify other symptoms, such as weight loss, insomnia, pressure sores, and nausea.
- Fear and anticipation of pain can also be demoralizing. "Will the pain return?" "Will it get worse?" "Will I be able to endure it?"
- Pain contributes much to anxiety about the dying process. Some people assume that dying is "all pain" and unavoidable so. This expectation can generate emotional distress, impaired communication, and, in some instances, suicide ("I'd kill myself first!").

The very fact that pain control has now become a major priority in terminal care owes much to the hospice approach. Until recent years, little dependable information was available on the type and extent of pain experienced by dying people. Today there is renewed interest in assessing pain and providing relief. Saunders (1993) has set the example with her demonstration that adequate pain relief can be given without dulling the patient's mental processes and her rejection of the fear that people with but a few months or weeks to live will be turned into "drug addicts."

Hospice physicians and nurses have become the state-of-the-art experts in pain control. Much of the hospice success in pain control derives from superior knowledge of available medications and their optimal use, but part of the success must be attributed to the hospice philosophy itself: people *should* be as pain-free as possible as the end of life approaches, to allow them the opportunity to complete projects, engage in leave-takings, or just find some enjoyment and meaning in each remaining day. This attitude translates into a refusal to "play the usual games" so often favored by physicians who would prefer not to associate themselves with dying patients at all. Hospice staff do not expect dying patients and their families to endure pain as long as possible, until forced to "beg" for relief.

The hospice team is particularly expert in helping people cope with unremitting pain. In general, the medical profession has given more attention to the relief of short-term or acute pain. Applying the same type of regime to a terminally ill cancer patient is a still-common mistake. Hospice practice and research have demonstrated that most people can receive significant relief from pain throughout the dying process. There are exceptions, and therefore clinicians and researchers are continuing to look for improved techniques. Most of the failures in pain relief, however, are failures to apply knowledge that has already become available (Levy, 1988). For example Kinzel et al. (1992) found that a sample group of hospital-based nurses and physicians did not have the correct facts about some important facets of pain relief in terminally ill people, even though they held generally favorable attitudes toward hospice.

Only 35 percent of nurses and 56 percent of physicians recognized that the total dose of narcotic to provide equivalent pain relief would be less with a regular dosing schedule than on an as-needed basis in this (a palliative care) setting. Only 10 percent of nurses and 38 percent of physicians were able to correctly order four narcotic analgesics according to potency. None of the physicians or nurses correctly identified 'more than 960 milligrams' as the correct response on a multiple choice question regarding the maximum safe dose of morphine sulfate that can be given orally over 24 hours. (p. 88)

Physicians themselves have reported that they do not have adequate education and training in providing relief from pain (Miller, Miller, & Single, 1997). This deficiency continues to be reconfirmed by additional studies. Sloan, Donnelly, Schwartz, & Sloan, 1997) presented common clinical symptoms of a patient with advanced cancer to thirty-three resident physicians, many of whom proved to be unable to manage the symptoms. Two of the specific findings are particularly noteworthy: The physicians (1) did not prescribe adequate medication to relieve the acute suffering of dyspnea (difficulties in breathing), and (2) tried to treat a lack of appetite with forced feedings. Patients with advanced cancer under the care of these physicians would have suffered the anxiety of dyspnea without relief because of the widespread fear in the medical profession that opioids, the drug of choice for this problem, would turn the patients into addicts. Inflicting forced feeding on a person with advanced cancer would add another torment without providing real benefit. One other finding also should be mentioned: physicians with more experience were no more competent than those with less experience. Basically, physicians who themselves were not skilled in managing pain and other symptoms were the models for younger physicians.

Findings such as these suggest that medical and nursing schools have not been providing adequate, up-to-date information on the most effective use of pain-relieving medications for terminally ill patients, nor have their graduates kept themselves current on this topic through continuing education. This picture becomes more disappointing, perhaps even alarming, when we add another of Kinzel and colleagues' results: "Ninety-two percent of nurses and 88 percent of physicians felt very or mostly competent in their ability to provide technically competent care to terminally ill patients." To the extent that this pattern of findings is representative, it looks as though typical hospital-based physicians and nurses have a level of confidence that is not supported by their actual knowledge of the effects of specific pain medication regimes on terminally ill people. Professional as well as public education about hospice procedures obviously remains a high priority.

Effective pain management requires more than textbook knowledge of drug effects (especially since some of the textbooks themselves are out of compliance with clinical experience). The needs and pain tolerance of a particular individual must be considered, and the course of treatment must be subject to prompt review whenever problems arise. A series of excellent articles in the palliative care literature offers insights into the process of selecting, monitoring, and evaluating analgesics in terminal care (McCaffery & Ferrell, 1991; Ferrell, 1991; Muir, Krammer, Cameron & Von Gunten, 1999). Another useful source of information can be found in a continuing series of publications from the American Pain Society and The World Health Organization (WHO).

Family members as well as professional caregivers often become become partners in pain relief efforts. Betty Rolling Farrell, a leading nurse-researcher located at the City of Hope Hospital (Duarte, CA), was able to identify many of the pain-related concerns experienced by family members (Ferrell, Ferrell, Rhiner, & Grant, 1991). For example, past episodes can lead to apprehension about what might happen next: "He was in very severe pain before his surgery and I just wait for it to start again. I'm so afraid." The use of a medication regime that does not control pain consistently or for an extended period of time also proves distressful: "Medications are given every hour. I need some rest. Something to last longer to relieve the pain" (Ferrell, et al., 1991, P. S67). Knowledgeable caregivers, whatever their professional background, acquaint themselves with the family's needs and concerns and help the family to become a part of the pain relief effort.

Another key to alleviating pain in terminally ill patients is to reduce the mental distress associated with illness, dependency, loss of function, and concern about the future. The personality and mental state of the patient and the interpersonal setting in which he or she is located can either increase or decrease sensitivity to pain. Some people have difficulty with the concept that pain can be all too real and at the same time related to one's mental and emotional state. In *Noninvasive Approaches to Pain Management,* Turk & Feldman (1992) do their best to clarify this concept:

> Although we will suggest that psychological factors may *modify the perception of pain and augment the experience of pain,* this is not the same as suggesting that psychological factors *cause* the pain. Nor is it to suggest that the pain reported is only imagined. Furthermore, we are not advocating that noninvasive approaches should be used *in place* of medical and surgical procedures. Rather, it is the intention to sensitize health care and especially hospice workers to the importance of considering the role of psychological factors in pain and to alert them to a set of strategies that may be useful to complement the usual pharmacological and surgical modalities already in their armamentarium. (1992, p. 3)

Specific suggestions for relieving pain without surgery or drugs include massage, application of heat, cold, menthol, and electrical nerve stimulation to the skin, careful positioning and exercising, hypnosis, and guided imagery. Often some special effort is required in learning how to use these techniques to their best advantage and in teaching them to family caregivers. However, most if not all of the techniques can be used safely by many caregivers and can provide comfort without themselves producing stress or side-effects.

Perhaps the next time we hear of a person seeking physician-assisted suicide we should think immediately of noninvasive pain alleviation techniques and respite care programs as alternatives.

Not all terminally ill people suffer pain. Hospice specialists report that as many as half of terminally people have no pain. We should quickly note, however, that a person may be free of pain at some phases of the illness but experience pain at another time. Studies of terminally ill people who are in a home care hospice program indicate a somewhat higher frequency of pain: between 68 percent and 85 percent, depending on the

particular study. Uncontrollable pain is experienced by about 10 percent of terminally ill patients who are admitted to hospice care programs (Dobratz, 1995).

Hospice programs have proven effective in controlling pain for most of the patients they serve. In the most typical situation, both pain and the fear of pain are substantially reduced shortly after hospice care begins. Hospitals and private physicians who follow WHO and hospice guidelines for pain relief have also been successful. A significant achievement of the hospice movement has been to encourage effective pain relief in the traditional medical context as well as in palliative care programs, although the latter are able to offer a broader spectrum of care and comfort services to dying people and their families.

Palliative care experts Jane M. Ingham and Kathleen M. Foley (1998) conclude:

> Despite the extensive body of knowledge available regarding cancer pain assessment and management, it often remains untreated, thereby diminishing the quality of patient care at the end of life. (1998, p. 89)

Ingham and Foley offer recommendations based on conclusions reached by the World Health Organization. These recommendations are presented in Box 5-1.

Other Symptoms and Problems

Pain is not the only problem that can beset a dying person. Other types of symptoms may include:

- Nausea
- Vomiting
- Dyspnea (respiratory difficulties)
- Pressure sores
- Insomnia
- Incontinence
- Weakness
- Fatigue
- Confusion
- Depression

Effective care requires attention to the prevention or alleviation of all of these problems. With the active participation of a family caregiver as well as the hospice professional staff and volunteers, it

---

BOX 5-1

WORLD HEALTH ORGANIZATION RECOMMENDATIONS FOR THE CARE OF TERMINALLY ILL PATIENTS

- Governments should establish national policies and programs for pain relief and palliative care for patients with advanced disease.
- Governments should ensure that such pain relief and palliative care programs are incorporated into the existing health care systems; separate systems of care are not desirable.
- Governments should ensure that health care workers are adequately trained in palliative care and pain management.
- Governments should review their national health policies to ensure that equitable support is provided for programs of palliative care at home.
- In the light of the financial, emotional, physical, and social burdens carried by family members who are willing to care for terminally ill patients at home, governments should consider establishing formal systems of recompense for the principal family caregivers.
- Governments should recognize the singular importance of home care for dying patients and ensure that hospitals are able to offer appropriate backup and support for home care.
- Governments should insure the availability of both opioid and nonopioid analgesics and the availability of medications that control symptoms.
- Governments should review the controls governing opioid use with a view to simplification so that drugs are available in the necessary quantities for legitimate use.

---

is often possible to relieve these symptoms—for a while. Despite the best care, however, a terminally ill person is likely to become weaker and more fatigued as the end approaches. It will also become increasingly difficult for the dying person to move about. Nevertheless, it has been found that hospice patients are somewhat less likely to be restricted to their beds until death is very close (Mor, 1987). But one must expect decline. Findings from the National Hospice Study (Mor, Greer, & Kastenbaum, 1988) indicate that the social quality of life remained high for hospice patients during their final weeks and days as compared with that of patients receiving traditional medical care. Despite the inescapable fact of continued physical deterioration, patients receiving hospice care maintained their intimate relationships and avoided the social isolation that has sometimes befallen dying people. But the data also suggested that the personality and values of the person before his or her terminal illness also had a major influence on experiences during the last weeks of life. The difference between hospice and traditional types of care sometimes seemed to be less important than individual dif-

ferences in personality and social support system. This finding can serve as a useful reminder that people as well as treatment approaches differ markedly.

There is some evidence that hospice patients were able to experience a situation close to their own preferences (given, of course, the severe problems associated with rapidly failing health). Recall the thought questions raised at the end of Chapter 5. You were asked first to describe the last three days of your life as you would like them to be. This question, suggested by Beatrice Kastenbaum, was included in the NHDS. The following types of answers were most common (in order of frequency):

- I want certain people to be here with me.
- I want to be physically able to do things.
- I want to feel at peace.
- I want to be free from pain.
- I want the last three days of my life to be like any other days.

The support offered by hospice care makes it possible for many patients to be at home and enjoy the company of the "certain people" who mean the most to them. Similarly, with the advice and support of hospice volunteers and staff, the patient could still control some activities of daily life. Remaining in their environment provided a context for feeling at peace and keeping something of the feeling of a comforting routine. The patients' goals and the goals of hospice care were identical.

It is interesting to note some of the least frequently mentioned wishes for the last three days of life. Only about one person in twenty cared about "completing a task" or being "mentally alert." Even fewer hoped to "accept death," and fewer still wanted to "know when death is imminent," "to be able to bear pain," or "live until a certain time or event." This collection of low-incidence items includes many of the most dramatic wishes that are sometimes attributed to the dying person. By far the greater number of terminally ill people simply wanted the comfort of familiar faces and the ability to continue to do a little for themselves and have a sense of peaceful routine. The goal of accepting death philosophically or demonstrating the ability to tolerate pain was seldom stated.

There is much in these findings that invites reflection. We might simply note here that (1) what most people wanted was no more and no different from what hospice care tries to achieve, and (2) it is wiser to learn from each individual what really matters than to attribute motives and themes picked up elsewhere. The question on sources of strength was also included in the NHDS survey. Following are the most frequent responses given by a subsample of NHDS patients:

• Supportive family or friends
• Religion
• Being needed
• Confidence in self
• Satisfied with the help received

There appears to be a good match in general between what terminally ill cancer patients hope for (apart from recovery) and what hospice care is designed to achieve by its philosophy and method.

Marjorie C. Dobratz (1995) observes that a dying person's quality of life depends much on the social support that has been available to that person. This connection has been well established by her own studies and those of other investigators. Now it has become apparent that one of the most important components of this social support is "how dying persons perceive their emotional and cognitive well-being." Dying people are most likely to experience their lives as meaningful and to adapt well to the challenges they face when they feel that others truly care for them. Dobratz further notes that when liberated from pain, hospice patients often show a remarkable capacity to retain their self-esteem. Competent management of pain, enhanced by loving attention from both family and hospice caregivers, is helping many a terminally ill person to find meaning and value in every day of life.

Your Deathbed Scene, Revisited

Think about the personal deathbed scene you imagined while reading the preceding chapter. Now that you have read more about the dying process and terminal care, it might be instructive to review your own expectations. If your death-bed scene was similar to those of most students, you portrayed a rather sanitized image that does not have much in common with the way that most people actually die. This is true particularly with respect to pain and other symptoms. Most dying people have pain—although it may be controlled by competent physicians and nurses—and most dying people have a variety of other symptoms as well.

By contrast, most college students portray themselves as dying without pain and without other symptoms (Kastenbaum & Normand, 1990). What does this discrepancy mean? At the least, it means that even those self-selected people who have chosen to enroll in a death-focused class have unrealistic ideas about their physical condition at the end of life. What else might this discrepancy mean? I leave this question to your own reflections.

In some other respects, the typical deathbed scene expected by college students does have some relationship to the actual deathbed scenes experienced by many people who have received hospice care: death occurs at an advanced age by a person who is at home, with the companionship of family and other loved ones. But while many college students have made a point of indicating that they wanted to "go quickly" and actually *would* "go quickly," most people actually die over a longer period of time. To be sure, some terminally ill people do "slip away quietly" in their sleep, but this passage is usually preceded by months of declining health and increased functional limitations. Realistically, most of us will live for some time with our final illness, and so will our loved ones. Each person must make his or her own decision about the desirable balance between wishful fantasy and reality.

ACCESS TO HOSPICE CARE AND THE DECISION-MAKING PROCESS

It is important to consider the hospice approach in some detail because of its compassionate philosophy, innovative techniques, and constructive influence on the entire health care system. And yet the choice to seek hospice care is made by "only" about a quarter of a million people a year in the United States. When we recall that there are about six thousand deaths each *day*, it can be seen that hospice is still a long way from serving the needs of all those who are terminally ill.

Perhaps this is as it should be. From its origins, hospice was intended as an alternative, not as a road that everyone must take. What are the factors that work against choosing the hospice alternative? Obviously, hospice is not selected when people either are not aware of its existence or when no hospice service is available to them. On some occasions, physicians express opposition to hospice, and their patients will feel obliged to comply with the doctor's preference. Other factors raise serious questions about the suitability of hospice care even when ignorance, unavailability, and professional bias are not involved. Three of the most common issues are as follows:

1. *How certain is the prognosis?* Those who decide to seek hospice care have become convinced that they have only a few months (or less) to live. Usually these people have "been through the mill" in diagnostic and treatment procedures. In choosing hospice, they are expressing a preference for the highest possible quality of life rather than continued efforts to prolong life that would be doomed to failure.

However, some people are not in the position to make that choice. Either there is still reason to hope that recovery or remission will occur, or it is difficult to predict how long they have to live with their terminal condition. Certainty of death within the near future is a difficult forecast to cope with, yet it does provide a firm basis for decision making. A person who could live a month or several years with a life-threatening condition may not be in a position to enter a hospice program, nor may a person who still has a "fighting chance" to recover.

2. *Does the course of this terminal illness lend itself to existing forms of hospice care?* Hospice programs have developed primarily around the needs associated with patients with incurable cancer and those afflicted with progressive neuromuscular conditions such as amyotropic lateral sclerosis ("Lou Gehrig's Disease"). There has always been a willingness to help people with other conditions as well. However, the more the nature and course of a terminal illness differs from the patterns associated with cancer, the more questions must be raised about the "match" between hospice resources and the individual's needs. Two types of conditions are especially likely to raise this question: (a) conditions in which a person might either live quite a while or die suddenly, and (b) conditions that involve extensive precautions against infection—either of or by the patient. Each hospice establishes its own scope of services, and most attempt to expand this scope as demands arise. Saunders (1993) speaks encouragingly of hospice's continuing efforts to meet the needs of people with a variety of terminal conditions other than cancer, and her opinion is being supported by increased attention to noncancer conditions in the palliative care literature (e.g., Kinzel, 1992a; 1992b). It would be wise, however, to look carefully into the abilities of local hospice organizations to meet the needs of those whose terminal illness is not cancer related or neuromuscular.

3. *Is the family situation conducive to hospice care?* The basic hospice model involves a dying person, that person's family and home, and the services provided by professional and volun-

teer caregivers. Ideally, there is an intact family that wants the dying person to be at home as much as possible and whose members are ready and willing to participate in the daily care. That each hospice patient must have a primary family caregiver (e.g., spouse or child) has become a requirement in the federal regulatory and funding system. The number of exceptions is increasing, however, and regulatory agencies appear to be a little more flexible in this regard. Hospices, neighbors, and others can sometimes be very creative in coming up with a primary caregiver and a home environment. One cannot count on these exceptions, however. In deciding about hospice care, attention must certainly be given to the availability and readiness of family support.

Gaining access to a hospice program does not have to be difficult. The easiest path is for patients who are eligible for Medicare (Part A) hospital insurance. The patient's physician and the hospice medical director must certify that the patient has a life expectancy of six months or less. When this certification has been made, the patient signs a statement that expresses his or her selection of hospice care for the terminal illness. This special hospice Medicare benefit then replaces the standard Medicare benefit. From the patient's standpoint, the coverage is quite extensive. The services of physicians, nurses, home health aide, homemaker, and pastoral counselor are all covered, as are rentals of medical equipment and medications. Generally, at-home expenses are fully covered, but there may be some expenses associated with in-hospital stays. (The hospice may provide services for which it does not receive full reimbursement, but that's another story.)

Access to hospice can be more difficult if a patient does not have a primary physician with whom a strong trusting relationship has been established, or is not eligible for Medicare hospital benefits. These and other possible obstacles often can be overcome after discussion with a hospice director or social worker. It is useful to allow some time to explore the situation, have one's questions answered, and find solutions to any problems that might stand in the way of access. According to a recent study by McNeilly and Hil-

lary (1997), the most common barriers to hospice service include:

- Physicians' difficulty with hospice admission criteria, reluctance to lose control of their patients, and, in some cases, restrictions on the number of pain control prescriptions they are allowed to write.
- Insufficient family cooperation with hospice. As one nurse commented, "Many times, the patient is ready for hospice and the family is not."
- Inadequate communication between managed care health staff and terminally ill patients and their families. As expressed by another hospice nurse:

> Doctors don't take the time to discuss with patients and families. This is particularly true for the county system and HMOs. Patients have seen so many doctors, they don't have a particular doctor. They feel so trashed, because they feel like they've been bumped from person to person, and now they have to choose hospice. Late referral of patients to hospice care. This is a persistent problem not only in the United States, but also throughout most of the world. Patients are sometimes referred to hospice when they have only a few days to live, thereby severely restricting the ability of palliative care providers to help them.

A special article in the prestigious *New England Journal of Medicine* has provided major documentation for the pattern of (too) late referral of terminally ill patients to hospice care programs. Physicians Nicholas A. Christakis and Jose J. Escarce (1996) analyzed information available for 6,451 hospice patients. They found that about one patient in six died within seven days of enrollment, and almost three in ten died within fourteen days. The median length of survival after enrollment was thirty-six days. (There were substantial differences by specific type of terminal condition; for example, those with kidney failure had the shortest average survival time, seventeen days, and those with chronic obstructive pulmonary disease had the longest, 76.5 days.) Survival after hospice admission was about ten percent shorter for men as compared with women. Enrolling patients in hospice care when they have

BOX 5-2
SHOULD I BECOME A HOSPICE VOLUNTEER? A DIALOGUE

- **Does my local hospice need volunteers?**
  Probably so. A hospice usually has a director of volunteers and will welcome your call.

- **What should I expect when I meet the director of volunteers?**
  A friendly but "professional" interview. The hospice has responsibility for exercising good judgment in the selection of volunteers.

- **You mean they might not accept me?**
  This is a possibility. Has someone very close to you died recently? Many hospices ask people who have had a recent bereavement to wait a while before becoming a volunteer. Or the interviewer may judge that you have a disorganized life style.

- **—hey, I'm going to get organized, starting tomorrow!**
  Fine! But the volunteer director will need to be convinced that you are a person who keeps appointments and does what has to be done in a reliable manner. And should you come across as a person who feels the need to impose your own religious beliefs on others—or use hospice in the service of your own fantasies and problems—you might receive a polite but firm refusal.

- **That won't happen to me. I'm taking this great class on death and dying, and I'm reading this really terrific textbook. So after I'm accepted as a volunteer, will they give me some guidance and supervision?**
  Definitely. You will be asked to attend a series of training sessions before you are activated as a volunteer. Most people find this a valuable learning experience. You will receive guidance and supervision all the way along the line, and you will always have somebody to call if problems arise.

- **What kinds of things would I do as a volunteer?**
  There are many possibilities. You might be a companion for a patient in his or her home for a few hours so that others in the household have the opportunity to shop or take care of business. You might drive the patient to an appointment or to visit an old friend. You might help the patient write letters. You might help prepare a meal when family or friends visit. You might help the patient or a family member complete a special project. And at times you might just "be there." A hospice volunteer can wind up doing many different things, depending upon the needs of the individual families (Willis, 1989). And some volunteers devote themselves to keeping the hospice system going rather than working with patients. They do office work, fund-raising, and other things that do not necessarily involve direct patient or family contact.

- **What are the other volunteers like?**
  I've been fortunate enough to know many hospice volunteers. As a rule, they are bright, mature, and neighborly people who have been rather successful in life. Many feel that through hospice they can give something back to other people. Some are health care professionals who believe strongly in the hospice philosophy.

- **Like nurses and medical social workers?**
  Yes, some volunteers are well-qualified professionals. Some have been very successful in other lines of work but are new to health and social care. And you will find other students as well—looking for an opportunity to help others while acquiring valuable personal experience.

- **Anything else I should know?**
  Before you contact hospice, reflect on your own motivation: a passing curiosity or a firm resolve to help others? Will you be available to serve as a volunteer after you complete the course? Even though hospice may ask you to give only a few hours of your time per week, people will be counting on you to come through. If you have further questions at this time, you might ask your local hospice to put you into contact with several of their experienced volunteers.

- **See you at the hospice office!**
  Go easy on those donuts.

but a few days left to live deprives them of the care and quality of life they might have experienced with a more timely introduction to hospice.

Many people have discovered a way to become active in the hospice movement by serving as volunteers. Interested? See Box 5-2.

SUMMARY

Hospice care is intended to provide comfort, relief, and a sense of security for terminally ill people and their families. It differs from traditional medical management in several important ways: (1) The staff has expertise in the control of pain and other symptoms. (2) Care is centered around the situation, needs, and desires of the dying person and family. (3) Family members and volunteers are included as part of the caregiving system. We saw that the hospice approach to terminal care has its roots in shelter houses established in the fourth century for the comfort of pilgrims, the ill, and the dying. After a period of neglect, hospice activity started again in the late nineteenth century and took its modern form with the establishment of St. Christopher's Hospice in London, in 1967. Connecticut Hospice in New Haven was the first such program in the United States, established in 1974. More than two thousand hospice programs are now in operation in the United States. Standards of care for hospice programs include not only the well-being of the patient, but also of the family and staff. Differences exist between full-service and partial-service hospices. Adult respite programs can provide a useful temporary alternative to hospital and home care. Case histories offer some idea of how hospice care is offered and its benefits for dying people and their families.

Hospice programs have usually served adults with advanced cancer or progressive neurological dysfunction. We looked at several other applications of hospice philosophy and practice: for children, people with AIDS, nursing home residents, prisoners, the homeless, and the impoverished. We also learned that hospice programs are developing rapidly throughout the world, finding welcome in nations with very different cultural and religious patterns.

Research and clinical experience indicate that hospice care often prevents and relieves suffering. Pain relief is most often the highest priority.

Unfortunately, what has been discovered about effective pain relief in palliative programs has not always been applied by physicians operating outside the hospice framework. Many physicians are still inadequately trained to provide effective pain relief for dying people, and many still have unrealistic anxieties about turning a person into a drug addict through the administration of morphine and related medications. Hospice care providers also understand that the relief of suffering requires relief of the mental distress that can be associated with illness, dependency, loss of function, and concern about the future. There is now a renewed call for the government to become more supportive of palliative care for dying persons.

We concluded by revisiting your deathbed scene, defining volunteers' role in hospice care, and discussing questions that arise regarding access to hospice care and the decision-making process.

REFERENCES

American Pain Society (1992). *Quality Assurance Guidelines for Relief of Acute Pain and Chronic Cancer Pain.* (3rd ed.). Skokie, IL: American Pain Society.

Brock, D. B. & Foley, D. J. (1998). Demography and epidemiology of dying in the U.S. with emphasis on deaths of older persons. *The Hospice Journal, 13,* 49–60.

Castle, N. G. (1997–1998). Innovations in dying in the nursing home: The impact of market characteristics. *Omega, Journal of Death and Dying, 36,* 227–240.

Castle, N. G., Mor, V., & Banaszak-Holl, J. (1997). Special care hospice units in nursing homes. *The Hospice Journal, 5,* 59–69.

Christakis, N. A., & Escarce, J. J. (1996). Survival of Medicare patients after enrollment in hospice programs. *The New England Journal of Medicine, 335,* 172–178.

Corr, C. A., & Corr, D. M. (1992a). Adult hospice day care. *Death Studies, 16,* 155–172.

Corr, C. A., & Corr, D. M. (1992b). Children's hospice care. *Death Studies, 16,* 431–450.

Cox, C. (1998). Hospice care for persons with AIDS: Findings from a national study. *The Hospice Journal, 13,* 21–34.

Daneault, S., & Labadie J. F. (1999). Terminal HIV disease and extreme poverty: A review of 307 home care files. *Journal of Palliative Care, 15,* 6–12.

Dobratz, M. C. (1995). Analysis of variables that impact psychological adaptation in home hospice patients. *The Hospice Journal, 10,* 75–88.

Ferrell, B. R. (1991). Managing pain with long-acting morphine. *Nursing 91,* October, pp. 34–39.

Ferrell, B. R., Ferrell, B. A., Rhiner, M., & Grant, M. (1991). Family factors influencing cancer pain management. *Postgraduate Medicine Journal, 67* (Suppl. 2): SG4-S69).

Gilmore, A. J. J. (1989). Hospice development in the United Kingdom. In R. Kastenbaum & B. K. Kastenbaum (Eds.), *Encyclopedia of death.* Phoenix: Oryx, pp. 149–152.

Ingham, J. M., & Foley, K. L. (1998). Pain and the barriers to its relief at the end of life: A lesson for improving the end of life health care. *The Hospice Journal, 13,* 89–100.

Jusic, A. (1997) Palliative medicine's first steps in Croatia. In C. Saunders & R. Kastenbaum (Eds.), *Hospice care on the international scene.* (pp. 125–129). New York: Springer.

Kastenbaum, R. (1995). Children's hospice. An Omega interview with Ida M. Martinson. *Omega, Journal of Death and Dying, 31,* 253–262.

Kastenbaum, R., & Normand, C. (1990). Deathbed scenes as expected by the young and experienced by the old. *Death Studies, 14,* 201–218.

Kastenbaum, R., & Wilson, M. (1997). Hospice care on the international scene: Today and tomorrow. In C. Saunders & R. Kastenbaum (Eds.), *Hospice care on the international scene.* (pp. 262–272). New York: Springer.

Kinzel, T. (1992a). Hospice care for the noncancer patient: A survey of issues and opinions. *Loss, Grief & Care, 6,* 77–84.

Kinzel, T. (1992b). End-state lung disease: A hospice approach to the psychosocial aspects of care. *Loss, Grief & Care, 6,* 137–146.

Kinzel, T., Askew, M., & Goldbole, K. (1992). Palliative care: Attitudes and knowledge of hospital-based nurses and physicians. *Loss, Grief & Care, 6,* 85–95.

Levy, M. H. (1988). Pain control research in terminal care. *Omega, 18,* 265–280.

Martinson, I. (1989). *Pediatric hospice care: What helps?* Alexandria, VA: Children's Hospice Institution.

Maull, F. W. (1998). Issues in prison hospices: Toward a model for the delivery of hospice care in a correctional setting. *The Hospice Journal, 13,* 57–82.

McCaffery, M., & Ferrell, B. R. (1991, June). How would you respond to these patients in pain? *Nursing, 91,* 34–37.

McGrath, P., Yates, P., Clinton, M., & Hart, G. (1999). "What should I say?" Qualitative findings on dilemmas in palliative care nursing. *The Hospice Journal, 14,* 17–34.

McNeilly, D. P., & Hillary, K. (1997). The hospice decision: Psychosocial facilitators and barriers. *Omega, Journal of Death and Dying, 35,* 193–218.

Meagher, D. K., & Leff, P. T. (1989–1990). In Marie's memory: The rights of the child with life-threatening or terminal illness. *Omega, Journal of Death and Dying, 20,* 177–191.

Miller, P. J., & Mike, P. B. (1995). The Medicare Hospice Benefit: Ten years of federal policy for the terminally ill. *Death Studies, 19,* 531–542.

Miller, K. E., Miller, M. M., & Single, N. (1997). Barriers to hospice care: Family physicians' perceptions. *The Hospice Journal, 12,* 29–42.

Mor, V. (1987). *Hospice care systems.* New York: Springer.

Mor, V., Greer, D., & Kastenbaum, R. (1988). *The hospice experiment.* Baltimore: Johns Hopkins University Press.

Muir, J. C., Krammer, L. M., Cameron, J. R., & Von Gunten, C. F. (1999). Symptom control in hospice—state of the art. *The Hospice Journal, 14,* 33–61.

National Hospice Organization (1994). *The basics of hospice.* Arlington, VA: National Hospice Organization.

Phipps, W. E. (1988). The origin of hospices/hospitals. *Death Studies, 12,* 91–100.

Roy, D. J. (1999). Palliative care Canada 1999—A question period. *Journal of Palliative Care, 15,* 3–5.

Saunders, C. Dame Cicely Saunders: An Omega interview (1993). *Omega, Journal of Death & Dying, 27,* 263–270.

Sloan, P. A., Donnelly, M. B., Schwartz, R. W., & Sloan, D. A. (1997). Residents' management of the symptoms associated with terminal cancer. *The Hospice Journal, 3,* 5–16.

Turk, D. C., & Feldman, C. S. (Eds.) (1992). *Noninvasive approaches to pain management in the terminally ill.* New York: Haworth.

Weisman, A. D., & Kastenbaum, R. (1968). *The psychological autopsy: A study of the terminal phase of life.* New York: Behavioral Publications.

Willis, J. (1989). Hospice volunteers. In R. Kastenbaum & B. K. Kastenbaum (Eds.), *Encyclopedia of death* (pp. 147–149). Phoenix: Oryx Press.

Wilson, M., & Kastenbaum, R. (1997). Worldwide developments in hospice care: Survey results. In C. Saunders & R. Kastenbaum (Eds.), *Hospice Care on the International Scene.* NY: Springer.

Wright, K. D., Jones, A., & Wright, S. E. (1999). Dying homeless but not alone: Social support roles of staff members in homeless shelters. *Illness, Crisis, & Loss, 7,* 233–251.

GLOSSARY

Amyotropic Lateral Sclerosis: A still-incurable neuromuscular disorder in which there is a progression of weakness and paralysis until vital functions are inoperative. Also known as "Lou Gehrig's disease," after the New York Yankee Hall of Fame first baseman.

Cachement Area: The geographical region served by a health care agency.

Hospice: (1) A program of care devoted to providing comfort to terminally ill people through a team approach, with participation by family members. (2) A facility in which such care is provided.

Living Will: An early type of advance directive intended to prevent the use of aggressive diagnostic and treatment methods when a terminally ill person is unable to express his or her wishes directly.

Medicare Hospice Benefit: A federal reimbursement program that enables eligible people to select hospice care as an alternative to traditional medical management during their terminal illness.

National Hospice Study: A major project (1982–83 that compared traditional and hospice care for terminally ill people in the United States. The Medicare Hospice Benefit was established as a result of this study.

Palliative Care: Health services intended to reduce pain and other symptoms to protect the patient's quality of life.

Remission: The disappearance or relief of symptoms.

Symptom: An observable sign of disfunction and/or distress (e.g., pain, fever).

Terminal Illness: Defined in the Medicare Hospice Benefit as an illness that is expected to end in death within six months or less. In other contexts, the specific definition of terminal illness is open to discussion and controversy.

What we most enjoy and treasure often can be part of our end-of-life experiences.

chapter 6

END-OF-LIFE ISSUES AND DECISIONS

I haven't decided anything. I haven't even decided if I should decide be-cause—well, who knows what will happen when it happens and anyhow I'm not a doctor, and anyhow...and anyhow...{In your work, do you help other people make decisions?} That's different! (Laughing). Other people's decisions are not the problem!
—A graduate student in social work

The central problem of requiring clear and convincing evidence boils down to the fact that all indications suggest that the vast majority of Americans would not want to be kept alive in a vegetative state. If this is true, then many more will be harmed by acting on the never give up presumption than would be harmed using a patient's dignity interest as a guide.
—James M. Hoefler, 1997, p. 157

After two years of nursing home care, Millie Morrisey developed pneumonia and respiratory distress. As had been its custom, the nursing home staff called an ambulance. Documentation of preferences—which included fore-going antibiotics, mechanical ventilation and tube feeding—were neither sought nor readily accessible in her chart. The hospital quickly admitted her to the ICU, initiated antibiotics and mechanical ventilation, and used physi-cal restraints so that she would not dislodge the tubes and lines to which she was connected. She mostly did not seem to understand what was happening and was agitated and tearful.
—Marilyn J. Field and Christine K. Cassel, 1997, pp. 93–94

FROM DESCRIPTION TO DECISION MAKING

How do we think and feel about death, as individuals and as a society? How do we deal with death-tinged situations in everyday life? How do we try to understand the dying process and provide comfort? These are kinds of questions that have concerned us up to this point. We have described and interpreted. There is another step to take, however—a big step. What should we *do?* What decisions should we make about the last phases of our own lives? And how should we approach the responsibility of assisting others who are making such decisions for their lives? This chapter focuses on end-of-life issues and decisions.

We have prepared ourselves somewhat for this challenge by observing how hospice care (*see Chapter 5*) attempts to provide safe conduct through the dying process (*see Chapter 4*). Each day many people face the decision either to continue with cure oriented treatment or choose symptom relief and comfort care. This end-of-life decision, like the others considered in this chapter, depends much on the adequacy of communication among health care professionals, terminally ill patients, and their families. Another type of end-of-life decision is considered in a separate chapter: physician-assisted death, also known as assisted suicide (*see Chapter 9*) raises legal, medical, and ethical issues that require special examination. In this chapter, we concentrate on the broad range of basic end-of-life decisions that we are likely to encounter either directly or indirectly.

We begin with a brief inquiry into the whole idea of planning for the end of our lives, and then we reflect on our own ideas and feelings as we trace the development of advance directives for controlling care during a terminal illness. After we have brought ourselves up to date with the most recent approaches, we look at the larger picture of society's evolving response to the care of dying people.

Should Everybody Participate in End-of-Life Decisions?

There has been a turnabout in public attitudes toward end-of-life decision making. The idea that we should have "the final say" in our own lives did not gather force until our society started a renewed dialogue about dying and death, stimulated by the increasingly widespread application of life support systems and the emergence of the hospice care movement. Furthermore, the idea of patient self-determination had to overcome the tradition of leaving such important matters as medical decision making to the experts. Those who did want to have a say had little backing from the legislatures, the courts, and the weight of professional and public opinion.

Today there is much more support and opportunity for us to express our wishes. Informed consent is an established principle. A variety of advance directives are available. Some individuals and organizations within the health care community have taken leadership in education for making and carrying out end-of-life decisions. In fact, there is now so much advocacy for patient decision making that it is useful to pause for a moment before heading into the main substance of this chapter. Are planning and decision making really for everybody? Are we promoting an initiative that offers people increased control over the last days of their lives? Or are we perhaps imposing a newly popular view that might actually be disturbing to some people?

The graduate student who admitted, "I haven't decided anything" had her reasons—at least three of them. She recognized that *we have limited control over the future.* We might be deceiving ourselves if we believe that making specific plans somehow guarantees that events will occur in just that way. Many others have found that their best-laid plans were voided by the odd jolts and bumps of life. She also recognized that *we might not know enough to make realistic decisions* about technical matters that are not within our own compass of information. The third reason had more to do with her own personality and current situation ("Other people's decisions are not the problem!"). She is among those *people who try to avoid making decisions as long as they can.* A self-described procrastinator when it comes to making decisions, she was also caught up in the demands of her professional education and felt that she could spare little time and energy for anything that could be put off until later.

People differ in their approaches to decision making (which has become a lively field of re-

search in its own right, apart from the specific issue of end-of-life choices). Some people find
decision making stressful. Others characteristically make and unmake decisions so that even a
major decision might not hold up a few days
later. Furthermore, the current emphasis on individual autonomy is particularly hard on people
who are accustomed to either relying on others
or coming up with a decision through family or
cultural processing. The idea that all individuals
should make decisions for themselves has a lot of
appeal in societies that laud individual personality and achievement. It may be difficult for main-
streamers to realize that not everybody shares
that view of life, and therefore not everybody
would be comfortable in taking a highly individualistic approach to end-of-life decisions.

Barbara A. Koenig (1997) has offered one of
the most articulate challenges to the prevailing
view:

> Innovations in health care ethics that emphasize
> advance care planning for death or a patient's
> "right" to limit or withdraw unwanted therapy
> appear to presuppose a particular patient. This
> ideal patient has the following characteristics:
> (1) a clear understanding of the illness, prognosis,
> and treatment options that is shared with mem-
> bers of the health care team; (2) a temporal ori-
> entation to the future and desire to maintain
> "control" into that future; (3) the perception of
> freedom of choice; (4) willingness to discuss the
> prospect of death and dying openly; (5) a balance
> between fatalism and belief in human agency
> that follows the latter; (6) a religious orientation
> that minimizes the likelihood of divine interven-
> tion (or other "miracles"); and (7) an assumption
> that the individual, rather than the family or
> other social group, is the appropriate decision-
> maker. (1997, p. 370)

This portrait of the "ideal" patient brings to
mind many people who would deviate from this
standard. In many world cultures, the family is
clearly the center of life. Loyalty, responsibility,
and meaning have their locus in the family. Furthermore, respect for the past may be no less important than what one achieves in the future.
This way of life may be accompanied by the
deeply held belief that people can do little to alter
their fate: it is in the hands of the gods. The

"ideal" patient, then, cannot live within the kind
of ethnic and religious heritage relied upon by
most of the earth's people through the centuries.
An overemphasis on individual decision making
runs the risk of making "deviates" or "failures" of
a great many people who are simply moving
along a well-trodden pathway as did many generations before them.

Does this mean that we should not encourage
individual participation in end-of-life decision
making? Not at all. It does mean that we are
most helpful when we are attentive and responsive to individual differences, whether founded
on personality or ethnic/religious background.
Madeleine Leininger (1978), a pioneering nurse-
anthropologist has written:

> Patients have a right to have their socio-cultural
> background understood in the same way they ex-
> pect to have their physical and psychological needs
> identified and understood.... Treating all patients
> alike is unsafe, unscientific, and a questionable
> way to meet health care.... A health care profes-
> sional should not begin to care for a patient before
> making a cultural assessment. (1978, p. 87)

It would be unfortunate if terminally ill people
were forced into either-or situations: make your
decision now, or we will make it for you! Patients
do not have to make decisions in a way that is
unfamiliar or unduly stressful for them. Human
service providers can learn how the patients
themselves interpret their situation and can help
them to navigate through the perils of terminal
illness in ways that are both effective in preserving comfort and function and consistent with
their own lifelong beliefs and practices.

Suppose, though, that we *are* interested in
having our own wishes expressed and honored.
How would we go about it? We would become
familiar with the opportunities afforded by advance directives.

THE LIVING WILL
AND ITS IMPACT

Advance directives are instructions for actions
to be taken in the future if certain events occur.
Why not just wait until those events do occur?
Because we might not be in a position to take
those actions ourselves. Our interest here is in

advance directives that deal with end-of-life decisions. I might not be able to speak for myself at the moment that medical personnel are trying to determine what they should or should not do with me. A document that provides my personal guidelines might be welcomed by the medical personnel—but, then, again, it might not, as we will see.

The Living Will is the first advance directive to have received general attention in the United States. It was introduced in 1968 by a nonprofit organization that was somewhat ahead of its time in the effort to educate the public and professionals about end-of-life options. (Then known as the Euthanasia Educational Council, it later was renamed Concern for Dying.)

People were encouraged to add other specific statements between the introductory text and the signature, although apparently few did. Alexander (1988) provides further information about the Living Will.

The Living Will has played a valuable role in stimulating both public and professional awareness of death-related issues. People have had to

---

BOX 6-1
MY LIVING WILL

To My Family, My Physician, My Lawyer, and All Others Whom It May Concern

Death is as much a reality as birth, growth, maturity, and old age—It is the one certainty of life. If the time comes when I can no longer take part in decisions for my future, let this statement stand as an expression of my wishes and directions, while I am still of sound mind.

If at such a time the situation should arise in which there is no reasonable expectation of my recovery from extreme physical or mental disability, I direct that I be allowed to die and not be kept alive by medications, artificial means or "heroic measures." I do, however, ask that medication be mercifully administered to me to alleviate suffering even though this may shorten my remaining life.

This statement is made after careful consideration and is in accordance with my strong convictions and beliefs. I want the wishes and the direction here expressed carried out to the extent permitted by law. Insofar as they are not legally enforceable, I hope that those to whom this Will is addressed will regard themselves as morally bound by these provisions.

DURABLE POWER OF ATTORNEY
(optional)

I hereby designate _____ attorney for the purpose of making medical treatment decisions. This power of attorney shall remain effective in the event that I become incompetent or otherwise unable to make such decisions for myself.

Signed _____

Optional Notarization: Date _____

"Sworned and subscribed to Witness _____

before me this _____ day _____ of _____ 20 _____,"

Witness Address _____

Notary Public Seal Address _____

Copies of this request have been given to _____

_____

(Optional) My Living Will is registered with Concern for Dying (No. _____).

examine their own thoughts, feelings, and assumptions. Communication has increased somewhat between individuals and their families, physicians, nurses, ministers, and lawyers. "What do you think of the Living Will?" "What do they mean by 'heroic measures'?" Questions such as these made it easier to open up dialogues on death and dying with the important people in our lives. Over the years, there has been a growing consensus in favor of the Living Will, even among people who have not completed one themselves ("I just haven't gotten around to it, I guess. OK, OK, I know I said the same thing last time!").

It is important to keep in mind that the Living Will does not include provisions for assisted death. Some people who support the Living Will as an expression of an individual's preferences do not support assisted death (Scofield, 1993). However, one sentence in the standard Living Will does walk the boundary: "I do, however, ask that medication be mercifully administered to me to alleviate suffering even though this may shorten my remaining life." This statement is counterbalanced by the qualification: "I want the wishes and directions here expressed carried out *to the extent permitted by law.*"

Suppose that you are a physician. The patient you are attending at this moment has previously entrusted you with a signed and witnessed copy of her Living Will. She is dying. She is also in physical and emotional distress. "I want to die," she tells you. It had been your intention to control her pain with morphine. A heavier dose would not only relieve her pain but also hasten an easy death. Would you feel justified in prescribing a lethal dose because it is consistent with the advance directive ("…even though this may shorten my remaining life")? Or would you feel that you were dishonoring your profession or even committing murder? Even physicians who were much in sympathy with the patient's request might feel uncertain about the legal and ethical implications of withholding procedures that might extend life. The living will, valuable instrument that it is, does not answer all of the questions for us, and, indeed, raises new questions.

Furthermore, the fact that a person has completed a Living Will does not guarantee that it will come to the attention of physicians and other health care personnel when it really counts. Having a document registered by the office of a New York–based organization does not necessarily mean that a physician in Pocatello or a paramedic in Nashville will have this information readily available.

RIGHT-TO-DIE DECISIONS THAT WE CAN MAKE

The Living Will stirred up interest, hope, and anxiety. As we will see later (*in Chapter 9*), serious questions arose about both the right to refuse treatment and the kind of evidence that should be required as proof of the person's intentions. The right to refuse treatment gained support as courts upheld the principle of informed consent: not only in terminal care situations, but in all health care situations, patients must receive adequate information about the nature of the procedures and the potential risks as well as benefits. It proved more difficult, however, to obtain agreement on the evidence required for proof of a patient's wishes. What, for example, if a person had not completed a Living Will document, but had expressed his or her wishes to a friend or family member? What if there had been a personal note (such as a diary entry) but not an actual document? As indicated by an opening quote, surveys indicate that most people would not want to be kept alive in a vegetative state (Hoefler, 1997). Should this mean that physicians should not try to do all they can to keep a person alive when the evidence for the person's wish is not fully established? What if this particular person is not like "most" people?

We consider now some of the major developments that owe much to the Living Will, but go well beyond. This includes the opportunity to review our own feelings and beliefs.

From Living Will to Patients' Self-Determination Act

The Living Will was soon accepted in principle by many people, although fewer have actually executed such a document. State legislatures hesitated for a little while, then complied with the public's request to have a legal foundation placed under the Living Will declaration. Most states have passed measures (often called "natural death acts") that provide legal status of Living Will–type documents.

Experience has shown, though, that the existence of a Living Will—even when supported by law—does not necessarily guarantee that the intentions expressed in this instrument will be respected in practice. Part of the problem can be traced to the health care system's previous unfamiliarity with such documents. Physicians and hospital administrators were not accustomed to having their patients tell them what they could and could not do. There is also the problem of integrating the Living Will into the health care communication system. Where should the document itself be located? How many copies should be made? How can an individual be sure that anybody will actually look at his or her Living Will when the time comes? These problems were especially common in the early days of the Living Will and are not uncommon today.

Perhaps the most persistent problem, however, has been the lack of clarity and detail in the Living Will itself. As we saw in Box 6-1, the Living Will uses a standard text. This text conveys the general intention to be spared medical intervention that would prolong life when "there is no reasonable hope of my recovery from extreme physical or mental disability." So far, so good. But how useful is this document to a paramedic, nurse, or physician who must make a critical decision and, often, make that decision quickly? Too often the Living Will has not met the needs of the situation. The health care provider may be committed to obeying a patient's expressed wishes. However, if that patient cannot speak for himself or herself in the situation, and the Living Will is vague and incomplete, the health care provider may have to proceed in accordance with the customary procedure. This could mean the insertion of a nasogastric tube and attachment to a ventilator.

It is now well recognized among health care professionals that the Living Will can be improved by the introduction of more specific language. We cannot be more specific in drawing up an advance directive, though, unless we have also thought in specifics. We might be inclined to avoid getting down to details. "What do I know about intensive care?" we might protest, or "How do I know exactly what the situation will be if I ever need to call on my Living Will!" These are good questions. Good answers might be: "Part of being an informed citizen today is knowing something about medical care options in our high-tech world," and "None of us know what the situation will be—which is precisely why we need to provide the best guidance possible to those who may in the position of caring for us in our critical moments."

Executing a Living Will might be an appropriate step for those who want to reduce the possibility of being maintained in a persistent vegetative state. The Living Will or other advance directive does not authorize assisted death. It does authorize withholding and/or withdrawing life support measures for a person who has lapsed into conditions such as those of Karen Ann Quinlan and Nancy Cruzan (*see Chapter 9*). After serious consideration, a person might also choose *not* to execute a Living Will. For example, some terminally ill cancer patients have decided against it because their spouses were upset by and opposed to this idea (Stephens & Grady, 1992). It can be useful to confront our own fears, hopes, and values by considering the possibility of establishing a Living Will. Whatever the decision we reach, we will probably know ourselves better and be in a better position to help family and friends who may also be considering this option.

We can begin immediately by responding to the questions presented in Table 6-1. These questions explore our readiness to consider and discuss end-of-life issues in general.

These questions go well beyond specific instructions for care during the terminal phase of life. We are asking ourselves to place our entire lives in perspective, especially our most significant human relationships. A document is only a document. The Living Will takes on authentic meaning when it is based on our thoughtful assessment of our lives as individuals and as companions to others.

In prefacing *The Rules and Exercises of Holy Dying*, Jeremy Taylor observed that:

It is a great art to die well, and to be learned by men in health, by them that can discourse and consider, by whose understanding and acts of reason are not abated with fear or pains: and as

TABLE 6-1

My Readiness to Explore and Discuss Personal End-of-Life Issues

Yes	No	
____	____	1. I feel ready to consider all of the issues related to the end of my life.
____	____	2. I intend to discuss at least some of these issues thoroughly with at least one other person whose views matter to me.
____	____	3. I intend to require of my physicians that they provide me with all of the information I need to guide my decision making in a prompt, comprehensive, and honest manner.
____	____	4. I intend to select or create a document that communicates my preferences regarding treatment during the terminal phase of life.
____	____	5. I intend to designate a person to represent my preferences and interests in the event that I become incapacitated.
____	____	6. I intend to review and, if appropriate, modify my will and other legal instruments to ensure that they represent my final wishes in an effective way.
____	____	7. I intend to review my most significant relationships and take whatever steps are needed to resolve lingering problems and to renew and strengthen mutual ties.
____	____	8. I intend to do all that is possible to provide the opportunity for meaningful leave-taking interactions with the people in my life.
____	____	9. I intend to convey my preferences regarding burial/cremation and funeral services to those who will be responsible for making the arrangements.
____	____	10. I intend to review and reflect upon what is of most importance to me in life, and to devote much of my remaining time and energies to these core values.

the greatest part of death is passed by the preceding years of our life, so also in those years are the greatest preparations to it. (1655/1960, p. iv–v)

Taylor's advice is perhaps even more relevant today because the options for technological prolongation of life have so greatly increased and, as we have seen, the legal and moral dimensions have also become more complex.

We are ready now for Table 6-2, which presents several of the key decision points that should be specified in a Living Will or other advance directive if we want to convey specific instructions to health care providers.

You will have noticed that the first three requests differ in important respects. Unfortunately, these differences are not made clear in the usual Living Will document. It might be stressful to think our way through each of these decision points, but doing so will reduce the stress and ambiguity for the health care service providers upon whom we depend to honor our requests. Put bluntly, we must make and communicate our own decisions in the clearest possible manner if we expect others to take responsibility for respecting these decisions.

Informed Consent and the Patient's Self-Determination Act

The Living Will is an optional document. We can avoid even thinking about it if we so choose. Until December 1, 1991, both health care providers and the general public could follow their own tendencies, either to confront or to ignore the right-to-refuse-treatment issue. The situation changed dramatically when the Patient's Self-Determination Act (PSDA) took effect. This is a federal law. It affects all health care agencies that receive any federal funding—in practice, then, it affects virtually all health care agencies. More significantly, it affects all of us who seek treatment through a hospital or other health care agency.

The PSDA introduced the following requirements:

1. Patients must receive information on their rights to receive or refuse treatment and to formulate advance directives.
2. An advance directive consists of a Living Will document designating a person to act in one's place if one is no longer able to act in one's

TABLE 6-2
Advance Directive Requests

Yes	No	
___	___	1. I want all life-sustaining treatments to be discontinued if I become terminally ill and permanently incompetent.
___	___	2. I want all life-sustaining treatments to be discontinued if I become permanently unconscious, whether terminally ill or not.
___	___	3. I want all life-sustaining treatments to be discontinued if I become unconscious and have very little chance of ever recovering consciousness or avoiding permanent brain injury.
___	___	4. I want to be kept alive if I become gravely ill and have only a slight chance of recovery (5 percent or less), and would probably require weeks or months of further treatment before the outcome became clear.
___	___	5. I want to have fluids and nutrition discontinued if other life support measures are discontinued

own behalf. (The designated person is given *power of attorney* for health care decisions.)

3. Patients must be informed about the institution's policy concerning advance directives.
4. Informational materials developed by the federal government must be produced and distributed to patients upon admission.

The Living Will has come a long way! Not only are all health care agencies required to give patients the opportunity to establish advance directives, but they must do so to be in compliance with the Joint Accrediting Association of Healthcare Organizations (Pugh & West, 1994–1995).

The PSDA is a forward-looking law that attempts to empower all of us in coping with life-and-death contingencies. It embodies the principle of *informed consent.* Courts have established that we have a right to refuse treatment. In deciding whether or not to exercise that right, we must have adequate information on the nature of the proposed treatment, its probabilities of success, and possible side effects. We also need to be informed about other treatment (or no-treatment) options and their probable outcomes. The PSDA, then, is a large-scale, government-mandated approach to providing sufficient information and opportunity for patients to participate in treatment decisions. At the least, the PSDA makes it more difficult to ignore a patient's values and preferences. It is also an intention of the PSDA to stimulate thought and discussion. We are encouraged to review our attitudes and options, clarify our values, and communicate with

each other regarding end-of-life issues. Health care agencies are encouraged to improve their sensitivity to the needs and desires of the individual and to become more familiar with the value issues inherent in end-of-life issues.

Those of us who choose to make an advance directive will also want to specify a person who can support the enforcement of our wishes should we be unable to do so. This person is given a *durable power of attorney for health care.* The specified individual does not have to be a lawyer; it could be any person we believe we can count upon to represent our views effectively should the occasion arise. The existence of an advance directive and the appointment of a person with the durable power of attorney for health care makes it much easier for the health care system to honor do-not-resuscitate or other requests to place limits on medical interventions. These measures demonstrate that we have made our decisions in a planful manner while mentally competent. It avoids the difficult situation in which people are unable to express their wishes as a result of massive impairment. For example, Karen Ann Quinlan (*see Chapter 9*) may have once told a friend that she would not want to be maintained in a persistent vegetative state, but there was no documentation that the courts or health care providers could rely upon. In such instances there is the issue of *substituted judgment.* What would this person tell us if able to express his or her wishes? Establishing a substituted judgment decision that meets with the approval of family, health care providers, and the court is a challenging, conflictful and sometimes unsuccessful process. The PSDA offers a more direct approach, one that should result in treatment decisions that respect the patient's values and wishes.

Unfortunately, there are signs that the PSDA has not yet made much progress toward achieving these goals. Pugh and West (1994–1995) have identified several flaws in the act. These include:

1. The Act does not require that a health care professional be assigned the responsibility to ensure that the provisions of the PSDA are carried out as intended.
2. Information sharing between health care facilities is not carried out in a timely and efficient manner.
3. There is no penalty for health care providers if they fail to honor advance directives.
4. Congress did not allocate monies for the federal educational campaign.
5. Advance directives are often too vague and difficult to interpret.

We have already suggested an approach to overcoming the last of the problems identified above. In practice, however, many advance directives remain too vague and difficult to interpret. Health care agencies have shown little initiative in educating the public on this matter. Furthermore, there is no evidence that health care agencies have expended much effort in educating their own staff members. PSDA seems to be regarded largely as one more burdensome regulation. Agencies must comply with it—at least on paper—but valuable time should not be wasted in staff education regarding the philosophy and practice of the PSDA.

Most hospitals call upon the admitting clerk to ask the patient, "Do you have a Living Will? Do you have a durable power or attorney for health care?" The admitting clerk is not usually a person who has been selected on the basis of superior communication skills, awareness of cultural diversity, and in-depth knowledge of end-of-life issues. The clerk asks questions and fills out forms all day long. The last thing this busy person wants is a lengthy philosophical and emotional discussion with an anxious patient and his or her family. Basically the clerk just wants to get these questions out of the way and move on.

For the patient, this interaction is also likely to be unrewarding, even puzzling and disturbing. Only about one patient in five has prepared a Living Will and/or designated a person to exercise the power of attorney (Greve, 1991). Many people have not previously discussed these issues with their next of kin. Some have no idea what all of this means and would rather not know. The point of admission to a hospital or long-term care facility is often a time of heightened fear and tension. Communication—with strangers—can be especially difficult. There are people in the health care system who recognize this reality and make a determined effort to communicate effectively at the point of admission. Others make the extra effort of attempting to persuade patients to consider their advance directive actions long before they may be called upon to express them in the hospital admission situation. By and large, however, the potential of the PSDA has yet to be realized because of interpersonal communication problems, flaws and unfulfilled promises in the implementation of the act, and the less than wholehearted response of the nation's health care system.

At present most people have not made advance directives and assigned durable power of attorney for health care. Depending upon the study, between 15 percent and 25 percent of the general population have established advance directives. It is difficult to draw conclusions about people who are already hospitalized because studies have come up with a range of between 1 percent and 40 percent for those who report that they have advance directives (Miles, Koepp, & Weber, 1996). Who is most likely to establish an advance directive and thereby reject aggressive life-sustaining treatment?

- People with terminal cancer
- People with AIDS
- People with better education
- People from higher socioeconomic classes

Interestingly, most health care professionals *do not* have advance directives for themselves. Researchers note:

A trusted person to receive and interpret the advance directive, and not simple self-assertion alone, is the foundation of most advance directives.... Most people hedge advance treatment preferences or otherwise express insight into the difficulty of precisely formulating an advance treatment preference.... Many people, especially elderly persons, would rather trust a proxy than express a preference. (1996, p. 1063)

By all accounts, the decision to establish an advance directive is a complex process for most people and can be influenced by the responses they receive from family, friends, and colleagues. Although off to a somewhat slow and cumbersome start, the Patients' Self-Determination Act is having some influence on our health-related communications and decision making. If the PSDA can be made to work as intended and more of us prove willing to think our way through end-of-life issues, surely there will be fewer lengthy courtroom struggles and possibly fewer occasions for home visits by Dr. Kevorkian.

Five Wishes: A New Advance Directive Option

Recently a new advance directive option has become available. Five Wishes was developed by Aging With Dignity, a nonprofit organization that can be reached at (850) 681-2010 and www.agingwithdignity.org. Why still another approach, given that we already have the Living Will, the PSDA, and natural death legislation in most states? There is a persuasive reason: many patients still hesitate to exercise their rights to limit curative treatment, and many physicians still hesitate to restrict themselves to palliative care. Often medical students are given only about three hours of class time to study the subject of working with terminally ill patients. It is not surprising that they become physicians who are uncomfortable dealing with dying patients and their families. Physicians seldom speak plainly to patients about the prognosis (probable outcome) of their illnesses when they are poor, preferring instead to talk about the details of treatment (Miyaji, 1993). Communication problems arise on all sides. For example, only about one of four hospital patients discusses advance directives (Silverman, 1995). For their part, hospitals often wait until the very morning of a major surgery

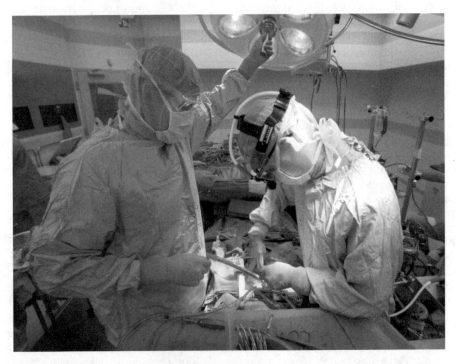

Open heart surgery is one of the many options that was not available until recent years. When should all possible treatments be tried, and when should attention turn instead to comfort care?

before giving patients the opportunity to consider and sign an advance directive.

There is considerable support for the idea that nurses or other health care personnel should serve as patient advocates to assist in the decision making process, but preparation and guidelines for this role remain undeveloped. Furthermore, terminally ill people and their families often find it difficult to present their concerns and desires in a clear and organized way. The possibility for misunderstanding between patient and physician is increased by communication difficulties on both sides.

Communication about end-of-life issues apparently has not improved as much as one might have hoped, in light of the increased attention given to this topic in recent years. Five Wishes is a new version of the Living Will, intended to help patients, families, and health care providers to communicate more effectively. Supported by a grant from the Robert Wood Johnson Foundation, it was found useful when introduced in Florida, and then revised with the assistance of the American Bar Association Commission on Legal Problems of the Elderly. It is applicable for use by adults of any age, although the emphasis was originally on helping elderly people make end-of-life decisions.

Basic facts about Five Wishes:

- It is a document that enables people to state clearly their preferences for end-of-life care.
- Identifying somebody who will serve as a health care agent is part of the decision package. (It is suggested that two other people be identified as substitutes in case the primary health care agent is not available.)
- The document is to be signed in the presence of two witnesses. (Notarization is required only in Hawaii, Missouri, North Carolina, and Tennessee.)
- Special witnessing requirements may be required for people who live in long-term care facilities, homes for the mentally retarded or developmentally disabled, or mental health institutions in the states of Connecticut, Delaware, Georgia, New York, and North Dakota.
- At present the Five Wishes meet requirements for a valid advance directive in Arizona, Arkansas, Colorado, Connecticut, Delaware, District of Columbia, Florida, Georgia, Hawaii, Idaho, Illinois, Iowa, Louisiana, Maine, Mary-

land, Massachusetts, Michigan, Minnesota, Mississippi, Missouri, Montana, Nebraska, New Jersey, New Mexico, New York, North Carolina, North Dakota, Pennsylvania, Rhode Island, South Dakota, Tennessee, Virginia, Washington, and Wyoming.

- The Aging with Dignity organization cautions that physicians in states not in the list above may be reluctant to honor Five Wishes. However, they suggest that it can nevertheless be useful to put one's wishes in writing and show and discuss the document with one's physician.

You have a legal and moral right to decide what kind of medical treatment you want or don't want when you are seriously ill and your death is expected. You also have a right to choose a person to make health decisions for you when you are no longer able to speak or think clearly. Five Wishes helps you exercise these rights. But remember, your doctor needs to know, and be willing to follow, your wishes. (1999, p. 2)

- A distinctive and valuable feature of Five Wishes consists of lists of possible actions. Each list includes many of the key decision points that might otherwise not come to mind and therefore provides the kind of specific guidance needed by physicians and other care providers willing to comply with the patient's wishes.

The Five Wishes

Following are slightly abridged versions of the information and instructions found in the official Five Wishes document. The complete document is available from Aging With Dignity at P.O. Box 1661, Tallahassee, FL 32302-1661, or the website provided on page 164.

Wish 1: The Person I Want to Make Care Decisions for Me When I Can't

If I am no longer able to make my own health care decision, this form names the persons I choose to make these choices for me. This person will be my Health Care Agent (or other term that may be used in my state, such as proxy, representative, or surrogate).

This person will make my health care choices if both of these things happen:

1) My attending doctor finds that I am no longer able to make health care choices, AND

2) Another health care professional agrees that this is true.

- your Health Care Agent should be at least 18 years or older (in Colorado, 21 years or older) and should not be:
- your health care provider, including owner or operator of a health or residential or community care facility serving you.
- an employee of your health care providers.
- serving as an agent or proxy for 10 or more people unless he or she is your spouse or close relative.

Identify the person you choose as your health care agent, providing name, phone number, and address. Identify two other people who you would choose if the first person is not available or willing to make the choices for you when the time comes. One can cancel or change the health care agent(s) identified in the form at any time.

I understand that my Health Care Agent can make health care decisions for me. I want my Agent to be able to do the following.

Please cross out anything you **don't** want your Agent to do that is listed below**:**

- Make choices for me about my medical care or services, like tests, medicine, or surgery. This care or service could be to find out what my health problem is, or how to treat it. It can also include care to keep me alive. If the treatment or care has already started, my Health Care Agent can keep it going or have it stopped.
- Interpret any instructions I have given in this form or given in other discussions, according to my Health Care Agent's understanding of my wishes and values.
- Arrange for admission to a hospital, hospice, or nursing home for me. My Health Care Agent can hire any kind of health care worker I may need to help me or take care of me. My Agent may also fire a health care worker, if needed.
- Make the decision to request, take away or not give medical treatments, including artificially provided food and water, and any other treatments to keep me alive.
- See and approve release of my medical records and personal files.
- Move me to another state, to carry out my wishes.

- Take any legal action needed to carry out my wishes.
- Apply for Medicare, Medicaid, or other programs or insurance benefits for me. My Health Care Agent can see my personal files, like bank records, to find out what is needed to fill out these forms.

Wish 2: The Kind of Medical Treatment I Want or Don't Want

I believe that my life is precious and I deserve to be treated with dignity. When the time comes that I am very sick and am not able to speak for myself, I want the following wishes, and any other instructions I have given to my Health Care Agent, to be respected and followed.

A. General instructions

- I do not want to be in pain. I want my doctor to give me enough medicine to relieve my pain even if that means that I will be drowsy or sleep more than I would otherwise.
- I do not want anything done or omitted by my doctors or nurses *with the intention of taking my life.*
- I want to be offered food and fluids by mouth, and kept clean and warm.

B. Meaning of "life-support treatment"

Life-support treatment includes: medical devices put in me to help me breathe; food and water supplied artificially by medical device (tube feeding); cardiopulmonary resuscitation (CPR); major surgery; blood transfusions; dialysis; and antibiotics.

If I wish to limit the meaning of life-support treatment, I write this limitation in the space below....

C. If I am close to death:

If my doctor and another health care professional both decide that I am likely to die within a short period of time, and life-support treatment would only postpone the moment of my death (**choose *one* of the following**):

___ I want to have life-support treatment.
___ I want to have life-support treatment if my doctor believes it could help, but I want my doctor to stop giving me life-support treatment if it is not helping my health condition or symptoms.

___ I do not want life-support treatment. If it has been started, I want it stopped.

D. If I am in a coma and I am not expected to wake up or recover (choose *one* of the following):

___ I want to have life-support treatment.

___ I want to have life-support treatment if my doctor believes it could be helpful, but I want my doctor to stop giving me life-support treatment if it is not helping my health condition or symptoms.

___ I do not want life-support treatment. If it has been started, I want it stopped.

E. If I have permanent and severe brain damage and I am not expected to recover:

If my doctor and another health care professional both decide that I have permanent and severe brain damage, (for example, I cannot open my eyes, I cannot speak or understand) and I am not expected to recover, and life-support treatment would only postpone the moment of my death (**choose *one* of the following**):

___ I want to have life-support treatment.

___ I want to have life-support treatment if my doctor believes it could help, but I want my doctor to stop giving me life-support treatment if it is not helping my health condition or symptoms.

___ I do not want life-support treatment. If it has been started, I want it stopped.

F. If I am in another condition under which I do not wish to be kept alive:

If there is another condition under which I do not wish to have life-support treatment, I describe it below. In this condition, I believe that the costs and burdens of life-support treatment are too much and not worth the benefits to me. Therefore, in this condition, I do not want life-support treatment. (Please write the condition or conditions in the space below, or leave the space blank if you have none)…

Wish 3: How Comfortable I Want to Be

I do not expect my wishes to place new or added legal duties on my doctors or other health care providers. I also do not expect these wishes to excuse my doctor or other health care providers from giving me the proper care asked for by law.

Please cross out anything that you **don't** agree with:

- I do not want to be in pain. I want my doctor to give me enough medicine to relieve my pain, even if that means that I will be drowsy or sleep more than I would otherwise.
- If I show signs of depression, nausea, shortness of breath, or hallucinations, I want my caregivers to do whatever they can to help me.
- I wish to have a cool moist cloth put on my head if I have a fever.
- I want my lips and mouth kept moist to stop dryness.
- I wish to have warm baths often. I wish to be kept fresh and clean at all times.
- I wish to be massaged with warm oils as often as I can be.
- I wish to have my favorite music played when possible until my time of death.
- I wish to have personal care like shaving, nail clipping, hair brushing, and teeth brushing, as long as they do not cause me pain or discomfort.
- I wish to have religious readings and well-loved poems read aloud when I am near death.

Wish 4: How I Want People to Treat Me

Please cross out anything that you **don't** agree with

- I wish to have people with me when possible. I want someone to be with me when it seems that death may come at any time.
- I wish to have my hand held and to be talked to when possible, even if I don't seem to respond to the voice or touch of others.
- I wish to have others by my side praying for me when possible.
- I wish to have the members of my church or synagogue told that I am sick and asked to pray for me and visit me.
- I wish to be cared for with kindness and cheerfulness, and not sadness.
- I wish to have pictures of my loved ones in my room, near my bed.
- If I am not able to control my bowel or bladder functions, I wish for my clothes and bed linens

to be kept clean, and for them to be changed as soon as they can be if they have been soiled.

- I want to die in my home, if that can be done.

Wish 5: What I Want My Loved Ones to Know

Please cross out anything that you **don't** agree with.

- I wish to have my family members and loved ones know that I love them.
- I wish to be forgiven for the times I have hurt my family, friends, and others.
- I wish to have my family members and friends know that I forgive them for what they may have done to me in my life.
- I wish for my family members and loved ones to know that because of the faith I have, I do not fear death itself. I think it is not the end, but a new beginning for me.
- I wish for all of my family members to make peace with each other before my death, if they can.
- I wish for my family and friends to think about what I was like before I had a terminal illness. I want them to remember me in this way after my death.
- I wish for my family and friends to look at my dying as a time of personal growth for everyone, including me. This will help me live a meaningful life in my final days.
- I wish for my family and friends to get counseling if they have trouble with my death. I want memories of my life to give them joy and not sorrow.

People are also given the opportunity to add wishes that are not on any of the lists. There is also a place to tell others "how I want to be remembered, please say the following about me…" Additionally, people can specify the type of funeral and memorial service they prefer.

Evaluating the Five Wishes

It is too soon to evaluate the effectiveness of Five Wishes in achieving its goals of improved communication and end-of-life care. The positive signs include its timeliness, entering the scene just as the medical community has started to show renewed dedication to improving terminal care. The quick approval of Five Wishes by many states is also an encouraging sign. The document itself offers far more detail than its predecessors and thereby encourages us to think about end-of-life health issues in a more detailed way. It is possible that this level of attention to detail, however, will discourage some people. Those who might be ready to sign a ready-made document with standard language might not be ready to think through the larger set of alternatives presented in the Five Wishes (and in the exercise offered in Box 6-2).

There may also prove to be a problem in the shift of focus that occurs with the last two wishes. The first three wishes focus on the decisions we might want to make about our own medical care. This is a straightforward proposition. The last two wishes, however, attempt to influence the way other people feel and behave. Experience suggests that people seldom are able (even if they are willing) to alter their feelings and behaviors simply because they have been asked or commanded to do so.

The problem does not affect all components of the the last two wishes. For example, there is not likely to be any difficulty with the wish "to have pictures of my loved ones in my room, near by bed." Nor is there fundamental problem in asking to have "people with me when possible" and having "my hand held and to be talked to when possible, even if I don't seem to respond to the voice or touch of others." We may begin to encounter difficulties, however, when others are asked to provide care with "cheerfulness, and not sadness." Some people are very sad indeed as they see a friend or family member in failing health; asking them to feel otherwise could increase stress. The wife who sits by her husband's side, holding his hand and trying to be "cheerful" may be so tense that she breaks down in tears the moment she leaves the room. Similarly, it may be difficult for family and friends "to look at my dying as a time of personal growth for everyone, including me." Some people do look at dying in this way, and some others are capable of doing so. But the realities of terminal illness and the marked differences among people in their attitudes toward life and death do not always contribute to such a positive view. If people believe they are being instructed to experience the terminal illness of a friend or family member "as a time of personal growth," this could increase their own anxieties and conflicts.

Much will depend on the sensitivity with which the Five Wishes are communicated and interpreted. The intention clearly is to support and enhance the relationships between dying people and those who have been most important to them. This good intention will have to survive a tendency we have seen in many other spheres—to turn a useful suggestion or guideline into a task, a command, a requirement for conformity. In other words, the Five Wishes will probably be as helpful as our ability to use them well.

A Right Not to Die?
The Cryonics Alternative

Relatively few people are aware of the *cryonics movement,* and fewer still understand precisely what is involved. It is worth mentioning here as a counterbalance to the current emphasis on the right to die. Some people who very much want to live believe that even high-tech modern medicine does not give them every opportunity. These people have opted for a radical alternative

Advocates of the cryonic approach believe that it may be possible to maintain "deceased" people at very low temperatures for long periods of time. Eventually medical breakthroughs will make it possible to rid people of the diseases and conditions that led to their "death." The bodies will then be restored carefully to normal temperature and the curative procedures undertaken. Some cryonicists believe that resuscitation should wait even longer—until science has turned the key that will enable us to halt or even reverse the aging process.

This scenario sounds like science fantasy and, in fact, has often been introduced in movies and works of fiction. Nevertheless, much of cryonics is grounded in demonstrable reality. Surgeons routinely lower patients' body temperature, especially for lengthy operations. Both human sperm and embryos have been maintained in a frozen condition until use—perhaps some readers of this book were given life in this manner by parents who could not conceive or safely deliver a baby in the usual way. Experiments have had some success in preserving body parts and even whole animals in a hypothermic state.

What about people? Yes, people have been placed in *cryostasis*, as this state is now known. The founder of the cryonics movement, R. C. W. Ettinger, estimates that about fifty people are currently in cryostasis, with the first publicized freezing being that of Prof. James Bedford in 1967. Ettinger's mother is one of the individuals most recently placed in cryostasis.

> At a temperature of –320°F, protected from decay and virtually unchanging, she will probably remain in her cryostasis for a long time—but not forever. One wonderful day—perhaps in fifty years, perhaps in a century—we expect to see her smile again, and greet us—physically young once more, but with her memories intact. She may be one of the first of our generation to achieve "immortality" [indefinitely extended life] through the skills of future medicine. (Kastenbaum, 1993, p. 163).

Stephen Bridge, director of the Alcor Life Extension Foundation, participated in transferring Professor Bedford from his original cryostatic cylinder to a new and more efficient vessel. Bridge reports that Bedford looked just as he did when he was placed in the first cylinder about seventeen years previously.

The cryonics procedure as such cannot begin until a physician has certified the patient as dead. To begin the procedure earlier would be in violation of existing law. From the viewpoint of the cryonicists, this person has become *deanimated* but has not lost the potential for restoration. A person who has been destroyed by an accident or other violent trauma would not be a candidate for cryostasis, because essential physical structures are not intact and cannot be replaced. Following the pronouncement of death, a team of cryonicists immediately starts the process of lowering the body temperature. Several injections are given to protect vital organs and a heart-lung machine is operated to circulate these medications. The deanimated person is then brought to the nearest available location in which further preparations can be made. Finally the encased and cooled body is placed in a cylinder filled with liquid nitrogen, a very cold substance that maintains its temperature without the need of electrical power. The cryonic organization maintains the level of liquid nitrogen (which is subject to evaporation over time) and ensures the integrity of the protective chamber.

Does cryonics work? Is it possible for a "deceased" person to be warmed back to life and have that life greatly extended? Nobody knows the answer to that question for sure. The cryonicists are optimistic but not foolhardy. They are not about to engage in reckless experiments. Instead, they are willing to wait until the expected scientific breakthroughs have made resuscitation a reasonable venture. There are many critics and skeptics, and many scientific challenges that must be overcome before the question can be tested. If this subject interests you, you might want to read the book that introduced the topic, Ettinger's *The Prospect of Immortality* (1966) and his current reflections on the cryonic movement (Kastenbaum, 1994–1995). Drexler (1991) provides a book-length examination of the emerging scientific work that pertains to cryostasis and resuscitation. A brief overview can be found in Kastenbaum (1993), and the Alcor Life Extension Foundation (1993) offers a compilation of current information.

Another question is almost as interesting: *should* cryonics work? Is it ethical for people to desire to live beyond their "deaths?" Some people cite global overpopulation as a powerful reason to discourage or even forbid cryonic restoration. One counterargument of the cryonicists is that as a society and as individuals, we already are investing tremendous resources in attempting to forestall death; why should we suddenly and arbitrarily draw the line at cryostasis?

Can we claim a right to die without also allowing people to claim a right to live? This seems to be the most significant question at the moment, while the actual outcome of cryonic efforts is still unknown. Can we advocate one right and deny the other? This is a problem worth keeping mind for most of us. Meanwhile, Ettinger is continuing to plan "rebirthday parties" for a number of people he has described as "slightly dead."

A Perspective on End-of-Life Decisions

Society is actively engaged in rethinking and restructuring the ways in which we treat each other near the end of life. This itself represents a major shift in attitudes and priorities, and it is a shift that either reduces or increases anxious tension, depending on circumstances. Both the general public and health care professionals may at times feel uncomfortable because the rules seem to have changed. People are now being asked to make decisions that formerly seemed to make themselves. Physicians were generally in the position of unquestioned decision makers. These decisions could be made on the basis of common practice, for example, do everything that might be done to extend life, even if there is little or no hope of success. On occasion the decision could be made—quietly and unobtrusively—to withhold or withdraw cure-oriented treatment to spare the patient further suffering.

Now physicians are expected to share decision making with patients and their families and to be responsive to other health care professionals and legislative measures as well. The expanded circle of people now involved in end-of-life decision making might feel either more anxious tension because of their heightened responsibilities or a sense of relief because their perspectives and needs have opportunities for expression.

The new social and medical climate for end-of-life decisions favors increased participation, communication, and patient's rights. We might therefore expect a widespread transformation—and consequently find ourselves surprised and disappointed when these principles are neglected, for example, as demonstrated by the SUPPORT study (*see Chapter 4*) and in the opening quotation about nursing home resident Millie Morrisey. Perhaps it would be useful to bear in mind the difficulty of changing entrenched old ways and the need to learn how to fulfill the promise of the new. The discouraging results of the SUPPORT study, for example, have led to renewed and more sophisticated efforts to improve physicians' responsiveness to patient and family needs at the end of life. More physicians have become active in this cause. And Millie Morrisey's distress was soon alleviated. The nursing home staff did become aware of her wishes and quickly removed the ventilator and offered her comfort care that resulted in a peaceful death a few days later (Field and Cassel, 1997). Furthermore, shaken by this experience, the nursing home made changes in its policies and practices to prevent a repeat occurrence.

Johan Sebastian Bach continued to compose his monumental *Art of Fugue* until very nearly his last breath.

We are in a difficult but promising situation: more people are concerned about making end-of-life decisions that respect patient and family wishes, but how to do this in an effective and timely way is a challenge that still must be addressed.

A broader perspective on end-of-life decision making must also take into consideration many factors beyond health care. Financial matters of-ten require attention. These actions can be as simple as locating and reviewing documents such as wills and insurance policies, or as complicated as working out debt payment plans and the distribution of financial resources to surviving family members. There may also be crucial personal situations to resolve. Does the terminally ill person want to overcome years of grudges and negative feelings toward a family member or friend?

Is it better to hold on to the anger or seek resolution? Or is it the terminally ill person's relationship with God that needs to find resolution one way or another? Still again, there may be a strong need to complete a project or mission. Near the end of his life, J. S. Bach (1685–1750) was so weakened by illness that his family tried to persuade him to remain in bed. He wouldn't have that. Instead he devoted practically every waking hour to *Art of Fugue*, one of the most remarkable compositions from one of the world's most remarkable composers. His mental and emotional powers remained at their peak despite his rapidly failing health. There are not many J. S. Bach's, with such a monumental project to complete near the end of their lives, but others among us have endeavors to which they are deeply committed.

End-of-life decisions can take many forms, so we are well advised to be sensitive to the special needs of every individual.

SUMMARY

The responsibility for end-of-life decisions was once largely in the hands of physicians and the health care system. Today there is more opportunity for patients and their families to participate in decision making. We observed at the outset, however, that not everybody feels prepared to take on the responsibility for exercising control over the types of medical interventions they want near the end of their lives. The "ideal" patient, from the standpoint of current thinking, is somebody who values having control over the future, stands ready to make significant decisions, and has a cultural heritage in which individual choice is salient. One should be careful about imposing mainstream concepts of individual choice and control upon people whose personalities or ethnic backgrounds are inclined in a different direction.

We saw that the first advance directive to gain wide attention was the *Living Will*. This document stimulated the discussion of end-of-life issues within families as well as within the health care, legislative, and judicial spheres. Within a few years, most states had enacted legislation based upon the Living Will concept that people should have the right to limit the kind of treatment they receive near the end of their lives. Courts established the *principle of informed consent*,

which supports individual choice. Nevertheless, neither the Living Will nor the measures enacted by legislatures could overcome the many obstacles to fulfilling the promise of advance directives. The federal government then enacted the *Patients Self-Determination Act*, with the intention of increasing patient participation and hospital compliance. This measure also has proven to be only a limited success. A new and more detailed advance directive, the *Five Wishes*, has shown promise in generating instructions that can be used effectively by health care personnel.

In trying to develop a perspective on end-of-life decisions, we noted that we are in a difficult transition period from the previous physician-oriented approach to one in which the wishes and needs of patients and their families are fully considered. We also noted that end-of-life decision making is not limited to health concerns, but also may include important relationship, spiritual, economic, and personal challenges.

REFERENCES

Aging with Dignity (1999). *Five wishes.* Tallahassee: Aging with dignity.

Alcor Life Extension Foundation (1993). *Cryonics: Reaching for tomorrow.* Scottsdale, AZ: Alcor Life Extension Foundation.

Alexander, G. J. (1988). *Writing a living will.* New York: Praeger.

Drexler, K. E. (1991). *Unbounding the future.* New York: Morrow.

Ettinger, R. C. W. (1966). *The prospect of immortality.* New York: Mcfadden-Bartell.

Field, M. J., & Cassel, C. K., (Eds.). (1997). *Approaching death. Improving care at the end of life.* Washington, DC: National Academy Press.

Greve, P. (1991, November). Advance directives—what the new law means for you. *Registered Nurse,* 63–67.

Hoefler, J. M. (1997). *Managing death.* Boulder: Westview Press.

Kastenbaum, R. (1993). Cryonic suspension. In R. Kastenbaum & B. Kastenbaum (Eds.), *Encyclopedia of death* (pp. 61–66). New York: Avon Books.

Kastenbaum, R. (1994–1985). Cryonic suspension: An *Omega* interview with R. C. W. Ettinger. *Omega, Journal of Death and Dying. 30,* 159–172.

Koenig, B. A. (1997). Cultural diversity in decisionmaking about care at the end of life. In M. J. Field & C. K. Cassel (Eds.), *Approaching Death: Improving care at the end of life* (pp. 363–382). Washington, DC: National Academic Press.

Leininger, M. (1978). *Transcultural nursing: Concepts, theories, and practices*. Toronto: Wiley.

Miles, S. H., Koepp, R., & Weber, E. P. (1996). Advance end-of-life treatment planning: A research review. *Archives of Internal Medicine, 156,* 1062–1067.

Miyaji, N. T. (1993). The power of compassion: Truth-telling among American doctors in the care of dying patients. *Social Science and Medicine, 36,* 249–264.

Pugh, D., & West, D. J., Jr. (1994–1995). Advance directives: A patient's perspective. *Omega, Journal of Death and Dying, 30,* 249–256.

Scofield, G. (1993). The Living Will. In R. Kastenbaum & B. K. Kastenbaum (Eds.), *The encyclopedia of death*. Phoenix: Oryx, (pp. 175–176).

Silverman, H. J. (1995). Implementation of the patient self-determination act in a hospital setting. An initial evaluation. *Archives of Internal Medicine, 5,* 502–510.

Stephens, R. L., & Grady, R. (1992). Case analyses of terminally ill cancer patients who refused to sign a Living Will. *Omega, Journal of Death and Dying, 25,* 283–290.

Taylor, J. (1665/1977). *The rules and exercises of holy dying.* New York: Arno.

GLOSSARY

Advance Directive: A document that specifies the type of health care an individual wishes to receive should that individual not be in a position to express his or her wishes in a critical situation.

Assisted Death: An action taken by one person to end the life of another person at the other person's request.

Cryonics: An approach that attempts to preserve a body at low temperatures until medical advances have made it possible to cure the fatal condition.

Durable Power of Attorney for Health Care: The transfer of legal authority to a person who will make health care decisions for a person who at that time is unable to make or communicate his or her own decisions.

Five Wishes: A new advance directive form (supported by law in some states) that provides an expanded set of specific choices.

Informed Consent: The principle that patients should be provided with sufficient information to make decisions for or against accepting a treatment.

Living Will: The first type of advance directive to be introduced, requesting that no aggressive treatments be attempted if the individual is in the end phase of life.

Mercy Killing: An earlier common term for what is now referred to as "assisted death."

Patients' Self-Determination Act: A federal law requiring that health care organizations provide patients with the informed opportunity to establish an advance directive to limit medical treatment in specified situations.

The "soup kitchen" became a fact of American life during The Great Depression that started in 1929. Unemployed men, unable to support their families and stressed by loss of occupation and self-esteem, were vulnerable to thoughts of suicide, as were those who had made and lost fortunes.

Emmy, Susie, Tammy—My Dear Ones
Don't think badly of me. I am finally doing the right thing. I did so many
things that were wrong or just plain stupid. Please remember one thing.
That I love you and always have and always will. None of this was your
fault. It was just time for me to get out of everybody's life so you can all have
a life. Love you, love you, love you.
Mom
The bills are all paid.
—Suicide note of a 37-year-old woman

I remember sitting at this adding machine in this insurance office. These la-
dies were bossing me around and I'm adding numbers.... I decided right
then: I already felt dead. Everything I did, I felt more dead. Nothing felt
alive and nothing would help. I just felt it would be more congruent to be
dead. Just not to have this body to keep being in.
—Karen, quoted by Richard A. Heckler, 1994, p. 67

I didn't found out it was suicide until I was eleven. A neighbor girl derided
my sister one day. "Your father killed himself! Your father killed himself!"
So my mother told Jeanne and me that it was time we knew—the neighbor
girl was right.
—Larry Lockridge, 1995, p. 431

His third try was to move out of the apartment that reminded him too much
of Sadie and the life they had once shared. Max relocated to a sunbelt state,
but he hated it. Surrounded by strangers and an alien environment, he felt
more isolated and lonely than ever. He finally went out and bought a hand-
gun and spent an evening staring at it.
—Kastenbaum, 1994

Police have concluded that a west Valley man was trying to kill himself and his pregnant wife when he drove across a dirt median on the Loop 101 freeway and crashed head-on into a semi-tractor trailer earlier this month, sources have told The Tribune.
—Yantis & Burgard, June 26, 1999

Can a dead woman kill herself? Yes, and dead men, too; it happens many times every year. Karen became emotionally numb to protect herself from her sorrows and stresses. Few people, if any, noticed. Feeling as though one were already dead may be protection from both life and death in the short term, but it can also be another step closer to a suicide attempt. The inner journey from experiences of loss and deprivation to the edge of suicide has been lucidly described by counseling psychologist Richard A. Heckler (1994), whose work will be considered in this chapter.

The man whose son did not learn that he had died by his own hand was Ross Lockridge, Jr., author of the best-selling book, *Raintree County*. The nation was shocked when he committed suicide soon after the success of his novel, a selection of the Book of the Month Club in 1948. Years later his son, Larry Lockridge, reflected that his father "believed only the negative reviews" of his book. What seemed to be a small event—the reprinting of a critical review from *The New Yorker* in his hometown newspaper—"triggered the suicide of an already very depressed person (who was) caught up in a web of events he couldn't negotiate" (1995, p. 434). To live his own life as a whole person, the son had to come to terms with his father's suicide—and the same can be said for thousands of others who have become survivors of suicide.

The media paid no attention to Max during his more than sixty years of meeting his occupational, social, and family obligations. Little notice would have been taken had Max ended his life with his new handgun. He would have become just one more statistic: anyone who cared about this topic would have already discovered that older white males have the highest suicide rate in the United States.

The woman who wrote a farewell note to her children had made two previous suicide attempts before taking a fatal overdose. She had been quiet and uncomplaining as she went about her responsibilities, so the family also went about its business and thought she would be all right. On the first anniversary of her death, the oldest daughter (age 13) made a serious but nonfatal suicide attempt. Individuals attempt and complete suicides, but self-destruction frequently is also a family matter.

Many deaths that are not recorded as suicides nevertheless were motivated by the intention to die. Unfortunately, some people also decide to take others with them. Motor vehicle accidents that are not entirely accidents and deliberate encounters with law enforcement officers are among the ways in which a suicidal purpose is sometimes carried out. This topic is explored both here and in *Chapter 9* with its emphases on murder and accidental deaths.

Suicide occurs at every age, from childhood onward. The victims are males and females, the affluent and the impoverished, the seeming failures and the apparently successful. People take their own lives in rural Vermont and urban San Francisco, in crowded Tokyo and sparsely populated Lapland. The scope of the problem is worldwide and not limited to any particular class of people, although some groups are more at risk than others.

We begin with a statistical profile of suicide attempts (also known as *parasuicide*) and completed suicides. More detailed attention is then given to gender differences; suicide among youth, elders, and Native Americans; and special circumstances in which there is a higher risk of self-destruction. We will then increase our understanding by acquainting ourselves with both cultural and individual meanings of suicide, paying special attention to the descent into suicide and the attempt itself. This background will prepare us to consider the challenge of suicide prevention.

THE STATISTICAL PROFILE

Suicide has been among the leading causes of death in the United States ever since fairly reliable statistics have been available. The most recent national data (1996) reveal that suicide is the ninth most common cause. Experts in the field of suicide prevention have long been convinced that the actual toll is even greater than the approximately 30,000 certified suicides recorded in the United States each year. It is not unusual for a death to be classified in some other way (e.g., "accidental") if the suicidal component has not been established beyond a doubt. Furthermore, many people still find it difficult to believe that a child might be capable of committing suicide, so the reported statistics among the very young may not be reliable. "Accidental death" was the cause of death listed for one 9-year-old boy who arranged to drown himself in his bathtub after making sure that nobody was home. He was a more than capable swimmer who had been under stifling family pressure all his young life. At the other end of the age spectrum, I have also seen the self-assisted death of ailing and socially isolated old men go into the records as arteriosclerosis or heart disease. Because insurance policies often have provisions prejudicial to suicide, sympathetic medical examiners have also been known to shade the facts when there is any ambiguity as to cause of death at any age. *The statistical profile, then, tends to underrepresent the actual incidence of suicide.*

Interpreting the reported suicide rate has also been made more difficult by changes in the classification procedures. Those responsible for determining the cause of death are obliged to use the International Classification of Diseases, Injuries, and Causes of Death (ICD). The ICD has been revised twice in ways that affect suicide statistics. In 1958 it was decided that all deaths associated with a self-inflicted injury would be classified as suicides unless a specific statement attesting to accidental factors was included. This resulted in an increase in the percentage of reported suicides. To someone not familiar with this change of procedure, it would look as though there had been about a 3 percent rise in suicide. In 1968 this procedure was again revised. It was decided that death associated with self-inflicted injury would not be classified as suicide unless the *intentionality* of the act was specified. Accordingly, this led to a drop of about 6 percent in the percentage of official suicides.

These shifts in classification procedure have nothing to do with the actual number of suicides and make it difficult to compare rates over time. Still another problem becomes evident when we examine the technique used to calculate the suicide rate. It is based on the following formula:

$$\text{Suicide rate} = \frac{\text{Number of suicides}}{\text{population}} \times 100{,}000$$

The overall suicide rate in the United States is 12.3, up slightly in recent years. (A suicide rate of 12 means that during a calendar year there were twelve suicidal deaths for every 100,000 people in the population.) The accuracy of the reported rate depends on the care with which population size has been estimated as well as the accuracy of cause-of-death classifications. Some subpopulations tend to be undercounted. Illegal immigrants, nonwhites, the young, and transients of any age are among those who are often underrepresented.

If suicide statistics are to be used appropriately, the suicide *rate* must be distinguished from the *total number* of suicides in a population. As the population continues to increase, more deaths by suicide are likely even if the rate remains constant: same rate>more people>more suicide. This consideration applies to smaller geographical regions as well. Has the development of a suicide prevention service actually reduced the rate in a particular city? The shifting population of the city (plus transients, minus youths away at college or in military service, and so on) can make it very difficult to answer this question. If all relevant information were available over a reasonable time period, it might be found that the true *rate* has declined, but even so, the actual *number* of suicides might not be appreciably lower. This is one of the reasons that it is difficult to evaluate the effectiveness of suicide prevention services. Finally, for many years population data were sorted crudely into "white" and "nonwhite" categories. Important differences within the "nonwhite" category tend to be merged and distorted, and it is, of course, a stupid policy to define people by their "nonwhiteness." This practice is changing, but much of the available data are limited to this once-traditional distinction. Recognizing all these difficulties, what messages do the suicide statistics (*see Table 7.1*) have for us?

1. *Bad economic times are associated with an increase in suicide rates.* The overall rate of suicide in the United States reached a peak during the Great Depression of the 1930s and then declined. A later period of recession was associated with another general rise in suicide. There is little reason to doubt that social and economic conditions can affect the suicide rate, but this effect may differ from one subgroup to another.
2. *Completed suicides come most frequently from the white male segment of the United States population.* (Asian male suicide rates have also been reported as high, but the database is less adequate for drawing conclusions.) *At every age, white males are at greater risk for suicide than white females or nonwhite males and females (with the possible exception of males of Asian ancestry).* The difference in suicide rates between white males and other groups is substantial: more than twice as common at all ages over the past half century.
3. *The white male suicide rate increases with age, but females and nonwhites reach their peak vulnerabil-ity earlier in adult life.* Although the rate is highest among older white men, the actual number of suicidal deaths is higher for middle-aged men because there are more of them. Even a lower rate represents more fatalities. *It is the increasingly higher white male suicide rate with advancing age that is mainly responsible for the overall increased suicide rate with age in the United States.*
4. *Suicide rates have increased among youth, with males predominating.* Taking one's own life has become the third leading cause of death among people between 15 and 24 years of age. Approximately a fifth of all suicides are committed by those under age 25.
5. *Other groups at greater risk for suicide include city dwellers, the divorced (of either sex), and those suffering from depression or life-threatening illness* (McIntosh, 1992). Some studies have identified other specific populations at risk, such as children who have lost a parent to death, but the evidence seems to be clearest for the groups just mentioned.

The male suicide rate has been moving upward since 1950 for both whites and blacks. The female suicide rate follows a different pattern for these years. There was an upsurge of suicide among white females around 1970, but with this exception the rate has remained at the same level for thirty-five years. Suicide among African American females also reached a peak around 1970. Although at this time suicide was still relatively infrequent among African American females, their rate had nearly doubled within twenty years. Since its peak around 1970, the suicide rate for this group has declined, but never down to the earlier levels. These patterns indicate that men have become increasingly vulnerable to suicide in recent decades, but that women have recovered from their higher rates of 1970. Gender differences in suicide rate are consistently large and will be explored later.

United States and World Suicide Rates

How does the suicide rate in the United States compare with other nations? The United States has consistently been in about the middle of the

TABLE 7-1

Suicide Rates by Age in the United States, 1996

Age group	Rate
All ages combined	12.1
5–14	0.6
15–24	13.8
25–34	14.9
35–44	14.5
45–54	14.1
55–64	14.2
65–74	18.2
75–84	23.4
85+*	25.5

Source: United States Department of Health and Human Services: National Center for Health Statistics.

*Data for this age group may be somewhat less reliable.

list of nations that report their data to the World Health Organization. Hungary often tops the list, at 37. Finland (27.8), Austria (27.8), Denmark (20.4), and Switzerland (19.1) follow Hungary as the reporting nations with the highest suicide rates. Industrialized nations report higher rates, but it is also in these nations that statistics are gathered more systematically and in which there is less pressure to avoid reporting suicidal deaths as such. Strikingly, nations with a suicide rate less than 3 per 100,000 are also among the very lowest in technological development. These countries are Colombia, Maritius, Dominican Republic, Mexico, Panama, Peru, Philippines, Guatemala, Malta, Nicaragua, Papua New Guinea, Jamaica, and Egypt.

Is there something about modernization that increases a nation's suicidality? Many observers have identified factors such as higher stress, reduced social integration, and the encouragement of dreams of material success and wealth that often fail to materialize. Recently, a *population increase theory* has received some impressive support and suggests that the situation is even more complex than previously realized. Zhang (1998) finds that low suicide rates are common in countries with rapidly growing populations consisting of many young people. The faster the growth, the younger the population, the fewer the suicides. It is a good idea to pause for a moment to consider this pattern. Very low suicide rates do *not* necessarily mean that people are well off and enjoying life. Rather, it can mean that the birth rate is explosive and not very many people survive into middle and later adult years. Many people are impoverished and have little protection from health and economic problems. What are we to think, then? In the United States and other modernized nations, there may well be a direct relationship between quality of life and suicide—we expect a lot, experience stress in trying to attain our goals, and may consider ourselves failures when personal relationships and accomplishments fall short. In less modernized nations, however, people endure a low quality of life with fewer hopes that can be thwarted. There are so many other life-threatening conditions that suicide hardly compares.

Much more must be understood about national differences. For example, Canada and the United States are comparable in many respects as well as being neighboring nations with much interaction. Studies have found, however, that Canadian youth have a more accepting attitude toward suicide than do their age peers in the United States (Leenaars and Lester, 1992). Is attitudinal difference related to the fact that the suicide rate for young people in Canada exceeds the high rate in the United States and is continuing to escalate? It has also been found that the young males most at risk for suicide in Canada are those who are divorced, unemployed, and without religious affiliations. Findings such as these suggest that the loss or lack of connectedness to others may be a critical factor in at least some of the national differences in suicide rates.

Lack of social support and connectedness may also be a key factor in differential suicide rates within the same nation. For example, the highest suicide rates in the United States are found in western states such as Nevada, New Mexico, and Arizona, especially in the rural areas that offer relatively few opportunities for social interaction and support. The lowest rates are found in high-density states such as Massachusetts, New Jersey, and New York, where it is very difficult not to bump into people all the time. On closer inspection, the situation proves much more complicated. Who chooses to live in Nevada and who in Massachusetts? Are stresses greater in the "most suicidal" states, or are social support systems less available? Clearly, we need both statistical analyses and studies that are more "up close and personal."

What About Suicide Attempts?

Up to this point, we have focused on completed suicides. It is much more difficult to estimate the frequency of suicide attempts, many of which never show up in official documents. Now we finally have a useful estimate of suicide attempts. Crosby, Cheltenham & Sacks (1999) conducted a large-scale telephone survey, asking people to report whether they had thought about suicide (ideation), made a suicidal plan, or engaged in an actual attempt. The key results are summarized in Table 7.2. It is clear that suicidal ideas and thoughts are not uncommon in the general population. This is important to bear in mind, because there is often a sequential progression: ideation>plan>nonfatal attempt>fatal

TABLE 7-2

Incidence of Nonlethal Suicidal Thoughts and Behaviors in the United States

Type of Suicidality	Percentage of Sample	Population Estimate
Ideation	5.6	10,500,000
Planning	2.7	2,700,000
Attempts	0.7	700,000
		(1,100,000 attempts)

Source: Crosby, Cheltenham and Sacks (1999)

attempt. Heightened awareness of the frequency of these earlier signs could save lives.

The Human Side

The impact of suicide cannot be gauged by numbers alone. Even attempts that do not result in death can have significant consequences. For example, family and friends are put on alert and may respond either by renewed efforts to help the individual or by further emotional isolation of the attempter because of their own heightened anxiety. The suicide attempt is sometimes viewed as a manipulative action and thereby arouses resentment and hostility—or it may win some temporary gains and concessions.

I have observed a tremendous range of responses to suicide attempts. In one instance, colleagues became more sensitive to the individual's sense of despair and were able to provide valuable help with both emotional support and practical actions to change a frustrating situation. In another instance, however, the parents refused to be "impressed" by their adolescent daughter's near-fatal attempt and, in effect, challenged her to "finish the job." She did. A suicide attempt (or threat) is likely to alter interpersonal relationships as well as the individual's own feelings. Completed suicide often leaves the survivors shaken. The guilt can be disabling. Furthermore, the survivors may feel that they cannot speak openly about the death to others and therefore become socially isolated.

The social cost of suicide is high, although impossible to calculate precisely. Occasionally one suicide seems to encourage another as some vulnerable people identify with the deceased and see self-destruction as an acceptable means of solving their problems. When the suicide of a young celebrity is reported vividly by the media, there may be a short-term increase in suicide attempts and completions by some people who have identified with the star and who have been having problems of their own. The public at large, however, does not appear susceptible to "suicide by contagion." The human side of suicide also includes children left without parents and therefore made more vulnerable to stress and self-doubts that can haunt them throughout their lives. Children with family members who attempted or completed suicide are more likely to make suicide attempts themselves at some point in their lives. Suicide has a ripple effect of stress and distress that starts with immediate family and friends and may continue to widen. Behind each number in the suicide statistics there are families, friends, and colleagues who will never be quite the same again.

THREE PROBLEM AREAS

A more detailed look at suicide among youth, elderly persons, and Native Americans will illustrate some of the many relationships between individual self-destruction and society.

Youth Suicide

The suicide rate among adolescents and young adults (ages 15 to 24) has almost tripled since 1950; it is estimated that about *half a million* serious attempts are made by American youths each year. In a society that is often characterized as youth oriented, it is enigmatic as well as alarming that completed and attempted suicide have become so prevalent among young people. Consider some of the additional facts:

1. *The increase in completed suicides is clearly greater for males, although female suicide has also become more common.* More suicide *attempts* are made by young women.
2. *Both sexes now turn to firearms and explosives as the most common method of self destruction* (even

more frequent among males). Some form of poisoning or overdosing is the second most common method used by young women. Hanging and strangulation are also more frequent among young women.

3. *Studies consistently find that suicide rates are higher among college students than among youth in general.* Some of this difference, however, is related more to age than to the college experience as such. Suicide rates generally increase with age, and the college student population tends to be older than the average person counted in the 15-to-24 age group. Furthermore, graduate students and others who are a little older than the overall college population are more at risk.

4. *Academic pressure seems related to suicide among college students, but not in a simple way.* Many undergraduates who committed suicide had a higher grade point average than their peers. Objectively, they were doing well. Subjectively, however, they had performed below their expectations—or what they took to be their parents' expectations. "I couldn't face Dad and that big scene there would be after all the money he had spent on my education and how he had wanted to be proud of me and blah, blah, blah!" This is how one student explained his near-fatal suicide attempt to a counselor, but many others have had similar experiences.

5. *Most of those who have gone on to commit suicide expressed their despondency to others and often made explicit comments about their intentions.* Clinicians have long held that many suicidal people do issue a cry for help. This seems to be true of many of the youths who see suicide as a possible solution to their problems. Every expression of suicidal intent provides an opportunity for a helpful intervention.

6. *The immoderate use of alcohol and other drugs occurs more often with suicidal people than with the general population at all ages.* A sudden change in drinking habits may be a particularly important

Depression and alcohol are two risk factors for suicide that often occur together.

factor because the risk of suicide increases when a person goes on a "jag." Alcohol and drug abuse have been identified as especially important factors in youth suicide. This was clearly illustrated in the pattern of substance abuse that preceded Kurt Cobain's suicide and was also found in the deaths of several other young rock-oriented singers. But alcohol and drug use also shows up in many of the death investigations carried out for youths unknown to fame: estimates are that alcohol or drugs are involved in between a third and a half of all youth suicides (Colt, 1991). A particularly lethal combination is the loss of a valued relationship through rejection, separation, or death (see below) when it is followed by increased alcohol use (Hendin, 1995).

7. *The loss of a valued relationship is one of the most common triggering events for youth suicide.* This can involve the death of a parent, breaking up with a lover, having a quarrel with a close friend, being disappointed in a role model, or learning that one's favorite dog or cat has died. Many people experience these kinds of losses and stresses without becoming suicidal. However, some have become more intensely sensitized to loss and stress and lack other coping resources. Past experiences of loss, rejection, and unworthiness make some youths more vulnerable to suicide when new interpersonal problems arise. Psychiatrist Herbert Hendin has worked with many college students who have "incorporated an emotional lifelessness that characterized their relationship with their parents. Most have learned to use school work in a defensive withdrawal from their families and from the world outside. This adaptation is often encouraged by their families, who find it easier to deal with the fewer demands of an emotionally muted child. (1985, p. 29)" It was not unusual for these people to have had depressed and suicidal thoughts for many years. The college experience, then, did not generate a suicidal impulse for the first time but may have provided an occasion for its expression.

8. *Heavy metal music attracts depressed and suicidal youth—it does not cause suicide* (Stack, 1994; Stack, 1998). Many heavy metal fans come from dysfunctional families, experience diffi-

culties in coping with the world, and are low in self-esteem. The angry pounding rhythms resonate with their feelings, reducing their sense of aloneness, but they have not been shown to contribute directly to suicide.

The role of the family in youth suicide should not be ignored. Leenaars and Wenckstern (1991b) have identified the following family characteristics that tend to be seen in families of suicidal adolescents and young adults:

1. The families often impose rigid rules.
2. Communication patterns within the family are poor: people do not really listen to each other.
3. One parent may establish too strong an emotional bond with the youth (e.g., "smother love") while at the same time not encouraging the youth's progressive growth toward responsibility and independence.
4. Long-term patterns of dysfunction exist within the family, for example, father or mother absence, divorce, alcoholism, mental illness. Adolescent females with suicidal tendencies also have a much higher rate of incest than does the population in general.

Leenaars & Wenckstern emphasize that "There are no evil, weak parents, only perturbed parents or, more accurately, perturbed and suicide-enhancing *families*" (1991, p. 101). A suicidal youth, then, may represent a distress call on the part of his or her entire family.

All of us may have the opportunity to help an adolescent or young adult find an alternative to suicide. This process begins with our willingness to take this measure of concern and responsibility. The next step is to become familiar with some of the most typical signs of suicide risk in this age group (*see Table 7.3*). We should keep in mind that all young men and women have their own unique biographies and their own distinctive coping styles. We should also avoid a mechanical approach to detecting possible suicidality, considering instead this particular person in his or her particular situation.

I would add two other observations. First, many suicidal youths are misguided by vague and wishful thoughts about death. The person often assumes that he or she will be able to witness

TABLE 7-3

Youth Suicide: Factors Associated with Higher Risk

- Other members of the family have made suicidal attempts.
- This person has made a previous suicide attempt.
- There have been recent changes in this person's behavior, including level of social activity, sleeping, eating, choice of clothes, and use of alcohol or drugs. The behavior change can take the direction of either withdrawal from previous interests and activities or a sudden burst of pleasure-seeking and risk-taking activities. The clue is that in either case, this person is acting very much differently than usual.
- The person experiences a sense of hopelessness, apathy, and/or dread. "What's the point of trying again?" "There's nothing I can do about nothing." "So, who cares anyway? I don't!"
- The person makes explicit or implicit statements about ending his or her life. "I've had enough of this crap!" "You're going to see me on the 10 o' clock news!" "I want it get it all over with, and I will!"
- The thought process has narrowed to the point that everything seems open or closed; there is little or no ability to acknowledge shades of meaning, and only extreme courses of action are envisioned. "I'll kill her, *or* I'll kill myself." "I can *never* get anything right." "He was the *only* person who understood me and I can't live without him." "There's *only one way* out of this mess."
- Abrupt flashes of anger interfere with activities and interactions. The person becomes touchy and unpredictable and seems to overreact to small frustrations or provocations. There may also be an increase in glowering resentment and uncooperativeness even if this does not explode into overt displays of anger. Aggressive and antisocial behavior occurs more often among males than females as a forerunner of a suicide attempt.

the response of survivors. "Look how upset they will be!" "They'll be sorry they treated me so bad." "They'll know I really meant it." I have also heard many expressions of the assumption that death is "just a trip," perhaps similar to a pleasant alcohol or drug high. They have not read Greyson's (1992–93) study in which he found that people who reported near-death experiences also reported very strong antisuicide attitudes. Another common belief on the edge of suicide is that death is a something better than life (as compared with the alternative view that death is the absence of life). A tendency to envision death as more rewarding than life may contribute to the decision to take one's life.

Second, it is important to remember that suicidal impulses do not have free reign. People of all ages also have strong reasons *not* to take their lives despite moods of discouragement and frustration. Thoughts of suicide are common in Hong Kong as well as in other nations in which this tendency has been investigated. Although as many as two in five adolescents report having considered suicide, most have not and likely will not make an attempt (Chan, 1995). One key to suicide resistance among these youth is the fact that they have powerful reasons for wanting to live.

It is worth reflecting on the reasons that do not seem to weigh strongly against suicide, as well as those that do. For example, it may be tempting to try to prevent suicide by emphasizing religious and moral beliefs, but it is more effective to direct attention to all the life experiences that lie ahead and the other reasons frequently cited by the Hong Kong teenagers, as well as by suicidal college students in the United States whose curiosity about and hopes for the future were their main reasons for not making a lethal attempt (Jobes & Mann, 1999). Inquiries into suicidal thought among young people should be balanced by inquiries into the hopes and values they hold that can be fulfilled only by overcoming challenges and growing into a rewarding adult life.

Do Children Commit Suicide?

Despite all of the attention given in recent years to youth suicide, very little has been directed to those who are even younger. It has often been assumed that few, if any, children commit suicide. This assumption has been coming under increasing critical scrutiny. In fact, there is now enough concern about childhood suicide to have prompted the writing of *Suicide Prevention in Schools* (Leenaars & Wenckstern,

TABLE 7-4

The 10 Most Important and 10 Least Important Reasons for Living, According to Chinese (Hong Kong) Adolescents

Most Important	*Least Important*
1. Courage to face life	1. Religious beliefs forbidding
2. Wanting to experience life	2. Being a coward, "no guts"
3. Not fair to leave parents by themselves	3. Fear of the unknown
4. Desire to live	4. Only God has right to take life
5. Not wanting to hurt family	5. Could not decide how to do it
6. Wanting to grow together with friends	6. Method would not work
7. Finding other solutions	7. Fear of going to hell
8. Having many things to do	8. Fear of method failure
9. Finding a purpose in life	9. Being thought of as weak
10. Learning to adjust and cope	10. Being morally wrong

Source: Adapted from Chan (1995) N = 277.

1991b) and other contributions to this topic. As we will see in Chapter 10, children do think about death, and it is no secret that children also think about the uncertainties and frustrations of life. Mishara (1999) has recently found that third graders have a clear understanding of suicide and that even younger children realize that people can and do take their own lives. We should not be entirely surprised that suicide makes its occasional appearance during the grade-school years and, more rarely, even during the preschool years. However, some people categorically deny that any person under the age of 13 or 14 could possibly intend to kill himself or herself.

> Adults prefer to believe that children do not commit suicide. It seems inconceivable that children could become so desperate and suffer so much at their young age that they would choose death over life. Guilt and anxiety make us blind to the truth, even when it cries out to us. We are also blinded by false perceptions about childhood. (Orbach, 1988, p. 23)

Israel Orbach and his colleagues have conducted a series of studies on "children who don't want to live." Orbach has identified a typical progression toward a potentially lethal suicide attempt.

> The process starts with a harmless attempt, by which children can assess the effect it has on their surroundings. At the same time, this attempt rep-

resents a test of their ability to cope with their fear of death. A second attempt often follows the first—especially if there is only a minimal response from the social environment. This second attempt is a little more bold and dangerous, and has more serious consequences. (1988, p. 27)

Orbach reports that angry parents have sometimes challenged their children to try harder to kill themselves the next time. And that is just what some children proceed to do. The observations made by Orbach and his colleagues indicate that children often give a number of verbal and nonverbal messages about their desperation and their intent before making a lethal suicide attempt. All too often, adults simply do not believe that the children mean what they say. His findings are consistent with those of Mishara, who notes that few young children report having discussed suicide with adults.

Detection of and response to suicidal thoughts and actions in childhood become even more important when we realize that this is also the foundation from which many suicides in adult life originate. For example, a young child who considers himself or herself unwanted and unloved may have thought of suicide repeatedly and even made one or more attempts that escaped notice. In adolescence or young adulthood, this person may encounter new experiences of rejection and disappointment that resonate with the earlier anxiety and self-destructive tendencies. This child whose suicidal orientation was ignored years before, may become part of the suicide statistics in adolescence or the early adult years.

The development of suicidal behavior in children and adults follows the same general pattern. This should not be surprising, because all suicidal adults were once children. The earlier phases of this pattern include a sense of intolerable pressure from the family, a depressed attitude, and various coping attempts that do not work very well and that result in accumulated frustrations and a loss of self-confidence. If this stressful situation is not altered, the idea of suicide appears and the child or adult now attempts to cope through one or more types of self-destructive behavior. If others do not respond in a helpful and effective manner, the individual feels increasing pressure and a sense of failure that confirms the feeling that suicide is the only solution. One further frustration, one further disappointment, one further loss or threatened loss of a relationship may be enough to convert the suicidal orientation into lethal action. Self-destructive behavior therefore can be seen as a process that is often set into motion as early as childhood but may claim its casualty at any later developmental level as well.

Do children commit suicide? In returning to this question, we must reply, "Yes, sometimes. But it is just as important to recognize that suicidal orientations may develop early in childhood and have their fatal outcomes later in life." Having faced this harsh reality, we are in a better position to be helpful both to the children who are at particular risk for development of a suicidal orientation and to the troubled families whose own anxieties are represented in the child's distress. Furthermore, there is much to work with in attempting to prevent the establishment of a self-destructive process. As Orbach and others have observed, even children who are experiencing high levels of stress have a desire to grow, to flourish, *to live*. Given understanding, protection, and caring relationships, many of those at risk for self-destruction can embrace instead the alternative of life.

Suicide among Elderly People

We left Max staring at his newly purchased handgun, wondering whether that was the way to solve his problems. Elderly white men remain the people most vulnerable to suicide. Since 1990, the largest increase in the suicide rate has been among people 85 years of age and older; furthermore, as already noted, there is a worldwide tendency for rising suicide rates among elders. The rates among white men increase from middle age onward. However, despite this vulnerability, suicide among the elderly often fails to receive sufficient attention. The victim may have been socially isolated for some time before death, or the community may be less disturbed by the act than when a young person is involved (Kastenbaum, 1995). Nevertheless, suicide in later life represents not only the premature death of a fellow citizen but also an implicit commentary on the place of elderly people in the United States. What is to be said about the current status of "the American dream" if, after a long life of responsible contributions, an elder finds himself or herself in a nightmare that suggests suicide as the only solution?

The presence of physical illness and other negative realities does not necessarily make self-destruction the plan of choice. My colleagues and I have worked with many older people who had reason to despair and to prefer the prospect of death over the harsh realities of life. Often these people were able to draw upon their own personal resources and find the strength and will to live within a relatively short time. The key in some cases was a short reprieve from a stressful situation or objective changes to improve their quality of life; in other cases, it was a therapeutic alliance and counseling. Stress and despair can be experienced at any age—and the same is true of recovery. Several other findings about suicide in later life follow:

1. *The major demographic risk factors include being white, male, over the age of 65, living alone, and residing in either a rural area or a transient inner city zone* (Osgood, 1992).
2. *Social isolation is a theme that runs through most of the risk factors.* Suicide rates for the elderly tend to be higher in areas in which divorce rates and interstate migration are also higher.
3. *Depression increases the risk of suicide* (McIntosh, 1994). This is *not* the same as concluding that depression causes suicide; people cope with

depression in many ways other than suicide. Furthermore, not all suicidal elders show an obvious picture of clinical depression.

4. *Physical illness is a major risk factor for suicide among elderly adults* (Richman, 1991). Again, it should be kept in mind that (1) many elders cope with physical problems without becoming depressed, and (2) depression may occur without a basis in significant physical problems.

5. *Alcohol use increases the risk of suicide among elderly adults.* Alcohol abuse is approximately twice as frequent among suicidal adults than in the population in general. Increased use of alcohol is often intended to ward off depression and suicidal thoughts, and it may succeed in doing so for a while. Eventually, however, alcohol and/or drug abuse tends to increase the probability of suicide because of the impact on social isolation, health, and clarity of thought.

6. *Failure to cope with stress increases the risk of suicide among elderly adults.* Persistent stress syndromes (*see also Chapter 11*) are likely to develop for individuals whose coping responses are overwhelmed by the life changes and crises often encountered in the later adult years. A lack of adequate social support systems can further expose the individual's limitations. Once it has started, the psychophysiological stress reaction is often difficult to terminate and itself can become a major stressor, sapping the individual's strength and producing anxiety.

7. *Loss of relationships increases the risk of suicide among elderly adults.* Bereavement and divorce are the most common types of relationship loss for elderly adults. Some older adults also experience a particularly harrowing kind of relationship loss when the spouse is afflicted with Alzheimer's disease or a similar dementing condition. The spouse is still there, but the familiar and mutually supportive relationship has altered radically.

The Lethality of Suicide Attempts in the Later Adult Years

Although there are important similarities in the self-destructive patterns of young and elderly adults, there are important differences as well. In general, older adults are at even greater risk for death when they make a suicide attempt.

The ratio of suicide attempts to deaths is much smaller for elders, especially males. Overall, elders have a 4:1 ratio of attempts to completions, as compared with young adults' ratio of 20:1. Several factors contribute to this difference:

- Both elderly males and females most often choose firearms as their mode of suicide (McIntosh, 1994). This is true for adults in general in the United States. However, the proportion of firearms use is even higher among elders: about three of every four elderly male suicides involve the use of firearms.

- Elders are less likely than younger adults to give clear warnings of their suicidal intent. This characteristic is particularly true of males, who seem less inclined to share their personal feelings and also seem to have a more limited social support network, especially if they live alone and have little participation in community activities.

- Elders are less likely to recover from suicide attempts that produce serious trauma but from which a younger person might survive.

Preventing Suicide in the Later Adult Years

We have already seen that misguided attitudes and assumptions have served as barriers to detecting and preventing suicidal orientations in children. The details are different, but the general situation is similar in the case of elderly adults. Many people remain so anxious about the prospect of their own aging that they feel that depression, helplessness, and suicide are only to be expected. For example, the middle-aged person who says "I'll kill myself before I get that old!" is not likely to be very helpful in understanding and preventing self-destructive behaviors of the elders in their lives. Our first priority, then, is to come to terms with our futures—those older people we ourselves will be one of these days, if we are fortunate enough.

If the motivation is there, we can do much to detect high suicide risk in elders and to help provide alternatives. Physicians and other human service providers often have interactions with elders who are one step away from suicide. Studies have found that up to half of the people who commit suicide had seen a physician within a month of their death (Murphy, 1995). It is probable that elders are overrepresented in this group because relatively few physicians are trained in detecting depression and suicidality. Increased awareness of this risk on the part of service providers can result in timely interventions.

Older adults who are at elevated risk for suicide often show several of the characteristics identified in Table 7.5. Again, we would not want to use this information in a mechanical manner, but rather to guide our further observations and interactions.

There is reason for optimism in the prevention of elder suicide. By and large, people do not reach their later adult years unless they have both resilience and skill. Max, for example, had demonstrated competence in school, work, and interpersonal relationships throughout his life. He had overcome many challenges, savored some successes, and adjusted to some disappointments.

The death of his wife was a severe loss to him. Along with the sorrow there was the question of how—and why—he should go on with his life. After several coping attempts had failed, Max decided to try a solution that is deeply engrained in the tradition of this nation: when all else fails, kill somebody (*see Chapter 8.*) However, after staring at that gun, Max realized that this was not his solution. Just as he was not a person who was made for sitting around in the sun, so he was not a person who dealt with problems in an explosive and violent manner. And so Max went on to find another solution.

He returned to his old neighborhood and drifted naturally over to the library that had been his home away from home in childhood. Max soon became first an unofficial assistant to the librarian and, eventually, a person whom the children and youth of the neighborhood sought out for advice and companionship. Max not only *felt* useful and connected again—he *was* useful and connected. He took the money he received from selling the gun and plunked it into the library's fund to help low income children purchase their own books.

We have been focusing on elder male suicide because this is the subpopulation that is most at risk. As we have seen, though, elderly women also tend to use lethal means when they attempt suicide. It is also probable that a large but undocumented number of elderly women hasten their deaths by not looking after their health and gradually withdrawing from social contact. Deaths of this type are known as *subintentional*. They are not certified as suicides, but those who are familiar with the situation often believe that the person contributed to the death in a significant although indirect manner.

Suicide among Native Americans

The white man's conquest and development of the New World was catastrophic to the ancestors of many of those now known as Native Americans. Although the infamous quotation "The only good Indian is a dead Indian" was in fact a misquote, there is no denying that American history expressed a genocidal component in some of its dealings with the nation's original inhabitants. It is equally troubling to think that the present high suicide rate among Native Americans is a continuing part of that heritage. Whatever the actual connection might be, it is a matter of record that genocide has in fact been followed by high rates of suicide.

The basic facts about suicide among Native Americans follow (McIntosh, 1993).

1. *The rate is exceptionally high.* Native Americans as a total group have the highest suicide rate of any ethnic or racial subpopulation.

TABLE 7-5
Elderly Adults: Ten Indicators of Possible Suicide Risk

1. Sad, dejected, or emotionally flat mood
2. Stooped, withdrawn, fatigued, lack of eye contact
3. Careless in grooming and dress
4. Restlessness, handwringing, constant motor activity
5. Inattention, lack of concentration, losing the thread of the conversation
6. Loss of appetite/weight
7. Sleep disturbance (insomnia or oversleeping)
8. Loss of interest in activities that previously were pleasurable
9. Loss of interest in other people
10. Preoccupation with vague and shifting physical complaints

Celebrating one's own cultural heritage and personal skills provides a strong counterforce against suicidality.

2. *Tribal differences in suicide rates are large and also vary over time.*
3. *Alcohol is a major factor in Native American suicide.* Although there is a strong association between alcohol and suicide for the general population, it is even stronger with Native Americans. Alcohol abuse has been related to high unemployment, prejudice, cultural conflict, and the loss of heritage, among other factors. Suicide is clearly a symptom of social stress and disorganization as well as a tragic outcome for the individual and his or her survivors.
4. *Unlike the general population, Native Americans are more at risk for suicide in youth than in old age.*

Rates for elderly suicide are low; the peak occurs in the late teens and twenties.

Thus, suicide is an even greater problem among Native Americans than in the general population. The average life expectancy remains relatively low for Native Americans. This unfortunate fact contributes to a youth-oriented structure in the population, and young Native Americans are the most susceptible to overt self-destruction. (If a life foreshortened by alcoholism is to be regarded as a form of indirect suicide, many older Native Americans must also be counted as victims.)

Data recently made available by the National Vital Statistics System identify the leading causes of death among American and Alaskan natives from 1993–1996. It is alarming to see that suicide not only is among the leading causes of death, but it also becomes salient very early in life. Suicide is the second leading cause of death for 10–14 year olds and remains in that position from ages 15–34. The lives of many American and Alaskan natives end in self-destruction just when life should be opening up with all of its opportunities and discoveries. Suicide is still the sixth leading cause of death in the 35–44 age range, but it becomes uncommon through the rest of the age range. Those who survive into their later adult years seem to be highly resistant to suicide—quite the opposite of the lifespan risk for suicide among whites.

It should be emphasized that suicide, motor vehicle accidents, and other forms of violent death did not become a salient part of Native American societies until they were exposed to prolonged and overwhelming stress and deprivation (Kozak, 1991). Programs that provide realistic opportunities for youth to pursue their goals and dreams and that strengthen tribal values are likely to result in a sharp decrease in suicide.

High-Risk Situations for Suicide

The risk of suicide is increased in some situations. Here are several important examples. Again, we keep in mind that these useful generalizations should not be substituted for knowledge of the way particular people deal with particular circumstances.

1. *People with HIV/AIDS are at a higher risk for suicide.* The American Foundation for Suicide Prevention estimates that the risk of suicide is up to twenty times greater for people with HIV/AIDS than for the general population. Some people become suicidal when they first learn of their HIV infection, others when HIV converts into AIDS symptoms. The suicide decision is sometimes made in a mental state compromised by the illness and/or by the use of drugs and alcohol. Nevertheless, much of the suicidality in people with HIV/AIDS has been based on a rational assessment of the situation—the feared loss of function and increase in suffering (Werth, 1995). We should not overlook the grief experienced by many people with HIV/AIDS who have lost friends from the same disease. Although suicide is a salient thought for many people with HIV/AIDS (Beckerman, 1995), many respond positively to counseling and social support.

The feeling of being isolated and rejected can contribute more to suicidality than the disease itself. As is the case with other life crises, people with HIV/AIDS often come to terms with their situation and continue to live meaningful and useful lives, and the improved survival outlook for people with HIV/AIDS in recent years is another protection against suicide.

2. *Gambling is associated with a higher risk of suicide.* The connection between gambling and suicide has often been observed. Solid data now confirm this relationship.

Las Vegas, the premier U.S. gambling setting, displays the highest levels of suicide in the nation, both for residents of Las Vegas and for visitors to that setting. In general, visitors to and residents of major gambling communities experience elevated suicide rates. In Atlantic City, abnormally high suicide levels for visitors and residents appeared only after gambling casinos were opened. The findings do not seem to result merely because gaming settings

The facts are clear: Suicide rates are higher in cities with major gambling enterprises.

Children who are bullied at school are more likely to become depressed and suicidal.

attract suicidal individuals. (Phillips, Welty, & Smith, 1997, p. 373)

The many advertisements I have seen for Las Vegas and other gambling destinations seem to have neglected mentioning that along with "gaming" (presumably a more positive word than "gambling") and entertainment, one also has the opportunity to become more suicidal. Is it socially responsible to glamorize and promote "gaming" when the link with suicide has been so clearly established? Or does social responsibility no longer matter?

3. *Schoolyard bullies and peer harassment increase suicidality.* Children and teens who have been pushed around, insulted, threatened, and mocked by classmates not only feel miserable as a result, but also are at a higher risk for depression and suicide (Rigby & Slee, 1999). This situation becomes even more dangerous when the victim feels that he or she has no social support from family, teachers, or friends. Bully and harassment victims report more suicide ideation. Additionally, you may have noticed

that youth who commit acts of violence (such as the Columbine High School killings) feel that they have been rejected and mocked by classmates and/or teachers. There is every reason to take notice of bullying and peer harassment, act to prevent this kind of behavior, and offer social support to the victims.

4. *"Suicide by cop" has become an established term because so many incidents have occurred around the nation.* The term was introduced in 1983 by Dr. Karl B. Harris, Chief Medical Examiner for the County of Los Angeles. He discovered many instances in which an armed suicidal person confronted a police officer in such a way as to force the officer to shoot in self-defense. In these cases, it was later discovered that the suicidal person's gun was unloaded or nonfunctioning; the idea all along had been to force the officer to engage in the police version of assisted suicide. This type of confrontation is very stressful for the officers, both at the time and afterward. A creative and effective alternative has been developed by some law enforcement units:

When deputies in the Antelope Valley were confronted earlier this month by an armed man who continued resisting after being shot with "beanbag" rounds, they did an unusual thing for law enforcement officers—they just went away. The man eventually returned home, without harming himself or anyone else. (Blankenstein, 1998)

The phenomenon of suicide by cop is a powerful reminder that we cannot deftly separate individual and societal responses, nor can we keep suicide and homicide in separate categories.

Balancing Individual and Cultural Influences on Suicide

It is obvious that we must keep a balance between individual and sociocultural factors. The realities of everyday life and prospects for the future may differ appreciably for a white, Anglo-Saxon, Protestant undergraduate; an elderly African American widow; and a youth living on a poverty-stricken reservation. The same act of desperation can flow from many sources. Pre-

ventive and interventive efforts will be more effective in some circumstances if they are focused on the individual; in other circumstances, a broader social policy approach may be necessary. We now examine some major cultural and individual influences on suicide.

SOME CULTURAL MEANINGS OF SUICIDE

The act of suicide has been interpreted in many different ways throughout human history. Most of these earlier conceptions are still with us and still busy competing with each other. In addition, we are being faced with relatively new situations, such as persistent vegetative states and the intensified advocacy for "death on demand" and physician-assisted death (*see Chapter 9*). New interpretations of suicide may emerge from the new challenges.

Suicide As Sinful

One of our strongest cultural traditions regards suicide as sinful. This position has been held for

"Suicide by cop" is a situation well known to law enforcement officers.

centuries by defenders of the Judeo-Christian faiths. Catholics, Protestants, and Jews generally have been taught that suicide is morally wrong. Condemnation of suicide has been emphasized by the Catholic Church since the fourth century. But why? What is it about suicide that is so appalling that it must be condemned and discouraged by all the authority that an organized religion can command? St. Augustine helped to establish the Catholic position by crystallizing two fundamental objections to suicide. The first depends upon articles of faith that are not shared by all followers of the Judeo-Christian tradition—namely, that suicide precludes the opportunity to repent of other sins. However, the other objection is based on the sixth commandment: "Thou shalt not kill." Suicide is not exempt from this commandment in St. Augustine's judgment of 426. However, he did have to volunteer some exceptions to his own rule:

> Abraham indeed was not merely deemed guiltless of cruelty, but was even applauded for his piety, because he was ready to slay his son in obedience to God, not to his own passion.... Samson, too, who drew down the house on himself and his foes together, is justified only on this ground, that the Spirit who wrought wonders by him had given him secret instructions to do this. (1971, I:xxii)

Perhaps the most uncomfortable exception granted by St. Augustine concerns Jepththah's execution of his daughter because he had promised God he would sacrifice "whatever first met him as he returned victorious from the battle." Although very influential, this church father's pronouncement has troubled some believers through the century by ruling against suicide yet justifying a father's killing of his daughter in order to keep his own reckless promise.

In the thirteenth century, St. Thomas Aquinas (1279/1971) reaffirmed Augustine's conclusion but added another objection. He argued that God and only God has the power to grant life and death. Suicide is sinful because it represents a revolt against the ordained order of the universe. The self-murderer is engaging in a sin of pride, of self-assertion in a realm meant to be ruled by deity. This point has also been advocated by a man whose ideas of human nature and society exerted great influence over the founding fathers of the United States. John Locke refused to include self-destruction as one of the inherent liberties: "Every one...is bound to preserve himself, and not to quit his station willfully." A person who abandons his station thereby transgresses the law of nature (1690/1971, p. 26). According to Locke, as the handiwork of God, we are possessions that are not at liberty to dispose of ourselves. This fierce moral condemnation of suicide allows few, if any, exceptions. Great suffering does not entitle a person to suspend the "law of nature" and take life into his or her own hands.

Individuals who accept this cultural tradition are likely to feel that there is more to lose by suicide. The survivors have more to lose as well. The suicide of a family member could bring a strong sense of shame as well as the feelings of loss and grief that accompany bereavement from death produced by other causes. Suicide, in other words, can be a moral stigma not only for the individual but also for those who become contaminated with it by association.

Condemnation of suicide as a violation of the sixth commandment, however, is difficult to square with the tradition of warfare and violent death that has been not only condoned but at times actively pursued by those who see themselves as defenders of the faith. Religious wars and the persecution of heretics repeatedly have violated the edict, "Thou shalt not kill." As Jacques Choron observes, "during the Middle Ages, mass suicide was frequent among persecuted sects of Christian heretics and non-Christian minorities.... The category of non-Christians included Moslems and Jews, who refused to be converted to Christianity and preferred to commit suicide" (1972 pp. 25–26). Violation of the sixth commandment therefore led directly to suicide. The persecuted victim might be regarded as a sinner for committing suicide, but the persecutors, acting in the name of their religion, would not be sinners if they either threatened the dissidents to the point of suicide or killed them outright.

The image of the crucifixion, so powerful in the Christian tradition, is a sacrifice of suffering unto death with strong suicidal connotations. Some of the early Christian thinkers, in fact, regarded the death of Jesus as suicide (Alvarez,

1970), as did deeply reflecting Christians of later times, such as John Donne (1646/1977). Choron (1972) suggests that suicide through martyrdom became all too tempting to those who tried to follow along Christ's pathway. It was glorious to die as a martyr! The Church found it advisable to protect some true believers from themselves, to reduce the attractiveness of death now that immortality had been proclaimed, and to discourage widespread emulation of the early martyrs.

Admiration of martyrdom has persisted, however, and so has the moral condemnation of suicide. (But keep in mind that martyrdom is not identical with suicide in general; it is a self-chosen death that occurs in a particular way in the service of a particular cause or idea and requires the "cooperation" of others.) As both Alvarez and Choron remind us, the Old and New Testaments do not directly prohibit suicide, nor do they even seem to find this action particularly remarkable.

Other influential voices within the Christian tradition have offered alternative interpretations. For example, philosopher David Hume reasoned along these lines:

> I am not obliged to do a small good to society at the expense of a great harm to myself; why then should I prolong a miserable existence...? If upon account of age and infirmities, I may lawfully resign any office, and employ my time altogether in fencing against these calamities, and alleviating as much as possible the miseries of my future life; why may I not cut short these miseries at once by an action which is no more prejudicial to society? (1826/1990, p. 43)

Suicide As Criminal

Is suicide a sin or a *crime*? The intertwining of church and state once made it easy to regard suicide as both criminal and sinful. Even Locke, with his radical ideas of equality and liberty, spoke of the person who would lift his hand against himself as an "offender," one who is "dangerous to mankind" and commits "a trespass against the whole species." Certainly the sinful and the criminal interpretations of suicide have something in common. Both regard self-destruction as a willful violation of the basic ties that relate the individual to the universe.

Through the years, however, the civil and divine realms of authority have become more independent of each other. This has also strengthened the view that suicide is a crime but not necessarily a sin. Suicide as crime has been an influential tradition up to the present day, although it has always been accompanied by dissident voices. The word *suicide* itself seems first to have entered use in about the middle of the seventeenth century. The earliest citation given by the *Oxford English Dictionary* attributes the following statement to Walter Charleton in 1651: "To vindicate ones self from...inevitable Calamity, by Suicide is not...a Crime."

Suicide is more likely to be punished by human authority when it is interpreted as a crime as well as a sin. If it were "only" a sin, perhaps answering to God would be quite a sufficient consequence. As crimes, however, suicide attempts have often brought severe punishment on top of the moral condemnation. Punishment has included torture, defamation, and impoverishment. Surviving family members have sometimes been punished also by having their possessions confiscated by the state.

The interpretation of suicide as crime is waning. Criminal laws either have been erased from the books or are not vigorously enforced. Another indication of attitude change can be seen in life insurance policies. It was once common for insurance companies to treat suicide as though it were a special kind of crime—one intended to defraud the underwriters. It is now possible to have death benefits associated with suicide, although with certain limitations and restrictions built into the contract.

Decriminalization of suicide is based upon the realization that such penalties have not served as effective deterrents, and that few people were willing to enforce the laws. It may also be in keeping with a social climate in which the meanings of life and death are being reevaluated in general. Law enforcement agencies have now become effective frontline resources for suicide prevention in some communities, liberated now from the legal responsibility of having to look upon the attempter as a criminal. Suicide remains on the books as a felony only in parts of Kentucky and South Carolina, old laws that do not seem to have been enforced in many years.

Suicide As Weakness or Madness

Some people who commit suicide can be classified as psychotic or severely disturbed, but others cannot. Individuals with diagnosed psychiatric conditions have a higher suicide rate than does the population at large, and people diagnosed as depressive psychotics tend to have the highest rates of completed suicides. If we are concerned with the probability of suicide in very large populations, mental and emotional disorders are relevant variables to consider—they can help us a little to identify people at risk and to make some predictions. However, psychiatric disorder is far from satisfactory as an explanation or predictor of suicide. Even when a psychopathological state is present, however, this itself does not explain, let alone motivate, the action. Many people go through disturbed periods without attempting suicide. It would be tempting to believe that a person has to be crazy to commit suicide, but this is simply not true.

What about the related explanation that suicide is the outcome of *weakness*? This view picked up additional support as a result of the survival-of-the-fittest doctrine (Darwin, 1859/1971). Since then, many groups have interpreted Charles Darwin's theory of evolution in terms of their own values and only secondarily on the scientific evidence as such. Those who favor a rough-and-tumble, highly competitive struggle for power have tried to rationalize these tactics by analogy with the so-called survival-of-the-fittest principle. This "social Darwinism" approach is meant to justify the raw pursuit and exploitation of power. Those who fall by the wayside just don't have "it." Seen in these terms, suicide is simply one of the ways in which a relatively weak member of society loses out in the junglelike struggle; suicide is one of nature's ways to preserve the species by weeding out the less fit. This interpretation is not necessarily one that would have been endorsed by Darwin himself, who had little control over how society chose to use or abuse his ideas.

This position is not taken quite as openly today as it was in the heyday of rugged individualism and naive social applications of evolutionary theory. Nevertheless, we can still see it in operation. "If you can't stand the heat, get out of the kitchen!" was one type of comment heard after a spectacular suicide in New York City, when a ranking executive of a major international corporation leaped to his death from offices high above Manhattan. Media coverage emphasized the length of time that his fallen body tied up traffic and other circumstantial aspects of the death. Little attention was given, then or later, to his state of mind, the meaning of his suicide, or the impact upon survivors. Other executives around the nation commented off the record that some people just can't take the gaff. There was a note of pride in such comments: "I am strong enough to cope with adversity; that other fellow wasn't." Is this a justified interpretation, or simply a way of covering our own fears and asserting our own superiority?

Suicide As "The Great Death"

The Buddhist tradition in China and Japan includes the image of *daishi*, which translates roughly as "The Great Death." Through their own example, Zen masters have shown how a person might pass admirably from this life. The discipline and devotion of the master appealed to the warrior. The *samurai* would seek *daishi* on the battlefield. This influence remained strong enough through the centuries to enlist the self-sacrifices of *kamikaze* pilots in World War II (although some of these young men still had their doubts about carrying through missions that meant almost certain death).

Suicide itself has been honored as a form of *daishi*. *Seppuku* is a traditional form of suicide in Japan, better known in the West as *hara-kiri*. The act itself consists of disembowelment, usually with a sword. In some situations, this form of death has served as an honorable alternative to execution. A person condemned to death would be given the privilege of becoming his or her own executioner. Voluntary *seppuku*, by contrast, might flow from a number of different motives on the part of the individual (e.g., to follow a master into the great beyond or to protest an injustice). Placing your entire life at the disposal of an honorable or noble motive was a much-admired action. In our own time, the self-immolation of Buddhist monks in Southeast Asia to emphasize their religious and political protests has also made a deep impression on observers.

Ritualized, honorable suicide of this "Great Death" type seems to integrate various levels of existence. By opening his abdomen, the individual is showing the world that his center of being (thought to be located there) is pure and undefiled. Specifically, the individual puts the sword to the *hara*, the (imagined) locus of breath control, and breath is regarded in many cultures as closely akin to both life itself and divinity. The act therefore involves a network of physiological, individual, social, and religious referents.

The association of suicide with desirable death has not been limited to Asia. It was one of the characteristic themes of the ancient Greeks and Romans:

> In Alexandria in the third century B.C. the philosopher Hegesias taught that life was so fleeting and full of cares that death was man's happiest lot. He lectured so eloquently that…many of his listeners committed suicide. Two centuries later, during the reign of Cleopatra, herself a suicide, there seems to have existed…a school that taught the best ways of committing suicide. Some "students" were rumored to have killed themselves during sumptuous banquets. Such excess anticipated the Roman Empire. For if the Greeks rationalized suicide, the Romans made it a fashion, even a sport. (Colt, 1991, p. 148)

And so the "same" action that later was considered a sin by some people and a crime by others was regarded by Romans of the classical period as perhaps the most noble and glorious thing a man (sic) could do.

Suicide As a Rational Alternative

The belief that suicide can bring a glorious death has a more subdued echo in another cultural tradition, also dating from ancient times. This is the attitude that suicide is an acceptable, rational alternative to continued existence. It is a view often conditioned by adverse circumstances. "Life is not always preferable to death" is the thought here. Individuals do not destroy themselves in hope of thereby achieving a noble

postmortem reputation or a place among the eternally blessed. Instead they wish to subtract themselves from a life whose quality seems a worse evil than death.

Renaissance thinkers often praised death as the place of refuge from the cruelties and disappointments of life. Erasmus (1509) is but one of the eminent humanists who observed what a distance there is between our aspirations for the human race and the failings discovered on every side in daily life. The newly awakened spirit of hope and progress soon became shadowed by a sense of disappointment and resignation that, it sometimes seemed, only death could possibly swallow.

Much earlier in history there is also evidence that the harshness of life made suicide an appealing option to many. Stoicism, a philosophical position that was enunciated in ancient Athens and Rome and has since become virtually a synonym for rational control, was in actuality

> …a last defense against the murderous squalor of Rome itself. When those calm heroes looked around them they saw a life so unspeakable, cruel, wanton, corrupt, and apparently unvalued that they clung to their ideas of reason much as the Christian poor used to cling to their belief in Paradise and the goodness of God despite, or because of, this misery of their lives on this earth. Stoicism, in short, was a philosophy of despair; it was not a coincidence that Seneca, who was its most powerful and influential spokesman, was also the teacher of the most vicious of all Roman emperors, Nero. (Alvarez, 1970, p. 66)

From ancient philosophers to contemporary existentialists, from victims of human cruelty and injustice to people whose lives just didn't seem to work out, a tradition has been maintained in which suicide is regarded as an option available to the reasonable person.

There have been many times in human history, misery was so general and the outlook so grim that it seemed natural to think seriously of suicide. The horrors of the plague years, for example, intensified by warfare and general social disorganization, led many to question the value of continued life. Nevertheless, careful attention should be given to the question of what it is that might make a suicide "rational." Brandt (1990) observes that what might seem rational from the standpoint of the individual contemplating suicide might not seem rational from another person's perspective. Furthermore, it can be difficult to determine whether or not a person is thinking in a rational manner when contemplating suicide—and impossible to do so after the fact.

The Judeo-Christian tradition has in general advocated life. There is intrinsic value in life. We should not dispose of life, no matter what the provocation or temptation. This message has been imperfectly delivered. At times it has been contradicted by actions of the true believers themselves. Nevertheless, enough of this spirit has come across to establish a challenging issue for all of us: Is life to be valued and fostered under all conditions because it has primary and intrinsic value? Or is the value of life relative to the circumstances? We encounter this issue repeatedly today, for example, in the prospect of health care rationing and the spectrum of right-to-die decisions.

A POWERFUL SOCIOLOGICAL THEORY OF SUICIDE

Emile Durkheim proposed a comprehensive sociological theory of self-destruction in 1897. *Le Suicide* (1897/1951) became a cornerstone for the emerging science of sociology and remains one of the most influential theories of suicide in our own day. It says much for Durkheim's perspicacity that his ideas and findings continue to command the attention of those who study and seek to prevent suicide.

His approach was audacious for its time. Suicide was not a matter of the individual's relationship to God, nor were moral values the primary focus. Instead, suicide could be viewed most accurately at a distance, and by a cool observer who was more interested in the overall pattern of self-destruction than in any particular life and death.

The Importance of Social Integration

Why, then, do people kill themselves? If we insisted upon a simple answer, Durkheim would point toward society. He then would acquaint us with the idea of *social integration*. All individuals are more or less integrated into their societies. Suicide risk depends much upon the extent of social integration between individual and society.

The culture itself shows more or less *social solidarity*, or cohesiveness. Society may be stable, consistent, and supportive, or it may be falling apart under stress. The individual, then, may be weakly or strongly integrated into a high- or low-solidarity culture, as shown in Table 7.6.

The crucial index for suicide can be found in the interaction between integration and solidarity. How much does the culture control the individual? Both a weakly integrated person in a cohesive society (low-high in Table 7.6) and a person trapped in a disorganized culture (high-low) are in difficulty because there is not enough group control. And with lessened group control, there is a heightened possibility of suicide. However, suicide can also result from too much control by society. Durkheim's theory, then, invites attention to both the cohesiveness of society and the social integration of any particular individual.

Collective representations is another important Durkheimian concept. All cultures have collective representations that convey the spirit or personality of the culture as a whole: the guiding themes, moods, or emotional climate. Under certain circumstances this group spirit can turn morose and self-destructive. This means that individuals who are well integrated into the culture may be especially vulnerable. They are more likely to absorb the pessimistic mood of the larger society and may act it out with fatal results. This aspect of Durkheim's theory suggests that the very forces that should hold a society together

TABLE 7-6

Types of Connection between Individual and Society

Individual's integration into society	Society's solidarity
High	High
High	Low
Low	High
Low	Low

can take on the opposite character and lead to what we might call *sociocide*. The mass suicide and homicide in Jonestown, Guyana, that resulted in the eradication of a unique community and more than 900 lives is one potent reminder that the sociocide concept should not be neglected.

Four Types of Suicide

Most of the attention to Durkheim today focuses on the four types of suicide he delineated, each thought to represent a distinctive relationship between individual and society. *The egoistic suicide is committed by people who do not have enough involvement with society. They are not under sufficient cultural control.* The executive who literally fell from on high is one probable example. Individuals whose talents, inclinations, or stations in life place them in a special category, relatively immune from ordinary social restrictions, are especially vulnerable to egoistic suicide. The celebrity in the entertainment field, the creative artist who follows his or her own star, the person in a relatively distinct or unique role, all may go their own personal ways until they can no longer be reached effectively by cultural constraints. Again, the recent example of Kurt Cobain comes immediately to mind. Intellectuals are also common in the category of egoistic suicide. They are more likely than others to pick up those collective representations described as sociocidic. Sensitive to underlying currents of melancholy and despair in the culture and, in a sense, lost in their own thoughts, they have little outside themselves to grasp when the suicide impulse arises.

Very different indeed is the *altruistic* suicide. Already mentioned were such examples as the *seppuku* tradition and the *kamikaze* combat death. *Suttee*, (Sati), the now-illegal Indian practice of a widow's giving her life at her husband's funeral, is another dramatic example. According to Durkheim, *altruistic suicide occurs when the individual has an exaggerated or excessive concern for the community.* This is usually the strongly integrated person in a high solidarity culture (high-high, Table 7.6). Altruistic suicides tend to be less common in Western societies but often are admired when they do occur. The soldier who volunteers for a "suicide mission" (one in which death is al-

most certain) in order to protect comrades or achieve a military objective can be considered both a hero and an altruistic suicide.

The third type is called *anomic suicide. Social breakdown is reflected most directly in the anomic suicide.* Here it is less a question of the individual's integration with society and more one of society's ability to function as it should. People are let down, cast adrift by the failure of social institutions. Unemployment is an important example: a person thrown out of work has lost a significant tie to society and through society's doing, not his or her own. Bad times, unemployment, suicide—a predictable sequence. Similarly, a person forced to leave his or her occupation because of age may enter an anomic condition that leads to suicide. When the rupture between individual and society is sudden and unexpected, the probability of suicide is thought to be especially high. This situation arises, for example, when the death of an important person drastically reduces the survivor's place in society.

For many years, this set of three suicide types dominated the picture. Recently, however, more attention has been given to a fourth type, which Durkheim introduced but treated more as a curiosity: *fatalistic suicide.* A person may experience too much control by society, he suggested. *A culture that stifles and oppresses some of its members may thereby encourage fatalistic suicide.* The individual sees all opportunities and prospects blocked. Durkheim spoke of slavery as a condition that engenders fatalistic suicide but thought that civilization had put this kind of oppression well into the past. Oppression and subjugation have not disappeared from the human condition, however, as totalitarian regimes continue to manifest themselves throughout the twentieth century.

Both the altruistic and the fatalistic suicide involve excessive control of the individual by society. In altruistic suicide, the individuals appear to share wholeheartedly in the collective representations. They die *for* their people. In fatalistic suicide they die in despair of ever being able to actualize themselves in a culture that affords little opportunity for self-esteem and satisfaction.

We move now from a sociological approach to the individual's own thoughts, motives, and lifestyle as factors in suicide.

SOME INDIVIDUAL MEANINGS OF SUICIDE

Just as the preceding discussion did not exhaust all cultural and sociological meanings of suicide, so this section can only sample some of the individual meanings. The intent is to convey something of the various states of mind with which people approach a suicidal action.

Suicide for Reunion

The loss of a loved one can be experienced as so unbearable that the survivor is tempted to "join" the deceased. Recently-bereaved people often experience the "presence" of the dead. This may be regarded as part of the normal response to the death of a loved person, and it may help to reduce the sense of abandonment. But desperate longing may impel a person to follow the dead all the way to the other side if the relationship has been marked by extreme dependency. "I can't go on without him." "I am not complete without her." "What's to become of me? I can't manage by myself." Many people have feelings of this kind. Sometimes these feelings are accompanied by suicidal thoughts. Reunion fantasies may have some temporary value while bereaved individuals reconstruct their lives, but they can also lead to suicidal actions.

Some sociocultural themes can encourage suicidal reunion fantasies and actions. Heaven is such a delightful place—and it is so miserable here. Death is not real; it is only a portal to eternal life. Insurance advertisements have depicted a deceased husband gazing down with approval from the clouds. Messages of this type encourage a blurring of the distinction between the living and the dead.

Children are particularly vulnerable to reunion fantasies because they are still in the process of attempting to establish their identities as individuals. A parent or older sibling who has "gone off to heaven" has left the survivor with painful feelings of incompleteness and yearning. Some adults remain relatively childlike in their dependency on others and feel very much the same way when separated by death. Suicide to achieve reunion seems most likely when the person lacks a fully developed sense of selfhood, whether because of developmental level or personality constellation; when death has removed a significant source of support; and when there are salient cultural messages that make death appear unreal and the afterlife inviting.

Suicide for Rest and Refuge

Worn down by tribulations, a person may long for a "good rest" or a "secure harbor." This motivation can have many outcomes other than suicide. A vacation far away from the grinding routine may restore energy and confidence. Somebody else may appear on the scene to share the load. Or the vexed and fatigued person may simply drop his or her responsibilities for a while. Alternatives such as these may not work out, however. Life may be experienced as too unrelenting and burdensome. The miracle of an ordinary good night's sleep may seem out of reach as depression deepens. Under such circumstances, the fantasy of a prolonged, uninterrupted sleep may take on a heightened allure. The sleep-death analogy is readily available in America as in most other cultures (*see Chapter 2*). It is tempting to take a few more pills than usual and just drift away.

This attitude toward suicide is also encouraged by individual and cultural tendencies that blur the distinctions between life and death. It falls well within the established cultural style of solving problems by taking something into our mouths (puff on a cigarette; suck on a pipe; swallow pills for headaches, indigestion, any form of distress). People with oral or escapist tendencies dominant in their personalities might be expected to be especially vulnerable to these lures of suicide.

Suicide for Revenge

The lover is rejected. The employee is passed over for promotion. Another child is preferred and pampered. The particular situation is not as important as the feeling of burning resentment and hurt left inside. And it may not have been the first time. Some people repeatedly feel that they are treated unfairly. Their achievements never seem to be recognized. No matter how hard they try, love and appreciation are withheld. Others may not recognize the state of mind with which such a person approaches a situation and how intensely hope and doubt, anger and longing are intermingled.

I felt crushed. Absolutely *crushed*. It was my first really good semester. No incompletes. No withdrawals. All A's and B's. And no "episodes." I kept myself going all semester. I really felt strong and independent. I knew I shouldn't expect too much when I went home, but I guess…I mean I *know* I expected a little appreciation. You know, like maybe Mother just smiling and saying, "Had a good semester, didn't you? I'm happy for you" or "I'm proud of you," though she would never say *that*.

This young woman felt that her achievement passed without notice, that, in fact, the family hardly noticed that she had come back home. Hurt and angry, she decided to get back by making a suicide attempt. If her family would not pay attention when she did something right, maybe they would when she did something wrong. "I wanted to hurt them—and hurt me—just enough." She slashed away at her wrist and arm. The self-wounding seemed to release some of her despair. She had not injured herself seriously, so she wrapped the wounded area in a bulky bandage. Nobody seemed to notice. A few days later, she removed the bandage, exposing the patchwork of fresh scars. There still was no obvious response from the family. Instead, they were enthusiastically anticipating the graduation and upcoming marriage of one of her cousins.

She felt even more crushed and low when she was passed over in the wedding arrangements as well: "I couldn't even be part of somebody else's happiness…I knew that revenge was stupid. But I *felt* like doing something stupid. Listen everybody: you're 100 percent right! I am a stupid person. And here is something really stupid to prove it!" She hurled herself from a rooftop.

I wanted to kill myself then. I think I did. But I also wanted to see the look on their faces when they saw that bloody mess on the sidewalk. I could see myself standing alongside the rest of them, looking at that bloody mess of myself on the sidewalk, and looking at their shocked looks…I didn't think what it would be like if I half-killed myself and had to live with a crushed body. Maybe that was the really stupid part of it.

She survived a suicide attempt that might have been fatal. She was also fortunate in that her injuries did not prove permanently crippling, although she was disabled for months. The physical pain and trauma relieved some of her emotional tension for awhile. Yet she felt that she might "have to" do it again, perhaps "next time for keeps." She did not need a psychologist to suggest that her suicide attempts were efforts to punish others by punishing herself. She was also perfectly capable of pointing out that both attempts had been aimed at forcing either love or remorse from the people who had been letting her down for so long. (At last report, this woman was alive, well, and somehow a stronger person for the ordeals she had undergone.)

The example given here illustrates several other characteristics often shown by a person who is on a self-destructive footing. This woman's fantasy included witnessing the impact of her suicide. *She had divided herself into murderer and victim.* The revenge fantasy would have lost much of its appeal had she recognized that she would never be able to confirm or appreciate the hoped—for impact. People who attempt suicide for reasons other than revenge may also act upon the assumption that, in a sense, they will survive the death to benefit by its effect.

She also experienced some tension release through the self-destructive action itself. It is not unusual for the sight of one's own blood to relieve built-up emotional pressures, if only for a while. Another woman who had slashed her wrists on several occasions told me, "I felt as if I had done something finally. I wasn't paralyzed anymore. I wasn't suffering helplessly. I took action into my own hands, and that felt good." Perhaps the experience of surviving this type of suicide attempt encourages the fantasy that one would still be around to feel better after a fatal attempt as well.

The low self-esteem of many suicide attempters is also evident in the instance given here.

Having a very unfavorable opinion of yourself may be linked with a variety of other motivations in addition to the fantasy of revenge. The combination of the revenge fantasy and low self-esteem appears to be a particularly dangerous one, however.

Suicide As the Penalty for Failure

A victim of suicide may also be the victim of self-expectations that have not been fulfilled. The sense of disappointment and frustration may have much in common with that experienced by a person who seeks revenge through suicide. But here the person holds himself or herself to blame. The judgment "I have failed" is followed by the decision to enact a most severe penalty, one that will make further failures impossible. It is as though the person has been tried and found guilty of a capital offense in his or her own personal court. A completely unacceptable gap is felt between expectations and accomplishment. Some people might take the alternative of lowering expectations to close the gap. Others might give themselves the benefit of the doubt in evaluating their accomplishments ("I really didn't do so badly, everything considered"). And others might keep trying to bring performance up to self-expectations. However, for some people a critical moment arrives when the discrepancy is experienced as too glaring and painful to be tolerated. If something has to be sacrificed, it may be themselves, not the perhaps excessively high standards by which the judgment has been made.

A sense of failure is prominent among many people who take their own lives. The psychological autopsy technique (a special kind of case review) often finds that adult male suicide has occurred after the person was fired, demoted, or passed over for promotion. Female suicides are more often related to real or perceived failures in relationships. Young female suicides often have a history of persistent troubles with men. Those who married and had children had further difficulties in meeting the responsibilities of the maternal role. Older women who took their lives often seemed to have lost or given up most of their social roles and obligations. For women younger than 50 years of age, work failure does not seem to be nearly as salient a factor in suicide as it is for men. Yet often the suicidal person has experienced repeated failure in both personal relationships and work life.

Fortunately, not every person who experiences failure commits suicide. This has led to Warren Breed's (1972) concept of a *basic suicidal syndrome*. Failure plays a critical role but takes on more lethal potential because of its association with the other factors. The syndrome includes *rigidity, commitment, shame,* and *isolation,* as well as *failure* itself. The individual tends to be rigid in that he or she cannot shift from one role or goal to another nor shift level of aspiration. There is only one goal, one level of expectation, and only one way to achieve it. There is also a strong sense of commitment—that is, an intense desire to succeed. The sense of *failure* involves more than performing below self-expectations. It also includes a sense of culpability, of self-blame. The feeling is likely to go beyond guilt. A person who has failed or erred still might have a chance for redemption. The suicidal syndrome is characterized by a generalized sense of *shame*. It is not just that the individual has failed at something—he or she feels totally worthless. "I am no good. Never will be. I am nothing." From all of these interacting factors, the individual may develop a sense of isolation. This syndrome has been found by Breed and his colleagues most conspicuously in white, middle-class adults, both men and women. It does not seem to hold for lower-class African American men who kill themselves.

It is going too far to speak of this as *the* basic suicidal syndrome. Breed readily acknowledges that other patterns are also associated with suicide. Several have already been sketched here. But the high-aspiration, shame-of-failure dynamics revealed by his research do come close to the meaning of suicide for many in American society today. It does not tell us, however, why one person with a basic suicidal syndrome commits suicide while another finds a different solution to his or her problems, nor does it explain how the syndrome develops in the first place. A sequence is at least suggested, though. An individual may not become suicidal all at once, but may start leaning toward an eventual act of self-destruction from an initial rigid setting of high aspirations. This is followed by failure, perhaps repeated failures, to a shamed and despondent pattern of isolating himself or herself from others. Further understanding of this sequence could prove helpful in identifying people who are at particular suicidal risk and providing them with timely assistance.

Suicide As a Mistake

Death may be the intended outcome of an overdose or other self-destructive action, but the person might not die. A serious attempt may fall short of its objective for a number of reasons: an unexpected rescuer may appear on the scene, a determined self-mutilation may happen to miss a vital spot, the overdose may induce vomiting instead of coma, even a loaded gun may fail to fire. The victim may "betray" himself or herself, as in the case of the bridge jumper who survives the often-deadly fall and then swims desperately for life.

But there can be a discrepancy between intention and outcome in the other direction as well. Some people kill themselves even though there is good reason to believe that they did not mean to. The victim had counted on being rescued. The overdose was not supposed to be lethal. Some kind of control or precaution had been exercised to limit the effect, and yet the outcome was death. We cannot automatically conclude that death was the intention any more than we can insist that a person did not intend to commit suicide because the attempt happened to abort. In suicide, as in most other actions, we do not always achieve the outcome we had in mind. The person may have wanted much to live, but a mood, a desperate maneuver, and a misjudgment brought life to a sudden close.

People who work with the suicidal recognize that an individual contemplating a self-destructive act frequently is of two minds. This is the impression, for example, of volunteers who pick up the phone when a call is made to a suicide prevention hot line. The very fact that a person would reach out for human contact in this way suggests some continuing advocacy for life. We have no way of knowing whether all people in a suicidal state of mind experience strong ambiva-

lence. However, many people with suicide on their minds do go back and forth about it, experiencing conflicting life-and-death tugs, even at the same time. A life-threatening act that emerges from a wavering or conflicting intention may itself show some apparent contradictions. Why would she have taken the overdose just a few minutes before her husband was due home if she were entirely of a mind to take her life? And yet she did take the pills, and if her husband happens to be delayed coming home this day, will this gesture have become indeed her final gesture?

Helping people to survive their own mistakes is an important part not only of suicide prevention but also of public health safety in general. Access to lethal means of self-destruction could be made more difficult, for example, thereby placing some time and distance between a momentary intention and a permanent error. Suicide rates dropped significantly in England when coke gas was no longer widely available as an easily available mode of suicide in the home or when its toxicity was reduced.

Mental health specialists have persistently advocated the construction of a lower-span sidewalk for the Golden Gate Bridge, a place that has become known widely as a "suicide shrine." Seiden (1977) followed up on more than 700 people who had approached either the Golden Gate or Bay Bridge with suicidal intentions and who were intercepted by alert citizens or police before completing the action. *Ninety-six percent of these people did not make subsequent fatal attempts, and all of the survivors favored construction of a barrier.* "If there had been a barrier every one of them reports they would have reconsidered" (1977, p. 274). The suicidal intention had been strong but ambivalent. The attempters had given society a chance to catch them before they made a fatal mistake. Seiden adds that "Considering the transitory nature of suicidal crises, the presence of a highly lethal and easily available means such as the bridge must be regarded as equivalent to a loaded gun around the house ready to be used in an impulsive outburst." Society could take a more active role in protecting people from those critical moments when the possibility of making a fatal mistake is on the horizon.

A Psychoanalytical Approach to Suicide

Since life seeks to preserve itself, how could a being actively pursue its own destruction? Freud first suggested (1917/1959) that suicidal individuals, turn a murderous wish against themselves. By destroying themselves, they symbolically destroy the other person. Suicide victims behave as though they are rooting out the inner representation of another person, a representation that might derive from early childhood when the distinction between self and other is incomplete.

Freud did not remain satisfied with this theory. Later (1923/1961) he offered a more philosophical concept: we do not have just one basic instinctual drive. Each of us possesses a pair of drives that have different goals. These are a life instinct, *Eros*, and a death instinct, *Thanatos*. These drives constantly interact in our lives. When Thanatos gains the upper hand, we may engage in a self-destructive action. Vulnerability to suicide exists for all humans because there are so many obstacles in our pathway to gratification and because much of our aggression is forced inward. This twin-instinct theory has not found much application in day-by-day interactions with people at suicidal risk, and researchers have yet to come up with convincing ways of testing the theory. However, the psychoanalytical approach does alert us to the long developmental career that precedes a self-destructive action. The young child, for example, may internalize the negative attitudes conveyed by cruel or thoughtless parents. This burdens the child with a superego that is excessively oriented toward criticism and self-destructive action. Chaotic and inadequate parenting may also jeopardize the child by leaving him or her with a brittle ego that fragments and shatters under pressures that most other people are able to withstand.

Many present-day clinicians and researchers have modified the early psychoanalytical approach to take sociocultural factors more into account. As we have seen, for example, some Native Americans are at exceptionally high risk for suicide and other self-destructive actions. Their low sense of self-esteem comes from the deprivation and discrimination experienced in their contacts with mainstream society. The child is in danger of growing up with a severe lack of confidence in his or her identity and worth, as well as with a tendency to keep aggressive impulses locked up under high pressure until efforts at control fail. This contrasts with the pride and satisfaction a child would have taken in being, for example, a Cheyenne in preceding generations, when the people were independent and possessed a favorable group self-image. These dynamics of low self-esteem and self-directed aggression can lead to fatal outcomes other than suicide, as witnessed by the high alcohol-related death rates on the same reservation. The psychoanalytical approach remains useful today, but it is not necessary to accept every interpretation nor to ignore other relevant factors.

The Descent Toward Suicide

How do people move toward suicide? Are there enough common features to help us identify and understand the states of mind that culminate in a suicide attempt?

Richard A. Heckler (1994) has drawn upon his own experiences as a counselor, as well as the research literature to offer a useful description of the events and states of mind that often precede a suicide attempt. The most basic and common experiences along the way to a possible suicide attempt—and possible death—are the following:

- An experience of loss and/or trauma that deprives the person of emotional support from others and sensitizes the person to the possibility of further losses. These hurtful experiences often occur early in life, when the person is most vulnerable and most in need of support and guidance. For example, the father may have abandoned the family, and this may have been followed by the mother's depression and drug addiction, and then her death.
- The person experiences the loss of hope for a satisfying life and the belief that the world is a coherent and rational place where good intentions and good actions have good consequences.
- The person has a sense of descending, sinking, falling slowly into a subhuman kind of exist-

ence. This is accompanied by low self-esteem and a feeling of helplessness—like trying to run through quicksand.

- Withdrawal and communication breakdown increasingly isolate the individual from others. There is often a mutual withdrawal from significant emotional interactions as family members and friends also find themselves unable to cope with the situation of loss and trauma.

- The pre-suicidal person now constructs a facade as protection against further emotional pain. Karen, as quoted in the beginning of this chapter, built a robot-like facade around her doubts, fears, and vulnerabilities. She was just there, doing her work, trying to be socially invisible to avoid interactions. In a sense, though, she was not there at all. Within the facade of a competent but distant and uninviting person, she experienced the deadening effect of this protective strategy and "just felt it would be more congruent to be dead. Just not to have this body to keep being in." Other people may construct other types of facades that offer from protection but also exact a high price in restricting the quality of life.

- If the descent continues, the person now enters a state of mind that Heckler believes can be described accurately as the *suicidal trance*. There is a greatly restricted range of thoughts and feelings. The person is aware of little but his or her own suffering. There is a deepening conviction that the only options available are to continue suffering or to free himself or herself from suffering through death.

- The person now thinks and feels as though trapped in a tunnel. Death increasingly seems to be the only logical and possible exit.

- The movement toward suicide is likely to be accelerated by the impression that death is somehow beckoning, offering release, even commanding the act of self-destruction. For some people, this takes the form of hallucinatory voices, but others are aware that it is their own mind making the decision.

- A precipitating event is likely to trigger the actual suicide attempt when the person is already primed toward death-as-release. Often this precipitating event is some form of rejection by another person.

The descent toward suicide can be halted at any of these points by understanding and helpful interactions, as well as by the individual's own resourceful efforts. The deeper the person has descended into the presuicidal sequence, however, the more difficult the challenge. Nevertheless, it is an encouraging fact that Heckler's case sample is drawn from people who did "wake up, alive." I was impressed by the courage and resourcefulness of many of the people, who fought uphill battles against despair before making suicide attempts. I have known some people like this myself, and perhaps you have, too. The private hells they have had to survive often were not at all of their own making.

FACTS, MYTHS, AND GUIDELINES

Some of the major social and individual meanings of suicide have been considered. Now we will evaluate some of the *myths* that have grown around the subject over the years. This will serve as a partial review and will also prepare us for a set of guidelines

Popular Myths about Suicide

- *A person who talks about suicide will not actually take his or her own life.* There is abundant evidence to show that this statement is not true. Approximately three out of every four people who eventually kill themselves give some detectable hint ahead of time, whether by less serious attempts or by oral statements (the latter are sometimes as direct as can be—e.g., "I'm going to blow my head off," "If things don't get better in a hurry, you'll be reading about me in the papers"). This is one of the most dangerous myths because it encourages us to ignore cries for help. As noted above, the rejection of the communication itself can become the last straw for a person contemplating suicide.

- *Only a specific class of people commit suicide.* It is sometimes held that suicide is a particular risk of either the poor or the rich. The poor are assumed to feel helpless and deprived, the rich to be bored and aimless. These simplifications fail to consider the complexity of the individual's relationship to society. People in all income brackets and social echelons commit suicide. An explanation limited to economic or class distinctions alone is not adequate and contributes to our blind spots in the identification of individuals at risk.

- *Suicide has simple causes that are easily established.* It would be closer to the truth to say that many of us are easily satisfied with hasty and superficial explanations. This chapter has emphasized *meanings* rather than *causes* of suicide, which are often far from simple.

- *Asking people about suicide will put that thought in their minds and encourage suicide attempts.* This is one of the most common of the mistaken assumptions. Many lives have been saved when communication on this topic was opened.

- *Only depressed people commit suicide.* This misconception is held by some professionals as well as by the public. People with a psychiatric diagnosis of depression do have a higher suicide rate than those with other psychiatric syndromes or those without known syndromes. But suicide may occur in any type of psychiatric disorder. The person may not even seem to be especially unhappy immediately before the fatal action. It is dangerous, then, to overlook suicidal potential on the basis of the assumption that only depressed people take their lives.

- *Only crazy or insane people commit suicide.* This mistaken proposition is related to the one just described. Psychiatrists disagree on the number of suicides associated with obvious mental disorder, but some of the most qualified researchers and clinicians find that suicide is not invariably related to psychosis. Rational people can feel overwhelmed by circumstances.

- *Suicidal tendencies are inherited.* It is true that more than one person in the same family may commit suicide. Some families do have a suicidal tradition that seems to perpetuate itself, but there is no evidence for a hereditary basis, even in special studies made of identical twins. The explanation for suicide has to be sought elsewhere—with particular attention to family patterns of communication.

- *When a suicidal person shows improvement, the danger is over.* The period following an apparent improvement in overall condition is actually one of special danger. Sometimes this is because the client has improved enough to be discharged from a mental hospital and therefore has more opportunity to commit suicide. It may also be related to a recovery of enough energy and volition to take action. Sensitivity and interpersonal support are especially needed when the person seems to be pulling out of a suicidal crisis.

- *People who are under a physician's care or who are hospitalized are not suicidal risks.* This is wishful thinking. Many people who commit suicide have received some form of medical or psychiatric attention within six months preceding the act. Suicides can and do occur in the hospital itself (Kastenbaum, 1995). Furthermore, the institutional situation itself can contribute to anxiety, low self-esteem, and other conditions conducive to suicide.

- *Suicide can be prevented only by a psychiatrist or mental hospital.* Some of the most successful suicide prevention efforts are being made by a variety of people in the community who bring concern, stamina, and sensitivity to the task. The human resources of the entire community may hold more hope than the limited cadres of professionals or institutions. It is neither necessary nor realistic to pass all of the responsibility to a few.

SUICIDE PREVENTION

We have already touched upon suicide prevention in several ways. Improving our ability to observe signs of possible heightened suicidal risk in children, youth, and adults is a useful first step. Recognizing that a number of common assumptions about suicide are not supported by fact is another useful step. Now we will consider some other contributions that we can make to suicide prevention as individuals and as a society.

Individual Guidelines to Suicide Prevention

Many suicides can be prevented. Perhaps you have already played a role in preventing suicide without realizing it. The companionship you offered a person during a crucial period or the confidence you displayed in a friend after he or she suffered a failure experience might have provided just enough support to dissolve a self-destructive pattern in the making. Whenever we bring sensitivity and a genuinely caring attitude to our relationships with other people, we may be decisively strengthening their life-affirming spirit.

How we should best proceed depends upon who the suicidal person is, who we are, and what kind of relationship we have to go on together. A few general guidelines can be offered, however:

- *Take the suicidal concern seriously.* This does not mean panic or an exaggerated, unnatural response. It does mean time, attention, and active listening.
- *Do not issue a provocation to suicide.* Strange though it may seem, people sometimes react to a suicidal person in such a way as to provoke or intensify the attempt. Do not be one of those "friends" who dares this person to make good his or her threat or who intimates that he or she is too "chicken" to do so. Do not belittle or joke away the suicidal state of mind—this might intensify the need to do something desperate so that others will appreciate how bad he or she really feels.
- *Go easy on value judgments.* "You can't do that—it's wrong!" This is sometimes the exclamation that would come most readily to our lips, but it is seldom a useful one. It is not helpful to inject value judgments when a troubled person is starting to confide self-destructive thoughts.
- *Do not get carried away by the "good reasons" a person has for suicide.* The interpersonal response to a suicidal individual sometimes involves much reading of our own thoughts and feelings into the other person's head. We may think, "If all of that were going wrong with *my* life, I'd want to kill myself too!" This conclusion might be at-

tributed to the other person all too hastily. For every person who commits suicide when faced with realistically difficult problems, many others find alternative solutions. It is possible to respect the reality factors in the suicidal individual's situation without lining up on the side of self-murder. This respectful, nonevaluative approach is taken by many of the people who pick up the phone when a crisis hot line call is put through.
- *Know what resources are available in the community.* Who else can help this person? What kind of help might this person find most acceptable? What services are available through local schools, religious groups, and mental health centers? Does your community have a crisis intervention service? How does it operate? Learn about and, if possible, participate in your community's efforts to help those who are in periods of special vulnerability.
- *Listen.* This is the advice you will hear again and again from people who have devoted themselves to suicide prevention. It is good advice. Listening is not the passive activity it might seem to be. It is an intent, self-giving action that shows the troubled person that you are there. And it is an opportunity for the person to discharge at least some of the tensions that have brought him or her to a certain point of self-destructive intent and to sort out other possibilities.

Systematic Approaches to Suicide Prevention

Many communities include crisis hotlines and other services that can be useful to both a suicidal person and his or her worried family, friends, and colleagues. Large metropolitan areas also have centers specifically dedicated to suicide prevention. Mental health specialists in clinics or private practice are also available in many areas.

Suicide prevention centers usually offer 24-hour telephone counseling services. Some also provide walk-in clinics where people may receive crisis counseling. Many of those who use these services are able to work through their crises without resorting to suicide. However, many people with high suicidality do not contact a center. Younger adults and women are more likely to seek help through a suicide prevention center than are older adults and men. Suicide prevention centers often try various types of public information and reach-out programs to encourage contacts from older adults and men. It is not easy to bring some of the people at greatest risk into the orbit of the suicide prevention center, so alternative ways of reducing suicide must also be pursued.

The community may decide to take other actions to reduce suicide risk. These programs range from making access to "jumping-off places" more difficult (Berman, 1990) to promoting both recreational and employment programs for youth. Reducing access to guns could be a particularly effective component of a community's suicide prevention efforts for elders because they are less likely to shift to other modes of self-destruction.

One of the most promising systematic approaches to suicide prevention is through educational programs (Leenaars & Wenckstern, 1991b). Educators and parents must first work through their own anxieties and become more familiar with the facts of suicide. Education directed to school children could be the most efficient way to increase the general public's ability to prevent suicide in the long run. It will be necessary, however, to study the effects of these programs carefully and to revise and improve them when indicated.

Please Note: Physician-Assisted Death, also Known as Physician-Assisted Suicide, is Examined in Chapter 9.

SUMMARY

We have seen that suicide takes many forms and that both thoughts and attempts are more common than we might have supposed. A statistical overview disclosed that suicide is the ninth most common cause of death in the general population of the United States, but is even higher for adolescents and young adults. The United States, with its suicide rate of 12.3 per 100,000, is in about the middle of the list of nations that report their data to the World Health Organization. Countries with the lowest suicide rates have rapidly expanding populations and struggle with impoverishment and disease. Special attention was given to youth suicide, and in particular to males and college students who are at a higher risk (see Table 7.3 for a review of high risk factors). We saw that children can also be suicidal to the point of taking their lives if their concerns are ignored by adults. Suicide rates are highest among elderly people, especially white males, and they are alarmingly high among young Native Americans and Alaskan natives. Several situations increase the risk of suicide: HIV/AIDS infection, gambling, and victimization by bullies and other peers.

Several meanings of suicide have been promulgated in our society: suicide as sinful, criminal, weakness or madness, "The Great Death," and a rational alternative. Sociobehavioral scientists and clinicians have offered their own explanations. Durkheim's pioneering sociological theory features his concepts of social integration, collective representations, and the altruistic, anomic, egoistic, and fatalistic types of suicide. Several individual meanings of suicide were discussed: suicide as reunion, rest and refuge, revenge, penalty for failure, and mistake. Freud's first theory explained suicide as anger toward others that has been turned inward. His second theory proposed warring life (Eros) and death (Thanatos) instincts, in which self-destructive tendencies may dominate because of problems experienced in early development.

Richard Heckler's description of "the descent toward suicide" added to our understanding of the sequence of problems, losses, and failed attempts at coping that can lead first to suicidal thoughts, then to attempts, and finally to death. We reviewed several popular myths about suicide (e.g., "A person who talks about suicide will not actually take his or her own life") for the express purpose of pointing out that these statements are *not* supported by facts. We concluded with a brief consideration of what we can do to prevent suicide as individuals and as citizens.

REFERENCES

Alvarez, A. (1970). *The Savage God*. New York: Random House.

Beckerman, N. L. (1995). Suicide in relation to AIDS. *Death Studies, 19,* 223–234.

Berman, A. L. (Ed.) (1990). *Suicide prevention. Case consultations.* New York: Springer.

Blankenstein, A. (1998: August 24). Handling suspects who seek "suicide by cop." *Los Angeles Times.*

Brandt, R. B. (1990). The morality and rationality of suicide. In J. Donnelly (Ed.), *Suicide. Right or wrong?* (pp. 185–200). Buffalo, NY: Prometheus.

Breed, W. (1972). Five components of a basic suicide syndrome. *Life-Threatening Behavior, 3,* 3–18.

Chan, D. W. (1995). Reasons for living among Chinese adolescents in Hong Kong. *Suicide & Life-Threatening Behavior, 25,* 347–357.

Choron, J. (1972). *Suicide*. New York: Scribner.

Colt, G. H. (1991). *The enigma of suicide*. New York: Simon & Schuster.

Crosby, A. E., Cheltenham, M. P., & Sacks, J. J. (1999). Incidence of suicide ideation and behavior in the United States, 1994. *Suicide & Life-Threatening Behavior, 29,* 131–140.

Dangelis, N., & Pope, W. (1979). Durkheim's theory of suicide as applied to the family: An empirical test. *Social Forces, 57,* 1081–1106.

Darwin, C. (1971). *Origin of the species*. Cambridge: Harvard University Press. (Original work published 1859)

Donne, J. (1977). *Biathanatos*. New York: Arno Press. (Original work published 1646)

Durkheim, E. (1951). *Suicide*. (J. A. Spaulding & G. Simpson, Trans.). New York: Free Press. (Original work published 1897)

Erasmus, Desiderius. *Encomium moria. The praise of folly.* (Original work published 1509)

Farberow, N. L. (Ed.) (1980). *The many faces of suicide*. New York: McGraw-Hill.

Farberow, N. L., & Shneidman, E. S. (Eds.). (1965). *The cry for help*. New York: McGraw-Hill.

Frederick, C. J. (1985). Youth suicide: An introduction and overview. In M. L. Peck, N. L. Farberow, & R. E. Litman (Eds.), *Youth suicide* (pp. 1–18). New York: Springer.

Freud, S. (1959). Mourning and melancholia. *Collected papers,* Vol. 4 (pp. 152–172). New York: Basic Books. (Original work published 1917)

Freud, S. (1961). *The ego and the id*. New York: W. W. Norton (Original work published 1923).

Greyson, B. (1992–1993). Near-death experiences and antisuicidal attitudes. *Omega, Journal of Death and Dying, 26,* 81–90.

Heckler, R. A. (1994). *Waking Up, Alive*. New York: Ballantine Books.

Hendin, H. (1985). Suicide among the young: Psychodynamics and demography. In M. L. Peck, N. L. Farberow, & R. E. Litman (Eds.), *Youth suicide* (pp. 19–38). New York: Springer.

Hendin, H. (1995). *Suicide in America.* (rev. ed.). New York: W. W. Norton.

Hume, D. (1826). On suicide. Quoted by G. H. Colt (1996). *The enigma of suicide* (p. 173). New York: Simon & Schuster.

Jobes, D. A., & Mann, R. E. (1999). Reasons for living versus reasons for dying: Examining the internal debate of suicide. *Suicide & Life-Threatening Behavior, 29,* 97–104.

Kastenbaum, R. (1994). Alternatives to suicide. In L. Tallmer & D. Lester (Eds.), *Now I lay me down. Suicide in the elderly.* (pp. 196–213). Philadelphia: Charles.

Kastenbaum, R. (1995). The impact of suicide on society. In B. L. Mishara (Ed.), *The impact of suicide.* (pp. 169–186). New York: Springer.

Kozak, D. L. (1991). Dying badly: Violent death and religious change among the Tohono O' Odham. *Omega, Journal of Death and Dying, 23,* 207–216.

LaFleur, W. R. (1974). Japan. In F. H. Holck (Ed.), *Death and Eastern thought*. Nashville: Abingdon.

Leenaars, A. A., & Lester, D. (1992). Comparison of rates and patterns of suicide in Canada and the United States, 1960–1988. *Death Studies, 16,* 417–430.

Leenaars, A. A., & Wenckstern, S. (1991a). *Suicide prevention in schools*. New York: Hemisphere.

Leenaars, A. A., & Wenckstern, S. (1991b). Suicide in the school-age child and adolescent. In A. A. Leenaars (Ed.), *Life span perspectives of suicide* (pp. 95–108). New York: Plenum.

Lester, D. (1972). *Why people kill themselves*. Springfield, IL: Charles C. Thomas.

Locke, J. (1971). *Concerning the true original extent and end of civil government*. In R. M. Hutchins (Ed.), *Great books of the Western world* (Vol. 35). Chicago: Encyclopedia Britannica. (Original work published 1690)

Lockridge, L. (1995). Least likely suicide: The search for my father, Ross Lockridge, Jr., author of Raintree County. *Suicide & Life-Threatening Behavior, 25,* 429–436.

Maris, R. W. (1981). *Pathways to suicide*. Baltimore: Johns Hopkins University Press.

Marshall, J. R., Burnett, W., & Brasure, J.. (1983). On precipitating factors: Cancer as a cause of suicide. *Suicide & Life-Threatening Behavior, 13,* 15–27.

McIntosh, J. L. (1983–1984) Suicide among Native Americans: Further tribal data and considerations. *Omega, Journal of Death and Dying, 14,* 303–316.

McIntosh, J. L. (1992). Epidemiology of suicide in the elderly. In A. A. Lenaars, R. W. Maris, J. L. McIntosh & J. Richman (Eds.). *Suicide and the older adult* (pp. 15–35). New York, Guilford.

McIntosh, J. L. (1993). Suicide: Native-American. In R. Kastenbaum & B. K. Kastenbaum (Eds.), *The encyclopedia of death* (pp. 238–239). Phoenix: Oryx.

Mishara, B. L. (1999). Conceptions of death and suicide in children ages 6–12 and their implications for suicide prevention. *Suicide & Life-Threatening Behavior, 29,* 105–118.

Murphy, G. E. (1995). 39 years of suicide research. *Suicide & Life-Threatening Behavior, 25,* 450–457.

Orbach, I. (1988). *Children who don't want to live.* San Francisco: Jossey-Bass.

Osgood, N. J. (1992). *Suicide in later life.* New York: Lexington.

Phillips, D. P., Welty, W. R., & Smith, M. M. (1997). Elevated suicide levels associated with legalized gambling. *Suicide & Life-Threatening Behavior, 27,* 373–378.

Prodis, J. (1994: April 18). Trial of 'suicide doctor' pits law vs. jury's emotions. Associated Press dispatch.

Richman, J. (1991). *Preventing elderly suicide.* New York: Springer.

Rigby, K., & Slee, P. (1999). Suicidal ideation among adolescent school children, involvement in bully-victim problems, and perceived social support. *Suicide & Life-Threatening Behavior, 29,* 119–130.

Robbins, L. N., West, P. A., & Murphy, G. E. (1977). The high rate of suicide in older white men: A study testing ten hypotheses. *Social Psychiatry, 12,* 1–20.

St. Augustine. (1971). *The city of God.* In R. M. Hutchins (Ed.), *Great books of the Western world* (Vol. 18). Chicago: Encyclopedia Brittanica. (Original work published 426)

St. Thomas Aquinas. (1971). *Summa theologica.* In R. M. Hutchins (Ed.), *Great books of the Western world* (Vol. 19). Chicago: Encyclopedia Brittanica. (Original work published 1279)

Seiden, R. H. (1977) A tale of two bridges: Comparative suicide incidences on the Golden Gate and San Fransisco–Oakland Bay bridges. *Crisis, 3,* 32–40.

Seiden, R. H. (1981). Mellowing with age: Factors influencing the nonwhite suicide rate. *Omega, Journal of Death and Dying, 13,* 265–281.

Shneidman, E. S. (1976). Current over-view of suicide. In E. S. Shneidman (Ed.), *Suicidology: Contemporary developments* (pp. 1–21). New York: Grune & Stratton.

Stack, S. (1979). Durkheim's theory of fatalistic suicide: A cross national approach. *Journal of Social Psychology, 107,* 161–168.

Stack, S. (1994).The heavy metal subculture and suicide. *Suicide and Life–Threatening Behavior, 24,* 15–23.

Stack, S. (1998). Heavy metal, religiosity, and suicide acceptability. *Suicide and Life-Threatening Behavior, 28,* 386–394.

Swanson, W. C., & Breed, W. (1976). Black suicide in New Orleans. In E. S. Shneidman (Ed.), *Suicidology: Contemporary developments.* (pp. 99–128). New York: Grune & Stratton.

Tabachnick, N. (Ed.). (1973). *Accident or Suicide?* Springfield, IL: Charles C. Thomas.

U.S. Senate Judiciary Committee (1991). *Report of the U.S. Senate Judiciary Committee.* Washington, DC: Government Printing Office

Wallace, S. E. (1973). *After Suicide.* New York: Wiley Interscience.

Werth, Jr., J. L. (1995). Rational suicide reconsidered: AIDS as an impetus for change. *Death Studies, 19,* 65–80.

Yantis, J., & Burgard, M. (1999: June 26) Crash on 101 murder, suicide. *The Tribune* (Tempe, AZ).

Zhang, J. (1998). Suicide in the world: Toward a population increase theory of suicide. *Death Studies, 22,* 525–540.

GLOSSARY

Altruistic Suicide: Committed by people who have extremely high or excessive concern for society (Durkheim).

Anomic Suicide: Committed by people who fail to receive support and meaning from society (Durkheim).

Collective Representations: The symbols and themes that convey the spirit and mood of a culture.

Daishi: An ideal or "great death" in Buddhist tradition.

Egoistic Suicide: Committed by people who are not under sufficient control by societal norms and obligations (Durkheim).

Fatalistic Suicide: Committed by people who are stifled and oppressed by society (Durkheim).

Genocidal: A systematic plan and/or action that targets an entire population for death.

Intentionality: An action that places one's life at risk when it has been established that the act was planned as self-destructive, as distinguished from accidental.

Parasuicide: Attempted suicide.

Samurai: Warrior who follows a strong code of honor (in Japanese tradition).

Seppuku: Suicide by ritualistic disembowlment (in Japanese tradition). Also known in West as *hara-kiri.*

Social Integration/Solidarity: The extent to which individuals are connected to a society that is more or less cohesive (Durkheim).

Stoicism: A philosophical tradition that emphasizes rationality and the ability to withstand despair and emotional provocations and temptations.

Suicidal Trance: A state of mind in which a person sees death as the only way to relieve suffering and gives little attention to anything else.

Suicide: Self-murder.

Suicide Rate: A measure computed by multiplying the number of suicides by 100,000 and dividing by the population number. Not to be mistaken for a percentage.

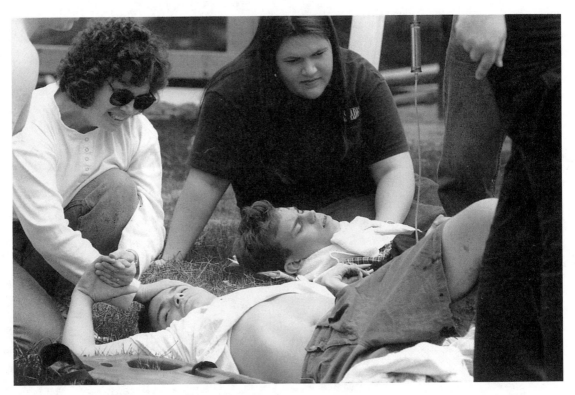

Victims of the shootings at Columbine High School (Littleton, Colorado, April 20, 1999) receive assistance.

chapter 8

VIOLENT DEATH: MURDER, TERRORISM, DISASTER, AND ACCIDENT

ATLANTA—A "day-trader" apparently upset over stock losses opened fire Thursday in two brokerage offices, killing nine people and wounding 12. He escaped, then shot himself to death five hours later when police stopped his van at a gas station.
—Shelley Hill, July 30, 1999

Benjamin Nathanial Smith, a 21 year-old student, who went on a rampage over the Fourth of July weekend, shooting Blacks, Jews and Asians in Indiana and Illinois; killing two people and wounding 12, the authorities say.
—Pam Belluck, July 7, 1998, p. A10

PORT HURON, Michigan: Four middle school students plotted to force their principal at gunpoint to call an assembly, then massacre those at the gathering several classmates testified Thursday. The four then planned to kill themselves, one student said during a preliminary court hearing for two of the accused students.
—David Goldman, May 18, 1999, p. A7

Kendra Nowak, whose newborn baby was discovered in a garbage bag in her Michigan home, was a physically and emotionally abused teenager. She was 19 and single when she gave birth in the home she shared with her mother. No one had even known she was pregnant.... Authorities said the baby had lived for two days but had been dead for a week when it was found.
—Charles Patrick Ewing, 1997, p. 85

Anthony Robles, 3, wouldn't get dressed one morning, so his grandmother's boyfriend threw him down, slamming the toddler's head against a concrete floor, police said. The boyfriend, 41, was baby-sitting the boy in the grandmother's Phoenix apartment, and the child's mother was in jail.
—Karina Bland, June 27, 1996

KLM eight seven zero you are cleared to the Papa Beacon, climb to and maintain flight level nine zero, right turn after takeoff.
—Control tower to pilot, Cushing, 1994, p. 19

In this chapter, we consider deaths that stun and enrage, deaths that challenge our ability to comprehend the way that the world works and the way that our own minds work. We have already considered one difficult question: why do people kill themselves? Now we must consider the larger spectrum of sudden and violent deaths. These deaths are experienced as painful losses by the survivors. Often they also lead to heightened fears and doubts: fears that still other sudden and violent deaths might occur, doubts that the world is as rational and safe a place as we would like to believe. Every society's death system is stressed by sudden and violent deaths. We have divided these events into the traditional categories of murder, accident, terrorism, and disaster. The distinctions are not always that clear-cut, however, and the definitions themselves may be subject to challenge. One person's "terrorism," for example, may be another person's legitimate "war." It is unpleasant to read—or write—about the human tragedies encompassed by this chapter, but to avoid doing so would be to avoid part of the reality of our relationship to death. Consider for a moment just the events already noted

- Mark Barton was described as "very calm and determined, no feelings" when he gunned down employees in two brokerage firms. He had become a new kind of gambler, a person who played the stock market addictively through the Internet. Stocks had tumbled that day. He had lost about $100,000. Other day traders have experienced heart attacks and other stress reactions on a bad day. Were this man's actions the harbinger of a new kind of domestic terrorist, a person who slaughters others instead of taking responsibility for his own actions?
- A new category has been added to the list of criminal offenses: hate crime. This refers to as-

saults against people and property, motivated by rage against a class of people. The people attacked have done nothing to harm the aggressor—other than to be of another race, nationality, or religious group as perceived by the assailant. The "ethnic cleansing" that devastated Burundi, Rwanda, Bosnia, and Kosovo has its counterpart in groups who encourage hate crimes in the United States.
- The nation was shocked when fourteen students and a teacher were massacred by two students at Columbine High School in Colorado. The attack had been elaborately planned and could have resulted in a great many more deaths, including those of police officers and other rescuers. Some of us brood about our real or imagined grievances, but what state of mind turns grievance into mass murder? And why have there already been several copycat attempts by other students?
- The love of a mother for her baby is often intense and persevering even when the circumstances are difficult. How is it possible, then, for a woman to destroy her baby—and why does this kind of murder seem to be occurring more often today?
- One of the most unthinkable types of death has also been showing up with increasing frequency in American homes. Incidents of child abuse, including those with severe and lethal outcomes, have increased sharply in recent years. What are we to make of the fact that adults are abusing, battering, and killing young children?
- Accidents are a different matter. By definition, accidents just happen. But more often than might be supposed, there is human error—especially lack of adequate foresight and communication—behind fatal accidents. The brief exchange between the control tower and a commercial jet pilot was followed a few sec-

onds later by a catastrophe that resulted in the loss of 583 lives, the worst accident in aviation history. With better communication, these people would still be alive.

We now consider death by violence in a more systematic way, beginning with murder and continuing to war, terrorism, disaster, and accident. We will learn not only about violent death but also about some characteristics of the society in which we live.

MURDER

Overview

A person who takes the life of another has committed homicide. If a court rules that this killing was intentional and unlawful, the act has been judged to be murder. All murders are homicides; some homicides are murders. You may have committed "justifiable homicide" if you used lethal force to protect your own life; you may be guilty of "negligent homicide" if your carelessness resulted in the death of another person. Distinctions of this kind can be very important in the judicial process. For the purposes of this chapter, however, we will use the simplest and most direct word, *murder*.

Murder: The Statistical Picture

Of nations providing information to Interpol (Table 8-1) the United States has the highest murder rate in the world. It is difficult to escape the implication that there is something particularly "American" about this high rate. Neighboring Canada shares the North American continent with us and is comparable in many respects—yet has a murder rate nearly two-thirds lower. Western European nations, with whom we might also compare ourselves, generally have murder rates even lower than Canada's. Politically troubled Northern Ireland is an exception, yet its 4.0 murder rate is only a little more than half as high as ours. And among the hard-pressed people of Chile, the relatively high murder rate is surpassed by that of the affluent and powerful United States.

Who are the killers, who are the victims, and what are the trends?

TABLE 8-1

Homicide around the World

Nation	Homicide Rate*
Austria	1.3
Canada	2.7
Chile	5.6
Denmark	1.2
Egypt	1.0
England	1.1
Finland	1.8
Greece	1.0
Hungary	1.9
Ireland	0.8
Italy	2.1
Netherlands	1.2
New Zealand	1.7
Nigeria	1.5
Northern Ireland	4.9
Portugal	3.0
Sweden	1.4
Switzerland	1.1
United States	*7.9***

Data Source: Information Plus: Gun Control (1989), drawn from Interpol reports.

*Number of murders per 100,000 population.

**6.8 in 1997, the most recent update.

- Murder rates in the United States show a general pattern of increase from midcentury into the 1990s but have declined since 1996. The lowest rate during this span was 4.0 per 100,000 in 1957; the highest was 10.2 in 1980. Preliminary statistics from the FBI indicate that the number of murders has continued to decline—by 8 percent from 1997 to 1998 (Burrell, 1999). However, there are still nearly 20,000 known homicides a year in the United States. The decline has been variously attributed to a healthy economy, more efficient police work, and a slightly smaller percentage of young males in the population.
- Suicide rates have been consistently higher in the southern states than in the nation as a whole. Southern states continue to account for approximately 40 percent of all murders.
- The risk of murder often varies markedly within the same state and even within the same community.

- Men are most often both the killers and the victims. When a female is the victim, the murderer is a male in nine of ten cases. When the victim is male, the killer is a male in eight of ten cases. About three of every four murder victims is a male.

- People are most at risk to become murder victims between the ages of 25 and 44.

- Most murders (about 90 percent) are committed by killers of the same race as the victims. This fact is worth emphasizing because interracial murders often arouse more fear and anger. It has been observed that newspapers and other media give more attention to interracial murders and thereby "push the panic button" for many people.

- Murder rates are higher among African Americans, who are also more frequently the victims of murder. "Blacks are overrepresented among convicted killers. Statistically, a black male is more likely to kill than is a white male. A black female is also more likely to kill than is a white female. It also must be remembered that most killers murder within their own race" (Holmes & Holmes, 1994, p. 4). Murder continues to be among the higher risks of death for black men into old age.

- At least three of five murders are committed by people who are relatives, lovers, friends, neighbors, or colleagues of the victims. Again, the media tends to spotlight killings by strangers (e.g., in the course of a robbery or a freeway sniping). But the fact remains that among both African Americans and whites, the killer and the victim usually are acquaintances, if not relatives or intimate companions. Furthermore, family violence that results in serious injuries as well as death continues to be rampant. The most common type involves violence between spouses or ex-spouses.

- Murders are most common in large cities— about three times more frequent than the national average. (Murder and other violent crime has decreased in large cities over the past few years, although public concern has not.)

- Handguns are the most often used weapons of murder. Firearms in general are involved in about seven of every ten killings. Knives and other cutting or stabbing instruments are the next most common lethal weapons. Knives, however, are the weapons most frequently used in murders committed by those of Asian or native American heritage.

- The overall trend in recent years has been for higher and higher murder rates in the United States. Most other causes of death have decreased during the same years. Although the murder rate has occasionally dipped during this period of time, the overall trend has been a marked increase.

- Arguments are the most frequent of the known provocations for murder, occurring about twice as often as in all other types of felonies combined. It must be kept in mind, however, that the provocations or reasons for murder remain unknown in many instances (Holmes & Holmes, 1994).

- Murder has become the leading cause of death for women in the workplace. Men are usually the killers. Some observers believe that male insecurity and rage may be intensified by increasing competition from women, especially during a time of high unemployment. Another possibility is that the workplace has become more dangerous for everybody because of the overall social climate of violence and ready access to firearms. Both men and women can become frustrated and angry in a variety of workplace situations, but men are more likely to respond with a lethal outburst.

Some experts believe that the number of murders and other violent crimes is closely related to the number of young males in the population. From this viewpoint, the recent reduction in murders can be attributed to the fact that "the baby boomers are getting older" (Walsh, 1996). If this is true, there may be some bad news coming, as perhaps already demonstrated in the outbreak of school shootings in the United States and Canada

> Within the next decade, the nation's 39 million children under age 10 will become teenagers, giving the nation its largest teenage population since the 1950s. More will be "at risk" than ever, coming from low income homes with a single parent. This is the calm in the crime storm. (1996, p. A24)

There is continuing concern about the increased number of teenagers with guns, a trend that started in association with the sale of illegal drugs. Some authorities believe that "the young people dealing drugs started carrying their guns around with them, to school and in their neighborhoods, and then other teenagers began copying them" (Butterfield, 1994, p. A-10).

Patterns of Murder in the United States

A man with a long criminal record ambushes and executes another criminal; this was his day's work. Another man nervously attempts his first holdup. Something goes wrong and he fires his gun at the clerk, then flees in panic. After a bout of drinking, a rejected lover breaks in upon the woman, her children, and her new friend. Cursing them all, he sprays the room with bullets from a semiautomatic rifle. An emotionally fragile woman hears voices that tell her what to do in her predicament. Obeying the voices, she strangles her child and then attempts to take her own life.

It is obvious that there cannot be any one, all-encompassing explanation for murder. It becomes important, then, to look at some of the specific patterns that murder takes in the United States. We will examine (1) violence and abuse in the home, with spouse, children or parents as victims; (2) young men with guns, including school shootings; (3) mass and serial killers; and (4) political murders (assassinations).

Domestic Violence

Law enforcement officers around the nation are well aware that they might encounter extreme violence when they respond to calls for family situations. As already noted, most killings involve people who know each other, often in very close relationships. The killer is usually a man, whether the murder grows out of a domestic or a criminal situation. Wives are the most common victims of intrafamilial killings, followed by husbands, sons, daughters, fathers, brothers, mothers, and sisters.

Men Who Kill Their Partners

Many women are subjected to repeated abuse and violence from their male partners. More than a thousand a month are killed, even though they had previously sought help from the police or the courts. In four out of five spousal homicides, the police had been called to the home at least once. Ewing asks and answers the questions that come directly to mind: why are so many battered women killed by their abusers, and why does the law fail to prevent these deaths?

> The overall likelihood that a battered woman will be killed by her batterer is directly proportional to the degree she resists being abused. Battered women who resist abuse or fight back are much more likely to be killed than battered women who suffer in silence. Battered women who leave or even try to leave their batters are the most likely of all to be killed. (1997, p. 22).

Many communities have responded to the desperate situation of battered women by providing shelters and counseling programs. This increase in community resources for battered women, however, has been accompanied by an increase in murders by their abusive partners. Ewing explains:

> Ironically, giving a battered woman a place to go makes it more likely that she will leave—or at least try to leave—her batterer, but that also increases the likelihood that she will be killed by him. The explanation lies in the dynamics of the battering relationship. Control is the ultimate issue in most of these relationships. Batterers have an obsessive if not a pathological need to control the lives of the women with whom they share intimate relationships. (1997, p. 22).

Is it a mistake, then, to offer haven and assistance to women who are trapped in an abusive and life-threatening relationship? Not really. Such assistance has helped some women to free themselves (and their children) from abusive relationships, literally saving their lives. However, the prevention of abuse and murder probably will require much more attention to the people committing these offenses, the male partners. Generally, these men have themselves been victims of abuse in their youth. They treat women and children as personal possessions, compensating for their own low self-esteem. It is not unusual for an abusive male to feel that he is being "the big man," who now has the dominant role that reverses the victim role he knew as a child.

Cultural tradition has given men enormous latitude for controlling the lives of their wives and children. Wife-beating was seldom treated as a criminal offense in a society in which women were required to abide by their husbands' decisions and were denied the right to vote for more than a century. Not so long ago, an employed woman could not have a credit card unless it was registered in the name of her husband or father. An abusive and potentially murderous male partner is still supported to some extent by the unwritten law that women are here only to serve men. Programs that provide assistance to families threatened by a pattern of male abuse are part of the solution, but the men themselves must be fully involved in preventive programs—an approach that requires real commitment to the idea of equal rights and responsibilities.

Women Who Kill Their Partners

Women may also kill, however, especially when they have suffered humiliation, abuse, and injury at the hands of a man.

> "I'm going to kill you, you bitch. I'm going to kill you this night!" Bella ran from side to side in the room, but couldn't get to the door because Isaac had blocked it off. Isaac forced her into a corner, holding her up with a hand in her hair, and began hitting her repeatedly with his fist. Bella could hear the children screaming and kept crying to them to get help. She was sure Isaac would kill her if no one intervened. Then he began to bang her head against the wall. Bella was too dizzy to resist anymore, and just hung on. The attack ended a few minutes later when a relative stopped by and restrained him. (Brown, 1987, pp. 61–62)

This violent episode is typical of many others experienced by the battered women in Angela Browne's study. The rages were often sudden and unprovoked. The insults and accusations had little if any basis in anything the wife had done, and the attacks themselves were savage. Many battered women described their husbands as having become entirely different people during the assaults: "He'd get a look in his eyes and start to breathe differently." "It was like dealing with a stranger." Repeatedly the victim of a man who

might become crazed with fury at almost any time, these women lived in fear for themselves and their children. Bella endured twenty years of severe abuse until one night Isaac went too far. He threatened to kill their oldest daughter when she came home. Isaac fell asleep first, however, and Bella and another daughter shot him and then set the house on fire. This removed one major threat from Bella's life but did not set her free. She was found guilty of murder in the first degree and sentenced to life imprisonment. Permanently disabled and in very poor health as a result of the repeated attacks from Isaac, she is considered to have a shortened life expectancy.

Each year there are approximately 1.5 million physical assaults upon women by their male partners. Many of these men are in a drugged or intoxicated state at the time. It is the women who usually suffer the injuries. Severely battered women seldom have behaved violently toward their mates—until a few such as Bella try to end their ordeals through murder. Most often, the battered women tried to placate their husbands and did what they could to avoid such episodes. Legal protection and social support for battered women is still quite inadequate in most places. This means that more women (and children) will continue to suffer, and more will be provoked to take extreme measures.

Unfortunately, "many states do not have self-defense laws, and in those states even the belief that one is in dire or fatal danger is not considered an adequate defense for the commission of homicide" (Holmes & Holmes, 1994 p.33). Even where a self-defense provision exists, a woman may be found guilty of homicide if she is judged to have defended herself too effectively against partner assault.

It is ironic that the United States, with its commitment to preventing and treating life-threatening diseases and its support of hospice care, has been so slow in protecting women from lethal attacks by their male partners. In a recent Arizona example, typical of many throughout the nation, a woman was repeatedly assaulted by her husband and the life of their infant daughter was placed in jeopardy. The health care system looked after her injuries, but the judicial system turned the husband loose after each incident—until he did kill her. What our society will do to save a life varies greatly with the person at risk, the situation, and the attitudinal context.

People Who Kill Children

Physicians, nurses, teachers, and other human service providers have something else to worry about these days: they see children who bear the physical and emotional marks of abuse. These injuries have been inflicted by their parents or by other adults in the home. A grade school teacher may have been speaking for many others when she told me:

> We don't want to notice. We don't want to suspect. We don't want to believe. But we have to notice, we have to suspect, and, more and more we have to believe…that this child is being very badly mistreated and is at risk for…everything. Including death. Including death.

It is no longer unusual to find police officers on the pediatric unit of a hospital. They have been called by a physician or nurse who recognizes a young child's injuries as being the results of abuse—beating, shaking, burning, being thrown against a wall or down a flight of stairs, or neglect—starvation, dehydration, lack of physical care. From a nurse on a unit devoted to the care of infants:

> The worst thing is that it happens at all. The next worst thing is that it is becoming almost routine. You see this incredibly beautiful baby. And you see what has happened to it. And you know that even though the baby makes it through this time, there very likely will be a next time. Some cases, as soon as we have our first look, we're on the phone to the police. Let me tell you, they hate it, too, maybe as much as we do.

In my home state of Arizona, Child Protective Services is overwhelmed by the magnitude of its responsibilities. The agency does not have the resources to respond promptly and adequately to all instances of child endangerment. Furthermore, the situations of many children at risk don't reach the attention of this agency or any other until there has been serious injury or death (Bland, 1996). Similar problems are being experienced throughout much of the nation (Associated Press, September 19, 1996). Reports indicate that the number of children abused and ne-

glected rose from 1.42 million to 2.61 million between 1986 and 1993, and the number of those who were seriously injured from 141,700 to 565,000. These children constitute a high-risk group for becoming victims of murder. The most recent data available reveal 1,215 documented cases of children in the United States who died from abuse and/or neglect; this is almost certainly an underestimate.

What is happening? Most observers attribute the rising abuse and murder of children to dysfunctional families. The inability of families to care for their children is in turn attributed to such factors as unemployment, alcohol and drug abuse, and the abandonment of mothers and children by the fathers. At least two additional factors may contribute as well, although here I must draw upon personal observation rather than adequate studies:

1. *Lack of parenting skills.* Many people who become threats to their own children have themselves had little opportunity to learn how to be caring and effective parents. Fortunately, these people often are motivated to improve their parenting skills when given the opportunity through education and counseling.
2. *The replacement father syndrome.* This is my name for a situation that is responsible for many instances of severe and repeated child abuse, all too often with a fatal outcome. A woman is left to cope alone with one or more children. She takes a new lover. For this man, the children are just in the way, unwanted distractions and responsibilities. But there is something else here as well: an impulse to destroy the children of the previous husband or lover. During an episode of stress or alcohol- or drug-clouded thinking, the new lover attacks the child. Attacks may also be premeditated and carried out in a deliberate way—sometimes with the passive acceptance, or even the cooperation, of the woman who does not want to lose her new man. When you come across reports of serious child abuse and murder, observe for yourself how often the perpetrator is the replacement father. Awareness of potential dangers to children in the replacement father situation might help to prevent such tragedies.

Neonaticide (the killing of a newborn baby) requires special attention. Most women who do so are young, white, unmarried, uneducated, and poor. They have very little in the way of social support and are suffering from depression and a sense of hopelessness. Sometimes they succeed in denying their pregnancies to themselves, as well as concealing it from others, until the last moment. Usually they have made no plans for either the birth or the care of the child—they are simply overwhelmed and trying to make the problem go away.

They are not likely to seek help, because they do not expect anyone to help them. Abortion is not a strong option for a person who is denying and concealing pregnancy, and it becomes less of an option as time goes by. Adoption is another possible option, but most of these young women do not feel sufficiently connected to and knowledgeable about society to explore this alternative (and, again, there is the denial/deception factor). How about leaving the baby someplace where there would be a good chance for its being quickly discovered and cared for? Some young women in this predicament do leave the baby at a clinic or child care center. Nevertheless, many unwanted infants are placed in a plastic bag and tossed in a trash or garbage bin. Why? Because it is convenient, because it lessens the chance that a connection will be made with the mother, and because the symbolism of trash and garbage res-

onates with the young woman's own feelings of worthlessness and horror. The mother is the person who will be held responsible for this death if the connection is ever discovered—but this killing must also be acknowledged as part of a larger pattern of deprivation, abuse, and failure to develop positive bonds with the community.

Children Who Kill Parents

Each year about 300 parents are killed by their children in the United States Katherine M. Heide (1992) has analyzed the pattern of parricide:

- Most of the murdered parents and stepparents are white and non-Hispanic.
- The victims are usually in their late 40s or 50s.
- Most of the killers are white, non-Hispanic males.
- A juvenile (under age 18) is more likely to kill a parent than to kill anybody else.
- Most of the juveniles who kill their parents were victims of severe abuse by those parents.

Heide identifies twelve characteristics associated with adolescents who kill their parents (Box 8-1). These characteristics pretty much speak for themselves.

Young Men with Guns

The guns that kill are almost always in the hands of men, and most of the men are young.

BOX 8-1
ADOLESCENTS WHO KILL THEIR PARENTS

1. A pattern of family violence
2. Failed efforts by the adolescents to get help
3. Failed efforts by the adolescents to escape from the family situation
4. Isolation and few social outlets
5. A family situation that became increasingly intolerable
6. Increasing feelings of helplessness
7. Inability to cope with increasing stress, leading to a loss of self-control
8. Little or no previous involvement with the criminal justice system

9. Ready availability of a gun
10. Alcohol abuse and/or alcoholism in the home
11. Evidence that the adolescent may have been in a dissociative state at or near the time of the killing
12. Evidence that the adolescent offender and other family members felt relieved by the victim's death

Source: Kathleen M. Heide (1992).

The role of the murderer has been passing to even younger men in recent years: those in the 15–24-year-old range now have the highest rate of committing homicides—as well as the highest rate for becoming victims of homicide. Nine out of ten law enforcement officers who are killed in the line of duty are victims of guns in the hands of young men.

Many killings occur during drug-related transactions; others occur as part of gang rivalries. The general public tends to pay less attention to these deaths than to murders that seem to be casual, random, and unpredictable. The belief that such killings are becoming more common has led to the present state of anxiety in which schools, public offices, merchants, and private individuals feel the need for increased security—a need that has resulted in more purchases of guns for self-protection. Actually, as previously noted, the murder rate has declined somewhat in the past few years, but we are still responding to the longer pattern of increase and to disturbing media coverage of violent killings. It is difficult to feel reassured by recent statistics when yellow police tape cordons off homes, shops, and streets where innocent people have been shot to death.

Perhaps the most alarming development has been the apparent increase in drive-by shootings. We must stay with "apparent" increase because law enforcement agencies generally have not tracked drive-by shootings as a special class of crime. Nevertheless, there are more reports than ever of gunfire from passing cars, sometimes resulting in death, always resulting in fear and anger. Following is an excerpt from an incident reported by a local newspaper:

Two teens charged with shooting bicyclists…last month exchanged high-fives after one shooting and joked about getting "20 points" for another, according to police reports. Michael James Sheehan and Damon Eli Richardson, both 18, were indicted Thursday on two counts each of aggravated assault and eight counts of endangerment…. Greg Whipperman, 35, and Robert Valdez, 33, were shot in the back while riding their bicycles in the early-morning hours…Sheehan and Richardson also are accused of participating in eight drive-by shootings earlier that morning as part of a drunken spree…. I just looked at him in my mir-

ror and saw him fall. And I was like, "Yeah, you hit him. Good shot!" (DeBruin 1994: April 6).

In this incident and many others, the assailants had been using alcohol or drugs. Substance-impaired judgment, however, is not enough to account for such potentially lethal attacks on people unknown to them. How, then, can we understand these incidents?

The approach I consider most useful investigates the following hypotheses:

1. The young males who engage in drive-by and other forms of gun violence have not developed a sense of identification with the human race at large. There is little awareness of how others think and feel, little empathy. To them, other people are objects. This arrested development of feelings for humanity is in all probability the outcome of earlier failures in socialization: they themselves were probably treated without understanding and compassion.
2. Peer acceptance, important for most young adults, is a dominating motivation for these men, who envision no other reward structure in their future.
3. Guns—and automobiles—provide remote devices for dealing death. One does not have to confront another human being, a confrontation in which mental and physical skills could determine the outcome. One can be a "man" by killing another human being as easily as one operates a remote control for the television set.

Every generation known to history has faced the challenge of socializing its young males and directing their spirit and energies into constructive uses. Our generation certainly has its work cut out for it.

School Shootings

A new dimension recently has been added to young men with guns—and bombs. It is not so new for students to engage in pranks and acts of vandalism. A successful businessman confessed to me that a few years back, he and several other students had placed "For sale" signs on the high school and then gone to the trouble of filling the swimming pool with gelatin (orange flavor, mainly). Most students with deeper grievances simply skip or withdraw from school. Personal animosities are settled—or at least expressed—through a scuffle after school. Nobody is seriously hurt, and sometimes the antagonists even become friends afterward.

Today the ready availability of guns and recipes for bomb making provide a much more dangerous avenue of expression for youth grievances. Furthermore, the victims are no longer limited to particular people who are perceived as having rejected or harmed the killers. A pair of angry adolescents might choose an entire set of fellow students (e.g., athletes, people of a different race), or just let loose on anybody unfortunate enough to be on the scene. One "quiet kid, pretty much like the others" might bring a rifle and a back-up pistol to school one day and fire at his classmates. But why? The following beliefs can help answer the question.

- *Killing is part of life in the United States.* The killing function of the death system is deeply embodied in U.S. history. For example, Lane (1997) notes that starting with colonial times, guns were far more common in the new land than they had been in England. Muskets were seen as necessary for protection against the French and hostile natives as well as for hunting. Guns and killing became even more significant in the aftermath of the Civil War. Rifles and handguns remain easily available today.
- *Killing solves problems.* A nasty relationship can be ended this way; so can an unsatisfactory drug transaction. Suicide is another way in which problems can be made to go away (although not for the survivors). The higher rate of male suicide is related to the most frequently chosen method—guns—as a "manly" response to stress. The 14 year-olds in Port Huron charged with plotting to massacre their students and teachers also planned to commit suicide afterward; this seems to be a common theme in school shootings. The 15 year old shooter in Heritage High School (Conyers, Georgia) had already stuck a revolver in his mouth before the principal arrived in time to talk him out of killing himself.
- *There is no other way to deal with rejection, frustration, and loss.* This belief is mistaken. Nevertheless, some teenagers become killers because

they cannot think of any other way to deal with a threat to their relationships with their girlfriends. Young people usually have not had much experience in coping with disappointment and frustration. Their thought processes are therefore likely to be truncated, even reduced to the fatal either/or: "Either she comes back to me or I have to kill—somebody, maybe everybody." A 15 year old arrested for killing his parents and two classmates and wounding twenty others explained: "I had no other choice." Take frustration, inexperience, and oversimplified thought processes and add the availability of weapons—the potential for a lethal outcome is there.

- *The world is divided between Us and Them (or just Me and All of You).* Anybody who has survived adolescence is likely to remember the "in groups," the students who seemed to get all the attention and all the breaks. Even people who were among the most popular students later report that they often suffered from feelings of uncertainty, anxiety, and being left out. Furthermore, the prejudices nurtured in society have the opportunity to play themselves out in the high-school years. Many adolescents take advantage of this opportunity to become friends with people who differ in racial, religious, or ethnic background. Others, however, bring with them deeply ingrained prejudices that can easily be triggered. The Columbine High School shootings, for example, had a racist component that has been associated with the influence of skinhead organizations. There are always others to blame and attack when things go wrong in one's own life.

We hear frequent calls for greater understanding between people of different races and backgrounds, more effective adult guidance, and decreased access to firearms. We should be listening, shouldn't we?

Mass and Serial Killers: Who Are They and Why Do They Do It?

Many killings appear to be understandable. A burglar picks the wrong home to burglarize and is shot dead. One drug dealer is ambushed by another in a turf dispute. A drunken brawl ends in death when one combatant goes for a knife. These killings disturb but do not puzzle us. Mass and serial killing, however, seem more remote from ordinary human experience. Who are these killers, and why do they kill so many? Mass killers are alarming to society both because of the many lives they destroy at one time and place and because their very existence appears to contradict our expectations of human feeling and conduct. We will see that there are similarities and differences between mass and serial killers and that both types of murder are indeed quite out of the ordinary.

A mass killing is one in which several people die in a single episode. Some examples of mass killing in recent years:

- Twenty-one shot to death at a McDonald's restaurant in California (1984)
- Sixteen family members shot to death in Arkansas (1986)
- Eighty-seven die of smoke inhalation and burns in a night club fire in New York City (1990)
- Twenty-two shot to death in a restaurant in Texas (1991)
- Three family members killed at home and nine shot to death in Atlanta brokerage offices (1999)

These examples of mass murder in the United States are typical in that all were the work of a lone killer (a male) and that most involved firearms. Furthermore, in most of these instances the killer knew few if any of his victims. He may have wanted to get back at a particular person he thought had treated him badly (as in the night club arson), but he had no compunction about slaying many others as well. The most recent of these mass killings (Atlanta) had a disturbing new element that will be discussed below.

The public perception of the mass murderer has proven to be accurate—that he is a person who feels rejected by society, angry at real or imagined mistreatment, and motivated to "get back" at all that has oppressed him, even though he has suffered no harm from the particular individuals he has killed. James Oliver Huberty personifies this description. He had lost his longtime job as a skilled worker when the plant had to downsize because of economic conditions. He moved to another state, found another job, but lost it. Over the years, he had often practiced shooting his rifles into the basement wall and occasionally frightened his neighbors by brandishing a weapon. One afternoon he told his wife he was going to "hunt humans." She assumed that James was just trying to upset her again. He kissed her goodbye and walked back to the McDonald's where he and his family had lunched a few hours earlier. He opened fire, killing twenty-one and wounding another nineteen before being felled by a police sharpshooter.

The available explanations remain inadequate, however, because many people have come from dysfunctional families and have later experienced rejection and hard times, but only a few become mass murderers. Holmes & Holmes (1994) find that mass murderers also have a strong suicidal streak: they are willing or even motivated to die at the scene of their crimes. This tendency contrasts with that of most serial killers, who intend to keep on killing as long as they can.

Some mass murderers are psychotic, but again, not all psychotic people become mass murderers. In general, mass murderers (and serial killers) do not attract much attention until they are apprehended or shot. Others have little sense of their own identity and are willing to become disciples of a charismatic person—such was the situation with Charles Manson and several of his followers. Their mass killing episodes may also be compared with the hate group dynamics expressed by Nazis and emulated by skinheads. The latter have caused many violent confrontations with people they have targeted as objects of their hatred, both in the United States and Germany, although not all of these have resulted in fatalities.

The mass murderer is always a man (Lane, 1997). He is typically a white male in his late twenties or thirties. Rarely is the mass murderer a hardened criminal, although a spotty history of property crime *is* common (Levin & Fox, 1985). The occurrence of mass murder often follows a spell of frustration, when a particular event triggers sudden rage; yet in other cases, the killer is coolly pursuing some goal he cannot otherwise attain (1985, p. 48).

A few special aspects about mass killers are worth keeping in mind:

1. Mass killers do not draw their violence from the Southern tradition of homicide. Although murder is most common in the South—and often appears to be the outcome of a lethal response to a challenge—relatively few mass murders occur in the South, nor do they take the form of a direct confrontation. There is reason to believe that Southerners have continued to provide more support for each other through neighborhoods, churches, and other community organizations, thereby reducing the sense of alienation that can lead to violence against others. "Even an unemployed or divorced man in the rural South was far less likely to be alone. His kin, congregation, or lodge were there to help" (Humphrey and Palmer, 1986–1987).

2. Boom cities attract many people whose high hopes fail to be fulfilled. The people become bitter, disillusioned, and ready to try something different to get rid of their frustrations and anger (as was the case with Huberty).

3. The age and race correlates of murder in general do not apply to mass or serial killers. Most murders are committed by young adults, and, as already noted, the rate is higher among African Americans. By contrast, most mass killers are white and in their thirties or forties.

4. Although only a few mass murderers prove to be psychotic, another type of deviant personality is well known to health professionals and law enforcement agencies: the person with an antisocial personality (also known as *sociopath* and *psychopath*). He or she is not out of touch with reality and does not hear voices that order him to kill. Basically, the antisocial personality does not feel affection or empathy for other people. This is the person whose mode of operation is to "use" other people without remorse. The antisocial personality is likely to have a low toleration for frustration and to explode in rage when things don't go his or her way. There is no real concern for other people.

Mark Barton, the Atlanta mass murderer, had some of the typical characteristics of a mass murderer, notably the low toleration for frustration and explosive rage when things go wrong. His interpersonal relationships were also deeply flawed; he was a father who neglected his children, kept to himself, and made few if any friends. He was clearly a person who had little affection or empathy for others. Barton was also white and in his middle years (44), like other mass murderers. However, he had worked as a chemist, had a middle-class lifestyle, and was not conspicuously on the outs with society. In fact, neighbors described him as a quiet, churchgoing man who worked all day on his computer.

Two ominous characteristics of Barton and his rampage awaken concern that more such mass killings might occur in the future. First, is it possible that people with limited social skills or empathy will further distance themselves from others by means of an all-consuming computer connection to the world—a "virtual" life rather than an actual one? This computer-mediated lifestyle might have just enough of a deadening effect on the user's sense of human bonds that the person finds it as easy to squeeze a trigger as to click on an icon. Second, day trading is already becoming an addictive form of gambling, one in which the stakes can go completely out of control. The high of making a "quick killing" on the stock market can be followed by the loss of one's entire savings and assets. Desperation becomes rage and rage becomes murder. There is much more to Barton's story: not only did he spray two brokerage offices with bullets, he also murdered his own family with a blunt instrument one or two days before. Furthermore, he was the main suspect in the deaths of his first wife and her mother, which occurred soon after he took out a large insurance policy on his mother. Barton, then, was not simply a man who became unhinged by losses on the stock market; he was already a manipulative and self-centered person with a habit of using and discarding other people for his own aims. This should come as something of a relief—most day traders will not become killers after a bad spell on the computer. However, we may not have seen the last of this kind of tragedy.

Serial killing occurs in other nations as well. Nineteenth-century London's "Jack the Ripper" is the prototypical serial killer. Like many other serial killers, "Jack" was a male who chose women for his victims. Prostitutes have long been at special risk for serial killing. Some serial killers, however, have attacked children or hospital patients, while others have selected almost any available target.

David Lester (1995) notes:

The motives of serial killers seem to have changed over the years. In preindustrial times, serial murderers tended to be depraved aristocrats preying on peasants; in the industrial era, seemingly respectable middle-class men killed prostitutes, homeless boys and housemaids. Today serial murderers are often people who exist on the margins of society, those who have failed to achieve their personal expectations, who are mainly of working- and lower-middle-class origins, and who attack middle-class victims such as college students. (1995, p. 187).

A recently apprehended serial-killing suspect who has been charged with eight slayings fits the pattern identified by Lester (Pearson 1999: June 22). Nevertheless, there has not yet been sufficient research to indicate why some people with dysfunctional family backgrounds and difficult life experiences become serial killers but most do not.

Holmes and Holmes offer the chilling estimate that "From our contacts with law enforcement officials all over the United States, we believe that a more accurate estimate may be as high as 200" (1994, p. 103). It is thought that many serial killers "limit" themselves to two or three murders a year and therefore draw less attention to themselves and are able to continue.

Serial killers receive a great deal of attention from the media. A series of bloody murders becomes a Monday night movie. Some killers report that they wanted to be famous, just like the people they have seen on television. Protests and criticisms have been voiced repeatedly about the tendency of the media to capitalize on serial killing and other forms of violent death. The media's usual response is to note that the public has a right to be informed and also, incidentally, that it sells newspapers and raises the viewership ratings. And so the death system keeps right on being the death system: the mass or serial killer becomes a commodity, and perhaps an inspiration to other potential killers.

Political Murder: Assassination in the United States

Abraham Lincoln…John F. Kennedy…Robert F. Kennedy…Martin Luther King, Jr. The assassi-
nation of these four leaders has become a disturbing part of American history. The murder of a political leader has both its private and its public side. A child loses a father, a wife her husband, the country a leader. A systematic examination of political assassinations in the United States has been conducted by James W. Clarke (1982), who researched the cases listed in Table 8-2. Some people take comfort in the view that a rational individual would not make an attempt on the life of a political figure. Attention has so often been given to the mental state of the assassin that one might conclude that this theory has been well established. Not necessarily. The mental illness theory does not account for all or even most of the assassination attempts.

Clarke found four types of assassins. They may be summarized as *Type I: Political Extremists; Type II: Rejected and Misguided People; Type III: Antisocial Personalities;* and *Type IV: Psychotics.* Three of these types were clearly in contact with reality and did not suffer from delusions, hallucinations, or other cognitive distortions. This is not to say that the assassins were without personal problems. Social isolation or disturbances of interpersonal relationships were characteristic of several types. They differed markedly in the primary motive for the assassination attempt. This can be seen most clearly when comparing the Type I and the Type IV assassins.

The public stereotype of the crazed assassin is represented by the men who threatened the lives of Andrew Jackson, James Garfield, and Theodore Roosevelt. These people were delusional and, at times, incoherent. Almost anybody would have easily recognized their distortions of reality and need for treatment. In keeping with their defects in reality test testing, Lawrence, Guiteau, and Schrank were confused and idiosyncratic in their motivation. Guiteau, for example, had a friendly attitude toward Garfield, but convinced himself that the president must be killed to "save the Republic." He later said that God had made him do it. It was clear that in this and in most other matters, Guiteau had a grossly distorted view of himself and the world.

By contrast, the Type I assassins were motivated by political objectives: "rational extremists," as Clarke puts it (1982, p. 262). Booth, Collazo, Torresola, and Sirhan were motivated by

TABLE 8-2

Political Assassination Attempts, United States

Year	Intended Victim	Assassin	Outcome
1835	Andrew Jackson	Richard Lawrence	Unharmed
1865	Abraham Lincoln	John Wilkes Booth	Killed
1881	James Garfield	Charles Guiteau	Killed
1901	William McKinley	Leon Czolgosz	Killed
1912	Theodore Roosevelt	John Schrank	Wounded
1933	Franklin Roosevelt	Giuseppe Zangara	Unharmed*
1935	Huey Long	Carl Weiss	Killed
1950	Harry S Truman	Oscar Collazo and Griselio Torresola	Unharmed†
1963	John F. Kennedy	Lee Harvey Oswald	Killed
1968	Martin Luther King	James Earl Ray	Killed
1968	Robert Kennedy	Sirhan Sirhan	Killed
1972	George Wallace	Arthur Bremer	Wounded
1974	Richard Nixon	Samuel Byck	Unharmed**
1975	Gerald Ford	Lynette Fromm	Unharmed
1975	Gerald Ford	Sara Moore	Unharmed

Source: James W. Clarke 1982.

*Chicago Mayor Anton Cermak was killed and four others wounded in the volley of shots fired at President Roosevelt.

†Security guards Leslie Coffelt and Joseph Downs were wounded; Coffelt died as he returned fire and killed Torresola.

**Byck killed two Delta pilots and wounded a cabin attendant in an aborted attempt to force the plane to crash into the White House.

their identification with nationalistic aims. Czolgosz thought that by killing McKinley he would be striking a blow for "the good working people," a class-oriented political motivation. None of these men was insane (legal framework) or psychotic (psychiatric).

The people Clarke classifies as Type III assassins will remind us of the antisocial personalities who committed mass murders. These men, such as Bremer, Byck, and Zangara, hated the society they felt had rejected and frustrated them. Unable to express feelings other than helplessness or rage, they cast about for a target that would symbolically represent these aspects of society they most disliked. They did not have personal animosity toward the leaders they attacked. Like the mass murderers, the Type III assassins showed no remorse. Although neither the typical mass murderer nor the Type III assassin is "crazy," each has a fundamental character flaw in the ability to feel and express ordinary human feeling.

Up to this point, we have seen that some assassins (Type III) have been the same kind of people who commit mass murders, and that a few others (Type IV) are, in fact, the psychotic killers celebrated in stereotypes, but that others (Type I) have been politically conscious people who took this extreme action thinking that it would further a cause to which they held allegiance. This leaves still another kind of assassin. Oswald, Byck, Fromm, and Moore were very anxious people who felt rejected and unable to cope with the demands of life. They wanted to be taken seriously by somebody and to prove themselves in some way. Although a Type II assassin might attach himself or herself to a political cause, the basic objective is personal: somehow to redeem one's own miserable life by a bold deed. As Clarke observes, the Type II assassins were misguided people, but not insane.

This attention to the psychological makeup of individual assassins should not distract us from more systematic factors. For example, the emergence of television has generated an unprecedented type and degree of coverage for spectacular events. How often do you want to see the stricken man crumple from the bullet? Would you like to see it in slow motion? Split-screen? Reverse angle? Whether the potential assassin's motivation is primarily political or personal, over the past several decades there has been the added incentive of having this event flashed before the eyes of many millions of people. Another point to consider is that some potential assassins have political grievances that are not in themselves irrational. We will encounter this problem again when we look at terrorism. To recognize that actual and significant political grievances can stimulate assassination attempts is not to condone such acts of violence. Instead, we may be better prepared as a society to prevent or respond to assassination attempts if we do not insist on believing that they are all the work of people who are mentally ill. A more general issue recurs here as it did when we considered mass murderers: can we continue to be an open and trusting society and still improve our ability to protect ourselves, our children, and our leaders from the killers?

TERRORISM

The bomb that killed 168 people and demolished the Alfred P. Murrah Federal Building in Oklahoma City on April 15, 1996, still resonates in the nation's memory. The Oklahoma City bombing is the terrorist attack with the greatest impact in the United States in our time. We will first size up terrorism at large and then return to this devastating episode.

Who Is the Terrorist?

Terrorism is "violence or threat of violence, in which civilians or locations habituated by civilians are targets or are frequently involved in the conflict" (Picard, 1993, p. 11). This is a useful working definition of terrorism. It makes clear the facts that (1) terrorism operates as a threat as well as an actuality, and (2) it usually claims civilians as victims. But who is the terrorist?

Is the terrorist a believer in the fundamentalist Shi'ite form of Islam who is prepared for his own death as he plans the massacre of others? Yes, sometimes. This was true, for example, of Raad Meftel Ajeel, the young man who crashed

through the gates of the U.S. embassy in Kuwait, dying as his cargo of hexogen and butane exploded. The identity of the two Shi'ites whose earlier and similar suicidal attack resulted in the death of 241 American and 58 French servicemen in Beirut has never been determined. This new form of terrorism had been introduced a few months prior to these attacks, on April 18, 1983, when a truck loaded with explosives killed forty-five people in Beirut. What was new about these attacks was the willingness of the terrorist to ensure the success of the mission by sacrificing his own life. Terrorism, in instances of this kind, combines murder with suicide and also resembles assassination in being motivated by a political or religious cause.

Yet terrorism itself is by no means either a recent development or a tactic used only by some Shi'ite extremists. Terrorism has had a long and diverse history. Some examples are listed in Table 8-3. Terrorism was a force as early as the eleventh century. The group of killers whose name is still invoked today—the Assassins—were members of a small but highly disciplined Middle Eastern religious sect that believed in the imminent beginning of a new millennium. Mistreated by those in control at the time (the Seljuks), the Assassins carried out lethal terrorist operations for about 200 years. Disguising themselves in various ways and choosing the dagger as their weapon, the Assassins killed a number of powerful leaders and succeeded in creating a climate of terror. They expected to die as they completed their missions.

During part of the same period, Christian Crusaders fought for possession of the Holy Sepulchre (which actually no longer existed). The Crusaders were not a terrorist organization, but they did abandon themselves to episodes of massacre and atrocity. The major example occurred when they broke through the defenses in Jerusalem and slaughtered many of the inhabitants, including women and children. The Jews of this city, who had played no particular role in the hostilities, were herded into a mosque and burned alive. Institutionalized terroristic killing as part of the Christian establishment awaited the formation of the Inquisition in 1231. The persecution of suspected heretics and dissidents spread through much of Western Europe. Thousands

Terrorism has taken lives and created tensions throughout much of the world.

TABLE 8-3

Some Terrorist Killers before the Twentieth Century

Terrorist Organization	Time	Place	Usual Methods
The Assassins	c. 11th–13th	Persia, Syria	Dagger
The Crusaders	c. 11th	Jerusalem	Burning alive
The Inquisition	c. 13th–17th	Europe	Burning alive
Tamerlane	c. 14th	Middle East	Burial alive
French Republic	1790s	Paris	Guillotine
The Thugs	c. 19th	India	Strangulation
Ku Klux Klan	1867–	United States	Lynching, guns, fire
Molly Maguires	1870s	United States	Explosives, guns
Narodnaya Volya	1878–1881	Russia	Guns, explosives
The People's Will	1869–1885	Russia	Bomb-throwing
Anarchists (individuals)	c. 1890s	Europe	Bomb-throwing

Sources: Dobson & Payne (1987), Hofstadter & Wallace (1971), Lacquer (1987), Lea (1906–1907), O'Brien (1973), Raynor (1987), Wakin (1984).

were burned alive, and many others died while being questioned and tortured. The later Protestant version of religious persecution was no less cruel and deadly. Many conquerors have utilized terror tactics not only to destroy enemies but also to undermine the will to resist. Tamerlane, for example, buried thousands of his victims alive. Terrorism has accompanied many other military campaigns throughout history.

For the word *terrorism* itself, we must turn to the French Revolution. The new government rounded up suspected "enemies of the people" and sent about 30,000 of them to the newly invented guillotine. Robespierre seemed to believe that by making so many public examples of people guilty of unacceptable thoughts or conduct, he would create a new type of society in which everybody lived in love and harmony. Like most other terrorist actions, the "reign of terror" failed to achieve its objectives, and Robespierre himself went to the guillotine.

Terrorism occurred in many places and circumstances throughout the nineteenth century. The Thugs (or *thuggees*) of India robbed travelers and strangled them with silk ties. The Thugs themselves regarded the killing as an honorable and sacred act of religious devotion. And, like many other murdering terrorists, Thugs professed to hold death in contempt. The terrorist tradition includes a pattern of belief and behavior

in which there is no compunction about killing others nor about meeting one's own death through violence.

The Ku Klux Klan (KKK) and the Molly Maguires exemplify terrorist groups that formed in the United States shortly before and after the Civil War. Started in 1867, at first the KKK attempted to protect Southern whites from some of the threats and abuses that followed their defeat. Before long, however, the KKK had become a terrorist organization intended to keep the freed African Americans "in their place." The KKK did not specialize in mass killing; instead, threats, beatings and property destruction were augmented by the occasional lynching. Perhaps the fact that the KKK often had the support of the local establishment (or actually was the local establishment under its robes) meant that the executions did not have to be numerous, but simply had to remind potential victims that "uppityness" would not be tolerated. Historians of violence in the United States believe that much of this tradition was generated by the KKK and similar organizations after the Civil War to keep African Americans in a powerless position. We may also think here of the long-standing excess of murder in the southern United States that continues to this day.

The Molly Maguires first made themselves known in the 1860s as some Irish Americans reacted to oppressive and dangerous circumstances. As one historian tells it:

> In Pennsylvania, the oppressors were mine owners who brutalized the miners and their families. The miners went down into the dangerous hell of the mines, often with their children along, digging up wealth for the owners and a marginal living for themselves. New waves of immigrants enabled the owners to keep wages low; workers were forced to live in company houses and buy at company stores in between periods of idleness when they earned nothing. Even while working, many a miner received, instead of his monthly pay, a "bobtail check" showing that he owed the company money. When workers tried to organize, the owners intimidated them, and when fledgling labor organizations protested or struck, they were crushed. (Wakin, 1984, p. 147)

The Molly Maguires threatened and beat mine owners, then used bombs to create an atmosphere of terror, killing several people they considered to be oppressors. This underground movement did arouse fear and direct attention to the miners' predicaments, but like so many other organizations that resorted to terror, it failed to achieve its basic objectives. Improved conditions for miners would still be a long time in coming—and clever detective work resulted in the conviction and hanging of nineteen Molly Maguires, probably more men than the group had itself killed during its decade or so of activity.

Terrorism can also be instructive: Did the Molly Maguires perhaps learn something from the ruthless methods of their bosses, and did both management and labor in the forthcoming years teach each other new lessons in brutal force? And did the prolonged exposure to threat and violence suggest something to the nineteenth century African American that is expressed in contemporary murder rates?

Twentieth-Century Terrorism

What will historians say about the so recently elapsed twentieth century? One fact will be impossible to overlook: the infliction of deprivation, cruelty, and death upon millions of people. Throughout all of human history, there have never been so many casualties of man-made violence.

Numbers can be numbing. We can grasp and respond to the death of one person, to the death of a family, perhaps to the death of all occupants of a jet liner. It is much harder to grasp both the individual and the mass tragedy when the victims are numbered in thousands…in millions. Table 8-4 looks much like any other table: some identifying information and a lot of numbers. But for any thinking, feeling human being, there can be nothing "so what" about the horrors represented here.

Survivors of all these campaigns of terror are still among us, and many can recall their experiences with vivid immediacy. For example, an aged woman in Arizona will never forget how her childhood and very nearly her life were destroyed when the Turks started their operation to eliminate the Armenian population. In her own neighborhood, the men were rounded up for "routine questioning" that turned out to be excruciating torture, followed by death. As it became clear that this was only the beginning of the terror, she and her family barely managed to escape. If this had proved to be the only example of large-scale terrorism in the twentieth century, its memory might have been more firmly impressed upon society in general. Approximately 800,000 people slaughtered—not killed in combat, but slaughtered!

Nothing in the ordinary experience of most people can serve as comparison. We know that thousands are killed in automobile accidents. We are aware of AIDS as a newly emerged life-threatening disease. We may have read the names on the Vietnam Memorial Wall. But years of highway fatalities, AIDS-related deaths, and Vietnam casualties are surpassed by what the armed forces of one nation did to the civilians of a differing ethnic group within a period of some months.

This, in the eyes of some observers, was only a "sideshow" to World War I and, as events would subsequently show, only one of numerous reigns of terror that have marked the twentieth century. The total number of estimated deaths from the various persecutions and massacres listed in Table 8-4 exceeds 22 million men, women, and children. This number is larger than the populations of Finland and Holland combined, larger than the cities of Chicago, Los Angeles, Montreal, New

TABLE 8-4

Examples of Large-Scale Terrorism in the Twentieth Century

Killers	Victims	Date	Deaths
Turks	Armenians	1915	800,000
Soviet Communist Party	Russian peasants	1929–1932	11,000,000
Soviet Communist Party	Russian "dissidents"	1937–1938	500,000
Nazis	Jews	1933–1945	6,000,000
Muslims*	Hindus, Sikhs	1946	
Hindus, Sikhs*	Muslims	1946	1,000,000
Sudanese Muslims	Sudanese, Africans	1955–1972	1,000,000
Indonesians	Communists	1965	600,000
Nigerians	Ibo	1966–1967	800,000
Khmer Rouge	Cambodians	1975–1977	2,000,000
Tutsi/Hutu†	Hutu/Tutsi	1972–1975	100,000
Hutu/Tutsi	Hutu/Tutsi	1994	500,000
Hutu/Tutsi (Burundi)	Tutsi/Hutu	1996	50,000+
Kosovo	Ethnic Albanians	1999	10,000

Sources: Amnesty International (1984), Associated Press (1994: April 16), Becker (1986), Conquest (1986), Grosscup (1987), Gutteridge (1986), Kuper (1981), Laqueur (1987), Morgan (1989), Payne (1973), Sterling (1981), *Time* (1994: April 18). All numbers are best available estimates.

*During the partition of India following War War II, Hindus and Sikhs moving east were slaughtered by Muslims, and Muslims moving west were slaughtered by Hindus and Sikhs.

†Terrorism, including massacre, was carried out both by the minority Tutsi and the majority Hutu peoples of Rwanda and Burundi. A new wave of ethnic/political violence erupted in April, 1994 with reports of massacres and total social disorganization.

York, Ottawa, and San Francisco combined. Without doubt, this total is also an underestimate. There is no really reliable estimate for the deaths suffered by Cambodians at the hands of the Khmer Rouge—in the hundreds of thousands, surely, perhaps more than a million. For the other totals, relatively conservative estimates have been selected. It could be argued that more than 30 million perished as the direct result of the various reigns of terror listed in Table 8-4—and this list is not intended to be complete.

As these words are being written, people with fresh memories of terror are just starting the process of recovery. Families who escaped from Kosovo and found welcome in Arizona are now returning to what is left of their homes and communities. More than 10,000 others were killed during an operation that was peculiarly described as "ethnic cleansing." Is a person's ethnicity "dirty"? Are robbery, torture, eviction, and massacre "cleansing?" The assault on ethnic Albanians in Kosovo is one more devastating chapter in the attempt to acquire or keep political power through the use of terrorism and lethal force.

It is not within the scope of this book to examine these events in detail. However, we can offer a few observations based securely upon the available evidence.

1. Terror has often been unleashed against people who share the same land and many of the same experiences and tribulations, but who are *perceived as being different in some significant way.* Most German Jews, for example, were law-abiding and patriotic Germans—but when Hitler pushed the anti-Semitism button, Germans who also happened to be Jewish were ostracized, then slaughtered. Hindus, Sikhs, and Muslims alike had shared the hardships of drought, famine, and colonial subjugation, but the mutual perception that their religious differences were all-important led to widespread atrocities and killings during the

The Holocaust took more than 6 million lives during World War II and left many others widowed and orphaned. Here are a few children who survived imprisonment in the Auschwitz (Poland) camp.

partition of India and the creation of Pakistan—and hostilities have resumed recently.

2. Killing is often preceded by ostracism, by *denying the other person's fundamental reality as a human being*. Our people are truly human; others are less than human. It would not re-

ally be killing a person to eradicate those vermin, waste those pigs. In this sense, the murder takes place first in the mind.

3. *Fear kills.* Reigns of terror have often been triggered or intensified because those in power have feared overthrow. The Stalinist

purge of 1937–1938, for example, was directed almost exclusively at Soviet citizens who were suspected of harboring politically unreliable thoughts. An alleged plot against the government of Indonesia aroused fear-driven hysteria of such magnitude that 600,000 fellow citizens were slaughtered in a short period of time, most of them innocent of any crime or criminal intention

4. *Cold-blooded "rationalism" kills.* In many episodes of terrorism, the attackers have shown themselves as frenzied and brutal people, caught up and distorted by high passions. But some of the most destructive terrorist operations have been systematically planned as "rational" ways to achieve political objectives. Did 11 million Russians actually die at the hands of fellow Russians in 1929–1932? Yes, that is no misprint. Stalin (who would later kill another half million in a devastating purge) saw to it that millions of peasants died so that he could achieve his economic and political aims. Most died from planned starvation, but others were killed outright. (And this incredible destruction of his own countrymen did not achieve its "rational" objectives either; terrorism seldom if ever does.

5. *Religious intolerance instigates and justifies terrorism.* Many people secure in their own religious beliefs have lived harmoniously with people of other faiths. Nevertheless, some of the bloodiest reigns of terror have been launched by people who were convinced both that they, and they alone, have the true religion and that they are therefore entitled to convert or destroy all others. True believers become some of the most dangerous people alive when they become killers. There is no hesitation, no reflection, no compassion. True believers often appear on both sides of religious/ethnic issues.

I have known several mental patients who heard voices or felt strong impulses that brought them to the edge of killing another person. They suffered terribly because they did not want to kill and yet they could not stand the pressure—so they sought help. I have yet to learn of a religious cult that asked for help to rid itself of murderous impulses.

6. *Terrorism fails.* Seldom has a terrorist organization or movement achieved its objectives by persecution and killing. The Nazis' "final solu-

tion," for example, was not only brutal and inhumane to the extreme, but it also contributed significantly to Germany's defeat. Many of that nation's leading scientists, physicians, and other professionals were Jewish. *Germany without Jews* (Engelmann, 1984) was a weakened nation. Furthermore, Germany was left with a heritage of guilt and shame over the participation of many people not in the Nazi movement or hierarchy who became *Hitler's Willing Executioners* (Goldhagen, 1996). In an earlier epoch, an arrogant and intolerant Spanish monarch banished the Moors from what had been their homeland for centuries. The conditions of this banishment were so harsh that more men, women, and children died than survived to move on elsewhere. This "purification" or "ethnic cleansing" plan dealt Spain a blow from which it has never recovered. Repeatedly, terrorism has failed to achieve lasting success; most often it has brought about violent discord among the terrorists themselves, retaliation from others, and the loss of opportunities for improving one's conditions by positive efforts.

Terrorism and the Death System Today

The pattern of terrorism has been changing in recent years. The newer terrorism is as deadly and devastating as ever, but we must give some attention to the ever-shifting context and meaning of terrorism in the international death system.

The Direction of Terrorism: Up or Down?

Twentieth-century terrorism has several important structural aspects. One of these involves the *direction* of terrorism: up or down? *Upward-directed terrorism* operations are conducted by people who consider themselves oppressed and disenfranchised. They use violence and the threat of violence, hoping either to recruit other supporters and force the establishment to grant concessions or to overthrow the regime. Upward-directed terrorism—the terrorism of protest—usually takes episodic forms, claims some innocent victims, creates a climate of fear, and leads to violent reprisals, some of which also kill innocent victims. From ancient times to the present, women and children have been particularly vulnerable, caught between factional violence and reprisals.

Downward-directed terrorism is employed by the regimes themselves, seeking to maintain or extend their power. The more totalitarian the regime, the more terrorism. The terrorism of oppression is generally more efficient and far reaching than the terrorism of protest. The entire apparatus of the government is available for this purpose, including paid spies and informers, controlled media, and military and paramilitary forces. Amnesty International continually reports on "disappearances," tortures, and killings still being carried out by many regimes today. There seems to be no limit to the brutality and violence that some governments will inflict on their own people.

Two facts stand out regarding upward-directed and downward-directed terrorism in the twentieth century: (1) Totalitarian regimes have very few episodes of protest terrorism. The streets are safe—until the regime decides to launch one of its own reigns of terror. Open societies are more vulnerable to protest terrorism. (2) The death toll from terrorism is much higher when the establishment itself turns killer. Protest terrorists may kill dozens of people, even, on rare occasions, hundreds. Stalin's Soviet Communist Party systematically killed millions of Russian peasants.

Three other structural considerations are closely related: technology, media coverage, and financing. Terrorism of all types has become capable of causing more deaths and by a greater variety of methods through the use of advanced technologies. It is no longer necessary to approach a victim with a dagger concealed under a robe. Plastic explosives, remote detonation devices, and many other technological innovations have added to the lethal potential of terrorism.

Mass media and terrorism have become an "odd couple." The media feasts on reports and rumors of terrorism, thereby augmenting the terrorists' own ability to create a climate of fear. Close observers of media coverage agree that television and the press often "construct" terrorist threats by their selective and at times exaggerated coverage (Dobkin, 1992; Picard, 1993; Weimann & Winn, 1994). Accordingly, various factions "play" the media to achieve their goals.

Some events are staged for their media value: "A bomb exploding here in rush hour will make television news around the world." This phenomenon is well expressed in the movie *Wag the Dog*. Meanwhile, the controlled media of totalitarian regimes carefully avoids mentioning atrocities conducted by its own government.

Financing is perhaps the least recognized major factor in terrorism today, especially on the international scene. Terrorism has become a fairly expensive proposition. Although some individual terrorists come from impoverished circumstances, the movements themselves are generally well financed and represent investments for which a substantial return is expected. A young bomber, for example, may be giving his life for somebody else's dream of wealth and power.

The New Target: Innocent Bystanders

The primary target of terrorist attacks has changed over the years. "Terrorism" usually targeted the person and property of specific adversaries, for example, a police station or a military patrol. In recent years, however, some of the most brutal regimes have collapsed as part of the breakdown of the communist bloc and the dissolution of the Soviet Union itself. There is still old-fashioned terrorism and equally lethal counter-terrorism in existing oppressive regimes. From the international standpoint, however, terrorism has now selected two new primary targets. In their analysis of extensive data on worldwide terrorism, Weimann and Winn (1994) find that police and military are no longer the chief targets of terrorist attacks. Furthermore, important installations such as hydroelectric plants and other utilities are seldom attacked. With a few exceptions, the top governmental leaders are also less frequently targeted. Who is the target then? Diplomats and ordinary citizens!

As victims, diplomats embody a different symbolic meaning from that of policemen. In those autocratic countries that historically faced domestic terrorism, police forces represented violent repression, the flouting of law by authorities, and the abusive application of raw power. Contemporary diplomats do not conjure up the same imagery. They are by contrast the embodiment of conciliation, codes of conduct, and constraints on the use of power. (Weimann and Winn, 1994, p. 34)

The targeting of diplomats is a profound violation of international law that has been for the most part respected even during periods of total war. It is also a way to slow the process of finding peaceful solutions to problems for those who want to retain the power of violence.

Attacks on ordinary citizens provide a symbolic way to mock powerful nations whose economic and military power do not necessarily protect individuals in the course of their everyday lives. Airlines were a favorite target until improved security measures made terrorist attacks more difficult and more dangerous to the perpetrators. Nevertheless, ordinary citizens and business people have become the most common targets of terrorist attacks in recent years. There are no more innocent bystanders.

The Psychological Side of Terrorism

What about the psychological side of terrorism? Following are several observations I would like to share with you:

1. The terrorist has often been portrayed or perceived as an alluring and powerful figure, a new kind of romantic. Robin Morgan (1989) has even suggested that the terrorist has become a contemporary version of the *Demon Lover:*

    He evokes pity because he lives in death. He emanates sexual power because he represents obliteration. He excites with the thrill of fear. He is the essential challenge to tenderness. He is at once a hero of risk and an antihero of mortality. (1989, p. 24)

From the standpoint of our own research, the image of the romantic and lethal terrorist seems to be another version of The Gay Deceiver—the worldly, strangely charming, sexy person who is willing to show us a good time, and then…! Morgan also sees the terrorist as an example of unrelenting male aggressiveness that has victimized women in many ways throughout the centuries. It is a matter of documented fact, however, that female terrorists have been every bit as deadly as their male counterparts.

2. One person's terrorist is another person's hero. The popular figure of William Tell represented a terrorist to the authorities of the time. You and I might find ourselves in sympathy with some people who have carried out terrorist activities against brutal regimes. In fact, the rebellious spirit has often been considered an American specialty, and the film industry has been supplying us for decades with heroes who saddle up against the forces of unjust authority. There is some danger, then, that the "terrorist" will be whoever those in control of the media choose to portray in those terms.

3. Some people clearly identify themselves with life, some with death. Death was a characteristic of the Nazi self-image (Friedlander, 1984); it can also be observed in the dress, speech, and behavior of some "skinheads" today. The terrorist, lacking a positive self-image and filled with a generalized rage toward society, may be using the coping strategy of "identifying with the aggressor." Who is the aggressor of aggressors? Perhaps Death qualifies for that role. Some terrorists may be attempting to disguise and transform their personal fear of annihilation by entering Death's service.

4. Freud's *death instinct* is a failed theory according to many critics, including the majority of psychoanalysts (Freud, 1923; Kastenbaum, 2000). Nevertheless, it is difficult to escape the idea that a propensity for destructiveness is rooted in human nature. The terrorist—whether member of a furtive cult or a high-ranking government official—is a constant reminder that our death system does not include only the caring, compassionate, and life-protecting passions of society. The killer has always been with us and, on some horrifying occasions, has been us.

From Waco to Oklahoma City and Beyond

Perhaps even this background analysis of terrorism does not quite prepare us for recent developments. The Oklahoma City bombing, with its 168 deaths, is the central event, but to many observers, this tragedy is linked with previous and subsequent acts of violence, as well as with the prospect of even further attacks on the lives of everyday citizens. The recent school shooting episodes may have been stimulated in some way by the Oklahoma City bombing. For the people of Oklahoma City and many others, the sorrow and anger must certainly focus on the personal losses they have suffered. For the nation as a whole, there is compassion for the victims and survivors and also a challenge to deeply rooted beliefs and expectations.

First there is the *weakening of the sense of security.* Since the Civil War, we have not experienced large-scale violence in our homeland. Organized crime, from the Prohibition era to the present, could be compartmentalized as "bad guys killing bad guys." Reports of international terrorism similarly could be dismissed as "foreigners killing foreigners." There was uneasiness about the increasing incidents in which drug-related killings and gang activities were resulting in the deaths of ordinary citizens, including children who happened to be in the line of fire. It was also recognized that some political extremists and emotionally disturbed people in the United States

were potential agents of destruction, bombs that could explode at any time. By and large, however, we felt that most of us who led law-abiding lives would be safe until Nature herself came calling with the mortality card. The Oklahoma City bombing demonstrated all too vividly that the shield of invulnerability was an illusion.

The second blow was to our assumptions about the source of terrorist danger. At first there was widespread suspicion that the Oklahoma City bombing was the work of international terrorists. It had to be some very bad people from someplace else. The evidence, however, pointed to two U.S. citizens, Timothy McVeigh and Michael Fortier. We could no longer feel that only extremist outsiders posed terrorist threats.

There is a growing meld between serial and mass murders committed by individuals and terrorist acts associated with an organized movement. For example, the serial killer who gave himself the name *Unabomber* used a terrorist tactic (explosive devices sent through the mail) and seemed to be carrying out a plan of destruction against certain human targets (three killed and twenty-two injured—all strangers to Theodore

Although critics sometimes speak of the United States as a "gun culture," firearms did not become common until weapon manufacture for the Civil War.

Kaczynski, the man arrested and accused of these crimes). He seemed to think of himself as a one-man organization ("It doesn't appear that the FBI is going to catch us any time soon,") and he made a point of striking again five days after the Oklahoma City bombing.

The Oklahoma City tragedy seemed to connect with isolated acts of violence by individuals, coming together to create a general picture of a menace from within our society.

The government itself is the enemy. Therefore it is more than acceptable—it is necessary and heroic to attack the government. This is an extreme proposition. The American public does not share this view or condone acts of violence toward people and property associated with the government. Nobody described the Oklahoma City bombers as "heroes." Nevertheless, for many years the government has been accused by some people as being overbearing, unresponsive, and intent on taking away individual liberties (notably, for example, by gun control measures). No evidence has come to light of any grand conspiracy against the government by local militias and other organizations. However, the perception that the government is the enemy of the people has generated

a situation within which acts of violence are more likely to occur—at the hands of people who see themselves as good citizens defending their rights.

The deaths of Branch Davidian men, women, and children in Waco almost certainly contributed to the Oklahoma City bombing. The Oklahoma City attack came on the anniversary day (April 19) of the mass deaths in Waco, Texas, in 1993. Timothy McVeigh was reportedly angered by the action of federal agents in Waco—although a great many other people shared this reaction. You may recall what happened at the group residence of the Branch Davidian sect members outside Waco, Texas. This religious community was under federal investigation for possible child abuse practices. Other complaints included a report that members had been stockpiling weapons and ammunition. However, the Branch Davidians apparently had violated no law in acquiring these weapons, nor had they been charged with acts of violence or terrorism. They were regarded as a group of people who practiced a communal version of Christianity that set them somewhat apart from mainstream society. They might or might not be guilty of law-breaking, but the

Fire consumes the Branch Davidian compound in Waco, Texas as the stand-off with federal forces erupts into violence.

group did not fit the profile of an aggressive and militant organization.

Leaders of the Branch Davidians were not cooperative with federal investigations. A stalemate developed in which a large force of armed federal agents occupied the field around the Branch Davidian compound. After fifty-one days of siege and unsuccessful attempts at negotiation, federal agents attacked the compound: four FBI agents were shot dead. Subsequently, the federal forces launched a stronger attack that included armored vehicles and tear gas canisters. The building caught fire. Eighty Branch Davidians, including seventeen children, died in this fire. The attack upon the compound was severely criticized from many quarters, although a criminal trial was unable to determine who fired the first shot. There were conflicting accounts of the entire situation, especially the cause of the fire. Now, years later, there is a new investigation into charges that the fire was started by flammable canisters used or approved by FBI agents. At the least, the massive use of force by federal agencies gave the impression of contributing to the deaths of the very children whose welfare was supposed to be their concern—and the deaths of their parents as well. Some people responded to the Waco tragedy as a terrible error in judgment on the part of the federal agencies involved; others took it as confirmation of their existing fears and suspicions.

Symbols of the government became attractive targets for the new breed of domestic terrorists. A major federal building made an especially attractive target. But why multiply the tragedy of Waco by taking the lives of people who had no conceivable relationship to the attack on the Branch Davidian compound? The old adage "Two wrongs do not make a right" does not seem to make an impression on either domestic or international terrorists.

The shock waves that follow a terrorist attack can lead to significant changes in the way a society thinks about itself and the rules it enforces. The United States is not without blood on its hands: the federal government has sponsored terrorist activity in other nations. Federal and local authorities have also carried out actions that deprived American citizens of their rights (such as the detention of Japanese Americans during World War II). Nevertheless, the United States remains one of the most open societies in the world. Threats of international terrorism have already led to security measures that impose somewhat on individual citizens—for example, the inspection of passengers and luggage for airline flights. The White House is not as approachable by either foot or vehicle since concrete barriers were constructed to foil assassination attempts. One also encounters security measures in entering many federal and state buildings. Additional security measures are being advocated. Canadian authorities, carefully observing developments in America and concerned about their own internal sources of danger, are also poised to increase security measures (Wilson-Smith, 1996).

Should we increase security measures and therefore become a little more like the image of a liberty-stifling nation that has aroused the fear and anger of people with terrorist potential? Drawing the line between responsible actions to reduce terrorism and preserving individual liberties is becoming an increasing challenge in today's death system (Robert, 1995).

Reflections on the Oklahoma City Bombing

We should not underestimate the emotional devastation of sudden death on survivors. Research on grief has made it clear that a sudden, unexpected death is much more difficult to bear; when the victims are children, the shock and pain are even greater. As a society, we have a long way to go in understanding the course of long-term grief and how best to provide support.

The mind-set that contributes to killing is another matter that deserves continuing attention. I have noticed three characteristics of people who band together to commit terrorist acts: First, they usually have had loss and trauma in their own lives. Often their anger and determination are fueled by harm that came in the past to family, friends, or other people with whom they identify. The cruel irony is that they are ready to kill others, including innocent bystanders, to exact "payback" for what has happened to them or to their people. This cycle of revenge killing has proven extremely difficult to terminate. Second, the expressed aims of terrorist programs often drop from view after the activities begin. The acts of destruction become ends in themselves, instead of means of achieving the ends. Third—and perhaps most significant—the terrorist has absolute conviction that he has the right to kill. There is no room for questioning values. There is no other side of the issue. This narrowed, intense, and impervious mind-set has something in common with that of people who prepare for suicide with the fixed idea that no other option is available. Recognizing, preventing, and ameliorating the terrorist mind-set might prove even more useful than constructing concrete barriers and introducing ever more invasive security measures—but we will have to learn more about our own minds as well to understand how inflicting death can seem to be the best way to improve life.

ACCIDENT AND DISASTER

Accidents and disasters have in common the fact that the deaths were not intentional. How much differences does this make? At the time of this writing, the cause of the explosion that sent TWA flight 800 into the sea and killed all 229 aboard has yet to be determined, despite months of intensive investigation. The most important fact is that some people died and others became grieving survivors. And yet the lack of intention does make a difference to us. Have lives been lost because something happened that was out of human control, or because of hostile and deadly intent? Part of our interest is related to what we think we should do next, for example, find and persecute a killer or correct a mechanical problem. But the question of intentionality is also important because it tells us something about the world in which we live and therefore affects our attitudes toward others and our personal sense of security.

Unfortunately, intentionality can be very difficult or even impossible to establish, as can be observed in many legal proceedings. Part of the problem resides in our lack of definitive knowledge of another person's state of mind. Another part of the problem is that the other person—or even ourselves—may not be quite sure of the intentionality. And part of the problem is that "intentionality" often is neither simple nor enduring. A person may have mixed feelings about taking a certain course of action, and these feelings might change several times during the course of that action and afterward.

Despite these difficulties, the concept of unintentioned death provides a useful pathway through the kinds of death that are customarily called *accidents* or *disasters*.

Accidents

We begin with a statistical overview of accidents. We then look more closely at the contexts and dynamics often associated with accidental deaths.

The Statistical Picture

Accidents have always been a major course of death. Today we are especially aware of the death toll from motor vehicle accidents. What might be surprising is the fact that the rate of accidental deaths has declined appreciably throughout the twentieth century. In 1910 the death rate for accidents was 84.4 (computed per 100,000 in the population). The rate remained at around this level for more than twenty years, then started a significant decline. In recent years, the rate has stabilized at less than half the 1910 level (in 1993 it was 34.9). Industrial accidents (such as coal mine explosions or collapses) and fires are among the types of accidents that take fewer lives today. Also, even though the *number* of motor vehicle fatalities has increased with the number of people on the road, the death rate has declined in recent years.

About 90,000 Americans die as the result of accidents each year. The National Safety Council estimates that an injury accident occurs every two seconds and a death every six minutes. A motor vehicle injury accident, the most common type, occurs every sixteen seconds and a motor vehicular death every thirteen minutes. The distribution of deaths by type of accident and age (see Table 8-5). reveals that motor vehicular fatalities are the most common type of accidental death in all age groups. It can also be seen that a very different kind of accidents—falls—becomes an increasingly high risk for elderly adults. Not all types of accidental deaths follow this pattern. For example, fires and burns are more often the cause of fatalities for very young children and people 75 years of age or over.

The vulnerability of elderly men and women is increased by pre-existing health factors. Elders are more likely to have one or more conditions that require medical treatment. They may also have more limited powers of recuperation from trauma and stress. Therefore an accident from which a younger person might recover is more likely to prove fatal to an elderly person.

The most recent data show that alcohol intoxication remains a major factor in motor vehicle fatalities. In 1997 about two out of every five motor vehicle deaths involved alcohol use.

How does the accidental death rate in the United States compare with that of other nations? Comparisons must be guarded because countries differ in the way they report accidental deaths. With this qualification in mind, it appears from World Health Organization data that the United States is among the safer nations but far from the most safe. Hong Kong (15.1) and Singapore (17.6) report extraordinarily low accidental death rates. Australia, Costa Rica, Iceland, Ireland, Japan, the Netherlands, and the United Kingdom have decidedly lower rates and Canada a marginally lower rate than the United States. There are nations with much higher rates, however—notably former members of the communist bloc, the Czech Republic, Hungary, and Poland.

The Human Side of Accident Fatalities

The statistical picture reminds us that all fatal accidents are not the same. The automobile passenger who is killed when broadsided by another vehicle was in a situation much different from that of the elderly pedestrian who slipped on an icy sidewalk, or the young child who drowned in the family pool when, for one tragic moment, nobody was standing watch. Important differences can exist within the same general type of fatal accident. For example, reckless driving is often responsible for fatal motor vehicle accidents in which a young person is behind the wheel. Poor maintenance of the vehicle is often a contributing cause as well. By contrast, the failure to take sufficient note of traffic conditions and slow reaction times are more often associated with fatal accidents for which elderly drivers are responsible. Additionally, single-car accidents are often associated with the use of alcohol or drugs and sometimes with a self-destructive intention as well (in which case the "accident" is not entirely an accident).

Some accidents are truly accidents. People behaving in a responsible manner may become victims of unforeseen equipment failures or unpredictable events. "Being in the wrong place at the right time" is sometimes a realistic expla-

TABLE 8-5

Accidental Deaths in the United States

Type of Accident	Number of Deaths	0–4	5–14	15–24	Age Group 25–44	45–64	65–74	75+
All	90,000	3,400	3,600	13,900	25,900	14,500	7,900	20,800
Motor Vehicle	42,000	1,000	2,000	10,600	14,200	6,900	2,900	4,400
Falls	13,500	90	80	230	900	1,300	1,500	9,400
Poisoning	6,500	40	30	280	4,300	1,100	300	450
Drowning	4,800	700	500	900	1,400	800	240	260
Fires and Burns	4,000	850	350	200	650	600	500	850
Suffocation	2,900	140	30	30	200	450	550	1,500
Firearms	1,600	40	180	550	450	210	60	110
Gas Poisoning	700	40	30	110	200	140	50	130
Other	14,000	500	400	1,000	3,600	3,000	1,800	3,700

Source: National Safety Council, 1993.

nation. On the other hand, some of the most devastating accidents have been primed by human error, indifference, or greed. In these instances, it is more accurate to speak of the lethal episode not as an *accident* but as a *probable outcome.*

Consider the following example. On April 27, 1865, the steamship *Sultana* started its voyage north from Vicksburg. Almost all of the passengers were Union soldiers, including hundreds who had been incarcerated in prison camps under conditions of extreme stress and deprivation. They were all exhausted survivors of a long and bitter conflict, finally on their way home. Early the next morning, the steam boilers exploded, the ship splintered, and passengers and crew were hurled into the cold waters of the Mississippi River. Of the 2,200 people aboard, 1,700 died almost immediately, and another 200 of exposure and injuries later. This was, and still is, the largest loss of life on an American ship, the casualties exceeding even those of the Titanic.

An accident? The *Sultana* was built to accommodate 376 people. About six times as many people were crowded aboard. Furthermore, there had been clear indications that the boilers were failing (Salecker, 1996). Greed and indifference to the safety of human lives had created a situation that markedly increased the *probability* of catastrophe. The tragic outcome is classified officially as an "accident," but this was far from an unpredictable event. The death toll was also increased by the fact that few of the passengers knew how to swim—largely because relatively few people in the United States at that time were proficient swimmers. Throughout the world, numerous other ships have gone down with a heavy loss of life because of overcrowding and neglect of safety measures. *It is a dangerous misrepresentation to classify as accidents fatal events that were shaped by human error, indigence, and greed. "Accident" implies that nothing could have been done to prevent the loss of life—thereby contributing to lack of prevention in the future.*

Airline catastrophes provide many examples in which human error has contributed significantly. Communication problems often are at the core, and these problems often occur because of ambiguity or other flaws in the entire system of communication that governs air travel. For example:

The captain of an American Airlines jet that crashed in Colombia last December entered an incorrect one-letter computer command that sent the plane into a mountain, the airline said Friday. The crash killed all but four of the 163 people aboard. (Associated Press, 1996: August 24).

The pilot had not made a careless error. He thought he was entering the coordinates for Cali, the intended destination.

But, on most South American aeronautical charts, the one-letter code for Cali is the same as the one for Bogota, 132 miles in the opposite direction The coordinates for Bogota directed the plane toward the mountain.

The ambiguity and confusion in the communication system included the fact that most computer databases used different codes for Bogota and Cali. The lack of standardization among computer databases led the captain to make one fatal keystroke. Even with the efficiency and potential of computerized processes, there is also the risk of fatal error.

KLM eight seven zero, you are cleared to the Papa Beacon. Climb to and maintain flight level nine zero, right turn after takeoff. (Cushing, 1994, p. 19)

This quotation from control tower-to-pilot conversation was given at the beginning of the chapter. The runway was crowded and visibility was obscured by fog on March 27, 1977, in a Canary Islands airport. The pilot informed the tower, "We are at takeoff." What the pilot meant by this message was that the plane was actually lifting off. However, the air traffic controller interpreted the message as indicating that the plane was still on the runway and waiting for clearance. The controller thought he was giving instructions on what course to take when the plane did become airborne—the pilot thought he had been given clearance to fly.

The KLM pilot interprets the clearance as permission to fly to the Papa Beacon, but the Tower appears to have intended it as permission to fly to that beacon only after having received further clearance to leave the ground. The subsequent collision with another aircraft that was still on the runway resulted in the loss of 583 lives, the worst accident in aviation history. The use of alternative unambiguous phrases for the clearance would have enabled the controller to advise some action that might have averted the collision. (1994, p. 10)

Cushing has found dozens of instances in which inadequate communication resulted either in fatal accidents or near misses. Improved awareness of the communication process and its hazards could sharply reduce the possibility of accidents in aviation and other transportation situations. The automatic assumption that we understand what the other person means and that the other person understands what we mean can produce what Cushing has aptly titled *Fatal Words* (1994).

Recently a state attorney general has taken an important step toward holding organizations as well as individuals responsible for preventable fatal accidents. Miami-Dade State Attorney Katherine Fernandez Rundle has filed criminal charges against ValueJet Airline and SabreTech in connection with a 1996 crash in the Florida Everglades that killed all 100 passengers and crew. The defendants are charged with having improperly labeled highly flammable oxygen generators as empty and then lying about it. A fire spread through the cabin, causing the crash and loss of life (Sharp, 1999: July 14). An accident is not an accident when it is produced through deliberate indifference to life.

We reduce the probability that a fatal accident will happen to others or to ourselves every time we check out our assumptions, monitor our communications, and resist the temptation to rush full speed ahead without charting the waters.

Natural Disasters

Not all unintentional lethal events can be classified simply as man-made or natural. The changes we make in our physical environment can either increase or decrease the probability of a disaster. Furthermore, our decision to live in an area with known environmental hazards is likely to increase the number of casualties, should such events occur. Oceanfront living has attracted many people to coastal regions that are vulnerable to punishing storms. The beauty and privacy of a home in the woods places some people at risk for forest fires. Perhaps most notably, some areas in California that are considered at greatest risk for earthquakes are also some of the most highly populated areas. Many people are well aware of these risks and have made conscious choices to remain in hazardous areas because of their positive features. Others do not seem to realize the danger until touched by a near disaster.

"Natural disaster" customarily refers to an episode that occurs within a limited period of time. Earthquakes, storms, floods, and fires are the most common types. These are dramatic events and most the casualties make themselves known shortly thereafter. But there are also slow, massive disasters: A fertile agricultural region becomes an arid desert because of poor farming practices. A forest that supports a diversified ecology is destroyed, resulting in long-term deprivation for the human as well as the animal population. A river dies. Fish disappear. A new blight or pest destroys crops. These events may occur over a period of years—sometimes centuries—and their impact on human lives may also occur gradually and in complex ways. It requires a perspective on long-term developments to understand slow, massive disasters and devise effective preventive or remedial measures.

Through the centuries, earthquakes have been responsible for the most devastating episodic disasters. The following earthquakes had the most fatalities, as gleaned from historical as well as more recent sources:

- 830,000 in Shaanxi, China: January 24, 1556
- 300,000 in Calcutta, India: Oct. 11, 1737
- 250,000 in Antioch, Syria: May 20, 526
- 242,000 in Tangshan, China: July 28, 1976
- 200,000 in Yokohama, Japan: Sept. 1, 1923
- 200,000 in Nan-Shan, China: May 22, 1927

As can be seen, the most destructive earthquakes known have been distributed throughout human history. It can also be seen that the scale of casualties can far exceed what has happened in the United States up to now. Consider earthquake-prone California. The earthquake that occurred during the 1989 baseball World Series in the San Francisco area led to sixty-two deaths. One person died in a Southern California earthquake in 1992. The Northridge earthquake of 1994 led to sixty-one deaths. These episodes were important not only for their actual casualties and devastation but also for their forewarning of earthquakes to come. In the United States, we have little or no grasp of the extent of fatalities, injuries, and destruction that can result when a powerful earthquake strikes a heavily populated area. Along with the great loss of life, a massive earthquake also creates a very large number of bereaved people who will have both short- and long-term needs for material and emotional support.

Every year throughout the world, people are battered by storms or trapped by flood or fire. Some families have lived for many generations in areas vulnerable to particular hazards and have developed both the stamina and the strategies to put their lives together afterward. Seafaring people and travelers crossing the desert have long been aware that their lives are at the mercy of the elements. Only in recent times has the idea of having somehow conquered and subdued the elements flourished. Nature is very much alive, however, and continues to follow her own rules.

SUMMARY

Sudden and violent death take the forms of murder, terrorism, disaster, and accident. The boundaries between these forms of violent death are not firm and stable, however, as we have seen repeatedly. When is armed attack war and when is it terrorism? When is an accident actually homicide? We have also seen that there are many connections between individual actions that result in death and societal beliefs and practices. The fact that the United States continues to have the world's highest murder rate necessarily calls attention to characteristics of our society as well as those of individuals.

We first acquainted ourselves with overall murder rates and the characteristics of the people most likely to be killers and victims. For example, most murders are committed by people who are of the same race as the victims, and in most cases the victims and the killers knew each other.

We then explored in more detail several types of murder. Domestic violence includes abusive men who kill their partners and women who kill the men who have been abusing them. The tragedy of adults who kill children—even newborn babies—was also examined, including the rising incidence of child abuse and neglect, the lack of parenting skills, and the replacement father syndrome. Domestic violence includes parricide as well: children who kill their parents. Often these murders were preceded by years of abuse at the hands of the parents. Young men with guns account for the largest number of murders. The recent wave of lethal school shootings is discussed as a new dimension to youth violence.

Mass and serial killing show related patterns that differ from usual murders. We identified the typical characteristics of mass and serial killers and noted the possible emergence of a new type in the recent Atlanta massacre by an enraged day trader who lost his money on a downturn in the stock market. Political assassination is still another type of killing that should be distinguished from others.

Terrorism was rampant throughout the twentieth century with perhaps 30 million people dead and many others tortured and abused. We looked at both the history and the current face of terrorism in the world and also in the United States, with special attention to the disasters at Waco and Oklahoma City.

In conclusion, we learned about disasters and accidents as the causes of violent death. The accident rate in the United States has decreased over the years, but it could be sharply reduced if intoxicated drivers were no longer at the wheel.

REFERENCES

Amnesty International. (1984). *Torture in the eighties.* London: Amnesty International Publications.

Associated Press (1994: Feb. 27). Report: Gun usage in offenses rises.

Associated Press (1994: April 16). Rwanda Massacre Reports.

Associated Press (1996: August 24). Colombia crash linked to pilot error.

Associated Press (1996: Sept.19). Abuse is up 98%, report on kids finds.

Becker, E. (1986). *When the war was over.* New York: Simon & Schuster.

Belluck, P. (1998: July 7). *The Arizona Republic,* p. A10.

Bland, K. (1996: June 27). Child Protective Services opens files on 27 deaths. *The Arizona Republic,* p. 6A.

Browne, A. (1987). *When battered women kill.* New York: Free Press.

Burrell, C. (1999: July 19). Violent crime at 25-year low. Associated Press.

Butterfield, F. (1994: Oct. 14). Teen-age homicide rate has soared. *New York Times.*

Clarke, J. W. (1982). *American assassins.* Princeton: Princeton University Press.

Conquest, R. (1986). *The harvest of sorrow.* New York: Oxford University Press.

Cushing, S. (1994). *Fatal words.* Chicago: University of Chicago Press.

Dangelis, N., & Pope, W. (1979). Durkheim's theory of suicide as applied to the family: An empirical test. *Social Forces, 57,* 1081–1106.

DeBruin, L. (1994: April 6). Suspects joked about shootings, police say. *Mesa Tribune,* pp. 1A, 4A.

Dobkin, B. A. (1992). *Tales of terror. Television news and the construction of the terrorist threat.* New York: Praeger.

Dobson, C., & Payne, R. (1987). *The Never-Ending War: Terrorism in the Eighties .* New York: Facts on File.

Engelmann, B. (1984). *Germany without Jews.* New York: Bantam.

Erasmus. *The praise of folly.* (Original work published 1509)

Ewing, C. P. (1997). *Fatal families: The dynamics of intrafamilial homicide.* Thousand Oaks, CA: Sage.

Foster, C. D., Siegel, M. A., Plesser, D. R., & Jacobs, N. R. (Eds.) (1989). *Gun control.* Wylie, TX: Information Plus.

Frederick, C. J. (1985). Youth suicide: An introduction and overview. In M. L. Peck, N. L. Farberow, and R. E. Litman (Eds.), *Youth Suicide.* New York: Springer, pp. 1–18.

Freud, S. (1923/1961). *The ego and the id.* New York: W. W. Norton.

Friedlander, S. (1984). *Reflections of Nazism.* New York: Harper & Row.

Gibbs, N. (1995: May 1). The blood of innocents. *Time,* 57–61.

Goldhagen, D. J. (1996). *Hitler's willing executioners.* New York: Alfred A. Knopf.

Goldman, D. (1999: May 28). Suspects' classmates detail massacre plot. Associated Press.

Grosscup, B. (1987). *The explosion of terrorism.* Far Hills, NJ: New Horizon Press.

Gutteridge, W. (1986). *Contemporary terrorism.* New York: Facts on File.

Halttunen, K. (1998). *Murder most foul: The Killer and the American Gothic imagination.* Cambridge, MA: Harvard University Press.

Hawkins, D. F. (Ed.), (1986). *Homicide among Black Americans.* Lanham, MD: University Press of America.

Heide, K. M. (1992). *Why kids kill parents: Child abuse and adolescent homicide.* Columbus: Ohio State Press.

Hill, S. (1999: July 30). Atlanta rampage leaves 13 dead. Associated Press dispatch.

Holmes, R. M., & Holmes, S. T. (1994). *Murder in America.* Thousand Oaks, CA: Sage.

Humphrey, J. A., & Palmer, S. (1986–1987). Stressful life events and criminal homicide. *Omega, Journal of Death and Dying, 17,* 299–308.

Hofstadter, R. & Wallace, M. (Eds.), (1971). *American violence: A documentary history.* New York: Random House.

Kastenbaum, R. (2000). *The psychology of death.* (3rd ed.). New York: Springer.

Kozak, D. L. (1991). Dying badly: Violent death and religious change among the Tohono O' Odham. *Omega, Journal of Death and Dying, 23,* 207–216.

Kuper, L. (1981). *Genocide.* New Haven & London: Yale University Press.

Lane, R. (1997). *Murder in America.* Columbus: Ohio State University Press.

Laqueur, W. (1987). *The age of terrorism.* Boston: Little, Brown & Co.

Lea, H. C. (1906–1907). *A history of the Inquisition of Spain* (Vols. 1–4). New York: Macmillan.

Lester, D. (1995). *Serial killers.* Philadelphia: The Charles Press.

Levin, J., & Fox, J. A. (1985). *Mass murder.* New York: Plenum.

Masland, T., et al. (1994: April 18). Corpses everywhere. Rwanda: Once more, tens of thousands slaughtered. *Newsweek,* 33.

Morgan, R. (1989). *The demon lover: On the sexuality of terrorism.* New York: W. W. Norton.

National Center for Health Statistics. (1988, March). *Vital statistics of the United States.* Vol. 2, *Mortality, Part A.,* 1950–1985. DHHS Pub. No. (PHS) 8–1233. Hyattsville, MD.

O'Brien, J. (1973). *The Inquisition.* New York: Macmillan.

Payne, R. (1973). *Massacre.* New York: Macmillan.

Pearson, M. (1999: June 22). Serial-killings suspect charged in deaths of father, daughter. Associated Press dispatch.

Picard, R. G. (1993). *Media portrayals of terrorism.* Ames, IA: Iowa State University Press.

Raynor, T. P. (1987). *Terrorism: Past, present, future.* (Rev. ed.). New York: Franklin Wats.

Robert, S. V. (1995: May 8). After the heartbreak. *U.S. News and World Report,* 27–29.

Salecker, G. E. (1996). *Disaster on the Mississippi.* Anapolis: Naval Institute Press.

Sharp, D. (1999: July 14). Criminal charges filed in 1996 ValuJet crash. *The Tribune* (Tempe, Az), p. 1A.

Smith, P. (1989). Perfect murders. *New Statesman and Society, 57,* 1–9.

Stack, S. (1979). Durkheim's theory of fatalistic suicide: A cross national approach. *Journal of Social Psychology, 107,* 161–168.

Sterling, C. (1981). *The terror network.* New York: Reader's Digest.

Swanson, W. C., & Breed, W. (1976). Black suicide in New Orleans. In E. S. Shneidman (Ed.), *Suicidology: contempo-*

rary developments (pp. 99–130). New York: Grune & Stratton.

Tabachnick, N. (Ed.). (1973). *Accident or suicide?* Springfield, IL: Charles C. Thomas.

Time (1994: April 18). Descent into mayhem. Tribal slaughter erupts in Rwanda, 44.

U.S. Senate Judiciary Committee (1991). *Report of the U.S. Senate Judiciary Committee.* Washington, DC: Government Printing Office.

Wakin, E. (1984). *Enter the Irish-American.* New York: Thomas V. Crowell.

Walsh, J. (1996: September 9). Killings down but 'crime storm' looms. *The Arizona Republic,* pp. 1A, 24A.

Weimann, G., & Winn, C. (1994). *The theater of terror.* New York & London: Longman.

Wilson-Smith, A. (1996: May 1). No safe place. *Maclean's,* 18–24.

GLOSSARY

Assassination: The murder of a public official or other political figure.

Branch Davidians: A Christian sect, some of whose members died in their compound near Waco, Texas, during an attack by federal agents.

Day Trader: A person who makes a continuing series of quick financial transactions through the Internet.

Death Instinct: A biological impulse present in all individuals that is aimed at reduction of stim-ulation and activity to the point of death; also known as *Thanatos.* It is countered by *Eros,* the impulse for growth, love, and new experiences (Freud).

Homicide: The act of killing a human being.

Interpol: International Police Organization, primarily an information-sharing agency.

Mass Killer: A person who murders a large number of people in a single episode.

Mosque: An Islamic place of worship, a temple.

Murder: The criminal act of killing a human being.

Parricide: Murder of a parent.

Rational Extremists: A type of assassin who is motivated by political objectives; often mistakenly believed to be psychotic.

Replacement Father Syndrome: Abusive and life-threatening actions by a new husband or lover against the children of the wife's previous mate.

Serial Killer: A person who commits murders on repeated occasions.

Terrorism: Violence or threat of violence in which civilians or places used by civilians are the targets.

Unabomber: The name given to himself by a person who sent explosive packages through the mails to kill or injure the recipients.

An influential movement in the United States urged death for babies with birth defects and others who were considered to be burdens on society. The Black Stork was a symbol often used by critics of this movement.

chapter 9

EUTHANASIA, ASSISTED DEATH, AND THE RIGHT TO DIE

I swear by Apollo the physician, and Aesculapius, Hygeia and Panacea and all the gods and goddesses, that, according to my ability and judgment, I will keep this oath and this covenant. I will give no deadly medicine to anyone if asked, nor suggest any such counsel, and in like manner I will not give to a woman an abortive remedy. With purity and with holiness I will pass my life and practice my Art.
—The Hippocratic oath, fifth century, B.C.

Death Counseling
IS SOMEONE IN YOUR FAMILY TERMINALLY ILL?
Does he or she wish to die—and with dignity?
Call Physician Consultant [Telephone No.]
—Classified newspaper advertisement, June 1987

Dr. Kevorkian kept telling him, "If you don't want to go through with this, you don't have to. You don't have to worry about hurting our feelings. I you want to postpone for a week, a month, a year, don't even hesitate." My son kept saying, "No, no, let's do it. I want to go. I want to go." So I helped him with his mask to get it all adjusted...Dr. Kevorkian told him, "Now anytime you feel comfortable and ready you just go ahead and pull it. The gas will start."
—Carol Loving, 1995–1996, p. 175

Gale, a 72 year old former merchant marine, was suffering from emphysema. There is no question that he asked to die, but there is clear evidence that Gale had a great deal of ambivalence after the gas mask was put on his face, asking twice that it be removed. Kevorkian's original record of the incident...found in a garbage bag outside his assistant's (Neal Nicole) house, indicated that Kevorkian removed the mask in response to Gale's first request, but did not remove it in response to the second.
—Kaplan et al, in press-a

What has become known as the *Hippocratic oath* is thought to have been drawn from the writings of a physician who practiced on the Greek island of Cos 2,500 years ago (Edelstein, 1943). This ancient document is still very much at issue today: can a physician violate the injunction to give no deadly medicine and still be a physician? Dr. Jack Kevorkian is not the only physician who has intentionally contributed to the death of his patients, but both his actions and his words have had a powerful influence on the right-to-die controversy. Some people have expressed a debt of gratitude to Kevorkian for relieving either their own suffering or, as was the case with Carol Loving, the suffering of a family member. Others, such as Kalman Kaplan and his research team, present evidence suggesting that Kevorkian has been setting a dangerous precedent and taking people's lives into his own hands. Furthermore, the shadow of involuntary euthanasia has been cast over the movement to provide assisted death. "Mercy killing" has had influential advocates and extended even to generations as yet unborn—and this in the United States as well as Nazi Germany. People who know their twentieth-century history have some concerns about any movement that would encourage and legalize the taking of a life. Are these concerns valid or misplaced?

In this chapter, we consider the related topics of euthanasia, physician-assisted suicide, and the right to die. We must also look at *The Black Stork* (Pernick, 1996) to become aware of the possible connection between eugenics, euthanasia, and assisted death. We have prepared ourselves for this challenge by studying end-of-life decisions (*see Chapter 6*), suicide (*see Chapter 8*), and killing (*see Chapter 8*). We begin with a further consideration of The Hippocratic oath and its implications, then acquaint ourselves with key terms and concepts. This is followed by attention to public attitudes toward the set of right-to-die issues and a review of some of the major cases influencing the right-to-die controversy. We will then be ready to look at the assisted-death issue in some detail, enhancing our knowledge by consulting the latest research findings. These are difficult issues to confront; perhaps most difficult is the challenge of keeping an open mind through it all.

"I SWEAR BY APOLLO THE PHYSICIAN": WHAT HAPPENED TO THE HIPPOCRATIC OATH?

Kevorkian's classified advertisement was a clear signal that "death with dignity" was becoming more than rhetoric. Here was a physician who was actually offering to perform a service that most of his colleagues did not even want to talk about. It was a service, in fact, that seems to be specifically banned by the Hippocratic oath.

We often assume that (1) all physicians have sworn allegiance to this oath right up to the present day, and (2) this covenant does in fact represent the core belief system for physicians from antiquity forward. Neither assumption is correct. Many physicians graduate from medical school without being asked to take the Hippocratic oath. Kevorkian is among those who, along with his entire graduating class, was not asked to take the oath, which he now characterizes as irrelevant. Furthermore, the Hippocratic oath has encountered opposition since its inception. Seeking release from the rigors, pains, and disappointments of life was considered reasonable and even honorable behavior by many in the ancient world. I think it likely that the prohibition against *giving* "deadly medicine" was specified because *taking* deadly medicine had become a widespread practice. The prohibition against abortion was also contested, with Aristotle as one of the leading dissenters.

We are mistaken, then, if we persist in the belief that medical opinion has ever been undivided on the physician's role in life and death decisions. Today some physicians may continue to rely on the Hippocratic oath, but many have never entered into this covenant, and all are confronted with new and complex problems that Hippocrates himself never had to deal with. Even physicians who are well attuned to the Hippocratic oath must find a way to reconcile these precepts with the difficult decisions they must make day by day.

Physicians who practice in the mainstream U.S. health care system are not likely to advertise their services as consultants for those who wish to die. Instead, they must work within the system. They must find a way to help their patients who seem beyond ordinary medical help and yet, at the same time, avoid violating either their own moral code or the law of the land. Timothy E. Quill (1993) has become an effective spokesperson for physicians who attempt to make responsible decisions within the system as it now exists. His approach comes down to: "How can I help this person in this situation?" He is not trying to overturn the establishment or to prove some abstract principle. His mission perhaps is stated best in the subtitle of his recent book: *Making Choices and Taking Charge.*

Whatever one's position on physician-assisted death, one cannot simply invoke the Hippocratic oath as the unquestionable authority. We must work things out for ourselves.

KEY TERMS AND CONCEPTS

We will improve our ability to deal with life-and-death issues by becoming more familiar with key terms and concepts.

Euthanasia: A literal translation would be happy (*eu*) death (*thanasia*). However, it would be more accurate to understand this original usage as "dying without pain and suffering." We do not have to assume that dying is a great pleasure. At first, the euthanasia concept referred to the individual's state of being: "She died peacefully." Later, euthanasia came to signify actions performed to hasten death. Today the term retains something of its original meaning: a peaceful, painless exit from life. But it has taken on another meaning as well: the intentional foreshortening of a person's life to spare that person from further suffering.

Many people have emphasized the distinction between a life foreshortened by doing something and one foreshortened by deciding *not* to do something. The term *active euthanasia* has been given to actions intended to end the life of a person (or animal) who is suffering greatly and has no chance of recovery. A lethal injection or the administration of carbon monoxide are clear examples of active euthanasia. *Passive euthanasia* refers to the intentional withholding of treatment that might prolong life. Deciding not to place a person with massive brain trauma on a life support system is an example of passive euthanasia, as is the decision not to treat pneumonia or an opportunistic infection in an immobilized and cognitively impaired long-term patient.

This distinction is consequential in the minds of many people because it is thought to bear on legal and moral responsibility. A health care provider or family member who feels that it is acceptable to "let him/her go" (passive euthanasia) might be deeply troubled by the prospect of giving direct assistance to death (active euthanasia). The legal system and society in general have been more tolerant of the "letting go" approach. Nobody is inclined to make trouble when health care providers and family members agree that it would be pointless to introduce further procedures that would only prolong suffering or a vegetative state. The instrument known as the Living Will, the legislation known as the Patients Self-Determination Act (PSDA), and the new procedure known as Five Wishes (*see Chapter 6*) have provided further support for the passive euthanasia approach.

There is still substantial opposition to active euthanasia Many physicians strenuously object to placing their services at the disposal of death. This may be based to some extent on the Hippocratic oath but more powerfully on what would happen to their reputations as individuals and as a profession. "Doctors are supposed to keep people alive. If doctors also kill people, who can trust them? They are working both sides of the street!" Some physicians and other health care providers are also strongly opposed on personal religious or moral grounds. Furthermore, there is no sheltered legal status for a person who engages in active euthanasia. Such a person (whether physician or family member) may be charged with a crime and have his or her fate placed at the disposition of a judge and jury.

Now that we have introduced ourselves to active and passive euthanasia, we might be well advised to put these terms aside. We will still hear and read about active and passive euthanasia because these were the original terms of the controversy. Today, however, most physicians and bioethicists speak instead of *withdrawing or withholding life supports.* This makes discussion simpler and more direct. Instead of dealing with the somewhat abstract and unwieldy concept of euthanasia, we can focus on whether or not certain practical actions should be done or undone.

There is another potential benefit here: *perhaps we can detach ourselves from the memory of horrors that have been perpetrated in the name of euthanasia.*

Many people among us remember how the political, medical, economic, and military forces of a modern nation all collaborated in the murder of millions of people. The holocaust that eventually claimed millions of lives was preceded by Hitler's policy of *Vernichtun lebensunwerten Lebens*, in which Nazi doctors participated in the "extermination of valueless life." The victims were fellow German citizens, non-Jewish, who were invalids, infirm, unable to care for themselves—a large proportion of the institutionalized population. Killing these helpless people required the willingness of physicians and other people who had been entrusted with their care.

This brutal program might have been rejected by German society had it been exposed for what it was. It was made more palatable, however, by the disguising of the murders as euthanasia. The Nazi leadership declared that these people were being put out of their misery. This was for their own good. And yes, it would also save the cost of feeding and housing them. Enough physicians believed (or pretended to believe) this explanation to make the program a success.

It has to be obvious that what the Nazis did to their helpless citizens had nothing at all to do with euthanasia. These people were not terminally ill. They were not suffering intractable pain. They did not ask to be killed. They were simply murdered, one by one, through a process that had a bureaucrat at one end and a physician at the other. Discovering that he could induce physicians, lawyers, and other responsible people to engage in "mercy killing," Hitler moved on to his genocidal assaults against Jews and Gypsies (Friedlander, 1995).

The Black Stork

An almost forgotten episode in U.S. history brings this issue even closer to us. A keen interest in both eugenics and euthanasia developed early in the twentieth century. Preventive medicine was starting to make the impact that would soon result in lower mortality rates and longer life expectancies. Why not go all the way? Why not keep defective people out of the population in the first place? Sterilization of people thought to have defective genes was the solution proposed by eugenicists. And why not let defective newborn infants die? And while we are at it, why not end the lives of patients as soon as it is clear that

they are incurable? Euthanasia was the solution favored by those who did not think eugenics went far enough. Some people combined both approaches, notably a prominent Chicago surgeon by the name of Harry J. Haiselden. He boasted of having allowed the deaths of at least six "defective" infants, thereby setting an example for weeding out those unfit for society.

The unsettling history of the co-existing eugenics and euthanasia movements in the United States has recently been told by Martin S. Pernick (1996). His interest in this neglected topic was aroused when he had the opportunity to see the only viewable copy of a 1915 film called *The Black Stork*. This movie was part of the campaign to persuade the public to support eugenics and euthanasia. Physicians who saved defective infants came under attack by eugenicists. These two movements received considerable support from the public, although they drew stinging criticism as well. By the 1920s, the euthanasia facet of the movement had run into serious difficulty—but not before it had attracted the enthusiasm of some German physicians and political thinkers.

> By the 1930s racial hygiene, eugenics, and euthanasia played a complex but central role in the evolution of Nazi ideology and in the legitimization of Nazi genocide. Depicting their intended victims as carriers of racial "diseases" constituted a key feature of Nazi propaganda.... Programs for killing incurably ill institutional patients, such as the operation code-named "T-4" that secretly gassed over 100,000 disabled Germans, pioneered the machinery and trained the medical personnel who were then transferred to run the death camps for the "racially diseased." (1996, p. 164)

Can there be any wonder that the terms *euthanasia* and *mercy killing* now lead to fear, suspicion, and anger on the part of those who know how it has been so cruelly misused? The Native American woman who told me of the forced sterilization of many women in her tribe was not being paranoid; she was simply reporting facts.

The Ventilator As Example of Life-and-Death Decisions

"Withholding or withdrawing" treatment provides a more useful frame of reference for dealing with most life-and-death decisions in the health care system today. Even so, thoughtful people might disagree on the course of action that should be taken. It is also possible to disagree on just how much significance should be given to the withholding/withdrawing distinction.

Consider, for example, the ventilator. This device is one of the most familiar pieces of equipment in the intensive care unit. It is frequently used in life support situations. Suppose that a patient has been attached to a ventilator for weeks or even months. Families and hospital staff now agree that this person has no chance for recovery and is receiving no quality-of-life benefit from the life support system. Somebody pulls the plug. In a little while, the patient is dead. This is an example of withdrawing treatment. Now suppose that a person has just been brought to the hospital after a massive stroke or with severe brain trauma from an accident. It is obvious to the medical team that the higher brain centers have been destroyed. Death will soon occur unless the unresponsive body is hooked up to a life support system. The decision is made against using a ventilator. The patient is soon certified as dead.

The patient dies in both of these scenarios. The "instrument" of death in both is the ventilator. *How much importance do you attach to the difference between withdrawing and withholding treatment?*

Are both methods equally moral and acceptable (or equally immoral and unacceptable?). What if it were up to you? Would pulling the plug be no more difficult than deciding not to connect the plug in the first place? Whatever your judgment and your decision, you are sure to find some experts agreeing and others disagreeing. We will return to this problem later.

Euthanasia, assisted suicide, physician-assisted death, medicide, and other such terms all differ from suicide by involving the actions of another person. A suicidal person carries out his or her own intention. All forms of assisted death, by definition, require that another person contribute actively to the outcome. *How much importance do you attach to this distinction?* If a person really wants to have his or her life ended, do the details matter? "Yes," you might argue, "because it places a heavy responsibility on another person." "No," you might argue, "because it is the intention and the outcome that count, not the particular method." Attempts to legalize assisted deaths in the United States may hinge on the outcome of these counterarguments.

Slippery Slope: We use the *slippery slope* argument when we oppose a particular instance of assisted death because it could contribute to widespread abuse in other instances. "I can understand and sympathize with this person's request to be put

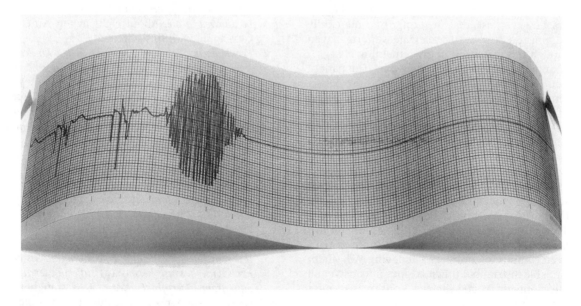

One criterion for determining death is the appearance of a flat line on an EEG read-out.

out of her suffering," we might say. "but if society consents to 'mercy killing' in this instance, tomorrow we will be asked to consent in a case where the right to die is not quite so clear. And so it will go, until we slide all the way down the slope."

Perhaps many people would give up too soon when confronted not only with a terminal illness but with other challenges and crises as well. Death would become too easy an out. We might even expect people to kill themselves or seek assistance in ending their lives. Perhaps physicians will be increasingly expected to participate in assisted death—and would that perhaps help to control the costs of health care in a graying society? And who can be sure that Nazi-style "euthanasia" might not come into fashion in the United States or elsewhere, again under the cover of deceptive terminology. There are sharp disagreements today regarding the applicability of the slippery slope argument to a particular life-and-death decision, and these disagreements are likely to continue for some time.

It is important to keep in mind that the Living Will, advance directives, and the Five Wishes do not include provisions for assisted death. Many people who support the Living Will as an expression of the individual's preferences do not support assisted death. However, one sentence in the standard Living Will does walk the boundary: "I do, however, ask that medication be mercifully administered to me to alleviate suffering even though this may shorten my remaining life."

Suppose that you are a physician. The patient you are attending at this moment has previously entrusted you with a signed and witnessed copy of her Living Will. She is dying. She is also in physical and emotional distress. "I want to die," she tells you. It had been your intention to control her pain with morphine. A heavier dose would not only relieve her pain but also hasten an easy death. Would you feel justified in prescribing a lethal dose because it is consistent with the advance directive ("...even though this may shorten my remaining life")? Or would you feel that you were dishonoring your profession or even committing murder? The Living Will, then, valuable instrument that it is, does not answer all questions for us and, indeed, continues to raise new questions.

OUR CHANGING ATTITUDES TOWARD A RIGHT TO DIE

Attitudes toward the right-to-die issue have changed appreciably in recent years and are still far from stable. We will track much of this pattern with the help of a national poll conducted by the Times Mirror Center for the People and the Press (1983). This poll was conducted just as attitudes appeared to be shifting toward more open discussion and acceptance of the right-to-die position. Although there have been several more limited polls since, we have not yet had a full-scale follow-up to the original survey. A caution: survey findings should not be used to answer questions of basic fact or morality. A ten-to-one vote against the law of gravity, for example, would not prevent unsupported objects from falling, and a nineteenth century survey would have found that most physicians believed that washing their hands was unnecessary and ridiculous. Nevertheless, surveys are important because our attitudes influence decisions and actions.

Survey Findings

First we will review the most general and clear-cut results of the Times Mirror survey.

1. *There are circumstances in which a person should be allowed to die.* About eight in ten Americans agree with this statement.
2. *People do have the right to make their own decisions about receiving life-sustaining treatment.* A six-to-one majority favors this statement.
3. *Doctors and nurses do not pay a lot of attention to the instructions they receive from patients about wanting or not wanting life-sustaining treatment.* Only one in five believed that physicians give their instructions careful consideration.
4. *The closest family member should be able to decide whether or not to continue medical treatment for a person with terminal illness who is unable to communicate and who has not made his or her wishes known in advance.* About 75 percent of the respondents agreed with this statement.
5. *It is sometimes justified for a person to kill his or her spouse because he/she was suffering terrible pain from a terminal disease.* This statement wins the support of seven out of ten people.

6. Most people (71 percent) know about the Living Will, but relatively few (14 percent) have actually made Living Wills for themselves.

7. *If suffering great physical pain or unable to function in daily activities because of an incurable disease, most people would ask their doctors to stop treatment rather than doing everything possible to save their lives.* About two out of three people agreed with this statement, excluding those with "don't know" responses.

8. *Right-to-die legislation—allowing medical treatment for a terminally ill patient to be withdrawn or withheld if that is what the patient wishes—*is approved by about eight people in ten.

   This set of findings reveals a strong consensus in favor of the individual's right to make decisions about life-sustaining treatment. Furthermore, it indicates a continuing movement toward the acceptance of suicide in certain circumstances, notably in the advanced stages of terminal illness. The public seems to be marching in step with the many state legislatures across the nation that have passed measures supportive of the Living Will. These survey results also suggest that the public is ahead of existing legislation in its willingness to consider assisted death an acceptable option.

   Despite the clear trends displayed in the findings already given, it is also clear that the public has not reached a consensus on all right-to-die questions. Following are several questions that elicited a more divided response from the national sample.

9. *Parents have the right to refuse medical treatment for an infant who is born with a severe handicap.* About half the respondents *disagreed* with this view, a third agreed, and the rest were divided between no opinion and "it depends." Although more people select the "should receive most treatment possible" alternative than any other, a substantial number do not endorse this view.

10. *The hospital or doctor should be held responsible if a patient's instruction to withhold life-sustaining treatment is ignored and the patient survives, but with severe disability.* Those who had clear opinions were divided six to five in favor of holding the hospital or physician responsible. Evidently we are a long way from a con-

sensus on what should be done in such a situation.

11. *A person has the moral right to end his or her own life if afflicted with an incurable disease.* Again, the public is closely divided on this question, with a seven-to-six edge for those who agree that there is a moral right to suicide under this circumstance—but see also the findings on the next two items.

12. *A person has the moral right to end his or her own life if he or she is an extremely heavy burden on the family or if living has become a burden to the person.* These were separate questions on the survey, but the responses were very similar: about two out of three respondents *disagreed.* They held that there is no moral right to end one's life because it has become burdensome to either self or family.

13. *A person has the moral right to end his or her own life if suffering great pain with no hope of improvement.* Given this circumstance, most people agreed that there was a moral right to end one's own life. The eight-to-five margin in favor indicated that the public makes a sharp differentiation between pain and the sense of being a burden as justification for ending one's life.

14. *I would tell my doctor to do everything possible to save my life if I had a disease with no hope of improvement that made it hard for me to function in my day-to-day activities.* This statement found the public almost equally divided in its response, with a very slight tendency toward disagreement. The differential (52 percent to 48 percent) is small enough to have arisen as a sampling artifact or error. The main point here is that "save life" and "stop treatment" attitudes are about equally current.

   The set of findings we have just reviewed (numbers 9–14) suggests a fairly complex pattern of attitudes toward the right to die in various situations. *The public did not—and probably still does not—support a sweeping, generalized approach.* Instead, people recognize that circumstances differ. Their approval or disapproval of a right to die depends much on these circumstances.

   This differentiated approach might be discomforting to policymakers, who might find it easier if a strong public consensus existed.

However, there is reason to be encouraged by the fact that many people do take the specific circumstances into account. This suggests that the public has become more aware of death-related issues and is willing to think carefully about the personal and medical realities involved, instead of relying upon broad generalizations.

Finally, let us consider a third set of findings that attempt to analyze public attitudes in a little more detail. *Do the respondent's age, sex, race, or religious beliefs make a difference in attitudes toward the right to die?*

15. *There is somewhat less support for the right-to-die position among people age 65 and older, non-whites, and those who report themselves as being very religious.* Age makes a particularly strong difference with respect to the moral right to commit suicide; people under the age of 30 are much more likely to hold that such a right exists. It should be added, however, that most people in the subgroups just mentioned do support many of the right-to-die options, but this support is not as widespread as in the general population.

16. *Born-again Christians and others who describe themselves as very religious are strongly opposed to parental decision making when a severely handicapped infant is born.* There are no differences between Protestants and Catholics with respect to parental decision making; the differences are found between individuals who see their religion as either very relevant or not very relevant to practical decision making in their lives.

17. *Family communication about death-related issues differs for daughters and sons.* Daughters were more likely to have discussed their mothers' preferences with them than sons were. Few adults, sons or daughters, have discussed these matters with their fathers.

18. *Women, people in the higher economic brackets, and those who have had significant personal experiences with death are more likely to discuss death with the people who are important to them.* Many adults in the sample report that they seldom communicate with anybody regarding death-related issues.

The Times Mirror survey results suggest that the U.S. public has become more open and knowledgeable about death-related issues over the past several decades, although not all have participated in this pattern of change. Perhaps this more straightforward orientation toward death owes something to the death education and counseling movement (*see Chapter 14*). It certainly owes something to the changing character of medical treatment and its associated psychological, social, and economic challenges.

What do physicians think about right-to-die issues? Most studies indicate a deep division of attitudes (Dickinson et al., 1997–1998). Physicians cannot present a united front on issues that are so crucial to both their personal lives and professional practice. It is likely that they will continue to struggle with the right-to-die dilemma for many years to come.

THE RIGHT-TO-DIE DILEMMA: CASE EXAMPLES

We have examined some of the key concepts and learned how they are viewed by the public. Now it is time to look at some of the specific human experiences that have influenced the present status of the right-to-die issue in the United States and that will also play a role in future developments. We begin with the case that made the question of assisted death one that the nation could not easily ignore.

The Ethics of Withdrawing Treatment: The Landmark Quinlan Case

A young woman became the center of national attention when she lapsed into a coma after a party on the night of April 14, 1975. One friend applied mouth-to-mouth resuscitation while another called the police, who also attempted resuscitation and took her to a hospital. She started to breathe again, but Karen Ann Quinlan did not return to consciousness. Traces of valium and quinine were found in her blood. Drug-induced coma was the preliminary diagnosis. Later this diagnosis was disputed and has never been fully clarified. Whatever the precipitating cause, Quinlan had suffered severe and irreversible brain damage as a result of oxygen deprivation.

Weeks and then months passed. Quinlan remained in the hospital. Her vegetative functions were maintained on a ventilator, with intravenous tubes providing fluids and nutrition. Her body gradually wasted away. After a few months, the once vital and attractive young woman had become a 60-pound shriveled form, curled into a fetal position. Talk of recovery and a miraculous return to life became less frequent as time went by. The hospital expenses continued to mount day by day.

Karen Ann was the adopted child of deeply religious parents. Joseph Quinlan maintained hope for nearly half a year. Finally his priest persuaded him that morality does not require that extraordinary means be used to prolong life. This communication did not resolve the moral issue, however; it simply exported it into other spheres. The Quinlans asked two physicians to turn off the ventilator. The physicians declined to do so.

Karen Ann Quinlan never regained consciousness after her 1975 accident. The question of whether she should be disconnected from the life support apparatus became the subject of intense legal, medical, moral, and religious debate.

They were not sure of the moral implications of such an action. They were also naturally concerned about the possibility of facing malpractice or even felony charges. As we have seen, physicians may still be troubled by these concerns today, after two decades of discussion and legal rulings. For physicians at that time, the request to "pull the plug" was almost equivalent to the first astronauts' walk in space.

What were the Quinlans to do? They pursued their request through the courts. The time-consuming legal process provided the opportunity for many opinions to be aired in the media, professional circles, and the courts. Some confusion was also generated. For example, there was a tendency to speak of Karen Ann as though she were already dead. The fact was that EEG tracings still showed weak electrical activity in the brain. A neurologist described her condition as a "persistent vegetative state." This phrase would be repeated many times about many other nonresponsive persons in the years to come. An attorney for New Jersey described a brief visit to her room:

> Her face is all distorted and she is sweating. Her eyes are open and blinking about twice a minute. She's sort of gasping. I've never seen anything like that.... I was there for seven minutes and it seemed like seven hours. (Kron, 1973, p. 22)

Medical testimony was given that Karen Ann would die within a short time if removed from the ventilator.

The court ruled against the Quinlans' request. In this ruling, the court specifically rejected the argument that religious freedom should be the basis for approving the removal of the life support system. This decision was appealed to the New Jersey Supreme Court. Here, for the first time, a court ruled that a ventilator could be turned off (in the popular mind, this was soon translated into "pulling the plug"). However, the court imposed a condition: physicians must first agree that Karen Ann had no reasonable chance of regaining consciousness. The New Jersey Attorney General decided not to challenge this decision. This meant that the United States Supreme Court was not asked at that time to make a precedent-setting decision for the entire nation. The Court's turn would come later in the Nancy Cruzan case, as we will see shortly.

Finally—fourteen months after she had lapsed into a nonresponsive state—Karen Ann was disconnected from the ventilator. She was expected to die quickly. However, her persistent vegetative state proved persistent indeed. Karen Ann remained alive (in some sense of the word) for more than ten years, until she succumbed to pneumonia in 1985. Many a thoughtful observer drew the inference that expert opinion is not always respected by the forces that govern life and death.

Karen Ann's predicament was not the first example of its kind, but it became the starting place not only for discussion but also for efforts to develop *due process* in right-to-die issues. It was recognized that medical technology now made it possible for many people to be maintained in a persistent vegetative state—and that human judgment would often suggest that medical technology *not* be applied beyond a point of no return. Guidelines were needed, and a system of checks and balances should be established.

It has been a long and winding road from the Karen Ann Quinlan dilemma to the present day. An estimated 5,000 to 10,000 Americans exist in persistent vegetative states. Some will remain unresponsive, yet alive, for years. Families and caregivers must deal with this difficult situation day after day. Since Karen Ann Quinlan's dilemma first captured public concern, there have been a number of proposed guidelines and systems of checks and balances. Court decisions have sometimes clouded and sometimes clarified our understanding. Meanwhile, physicians and other health care providers have responded in various ways to their new challenges. One of these responses became the subject of a continuing controversy. The principals in this drama were a young physician and a young woman who became known as Debbie.

"It's Over, Debbie": Compassion or Murder?

The Quinlan case was characterized by a long period of consultations, discussions, and legal proceedings. Many people participated in the decision making, and many facts were brought forward for public as well as family and professional scrutiny. More recently a very different case was reported in a leading medical journal. No author's name was attributed to "It's Over, Debbie," when this brief report was published in the *Journal of the American Medical Association* (Anon, 1988). The article was offered as a personal experience and consisted of only three paragraphs. This is the story:

A presumably young physician—a resident in gynecology—was on duty when called in the middle of the night. The request came from a nurse on the gynecologic-oncology (cancer) unit. This was not the physician's usual duty station. The doctor "trudged along, bumping sleepily against walls and corners and not believing I was up again." Upon reaching the unit, he picked up the patient's chart and was given some "hurried details" by the nurse. A 20-year-old patient was dying of ovarian cancer. An attempt had been made to sedate her by using an alcohol drip, but this had led her to vomit "unrelentingly."

Entering the patient's room, the resident saw that she was emaciated and appeared much older than her actual age. "She was receiving nasal oxygen, had an IV, and was sitting in bed suffering from what was obviously severe air hunger." There was another woman in the room who stood by the bed, holding the patient's hand. The physician had the impression that "The room seemed filled with the patient's desperate effort to survive." The physician also observed that the patient was breathing with great difficulty. The article states that she had not eaten or slept in two days, nor had she responded to chemotherapy. Presumably this information had been gleaned from the doctor's quick glance through the patient's chart.

Trying to take in the whole situation, the resident felt that it was a "gallows scene, a cruel mockery of her youth and unfulfilled potential. Her only words to me were, 'Let's get this over with.'"

At this point, the physician returned to the nurses' station to think things over and decided to "give her rest." The nurse was asked to draw morphine sulfate into a syringe. "'Enough,' I thought, 'to do the job.'" The physician returned to the patient's room and told the two women that he was going to give Debbie "something that would let her rest and to say good-bye." Within seconds of the intravenous injection, the pa-

tient's breathing slowed, her eyes closed, and her distress seemed to be at an end. The other woman stroked Debbie's hair as she slept.

The doctor "waited for the inevitable next effect of depressing the respiratory drive." Four minutes later, the breathing slowed further, sputtered, and came to an end." The dark-haired woman stood erect and seemed relieved. "It's all over, Debbie."

This brief report raised a furor among the readers of this widely read and respected medical journal. The media picked it up and the public was immediately drawn into the controversy as well. The response was divided, but critical reactions dominated.

The following are what I see as the most salient questions raised by this incident:

1. The physician had no prior acquaintance with the patient or her companion. This means that the life-and-death decision was made and carried out by a stranger. *Should a physician assist the death of a patient with whom he or she has no previous relationship and no background of knowledge?*

2. The decision was also made very quickly and without consultation. *Did the decision have to be made that quickly? Does a physician have the responsibility to get a second opinion before taking a life?*

3. The physician was fatigued. *Should physicians be able to take their own state of mind and body into account when on the verge of making important decisions?*

4. The physician's anxiety was heightened by the fact that the patient was also young—it became more difficult, then, to establish a sense of emotional distance: this terrible thing could also happen to the physician. The physician seems to have projected his own thoughts and feelings on the patient. The "gallows" and "cruel mockery" images emerged from the physician's own mind and may have had little resonance with Debbie's own thoughts. *Should physicians be required to demonstrate competency in dealing with their own emotions before being entrusted with other people's lives?*

5. At first the physician felt that "the room seemed filled with the patient's desperate effort to survive." A few minutes later, the

physician ended Debbie's life. There was no indication in the published report that the physician ever tried to reconcile the impression with the action. *Should physicians be required to demonstrate the ability to monitor their own thoughts in an alert and critical manner before being entrusted with other people's lives?*

6. The nurse was ordered to prepare a lethal injection. Is it morally defensible to order another person to participate in an assisted death? *Should the nurse have been given the opportunity to express her feelings and philosophy? Did the nurse have the responsibility to refuse this order and inform the physician that she was going to report this incident immediately?*

7. The physician ordered a lethal dose of medication instead of a dose that might have provided relief without ending her life. This alternative does not seem to have been considered. *Does a physician have the right to end a life before attempting to relieve pain and other symptoms by nonlethal means?*

8. The patient's distress had been intensified by a procedure (the alcohol drip) that had produced new symptoms without alleviating the existing symptoms. *Did this hospital routinely fail to provide adequate pain relief because of ignorance, indifference, or the fear of making an addict out of a terminally ill patient? Was it the failure of the hospital's overall symptom relief program that placed both the young resident and the young woman in this extremely stressful situation?*

9. Debbie spoke only one sentence to the doctor. Did the doctor try to converse with her or her companion? *Did the doctor hold her hand, establish eye contact, and attempt to have at least a little more guidance from her before making the decision to end her life? Should doctors be required to demonstrate communication competence in critical care situations before being entrusted with other people's lives?*

10. The doctor told the two women that he was giving Debbie something that (1) "would let her rest" and (2) would "let her say goodbye." What actually happened, according to the report, was that Debbie closed her eyes and died shortly thereafter, without having the chance to say goodbye or anything else. *Was the physician actually concerned with enabling leavetaking communication between Debbie and her companion? Did the physician really*

believe that death and "rest" are identical outcomes? Or did the physician misrepresent what he was actually doing in order to reduce his own anxiety level? What responsibility to truth and open communication should be expected of physicians in critical care situations?

An Arrow through the Physician's Armor

One of the painful lessons in this particular episode involves the role of the physician's own physical, mental, and spiritual state and the nature of the health care system. A tired and probably overworked physician found himself in a stressful situation that neither medical training nor personal experience had equipped him to master. His own insulation from dying and death was pierced momentarily by the sight of another young person in such a painful and vulnerable condition. The physician felt an urgent need to relieve Debbie's anguish as well as his own sense of personal vulnerability and inability to restore her health.

The physician had several options. These included taking other measures to relieve the patient's distress and discontinuing those that were adding to her distress. The physician could have consulted with others—the nurses who had been caring for Debbie as well as more experienced physicians. Certainly the physician could have made more effort to learn who Debbie was and what she wanted. It is not unusual for people to wish themselves dead when experiencing acute distress—but to be grateful later that another alternative had been found.

All of these options required time and patience—and time was not what this tired, poorly prepared, overmatched, and anxious physician could afford. The decision to end Debbie's life was influenced by the physician's urgent need to terminate a situation in which he or she felt powerless, vulnerable, and depressed. The needs and feelings of other people were barely considered, nor did the physician feel obliged to think of the philosophical, religious, sociopsychological, and legal factors that might lead one to hesitate before taking another person's life.

Much of the critical response called attention to the physician's disregard of standards and due procedure. Other doctors were aware that their own image and reputation were endangered by such episodes. The ease with which one young physician disposed of Debbie's problems by disposing of Debbie in the middle of the night seems to be a prime example of how slippery the slope can be.

We should keep in mind, however, that the anxieties of doctors (or hospital administrators) can lead to the opposite outcome as well: bodies being maintained on life support systems despite the obvious futility of this procedure and despite the family's and even the patient's own expressed wishes. The legal justice system in our society, for all of its flaws, does at least allow time and require evidence. Decisions hastily made in the middle of the night by doctors who are poorly trained in self-monitoring and interpersonal communication afford few, if any, safeguards.

Does a Person Have to Be Dying to Have the Right to Die?

This odd phrase brings us to one of the issues that is becoming increasingly important. Much of the right-to-die controversy at first centered around people who were either locked into a persistent vegetative state (e.g., Karen Ann Quinlan) or alert, responsive, but with little time to live (e.g., Debbie). As we have seen, there is increasing public support for the right to terminate life-sustaining procedures when a person is in either of these conditions. But what are we to think about a case such as the following? *As you read about this case, consider what decision you would have recommended at each point—and why.* Test your own decision-making skills and life-and-death philosophy.

Elizabeth Bouvia

A 26-year-old woman has earned a degree in social work and is seeking employment. Her husband leaves her. She becomes depressed and anxious. If she also becomes suicidal, would you recommend:

____ Everything possible should be done to prevent her from committing suicide.

____ Somebody should listen to her, offer advice and support, but not otherwise intervene.

____ Some other course of action should be taken, namely_____

_____

Why did you make this particular recommendation? _____

_____

_____

Now we add some further information. This woman is also afflicted with cerebral palsy. She retains just enough muscular control to operate an electrically-powered wheelchair, to speak, and to chew and swallow food when someone feeds her. Suppose that she expresses a strong wish to end her life—what course of action would you recommend?

____ Everything possible should be done to prevent her from committing suicide.

____ Somebody should listen to her, offer advice and support, but not otherwise intervene.

____ Some other course of action should be taken, namely _____

_____

Why did you make this particular recommendation? _____

_____

_____

There is a new development. The state will no longer provide transportation assistance for this woman. This makes it almost certain that she will not be able to find and keep a job. She is now deprived of the opportunity to pursue the career for which she prepared herself and the chance to support herself. As a result of this discouraging development, she expresses a strong wish to end her life. What course of action do you recommend?

____ Everything possible should be done to prevent her from committing suicide.

____ Somebody should listen to her, offer advice and support, but not otherwise intervene.

____ Some other course of action should be taken, namely _____

_____

Why did you make this particular recommendation? _____

_____

_____

Nobody has agreed to help her commit suicide (remember that she does not have the physical ability to do so herself). She is desperate. What can she do? She arranges to have herself admitted to a hospital so she can be left alone and gradually starve herself to death. When she is admitted to the hospital, attempts are made to change her mind, but her purpose holds firm. At this point, what course of action would you recommend?

___ Force her to take nourishment against her wishes.

___ Allow her to carry through her plan, while also providing her with companionship and the opportunity to discuss and reconsider her options if she so chooses.

___ Some other course of action should be taken, namely_____

_____

Why did you make this particular recommendation?_____

_____

_____

Now let's see what actually happened. Riverside (California) General Hospital refused to accept Elizabeth Bouvia's plan and brought the issue to court. The judge declared that Ms. Bouvia was fully competent and had made a decision that was both competent and sincere. But—he decided in favor of the hospital's position!

> The decisive point was that Ms. Bouvia was "not terminal" but "had a life expectancy of 15 to 20 years." He concluded, "The established ethics of the medical profession clearly outweigh...her own rights of self-determination." Therefore, "forced feeding, however invasive, would be administered for the purpose of saving the life of an otherwise non-terminal patient and should be permitted. There is no reasonable option." (Annas, 1984, p. 20)

George Annas, a professor of health law, argues that this was a poor decision that gave legal force to "brutal behavior." His key point is that medical care requires *consent* and is really no care at all when it is imposed against the patient's wishes. He reports that "four or more attendants wrestle her from her bed in the morning and restrain her while a nasogastric tube is rudely forced through her nose and into her stomach" (p. 24). Hospital officials insisted that its staff should not be asked to become accessories to a

suicide. (Apparently there was no concern about asking the staff to participate in a group assault on a helpless person.)

The impasse was resolved when Ms. Bouvia checked herself out of the hospital and was admitted to a nursing home that promised not to force food upon her. Once settled into the (unidentified) nursing home, Ms. Bouvia outlived the media's interest in her. She decided not to starve herself to death after all because this had proven to be too stressful a process.

Ms. Bouvia's predicament—and the predicament of all who became involved in the situation—illustrates what can happen when various rights come into conflict. Following are some of the rights that were asserted or implied:

1. The right to end one's own life—for any reason that seems significant to that person.
2. The right to end one's own life when not terminally ill but is facing years of infirmity and isolation.
3. The right to ask or require other people to help end one's life.
4. The right of society to oppose the wish of a person to end his or her life.
5. The right of "experts" (e.g., physicians, lawyers, judges) to do what they think is best for a person, even if this directly contradicts what that person seeks for himself or herself.

No judicial decision can resolve all of the issues raised by competing claims of rights. Some of these issues are linked with our deepest personal values and beliefs and may therefore be highly resistant to change as per court order. In this instance, many people were outraged by the court's support of physical intervention to force Ms. Bouvia to take nourishment. The basic sense of fair play and compassion seemed to be violated when a disabled individual, innocent of any crime, could be so abused by the system, and with a judge's consent. In situations such as these, judicial rulings might be "proper" on their own terms but are more likely to create than solve problems because they run counter to society's view of how people should treat each other.

Reflect a moment on the recommendations you made at various points in the development of Ms. Bouvia's predicament. What perspective did you take? Were you placing yourself in Ms.

Bouvia's situation, trying to see the situation from her standpoint? Or did you see yourself instead as a hospital administrator or as the nurse responsible for her care? The priorities and pressures of the situation take on a different pattern as we shift perspective. It is a constant challenge to put ourselves in the positions of all people who may be involved in a life-and-death predicament. Even the question of "which right is the rightist?" may be answered in a different way, depending upon our particular involvement and stake in the situation.

Ms. Bouvia's experience leaves us with three fundamental problems that neither society at large nor medical and legal experts have fully resolved: (1) If we have a "right to die," must this be limited to terminal illness and, if so, why? (2) Are there limits to the power that the state can legitimately exercise over an individual who wishes to die? (3) Is it acceptable to ask others to help us die? Responsible people continue to disagree.

Competent to Decide?

The issue of consent to treatment—or to the withholding or withdrawal of treatment—has already come to the fore. Consent would have no meaning, however, if the individual were unable to comprehend the situation, the options, or the consequences. Due process requires a determination of competence before the issue of consent can be addressed. What should be done when it is ruled that the individual is not competent?

Joseph Saikewicz was a 67-year-old resident of the Belchertown State School (Massachusetts). He was considered to be profoundly retarded, with a mental age of less than 3 years. Because of this intellectual deficit, he was not considered competent to enter into legal contracts or make other significant decisions regarding his own welfare. A representative of the state would make decisions in his behalf. Saikewicz was robust, ambulatory, and usually enjoyed good health. He was able to make his wishes known only through gestures and grunts. He had adjusted fairly well to the sheltered institutional environment but was vulnerable and disoriented in other settings.

The need for decision making arose when Saikewicz was diagnosed as suffering from acute myeloblastic monocytic leukemia, a form of the disease that was considered incurable. Chemotherapy produces a remission in some patients, but this usually lasts only for several months. Unfortunately, the course of treatment can produce serious side effects. According to the medical testimony, "a patient in Saikewicz's condition would live for a matter of weeks, or perhaps, several months.... A decision to allow the disease to run its natural course would not result in pain for the patient, and death would probably come without discomfort" (Robbins, 1983, p. 38).

If Joseph Saikewicz had been capable of comprehending his condition, he would have been able to decide whether or not he wanted chemotherapy, with its prospect of extending survival for several months but also making him feel sicker. Because he was not capable of making this decision, it fell to the medical and administrative officials and eventually the courts. In this instance, a Massachusetts probate judge ordered that all reasonable and necessary supportive measures should be provided to Saikewicz but that he was *not* to be subjected to chemotherapy. This decision was based on the consideration that *the state had no applicable interests or claims that outweighed Saikewicz's right to be spared the discomfort of a treatment that could not save his life.* The patient remained in his familiar institutional home until he died of pneumonia, a complication of the leukemia. Reportedly, he died without pain or discomfort.

Unlike the judicial decision that gave precedence to social institutions over the individual's (Bouvia) own wishes, this ruling supports the position that the state does not necessarily have either the right or the obligation to subject a person to treatment simply because the treatment is available. Each new case that comes up for judicial review will have its own distinctive features. This means that even when competency or incompetency has been clearly established, the ruling may be affected by other factors. Furthermore, a judge may find cause to make a ruling that departs markedly from the decisions made in previous cases of a somewhat similar nature.

Joseph Saikewicz was known to have been incompetent to give or withhold consent because of his lifelong intellectual deficit. Nobody challenged the classification of mental incompetence. This determination is not always so easy and free of dissent. For example, I have observed shifting levels of competence in aged residents of long-term care facilities. There are times when the person appears disoriented, out of touch with both the institutional environment and the larger world. On other occasions, the same person is alert, aware, and able to express preferences and intentions. Furthermore, this variable competency may be influenced much by how the person is being treated and what is going on around him or her. A change in medication (even in the dosage of the same medication) can result in either a spell of disorientation or a recovery from the fog. A person who has withdrawn from social interaction and has little to say may be assumed to be mentally incompetent when, in fact, he or she is suffering from a depressive reaction—or can no longer pick up conversations but is hesitant to ask for a hearing aid! If we assume that "old and institutionalized" means "incompetent," we might slide into the habit of making decisions without the person's participation. When such a pattern has developed, it is only a small step to assume that the person is mentally incompetent and unable to participate in a life-or-death situation.

On the other end of the age spectrum, we have already noted (*see Chapter 10*) that children tend to be excluded from participation in decision making about their own care. The child is not considered competent to give or withhold informed consent for medical procedures in general. Does this mean that every possible treatment must be given to (imposed on) a child? And who should decide? A noted bioethicist has offered this rationale for decision making:

> (1) Since children are not persons strictly but exist in and through their families, parents are the appropriate ones to decide whether or not to treat a deformed child when (a) there is not only little likelihood of full human life but also great likelihood of suffering if life is prolonged, or (b) when the cost of prolonging life is very great. Such decisions must be made with a physician who will be able to help the parents with the consequences of their decision. (2) It is reasonable to speak of a duty not to treat a small child when such treatment would only prolong a painful life or would in any event lead to a painful death. (Engelhardt, 1989, p. 151)

Engelhardt's position is an attempt to establish a new form of due process that will offer more protection for a child's welfare when life-or-death decisions are required. It is troubling, though, to find that expense and suffering are equated as variables: do not prolong life if this would prolong suffering or when it would cost too much. Cost is obviously an important practical consideration, especially in our present health care system. But are we ready to make cost functionally equivalent with suffering? At this point in his argument, Engelhardt seems to have exchanged the urgency of human suffering for a distancing policy formula. Even more troubling is the assertion that "children are not persons strictly but exist in and through their families." Images of infanticide and child abuse come to mind, as well as the perplexing question of when and how a child does become a person. Obviously, society has a long way to go in rethinking the nature of personhood and the rights of the child before we can deal wisely with life-and-death issues involving the young.

A Supreme Court Ruling: The Nancy Cruzan Case

Fifteen years after the Quinlan case brought the right-to-die issue to public attention, the United States Supreme Court issued its first direct ruling on the subject. Nancy Cruzan, 26, had been critically injured in an automobile accident on January 11, 1983. When discovered by paramedics, Cruzan was lying face down in a ditch—no respiration, no heartbeat. The paramedics were able to revive both her respiration and her cardiac function, but the young woman remained unresponsive. Physicians judged that she had suffered trauma to the brain and oxygen deprivation.

Three weeks later, she could grimace, display motor reflexes, and take a little nourishment by mouth. She may have had slight responsivity to pain and sound. Nevertheless, Nancy Cruzan did not respond to conversation, express thoughts and needs, or engage in either verbal or nonverbal communication. Surgeons implanted a feeding tube with the permission of her husband. It was not necessary to use a ventilator because she continued to breathe on her own. Rehabilitation efforts were attempted but failed. No improve-

Nancy Cruzan, another accident victim who suffered a permanent loss of consciousness, had her case brought before the United States Supreme Court.

ment was noted or expected, but the young woman remained alive and the state of Missouri continued to pay for her care.

Two options were considered at this point: continue to support Cruzan's life by tube feeding and nursing care, or withdraw these services, thereby leading to her death. There could also have been the option of a lethal injection or other direct life-terminating procedure, but it was not endorsed by those involved with the situation. Nancy Cruzan's parents asked hospital personnel to discontinue the tube feeding and hydration. It was understood by everybody involved that this action would result in the young woman's death. The hospital declined to honor the request without court authorization. As it turned out, this request would go all the way to the U.S. Supreme Court (1989). This is a summary of what happened:

1. The trial court ruled that Nancy Cruzan had a fundamental right to refuse or accept the withdrawal of what it termed "death prolonging procedures."
2. It was also ruled that she had expressed her general intent in a conversation with a close friend a year previously. Nancy had told her friend that if very ill or seriously injured, she would not want to continue her life unless she could live "at least halfway normally."
3. The Missouri attorney general appealed this ruling to his state's supreme court. By a 4-to-3 margin, the lower court's ruling was overturned. The life support procedures would have to be continued. A key point in this decision was the fact that Nancy had not prepared a Living Will or any other document that established her intent beyond a reasonable doubt.
4. The U.S. Supreme Court agreed to consider the parents' appeal of the Missouri Supreme Court decision. The Court recognized the principle that "a competent person has a constitutionally protected...interest in refusing unwanted medical treatment" (1989, p. 183). Nevertheless, by a 5-to-4 margin, the nation's highest court refused to overturn the decision. Each state has the right to establish due process in order to safeguard the rights of all involved. Nancy Cruzan had the right to refuse "death prolongation" procedures, but the state of Missouri had the right to require what it considered to be clear and convincing evidence that

this would really have been Ms. Cruzan's intentions if she could now express herself.

5. On the surface, it appeared that after six years of nonresponsive existence, Nancy Cruzan would have to continue in that condition for an indefinite period of time, despite the sense of sorrow and futility on the part of family and staff and the ever-mounting expense. The Supreme Court, however, had created a way out of the dilemma. The state itself could reconsider the evidence and approve withdrawal of life support activities. And that is just what happened. Nancy Cruzan's physician had opposed the withdrawal of life support. But he had seen enough. A court-appointed guardian asked the physician if he still thought it was within the patient's interest to continue the tube feeding and hydration. "No, sir. I think it would be personally a living hell!" A Jasper County judge ruled that the parents' request could be honored. There were no further legal challenges this time, although a throng of protesters (not people who had known Nancy Cruzan personally) voiced their disapproval. The young woman died quietly twelve days after the tubes were removed (December 26, 1990).

What has been established by and learned from this ordeal? The U.S. Supreme Court did affirm—though indirectly—the principle that a competent person has the right to refuse treatment that would only prolong suffering. The Court also upheld the right of local jurisdictions to require due process in determining how particular cases should be evaluated. The Cruzan versus Missouri decision, however, did not address all of the issues that can arise in right-to-die cases; it did not even address all the salient issues in the Cruzan case. As we will see later in this chapter, more recently the courts have been called upon to rule on legislation that supports right-to-die decisions. It is likely that this process of legislative action and juridicial review will continue for many years.

Meanwhile, we might accept the challenge to draw our own lessons. For example, we can see the usefulness of articulating our wishes regarding end-of-life issues in some form of advance directive. Nancy Cruzan's situation would have been resolved sooner and with less stress for everybody

concerned had she executed a Living Will—but how many 23 year olds do you know who have actually done this? We may choose to disagree with the Missouri court's refusal to consider several serious conversations that Nancy Cruzan had with other people within a year of her accident, conversations in which she consistently spoke of her belief that it is best to "let go" in such situations and leave it up to God. "The testimony of close friends and family members... may often be the best evidence available of what the patient's choice would be" (1989, p. 203). Or we may choose to be more cautious, realizing that friends could possibly have misinterpreted these conversations.

We can also see that the decision to withdraw life support is a difficult one when respiratory function, cardiac function, and motor reflexes persist without external aids. The Missouri State Supreme Court emphasized that "Nancy is diagnosed as in a persistent vegetative state. She is not dead. She is not terminally ill. Medical experts testified that she could live another thirty years" (1989, p. 180). We need to be well informed and secure in our understanding about what it means to be alive and a person.

Finally, we are left with the question of perceived social value. Both Karen Ann Quinlan and Nancy Cruzan were young people who seemed to have full lives ahead of them. What about elderly people who find themselves in similar predicaments? Hemlock Society author Donald W. Cox notes:

> On November 30, two weeks prior to Judge Teel's order to remove Nancy's feeding tube from her stomach, the Court of Common Pleas in Lackawanna County (Scranton), Pennyslvania held that a sixty-four-year-old incompetent woman in a persistent vegetative state was entitled to have a naso-gastric feeding tube withdrawn. The hospital removed the tube and the woman died peacefully and quietly, in sharp contrast to the front-page publicity that enveloped Cruzan's death a few weeks later. (1993, p. 86)

Many elderly men and women have died in this manner. Others have died when health care personnel have decided against starting life support procedures. As a nation, we seem to place less value on the lives of older adults. We assume that old people are supposed to be depressed and therefore seldom intervene therapeutically (Hinrichsen, 1993). And when older people seem ready to die—well, that's what they're supposed to do, right?

DR. KEVORKIAN AND THE ASSISTED SUICIDE MOVEMENT

Society at large and the health care system in particular continue to struggle with the idea and practice of assisted death. Dr. Kevorkian's activities remained in the media spotlight until they reached a crescendo, when the television program *60 Minutes* featured a video that showed him giving a lethal injection to Thomas Youk. He challenged prosecutors to try him for murder. They did so—successfully—and Kevorkian was subsequently convicted of second-degree murder and imprisoned. He decided against going on the hunger strike he had threatened and, at last report, was serving time in a Michigan penal facility. Kevorkian's words, actions, and personality have dominated the subject of assisted death in the United States for more than a decade. Nevertheless, we must look at the broader picture here, starting again with terminology.

Kevorkian has often described his services as *assisted suicide*. This term locks in a particular interpretation (suicide) with which not all proponents of assisted death agree, and with which most suicidologists disagree. We will use the more neutral term, *assisted death*, which provides maneuvering room for a variety of interpretations. It should be noted that the most common term now in use is *physician-assisted death*. Despite its popularity, this term is unnecessarily limiting: people other than physicians can assist death.

Assisted death will be examined briefly within several contexts: (1) the medico-legal situation in the Netherlands (Holland) and Australia; (2) Kevorkian's philosophy and practice; and (3) recent alternatives and developments, including Compassion in Dying and the Oregon Death with Dignity Act, another new approach.

The Netherlands: A Social Experiment Watched Closely by the World

In recent years, the Netherlands' medico-legal system has been the focus of interest for both ad-

vocates and opponents of assisted death. This enterprising and often surprising nation has provided the most tolerant social climate for assisted death. Dutch courts established a tradition of sanctioning cases of medically assisted death brought before them during the 1980s (Gomez, 1991). These were individual court decisions—interpretations of the existing laws—in individual situations. These decisions did not meet with total approval on the part of all legal experts, health care professionals, and the general public. There was—and continues to be—critical and passionate dialogue between advocates and opponents within the Netherlands.

Physicians who engaged in assisted deaths remained apprehensive during this time because the laws still considered such acts to be criminal. A court might decide to enforce the laws because of individual circumstances of the case or a shift in judicial and/or public opinion. (Actually, no Dutch physician ever was sent to prison for ending a patient's life.)

In February 1993, the Netherlands enacted a law that made it legal for a physician to assist in ending a patient's life (Cox, 1993). The physician has to behave in compliance with a set of rules that includes the requirements that (1) the patient is terminally ill; (2) the patient has made an explicit request for life termination; and (3) the physician informs the coroner of this action and provides a detailed check list regarding the patient's situation and the physician's own actions. At the moment, the Netherlands is the only nation with a law that clearly sanctions (medically) assisted death. With the passage of this legislation, physicians have no concern about facing criminal charges—including murder—as long as they stay within the guidelines.

The issue is not so easily resolved, however. Some physicians and other health care providers in the Netherlands, as elsewhere, are opposed to assisted death for personal and/or moral reasons. Others are worried about the adequacy of the decision-making process: do the people involved always communicate adequately with each other and have full knowledge of the available options? Still others accept the legalization of assisted death in its present form but harbor concerns about the possible extension of this practice into other spheres, fearing that their nation may have already taken a dangerous step down that slippery slope. This fear was intensified on April 29, 1995, when an infant born in terrible pain with a spinal column defect was injected with a muscular relaxant that stopped her breathing. The baby girl's parents had authorized the procedure, and it was carried out by her physician. The Dutch Ministry of Justice prosecuted the physician on the charge of premeditated murder. The physician was found guilty—but not convicted. The trial was intended not to punish this physician but to establish new guidelines for assisted death (or, as some still prefer, *euthanasia*) for newborns with severe disabilities.

This case was important not only because it involved a newborn person, but also because (1) the decision was in the form of substituted judgment and (2) despite her serious physical defect and pain, the infant was not terminally ill. The little girl could not speak for herself. Is it reasonable and moral for anybody, even her parents, to make the decision to end her life? Or is the acceptance of this act of assisted death a dangerous slide further down the slippery slope that could result the in widespread killing of newborns and perhaps others who do not meet somebody's criteria for being an acceptable person? Few doubted that the parents loved their child and wished to spare her futher pain and suffering, but many feared the possible encouragement of other and more dubious acts of ending the lives of people who could not speak for themselves.

The most sever criticism of euthanasia in Netherlands comes from some of those within the country who have observed this practice in action. Dutch palliative care physician Ben Zylicz reports that there are frequent violations of the guidelines that have been established to protect abuses. In one recent year more than 200 patients who were fully or partly competent were killed although they had not requested death. He also points out that there are only 70 palliative care beds in the whole country. Zylic notes:

Few Dutch physicians have been trained in pain management and symptom control, and consequently, euthanasia is the only solution they know if the patient's suffering becomes too great. If you accept euthanasia as a solution to difficult and unresolved problems in palliative care, you will never learn anything (IAETF, 1998, p. 11).

In turning to the Netherlands experiences with assisted death, then, we find perhaps more problems than answers. And the answers, when forthcoming, sometimes are unexpected. For example, an institutionalized Dutch woman requested assisted death. The request was denied, but she was told that the institution could not force her to eat. She took no food and only a little water for several days and continued to express her wish to die. The institution then respected her decision and stopped offering her food. Well, they did give her some apple juice.

To the surprise of those who attended to her needs, her physical situation had not really deteriorated after three weeks. It was discovered that the contents of apple juice can keep people alive well over a hundred days and that, if she kept drinking apple juice, she would probably not die from starvation at all. A week later the nurses happened to serve the residents a hot meal with french fried chicken. At the smell of this dish the woman all of a sudden asked whether she could have some, too. Ever since she has been eating her meals again and for many months afterward she happily participated in all different kinds of activities the nursing home had to offer. (Meijburg, 1995–1996, p. 192)

Gradually the woman's physical condition deteriorated and "she died a natural death." This is one of many vignettes suggesting that there may be a lot of unknowns and good deal of ambiguity in the interaction between a person requesting assisted death and those who must respond to this request in some way. Perhaps it is not surprising that physician-assisted death remains a deeply divisive issue in the nation that has been most receptive to the idea.

Australia: Yes, and Then No

The assisted death/right-to-die controversy is raging in many nations today. Australia provides another instructive example. The first law that specifically legalized euthanasia and assisted suicide was enacted by the Northern Territory Parliament, taking effect July 1, 1996. Less than a year later, the Australian Senate overturned this law and forbade its territories from passing any measures that would make assisted suicide legal. Clearly the nation was in turmoil over this issue.

As in other nations, the case for assisted death was made on behalf of terminally ill people whose suffering had not been relieved. And again, as in other nations, the controversy served to alarm and educate the public about the situation experienced by terminally ill people. Should this person be granted her wish to avoid further suffering by assisted death, or is should physicians be more conscientious and effective in providing relief for pain and other symptoms?

An additional pair of questions soon came into focus: what physician would agree to terminate a life, and what physician would be qualified to do so? Only one Australian physician, Dr. Philip Nitschke, agreed to take on this responsibility, and then only after discovering that none of his colleagues would step forth. The several terminally ill people seeking assisted death under the new (and later revoked) law and the one physician willing to respond to their wishes became the center of heated controversy that has not yet abated (Nitschke, in press; Street & Kissane, in press). There is also increasing concern in the United States regarding the qualifications required of a physician who executes a patient's request for assisted death. Are all physicians qualified? What kinds of skills and experience are needed? This issue is a long way from being resolved at present.

Assisted Death in the Kevorkian Manner

Assisted death in the Kevorkian manner should be seen within its socio-medical context. Consider first the principle objections of medical practitioners to any form of assisted death:

- *Taking a life is inconsistent with the responsibilities and values of a physician.* Nothing could more contradict and undermine the mission of the healer.
- *Religious convictions forbid taking a person's life under any circumstances, with the possible exception of self-defense.* Some physicians could not even begin to consider the possibility of assisting death because of their deeply-held religious convictions.
- *The life might be mis-taken.* Nature does not always behave as physicians expect. The impulse to relieve suffering might result in ending a life that had potential for recovery.

- *Serious legal consequences might be expected to befall any physician who engaged in assisted death.* Malpractice suits and criminal charges would destroy the life of a physician reckless enough to take such action.
- *The dying person accuses the physician of being a failure.* Or, rather, it is the physician's self-accusation when the limits of medical art and science are exposed by incurable illness. Physicians were avoiding their dying patients in general. They certainly did not want to see their patients' unrelieved suffering and perhaps hear their cries for help.

When Kevorkian started his one-person campaign in 1990, he had practically no support from either medical organizations or court rulings. Furthermore, he well understood that he could not reduce the suffering of all terminally ill people by his own efforts. His hope was to arouse the sympathetic interest of the public and thereby force the medical profession to change its position regarding assisted death. This plan required Kevorkian to reveal rather than conceal his actions. He was therefore placing himself at risk of censure from the public and the media as well as the medical profession and the law.

Kevorkian has been eminently successful in arousing public opinion on this subject. Attitude polls have produced shifting and variable results. In the mid-1990s, most national surveys recorded an increase in public support; later polls have had more variable results. In the United States as in other nations, opinion is divided among the general public and among health care providers. Some individual physicians have come forth in support of Kevorkian's efforts, but powerful organizations such as the American Medical Association have taken a stand against physician-assisted death.

People who have known Kevorkian over the years characterize him as a very intelligent man with a keen grasp of medical history. Families who have sought his services speak of him as a compassionate and understanding person. Critics remark on Kevorkian's verbal attacks on those who do not agree with him, his apparent delight in publicity, and his "lone wolf" approach. Although principles are more important than personality in the long run, what are perceived as positive and negative features of Jack Kevorkian,

M.D. have influenced the reception to his words and actions.

Kevorkian's Agenda

Kevorkian would add planned death to the list of shattered taboos, now that legal sanctions against abortion and suicide have weakened. The agenda he presents also includes the establishment in communities across the nation of centers in which people could have assisted deaths upon their request and biomedical research could be done on dying and death. These *orbitoria*, as he calls them, would go much further than previously possible toward understanding the nature of death. Perhaps you recall Kevorkian's long-term interest in the changes that occur around the time of death (*see Chapter 2*). He also is a strong advocate for organ donations and has attempted repeatedly to establish a program through which condemned prisoners could donate their body parts.

As we can see, Kevorkian's agenda is broader and more complex than that usually presented in the headlines and sound bites. The media emphasis has been upon his controversial approach to relieving the pain and suffering of individuals through assisted death. Beyond this objective, Kevorkian is also attempting to complete what he sees as the long process of breaking away from concepts and values that once were dominant in Western society but that he believes no longer should rule our decisions. This stance puts him into conflict with much (though not all) of the religious, legal, and medical establishments.

Further, he would extend biomedical science into a zone that makes many people very uncomfortable. His advocacy for research into the central nervous systems of dying and dead people is reminiscent of the violent disputes that erupted when physicians first attempted to study cadavers. Postmortem examinations were prohibited by church and state. Physicians had to obtain cadavers through shady practices and conduct their examinations under risk of discovery and punishment. There is no question that major advances in medical knowledge derived from studying the dead, especially as this practice gradually won approval. However, this history does not mean that much of value would also be learned from the types of biomedical studies that Kevorkian has in mind, nor does it mean that these studies should be approved and supported. It is useful to be aware of this historical parallel, however, if only to recognize that Kevorkian has more on his mind than pain relief for suffering individuals.

Kevorkian's Method

One of the quotes opening this chapter is from a newspaper advertisement placed by Kevorkian after he had been inspired by a visit to the Netherlands and felt ready to offer assisted suicide in the United States. He no longer has to advertise. As one woman put it, "He was the court of last resort" (McMahon, 1995–1996, p. 166). People turned to Kevorkian when there seemed to be no hope for improvement in their condition or relief from suffering. There follows a discussion with a patient and family members. Some of these sessions were recorded on videotape. Kevorkian has repeatedly emphasized that he puts no pressure on the patient to make the final decision quickly or to make that decision in the direction of assisted death. The report offered by Carol Loving in an opening quotation is consistent with this statement. She further describes the final scene:

> The last things we said, we said these things a thousand times—but you can never say "I love you" enough, and he said to me, "Aren't you going to hold my hand?" I said, "Yep." I took hold of his hand and turned his CD player on, and he just pulled that clip and started breathing as deep as he could....
>
> The moment of his death was quite evident to me. My son let out this incredible sigh of relief.... (1995–1996, pp. 175–176)

The death of Nick Loving was accomplished through an apparatus constructed by Kevorkian, which he sometimes referred to as the "Mercitron" but which is better known in the media as "the suicide machine." Whether Kevorkian used this or some other procedure for a particular patient, it was the patient who took the decisive action. It is for this reason that Kevorkian can speak of having "assisted" at a death. The fact that he did not himself take the final action also served as protection against charges of murder. He forfeited this protection and crossed the line he himself had specified when he gave Thomas Youk a lethal injection.

Evaluating Kevorkian's Approach

Physician-assisted death as advocated and practiced by Kevorkian has been subjected to many criticisms. There is the religious-moral objection that here is a physician playing God. Only God can give life and only God should take it. This objection is potent for those who hold a religious belief of this type, and it is also influential for others who think that, for whatever reason, Kevorkian has stepped across a line that should be respected. There is also the objection, already noted, that the physician must always be on the side of life.

Additional problems demand attention when we look at the data for the deaths that Kevorkian has acknowledged facilitating. The most detailed presentation and analysis of these data are provided in two articles written by Kalman J. Kaplan, director of a suicide research center in Chicago, and his research team (Kaplan, in press-a; Kaplan, in press-b). The most important data come from the medical examiners who have investigated the cases in detail. Information of this kind was available for ninety-three cases.

1. *Most of the people whose deaths were assisted by Kevorkian were not terminally ill.* Only 28.3 percent were terminally ill. Because the majority (69.9 percent) were not terminally ill, significant questions must be raised: How adequate was Kevorkian's medical assessment of the patients? How valid is his claim for relieving the suffering of dying people if most were not dying? Do these data confirm the fears of a very slippery slope? In other words, did the availability of "death on demand" lead to premature death?

2. *The gender bias in Kevorkian's clientele suggests that his practice is encouraging and increasing suicidality among women.* We turn again to Kalman's data. Before the Michigan law against assisted suicide was signed by the governor, all of the deaths had been women. During the period that Kevorkian was dealing with legal proceedings against him, he participated in the deaths of eleven men and nine women. As soon as he was acquitted on charges of as-

sisted suicide, Kevorkian returned to the original pattern in which by far the greater number were women. In the general population, women are much less likely than men to commit suicide. The reverse is true among Kevorkian's assisted-death patients.

3. *The people assisted to death by Kevorkian fit the general profile of suicide attempters rather than terminally ill people.* For example, they had a high incidence of depression and dependency and a low incidence of the conditions that are the most common causes of death in the United States. The implication is that Kevorkian either stimulated or was the receptive target for unhappy people who might otherwise have either attempted nonfatal suicide attempts or found other ways to deal with their situations. Another disturbing implication is Kevorkian's inability to diagnose or treat their depression. Many people with depressive episodes or tendencies are effectively treated every day. Some of these people do express the desire to end their lives in order to end their miseries. Competent medical help has often contributed to a restoration of their spirits—but competent medical help with their lives is not what they received from Kevorkian.

4. *Kevorkian functioned without adequate medical information and consultation.* He seldom asked for a second opinion—and did so less and less as he continued his practice. This was especially unfortunate because Kevorkian did not have expertise in many of the specific medical conditions that affected his patients, nor in psychiatric evaluation or palliative care (*see Chapter 5*). Part of the problem came from the unwillingness of other physicians to cooperate with him. He could have done much more, however, to make sure that his patients had the advantage of medical and psychiatric expertise before assisting them to death.

5. *Death is much too extreme a solution to the relief of suffering.* For people who are in severe pain (most of his patients were not), there are alternatives. It is interesting to take an international example here. There was a sharp negative response after an eminent Japanese physician administered a lethal drug to one of his patients. A critic, the director of a hospice, wrote:

BOX 9-1
KEVORKIAN'S STANDARDS AND ACTIONS

Kevorkian's Standards	*Kevorkian's Actions*
• Call for psychiatric consultation.	• Rarely called for consultation.
• Call for pain specialist consultation.	• Rarely called for pain specialist.
• 24-hour waiting period after final request.	• Most deaths in less than one day.
• Extensive patient counseling.	• Brief conversations; no professional counseling.
• Stop the process if any sign that patient is ambivalent.	• Some patients were clearly ambivalent, but assisted death carried out.

Even if there is so much pain that it cannot be eliminated through the use of painkilling drugs like morphine, it is possible to enable the patient to sleep without feeling the pain by using large doses of tranquilizers or anesthetics. Physical pain is not a reason for permitting euthanasia. (Kato, 1996)

Philosopher Histake Kato reported an incident in which a friend of his was in excruciating pain during an attack of pancreatitis. The first doctor he saw did not take painkilling measures. His friend switched to another hospital, where the pain was removed. "In other words, both doctors who have the best know-how about eliminating pain and doctors who have no know-how at all exist side by side in the Japanese medical system" (1996).

Kevorkian has not established his credentials for the up-to-date and effective relief of pain, and he has shown little familiarity or interest in the hospice movement. It is therefore entirely possible that people have been driven to seek assisted death through medical failure to relieve pain—and that Kevorkian has not offered an alternative other than death.

6. *Despite his disclaimers, it appears that Kevorkian has rushed people into assisted death without adequate safeguards and consideration.* The case of Mr. Gale has already been mentioned. His very first case, Janet Adkins, was a woman in good health, suffering no pain and, in fact, playing tennis with her teenage son. Kevorkian seemed to become her instrument of destruction at the prompting of her husband. Kevorkian seems to have strayed from his own criteria in other cases as well (See Box 9-1). Data show that as time went on, Kevorkian moved more rapidly from his first meeting with the patient to the death. He increasingly violated the criteria he had himself insisted upon in his public statements.

7. *Kevorkian uses "silencing" techniques to defend his actions.* This pattern is clear in his book and in many of his presentations through the media. It is only the physician who should assist deaths. It is only the physician who understands. This attitude dismisses the experiences, values, knowledge, and feelings of a great many other people, including clergy, nurses, social workers, attorneys, sociologists, anthropologists, and philosophers. Kevorkian is open to the charge of excessively medicalizing dying and death.

Oakland County (Michigan) Judge Jessica Cooper offered her own evaluation of Kevorkian's activities when she sentenced him to a term of ten to twenty-five years when he was found guilty of second degree murder:

This trial was not about the political or moral correctness of euthanasia. It was all about you, sir. It was about lawlessness. It was about disrespect for a society that exists and flourishes because of the strength of the legal system. No one, sir, is above the law. No one. You were on bond to another judge when you committed this offense; you were not licensed to practice medicine when you committed this offense,

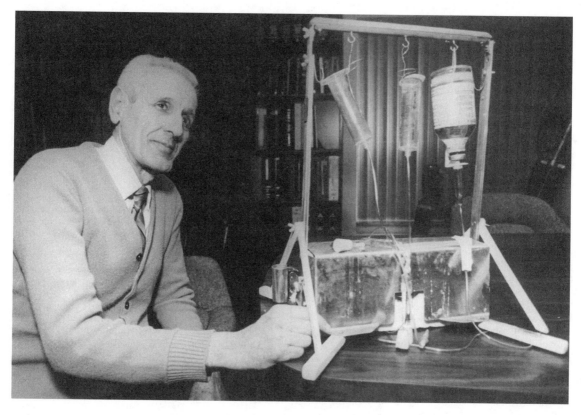

Jack Kevorkian with his suicide machine. Kevorkian was "present" at the death of more than a hundred people before being found guilty and imprisoned.

and you hadn't been licensed for eight years. And you had the audacity to go on national television, show the world what you did and dare the legal system to stop you.

Well, sir, consider yourself stopped.

www.catholic.org/euthanasia/kevsen.html

Compassion in Dying: An Alternative Model

A different approach to assisted death was introduced by Compassion in Dying, a nonprofit organization based in Seattle (P.O. Box 16483, Seattle, WA 98116, telephone (206) 624-2775). It has become a model for other organizations that attempt to meet the needs of terminally ill people who express a desire for death without violating legal or ethical principles. The guidelines and safeguards established by Compassion in Dying are summarized in Box 9-2.

Compassion in Dying emphasizes time, communication, and counseling. Representatives of the organization help patients and families to consider their alternatives. Founder and director Ralph Mero reports that hospice care is one of the alternatives explored.

The development of the hospice movement is one we strongly support. Many patients are able to endure the process of dying because of the generous provision of morphine and other pain medications which hospice offers. We have an experienced hospice nurse on our Board of Directors, and we value the advice we receive from hospice personnel. Most of our patients have been certified by their physicians as eligible for hospice care, and some were enrolled in hospice

---

BOX 9-2
COMPASSION IN DYING: GUIDELINES AND SAFEGUARDS

Guidelines

Eligibility
- Limited to adult, mentally competent patients who are terminally ill.
- Patient's condition must cause severe, intolerable suffering.
- Patient must understand condition, prognosis, and alternatives.
- Independent physician must examine patient, review records, and consult with primary care physician to verify eligibility.

Quality of Care
- Request for hastened death must not result from inadequate comfort care.
- Request must not be motivated by economic concerns or lack of health insurance.

Process of Requesting Assistance
- Request must originate with the patient.
- All requests will be kept confidential.
- Any indication of uncertainty cancels the process.
- Requests cannot be made through advance directives.

Mental Health Considerations
- Professional evaluation may be required to rule out emotional distress.
- Patient must understand and take responsibility for the decision.

Family and Religious Considerations
- Family must give its approval.
- Spiritual or emotional counseling may be arranged.

Safeguards (partial list)
- Patient must provide three signed written requests.
- There must be a 48-hour waiting period between second and third requests.
- Compassion in Dying representatives meet in person with patient and family.
- Any sign of indecision on the part of the patient, or opposition by the immediate family, cancels the process.
- Review team meets regularly to confirm eligibility and decide whether assistance is warranted.
- The patient may request that Compassion in Dying be present at the time of the death.
- Actual means of hastening death are prescribed by patient's physician and vary according to underlying condition.

---

programs when they contacted us. (Kastenbaum, 1994–1995)

How does Compassion in Dying respond to the slippery slope question?

COMPASSION can hardly be accused of providing "death on demand." We usually spend at least a month with patients between initial contact and time of death. Our somewhat complicated protocol slows down the process toward suicide to the degree that some patients feel it is not happening fast enough.... COMPASSION seeks to demonstrate that assistance with suicide can be provided carefully and thoughtfully, under the guidance of sensible constraints, and in a manner which will not jeopardize the wellbeing of vulnerable persons. If anything, our work enables some persons to postpone suicide or avoid it all together. *Just the knowledge that control has been regained may be enough to permit some patients to en-* *dure their illness until natural death.* (Kastenbaum, 1994–1995)

We can see now that people who favor the sanctioning of assisted death may take markedly different approaches. Please see Table 9-1 for a summary of some of the major differences between the Kevorkian and the Compassion in Dying Approaches.

New Developments in the Legalization of Assisted Suicide

Two recent developments are supportive of assisted suicide. The Oregon Death with Dignity Act was passed by a 51.3 percent to 48.7 percent majority by that state's voters in November 1994. This was the first such measure to be passed in the United States, after a similar measure was narrowly defeated in the state of Washington, as earlier described.

TABLE 9-1

Two Approaches to Assisted Death in the United States

	Kevorkian		Compassion in Dying	
	Yes	*No*	*Yes*	*No*
• Patient must be terminally ill.		√	√	
• Emotional distress is evaluated by mental health professional.		√	√	
• Consultation by a second physician is required.		√	√	
• Patient confidentiality is maintained.		√	√	
• Close contact is maintained with hospice organizations.		√	√	
• Provides the means of death.	√			√

Sources: Mero interview (Kastenbaum, 1994); Kevorkian (1991); print and television media reports.

The act applies only to terminally ill adults in Oregon. This obviously would have excluded most of the people at whose deaths Dr. Kevorkian assisted because, they were not terminally ill. The issue of assisted death for children has yet to be addressed in any definitive manner and is seldom even discussed. Eligibility for assisted death in Oregon requires that the person be older than 18 years and have an incurable and irreversible disease that will probably produce death within six months. This rules out people who have progressively deteriorating conditions but who are not at a high risk for death at present.

Numerous procedures and safeguards are built into the law to prevent its abuse. These include a fifteen-day waiting period after the request has been made, and a repeat of the request before a physician can write a prescription for a lethal dose of medication. Despite these and other safeguards, physicians and ethicists are already concerned about possible loopholes and flaws. For example, cancer research specialists Ezekiel J. Emanuel and Elisabeth Daniels (1996) fear that the law may permit assisted death before all treatment options have been exhausted. There is little doubt that legislation modeled on Ballot Measure 16 will soon be presented for consideration in many other states. Early findings indicate that physicians in Oregon have granted about one of every six requests for a prescription for a lethal medication. Effective palliative care, however, has led some terminally ill patients to change

their minds about assisted suicide. (Gazini et al., 1999)

The Oregon Death with Dignity Act has faced repeated challenges. At present efforts to prohibit federal funding for medical assistance are distressful to those who believe that low-income people would once again be deprived of care. Information has been held confidential regarding the few people who have made use of this measure for physician-assisted death. No adequate basis exists at present for evaluating this program.

Meanwhile, other states (notably California) have become active in supporting and opposing legislation that would legalize physician-assisted death. An increasingly educated public seems to be looking carefully at particular measures and discussing the options more openly and thoroughly. Legislators are aware that assisted death is one of the "hot potato" issues with voters and frequently are caught between their personal views and their desire to please constituents. Overall, the right-to-die situation is still far from settled.

SUMMARY

There was a time when few people discussed "the right to die" from a theoretical perspective. Today many people are intensely involved in this issue on both a personal and a practical level. Should terminally ill people have the right to ask a physician to end their suffering by ending their lives? This question has become complicated by factors such as: (1) memories of the abuse of eugenics and so-called "euthanasia" through the past century; (2) differing interpretations of the power of the Hippocratic oath; (3) concerns about the adequacy of care offered to terminally ill people by physicians; (4) concerns about the failure to take advantage of palliative care (hospice) options now available; (5) the attempt to broaden physician-assisted suicide to include any person who wants to die, whether terminally ill or not; and (6) the gap between theory and practice in carrying out physician-assisted death. Moral and religious considerations play a significant role throughout these issues. While defining our key terms, we explored the unsavory side of some past euthanasia programs, then looked at current attitudes toward the right to die. We next acquainted ourselves with some of the most important individual cases that brought the right-to-die issue to national attention and led to the first round of rulings and decision making. Although each case was unique, all revealed the complexities and ambiguities that often confront us in life-and-death situations.

We devoted sustained attention to physician-assisted suicide, starting with brief looks at developments in the Netherlands and Australia and then focusing on the approach taken by Jack Kevorkian, M.D. Making use of newly analyzed data, we learned that there are many troubling questions about the practice of physician-assisted death as carried out by Kevorkian. Finally, we looked at alternative approaches such as Compassion in Dying and the Oregon Death with Dignity Act. We will consider these challenging issues again in Chapter 15 as we try to develop a plan for living in a meaningful and responsible way with the knowledge of mortality.

REFERENCES

Annas, G. J. (1984). When suicide prevention becomes brutality: The case of Elizabeth Bouvia. *The Hastings Center Report, 13*, 20–21.

Anonymous. (1988). It's over, Debbie. *Journal of the American Medical Association, 259*, 272.

Cox, D. W. (1993). *Hemlock's cup.* Buffalo, NY: Prometheus.

Dickinson, G. E., Lancaster, C. J., Sumner, E. D., & Cohen, J. S. (1997–1998). Attitudes toward assisted suicide and euthanasia among physicians in South Carolina and Washington, *Omega, Journal of Death and Dying, 36*, 201–218.

Edelstein, L. (1943). *The Hippocratic oath: Text, translation, and interpretation.* Baltimore: Johns Hopkins University Press.

Emanuel, E. J., & Daniels, E. (1996). Oregon's physician-assisted suicide law. *Archives of Internal Medicine, 156*, 825–829.

Engelhardt, H. T. (1989). Ethical issues in aiding the death of young children. In R. M. Baird & S. E. Rosenbaum (Eds.), *Euthanasia. The moral issues* (pp.141–154). Buffalo, NY: Prometheus.

Friedlander, H. (1995). *The origins of Nazi genocide.* Chapel Hill: The University of North Carolina Press.

Gazini, L., Nelson, H. D., Schmidt, T. A., Kraemer, D. F., Delorit, M. A., & Lee, M. S. (1999). Physicians' experiences with the Oregon Death with Dignity Act. *New England Journal of Medicine 342*: 557–563.

Gomez, C. R. (1991). *Regulating death.* New York: The Free Press.

Greve, P. (1991: November). Advance directives—what the new law means for you. *Registered Nurse*, 63–67

Hinrichsen, G. A. (1993). Depression. In R. Kastenbaum (Ed.), *The encyclopedia of adult development* (pp. 106–111). Phoenix: Oryx

International Anti-Euthanasia Task Force (1988). *IAETF Update, 12*: 11–12. www.iaetf.org/iua15.htm#63.

Japan Times. (1996: June 21).

Kaplan, K. J., Lachenmeier, F., Harrow, M., O'Dell, J. C., Uziel, O., Schneiderhan, M., & Cheyfitz, K. (in press-a). Psychosocial versus biomedical risk factors in Kevorkian's first 47 physician-assisted deaths. *Omega, Journal of Death and Dying.*

Kaplan, K. J., O'Dell, J., Dragovic, L. J., McKeon, C., Bentley, E., & Telmet, K. J. (in press-b). An update on Kevorkian-Reding 93 physician-assisted deaths in Michigan: Is Kevorkian a savior, serial-killer or suicidal martyr? *Omega, Journal of Death and Dying.*

Kastenbaum, R. (1994–95). Ralph Mero: An Omega interview. *Omega, Journal of Death and Dying, 29*, 1–16.

Kato, H. (1996: June 25). Doctors need re-educating. *Sankei Shimbun.* Kyoto.

Kevorkian, J. (1991). *Prescription: Medicide.* Buffalo, NY: Prometheus.

Kevorkian sentenced 10–25 years in prison (1999) Retrieved 1999 from the World Wide Web: http://catholic.org/euthanasia/kevsen.html.

King, N. M. P. (1996). *Making sense of advance directives.* (Rev. ed.). Washington, DC: Georgetown University Press.

Kron, J. (1973, Oct. 6). The girl in the coma. *New York Magazine*, 17–24.

Leenen, H. J. J. (1990). Euthanasia, assistance to suicide, and the law: Developments in the Netherlands. *Health Policy, 8*, 197–206.

Lifton, R. J. (1986). *The Nazi Doctors.* New York: Basic Books.

Loving, C. (1995–1996). Nick Loving & Dr. Jack Kevorkian: An Omega interview with Carol Loving. *Omega, Journal of Death and Dying, 32*, 165–178.

Marker, R. (1993). *Deadly compassion.* New York: Morrow.

McMahon, P. (1995–1996). Nick Loving & Dr. Jack Kevorkian: An Omega interview with Carol Loving. *Omega, Journal of Death and Dying, 32,* 165–178.

Meijburg, H. H. V. D. K. (1995–1996). How health care institutions in the Netherlands approach physician assisted death. *Omega, Journal of Death and Dying, 32,* 179–196.

Miles, S. H., Koepp, R., & Weber, E. P. (1996). Advance end-of-life treatment planning: A research review. *Archives of Internal Medicine, 156,* 1062–1067.

Nitschke, P. (in press). "Desiring death, dispensing death" by Annette Street and David Kissane: A commentary. *Omega, Journal of Death and Dying.*

Pernick, M. S. (1996). *The black stork.* New York: Oxford University Press.

Pugh, D., & West, D. J., Jr. (1994–1995). Advance directives: A patient's perspective. *Omega, Journal of Death and Dying, 30,* 249–256.

Quill, T. E. (1993). *Death and dignity.* New York: The Free Press.

Robbins, B. (1983). *Last wish.* New York: Linden Press/Simon and Schuster.

Street, A., & Kissane, D. (in press). Desiring death, dispensing death. *Omega, Journal of Death and Dying.*

Times Mirror Center for the People and the Press (1983). *Reflections of the times: The right to die.* Washington, DC: Times Mirror Center for the People and the Press.

United States Supreme Court (1989). Missouri vs. Cruzan. In R. M. Baird & S. E. Rosenbaum (Eds.), *Euthanasia. The moral issues.* (pp.179–212). Buffalo, NY: Prometheus.

Weingarten, P. B. (1993). Concern for dying. In R. Kastenbaum & B. Kastenbaum (Eds.), *Encyclopedia of death.* (pp. 56–57). Phoenix: Oryx.

GLOSSARY

Advance Directive: A document that specifies the type of health care an individual wishes to receive should that individual not be in a position to express his or her wishes in a critical situation.

Assisted Death: An action taken by one person to end the life of another, at the other person's request.

Competence: The mental ability to make a rational decision about important matters in one's life (a legal concept).

Durable Power of Attorney for Health Care: The transfer of legal authority to someone who will make health care decisions for a person who at that time is unable to make or communicate his or her own decisions.

EEG Tracings: Electrical activity of the brain as displayed on a moving scroll or computer monitor.

Euthanasia: Originally, a pleasant death, one without suffering. Later applied also to actions taken to end a life. "Active" euthanasia involves an action that ends the life; "passive" euthanasia refers to the withdrawal or withholding of actions that might prolong life.

Hippocratic Oath: A code presenting ethical principles for the practice of medicine, attributed to a Greek physician of the fifth century B.C.

Informed Consent: The principle that patients should be provided with sufficient information to make decisions for or against accepting a treatment.

Living Will: The first type of advance directive to be introduced, requesting that no aggressive treatments be attempted if the individual is in the end phase of life.

Mercy Killing: An earlier common term for what is now referred to as "assisted death."

Orbitoria: Clinics or centers at which assisted death would be provided at patients' request and in which biomedical studies would be conducted.

Patients' Self-Determination Act: A federal law requiring that health care organizations provide patients with the informed opportunity to establish an advance directive to limit medical treatment in specified situations.

Slippery Slope Argument: Holds that accepting assisted death for any person will lead to a moral "slide" that will increase the demand and approval of death for many other people.

Ventilator: A machine that provides respiration for people who are unable to breathe adequately on their own.

Many children occasionally seek comfort from a parent at bed time. This need is stronger in children who have lost a parent or other loved one and fear further abandonment.

chapter 10

DEATH IN THE WORLD OF CHILDHOOD

Until children reach the age of five or six, they can't begin to understand what death really means.
—Philadelphia Child Guidance Center, 1993, p. 73.

How was the frog? The frog was dead, dead, dead. What else could it be? We buried it a whole summer ago!
—A 3-year-old girl's report after she and her older brothers checked out the place where they had held the funeral and burial for a frog briefly known the previous summer.

I love the juice, but the sun goes up; I see the stars
and the moonstar goes up,
And there always goes today. And the sun
Love people. But one always dies.
Dogs will die very sooner
Than mummies and daddies and sisters and
brothers because
They'll not die till a hundred and
Because I love them dearly
—Hilary-Anne Farley, age 5, in Lewis, 1966, p. 143.

He's been sick a lot this year.... But I kind of get used to him being sick.... I really want to know what it's like to stay home and watch and take care of my brother for a whole day when he's sick. And I know what to do. Every night you [a person with cystic fibrosis] have to get on this machine. And it's because you get all this mucus in your lungs and it's hard to breathe. And when you get sick, you really get sick.... And sometimes you die at an early age. But I don't think that will happen to Jason, because he's in pretty good shape. That's about it.
—Regan, 11-year-old sister of 9-year-old Jason, Bluebond-Langner, 1996, pp. 78–79.

Is there a contradiction here? Are children protected from anxiety and sorrow because they do not grasp the concept of death? Or is this vision of childhood innocence actually a product of adult fantasy and wish fulfillment?

In this chapter, we will see that children are much more observant of death-related phenomena than many adults—including child development experts—have supposed. We will also see that adults are well advised to be alert to differences in the way that children interpret dying and death. The ability to enter a child's world of life and death can be immensely valuable in responding to the needs of children as illness, death, and grief enter their lives in one form or another.

The Philadelphia Child Guidance Center specialists have many useful suggestions to make about fostering the emotional health of children. However, they have little to say about young children's encounters with death. It is not much of a concern:

> Lacking the ability to appreciate the permanence and gravity of death, very young children are not likely to respond to a specific death with strong emotions.... A child this young does not appear to experience the type of immediate, prolonged, and demonstrative grieving period for a dead loved one that an older child or adult typically does, nor should she or he be influenced to do so. (1993, p. 74)

This dismissal of young children's sensitivity to death and loss is just plain wrong.

The 3-year-old girl and her brothers were curious about the difference between being alive and dead. Almost all children share this curiosity, and many conduct their own little experiments, often without their parents' knowledge. Burying the frog in the first place (please note that it was dead at the time!) was a way of acquiring a sense of partial control over the mysterious phenomena of coming into being and disappearing into nonbeing. The funeral service was not simply an imitation of adult rituals, but also a way of feeling themselves into the birth-death-rebirth cycle. None had expected, but all had hoped that perhaps the frog would be alive and kicking again. Already sensitive to the fragility of life, these three healthy children were vicariously burying and attempting to restore a little of themselves through the fate of the bog dweller.

Hilary-Anne Farley, a Canadian girl only 5 years of age, created a poem that confronted the universal tension between love and death, the very themes that have stimulated so much adult poetry and philosophy through the centuries. She is bursting with love but is acutely aware that time and loss are inevitable: "And there always goes today;" "But one always dies." Does this sound like a child who has no clue about the reality and universality of death? She even recognizes differential longevity and the ambiguity of time. Here is time as the enemy that takes people away, but here also is time as insulation between now and death ("They'll not die til a hundred"). Young Ms. Farley calls upon the force of her love and her need to protect her family from death. They will live until a hundred "Because I love them dearly." Wish fulfillment? Of course. But the poem as a whole resolutely faces the reality of death and loss.

Regan and her family lived every day with Jason's illness and with the prospect of his early death. She adjusted to this situation as did everybody else in the family: life has to go on, and people have to do what they have to do. She was well informed about her brother's condition and had personal knowledge of somebody who had died young of the same medical condition, cystic fibrosis. Her brother had not died—yet. He was not dying—yet. Nevertheless, Regan's own childhood experiences were shadowed by the possibility of her brother's death and by the family's daily efforts to carry on "normally" despite their burden of anxiety.

It is understandable that parents and other adults want to protect their children from the anxiety and sorrow associated with the death of a loved person, and from intimations of their own mortality. This impulse to shield children from threatening realities is almost certainly bound to fail, however. No child is spared the possibility of losing loved ones. No child is exempt from life-threatening risks. No child grows up without noticing that sometimes what is here today is gone tomorrow. Whether we are ready to accept it or not, death is part of a child's world.

Our exploration begins with the adult's conception of children's conception of death. Next we explore children's understanding of death as observed in both research and natural settings. This is followed by learning how children cope with the death of others and how we can be

Children often learn of death through the loss of a pet. Here a father helps his daughter with the funeral for her goldfish.

helpful to them in their grief experiences. Some children also must cope with the possibility of their own death. We will learn much from listening to what these children themselves have said. We then examine our society's tradition of excluding children from participating in life-and-death decisions that are of personal concern to them. The chapter concludes with guidelines for sharing children's death concerns.

ADULT ASSUMPTIONS ABOUT CHILDREN AND DEATH

How was the subject of death treated in your home when you were a child?

This is the first of several questions raised in Box 10:1: Exploring Your Experiences with Death in Childhood. Please turn to these ques-

tions now. They will help you to bring your childhood experiences forward into the present moment. The activity of writing down your memories will also help you to compare your experiences with those of other people and to think about how these experiences may have influenced your life.

Following are some of the most frequent responses to the first question:

- They sat in dark rooms and became quiet.
- Very hushed and away from us as children. There were two deaths and three near deaths, from when I was 7 to when I was 10. I felt like I was left out of all of them. No one ever explained anything to me.
- I don't remember any conversations about death with my parents. My Mom went back

---

BOX 10-1
EXPLORING YOUR EXPERIENCES WITH DEATH IN CHILDHOOD

Write your answers on a separate sheet of paper.

1. How was the subject of death treated in your home when you were a child? What questions did you ask of your parents? What answers did you receive?

2. What most interested or puzzled you about death when you were a young child?

3. Do you remember the death of a pet or other animal at some time in your childhood? What were the circumstances? How did you feel about it? How did other people respond to your feelings?

4. Do you remember the death of a person at some time in your childhood? What were

the circumstances? How did you feel about it? How did other people respond to your feelings?

5. Can you identify any ways in which childhood experiences with death may have influenced you to this day?

6. What do you now think is the best thing a parent could say to or do with a child in a death situation? Why?

7. What do you now think is the worst thing a person could say to or do with a child in a death situation? Why?

East for my uncle's funeral and my grandparents funerals, but I did not go.

• Death was not something that was discussed with children. When my grandfather died, though, it was chaotic. The adults talked to each other about how the death took place. Everyone offered opinions of how the wake and funeral should be carried out. There were arguments and disagreements. All of us kids were completely left out.

• Since I come from a Christian home, death was addressed often as a concept and limited to an afterlife. When someone actually did die it was put in perspective with God at the center. For example, "He or she is in a better place…" At times I found this very comforting; at other moments I felt put off by their rehearsed responses.

• After the cat died, we were told about death in that the life is gone. No more movement, no more breath, etc. It seemed to make sense.

Some people remember being given straightforward, naturalistic information, such as that given after the death of the cat. Most often, however, families seemed to be following a rule of silence so far as communicating about death with children is concerned. Book (1996) has taken this "rule of silence" seriously in her exploratory study of family

narratives. Previous analyses by Shimanoff (1980) have shown that families develop both explicit and implicit rules to govern their conversations. Applying this approach to death-related communications, Book found that a primary family rule often was: "Do the right thing." This was a "coded" rule in that it really meant: "Don't say what you think about death; don't say what you feel about death." Studies of family communication tend to support the impression that children are seldom given the opportunity to participate in open discussion on death-related topics.

Studies also confirm the general impression that many adults do not understand how children of a particular age or developmental stage think about death. Usually this misunderstanding takes the form of underestimating both the child's concern and the child's ability to observe and ponder the phenomena of death. Blano (1988), for example, found that not only do adults misread their children's understanding of death, but, as a consequence, also tend to respond inappropriately when interacting with children in death-related situations.

Why do adults often have such difficulty in communicating with children about death? Perhaps it has something to do with the adults' own fears, doubts, and conflicts. Even in this era of hospice care, grief support groups, and university seminars, many people continue to avoid thinking and speaking of death whenever they can. And perhaps Sigmund Freud (1914)was on the mark when he suggested that, having lost their own childhood innocence, adults want very much to believe that their children live in a fairy tale world, safe from the stings of reality.

It is time now to learn how children think and feel about death. This information can help us to develop more effective ways of responding to their needs and our own.

CHILDREN DO THINK ABOUT DEATH

The most basic fact has been well established: children, even young children, do think about death. Evidence comes from many sources.

Early Experiences with Death in Childhood

One of America's first distinguished psychologists, G. Stanley Hall (1922), was also among the first to study aging and death. Hall and his student, Colin Scott, asked adults to recall their earliest experiences with death. These childhood experiences evidently had made a lasting impression because they were recalled in vivid detail:

> The child's exquisite temperature sense feels a chill where it formerly felt heat. Then comes the immobility of face and body where it used to find prompt movements of response. There is no answering kiss, pat, or smile.... Often the half-opened eyes are noticed with awe. The silence and tearfulness of friends are also impressive to the child, who often weeps reflexly or sympathetically. (1922, p. 440)

Hall adds that funeral and burial scenes sometimes were the very earliest of all memories for the adults he studied. More recent studies also find death experiences to be common among adults' earliest memories, as I have also found in some of my own research For example, an Italian-American butcher shared his earliest memory with me:

> I was still in the old country. We all lived in a big old house, me, my family and all kinds of relatives. I remember it was just a few days after my

fourth birthday, and there was grandmother laid out on a table in the front room. The room was full of women crying their eyes out. Hey, I didn't want any part of it, but somebody said grandmother was just sleeping. I doubted that very much. Grandmother never slept on a table in the front room with everybody crying their eyes out before. But what I really remember most is what I want to forget most. *"Kiss* your grandmother!" Yeah, that's right. They made me walk right up and kiss grandmother. I can still see her face. And I can still feel her face. Is that crazy? I mean, after all these years, I can still feel her cold dead face and my lips against it.

Although this man was the owner of a specialty meat shop and its chief butcher, he reported feeling panic on those few occasions when he has been in the presence of a human corpse. The early childhood experience with death had somehow become part of his adult personality.

A study of college students asked explicitly for the respondents' "earliest death-related memory" (Dickinson, 1986). Most of the memories centered around the death of a person, whether relative (70 percent) or nonrelative (15 percent). By far the greatest number of death memories involved the loss of a grandparent (48 percent); parental death was reported by 6 percent of the respondents. Dogs were the pets whose deaths were most often recalled (7 percent), but the following reflections on another type of pet also illustrate that childhood experiences may have long-term consequences:

> As a young child, I would receive ducks and chickens as an Easter present. One of these chicks was able to survive the playing and was able to grow into a nice white hen. She was my pride and joy, following me and coming when I called. The hen stayed at my Grandmother's. One Sunday dinner the main course was "fried chicken." It took me several minutes to realize just what had happened. To say the least, I was devastated and do not eat chicken to this day." (1986, p. 83)

In a follow-up study, the same investigator (Dickinson, 1992) found that college students still had intense memories of their early childhood experiences with death. It was startling to learn how anger—"outright hatred at times"—continued to be felt toward "a parent who had killed the [pet] animal, whether it was a parent who had accidentally run over the animal or the vet who 'put the animal to sleep'" (p. 172). The explanations given to them by their parents in childhood were often felt to be unsatisfactory. Most often the children had been told that a deceased person had gone to heaven. Some had been reassured because heaven was said to be a happy place. One 4-year-old girl, however, became upset when her father told her that her kitten "went to heaven to be with God." She responded: "Why does God want a dead kitten?" A 3-year-old also became angry when told that her grandmother had gone to heaven: "I don't want her in heaven. I want her *here!*" Not only are young children affected by death-related events, but they may recall these experiences with intense emotions many years later.

The childhood loss and death theme was evident again in research interviews that several students and I conducted with residents of Sun City and Sun City West (Arizona). These people were asked not for their earliest experiences with death, but for their earliest memories of any kind. The respondents went back at least sixty years and sometimes more than eighty for their memories. Many incidents were pleasant to recall; others were odd and hard to explain. However, more than one person in three reported an earliest memory that conveyed some encounter with death, loss, or separation:

- "The green chair nobody sat in any more. I remember going into the room and out of the room and back into the room time after time. Maybe Grandfather would be sitting in his chair the next time I entered the room. I know I was four because I just had a birthday with four candles—on the cake."
- "There were lots of people in the street, and there had been some kind of accident. I wanted to see what. A horse was on the ground and there was a twisted up, tipped over cart behind it. Somebody, a man, was saying they ought to shoot it. I got one look and then somebody pushed me away or led me away. I don't know what I thought about it at the time, but I can still see that horse."

Studies such as these indicate that the young child's experiences of death and loss may become life-long memories

for the adult. Perhaps you also found some death or separation memories coming to mind when you answered the questions about your own childhood experiences. Some readers of this book have taken their early memories as the starting point for their personal research. One young woman, for example, recalled having felt very much alone and frightened, "and there was something about the ocean and the beach in it." No other details came to mind from this memory, which seemed to have taken place just before her kindergarten days. She decided to ask her parents what had actually happened. They were reluctant, but:

> …then we had one of our best talks ever! Mom had had a miscarriage and the doctor had said she couldn't have any more babies or she might die herself. It never occurred to them to say any of this to a little kid like me. But while we were talking I suddenly remembered them getting rid of baby things, a crib and all, giving them away, and my mother looking real strange and distant. And that was when they sent me to live with a family I didn't like much so they could also get away a few days, together, and try to feel normal again. I can understand that perfectly now. But then, it was like they were going to get rid of me, too! And in my little kid's mind, the beach and the ocean were part of it all. Maybe they were going to leave me all by myself on the beach, or maybe a big wave was going to come and get me!"

This student had developed a pattern of avoiding beaches and large bodies of water, although she was also attracted to these places. The frank conversation with her family not only helped her understand the unpleasant and unaccountable early memory, but also dissipated her anxieties about going to the beach. Many other students have found it possible to gain a better understanding of some of their ways of thinking simply by bringing early memories to mind. A graduate student of social work reported that "I think I know now why I'm so crazy about stuffed animals! I had my favorite kitten squashed by a truck, and then the mother cat, too, by some kind of vehicle. And then, all in the same short period of time, a coyote killed our old family dog. Stuffed animals have a much better life expectancy!"

Your childhood memories of death-related experiences may be quite different from these. It would be going much too far to say that a particular childhood experience "causes" us to behave or feel in a particular way in adult life. Nevertheless, it is clear that childhood experiences tinged with death, loss, or separation can become significant influences on the way we see life and cope with death. Most of us carry in our memories our own personal historical evidence for childhood encounters with death.

Death in the Songs and Games of Childhood

Cultural history provides examples on a broader scale. The "innocent" songs and games of childhood through the centuries have often centered on death themes. The familiar "Ring-around-the Rosie" song and game achieved popularity during the peak years of the plague in fourteenth-century Europe. The "rosies" referred to one of the symptoms of the disease; the "all fall down" is self-explanatory. The children who enacted this little drama were acutely aware that people all around them were falling victim to the plague. We can imagine the security they sought by joining hands. The ritual impersonated the trauma and separation of death. Helpless passivity and fear were transformed into a group effort to actively master the threat. Today this game may seem quaint and innocuous, but in its heyday, "Ring-around-the-Rosie" represented both an acknowledgment of the prevalence of uncontrolled death in the environment and the impulse to share and master death-related anxiety.

The death theme is explicit in many hide-and-seek and tag games. Even the adult most unwilling to admit children's awareness of death would have a difficult time dismissing the tag game known as "Dead Man Arise!" This type of game has many names and local variations. In Sicily, for example, children play *"A Morsi Sanzuni."*

> One child lay down pretending to be dead while his companions sang a dirge, occasionally going up to the body and lifting an arm or a leg to make sure the player was dead, and nearly stifling the child with parting kisses. Suddenly he would jump up, chase his mourners, and try to mount the back of one of them.... In Czechoslovakia... the recumbent player was covered with leaves, or had her frock held over her face. The players then

made a circle and counted the chimes of the clock, but each time "Death" replied, "I must still sleep." This continued until the clock struck twelve when, as in some other European games, the sleeping player sprang to life, and tried to catch someone. (Opie & Opie, 1969, p. 107)

In tag games the person who is "It" must not peek or move while the other players conceal themselves. The touch of "It" is both scary and thrilling—almost a training ground for future Count Draculas. Even the slightest touch has grave significance: The victim is instantly transformed from lively participant to death personified ("It"). Further resemblances to death are suggested in variations in which the victim must freeze (enter suspended animation?) until rescued by one who is still free (alive?).

Historical observations strongly suggest that concern with death has been a common theme in children's play through the centuries, and I have not even spoken of all the zestful destruction games that have replaced each other over the years—zapping today's space invaders are the children of cops-and-robbers and the grandchildren of cowboys-and-Indians, whose more remote ancestors as children fought to the mock death as Saracens and Crusaders.

Our technologically advanced society has provided children and adolescents with ready-made games whose object is to inflict death in violent and humiliating ways. A coalition of parents persuaded major retail stores to remove the most extreme of these games from their shelves. Nevertheless, it remains a paradox that death games should be such a popular item in a society that finds it so difficult to think of and communicate about death with its children.

Research and Clinical Evidence

That death is a familiar theme to children has been verified by studies conducted in various parts of the world, using a number of different research strategies. It is the rule rather than the exception for children to include death among their interests and concerns. Following are a few examples from my collection of verified observations:

- A boy, aged 16 months, was taken to a public garden by his father, an eminent biomedical

Children who have been touched by death, especially sudden and violent, may find expression for their feelings in games of destruction.

scientist. This was a regular visit, one of their favorite expeditions together. The boy's attention was captured by a fuzzy caterpillar creeping along the sidewalk. Suddenly, large adult feet came into view, and the caterpillar was crushed (unwittingly) by another visitor to the garden. Immediately the boy showed an alarmed expression. He then bent over the remains, studying them intently. After a long moment, he stood up and informed his father, in a sad and resigned voice, "No more!" *"No more!"* Can there be a more direct and concise comment? From that moment the boy expressed an aversion to being in the public garden, looking with distress at fallen blossoms that he had not previously seemed to notice. It took several comforting attempts from his father before he would again visit this place of beauty and death.

- An 18 month old discovered a dead bird on the ground as he and his father walked through the woods. The boy crouched over by the bird, his face taking on an expression of the classic Greek mask of tragedy. "Bird!" he said. "Yes," his father replied, "A bird; a dead bird." For the next several days, the boy made sure to visit the dead bird, looking at it very carefully but not saying anything. One day there was a

crisp autumn breeze, and leaves floated down from the trees. The boy picked up a leaf and handed it his father—insisting with great determination that his father place the leaf back on the tree. The father said this could not be done, but, with the boy's insistence, he tried. The leaf would not stay put. The father tried again and again. The boy then looked sad and turned away. He never asked again to have a leaf restored to its tree, nor did he look again at the dead bird.

There was no doubt in the minds of these very young children that death was something special that required special thoughts and actions. Older children continue to come to grips with the sorrow of loss:

- An 8-year-old boy was improvising—loudly—at the piano. His father approached him with the intention of asking him to cease and desist, but noticed that the pianist was in a mood of deep contemplation, not just idly banging away. "What are you playing?" the father asked. The boy replied, "A funeral song for Lovey" (the family cat, recently killed on the highway). As the boy continued his improvisations, he explained the meaning of each passage. "This is Lovey sharpening her claws on a tree.... This is

Lovey when she has just heard the can opener.... This is Lovey curled up and purring."

Again, there can be no doubt that this child understood something of death's significance and, furthermore, felt the need and obligation to perform some ritual in honor of the deceased. From direct observation, clinical experience, and systematic research, there is ample evidence that children do think of death. It is useful to keep this basic fact in mind, because the situation becomes more complicated as the specific nature of their death-related thoughts is considered in some detail. Attempts have been made to present our knowledge of children's thoughts and feelings about death within some familiar model of human development. DeSpelder and Strickland (1996) utilize perhaps the two most popular accounts of early development, those of Erik Erikson (1950) and Jean Piaget (1973), along with the heuristic concepts of Freud. Unfortunately, the facts and the models do not really fit together very well. Piaget made a powerful contribution to the understanding of child development with his cognitive-adaptational approach. This approach, however, systematically avoids phenomena associated with change, loss, inconstancy, and impermanence—a magnificent structural denial of death. Freud changed his mind about the meaning of death in human development as he grew older (Kastenbaum, 2000), but both the earlier and the later view go in different directions than those taken by most empirical research. Erikson's theory illuminates many facets of human development but does not warm to death until it encompasses the later adult years. This situation means that we cannot relax into a simple and fixed model of the role of death thoughts and feelings in children's psychosocial development. We must labor with the facts as they present themselves and see whether perhaps a useful theoretical model might yet emerge.

Research Case Histories

Research findings usually are conveyed through statistics, and appropriately so. This custom, however, often fails to convey the reality of individual differences as well as the patterning of thoughts and actions within the individual. Three brief case histories drawn from my research will enable you to glimpse individual and family patterns. A general review of research findings follows. For the present purposes, this section concentrates upon data obtained in structured interviews with the mothers of schoolchildren.

Teresa

Teresa was a 7 year old described by her mother as a quiet girl who enjoys her own company: "She's just a very nice girl, not afraid to express any emotions at all." Teresa was especially interested in plants and how they grow, and was much involved in her family as a unit. The following is an interview with Teresa's mother.

INTERVIEWER: Has death come into Teresa's life?

MOTHER: My mother died, her grandmother, in January of this year... we all knew she was dying. I told Teresa and I told June [her sister] that she was dying. They wanted to know, "What is dying, where is she going to go, why is she going, why is she leaving me? She's my Grandma! I don't want her to die!"...And she was just very curious about the whole business of the wake and the funeral and "Why do we have to do this, why do we have to do that." The big thing was, "I don't want to see other people sad, because it makes me sad."

INTERVIEWER: How did Teresa respond to the death when it actually came?

MOTHER: She comforted me. She came to me. She would cry when I cried. She would put her arms around me and she would say, "Please don't cry; everything will be all right. Grandma isn't suffering anymore. Grandma is happy now."

The death was experienced as a major loss by everybody in the family. Grandma was 54 at the time of her death and had been very close to the whole family although not living with them. "My mother was my best friend and she was also my children's best friend," Teresa's mother said.

INTERVIEWER: What did Teresa understand about Grandma's death?

MOTHER: She understands that she [Grandma] was put in the ground in that cold outer casket, but Teresa realizes that she is not there. She's in spirit, beside her, watching and loving her always. And Teresa sees a bird—my mother was a bird freak—and she said, "I wonder if Grandma can see that bird?" You know, she's very much into, very aware that Grandma is around her, spiritually, not physically.

INTERVIEWER: What did Teresa not understand about this death?

MOTHER: She still doesn't understand…why. You know, why take her from us now, she wasn't old; she was a young woman. Why was she so sick, you know. What did she do? Did she do something bad?

INTERVIEWER: Does Teresa have any death concerns or fears?

MOTHER: I think she'd be very much afraid of losing me at this point because since my mother has died she's becoming extremely touchy with me; she gets a little bit upset when I have to go out, you know. "Please come back soon!" I think she relates it to losing me, to maybe her fears of losing her own mother.

INTERVIEWER: How have you answered her questions about death?

MOTHER: Well, as far as the religious, we don't get into it at my house, you know. I don't want to get into hell and heaven and that, because I don't want them to get hung up on it.… I really don't think we discussed it, you know, before it actually hit us; we never really discussed it with the children.…

INTERVIEWER: Has it been difficult to discuss death with Teresa?

MOTHER: Not with Teresa, not at all. With June, yes, but not with Teresa.

INTERVIEWER: How do you feel in general about the way Teresa thinks about death?

MOTHER: I think she's got her head pretty well together. She's really probably done better than I have.… Two or three months after my mother died, I was sitting by myself, having my crying jag and getting it all out, and Teresa got up out of bed. You know, I was sitting in the dark. I just knew it was coming. I had put them to bed. So she got up, and she came beside me and she said, "Mama, I know why you're crying." And I said, "Why, Teresa?" And she said, "Because you miss your mother." And I said, "You're right." And Teresa said, "But you always have to remember, how good she was to us, remember she used to take us uptown and buy us ice cream and she used to sing us songs and remember when she bought me this bracelet." And within a matter of, say, three minutes, I felt so relieved, like, you know, tons had been lifted off me; from this 7-year-old child, you know, really laying it on me and telling me, come on, you know, you got to go on living. And the oldest one [June] will not discuss it at all. You know, it's too bad.

INTERVIEWER: Do you have any questions of your own about what to do with a child in things related to death?

MOTHER: There are things I don't know, and so I wouldn't know how to explain it to them. I don't know how to make it easier for them.… This is a society where everybody dies—why do you grieve then? Why is there a wake, why is there a funeral? There are things I don't understand so I'm sure they don't understand, you know, why the pain?

INTERVIEWER: Should parents and children discuss death together?

MOTHER: *It's very important, so very important! I can remember my own first experience with death and how frightened I was of it.* I think it's something that should be talked about in a family and…I'm having a hard time expressing myself, but I really think that when people die, that we love, we shouldn't have to grieve…why do they put us through the wakes, the funeral? This is what we saw when we were children; we saw grieving after death—and my children will grieve over death.

INTERVIEWER: What is the worst thing a parent could say or do with a child in a death situation?

MOTHER: I would hate to stifle emotions. I would hate to say, "Stop all that crying!" Or, the other thing is, "He's gone away for a vacation. He's left us, but he'll come back." That's a bunch of lies and children see through these things.

INTERVIEWER: What is the best thing a parent could say or do with a child in a death situation?

MOTHER: Let the children see what goes on. Let them be totally involved with the family, to be able to express with the family their own emotions and to be totally included in what goes on instead of shifted off to a friend's house.

INTERVIEWER: How curious about death were you when you were Teresa's age?

MOTHER: I wasn't at all…until I was about 10 years old…I lost my cat and I remember, I cried all day upstairs in my room because I thought: This is death. I'm going to lose my mother. And I cried and cried and I was so scared and I had nightmares.

INTERVIEWER: How was death handled in your home when you were growing up?

MOTHER: It wasn't. I said to my mother once, "I'm so afraid that you are going to die." And she just said, "I'm not going to die"…. And…she died. (These words were spoken very softly and sadly.)

INTERVIEWER: Was that the way she should have handled it, or what do you think she should have done instead?

MOTHER: I think that she should have drawn more out of me and really given me time that I needed, and maybe have said—well, I don't know what you can say to a child to make it any easier when there is a threat, a scare of losing a parent, but just be able to sit down and discuss it.…

INTERVIEWER: What are your thoughts and feelings about death now?

MOTHER: Since my first death was my mother, I think it was very hard.… I just accept the fact that she is dead and I will no longer see her, but I just hang on to the thought that she's not suffering and that she knew she was dying even though nobody told her.… She said more with her eyes, more than anything else in the world. I feel very…I feel peace within myself.

INTERVIEWER: Did she tell you her thoughts or feelings at all?

MOTHER: No, she was aphasic…and paralyzed. She couldn't talk. The only thing she could do was move one arm and one hand and the night before she died, we went in there and they took her out of the special care unit and just took off the respirator and let her die and she just kept pointing up to heaven. She knew she was dying and she just…made us feel at ease. Because I was glad she knew, and she knew that I knew so we wouldn't have to play the game: "Okay, Ma, we'll get you out of here in a couple of weeks." It was kind of peace, you know, that we shared.

INTERVIEWER: Is there anything you would like to add?

MOTHER: I think we should teach children about death in schools. I don't mean we shouldn't teach them at home, but in school, too. Let people know what often happens in grief, so they won't be so surprised.… Should start early because it's like sex education, you know, you almost don't talk about it until it happens, until there is a problem.

Stanley

Stanley is another 7 year old who is described by his mother as "just the nicest boy a mother could ever want. Does what you tell him to—

most of the time.... His life is pretty much centered around the family and his dog."

INTERVIEWER: What does Stanley understand about death?

MOTHER: That whoever would die they're not going to see again and that's about all. As far as feeling for the person, he hasn't come to that stage yet.... We have a dog and if he died I wouldn't know what he would feel. I really don't. I would say he would be too little to think much about it.

INTERVIEWER: What does Stanley not understand about death?

MOTHER: What the purpose of death is. Why we were put on the earth for a reason and why we're going to die. Stanley is definitely too little to understand why somebody's laying in a casket. Especially if it is somebody young. Why is that person dead? You try to explain to him that God put him on this earth but He called him back. He wanted him back. I don't think he can comprehend that at all.... When a little boy dies, I tell him the little boy was very sick and God wanted him back.

INTERVIEWER: How have you answered Stanley's questions about death?

MOTHER: Sometimes I tell him that the person was very old and very sick. If it was a little boy, that the little boy was very sick and God wanted him back.... God put us here but He isn't going to let us stay here. We're all here temporarily and even though you boys are little doesn't mean you couldn't die tomorrow. Even Stanley, I told him, you could die tomorrow. I could die tomorrow. We don't know when. God doesn't tell us. It doesn't mean that just sick people die. Anybody can die—people get hit by cars.

INTERVIEWER: What is the worst thing a parent could say or do with a child in a death situation?

MOTHER: To hide it from them. If you want to cry, cry. That's the best thing. Make him experience it with you. Why

not? They've got to be exposed to it the way it is.

INTERVIEWER: How was death handled in your home when you were growing up?

MOTHER: *My parents shielded us from all of that.... We never got the answers we really wanted, so as a result we stopped asking.* That was about anything, even about death.... But death can bring people together, it's just that in our family it didn't. Would have been nice if our parents had let us join in, instead of getting our relatives to babysit us while they went and did it all...going to the funerals and all of that...I would have liked to have been at their side.

INTERVIEWER: What are your thoughts and feelings about death now?

MOTHER: I'm very conscious about death now. It panics me, truthfully, it really panics me. I know we can't live forever. If I knew I was dying, I just wouldn't want to wake up in the morning, that's all. That's how I would want it to be for me and yet it's probably the easy way out. I'm not too happy about other people dying either.... Dead people are supposed to be with God. We're supposed to be happy but we still can't. Part of us says we are—part of us says we're *not!*

Brian

Brian is 8 years old and "a bright boy with lots of curiosity. He's especially interested in rocks and minerals, gems, animals, underwater stories. He reads about them all the time, and talks about anything. But not death."

INTERVIEWER: What does Brian understand about death?

MOTHER: Oh, he understands it...I think. But he doesn't really like to talk about it. He doesn't like the idea that any of us will die. Like he said to me, "You'll never, never die, Mom." I tried to explain to him, well, that's not true, that I will die and so will Daddy, and when that time comes he must accept it because that's part of living. He understands what I'm saying. You can see that from the look in his eyes. But it makes him very, very sad, and he'll go, "I don't want to talk about that, I'd rather not—*please*, Mom!"

INTERVIEWER: What does Brian *not* understand about death?

MOTHER: Only one thing I can think of. His Daddy likes to hunt. He goes deer hunting and he killed, you know, a young deer. Brian couldn't quite understand that. He thought the deer was so beautiful and to kill him.... Well, we had to tell him *why* he killed the deer, and the deer hurt, and if he wasn't killed, if so many deer weren't killed a year, the balance of nature would be off.

INTERVIEWER: Does Brian have any death concerns or fears?

MOTHER: Losing one of us that he loves. He's very, *very* close to Cris [his sister] so, of course, he doesn't want her to leave the house. He's often said this. If she doesn't come home when she said she's supposed to come home he'll call me and say, "I'm awfully worried because she's out in the car, if she has an accident and gets killed, Mom, I don't know what I'll do." And I mean *upset*. I've seen him cry and tears going down his face and he'll say, "I would just die if my Crissy dies."

INTERVIEWER: What is the worst thing a parent could say or do with a child in a death situation?

MOTHER: Well, I'm going to say this from experience. *I think the worst thing to do is not let the child grieve.* To tell them they can't cry...bottling up these emotions does something to that person and carries on into their adult life. It does irreparable damage if you ask me, and I guess you did.

INTERVIEWER: How was death handled in your home when you were growing up?

MOTHER: Nobody prepared me for it, nobody answered my questions, nobody told me one thing or the other. "I don't want to talk about it," would be the answer, or, "I don't know why you ask me such foolish questions."

INTERVIEWER: What are your thoughts and feelings about death now?

MOTHER: Now, it's much different. I feel the more I think of it, the more at peace I feel with the fact that death is going to come. When I was younger I was hoping, oh, I'd never die, and now I know that I am, and the time comes I don't think I'll be afraid to die.... I have more acceptance of the fact of death now than I did when I was— even ten years ago or even five years ago.... I think it comes with time, you're more at peace with yourself. Even so, having children makes death more important in a way, too, your responsibility to them.

Reflections and Questions

Each person—child or adult—has a distinctive relationship with death that is based on both the individuality of his or her personality and the unique situations encountered in the course of development. Young as they are, Teresa, Stanley, and Brian already differ in their experiences and concerns. A thorough analysis of their orientations toward death would have to take into account both their individual personalities and what they have in common as children growing up at a particular time in history. Following are a few reflections and questions on these research case history excerpts:

1. Death has specific connotations to children. *It is not just death in general, but the death of particular people or animals that enlists their concern: Grandma for Teresa, Crissy and the deer for Brian.* The possibility (Crissy) as well as the actuality (Grandma) of death can stimulate thought and feeling. Stanley is confronted with specific death concerns by his mother ("you could die tomorrow. I could die tomorrow"). Many studies have focused on the ability of children to formulate abstract conceptions of death. Although this is a significant question, it should not lead us to forget that thoughts of death

most often arise around *specific* incidents and contexts. Children do not have to comprehend death in its most abstract aspects to recognize that it threatens their relationships with the people who are important to them.

2. Could we understand the differing death orientations of Teresa, Stanley, and Brian if we focused only on the children themselves? It is doubtful. *Experiences, attitudes, and ways of coping with death are part of the intimate flow of life between children and their parents.* The influence can go in both directions. Brian's questions about the slain deer, for example, and his apparently exaggerated fear for Crissy's well-being present challenges for the parents' own attitudes toward death.

3. *There may be several different orientations toward death within the same household.* Teresa and June, for example, differ in their openness to the discussion of death. A specific death may have varying effects on the children, depending upon their developmental phase, personality, and position in the family. It is important to become well acquainted with the entire family constellation if we want to understand the implications of one particular child's view of death. From other data it was clear that Brian, as the only boy in the family, wanted very much to be like his father—but does this mean he, too, will have to go deer hunting? If he were not first in the "line of succession," perhaps the slain deer would have taken on a different meaning.

4. Teresa's mother is a sensitive person who favors an open communication process and who reflects thoughtfully on her own behavior as well as her children's. This does not mean, however, that she has been able to cope with death-related problems to her own complete satisfaction. She has unresolved questions in some areas (the value of funerals and the grief process in particular). Although her own unresolved concerns lead to some difficulty in helping her children, Teresa's mother shows flexibility and the ability to learn from experience. By contrast, Stanley's mother does not seem to have sorted out her own assumptions about life and death. When Stanley notices a death-related incident, his mother is not likely to use this as an occasion to reflect on her own thoughts and values or really share the experi-

ence with her son. Instead she relies upon passing along a received dogma that has been familiar to her since her own childhood—but never much thought about. The abstraction level and tone of her explanation were of doubtful help to Stanley. *Parents who are not able to cope with a child's death-related curiosity on a simple, naturalistic level because of their own discomfort may be perpetuating the anxieties for still another generation.* Imagine Stanley's thoughts after his mother's explanation: "God does not want healthy people? Is it wrong to want people to live? Is God the enemy who takes my friends away? Do I have to get very sick and die to be loved by God?" I have, in fact, heard reflections of this type from children whose curiosity about death was answered by verbose patter that seemed to place the blame on God. On the topic of death, as on any other topic, it is useful to understand something of the child's frame of reference before unloading one of our "standard explanations."

5. Although Teresa's mother had a warm and loving home life in her own childhood, the topic of death had been glossed over by her parents. This has made it more difficult for her to cope both with the death of her mother—who had promised she was not going to die—and with the feelings of her own daughters. Brian's and Stanley's mothers likewise grew up in homes where death was not to be discussed with the children. This background of death avoidance in the childhood home is typical for the mothers in our study. Today's young mothers in general seem to be more aware of the value of discussing death with their children as part of their general preparation for life. However, most often they have not benefited from such good examples in their own homes while growing up. *We now have a transitional generation of parents who are trying to relate to their children in an area that was off-limits when they themselves were young.* This leads to second guessing of their own responses: "Did I say the right thing?" Eventually, however, the new openness should make death a less divisive topic between parents and children in generations to come.

It is not by accident that the research case histories sampled here are based on the mothers' reports. Children have fathers, too,

---

BOX 10-2
LESSONS FROM THE RESEARCH CASE HISTORIES

- It is the death of *particular* people or animals that enlists the child's concern.

- Death-related experiences, attitudes, and behaviors are part of the intimate flow of life between children and their parents.

- There may be several different orientations toward death within the same household.

- Parents whose own discomfort interferes with their response to their children's death-related

curiosity are likely to perpetuate these anxieties for another generation.

- There is now a transitional generation of parents who are trying to communicate in an open manner with their children, although their own experience was of family silence about death.

---

but they have been less willing to discuss this subject with me. Family death education seems to be viewed as something for mothers to handle. This situation appears to exist in many other nations as well. Okafor (1993) has recently observed that in Nigeria, family death education is also the province of the mother—whether or not she is fully prepared to carry out this role.

CONCEPTS OF DEATH: DEVELOPING THROUGH EXPERIENCE

It is clear that death has a place in the thoughts of children. But just what do children make of death? And how do their ideas develop from early childhood onward? Early studies emphasized the importance of maturation. Children seemed to understand death more adequately as their general mental abilities continued to develop. More recent studies indicate that life experiences also play a significant role. A 13 year old, for example, generally shows an understanding of death that is more accurate and complete than a 4 year old's. But is this because the older child has developed more advanced cognitive structures? Or is it simply because the older child has had another nine years of life experience from which to learn?

Recent studies indicate that the child's understanding of death is influenced by both maturation level and life experience, although much

remains to be learned about the interaction of maturational and experiential factors. This is similar to the general state of knowledge in developmental psychology. The specific interplay between maturation and experience is difficult to establish whether we are concerned with concepts of death or any other facet of the child's overall comprehension of reality.

"Auntie Death's" Pioneering Study

Our understanding of the way children think about death has been greatly influenced by one of the earliest studies, one that is worth reviewing in detail.

Hungarian psychologist Maria Nagy (1948/1969) invited 378 children, ranging in age from 3 to 10 years, to express their death-related thoughts and feelings. They represented a variety of social and religious backgrounds, and there was an equal number of boys and girls. The older children were asked to draw pictures and to "write down everything that comes to your mind about death." Children of all ages were engaged in conversation on the subject. As she reviewed the children's words and pictures, Nagy found that three age-related stages could be established (see Table 10-1).

- *Stage 1.* Stage 1 includes the youngest children, from the third until about the fifth year. These very young children expressed the notion that *death is a continuation of life but in a diminished form.* The dead are simply less alive. They cannot see and hear—well, maybe they can, but

TABLE 10-1

Stages of Death Comprehension
in Childhood (Nagy)

Stage	Age Range	Interpretation of Death
1	3–5	*Death is separation.* *The dead are less alive.* *Very curious about death.*
2	5–9	*Death is final—but one might* *escape it!* *Death is seen as a person.*
3	9–adult	*Death is personal, universal, final,* *and inevitable.*

not very well. They are not as hungry as the living. They do not do much. Being dead and being asleep are seen as similar conditions. The youngest children also thought of *death as temporary.* The dead might return, just as the sleeping might wake up. It was also clear that the theme of death as departure or separation was uppermost in the minds of many children.

Nagy noticed another characteristic of her youngest respondents' orientation. The preschoolers were very curious. They were full of questions about the details of the funeral, the coffin, the cemetery, and so on. Children's active engagement with the challenge of comprehending death was also noted repeatedly by Sylvia Anthony (1940/1972) in her study. This effort is related to another of Nagy's observations that has not received all of the attention it deserves. Even though these very young children did not seem to understand death adequately by adult standards, what they did think about it was powerful enough to arouse negative feelings (Brian's anxiety comes to mind, as do the childhood experiences of all three mothers in the case history excerpts). For Nagy's respondents, death at the very least did not seem to be much fun—lying around in a coffin all day, and all night, too. The dead might be sleeping, which is acceptable but boring, or they might be scared and lonely, away from all of their friends.

The combination of what the young child knows and does not know about death can arouse anxiety. "He would like to come out, but the coffin is nailed down," one 5 year old told "Auntie Death," the name bestowed on the psychologist by the chil-

dren. This comment suggests the fear of being buried alive that in some times and places has also been prevalent among adults. It also suggests that people are being cruel to the deceased by nailing down the coffin. The possibilities for further misinterpretations and ill feelings based on this limited conception of death are considerable, especially if the adults on the scene fail to understand how the child is likely to interpret death-related phenomena.

- *Stage 2.* The next stage begins at age 5 or 6 and persists until about the ninth year. The child now recognizes that *death is final.* The older the child within this age range, the more firm the conclusion. The dead do not return. Another new theme also emerged during this stage in Nagy's sample. Many of the children represented death as a person. Interestingly, *personification* is one of humankind's most ancient modes of expressing the relationship with death. One 9 year old confided:

> Death is very dangerous. You never know what minute he is going to carry you off with him. Death is invisible, something nobody has ever seen in all the world. But at night he comes to everybody and carries them off with him. Death is like a skeleton. All the parts are made of bone. But then when it begins to be light, when it's morning, there's not a trace of him. It's that dangerous, death. (Nagy, 1948/1969, p. 11)

The association of death with darkness is an ancient habit of mind, expressed by people in the earliest civilizations that have left us record. The other side of this idea is the equation of light with life. It is not unusual for a child's conception of death to include elements that once were the common property of adults.

The personification of death as a skeleton was fairly common in Nagy's sample of 5 to 9 year olds. For Nagy's respondents, death personifications often were fearful, representing enormous if mysterious power. Some stage 2 children added threats or lethal wishes to their personifications. As Nagy reports, "Kill the death-man so we will not die" was a frequent comment. Some children also depicted death as a circus clown—supposedly the embodiment of mirth and good times. Other children saw dead people as representing death, while still others personified death in the form of angels. Even angelic death, however, did not remove the sting of fear. "The death angels are great enemies of people," declared a 7-year old. "Death is the king of the angels. The angels work for death."

There is at least one more significant characteristic of stage 2, according to Nagy. *The realization of death's finality is accompanied by the belief that this fate might still be eluded.* The clever or fortunate person might not be caught by the "death-man." This idea also shows up in specific modes of death. A child might be killed crossing the street, for example. But if children are very careful in crossing the street, they will not be run over, and therefore they will not die.

In other words, children in this age range tend to see *death as an outside force or personified agent.* "It's that dangerous, death." However, the saving grace is that you do not absolutely have to die. Death is not recognized as universal and personal. Perhaps, just perhaps, you can be lucky or clever enough to elude it.

- *Stage 3.* The final stage identified by Nagy begins at about age 9 or 10 and is assumed to continue thereafter. By stage 3 the child understands that death is *personal, universal, and inevitable as well as final.* All that lives must die, including oneself.

Discussion of death at this age has an adult quality: "Death is the termination of life. Death is destiny. We finish our earthly life. Death is the end of life on earth," declared one 9-year old boy. A 10-year old girl added a moral and poetic dimension: "It means the passing of the body. Death is a great squaring of accounts in our lives. It is a thing from which our bodies cannot be resurrected. It is like the withering of flowers."

This new awareness is compatible with belief in some form of afterlife, as with the 9-year old boy who said, "Everyone has to die once, but the soul lives on." In fact, it might be argued that the child does not really have a grasp of afterlife concepts until death itself is appreciated as final and inevitable.

Evaluating Nagy's Contribution

Nagy's findings remain useful today, although the tendency to personify death between ages 5 and 9 seems to have diminished greatly, according to most follow-up studies. Perhaps this is a change wrought by the new childhood, with its exposure to mass media, high technology, and postmodern changes. "Death is like the computer's down and you can't get it started again," one 7-year-old told his mother recently. There also seems to be a tendency for children in America today to move through the stages at an earlier age than did the children studied by Nagy. This may be part of a larger trend in which some aspects of children's cognitive development have been accelerated through exposure to the diverse experiences they encounter in "the information age."

A recent study has turned up indications that young children today may be integrating technological developments into their dawning conceptions of dying and death. This characteristic is evident in a drawing by 5-year-old Michael (Figure 10-1). The researcher notes that:

> Michael…is concerned with burial, fantasy, and the world beyond. He integrates modern technology into his account of how God converts the dead into angels after hauling them up to heaven. His description of how people die is very concrete and practical, in keeping with what might be expected at this age. (Deveau, 1995, p. 86)

In the picture, according to Michael, "God uses a machine that turns them into an angel." People die "when they eat bad food, the bad food sticks to their heart and the blood can't get in the heart and then you have a heart attack…or something like that."

It is also probable, as Deveau has suggested, that the stages are not absolute and fixed, but, rather, represent temporary "resting places" in the child's continuing attempt to come to terms with death both cognitively and emotionally.

Maria Nagy's portrait of children's development of death concepts has served as a useful guide for half a century. Nevertheless, much can be added to Nagy's approach. We will now look at some of the major additions.

Are Concepts of Death Related to Cognitive Level, Gender, and Social Class?

Nagy organized her findings around the chronological age of her young respondents.

FIGURE 10-1
Michael's God Machine. Reprinted with permission from D. W. Adams & E. J. Deveau (eds.), Beyond the Innocence of Childhood. Vol. 1; "Perceptions of Death Through the Eyes of Children and Adolescents," Amityville, NY: Baywood, 1995.

This approach worked well, but later researchers have introduced a useful refinement. All children are not alike at a particular age. Some are further along in their physical, mental, social, and emotional development. A new critical review of the literature (Kenyon, in press) concludes that children with superior intellectual and verbal skills demonstrate more advanced concepts of death than do other children of the same age. Kenyon cautions, however, that children with limited verbal ability may also comprehend death concepts well but have difficulty in communicating their understanding. Kenyon discovered few effects of gender or socialeconomic status, with the exception that boys are more likely than girls to depict violent causes of death.

Does Anxiety Influence Children's Thoughts about Death?

Death is an emotionally laden subject for both children and adults, as we have glimpsed in the research case histories. Anxiety in general serves as an alarm signal for us—there's something potentially dangerous in this situation. A quick surge of anxiety can be helpful in directing our attention to the source of possible danger. Persistent or intense anxiety, however, tends to have dysfunctional effects on our perceptions and cognitions (Freeman & DiTomasso, 1994). If anxiety can influence adult thought processes, what effects might it have on children's incomplete and rapidly changing view of the world?

Considerations such as these have led a number of researchers to examine the influence of anxiety and related emotions on children's conceptions of death. *Separation anxiety* has been the central theme here. Bowlby (1980) has shown that separation from the parent is a source of disturbance for the young of many species, including but by no means limited to our own. Much of the communication between parent and young is intended to maintain or restore contact and security. Separation anxiety often rushes to the surface in adult humans. Even brief separations (e.g., a child going off to school) can lead to fears of abandonment and loss on the part of both individuals. Because children are naturally dependent on adults, it is a reasonable hypothesis that they are highly susceptible to separation anxiety. Within this context, all separations may be tinged with death anxiety, and death itself may be interpreted primarily as separation.

A series of studies by Israel Orbach and his colleagues lend much support to this theory. The most recent of these studies provides a useful example (Orbach et al, in press). Their respondents were boys and girls at three levels: first grade (ages 6–7), second grade (8–9), and fifth grade (10–11). All of the children were asked to indicate their understanding of the deaths of a brother, a cousin, and "Johnny," an unfamiliar child. The first graders perceived the death of a brother or a cousin less accurately than the death of "Johnny." One might suppose that "death is death" no matter the person or the situation. For these young children, though, the anxiety associated with the thought of a brother's or cousin's death was associated with a less mature conception than the death of a person they did not know. The effect of separation anxiety on death concepts appears to have diminished, but not entirely disappeared, by the time children have reached fifth grade. These boys and girls demonstrated accurate conceptions of death for both "cousin" and "Johnny." However, they still seemed to be so troubled by the thought of the death of "brother" that their thoughts were relatively less accurate and mature.

There are two major implications here. First, separation or death anxiety requires the use of defensive strategies. A readily available strategy is to modify the way one thinks about death. Therefore a young child's immature-seeming concept of death may represent defensive strategies for avoiding emotional pain. We might be underestimating this child's ability to understand the finality, universality and inevitability of death if we neglected the anxiety-defense dynamics. Second, the force of logic and intellect gradually liberate themselves from separation or death anxiety. This does not mean that the older child is free of separation or death anxiety. It does mean, however, that the child can now think at his or her most mature level when confronting the fear of losing a loved one. *Do we ever completely free our thought processes of death anxiety?* This is an unanswered question.

This inquiry into the emotional side of children's death conceptions may help to illuminate the challenges and conflicts that adults experience as well. For example, Lonetto (1980) asked children to draw pictures about death and then talk about them. Like Orbach, Lonetto found that the younger children expressed more separation anxiety. But he also observed that the older children were more disturbed by other aspects of death. "The happy smiles of the dead depicted by the younger children have all but faded away in the representations given by 10-year-olds, who show the dead with closed mouths and eyes" (p. 146). The older children were more likely to depict death as scary and horrible, and they also focus more on their own possible deaths as compared with others.

By age 11, there was more use of abstract symbols in the drawings, indicating a new way of coping with death. They could hint at death and represent its meanings (e.g., a valentine with tears pouring down its face) without having to draw all the unpleasant details. Interestingly, the use of black as the only color became dominant among the older children. This also showed up in their verbal comments. Jenny, age 11 years, 10 months, said:

> Death is blackness...like when you close your eyes. It's cold and when you die your body is cold. Frightening, I don't want to die...I wonder then, how I'm going to die...I feel scared and I try to forget it. When I feel like this, I try to forget it and just put something else into my mind. (1980, p. 154)

An 8-year-old boy in Lonetto's study offered this solemn meditation:

> When my pet died I felt sorry for him. Because he was only a kitten. When my mom buried him he might be turned into bones. When people die they just turn into bones too. When you die you cannot talk, see, write or anything like that. When you die they bury you in a little yard. I think everybody will die. (1980, p. 119)

We seem to pay a price for developing more mature and realistic conceptions of death. It is more difficult to fall back on the idea that dead people "are happy." Jenny has already put a new defensive strategy into operation, one that characterizes many adults as well: "I try to forget it and just put something else in my mind."

Developmental studies and observations made in natural settings all indicate that children are aware of death from an early age. A child does not begin with the realization that death is inevitable, universal, and final but does quickly grasp the implications of separation and loss. It is likely that the questions posed to a child's mind by death stimulate the desire to learn more about the ways of the world and contribute to overall mental development. Chronological age is a rough indicator of the cognitive level of a child's view of death; independent measures of the child's verbal conceptual development provide a more refined indicator.

Cultural Influences on Children's Concepts of Death

What children emphasize most in their thoughts about death may depend upon cultural influences. For example, children in Sweden and the United States had similar concepts of death at the same age. However, United States children more often depicted violent causes of death, while Swedish children more often depicted chapels in cemeteries, tombstones, crosses on church steeples, caskets, and other cultural symbols. Researchers Wenestam and Wass (1987), speculate that the much greater frequency of violence and death on U.S. television as compared with Swedish television may have a strong bearing on these differences in children's representations of death.

The role of religious beliefs and expectations is suggested by a study of Muslim girls, ages 6 through 10, in South Africa (Anthony & Bhana, 1988–1989). These children's conceptions of death were similar to those of children of the same age in Western nations. There were, however, interesting differences as well. For example, the realization that death is universal and inevitable seemed to be grasped at an earlier age by Muslim children. But this did not mean that they also accepted the irreversibility of death. "They believe that the dead come alive again under certain circumstances, such as when angels question them in the grave. It can, thus, be seen that the responses of the children are characteristic of their cultural and religious environments" (1988–1989, p. 225). The Muslim children were also more likely to believe in the importance of praying for the dead. No doubt there are many other variations in children's thinking about death as they respond to the ideas, actions, and symbols of their cultural backgrounds. Kenyon (in press) finds that the type and frequency of exposure to death seems to influence the speed with which children develop their concepts. This includes not only direct exposure to death, but also the effects of religious teachings and media.

We do not yet know how and to what extent children may have been affected by reports of the

Bombs and artillery shells ravaged Sarajevo and took many lives. Children find the opportunity for their own snowball war.

Oklahoma City bombing, the midair explosion of TWA Flight 800, the bomb that exploded during the Olympic Games in Atlanta, the school shootings, and other recent episodes of violence. Children in some other parts of the world have been facing personal threats from warfare, terrorism, and the diseases and malnutrition that are bred in these circumstances. The upheaval in Kosovo is an example that received worldwide attention. The children of Kosovo are just starting to return to the safe and normal routines that most of us take for granted, but many have already had unforgettable experiences of life-threatening episodes or loss of a loved ones. To a child in Burundi, Guatemala, the Sudan, and all too many other places, the death of others and the possibility of one's own sudden death are intrinsic to their experiences.

Those who have grown up in a hazardous and unpredictable environment may take sudden death as the norm. Among refugees of the war in Lebanon, it was observed that children made lethal weapons their playthings and often gunned each other down (Cutting, 1988). Observations of this type have also been made in other war-torn settings. The idea of killing might be part of any child's development of the overall concept of death (Anthony, 1948/1972). For children to emphasize and enact the role of killer, however, suggests that situational factors can have a very strong impact.

Over a longer arch of time, children born before and after the conquest of fatal childhood diseases and the introduction of television might differ in their experiences and concepts of death. My father occasionally spoke of his brothers who died of diphtheria in childhood. Many other long-lived adults have memories of the deaths of family members from contagions and infections seldom encountered today. Every new generation of children brings somewhat distinctive experiences to its understanding of death-related issues.

HOW DO CHILDREN COPE WITH BEREAVEMENT?

For some children, death has already become a reality. They have lost a person who had been very important in their lives. We look now at the effects of bereavement on children and the ways in which they attempt to cope. We will see that an increasing number of American children may be at risk for prolonged and disturbing grief reactions as a result of a traumatic bereavement.

A Death in the Family: Effects on the Child

A death in the family often draws attention and energy away from the needs of the children. When a parent dies, for example, the surviving parent's grief can interfere temporarily with the ability to care for the emotional or even the physical needs of the children. It can be very difficult for lone parents to manage both their own sorrow and the needs of their children.

Sometimes it is a sibling who dies. In this situation, the parents may be so involved in the plight of the dying child that other children are neglected. The surviving children may face two sources of stress. First, as already mentioned, the grieving parent may not be able to provide as much emotional support as well as guidance through the problems of everyday life. Second, the surviving children have their own anxieties and sorrows to suffer through. They may feel isolated if the adults fail to recognize their distress signals. Sensitive adults take into account both the child's developmental level and the role that the deceased person played in the child's life. What does this child understand about separation and death? Does the child understand that death is final and universal? Was the deceased person an older sibling whom the child had looked up to? Was the deceased a younger sibling whom the child had resented as a competitor for parental attention? Does the surviving child believe that she could join the lost sibling if she managed to get himself killed?

Furthermore, attention should be given to the quality of the child's personal and family situation prior to the bereavement. Had this been a tightly knit family in which the child enjoyed a strong sense of love and security? Was it a broken or bent family characterized by anxiety and insecurity? The impact of bereavement is influenced by the child's developmental level, the specific loss that has been experienced, and the previous pattern of family security and affection.

Bereaved children may express their distress in ways that do not seem closely associated with the loss. Serious problems in school may appear for the first time. Children may turn on playmates with sudden anger. Fear of the dark or of being alone may reappear. There are many ways in which a child's life pattern can show the effect of bereavement without an obvious show of sorrow. These children may be further inhibited from direct expression if commanded by the surviving parent to be "brave." Tears are then stigmatized as signs of weakness and disobedience.

Young children tend to express their memories of a lost parent through specific activities that had linked them together. An adult can preserve a valued relationship by replaying memories in private or sharing them with others. But a 2-year-old boy who loses his father is more likely to express his longing and sadness through actions.

> For weeks he spent much of his time repeating the daily play activities that had constituted the essence of his relationship with his father. He also insisted, over and over, on taking the walks he had taken with his father, stopping at the stores where his father had shopped, and recalled specific items. (Furman, 1974, p. 55)

The toddler's need added to the mother's emotional pain, but she recognized that it was the best way he had to adjust to the loss.

In remembering the deceased person, young children are likely to focus on a few strong images, in contrast to the bereaved spouse, who has many recollections from all of the years of marriage. A young child carries much of the remembrance of the lost parent in the form of scenes and activities in which intense feelings have been invested. Years after the death, the child may suddenly be overwhelmed with sadness when he or she encounters a situation that touches off a precious memory.

The mental image of the lost parent often remains with children long after the death. Adults sometimes make it easier on themselves by assuming that a child forgets quickly. The child may contribute to this assumption by showing an apparent lack of grief and mourning—what adults *perceive* as a lack of response. For example, the child goes back to watching television, a behavior that suggests to the adult that he or she probably doesn't understand what has happened. This assumption is contradicted by most clinicians and researchers who have observed childhood bereavement in detail. Although "some children could bear an astonishing amount of pain alone…most needed a loved person who could either share their grief or empathize with them and support their tolerance and expression of affect" (Furman, 1974, p. 57). The silent sadness of the bereaved child can be painful for the adult to acknowledge. But how are we to support and comfort unless we can accept the reality of the child's suffering?

It can be even more difficult to accept the child's response when it includes anger. The surviving parent may be horrified to hear criticisms of the deceased parent coming from the children. This may happen precisely at the time that the widowed spouse is at the peak of idealizing the lost husband or wife. And yet the expression of anger may be a necessary part of the child's adaptation to the loss. Such expressions do not mean that the child does not love and miss the lost parent—quite the opposite. One of the reasons some adults find it very painful to accept the child's expression of mixed feelings toward the deceased is that these feelings are within them as well. Whoever helps a bereaved spouse express grief openly and begin the long process of recovery is also helping the children by returning the strength and sensitivity of their remaining parent.

Most studies of children's parental bereavement have concentrated on the loss of the father. Several consistent differences have been found in the behavior of children who have suffered parental bereavement as compared with children who have both parents living.

Children whose father died tend to exhibit the following characteristics:

- Are more submissive, dependent, and introverted
- Show a higher frequency of maladjustment and emotional disturbance, including suicidality (suicide in children is considered in *Chapter 7*)

- Show a higher frequency of delinquent and criminal behavior
- Perform less adequately in school and on tests of cognitive functioning

Often a child's response to the death of a parent is not what it might seem to be on the surface:

> Kevin, age eight, revealed markedly little anxiety or sadness when questioned directly about how he was doing following the death of his father. However, when asked about any dreams he may have had about the death, he related several highly distressing dreams. In one a boy saw his deceased father. At first the boy felt excited, but then awoke feeling sad that his father wasn't really alive. The boy drilled a hole in his own head, took out the brain cells that contained memories of his father, and in that way "he would never think of him again, never have to feel sad again." (Kalter, Lohnes, Chasin, Cain, Dunning, & Rowarn, in press)

The more fully we can enter into a child's private world of hurt and fear, the better position we are in to provide understanding and comfort.

This general pattern does not mean that all bereaved children experience the difficulties listed above. The surviving parent and other social supports can help to protect the child, as can the personal resources the child has already developed. Nonetheless, parental bereavement must be regarded as a potential problem in many areas of a child's life.

Age at time of bereavement is an important variable. Children 7 years and younger tend to have more difficulties in the period immediately after bereavement.

Posttraumatic Stress Disorder (PTSD) following a Violent Death

It has been well established that a sudden, unexpected death has a more severe impact on the survivors (*see Chapter 11*). This impact can be further intensified by especially threatening features of the death—e.g., a drive-by shooting, a suicide, or mutilation of the corpse in an accident. There is growing awareness among mental health experts and researchers that often children are among those affected by sudden and violent deaths. Some teachers and school systems have already developed programs and techniques for reaching out to children who have been exposed to traumatic death. It would be useful to bring this awareness to all school systems as well as parents and the general public.

Central to this awareness is the syndrome known as Posttraumatic Stress Disorder (PTSD), which was officially recognized as a diagnostic entity in 1980 and is described in detail in the American Psychiatric Association's *Diagnostic and Statistical Manual of Mental Disorders* (1987). The phenomenon itself has been known for many years: a person comes through extremely stressful situations and then, at a later time, suffers "flashbacks" in which the traumatic events are re-experienced. During these episodes, the individual behaves in seemingly irrational, bizarre, and perhaps dangerous ways—not at all in keeping with his or her previous personality. These episodes often are frightening to family, friends, and the individual experiencing them.

The definitive description of PTSD is given in Table 10-2.

The general awareness of PTSD in adults, an awareness stimulated to a large extent by the experiences of some people who served in the Viet-

TABLE 10-2

Diagnostic Criteria for Posttraumatic Stress Disorder

A. The person has experienced an event that is outside the range of usual human experience and would be markedly distressing to almost anyone (e.g., serious threat to one's life or physical integrity; serious threat or harm to one's children, spouse, or other close relatives and friends; sudden destruction of one's home or community; or seeing another person who has recently been, or is being, seriously injured or killed as the result of an accident or physical violence).

B. The traumatic event is persistently re-experienced in at least one of the following ways:
   (1) Recurrent intrusive distressing recollections of the event *(in young children, repetitive play in which themes or aspects of the trauma are expressed)**
   (2) Recurrent distressing dreams of the events
   (3) Sudden acting or feeling as if the traumatic events were recurring (includes a sense of reliving the experience, illusions, hallucinations, and dissociative [flashback] episodes, even those that occur upon awakening or when intoxicated)
   (4) Intense psychological distress at exposure to events that symbolize or resemble any aspect of the traumatic event, including anniversaries of the trauma

C. The person shows persistent avoidance of stimuli associated with the trauma or numbing of general responsiveness (not present before the trauma), as indicated by at least three of the following:
   (1) Efforts to avoid thoughts or feelings associated with the trauma
   (2) Efforts to avoid activities or situations that arouse recollections of the trauma
   (3) Inability to recall an important aspect of the trauma (psychogenic amnesia)
   (4) Markedly diminished interest in significant activities *(in young children, loss of recently acquired developmental skills such as toilet training or language skills)**
   (5) Feelings of detachment or estrangement from others
   (6) Restricted range of affect, e.g., unable to have loving feelings
   (7) Sense of a foreshortened future, e.g., does not expect to have a career, marriage, children, or a long life

D. The person experiences persistent symptoms of increased arousal (not present before the trauma), as indicated by at least two of the following:
   (1) Difficulty falling or staying asleep
   (2) Irritability or outbursts of anger
   (3) Difficulty concentrating
   (4) Hypervigilance
   (5) Exaggerated startle response
   (6) Physiological reactivity upon exposure to events that symbolize or resemble an aspect of the traumatic event (e.g., a woman who was raped in an elevator breaks out in a sweat when entering any elevator)

E. Duration of the disturbance (symptoms in B, C, and D) is at least one month

*italics added

nam War. Recognition of PTSD in children who have experienced traumatic bereavements or other encounters with death is now starting to receive some of the attention it deserves (e.g., Barrett, 1995; Webb, 1993). Children whose PTSD is not recognized may become dysfunctional in various realms of their lives, including ability to pay attention, concentrate, and participate in rewarding friendships. Such a dysfunctional pattern is especially harmful in childhood, when so many basic personal and interpersonal skills are being developed. No less important, the child with PTSD is likely to be frightened, as shown by the following brief excerpt from a psychotherapy session with Nancy Boyd Webb in which Susan, age 9, shares her reaction to the automobile death of a schoolmate.

SUSAN: I'm having bad dreams that wake me up every night. Then in the morning I don't want to get up. I'm tired all the time, even when I go to bed at eight o'clock.

WEBB: That sounds pretty bad! Can you tell me what the dreams are like?

SUSAN: I dream that there is a gorilla in my closet and that he is going to sneak up to my bed and grab me and then take me away and roast me on a barbecue.

WEBB: That must be pretty scary! Does the dream wake you up?

SUSAN: Yes, and then I run into my mom's bed. (Webb, 1993, p. 196)

Children can be helped to overcome PTSD, but first we must be observant enough to recognize their distress and its possible connection to a disturbing death-related experience.

Long-Term Effects of Childhood Bereavement

The effects of childhood bereavement are not limited to childhood. Loss of a significant person in childhood can have an important effect on subsequent development. Major physical and mental illnesses occur more often in the adult lives of those who were bereaved as children. Other children develop in ways that perhaps can best be described as unusual. For example, some children take on the identity of their dead sibling or, more rarely, a dead parent. This is most likely to happen when the family had given preference to the child who is now deceased and then responds with approval to the impersonation. This borrowed identity may seem to serve its purpose well for a period of time, but it is likely to generate significant problems at some point in adult life.

Zall (1994) found that mothers whose own mothers had died in childhood showed symptoms of depression, worried about their own death, were overprotective and perfectionist. Despite these problems, however, many proved to be effective mothers themselves. They seemed to respond to the challenge of the parental role by completing their unfinished grieving over the deaths of their mothers. One of the women who exemplified this positive outcome offered the following comments:

> For many years I didn't want children. I decided to take the risk, with my husband's encouragement, and the experience of motherhood has been the most challenging and even more delightful than I ever dreamed. Because of my early loss and fear of dying and leaving my children, I have been extremely conscientious about teaching the children to separate from me very early in their lives. I tend to spend a great deal of time with them. (Zall, 1994)

Parental bereavement can be found in the childhoods of many people who made exceptional achievements in adulthood. Consider, for example, Charles Darwin. All through his life, Darwin retained the memory of his mother's deathbed, her black velvet gown, and the worktable. Curiously, though, he remembered hardly anything of her appearance and his conversations with her. Darwin's memory of his mother's death when he was 8 years old was vivid but fragmentary. He remembered being sent for... going into her room...being greeted by his father...crying afterward.... Even stranger, Darwin had much more detailed recollections of the funeral of a soldier that he attended a few weeks later.

Biographer Ralph Colp, Jr. (1975) was struck by Darwin's apparent repression of many of his memories of his mother and her death while details of the soldier's death remained fresh in his mind. Colp finds that death-related themes were closely interwoven with Darwin's work throughout his life. These themes showed up even in the notes he made in the margins of books, as well as in his dreams. One of the major themes disclosed was a "keen instinct against death." Colp and others believe that there is a connection between Darwin's ardent advocacy of life and his fascination with the evolution of new life forms.

Darwin's own observations confronted him with a challenge on both the personal and the scientific levels. His growing awareness of a process of natural selection, in which entire species die off, resonated with the feelings he still carried from the time of his mother's death. In his middle adult years, Darwin expressed fear of sudden death and regarded his theory as an indirect form of continued personal survival. Darwin had more bereavements to suffer in his adult life, notably the death of his much-loved daughter, Annie.

Above all, Darwin's personal experiences with death and his scientific perspective on the destruction of entire species contributed to his ardent love of life. Unable to believe in any doctrine of survival of death, Darwin had to bear with his own "intolerable vision of slow and cold death—death irrevocably, and, finally, ascendant over all life" (Colp, 1975, p. 200). Yet he also had the example of his father to inspire him. The elder Darwin had lived to age 83, with a lively mind right up to the end. Vivid memories of a father who was strong and admirable throughout a long life helped to sustain him during the course of his own life's work that was so burdened with death-related experiences and observation.

Near the end of his life, Darwin felt too ill to pursue major research, but he returned to the first creatures that interested him as a young boy—worms. He had enjoyed fishing and had mixed feelings about sacrificing worms to this cause. As an elderly man Darwin did little studies of worms. In Colp's words, "Thus, the old man, who as a boy had killed worms, now, night after night, observed how he would soon be eaten by worms" (1975, p. 200). This line of thinking was not altogether as morbid as it might sound. It was, after all, a continuation of Darwin's incessant fascination with life and death. Scientist Darwin respected worms as coinhabitants of planet Earth, who have a key role in maintaining the living ecology by literally passing the earth through themselves. That he, too, Charles Darwin, would become part of the worm and part of the earth again was not a cliché or a horror story but an acceptable aspect of our natural history.

Ten thousand examples would provide 10,000 different stories of the direct and indirect ways in which childhood bereavement influences the entire life course. The way each story turns out years later is likely to depend much on the kind of attention and support the child receives. We look now at some approaches that have proven useful.

HELPING CHILDREN COPE WITH BEREAVEMENT

1. *Develop and maintain an open communication pattern with children.* It is unrealistic to wait until a crisis situation has developed before including children in the discussion of significant issues. A child who is shunted aside whenever there are "important things" to talk about will have little opportunity to learn the communication skills that are required for dealing with difficult situations. Although limited by their levels of maturation and experience, children observe, think, and make choices. A family in which children feel that they can communicate about anything and everything with their parents and receive a careful and sympathetic hearing is a family that will be able to cope more resourcefully together when faced with bereavement or other stressful life events.

2. *Give children the opportunity to choose attending the funeral.* Adults often assume that children either would not understand funerals or would be harmed by the experience. These assumptions may be based on an underestimation of children's cognitive ability as well as their need to be a part of what happens. Findings from the Harvard Child Bereavement Study (Silverman & Worden, 1992) have confirmed that parents tend to give only the illusion of choice: "You don't want to go, do you? No, I know that you don't." As the study also found, children appreciate the opportunity to make their own decisions. In some cases, families encouraged children to make specific recommendations about the funeral, e.g., "outside, with lots of flowers, and with bright

colors so we can remember all the good things." Furthermore, those who attended the funeral were better able to cope with the loss of the parent. The researchers conclude that "funerals meet similar needs in children and in adults. By being included in the family drama, children felt acknowledged and thereby supported by their families, thus setting the stage for legitimating their roles as mourners.... The funeral becomes an opportunity to say good-bye, to feel close to their parent for one last time, and for the community to join them in doing this" (1992, p. 329). A new study provides additional support for the thesis that children who participate in funerals and other memorial rituals experience fewer emotional problems over the course of time (Fristad, Cerel, Goldman, Weller, E., & Weller, R., in press). However, attending graveside burial ceremonies or returning to visit the grave site was not often experienced as helpful. Contemporary funerals may be more supportive than those remembered by adults from their own childhood (Irion, 1990–1991). Nevertheless, a child who has decided against attending the funeral should not be forced to do so against his or her wishes.

3. *Check out what the child is thinking and feeling— do not assume that we know what the death means to him or her.* For example: "With children *never* interpret a head nod when you are explaining something to them as you would with an adult. They have learned the gesture from adults, but frequently it is for the child simply the easiest way to get the 'helping' adult to leave them alone...always gently ask the child to tell you what they have just heard and to explain it to you in their own words" (Hersh, 1995, p. 91).

4. *Encourage the expression of feelings.* This point was made by many of the mothers in our own study. Mental health professionals agree. A grieving child's thoughts and feelings are a part of reality that cannot be wished away or kept under wraps without adding to the already existing emotional burden. Young children are likely to find valuable means of expression through play and drawings, often accompanied by storytelling. Feelings can also be expressed through a variety of physical ac-

tivities, including vigorous games through which tension and anger can be discharged. Children of all ages can benefit from open communication with their surviving parent and other empathic adults. An especially valuable way for children to express their feelings is to help comfort others. Even very young children can do this. For example, one child attending a funeral later reported that "At the end while I was crying, my little cousin came up to me and gave me a hug and said it was okay. She was only three" (Silverman & Worden, 1992 p. 329). Comforting and altruistic behavior can begin very early in life.

5. *Provide convincing assurance that there will always be somebody to love and look after the child.* The death of a parent arouses or intensifies fears that the surviving parent and other important people may also abandon the child. Verbal assurances are useful but not likely to be sufficient. Children may become anxious when the surviving parent is out of sight or has not come home at the expected time. Sending the children away for a while is a practice that often intensifies the anxiety of abandonment. Adult relatives and friends who spend time with the children after their bereavement are helping the surviving parent to provide reassurance that there will always be somebody there for them.

6. *Professional counseling should be considered if the bereaved children are at special risk.* The death of both parents, for example, constitutes a special risk, as does a death for which the children might feel that they are somehow to blame. There is one special risk that arises for thousands of children each year:

> Mom told us to sit down and she said, "Girls, your Dad died." We both cried right away. We went down to the garage where everybody was. People began holding us and trying to make us feel better. No one knew what to say. We felt like everyone was just staring at us. It was like a big, bad dream. And to make matters worse, we found out from our Mom that Dad had killed himself.... It still is hard for us to understand. We were only five and nine years old. (Carolyn and Kristin in Dahlke, 1994, pp. 116–117)

The two girls had to contend—suddenly—with both the death of their father and the puzzle and possible stigma of his suicide. Their consuming question was: "If Daddy loved me, why did he leave me?" This became the title of a little book that the girls wrote together over a period of time. In addition to their supportive mother, Carolyn and Kristen had the skilled services of a professional counselor, David Dahlke. Every page of the girls' book reflects their personal growth experience as they explored their thoughts, feelings, values, and choices with the counselor's assistance.

Dahlke offers a detailed account of the counseling process along with the girls' own thoughts and comments by the mother. We learn, for example, that the children became afraid that if mother married again her new husband would also commit suicide. We also learn that the possibility of the father's suicide had already affected them before the act took place. As Carolyn reported, "I felt Dad threatened suicide a lot. I asked him, 'What if you kill yourself?' and he said, 'I won't do that!'...But he did. He lied to us.... Dad was mixed up."

Carolyn and Kristin showed both insight and resilience as they dealt with their loss and all of the questions it raised. Other children who suffer parental bereavement under especially traumatic and stressful conditions can also receive valuable assistance from qualified counselors.

THE DYING CHILD

Children sometimes think about death, loss, and separation even when there has been no obvious event to arouse their curiosity or concern. Writing about his own childhood, Spalding Gray recalls

the time when I woke up in the middle of the night and saw my brother Rocky standing on his bed, blue in the face and gasping for air, crying out that he was dying. My mother and father were standing beside the bed trying to quiet him, and Mom said, "Calm down, dear, it's all in your mind." And after he calmed down, my father went back to bed, and my mother turned out the light and sat on the edge of Rocky's bed in the dark.... We were all there, very quiet, in the dark, and then Rocky would start in, "Mom, when I die, is it forever?" And she said, "Yes, dear." And

then Rocky said, "Mom, when I die, is it forever, and ever, and ever?" and she said, "Uh-huh, dear." And he said, "Mom, when I die is it forever and ever and ever...?" I just went right off to this. (1986, p. 14)

Many other healthy children also may have moments when they imagine themselves dying and worry about what it means to be dead. It should not be surprising, then, to learn that children who actually are afflicted with life-threatening illnesses are keenly aware of their predicaments.

Sometimes the failure to communicate adequately with dying children arises from a death taboo. This was documented in a study that compared children suffering from uncontrolled leukemia with other children who were hospitalized with orthopedic conditions that posed no threats to their lives. All the children were Chinese. Those with leukemia were more tense, detached, and guarded. Given projective tests, the life-threatened leukemic children also expressed stronger feelings of being isolated and abandoned, while at the same time tending to deny the seriousness of their illness.

The authors, themselves Chinese, observed that in their ethnic group parents are especially reluctant to discuss death with their children (Lee, Lieh-Mak, Hung, & Luk, 1983–1984). Death is a taboo subject in general and even more so when children are involved. The child, whether healthy or fatally ill, is left to develop and test death concepts with little or no adult guidance. Inadvertently, the parents convey the impression that they are rejecting their dying children—why else, wonder the children, would their parents spend so little time with them and seem to take so little interest in their illness? Wherever such a taboo prevails, both the dying child and the parents are likely to suffer additional anguish because of the communication barrier.

Fortunately, there are also many examples of sensitive communication within families that face the impending death of a child. Shira Putter, who died at the age of 9 from a rare form of diabetes, has left a diary that offers the opportunity to learn how a child may interpret his or her own situation (Grollman, 1988). Problems in communication did arise along the way. At one point Shira was feeling that "Daddy doesn't care about me. I know he comes to visit me practically every day, but once he comes he always seems so far away. It's like he can't wait to leave again." She was reluctant to share this concern with her mother because "I didn't want her to get upset." But she did tell her mother, who then explained "that Daddy does love me and that was part of the problem. He loves me so much that it hurts him to see me sick and in pain. She asked me to please try to understand" (1988, p. 12). This little episode put everybody more at ease, including Daddy, and restored the usual family pattern of warm and caring interactions.

Dying children may hesitate to share their concerns because of the fear that this will only make their parents feel worse. On other occasions, Shira did remain silent when she could see that her parents were upset by new complications in her condition. So, far from being unaware of the perils they face, children may take a kind of parental role themselves and try to protect adults from anxiety and sorrow.

Firsthand accounts of the child's experience of terminal illness are also valuable in reminding us that each day can bring some new threat or challenge. Shira, for example, had to cope with the fact that her favorite doctor took himself off her case because he was so upset by her continued physical decline. The fear of abandonment by the most important people in their lives is often a major concern of dying children—and too often based upon the way that some adults do distance themselves from the children.

Shira and her family were able to maintain their closeness and mutual support until the very end. In one of her last diary entries, Shira writes of their Passover celebration. "In a way, it seemed like any other Passover. We said all the prayers. We sang all the songs. But when we were reciting the blessing, thanking God for letting us celebrate this special occasion, everyone started crying. Then, for about a minute, we all stood together quietly, holding hands. It was as if, without saying anything, I was telling everyone what was in my heart. That I loved them and wanted to be with them, but I couldn't make it much longer. That I wasn't afraid of dying anymore, so they had to let me go. They just had to" (1988, p. 70).

Myra Bluebond-Langner (1977, 1988) has provided valuable information on dying children's thoughts and feelings. She spent many hours with hospitalized children, listening to them and observing their interactions with parents and staff. There was no question about the children's keen awareness of their total situation. One morning, for example, Jeffrey made a point of asking Bluebond-Langner to read to him from the classic children's book, *Charlotte's Web* (White, 1952). He wanted to hear again "the part where Charlotte dies." This chapter, "Last Day," offers a combination of humor, drama, and consolation. "Nothing can harm you now" is one of its thoughts. Another is: "No one was with her when she died." When Bluebond-Langner completed her reading of the chapter, Jeffrey dozed off. He died that afternoon.

Many of the terminally ill children observed by Bluebond-Langner passed through five stages in the acquisition of information:

1. I have a serious illness.
2. I know what drugs I am receiving and what they are supposed to do.
3. I know the relationship between my symptoms and the kind of treatment I am getting.
4. I realize now that I am going through a cycle of feeling worse, getting better, then getting worse again. The medicines don't work all the time.
5. I know that this won't go on forever. There's an end to the remissions and the relapses and to the kind of medicine they have for me. When the drugs stop working, I will die pretty soon.

The children soon became sophisticated about hospital routines. They learned the names of all their drugs and how to tell one kind of staff member from another. Little escaped them. Staff members would have been astonished had they realized how much the children picked up on hospital processes and purposes. Most of all, perhaps, the children learned from each other. They would notice that they were now on the last drug that another child had received before his or her death or that people were now starting to treat them differently, meaning that something important had changed in their condition.

Recent studies such as these make it clear that seriously ill children work hard on understanding what is happening to them. They are aware of the possibility of death but must also give attention to the specific changes taking place in their bodies, the kind of treatment they are receiving, and how their family and friends are responding to them. A parent, teacher, physician, or nurse who assumes that a sick child is too young to understand anything is probably making a serious mistake. Consider this sequence reported by Barbara M Sourkes:

A 3 year-old boy played the same game with a stuffed duck and a toy ambulance each time he was hospitalized. The duck would be sick and need to go to the hospital by ambulance. The boy would move the ambulance, making siren noises.

THERAPIST: How is the duck?
CHILD: Sick.
THERAPIST: Where is he going?
CHILD: To the hospital.
THERAPIST: What are they going to do?
CHILD: Make him better.

During what turned out to be the boy's terminal admission, he played the same game with the duck. However, the ritual changed dramatically in its outcome.

THERAPIST: How is the duck?
CHILD: Sick
THERAPIST: Is he going to get better?
CHILD (shaking his head slowly): Ducky not get better. Ducky die. (Sourkes, 1996, pp. 157–158)

Two days later the boy drew a picture of "a vibrant firefly, smiling broadly as it emerges from the blackness into the...light." He explained: "Fireflies glow in the dark and show others the way." He died that evening.

Further insight into the world of a dying child is offered by Judi Bertoia (1993), an expressive therapist who worked with 7-year-old Rachel. This young girl was losing her battle with leukemia. Rachel expressed her thoughts and feelings through her drawings as well as her conversations with Bertoia. There could be little doubt that Rachel understood much of what was happening to her—one had only to view the crumbling houses and distorted bodies that were among her drawings. All was not fear and dread, however. Rachel showed a continued growth in knowledge and emotional material as time went on. Bertoia noted that Rachel's increasing understanding progressed in the stages that had been reported by Bluebond-Langner in her studies of dying children. Rachel also expressed her distinctive individuality through the drawings: she could not be reduced to a "type" or "stage," she was always Rachel, trying to understand and cope with her life-threatening illness in the best ways she knew how. And who can do any better than that?

Care of the Dying Child

Along with emotional support and sensitive communication, dying children are also likely to need a variety of medical, nursing, and other support services. In recent years, the hospice approach to terminal care has been extended to include children. The basic philosophy is the same as with hospice care in general: to help dying people enjoy the highest quality of life possible under the circumstances. This is accomplished by skillfully controlling pain and other symptoms, and by working with the family to support their own caregiving efforts.

Although circumstances may arise in which a hospital stay seems to be necessary, the focus is usually on home care. Children as well as adults often feel most secure within their own homes. Because sometimes neither the hospital nor the home seems to be the best place to care for a dying child, some hospice organizations have also established respite care facilities. These are usually small, homelike centers in which the child can receive care for a few days or weeks while the family copes with other problems.

Whether the child is at home, in a respite care center, or a hospital-based hospice service, the overall philosophy remains the same: give comfort, relieve distress, help the patient and family preserve their most basic values of life during this difficult time. At present, there are relatively few children's hospice programs, but a growing number of pediatric caregivers are applying hospice principles and techniques. Up-to-date information can be obtained by writing or calling Children's

Hospice International (1101 King Street, Suite 131, Alexandria, VA 22314; (703) 684–0330).

Whether or not a hospice approach is used, the care of a dying child is likely to be enhanced by attention to the following needs which have much in common with the situation of the bereaved child:

1. The opportunity to express his or her concerns through conversation, play, drawing, writing—whatever modality is most effective and natural for the particular child. Such creative activities as modeling clay figures or drawing pictures of the family may help to transform inner feelings into a tangible communication that can be shared with others. The very process of creative transformation—feelings into art—can itself have therapeutic value. Resentment and anger may be expressed on occasion in the child's play or art; this is usually part of one's natural response to overwhelming circumstances, and the opportunity to "get it out" often proves valuable.

2. Confirmation that he or she is still a normal and valuable person, despite the impairments and limitations imposed by illness. Sensitive parents and other caregivers will find ways to affirm and strengthen the child's basic sense of self. They will not allow "dyingness" to overshadow every interaction, every plan, every project. Instead, opportunities will be found for the child to do things that are still within his or her sphere of competence and to stay involved with roles and activities that have brought pleasure. One 10-year-old boy, for example, taught his younger siblings how to play chess while he was dying of leukemia; a girl, also 10, kept the statistics and figured the batting averages for her softball team after she herself could no longer play. With the availability of home computers, it is now also possible for children to enjoy computer-assisted learning programs, drawing, writing, and games with relatively little expenditure of energy.

3. Assurance that family members and other important people will not abandon the dying child, no matter what happens. Nonverbal behavior is a vital component of interaction that can either affirm or undermine the family's words of reassurance. As illustrated by Shira's

diary, children are quite aware of discomfort, tension, and conflict on the part of the adults in their lives. By their everyday actions as well as their words, parents and other caregivers must continue to convey their dedication to being with—to *staying* with—the dying child, come what may.

4. Reassurance that he or she will not be forgotten. Often a dying child has a fear of not being a part of what will happen in the family when he or she is no longer there. The child may also fear being replaced in the family constellation by another child, instead of remembered and valued for his or her uniqueness. In some situations, it may be useful to use mental imagery exercises to help the child prepare for impending separation and to participate in the future through imagination (LeBaron & Zeltner, 1985). Children may also come up with their own ways of feeling a part of the future, requiring of the adults only their sympathetic attention and cooperation. For example, a child may wish to give some favorite toys to a sibling or friend, or to make a cassette that can be listened to on birthdays or other special occasions.

In addition to these common needs and themes, each child with a life-threatening illness is almost certain to have distinctive ideas, hopes, and apprehensions. What special wish or secret fear is on the mind of this particular child? There is no substitute for careful listening and observation and for respecting the individuality of each child.

Siblings of the Dying Child

Anxiety and sorrow about the dying child can lead to neglect of other family needs. Parents may not give adequate attention to their own health, for example. The continuing stress can lead to a narrowing of attention, a concentration on "just what most needs to be done," and increased irritability and distraction even on the part of the most devoted parents. And, as recent findings suggest, the brothers and sisters of dying children may be at particular risk during this difficult period.

A leading researcher in this area has written that "The well siblings of terminally ill children live in houses of chronic sorrow. The signs of sorrow, illness, and death are everywhere, whether or not they are spoken of. The signs are written on parents' faces: 'My mother always looks tired now,' and 'Even my Dad's crying a lot.' The signs are there in hushed conversations: 'You learn everything by listening in on the (phone) extension" (Bluebond-Langner, 1988, p. 9).

The following problems are among those observed in well siblings in the course of Bluebond-Langner's research (1988):

1. Confusion about what role they are supposed to play in the family. Should they try to be like the sick child? Should they try to become "assistant parents"? Or should they become invisible, "just blend into the woodwork and get out of the way"?

2. A feeling of being deceived or rejected by their parents: "They don't tell me the truth.... Nobody really cares about me any more...."

3. Uncertainty about the future. "What's to become of all of us?.... Does it do any good to have plans any more?"

4. Changes in the relationships among the siblings. For example, the illness and hospitalization of the sick child may deprive the others of a companion. "Siblings often find that they cannot give reciprocally to one another.... For example, while Jake lay dying, complaining of his back hurting him and not being able to breathe, his brothers offered to rub his back. He pushed them away saying, 'no, no, not you. Only Mommy now.' The ill child's alliances shift from a closeness to both the parent and the sibling to a closeness with the parent divorced from that of the sibling" (Bluebond-Langner, 1988, p. 13).

5. Feelings of guilt and ambivalence. The well siblings are distressed by the suffering of the sick child but may also feel relieved—and feel guilty about feeling relieved—that they are not the ones who are dying.

6. Frustration in not being able to express their feelings and fears to their parents, who are so preoccupied with the dying child and with their own feelings.

Not all well siblings had all of these reactions, nor did these feelings occur all of the time. In some families, few obvious problems developed until the sick child had become extremely frail and disabled. Until that time, the parents had managed to find some time and energy for the other children and keep a semblance of normal family life going. But the well siblings themselves often took account of changes in the sick child's condition and needs. They recognized that the sick child now required a great deal of attention from the parents, and they were less likely to feel rejected or in competition.

Compassionate relatives, friends, neighbors, and teachers can lighten the burden by giving attention to the well siblings during and after the terminal process and by unobtrusively helping the parents in coping with the responsibilities of everyday life. A family with a dying child certainly needs and deserves sensitive, understanding, and mature companionship from the entire community.

The Stress of Working with Dying Children

Everybody who is called upon to provide care for a dying child is vulnerable to anxiety and sorrow—sometimes a sense of guilt as well because they are unable to save the child. Unfortunately, not much has yet been done to prepare health care professionals for this challenging kind of work. Papadatou (1997) believes that the medical profession's traditional emphasis on diagnosis and treatment of the disease has contributed to neglect of the dying child as a person—and neglect as well of the feelings of those who work closely with the dying child. Papadatou describes an innovative educational program for pediatric nurses at Children's Hospital in Athens, Greece. Pediatric nurses are provided with close and supportive supervision as they work with dying children and their families. They are given the opportunity to discuss their cases with a psychologist and to work with a supportive professional team. A sensitivity group experience is included, and their personal reflection is enhanced as they keep journals of their experiences. These and other techniques now being evaluated in Athens might well provide a new model that will help to prepare nurses throughout the world to provide care for dying children while also reducing their own stress. A follow-up study (Papadatou et al.,

1999) revealed that friends and relatives are seldom prepared to support nurses who are experiencing stress related to their work with dying children. Mutual support—nurse to nurse—seems to be a more effective approach at present.

SHARING THE CHILD'S DEATH CONCERNS: A FEW GUIDELINES

Adults may hope to shield children from death concerns, but it is in the child's own interests to identify and understand threats to his or her well-being. This has been all too true in situations in which children have been left to survive as they can with little assistance from the adult world. But it remains true even within the harbor of a loving family. Our children will encounter death in many forms—close and distant, imaginary and realistic. Many parents today received little guidance in death-related matters when they were young. It is not unusual, then, for adults to face inner struggles when called upon to respond to a child's questions.

This is not a "how-to" book, but it might be useful to present a few guidelines that have been helpful in relating to children on the subject of death.

1. *Be a good observer.* Notice how the child is behaving. Listen to what he or she is really saying. Do not rush in with explanations, reassurances, or diversions unless there is some overriding necessity to do so. You will be more helpful to the child if you are relaxed, patient, and attentive enough to learn what questions or needs the child actually is expressing rather than those you might assume to be there. For example, the child who suddenly asks a parent, "Are you going to be dead?" might have been thinking about something Grandmother said last week or any number of other happenings that aroused this concern. Taking a moment to learn how this question arose in the child's mind could also help to provide an appropriate response.

2. *Do not wait or plan for "one big tell-all."* Maintain a continuing dialogue with the children in your life as occasions present themselves. The death of pets, scenes in movies, newspaper articles, or television presentations—whatever

brushes with mortality the children have—all can offer the opportunity for discussion. This does not mean, of course, that parents should remain poised to jump on a death dialogue opportunity. But it is more natural and effective to include death as one of the many topics that adults and children can discuss together. We are more likely to be helpful when we are not ourselves caught up in the midst of a death situation. Combine a child who has been kept ignorant about death with an adult who is grief stricken or uptight and you have something less than the most desirable situation.

3. *Do not expect all of the child's responses to be obvious and immediate.* When a death has occurred or is impending, the child's total response is likely to unfold over time and to express itself in many ways. Changes in sleeping habits, mood, relationships with other children, and demands on adults may reflect part of the child's reaction to the death, even though the connection may not be obvious. Be patient; be available.

4. *Help the child remain secure as part of the family.* Sometimes adults have the panicked impulse to remove children from the scene when death has come too close (e.g., sending them off to a relative or neighbor). Examine such impulses before acting on them. Whatever practical decisions you reach, consider what the children might learn from the opportunity to participate in the family's response and what lingering questions, misinterpretations, and fears might remain if they are excluded.

5. *Use simple and direct language.* This is much to be preferred over fanciful, sentimental, and symbolic meanderings. Too often what adults say to children becomes a sermon, peppered with words and concepts that mean little to them. Try to provide children with accurate information. See whether they understand what you have said (e.g., by having them explain it back to you) and make sure that you have responded to what they really wanted to know in the first place.

6. *Be accessible.* The child's sense of comfort will be strengthened by the very fact that you are available to talk about death when the need arises. Your expression of feelings that are natural to the situation (worry, sorrow, perhaps

even anger) is not likely to harm the child, but rather will provide a basis for sorting out and expressing his or her own feelings.

7. *Be aware of all children in the family.* In some situations, one child may be central (e.g., seriously or fatally ill). It may seem natural to concentrate the family's resources and attentions on that child. Other children in the family continue to need love and reassurance, however, and to participate somehow in the total process.

8. *Don't break the relationship.* What a child feels or thinks about death at a particular moment might disturb or anger adults. We do not want to see or hear certain responses. Losing the closeness and support of important adults is a great danger to the child. This, in fact, is one of the reasons children may not share their thoughts and feelings with us. We do not have to approve or agree with everything the child tells us about death, but we do have to maintain a supportive relationship.

THE "RIGHT" TO DECIDE: SHOULD THE CHILD'S VOICE BE HEARD?

The "right-to-die" issue has generated controversy within the general public as well as the health care and judicial systems. We have touched on this issue a number of times throughout the book and examine it in detail in *Chapter 9*. It will also be useful to look briefly at this issue now, while we are still focused on the child's relationship to death. For our example, we will take the poignant case of Marie, who was a patient for most of her young life. Marie had little opportunity to experience a normal childhood because of severe kidney disease and the effects of treatment.

> During Marie's short life, she experienced numerous hospitalizations and separations from her family, who eventually abandoned her. Massive nosebleeds…terrified her mother and led to seven emergency hospitalizations and transfusions. Marie's lonely, monotonous hospital days were interrupted only by traumatic episodes which affected her both physically and emotionally. (Meagher & Leff, 1989–1990, p. 178)

Marie was especially fearful of and stressed by the kidney dialysis sessions. She would be put in restraints for this procedure, producing significant and unrelenting discomfort. "Marie's mother would not be waiting for her after the ordeal had ended. Sedatives would not be used to ease the passage of time." In fact, Marie did not receive medication for her pain whether in or out of dialysis. A dialysis nurse stated that giving her sedatives would only "spoil" Marie—she must learn to cope with pain. When Marie cried out for relief from pain, her pediatricians went through an elaborate placebo procedure, attempting to deceive the girl rather than offering actual medications. The placebo stunt did not relieve Marie's pain, and no other relief was offered. Marie's agony, her anger, and her fear all intensified until she became comatose and died.

How could this little girl have been allowed to suffer so long and so greatly? Did this pattern of "care" represent a violation of her rights? We might feel very strongly that the medical regime had been abusive and unsympathetic—*but do children have rights?* Specifically, do children have the right to participate in decisions regarding the quality of their own lives and the prospect of their own deaths? These questions have been avoided by many of the philosophers, policymakers, and physicians who analyze treatment decisions from ethical and legal standpoints.

Meagher and Leff are firm in their own opinion: "Marie has the absolute right to expect that any procedure or course of treatment be in her best interest" (1989–1990, p. 283). She has the right to be spared the pain and stress of undergoing procedures that offer no reasonable probability of extending her life for a sustained period. She would seem to have the right "at least to participate in the decision to refuse treatment or to withhold further interventions." However, as Meagher and Leff are quick to point out, the law does not agree with this conclusion. A person must be competent in the eyes of the law in order to make decisions, and "competent" is invariably part of the phrase, "competent adult" (Brock, 1993; Veatch, 1993).

I find it unsettling that the basis for determining competency differs for children and adults. The competency of adults is determined on a case-by-case basis: some adults are competent, others are not, and this status may change with time and circumstance. By contrast, children are considered not competent as a class. This two-track system of legalistic logic has a powerful effect on the policies enacted in our society's death system. It should be challenged, don't you think?

Historian Viviana A. Zelizer (1994) has compiled evidence for an interesting transition in society's image of the child. She finds that until fairly recent times, children were valued chiefly for their contribution to the economy: cheap labor at home, in the fields, and in factories. The modern image of the child started to emerge around the turn of the twentieth century as children became less an economic asset and valued instead as "emotionally priceless." Our heritage, then, features children as a cheap and expendable source of labor, responsible for obeying adult authority and having few, if any, intrinsic rights. Several generations later, it appears that society has yet to adjust its moral and legal perspectives.

SUMMARY

Adults often believe—or want to believe—that children do not understand death and should be protected from all death-related situations. The facts are quite different. Children are naturally curious about loss, disappearance, and death. Furthermore, no child is too young to experience the anxiety associated with separation experiences. Most studies indicate that children do not have a firm grasp of death's finality, irreversibility, and universality until about age 10. Nevertheless, even very young children have moments of sudden discovery (e.g., the frog was "dead, dead, dead. What else could it be?"), and the mystery of death is very much in their minds throughout their developmental process.

Many of today's parents grew up in homes in which death was never to be discussed, especially in the presence of children. This increases their difficulties in communicating about death with their own children. We learned something about the interaction between parents and children on the subject of death through a sampling of research case histories. It was clear that experiences, attitudes, and ways of coping with death are part of the intimate flow of life between children and their parents, and also that the death

of particular people or animals evokes a child's concern.

Studies indicate that the young child's experiences of death and loss often become lifelong memories for the adult. Psychologist Maria Nagy ("Auntie Death") found three stages of progressive understanding of death in her pioneering research: The youngest children think of death as a continuation of life in a diminished form. The realization that death is final occurs in the next stage, at about age 5, but there is still hope that one can be smart or lucky enough to elude death. By age 10 (stage 3), most children understand that death is personal, universal, and inevitable, as well as final.

More recent studies emphasize the relationship between separation anxiety and children's thoughts of death. For children, as well as adults, thoughts about death are often, possibly always, tinged with anxiety. Children in various cultures show basic similarities in their conceptions of death, but they also exhibit some culture-specific characteristics.

REFERENCES

Anderson, B. (1995). Do children belong at funerals? In D. W. Adams & E. J. Deveau (Eds.), *Beyond the innocence of childhood.* (Vol. 1., pp. 163–178). New York: Baywood.

Anthony, S. (1972). *The discovery of death in childhood and after.* New York: Basic Books, Inc. (Revision of *The child's discovery of death.* New York: Harcourt Brace and World, 1940).

Anthony, Z., & Bhana, K. (1988–1989). An exploratory study of Muslim girls' understanding of death. *Omega, Journal of Death and Dying, 19,* 215–228.

Barrett, R. K. (1995). Children and traumatic loss. In K. J. Doka (Ed.), *Children mourning; mourning children.* Washington, DC: Hospice Foundation of America, pp. 85–92.

Bertman, S. L. (1979–1980). The arts: A source of comfort and insight for children who are learning about death. *Omega, Journal of Death and Dying, 10,* 147–163.

Bertoia, J. (1993). *Drawings from a dying child: Insights into death from a Jungian perspective.* London: Routledge.

Blano, M. K. (1988). *A study of the level on which adults understand and respond to children in death-related situations.* Doctoral dissertation, Georgia State University.

Bluebond-Langner, M. (1977). Meanings of death to children. In H. Feifel (Ed.), *New meanings of death.* (pp. 47–6). New York: McGraw-Hill.

Bluebond-Langner, M. (1988). Worlds of dying children and their well siblings. *Death Studies, 13,* 1–16.

Bluebond-Langner, M. (1993). Children, dying. In R. Kastenbaum & B. Kastenbaum (Eds.), *Encyclopedia of death.* New York: Avon, pp. 46–48.

Bluebond-Langner, M. (1996). *In the shadow of illness.* Princeton, NJ: Princeton University Press.

Book, P. (1996). How does the family narrative influence the individual's ability to communicate about death? *Omega, Journal of Death and Dying, 33,* 323–342.

Bowlby, J. (1980). *Attachment and loss.* New York: Basic Books.

Brock, D. W. (1993). *Life and death: Philosophical essays in biomedical ethics.* New York: Cambridge University Press.

Colp, R. J. (1975). The evolution of Charles Darwin's thoughts about death. *Journal of Thanatology, 3,* 191–206.

Cutting, P. (1988). *Children of the siege.* New York: St. Martin's.

Dahlke, D. (1994). Therapy-assisted growth after parental suicide: From a personal and professional perspective. *Omega, Journal of Death and Dying, 22,* 113–152.

Deveau, E. J. (1995). Perceptions of death through the eyes of children and adolescents. In D. W. Adams & E. J. Deveau (Eds.), *Beyond the innocence of childhood.* (Vol. 1, pp. 55–92). New York: Baywood,

DeSpalder, L. A., & Strickland, A. L. (1996). *The last dance.* Palo Alto-Mayfield.

Dickinson, G. (1986). First childhood death experiences. *Omega, Journal of Death and Dying, 25:* 169–182.

Erikson, E. (1950). *Childhood and society.* New York: W. W. Norton.

Farley, H-A. (1966). Sun goes up. In R. Lewis (Ed.), *Miracles.* New York: Simon & Schuster.

Freeman, A., & DiTomasso, R. A. (1994). The cognitive theory of anxiety. In B. J. Wolman & G. Stricker (Eds.), *Anxiety and related disorders.* New York: Wiley-Interscience, (pp. 74–90).

Freud, S. (1914). On Narcissism: An introduction. In *Collective works* (Vol. 4, pp. 30–59). London-Hogart.

Fristad, M. A., Cerel, J.., Goldman, M., Weller, E. B., & Weller, R. A. (in press). The role of ritual in children's bereavement. *Omega, Journal of Death and Dying.*

Furman, E. F. (1974). *A child's parent dies: Studies in childhood bereavement.* New Haven: Yale University Press.

Gray, S. (1986). *Sex and death to the age 14.* New York: Vintage Books.

Grollman, S. Shira. (1988). *A legacy of courage.* New York: Doubleday.

Hall, G. S. (1922). *Senescense: the last half of life.* New York: D. Appleton.

Hersh, S. P. (1995). How can we help? In K. J. Doka (Ed.), *Children mourning; mourning children.* Washington, DC: Hospice Foundation of America, pp. 93–96.

Irion, P. E. (1990–1991). Changing patterns of ritual response to death. *Omega, Journal of Death and Dying, 22,* 159–172.

Jenkins, R. A., & Cavanaugh, J. C. (1985–1986). Examining the relationship between the development of the concept of death and overall cognitive development. *Omega, Journal of Death and Dying, 16,* 193–200.

Kalter, N., Lohnes, K. L., Chasin, J., Cain, A. C., Dunning, S., & Rowarn, J. (in press). The adjustment of parentally bereaved children: Factors associated with short-term adjustment. *Omega, Journal of Death and Dying.*

Kastenbaum, R. (2000). *The psychology of death.* (3rd ed.). New York: Springer.

Kenyon, B. L. (in press). Current research in children's conceptions of death: A critical review. *Omega, Journal of Death and Dying.*

Kevorkian, J. (1991). *Prescription: Medicide.* New York: Prometheus.

LeBaron, S., & Zeltner, L. K. (1985). The role of imagery in the treatment of dying children and adolescents. *Journal of Developmental Behavioral Pediatrics, 5,* 252–258.

Lee, P. W. H., Lieh-Mak, F., Hung, B. K. M., & Luk, S. L. (1983–1984). Death anxiety in leukemic Chinese children. *International Journal of Psychiatry in Medicine, 13,* 281–290.

Lonetto, R. (1980). *Children's conceptions of death.* New York: Springer.

Meagher, D. K., & Leff, P. T. (1989–1990). In Marie's memory: The rights of the child with life-threatening or terminal illness. *Omega, Journal of Death and Dying, 20,* 177–191.

Nagy, M. H. (1948/1969). The child's theories concerning death. In H. Feifel (Ed.), *The meaning of death.* New York: McGraw-Hill. (Reprinted from *Journal of Genetic Psychology, 73,* 3–27, 1948.)

Okafor, R. U. (1993). Death education in the Nigerian home: The mother's role. *Omega, Journal of Death and Dying, 27,* 271–280.

Opie, I., & Opie, R. (1969). *Children's games in street and playground.* London: Oxford University Press.

Orbach, I., Weiner, M., Har-Evan, D., & Eshel, Y. (in press). Children's perception of death and interpersonal closeness to the dead person. *Omega, Journal of Death and Dying.*

Papadatou, D. (1997). Training health professionals in caring for dying children and grieving families. *Death Studies, 6,* 575–600.

Papadatou, D., Papazoglou, I., Petraki, D., & Bellali, T. (1999). Mutual support among nurses who provide care to dying children. *Illness, crisis, and loss, 7,* 37–48.

Philadelphia Child Guidance Center (1993). *Your child's emotional health.* New York: Macmillan.

Piaget, J. (1960). *The child's conception of the world.* Patterson, NJ: Littlefield, Adams.

Piaget, J. (1973). *The child and reality: problems of genetic psychology.* New York: Grossman.

Shimanoff, S. B. (1980). *Communication rules: Theory and research.* Newbury Park, CA: Sage Books.

Silverman, P. R., & Worden, J. W. (1992). Children's understanding of funeral ritual. *Omega, Journal of Death and Dying, 25,* 319–332.

Sourkes, B. M. (1996). *Armfuls of time: The psychological experience of the child with a life-threatening disease.* Pittsburgh: University of Pittsburgh Press.

Vandewiele, M. (1983–1984). Attitudes of Senegalese secondary school students toward death. *Omega, Journal of Death and Dying, 14,* 329–334.

Veatch, R. M. (1993). Foregoing life-sustaining treatment: Limits to the consensus. *Kennedy Institute of Ethics Journal, 3,* 1–20.

Webb, N. B. (1993). Traumatic death of friend/peers: Case of Susan, age 9. In N. B. Webb (Ed.), *Helping bereaved children* (pp. 189–211). New York: Guilford,

Wenestam, C. G., & Wass, H. (1987). Swedish and U.S. children's thinking about death: A qualitative study and cross-cultural comparison. *Death Studies, 11,* 99–122.

White, E. B. (1952). *Charlotte's Web.* New York: Harper & Row.

Zall, D. S. (1994. The long term effects of childhood bereavement: Impact on roles as mothers. *Omega, Journal of Death and Dying, 29,* 219–230.

Zelizer, V. A. (1994). *Pricing the priceless child.* Princeton, NJ: Princeton University Press.

GLOSSARY

Affect: Emotion.

Aphasic: Unable to speak, most often a consequence of a cerebrovascular accident (also known as *stroke*).

Bereavement: The loss of a loved one through death.

Cystic Fibrosis: A hereditary disorder in which lungs and other organ systems are blocked by abnormal mucus secretions. A life-threatening condition.

Death Anxiety: Emotional distress and insecurity aroused by encounters with dead bodies, grieving people, or other reminders of mortality, including one's own thoughts.

Dissociative Episodes: Experiences that are not well integrated into the individual's basic personality and that therefore may be interpreted as coming from some other source.

Heuristic: A stimulus to further achievements, events, or knowledge.

Introversion: The personality characteristic of turning one's attention energies inward, as contrasted with *extroversion,* the direction of one's interests toward other people.

Leukemia: A progressive disease that produces distorted and dysfunctional white blood cells, increasing susceptibility to infection, bleeding, and anemia. Sometimes a life-threatening condition.

Personification: Representing an idea or feeling as a human or humanlike form.

Plague: The plague that resulted in the deaths of at least one-fourth of the population of Europe in the late fourteenth century. Generally considered to have been bubonic disease, carried by rats and fleas as well as stricken humans. Also known as "The Black Death."

Posttraumatic Stress Disorder: A response (sometimes delayed) to a death that has occurred under highly stressful conditions. The traumatic event is re-experienced repeatedly, and other disturbances of feeling, thought, and behavior are also likely to occur.

Separation Anxiety: Emotional distress and insecurity aroused by loss of contact with a valued and protective person (also observed in animal behavior).

Sibling: A brother or sister.

Trauma: A wound, injury, or emotional shock that produces injury.

Military cemeteries honor those who have served their nation in uniform. Prisoners of war and those still missing in action are commemorated in this field.

chapter *11*

BEREAVEMENT, GRIEF, AND MOURNING

My father died at age eighty-six following a lengthy bout with lung cancer and heart problems...My mother and I had a room in the hospital so we could care for him. His request to me the night before he died was, "I want you to care for Mother. I know it won't be easy, but all I'm asking is that you do this the best you can." Those words are as clear today as they were sixteen years ago. They haunted me when Mother died. I had failed to take care of her.
—Bozeman, 1999, p. 94

I used to wish that she would die. I remember before I brought her home from the hospital thinking, God, I wish she would just die and then I wouldn't have to bring her home and go through this and put the kids through this. And I just couldn't have been more wrong.
—Milo, 1997, p. 457

Fate has ordained that the men who went to the moon to explore in peace will stay on the moon to rest in peace. These brave men, Neil Armstrong and Edwin Aldrin, know that there is no hope for their recovery. But they also know that there is hope for mankind in their sacrifice. These two men are laying down their lives in mankind's most noble goal: the search for truth and understanding.
—Woodward, 1999, Associated Press dispatch

We have loved. We have lost. We have grieved. We have mourned. These are universal elements of the human experience, from the most ancient times to the present. Few people escape the sorrow and stress of loss. Individual grief has not been abolished by mass communication, computers, and all the scientific and technological innovations that we take with us into a new millennium. In this chapter, we examine one of our strongest links with the whole procession of the human race on earth: the capacity to suffer deeply and yet to renew our commitment to life when separated by death from a beloved person.

Life does go on for the survivors, but the process of transition is seldom painless or easy. Some people suffer greatly and, years later, still experience

Children who have lost a mother or father through death often have a need to revisit the places they had seen with their deceased parent.

difficulties related to their loss. The loss of an animal companion can also hit us hard: "The house is so empty without Ruffy. I could cry. I guess I do cry." We may question our ability or our desire to go on without the person we have lost. The familiar routines of everyday life may seem distant and meaningless: "I saw everything that was going on around me, but I couldn't touch it or feel it. It was as though there was a wall of glass between myself and the rest of the world." Our attention, concentration, and memory may falter. Friends, finding us preoccupied and unresponsive, may decide to leave us alone with our own thoughts. On the other hand, friends may marvel

at "how well" we are doing, "how strong" we are; little do they realize the doubts and anxieties we are concealing through "acting normal." Furthermore, our physical health may be in jeopardy. Perhaps we are sleeping poorly, failing to take adequate nourishment, and neglecting our own well being. Some of us may be on the verge of a drinking problem, while others may be developing suicidal ideation—risks that the people around us may or may not recognize.

Grief is painful, but we usually get over it in a year or so—right? Wrong! Jeanine Cannon Bozeman, a professor of social work at New Orleans Baptist Theological Seminary, describes the lasting

Grief and depression after a loss can make it difficult for a person to interact with others.

impact of her mother's death upon her. After sixteen years, she reports still having difficulty in accepting this loss and in forgiving the driver of the car in which her mother had been a passenger. Is sixteen years a long time to grieve? I have known people who are still caught up in deaths that occurred more than half a century ago, feeling that there just might have been something else they could have done, should have done. Grief does not necessarily have time limits, despite what we might have been told.

In this chapter, we look carefully at the grief and recovery process for parents who have lost children and children who have lost parents. We also consider husbands who have lost wives and wives who have lost husbands, and siblings who have lost siblings. Sometimes the shaken and sorrowing survivors do not seem to have the right to grieve—they were not family, yet the pain is there. Accordingly, we also look at hidden or disenfranchised grief.

There are also circumstances in which none of us "supposed" to grieve, because the person who died was not considered really a "person" in the full sense of the word. This was the subject of research by Elisabeth Moulton Miro, who found that mothers had formidable challenges to master in both the life and the death of their developmentally disabled children.

> They succeeded in making sense of what others might define as "tragedy" twice: once to accommodate a child with a disability in their world and once again to assimilate the death of that…child into their view of a world that has meaning and purpose. (Milo, 1997, p. 455)

We will be attentive, then, to the way society and individuals regard the person who has died and to the questions of value and meaning that can become insistent after a death.

Fortunately, "These brave men, Neil Armstrong and Edwin Aldrin," did not die on the moon. But what if the historic Apollo XI space mission had failed? How would the public respond to the strange fate—alive but without hope of rescue and, therefore, waiting for death? President Richard M. Nixon had a speech ready for this contingency by July 18, 1969, two days before the moon landing. Nixon and other officials were realistic about the risks involved in the

mission. They were also aware that the public might respond with a mighty wave of anger as well as sorrow and confusion should the astronauts become casualties. The grief of an entire population can be a powerful force—one that is capable of strong and unpredictable consequences. Throughout history, people in positions of leadership and control have had to cope resourcefully with public grief—or become casualties themselves.

All of the above assumes that we have a sound understanding of bereavement, grief, and mourning. We begin by clarifying these basic concepts. Then we look at some of the major theories that have been proposed and their implications for helping grieving people. The ways people actually cope with loss will be examined in some detail, drawing upon the most useful of both classic and current research. This includes the impact of grief on the survivors. Although we will discover common patterns and themes, we will also become aware of great individual differences and of the role played by sociocultural expectations. Finally, we will build upon these observations to improve our ability to recognize and respond helpfully to the grief experience, whether in ourselves or others.

DEFINING OUR TERMS: BEREAVEMENT, GRIEF, MOURNING

Bereavement, grief, mourning—the words themselves are not adequate to convey the transformation a death can bring upon the survivors. But let us at least begin with these words and see how they can best be understood.

Bereavement: An Objective Fact

Bereavement is an objective fact. We are bereaved when a person close to us dies. The term is usually applied when the person who has died is part of our family or a close friend. There is no hard and fast rule about how far this term should be extended. The death of a co-worker, for example, might or might not be considered a bereavement, depending on the relationship that had existed. Bereavement conveys the idea of a forcible separation that results in the loss of something we once had. If we have, in fact, lost a relationship with another person, we have had bereavement enter our lives.

Bereavement is also a change in status. The child may have become an orphan, the spouse a widower or widow. The *experience* and *consequences* of bereavement can take many forms. The fact itself, however, is simple: a person close to us has died. Bereavement status can only suggest what the survivors might be experiencing and how they have adapted to the loss. It is an objective fact that serves as a clue to possible psychological, social, and physical distress.

Bereavement is also an outcome of large-scale social phenomena. Widowhood and orphanhood are major consequences of war. The effects of war are to be gauged not only in territories seized or relinquished but also in the short- and long-range effects of bereavement. British, French, and Germans who survived World War I (the "War to End All Wars") felt that the cream of their youth had been destroyed. This was not an exaggeration. Each nation was not only deprived of the talents and energies of these men but also was left with a population of survivors who could not be expected to pick up their lives as usual when the war ended. How much of human history since World War I has been affected by the slaughter and bereavement of that one major conflict alone? And what has been the effect of other wars before and after? The consequences of mass bereavement must surely exert a powerful effect on the quality of life for many years thereafter.

War is just one of the more obvious large-scale events that influence who is bereaved and when. Bereavement points to many other social phenomena as well. The number of widows in American society, for example, has been increasing in recent decades. The increase in adults who have outlived their mates is one of the reasons that *loneliness* has become such an important topic for research and intervention. Widowed people are more likely to be socially isolated than others. In turn, social isolation tends to be associated with low morale and difficulties in coping (Lopata, 1993). Although bereavement by itself is only a bare objective fact, it is also a fact that tends to generate increased vulnerability and stress.

Grief: A Painful Response

Grief is a response to bereavement; it is how the survivor feels. It is also how the survivor thinks, eats, sleeps, and makes it through the day. The term itself does not explain anything. Rather, when we say that a person is griefstricken, we are only directing attention to the way in which his or her total way of being has been affected by the loss. Grief requires careful understanding on a person-by-person basis; it is not a word that can be taken as a simple explanation of what is being experienced and why.

Furthermore, grief is not the only possible response to bereavement. There may be anger or indifference, for example. Some individuals show what psychiatrists term a *dissociative flight* from the impact of death—a pattern of denial that can become so extreme that it forms the core of a psychotic reaction. Some people clearly recognize their loss but appear unable or unwilling to grieve. We cannot assume, then, that a bereaved person is experiencing grief at a particular time. Nevertheless, the grief response is so frequent and so painful that it is of primary importance for those who wish to understand and comfort the bereaved.

There is a classic description of the physical symptoms of acute grief:

> The picture shown by people in acute grief is remarkably uniform. Common to all is the following syndrome: sensations of somatic distress occurring in waves lasting from 20 minutes to an hour at a time, a feeling of tightness in the throat, choking with shortness of breath, need for sighing, an empty feeling in the abdomen, lack of muscular power, and an intensive subjective distress described as tension or pain. (Lindemann, 1944, p. 145)

Other symptoms also commonly seen were insomnia, failures of memory, absentmindedness, problems in concentrating, and the tendency to do the same things over and over again.

This classic description by psychiatrist Eric Lindemann should be seen in context. He was working with people who had been stunned by the sudden death of loved ones in the Cocoanut Grove fire (in Boston, 1942) in which 400 people perished in less than fifteen minutes and others died later of severe burns and smoke inhalation. Subsequent experience indicates that the total symptom picture seen by Lindemann may not be expressed by every person who has an acute grief reaction, but his description still conveys a vivid sense of what it is like to be overwhelmed by grief and continues to be the most widely quoted source.

Grief affects all spheres of life. A grieving person's body doesn't work very well. Many clinicians and researchers believe that the physical side of grief is so severe that it can properly be considered a disease process. This concept was first advanced by George Engel (1963), who suggested that an intensive or sustained grief reaction can precipitate serious illness, even death, in bereaved individuals who have underlying physical problems. Current theory and research continues to provide support for considering grief to be a physical disorder as well as a personal crisis (Averill & Nunley, 1993). It is the whole person who grieves, and this person is part of a network of interpersonal relationships. Grieving, then, takes place both within and between people, and it shows its effects in all spheres.

Neuroendocrine Changes in Grief

The grief experience operates as a stressor. The biochemical and physiological concomitants of grief place additional strain on the weak links in a bereaved person's physical systems, with the particular type of somatic reaction that develops depending on the particular weak link or defect that preexisted in the bereaved (Kim & Jacobs, 1993). Individuals differ in how they deal with loss psychologically. These differences in cognitive, behavioral, and relational responses influence the neuroendocrine system's response to the stress of grief. In all likelihood, our psychological and neuroendocrine responses to stress are always influencing each other.

Each response to the loss can itself contribute to further distress. For example, if we become withdrawn and inactive, we might become more vulnerable to opportunistic infections because of lowered body tone. Furthermore, new problems continue to arise as a survivor attempts to adjust to an altered life situation. The homeostatic mechanisms of the body continue to try to moderate the stress as the event of bereavement is followed by a period of active grieving. This protective response can result in *adaptation to chronic stress*. It is possible, then, for the protective response of the neuroendocrine system to contribute to a new form of homeostasis, one that assumes the continued existence of stress. Some grief responses become increasingly difficult to "get over" because our central nervous system has dedicated itself so effectively to moderating the effect of the stress. In other words, survivors may have to deal with their physiological response to stress, as well as the stress itself.

Abnormalities in neuroendrocrine functioning have been found among some grieving people. For example, the production of cortisol seems to be increased in people who experience persistently high levels of separation anxiety. The chronic stress of grief seems to stimulate the neuroendocrine system on an intermittent basis. This on-and-off pattern of stimulation might lead to health problems if the grief response continues unabated. There is still much to learn about the relationship between neuroendocrine activity during the grief process and long-term health effects.

We are not alone in responding physiologically as well as psychologically to the stress of separation. Infant monkeys show significant immunological and other physiological changes when they are separated from their mothers for even a short time. Laudenslager, Boccia, & Reite (1993) have made additional observations that could improve our understanding of the human response to loss as well. These researchers noticed, for example, that the behavior shown by the young monkeys was closely related to the magnitude of the physiological changes taking place within their bodies. The infant monkeys who were most agitated, slouching, and withdrawn were also those whose immune systems were most affected by the stress of separation. However, when the mother and infant were reunited, the young monkeys' immune systems returned to normal. (It would be interesting to know what was happening to the mother's immune system during this time as well!)

Furthermore, the young monkeys showed less behavioral and physiological stress during maternal separation if they were kept in a familiar environment and could see their peers. Familiar surroundings seem to have some value in buffering the effects of the loss experience. From other studies, it has also been found that when the young of various species have had a history of being held and petted, they are somewhat less vulnerable to the effects of stress, and they seem to have a more effective immune system. Monkeys as well as humans, experience both behavioral and physiological stress when separated from their "significant others"—and monkeys as well as humans can cope with this stress more successfully when provided with social support before and during the grief process.

Physical aspects of distress can be intensified by what a person does or fails to do in response to the loss. Going without proper nutrition and rest and general neglect of self-care is a dysfunctional pattern that sometimes accompanies the grief syndrome described by Lindemann and others. Both behavioral and physiological responses to the stress of loss, then, can place the bereaved person at heightened risk. And just how high is this risk? Are grieving people themselves at special risk for death? We will be considering this question later in the chapter.

Personal Responses to the Stress of Grief

The mind of a grieving person may not work as well as usual. Problems with attention, concentration, and memory increase the person's risk to self and others. A person who usually is alert and responsible becomes an inattentive driver, a parent who fails to notice household hazards, or a worker who becomes careless on the job. It is the emotional side of grief that often besets the survivor with the greatest distress, however. The person may be tossed between opposite extremes of reaction.

> When I got home from the morgue, I was just out for the rest of the day. I just couldn't help myself. I thought I would have a nervous breakdown, and my heart was going so fast. The man at the morgue said, "Well, if you don't stop crying, you're going to have a nervous breakdown." But all I could do was cry. That's all I could do. And I told him, "If I don't cry, God, my heart will burst."

I had to cry, because he wasn't going to be back no more. (Glick, Weiss, & Parkes, 1974, p. 17)

This woman had just found herself transformed from wife to widow. She first experienced shock, could not feel or think at all. And then she could not stop herself from feeling and crying. She feared for her self-control, even for her sanity. People in acute grief sometimes feel that they are "going crazy," that they will keep "getting worse and worse and then just fall all apart." People who have previously experienced such intense grief and have since found their way back can be very helpful to those who are in the midst of such experiences.

Distress does not end with the first wave of shock and grief. It is not enough to realize that a loved one is dead. One now faces the further realization that life is supposed to go on. Depending on the individual and the situation at the time of the death, there may be further waves of confusion, anxiety, rage, and other painful inner states. The sense of numbness can also return, sometimes to linger as though it would never go away.

That grief can return in wave after wave of distress was discovered in an important study of nineteenth century American diaries. Paul C. Rosenblatt (1983) found that recurring experiences of grief were common to the bereaved. A period of time would go by in which thoughts and feelings turned to other matters. Suddenly the memories would come flooding back, sometimes as painful as ever. People who felt they had recovered completely from the pangs of grief might be engulfed in a wave of distress months or years later. Some of the diary entries expressed a more profound sense of grief years after the loss than they had at the time.

> I think of Ma so much, & the horror of her taking never leaves me. Why should that condition come to her. Why should she keep it secret so long. What would have prevented it. (1983, p. 23)

This entry was written two and one-half years after the death of this man's wife. He had expressed no sense of grief for her in some time.

Many occasions could renew the sense of grief:

> I think of Henry every time I sit at table and see his place is vacant.

[Sitting again] in our old pew, I could not help thinking of my dear parents and before I could stop myself was crying bitterly. (1983, p. 27)

Anniversaries, places that rekindle a memory, and people who remind us of the lost person, all have the power to start a new wave of grief long after the death. Grief, then, is not only a formidable emotional state, but one that may return at various times. Most people seem to recover well from their first intense grief episode. The vulnerability often remains, although subsequent episodes are likely to be much briefer—an image, a sudden pang, a catch of the breath, a readiness to weep… and then, after a pause, a going on with life.

Mourning: A Signal of Distress

Mourning is the culturally patterned expression of the bereaved person's thoughts and feelings. Bereavement is a universal experience. No society, ancient or contemporary, has been spared the loss of people it valued, loved, and depended on. The ways people express their loss are not universal, however. These expressions vary somewhat from culture to culture and also change over time, as we will see.

From World War I to the Gulf War and Columbine High School

Geoffrey Gorer (1977) observed striking changes in mourning behavior within the same culture during his own lifetime. When his father died aboard the *Lusitania,* capsized by a torpedo in 1915, his mother became "a tragic, almost a frightening figure in the full panoply of widow's weeds and unrelieved black, a crepe veil shrouding her…so that she was visibly withdrawn from the world." But within a few months the death toll from World War I had become visibly represented throughout all of England: "Widows in mourning became increasingly frequent in the streets, so that Mother no longer stood out in the crowd." Eventually, signs of mourning were modified, reduced. Too many people were being touched too closely by death. The functioning of society as a whole would have been impaired had every bereaved person pursued every step of the traditional mourning ritual, which included a long period of withdrawal from everyday life. The previous tradition of mourning maintained its place so long as death was occasional; a new pattern had to be de-

veloped when death was rampant in everybody's neighborhood almost all the time.

Sometimes individual bereavement and grief come across clearly even in a complex and diversified society such as the United States. The gold star in the window of many a home in the United States during World War II indicated that a very particular life had been lost. But that particular death represented part of a national, shared cause. Each "gold star mother" had her special bereavement, but collectively they signified a loss felt by the entire nation. Where are the gold star mothers for Americans who died in Vietnam? Acknowledgment, sympathy, and support for families grieving for loved ones killed in Vietnam have been much less in evidence than they were in most previous military engagements (but see the delayed response in the form of the Vietnam Memorial Wall, *Chapter 12*). By the time American armed forces had withdrawn from Vietnam, the war had lost much of its sense of being a national, shared cause.

The Gulf War produced another type of mourning response. Death was notably absent from the messages about the Gulf War that reached viewers and readers in the United States (Umberson & Henderson, 1992). Smart bombs "serviced" their targets, while not-so-smart bombs resulted in "collateral damage." The attempt to eliminate images of death from Gulf War reports may have contributed to the public's difficulty in mourning those who died on all sides of the conflict. It was a little different with Kosovo. The remarkable absence of U.S. combat casualties throughout the military operation in Kosovo spared families grief and mourning, although not the anxiety of separation. The psychological distance between attack and result in air strikes, along with NATO's efforts to prevent civilian casualties, also served as insulation. The fantasy of a war without (obvious) death was shattered repeatedly, however, as video reports documented both the atrocities committed by Serbian forces against the civilian population of Kosovo and NATO's own lethal errors. Grief and mourning perhaps take on a different form when an expectation or illusion of safety has been destroyed.

The Oklahoma City bombing aroused both sorrow and anger throughout the general public. *Spontaneous memorializations (see Chapter 12)* occurred soon after the mass deaths and on the an-

NATO troops inspect the site of a mass civilian grave in a Kosovo village. It was estimated that 160 boys and men had been killed here, but their bodies were removed as NATO troops approached.

niversaries of the attack. However, there has also been an intense privatization of the experience. Many of the rescuers are still trying to deal with the personal impact of their experiences, with little support either from their organizations (most often firefighting agencies) or society at large. There are few, if any, modalities available to them for expressing their thoughts and feelings through accepted mourning practices.

Two suicides occurred among friends of Columbine High School shooting victims. The most recent was a basketball star who hanged himself in his garage as a CD played repeatedly, "I'm too depressed to go on." His grief proved much more intense than his outward signs of mourning.

There are also occasions when the death of a prominent and respected person is expressed through forms of general mourning. The flag stands at half mast. The train bearing the coffin rumbles slowly across the nation, observed by silent crowds. The city swarms with people as the old leader who for so long has been a part of the national identity (e.g., Churchill, deGaulle, Franco) is given a historic funeral. Millions of people may focus their eyes and thoughts on the funeral of a celebrated person whose death seemed to come much too soon, as with Princess Diana (*see Chapter 12*).

Culturally Varied Patterns of Mourning

Mourning occurs on a smaller and more personal scale for most of us in private life. Still, the ways in which we express the recognition of death reflect the attitudes and customs of society.

Nations with populations as varied as that of the United States offer many patterns of mourning—compare those of Americans of African, Chinese, Korean, Japanese, Italian, or Central European-Jewish heritage, for example. Furthermore, traditions of mourning are subject to change, some more rapidly than others. For example, in the closing years of the twentieth century, many people were either been uprooted from their native lands or had chosen to move elsewhere in search of opportunities for an improved quality of life. As part of this overall change in life circumstances, people are likely to experience new sources of stress along with the challenge of acculturation. One of the outcomes may be the need to modify their traditional expressions of mourning. This challenge can be illustrated by comparing the mourning practices of the Hmong in their homelands with the practices of those relocated to the United States.

Hmong Mourning Practices in Laos and in the United States

The Hmong people have been known to history for almost 5,000 years. Those who selected Laos as their home became involved in that nation's violent political upheavals during the 1960s. Many fled in fear for their lives in the mid-1970s, and of these refugees, about 120,000 relocated in the United States.

Hmong mourning practices are closely related to their religious beliefs. This belief system holds that a spiritual world coexists with the physical world. A newborn infant is under the care of spirit-parents before its birth and must therefore be inducted into the world of the living through an appropriate ritual. Ancestor-spirits are among the many types of spirits that interact with the world of living people. These spirits can either help or harm the living. It is important, therefore, to show all possible respect to the dead. Failure to treat the dead with respect could lead to adverse effects on the health and prosperity of surviving family members. Specific funeral and mourning practices differ because the Hmong, like many other people, have become somewhat diversified over the course of their history.

In Laos and other Hmong homelands, the process of showing respect for a deceased person through funeral and mourning practices is com-

plex and elaborate. We can begin to appreciate the significance attached to appropriate mourning by focusing on the large number of helpers required. Bliatout (1993) has identified the following types of helpers who must be available:

- *Guide to the spirit world.* This person will recite the *Qhuab Ke* verses from memory. Included in this recitation must be a mention of every place in which the deceased lived. Unless this recitation is offered, the deceased will not know that he or she has died, and also will not be able to find his or her way back to the place of birth. It is crucial to return to one's birthplace because the placenta has been buried there and is needed if the soul is to make it safely back to the spirit world.
- *Reed pipe player and drummer.* Usually two musicians are required. Their music verifies the fact that a death has occurred and provides safe passage to the soul of the deceased from one world to the other. The performance makes great demands on the stamina of the musicians, and the instruments themselves are sacred. Mourning has not properly started without this music.
- *Counselor to the family.* An elder is selected to sing comforting traditional songs to the family on the evening before the funeral.
- *Counselor to the dead.* Only deceased elders receive this special attention, in which texts are recited to help the soul on its journey between the world of the living and the world of ancestral spirits. Funeral, safe passage, and mourning rituals are more elaborate in general for elders than for younger members of the society.
- *Funeral director and an assistant.* These two serve mainly as coordinators to make sure that all tasks are being carried out properly by others.
- *Shoemaker.* This person constructs special shoes from woven hemp. "These special shoes turn up at the toe; without them, the souls will be unable to cross the big river, walk the treacherous paths, step over valleys of snakes…and arrive at the spirit world" (1993, p. 87).
- *Stretcher-maker.* This person creates a symbolic horse from bamboo thatch and two long wooden poles. The deceased will lie on this pallet for several days until the burial.

- *Geomancer* (a kind of shaman) discovers the best time for the burial to take place.
- *Food server.* This person is specially trained to communicate with the souls of the deceased.
- *Warrior.* The warrior shoots arrows or fires his gun in the air and engages in other rituals to help protect the deceased on his or her journey.
- *Coffin makers.* They must locate just the right tree to cut down and use. There must be no metal in the coffin, or any material other than the specific wood required.
- *Sacrificial ox slayers.* They must choose the right ox or oxen for this purpose. A whole day may be devoted to rituals associated with the sacrifices.

This list of helpers is incomplete, but the point has surely been made. For Hmong living in their homelands, the death of a family member cannot be mourned appropriately unless the funeral process involves many people carrying out specified roles with specified materials in specified ways. The funeral and mourning processes blend all along the way. And the process is an extensive one: for example, the Thirteenth Day End ritual must be performed after that amount of time has passed since the burial. On this occasion the soul is finally released from its body and is free to journey to the spirit world. In the meantime, nobody works at normal tasks other than food preparation and other basic life support activities.

What happens when Hmong relocate to the United States? As you can easily imagine, a great many problems arise. Following is a sampling of the problems that Bliatout has identified:

- *The American medical system urges or require autopsies in some cases.* "This is considered one of the most horrible things that can happen to a Hmong person, as it is believed that the person will be born mutilated in the next life" (1993, p. 96).
- *Often there is no opportunity for the Hmong to wash, dress, lay out the body themselves, or provide the symbolic (stretcher) horse.* This can lead to fears that one is not serving the deceased properly and therefore interfere significantly with the grieving and mourning process.
- *The reed pipes and funeral drum may not be allowed because they might disturb the neighbors!*

Again, mourners may fear that they are jeopardizing the safety of the deceased soul as well as their own lives because of this failure to honor and protect their dead. The sacrifice of oxen, the firing of guns, and other traditional rituals are also likely to be banned or to become impractical in their new environment.

- *Some Hmongs convert to Christianity and adopt lifestyles associated with our industrial-technical, mass media culture.* This can lead to a rift within and between Hmong families which, in turn, is likely to interfere with their established patterns of communal mourning.

The Hmong story—still in the process of transition—has many other parallels in our pluralistic society. Few if any ethnic/racial traditions of mourning are immune from influence and challenge.

Appreciating Universality and Diversity in the Response to Bereavement: An African American Example

The core experience of grief is much the same throughout the world. Expressions of mourning, however, may be specific to a particular culture. It is therefore possible for people in one culture to conclude that people elsewhere do not feel deeply when they are bereaved, when the fact is that the others simply express their grief differently. The mistaken assumption that life is cheap in Asia, for example, has been fostered by misinterpretations of culturally expressed modes of mourning. Our difficulties in comprehending what another person is experiencing when bereaved often are compounded by cultural differences, but our own culture has also displayed a lack of understanding about what the bereaved person goes through.

Pulitzer Prize–winning poet and novelist Alice Walker has described some of her own experiences that help to illuminate both what is universal and what is distinctive about a particular culture's response to grief. In a book written primarily for children—*To Hell with Dying*—Walker tells of her love for an old man by the name of Mr. Sweet. He was not the usual type of elderly person who would be invited to be the main character in a children's story: "Mr. Sweet was a diabetic and an alcoholic and a guitar player and lived down the road from us on a neglected cotton farm" (Walker, 1988, p. 1). Nevertheless, he was a continual source of delight and instruction for Walker and her older brothers and sisters. One of Mr. Sweet's specialties was dying. He seemed very close to death on several occasions but was rescued by the Walker children who, on a signal from their father, would "come crowding around the bed and throw themselves on the covers, and whoever was the smallest at the time would kiss him all over his wrinkled brown face and begin to tickle him so that he would laugh all down in his stomach, and his mustache, which was long and sort of straggly, would shake like Spanish moss and was also that color" (1988, p. 3).

As told by the adult Alice Walker, Mr. Sweet had long ago learned that the careers he wanted for himself—doctor, lawyer, or sailor—were at that time out of reach for a poor African American boy. In this sense, he might have been living in grief all his life, having lost his childhood vision of an exciting and rewarding career. However, he had in fact developed a very individualistic career of bringing joy to the children in his rural neighborhood. Alice Walker, belonging to a new generation, moved away for the college education that eventually contributed to her notable career as a writer. And, using these writing skills, she has given us a portrait of love and grief during a period of time in American history when many people of African heritage were denied equal access to opportunity, while others were crossing into the mainstream, though not without stress and pain.

The smiles and tears of *To Hell with Dying* have universal resonance—but the *particulars* of the experiences shared by Mr. Sweet and the Walker family reflect the unique patterns of life in a rural African American community during a recent period of our own society. An outsider, for example, would have no way of knowing that the old guitar in a young woman's hands was a tangible expression of both loss and continuity, grief and love.

How do Africans cope with grief and mourning when they are in their homelands? There are as many answers as there are varied heritages, but an instructive example comes from the Yoruba of western Nigeria. A culture with a long history

and firm identity, the Yoruba include about twenty-five million people in Nigeria, with about another five million in other nations, including the United States (Adamolekun, in press). There is a strong tradition of support for people in mourning. Even the salutations or greetings that one person gives to another play a role in this support system. Every person in mourning is greeted by other members of the community with expressions of concern, support, and encouragement. These expressions are specific to the kind of bereavement experienced (e.g., a spouse, parent, or child), how the death occurred (e.g., long illness or sudden accident) and the age, gender, and situation of the mourning person. This careful differentiation of message makes it clear that the society is aware of the distinctive loss. All of the salutations acknowledge the pain of the loss, and many congratulate the mourner for having the courage to bear up under this sorrow. An example of making the salutation relevant to the mourner's specific situation is the reminder to take good care of oneself in order to meet obligations for the family.

> This is more pertinent when a young widow is so overwhelmed with her grief that she feels she were dead or even tries to harm herself physically. Other survivors, like brothers, sisters, cousins, and nephews are sometimes prevented, through some phrases, from hurting themselves. This is more so when death is sudden and the deceased is in the prime of life. (In press)

The Yoruba response clearly shows that the community is aware of the grieving person's loss, recognizes the sorrow and stress, and encourages the person to go on with life. This supportive, communitywide support is seldom evident in the United States and other urbanized, technologically driven nations, where there is little patience with the mourning process.

Perhaps you have a cherished possession that reminds you of a person who is no longer with you. And perhaps, like those of Alice Walker, the memories represented by this object or picture help to nourish your sense of personal identity across the years of your life. Getting rid of Mr. Sweet's old guitar might seem like a good idea—we wouldn't have to look at it and have our sorrows rekindled. But this might also deprive us of a precious link to the past and to those who have meant much to us. And perhaps you agree that it is both more natural and more helpful to acknowledge the mourner's grief directly rather than avoid the subject or, even worse, avoid the person.

THEORETICAL PERSPECTIVES ON GRIEF

It is mainly grief that will concern us throughout the remainder of this chapter. Bereavement is a significant event in the life of the survivors, and mourning is a significant process of interaction between survivors and their society. Grief, however, is the major source of emotional distress for individuals and can lead to both long-term dysfunction and increased risk of death. Theoretical perspectives on grief can help us to make sense out of the sometimes puzzling responses and outcomes that can be observed in the wake of a death. Theory might also guide us in making more precise and sensitive observations. Most important, a sound understanding of grief can contribute much to efforts intended to help survivors cope with their losses.

The Griefwork Theory

For most of this century, one theoretical perspective has dominated the thinking of service providers, researchers and educators. The *griefwork theory* was introduced by Sigmund Freud (1919/1957) following the mass death and bereavement of World War I. Freud was shaken to discover that nations priding themselves on their highly cultivated civilization could behave so brutally toward one another. From his personal sorrows as well as his observation of widespread grief and mourning, Freud offered the following propositions:

1. *Grief is an adaptive response to loss.* It is not just an expression of emotional pain. Grief is also a kind of work that must be performed. Our "pay" for this work is the restoration of our own peace of mind and social competence.

2. *The work of grief is difficult and time consuming.* We cannot take a few days off and pick up normal life as though the loss had not occurred. Both the bereaved person and society should appreciate this fact. Demanding that one's self or others should quickly snap back to the earlier pattern of life can only be stressful and increase the difficulties in carrying out griefwork.

3. *The basic goal of griefwork is to accept the reality of the death and thereby liberate oneself from the strong attachment to the "lost object."* Some people make strong emotional investments in each other, for example, parent and child, husband and wife. Freud used the term *cathexis* in discussing these vital interpersonal bonds. We must somehow recover the emotional investment we made in the deceased person so that we can reinvest it in other relationships and values. How do we go about the detachment (*decathexis*) process? We must accept the fact that the loved one is really and truly lost to us. We cannot keep clinging to memory, hope, or fantasy. This acceptance must be accomplished on a deep emotional level; it is not enough to have only an intellectual acknowledgment of the loss.

4. *Griefwork is carried out through a long series of confrontations with the reality of the loss.* Survivors must deal with all of the feelings, memories, and daily life encounters that bring to mind their attachment to the deceased person. Often they must confront the same point of attachment over and over again. For example, a survivor might have to listen repeatedly to a particular song that was a favorite of the deceased person before this song loses its power to overwhelm him or her with anxiety and sorrow.

5. *The process is complicated by the survivor's resistance to letting go of the attachment.* We want to stay in touch with the "lost object" in any way we can. The need to hold on to the attachment tends to sabotage our efforts to accept the loss and return to normal life.

6. *The failure of griefwork results in continued misery and dysfunction.* Time itself does not heal. In fact, we do not reenter the mainstream of time until we have liberated ourselves from attachment to the deceased person. Survivors who remain intensely attached to the deceased person over a prolonged period of time are considered to be suffering from *pathological grief*. (It was once thought that grief should

be resolved within the first year of bereavement; most observers now are more flexible in their expectations.)

Freud's griefwork theory filled a major gap at the time that it appeared. Through the centuries poets, dramatists, novelists, artists, and composers had recognized grief as a central component of the human condition. It was not until the griefwork theory, however, that the sociobehavioral sciences had a conceptualization that took grief seriously, described some of its main characteristics, and offered guidance for helpful interventions. Whether or not one is convinced by the griefwork theory, it deserves much credit for encouraging sensitive attention to the experiences of bereaved people.

Interpersonal Applications of Griefwork Theory

Freud's original theory emphasized the intrapsychic response to loss—how we attempt to deal with our own thoughts and feelings. Some later contributors have called more attention to the interpersonal context of griefwork: how a loss affects our relationships. John Bowlby and Colin Murray Parkes stand out for the quality of their research and the heuristic value of their observations.

Bowlby (1969, 1973, 1980) offers a broad framework for understanding both attachment and loss. The current interest in attachment behavior and bonding owes much to his investigations. Bowlby makes a strong connection between the biological need for survival and the phenomena of grief and mourning. Both animal and human behavior provide him with many examples. The vulnerable young of many species exhibit distress and attempt to draw their absent mother to their side by whatever sounds and other communication signals they may have in their repertoire. The mother also seeks her missing young by calling or signaling to them. Neither the young nor the mother can relax until they have rejoined each other.

Adults also show the need for attachment when there is danger afoot. For example, citing a study of baboons, Bowlby notes that "not only infants but adults also when under stress are strongly disposed to cling to a companion. Thus

an adult female, when alarmed, clings to the back of her husband or is embraced by him. Conversely, when he is under stress during a fight, a male is likely to embrace one of his wives.... The persistence into adult life of patterns of behaviour seen first and at greatest intensity during infancy is found, then, to be a regular species of the behavioral repertoire of other primate species" (1969, p. 130).

Adult grief, then, resonates with our early experiences of separation. Every dog has been a frightened puppy, every cat a stressed kitten, and every adult human an anxious baby. We have all had the anxiety of separation experiences in our life histories, even if these were but fleeting episodes. The depressive state of a bereaved spouse has its precedent in the infant who felt abandoned and vulnerable. The feeling that "I can't live without you" may have its roots in the sense of vulnerability and anxiety that also accompanies separation between parent-young and mate-mate in many other species.

Why is griefwork so difficult for many survivors? Bowlby's answer is provided through his general theory of *attachment behavior*. The goal of attachment behavior is to maintain the security provided by a significant interpersonal relationship. Any situation that seems to threaten this bond will call forth:

> action designed to preserve it; and the greater the danger of loss appears to be, the more intense and varied are the actions elicited to prevent it. In such circumstances all the most powerful forms of attachment behaviour become activated—clinging, crying and perhaps angry coercion. This is the phase of protest and one of acute physiological stress and emotional distress. *When these actions are successful the bond is restored, the activities cease, and the states of stress and distress are alleviated.* (1980, p. 42)

I have added italics to the last sentence because here is a valuable insight for understanding the intensity and persistence of grief responses. In some situations, our response to a threatened loss of relationship proves effective. We communicate our concern, we prepare ourselves for effort and struggle, we put ourselves on full alert. However, when it is death that separates us from a loved person, none of our efforts prevail. The persistent absence of the deceased person may be accompanied by persistent stress. What is the survivor to do when efforts to restore the relationship by yearning, remembering, crying, praying, and raging have failed? The survivor may keep trying and trying:

> Evidence shows that, at perhaps increasingly long intervals, the effort to restore the bond is renewed: the pangs of grief and perhaps an urge to search are then experienced afresh. This means that the person's attachment behaviour is remaining constantly primed.... The condition of the organism is then one of chronic stress and is experienced as one of chronic distress. At intervals, moreover, both stress and distress are likely again to become acute. (1980, p. 42)

This description is consistent with ongoing research into neuroendocrine responses to the stress of bereavement. Our response to the stress of loss may itself become the source of continuing stress. Griefwork is so difficult because it must overcome our strong tendency to try to restore the lost love object through fantasies and emotions. We need patience and persistence—and some help from our understanding friends.

Parkes' contributions focus directly on the interpersonal dimensions of bereavement, grief, and mourning. He has conducted some of the most important studies of the *psychosocial transitions* involved in coping with the loss of a loved person. How do people attempt to get on with their lives among other people after bereavement? And under what conditions does griefwork fail, leaving the survivor in a state of prolonged social and personal dysfunction? These are examples of the questions that Parkes has been trying to answer. From his many observations Parkes has identified three basic components of griefwork:

- *Preoccupation with thoughts of the deceased person.* This represents a continuing search process (reminding us of the attachment-seeking signals and behaviors described by Bowlby in many species).
- *Repeatedly going over the loss experience in one's mind.* This is a painful process in which the survivor seems to be testing out the reality of the loss (did this terrible thing really happen?).

- *Attempts to explain the loss.* It is somewhat easier to accept the reality of a death and get on with one's own life if the loss somehow makes sense, had a reason behind it. During this part of the griefwork process the survivor is asking self and others "Why, why, *why?*" (Parkes, 1972)

Evaluation of the Griefwork Theory

The griefwork theory has offered valuable insights and stimulated useful research. There is little doubt that our understanding of grief has been enriched by the contributions of Freud, Bowlby, Parkes and others who have cultivated this approach. Nevertheless, there is also reason to believe that the griefwork theory has its limits.

Margaret Stroebe, a leading researcher of grief responses, has recently challenged griefwork theory: "Not only is there very little scientific evidence on the griefwork hypothesis, but studies that bear on the issue yield contradictory results" (1992–1993, p. 23). In other words, clinicians, researchers, and educators (as well as the media) may have accepted the griefwork theory prematurely and without adequate examination. "Taken as a whole, the empirical evidence...does not back the strong claims made by theorists and clinicians in favor of the griefwork hypothesis. There are insufficient studies; there are methodological shortcomings; and there are inconsistent findings. Overall...the griefwork hypothesis has neither been confirmed nor disconfirmed empirically" (1992–1993, p. 27).

Stroebe and her colleagues have been contributing important findings from their own study of recovery from conjugal (spousal) bereavement. The widows and widowers were contacted several times over a two-year period. "Working through grief seems to further adjustment for some, but not all bereaved persons" (1992–1993, p. 28). Many people had not devoted themselves to griefwork, yet were functioning well and free of depression. This outcome seems to question the proposition that it is absolutely essential to detach oneself from emotional bonding to the deceased person through a long, difficult, and painful process.

Nevertheless, the absence of griefwork was related to adjustment problems for some individuals—mostly widowers who attempted to distract themselves from the loss. In light of these findings, it would be useful to give more attention to individual differences in personality and coping styles. A recent review of the literature affirmed that "Apparently, not all bereaved persons need to express themselves in the same way or share the same experiences in order to manage the difficulties of this highly stressful process" (Lund & Caserta, 1997–1998, p. 288). There are also marked cultural differences. As Stroebe points out, bereaved people in Bali are expected to distract themselves and participate in cheerful interactions, while those in Egypt are encouraged to share their pain and sorrow with others. Quite possibly there is more than one way to cope effectively with the loss and stress of bereavement, with both personality style and sociocultural expectations having their influence.

Other Theoretical Approaches to Understanding Grief

There are now alternatives to the long-dominating griefwork theory. Most of these approaches have been suggested by counselors and therapists as a result of their clinical observations. Each emphasizes certain aspects of the total grief-and-recovery process, and all have been subjected to systematic research. We do not have adequate evidence to conclude that any one of these approaches is the most accurate, comprehensive, or useful. Nevertheless, each offers something useful to think about as we try to understand the grief process.

Task Theories

A person must accomplish certain tasks to move through the grief experience and return to a meaningful, satisfying, and effectively functioning life. This premise is the foundation for theories offered by Eric Lindemann (1944), William Worden (1991) and Teresa Rando (1992–1993). The tasks identified by each of these writers are shown in Table 11-1. I have taken the liberty of using the same words to summarize their theories when they mean essentially the same thing.

You will notice that the Lindemann and Worden theories remain very much under the influence of Freud's griefwork approach. Rando, however, is more in line with Straube's observations. For Rando, the grieving person does not have to set aside attachments to the deceased to quite the extent recommended by Lindemann and Worden. Rando's basic message might be stated: "We can still keep a cherished memory of our relationship with the lost person while we remake our lives and cultivate other relationships and activities."

We might want to notice something else about all of the task theories:

- They import the attitudes of middle-class, achievement-oriented society into the grief

TABLE 11-1

Three Task Theories of the Grief Process

Lindemann	Worden	Rando
1. Accept the loss.	Accept the loss.	Accept the loss.
2. Work through the pain.	Work through the pain.	React to the separation.
3.	Adjust to life without the person who has died.	Remember and reexperience the lost person and relationship.
4.	Place the lost person in the past.	Give up the attachment to the lost person & the life that used to be.
5.		Move into the new life but remember the old.
6.		Reinvest emotions and energies in other relationships & activities.

process. What is life? A series of tasks to be completed. What is grieving? The same. This is a culturally shaped viewpoint, so it may feel plausible and appropriate when applied to those who share this belief system. But one does not have to think of either living or grieving as tasks, no matter how familiar this idea might be.

- The theories are prescriptive. They emphasize what we *should* do. The theorists are all expert observers whose writings promote understanding of the grief process. Nevertheless, the descriptive and the prescriptive are mixed and can be difficult to disentangle.

Stage Theories

The Kübler-Ross (1969) stage theory of dying has also been applied frequently to grieving. Several other stage or phase theories have been identified by DeSpelder and Strickland (1996). All of the theorists specify that the first response to bereavement is shock, numbness, and disbelief. All specify the reestablishment of physical and mental balance as the final phase. They differ in their descriptions of the middle phases of the grief process as well as in the number of phases involved.

It is clear that many grieving people experience some of the feelings and attempt some of the coping strategies included in the various stage theories. It is not clear, however, that everybody in fact does go through all of these stages or under what conditions reintegration either is established or fails to be established. Like the task theorists, the stage theorists provide useful observations and guidelines but have not yet come up with independently verified models of the grief process. Unfortunately, few studies have been conducted to test the validity of these theories.

An Integrated Individual-Family Model

A recently proposed theory has taken a fresh and promising approach. Nancy L. Moos (1995) emphasizes the importance of family dynamics. In most circumstances, the grieving person is part of a family. The interaction patterns among the individuals in the family may be as important as,

or even more important than, the "tasks" or "stages" that occupy individuals.

Moos has provided a useful comparison of individual and family symptoms of grief (Table 11-2).

The individual symptoms are familiar in grief research and are taken into account in all theories. However, less attention has been given to interaction processes within the family. Moos focus on changes in communication patterns within the family and between the family and outsiders. For example, there is some evidence that family members who usually communicate with each other in *dyads* (pairs) may have difficulty in maintaining this interactive pattern when caught up in their grief. The emotional bond among family members can be threatened as individuals retreat into their own distress or form relationships with others outside the family.

Moos' interactive model of grief is worth serious attention by service providers, educators, and therapists. At the very least, she has reminded us that we respond to bereavement as families and communities as well as individuals.

HOW DO PEOPLE RECOVER FROM GRIEF?

We have already seen that there are more ways than one to cope with the stress and loss of bereavement. In this section, we explore these patterns in somewhat more detail. First we consider what has been learned about the death of a spouse. Next we will turn to responses to the death of children, and then to the grief and death of elderly adults and to survivors of traumatic or stigmatized death. Finally, we will complete our examination of the impact of grief by looking at the most extreme outcome: death of the bereaved person.

When a Spouse Dies

Most people experience emotional pain when a person close to them dies. The death also leaves an empty place in their lives and alters their responsibilities and sources of support. How do people cope with this situation? We will draw primarily from the results of two important studies. The first is the classic Harvard Bereavement

TABLE 11-2
Individual and Family Symptoms of Grief

Symptoms of Individual Grief	Symptoms of Family Grief
Somatic (Physical)	*Communication*
• Tightness in throat	• Noticeable increase or decrease in communication
• Shortness of breath	• Particular types of communication increase or decrease
• Disturbed sleep patterns	• Changes in patterns of communication, i.e., who talks to whom and in what way
• Loss of energy	• Reconnection or cutoff of certain family members
• Changes in appetite	
Intrapsychic	*Structural*
• Numbness, disorientation	• Confusion in family hierarchy
• Sadness, depression	• Dyads becoming triads
• Anger, fear, depression	• Role confusion
• Anxiety, guilt	• Acting out of members
Behavioral	*Extrafamily Relationships*
• Crying	• Isolation
• Loss of interest	• Withdrawal from friends/support network
• Restlessness/hostile outbursts	• Overprotection of members

Adapted from: Moos, 1995.

Study, the second a valuable new study directed by Morton Lieberman (1996).

The Harvard Bereavement Study

The Harvard Bereavement Study provides an empirical foundation for understanding the experiences of those who have lost a spouse through death. The material presented here is drawn from *The First Year of Bereavement,* by Ira Glick, Robert Weiss, and C. Murray Parkes (1974), and from Parkes and Weiss's (1983) follow-up study, *Recovery from Bereavement.* The participants were forty-nine widows and nineteen widowers, none of whom were more than 45 years old. They were first interviewed while they were still newly bereaved.

The Immediate Impact of Bereavement

Most women who had been expecting their husbands' deaths felt that they had been grieving *before* the event actually came to pass. This is a phenomenon that Lindemann calls *anticipatory grief,* which has been discussed increasingly in the past few years (e.g., Rando, 1989). Often a

woman expressed relief that her husband's long period of suffering had ended. However, the anticipatory grief did not eliminate the impact of the actual death; the wife felt pained and desolate when the end did come. Those who found themselves suddenly transformed into widows tended to suffer more intensively, however. They felt overwhelmed, anguished, as though there were no limits to the catastrophe that had befallen them. A newly and suddenly bereaved woman might feel so numb that she feared she would never again move, act, or think, or she might cry as though she would never be able to stop. Both states might alternate in the same person soon after she had learned the news. Although these reactions were not limited to the women who experienced sudden bereavement, usually they were more intense under these circumstances. Many subsequent studies have confirmed that sudden bereavement is especially stressful to the survivors.

Husbands who became widowers usually responded to the impact of the death very much as widows did. The men differed, however, in the ways interpreted their feelings and related the death to their entire life patterns. Although the women often emphasized a sense of abandonment, the men reported feeling a sort of *dismemberment*. The women would speak of being left alone, deprived of a comforting and protecting person. The men were more likely to feel "like both my arms were being cut off." The authors suggest that these different emphases are related to what marriage had meant for widow and widower. Marriage had sustained the man's capacity to work. For the woman, marriage had provided a sphere of interpersonal engagement. This meant that the newly widowed woman could more readily find some expression of her interpersonal needs by going to work, whereas the man was more likely to become disorganized in his existing work patterns.

Emotional and Physical Reactions Soon after Bereavement

Bewilderment and despair often continued beyond the first impact of loss. There were still periods of weeping, although widowers were more apt than widows to feel choked up rather than to express themselves through tears. Many physical symptoms appeared and sometimes lingered for weeks or months. Aches and pains, poor appetite, loss of stamina, headaches, dizziness, and menstrual irregularities were reported by many widows. Sleep disturbances were especially common and distressful. A widow would go to bed hoping to forget her cares for a while and to wake up the next morning with more energy and a brighter outlook. Often, however, she would wake up instead in the middle of the night and remain tormented by grief and the reality of her partner's absence. Instead of offering temporary relief from sorrow, the night often held anxieties of its own. Some women tried to knock themselves out by working hard and staying up late. Others turned to sleeping medications. The dread and emptiness of facing the night alone were relieved for some of the bereaved by having close friends or relatives who could listen to them and keep them company until sleep finally took over.

Most of the widows tried hard to maintain emotional control. This was a difficult effort. Often the newly bereaved woman would long for somebody else to take over and organize life for her. Although some widows expressed this need

directly, most attempted to resist it. The typical widow doubted her ability to meet the challenges but still assumed a stance of responsibility and competence. Each woman had to find her own balance between the desire to receive help and the fear of becoming dependent on others. Most women avoided a state of general collapse during the first few weeks after bereavement. However, some had increasing difficulty later. Delayed stress reactions were not rare.

The widowers were more likely than the widows to be uncomfortable with direct emotional expression of their distress. The typical widower attempted to maintain control over his feelings because he considered it unmanly, a weakness, to let go. The men also tended to emphasize realism. Such statements as "It's not fair!" were seldom made by men, although fairly often by women. The men seemed to require more rational justification for their reactions to bereavement. Although less troubled by anger than the widow, the widower did have difficulty with guilt. He was more likely to blame himself. "I wasn't sensitive enough to her," "I should have made things easier." When a wife died during childbirth, the widower sometimes felt guilty about his responsibility for the pregnancy. The widower's guilt reaction, however, tended to subside fairly soon, although the need for rational control over all responses to the death persisted.

Leave-Taking Ceremonies

The realities of daily life continue during the process of grief and recuperation. One of the major demands of the period soon after bereavement is the necessity to bid farewell to the lost spouse through some type of funeral process. The leave-taking ceremonies went well for most of the bereaved in this study. They often found it helpful to hear from others that they had done their part to ensure a proper farewell. This bolstered their sense of confidence in managing difficult affairs despite their shock and suffering. The widows were usually seen as the central and responsible individuals even though they were provided with significant assistance. The widow was seen by all as the final authority on what should be done, regardless of different wishes that, for example, the husband's family might have. In this way, the widow began to gain public acceptance as the new head of the family, a transition not usually involved when the bereaved person was the husband.

"These ceremonies were of great emotional importance for all respondents; there was nothing of empty ritual in widows' participation" (Glick et al., 1974, p. 102). The widows often felt that in arranging the ceremonies, they were able to continue the expression of their love, devotion, and attachment. "And those widows who felt their marriages had been only too deficient in these respects saw in the ceremonies of leave-taking a last chance to repair the lack" (p. 201).

Widows usually saw funeral directors as supportive and caring people rather than as obtrusive businessmen. Nevertheless, there were painful moments despite the support available. Some widows suddenly felt the full pangs of their late husband's death at a particular point during the funeral process, such as the last viewing of the body. The funeral emphasized the reality of the death, cutting through the haze of unreality in which many of the newly bereaved functioned despite their outward control and competence. The complete realization of the death, however, did not seem to dawn upon the bereaved at any one moment in time, although some of the moments were critical steps toward this realization.

The role of the clergy in the leave-taking ceremonies was not as prominent as might have been expected, at least from the widow's perspective. Most widows seemed to be operating on very limited emotional energy. They neither sought out nor took in what the clergy might have had to say. Understandably, the widows tended to be absorbed in their own feelings. Many of the widows were religious, however, and seemed to find some comfort in the clergy's repetitions of traditional beliefs about the continuation of soul or spirit after death.

The leave-taking ceremonies did not seem to be quite as important to most of the widowers in this study. They gave less attention to the details and did not express as much gratitude toward funeral directors. They were also more likely to feel that the cost of the funeral was too high. The emotional significance of the funeral itself may have been relatively less important for the men because they were primarily concerned with how they would manage in the months to come.

The funeral and all that it involved was something that they had to "get through" rather than the milestone it represented for many widows. These differences of emphasis should not obscure the fact that the leave-taking ceremonies were important to all of the bereaved, whether men or women.

Grief and Recovery: The First Year

And after the funeral? The study found what many have observed in their own lives: the long months after the funeral often seem to be the most difficult ones for both widow and widower. For a short time there is concentrated attention upon the needs of the bereaved. But the deceased spouse remains dead and the bereaved person's emotional and pragmatic problems continue day after day.

The Widows' Response

The widows in this study were left with the realization that they had to reorganize their lives, but now they lacked the clustering of help that had been available to them in the first days after bereavement. Most did not show much mourning behavior during this period, but they continued to grieve almost constantly. Typically, they withdrew somewhat from ordinary social life to signify their mourning status but seldom did anything conspicuous to emphasize it. The widows seemed to feel that they should not burden others with their sorrow. They felt that a "decent" amount of time had to pass before they could re-enter ordinary life and yet did not feel comfortable with a full-blown expression of mourning such as is customary in some societies.

Feelings of sorrow and anxiety remained intense even though the widows no longer spoke of their grief. Many engaged in *obsessional reviews*. Events surrounding the husband's death were relived over and over. The women often realized that this process was taking up much of their time and energy. They wanted to turn off the obsessional review but often could not do so. As Glick and his colleagues suggest, the "worry work" of obsessional review may help a survivor to integrate the realities of her loss into her ongoing life. Mulling over the death, in other words, is a component of griefwork. And, as we have seen from Stroebe's recent studies, griefwork seems helpful to some survivors.

The obsessional reviews described in this study often were concerned with what *might* have happened instead of what actually did happen. How could the accident have been avoided? How might it all have turned out differently? In this way, the review provided an outlet for temporary escape through fantasy but came back with renewed realization that there was in reality no way to undo the past. Additionally, the widows frequently searched for meaning through these reviews. *Why* had their husband been taken away? It was not the name of the disease or the technical reason for the accident that concerned the widow, but the need to make sense of the death. If "Why *me*?" is the question some people ask when they learn of their own terminal illness, "Why *him*?" seems to be the survivor's parallel question. These questions often lost some of their intensity, but the question of meaning continued to linger. There was no evidence that persuasive answers were found by the bereaved, at least within the time period encompassed by this study.

Frequently the widows were immersed in memories of their husbands. These were usually comforting thoughts. Although it remained painful to review the events leading up to the death, memories of the husband himself and of shared experiences generally were positive. This was especially true in the early weeks and months. A tendency to *idealize* the lost spouse was observed here, as it has been in many other studies. The deceased husband was the best man who ever lived, a wonderful husband, a marvelous father—he had no faults whatsoever. Later a more balanced view usually emerged. The widow would still think about him frequently and positively, but now some of his quirks and imperfections gained recognition as well.

Surges of anger—sometimes very intense—occasionally broke in between the early tendency to idealize and the later, more balanced view. For example, the widow might find herself suddenly angry at the husband for leaving her with the children to raise by herself. Some women then became even more upset when they caught themselves with harsh feelings toward the dead spouse and reacted with guilt or confusion. These

invasions of negative feelings into the idealized memories seemed to be part of the long process of developing a realistic attitude that the widow could live with through the years.

Often the widow's feelings about her husband went beyond vivid memories. *She might have a strong sense that he was still there with her.* This impression made itself felt soon after the death or a few weeks later. Once the widow developed the experience of her husband's presence, it was likely to remain with her off and on for a long time. This sense of remaining in the presence of a significant person who has died has been observed by many other clinicians and researchers as well (Berger, 1995; Lindstrom, 1995). The current study adds the finding that the sense of presence was especially persistent for women whose bereavement came without advance notice. The sudden loss of a spouse, allowing no opportunity for emotional preparation, seemed to lead to more extensive haunting experiences. For most of the widows, it was comforting to feel that the husband was still there somehow. But even when the sense of his presence had all the vividness of hallucination, the widow knew the difference. She knew that her husband was really dead, even though her sense of his presence was also real in its own way. It was neither unusual nor crazy for a widow to feel this sense of presence.

During the first year of the widow's bereavement, there was a gradual movement away from absorption in the loss and toward reconstruction of her life. This was not a smooth process by any means. By the end of a year, though, most of the widows had found more energy to channel into the obligations and opportunities of daily life. They might still experience episodes of anguish known only to themselves (e.g., when a situation reminded them poignantly of what they had lost). There was seldom a decisive severing of thoughts and feelings about the past. Instead, the widow continued to feel a sense of attachment to her deceased spouse but had called back enough emotional energy to cope more adequately with her current life situation.

Widows with children at home usually recognized their responsibilities clearly and felt that the need to provide parental care helped to keep them from becoming lost in their own grief. They attempted to help the children feel that the world was still a good place, that life could and would go on. Often there was a new resolve to be a good mother. These efforts were complicated by conflicting needs and values: the widows felt the need to be straightforward and realistic with the children, yet to shelter and protect them and keep their spirits up. The conflict became acute in some situations, such as in trying to tell the children what had happened to their father and why. Often unable to answer that question themselves or to keep themselves from asking it, the widows were in a difficult position in trying to provide answers to their children. That the children were at various ages and levels of cognitive development also complicated the communication process (*see Chapter 10*).

The Widowers' Response

The widowers in this study seemed to accept the reality of the death more rapidly and completely. Although the bereaved man was almost as likely to feel the presence of his wife soon after the bereavement, as time went by this phenomenon became much less common than it was for the widows. The man's need for control and realism expressed itself also in the tendency to cut off obsessional review after just a few weeks. The widower did not seem as tolerant of his impulse to dwell upon the past; he pushed himself right back to immediate realities, although, like the widow, he too felt a desire to replay the circumstances of the death.

What has often been noticed about the attitudes of men in American society showed up in the aftermath of bereavement as well. The widowers were not only control and reality oriented but also less likely to speak openly about their feelings. They did not usually seek out the opportunity to share either the events themselves or their personal reactions, although most men would respond to direct questions by the interviewers. Moreover, society responded to the widower by trying to replace some of the practical support he had received rather than providing him with an emotional outlet. Women most often were the providers of this kind of assistance.

When widows and widowers were compared at the same points in their bereavement, it usually *seemed* that the men were making a more

rapid adjustment. However, the researchers had reason to doubt that the widowers were actually recovering more rapidly. It was true that they did return more quickly to their previous roles and functions; they were also even less likely than the widows to go through a period of conspicuous mourning. The typical widower gave no outward sign of his grief. Yet a close look at the quality of the widower's personal life, including the occupational sphere, indicated a decrease in energy, competence, and satisfaction.

The widower usually made a more rapid *social* recovery but a slower *emotional* recovery than the widow. A year after his wife's death, the widower was much more likely than the widow to feel lonely and depressed.

Types of Recovery from the Impact of Marital Bereavement

People who did not have the opportunity to prepare for the spouse's death suffered more distress, not only immediately, but for some time afterward Parkes (1972). More than a year later, the spouse who had experienced sudden, unexpected bereavement was more socially withdrawn than the person who had known in advance that the spouse would die. He or she remained more preoccupied with the details of the death, had more difficulty in accepting the reality of the loss, and in general experienced more disorganization in daily life. Such a person was likely to be anxious and have a pessimistic future outlook.

The effects of bereavement are intensified by the shock of the unexpected. Furthermore, we cannot rely upon the passage of time by itself to facilitate recuperation from the trauma. Social support is needed both in the early period of acute bereavement and over the many months and even years required to adjust to the devastating loss.

Parkes also found that the response to early bereavement provides useful clues as to how the individual will respond as the months go by. *Those who were most disturbed a few weeks after the death usually were the ones who continued to be disturbed a year later.* The person who had strong feelings that the death was unreal and who tried to behave as though the spouse were still alive also was likely to have more difficulty than others over an extended time.

The death of a spouse by cancer often was associated with more rapid and less distress-ridden recovery of the survivor. This may be, as Parkes notes, because incurable cancer is a condition that provides time for both the terminally ill individual and the family to adjust to the prospect of death. (It should be understood that we are speaking here only of those people whose cancer proved fatal; it is erroneous to equate "cancer" in general with "terminal illness.")

The quality of the marital relationship influences the grief and recovery process. When the partners had very mixed feelings toward each other, the experiences associated with bereavement often were more disturbing. Similarly, it was harder for the survivor to adjust if the relationship had been based on a clinging dependence. If soon after bereavement the surviving spouse felt cast adrift, empty, and helpless because the mate was no longer around to make life run properly, difficulties in adjustment were likely to be more prolonged.

Unresolved Grief

Bereaved people who were coping well after two years had made progress in achieving a revised identity. All of the bereaved people in this study had to face the question of who they are now, having lost part of their identities with the loss of their spouses. By contrast, those still in despair had not formed a conception of the death that they found coherent and acceptable, nor were they able to modify their self-images in preparation for a new life without the husband or wife. Furthermore, they were more likely to use tranquilizers, to drink and/or smoke heavily, and to wonder whether anything in life was worthwhile. A question still remained: why do some people fall into one pattern and some into the other? Careful study of individual case histories led the investigators to the concept of *unresolved grief.* Parkes and Weiss (1983) found three syndromes, or types, of unresolved grief:

- The *unexpected grief syndrome* occurs in some people when the spouse dies without warning; therefore they do not have the opportunity to prepare themselves for the overwhelming loss.

Disbelief and intense anxiety often become not only the first but also the continued response.

- The *conflicted grief syndrome* can occur when death ends a troubled relationship, often one in which separation or divorce had been contemplated. Some of the marriages in the study involved alcoholic men whose behavior had created a climate of fear and disorder. Other marriages leading to the conflicted grief syndrome had been marked by depression and the withdrawal of the survivor. The unresolved grief experienced by survivors of a troubled marriage appears in a sense to be a continuation of the frustrations and disappointments that had characterized the relationship while the spouse was alive.

- The *chronic grief syndrome* is marked by the survivor's strong feelings of dependency. Although some distress may be experienced around the time of the death, the more compelling and lasting response is a deep sense of yearning for the lost one. Yearning for the deceased is often a part of any grief experience, but for people with this syndrome it becomes predominant. The survivor has unusually powerful dependence on the deceased spouse and does not feel personally capable of taking on the responsibilities of life with his or her partner gone.

Awareness of the nature of the marriage relationship that has been sundered by death and by the circumstances of the death itself (sudden or anticipated) could, then, improve our ability to identify those who are at particular risk for intense and prolonged distress.

Whatever the particular circumstances of the death, however, the grief process can be so disabling that the bereaved person is essentially out of commission for an extended time. Suicide attempts and severe depressive reactions requiring psychiatric treatment are among the risks. There is a need to distinguish between "normal" bereavement—enough of an ordeal itself—and responses that are exceptionally intense, debilitating, or prolonged. Most of the bereaved men and women in the Harvard study made their way through their distress without reaching extremes of despair or self-destructiveness. Similar findings have emerged from other studies. Nevertheless,

Although emotionally painful as reminder of the loss, a cemetery visit can also be a consoling way of affirming one's love.

we should not lose sight of the fact that some people do remain locked in their grief and mourning for an extended period of time, to the extent that they cannot derive satisfaction from their own lives or meet the needs of others.

Doors Close, Doors Open: The Lieberman Study

A recent in-depth study by Morton Lieberman has further illuminated the process of recovery from the death of a spouse. Lieberman and his colleagues interviewed 600 widows and 100 widowers. His findings are well expressed in the title of his book, *Doors Close, Doors Open* (1996). For

many widows and widowers, the loss of their partner both ended one phase of their life and initiated another.

This phenomenon can be seen clearly in the experiences of Andrew, a retired judge:

Right after her death, it seemed as if I went into a trance. Martha was so much a part of my life. Now it's almost six months and I'm still tortured by memories of her, particularly when I'm around the house and come across some of her personal things. All of her clothes are still in the house, as are her mementos. I keep them there to remind myself of how lucky I was to have a

woman like that.... Losing her has made me realize that there are still parts of myself that I don't
understand. (1996, p. 184)

His wife had been seriously ill for three years
prior to her death. Andrew had devoted himself
to her care and made it possible for her to stay at
home until the very end. Despite this proof of his
devotion to Martha, Andrew felt that he had
taken her too much for granted as he pursued his
career interests. Along with the regrets and the
sorrow, the new widower felt very much alone in
the world: "Martha was my best friend." A door
in his life had closed behind Andrew, separating
him from the relationship that had most enriched
and sustained him.

Andrew reached the threshold of a new door,
however, as he started to reflect seriously on the
meaning of his life, religion, and the prospect of a
hereafter. He decided to take a greater interest in
other people and their interests instead of centering so much on himself. In a sense, the loss of his
wife served as a wake-up call to Andrew. He did
not have to continue in the pattern he had followed for so many years, including traveling and
speech giving. He could study the Bible, interact
more fully with other people, and see the world
through reawakened eyes. Lieberman describes a
follow-up meeting with Andrew:

When I saw Andrew a year later, he looked much
younger than I remembered him, and his sports
coat and tie were more colorful than the grays
that had predominated.... The reasons for these
changes soon became clear: "Since we last talked,
my life has changed completely. I'm married now
to a woman named Claudia, whom I met about
nine months ago.... Not only is she attractive,
she's brilliant. I'm deliriously happy, and I've
changed totally. I got rid of all my clothes and
went out and bought all new ones. I sold my
house and all the old furniture and moved into a
new home with Claudia. I even bought a new car.
(1996, p. 185)

Andrew no longer was a traveling and speech-
giving man. He now did volunteer work at a hospice, taught Bible class to teenagers, and showed
more concern about the welfare of others than
about his own success. Interestingly, however,
his quest for meaning through looking inward
came to an end when he found Claudia and new
happiness.

People found many ways to recover from grief.
Remarriage, although gratifying to Andrew and
some others, was not necessarily the most successful move. Lieberman found that those who
remarried within the first two years of the death
did not feel any happier, any more in control of
their lives, or any higher in self-esteem than those
who remained single during that time. Individual
personalities and circumstances are of primary
importance: remarriage is an option to consider,
but not a panacea for all widowed people.

Lieberman also discovered that not all "help"
from other people was actually experienced as
helpful by a widow or widower. There are usually expectations that certain people will come
forth to provide support during this difficult period. If these people do not respond as expected
or hoped, the widowed person may feel hurt, rejected, and angry. A stranger or a human services
professional might offer potentially valuable support, but this will not "count" as much to the
widow who feels she has been let down by her
own family, friends, or colleagues. Adult children
are especially valued as sources of help by older
widows and widowers. This help includes practical
assistance, such as home maintenance, shopping,
and coping with insurance and other financial
transactions.

Lieberman's research adds strong support to
the proposition that we should attempt to understand individual patterns of response to grief
rather than relying too heavily on generalizations
about phases, stages, and tasks. Furthermore,
some people show remarkable personal growth
as they make their way through the painful process of grief recovery, while others continue to
struggle. The methods and findings of Lieberman's study (only partially described here) provide a valuable guide for further understanding.

The Family That Has Lost a Child

Losing a child to death is one of the most painful of all human experiences. The immediate anguish may be followed by many years of sorrow.
Acquaintances of grieving family members are almost certain to observe the powerful impact that

follows soon after a child's death. What others might not realize, however, is that the distress continues long beyond this acute phase and that the lives of the grieving family members may be altered in many ways.

When the emotional response to a loss remains a dominant aspect of a person's life over a long period of time, it is sometimes referred to as *chronic grief.* This is a useful descriptive term because it differentiates between the intense immediate response (*acute grief*) and responses that sometimes can persist through an extended period of time. Unfortunately, however, *chronic* is often taken to mean that a condition is unalterable and permanent. It might then seem that a family suffering prolonged grief after the death of a child is destined to remain in this painful state forever. But this is not necessarily true. There is no reason to rule out in advance the possibility that chronic grief can be relieved and the survivors once again find meaning and pleasure in life—although never forgetting their loss and never being quite the same.

Shadow Grief: Perinatal Death

The sorrow of a child's death often seems to follow a family like a shadow. After observing the reactions of mothers who had lost a baby before or soon after birth, Peppers and Knapp (1980) introduced the term *shadow grief.* Years after the death, many of the mothers were still feeling the anguish. In a later study, Knapp (1986) found the same phenomenon among parents who had lost older children to death. They were no longer completely dominated by grief, but the shadow or cloud had a way of making itself known as they moved through life. Knapp offers a description of this state of mind:

> Shadow grief does not manifest itself overtly; it does not debilitate; no effort is required to cope with it. On the surface most observers would say that the "grief work" has been accomplished. But this is not the case. Shadow grief reveals itself more in the form of an emotional "dullness," where the person is unable to respond fully and completely to outer stimulation and where normal activity is moderately inhibited. It is characterized as a dull ache in the background of one's feelings that remains fairly constant and that, un-

der certain circumstances and on certain occasions, comes bubbling to the surface, sometimes in the form of tears, sometimes not, but always accompanied by a feeling of sadness and a mild sense of anxiety. (1986, pp. 40–41)

Knapp's findings are consistent with observations that many others have made. Parents who have lost a child often feel that their own lives also changed at that moment. Furthermore, they may not want to relinquish the grief. The pain is part of the memory—and the memory is precious. Few people would choose to experience the intense anguish of acute grief. But the twinge of sorrow and the sharp but passing pain of memory may be something that both the individual and the family need to keep their lives whole (or as whole as they can be) following the loss of a child.

It is significant that shadow grief was first recognized in a study of mothers who had lost newborn infants. The death of so young a child is often given relatively little attention by society. The lack of communal recognition and support tends to leave the parents alone in their grief. Some newspapers even prohibit the publication of newborn death notices, and there are no sympathy cards on the market for this specific loss (Nichols, 1989). It is difficult to reconcile society's pattern of neglect of *perinatal death* with both the intensity of the parents' grief and the number of people who suffer such loss. The term refers to infants who die at any point from the twentieth week after conception through the first month after birth. Premature birth is still the most common cause of perinatal death, although advances in medical and nursing techniques have saved some neonates who otherwise would have died. Deaths also occur for a variety of other reasons (e.g., a genetic defect or a prenatal infection), and sometimes for reasons that are never clearly determined. We cannot exclude socioeconomic causes, either. Even in the United States—a technologically advanced society whose resources are the envy of much of the world—many pregnant women still do not have access to perinatal health services. Others do not seem to realize that such services are available and could improve the odds in favor of a healthy mother and a healthy baby.

Complications of Perinatal Grief

Grief over a perinatal death is similar in many respects to grief over any loss. There are, however, some circumstances and consequences that are more likely to be present. For example, the mother may still be sedated or exhausted at the time she learns of her child's death. She is also likely to be ready to mother her baby, both physically and emotionally. This total readiness, including lactation to provide breast milk, now has no opportunity to express itself directly. Another significant problem can arise in families that have other children. As Nichols observes:

The cliché "you have your other children" suggests that the other children are a source of comfort and perhaps could even take the place of the one who has died. Frequently nothing could be further from the truth for grieving parents. No other child replaces the one who died. Further, children can intrude upon the grief of parents simply because they are naturally being themselves. In addition, many parents do not know how to tell their children about the baby's illness or death, nor do they know how to help the children. (1989, p. 120)

Sensitive caregivers have learned that their first step is to recognize that a significant loss has occurred (or is about to occur, if the infant is still alive but not expected to survive). We can be more helpful to the parents and siblings when we ourselves comprehend the meaning of this loss. The family that has experienced perinatal death often feels misunderstood and abandoned by others.

Most bereaved parents tell us that the support they received from others at the time of the baby's death did not continue very long. They think that others do not continue to "live" their grief as they do. Others expect them to recover within a few short weeks. (Cordell & Thomas, 1997, p. 299)

Even more devastating is the experience of having more than one baby die, either during gestation or soon after. It is estimated that this happens more than twice as often among low-income African Americans than it does to whites in the United States (Guyer, Martin, MacDorman, Anderson, & Strobino, 1997). Fortunately, mothers who feel that they were treated with competence and compassion at the time of the first perinatal death may be able to cope as well as possible with a subsequent loss (Kavanaugh, in press).

Particularly effective responses have been shown by some nurses and physicians in situations when the mother and baby are still in the hospital, but the baby is almost certain to die soon. The family is encouraged to interact with the infant in a natural and loving way. Photographs may be taken of parents holding the baby, and various memorabilia (such as the child's first footprints or a lock of hair) given to them. It is encouraging to report that some physicians have taken leadership in developing "bereavement protocols" that help to prepare the entire staff to provide emotional support for family members (Weinfeld, 1990). Group counseling has also proved helpful (Cordell & Thomas, 1997).

Effects of a Child's Death on the Parents' Worldview

At whatever age it occurs, the death of a child not only brings the direct emotional pain associated with this loss, but can also unsettle the parents' overall philosophy of life. It is not unusual for religious people to wonder why God would allow such a thing to happen, and to follow this with anger or doubt. The perceived link between past, present, and future may also be disturbed. We usually expect "the next generation" to be just that. In some cultures, one of the strongest motivations for having children in the first place is to project the "family soul" ahead into future generations and thereby alleviate the parental generation's own death anxiety (Kastenbaum, 1974). If issues of this kind remain unsettled they can generate additional tension within the family, sometimes contributing to separation or divorce.

The death of a child raises questions about the parents' core assumptions regarding the nature and purpose of life. The loss and sorrow that follow the death of the child may be intensified by a crisis of belief or faith. The parents may feel that the world no longer makes sense, that there is very little that one can count upon. There is now some evidence that preserving an emotional connection with the deceased child helps to prevent the destruction of the parents' worldview. Klass (1992–1993) is among several researchers who have found that the "inner representation" of the dead child continues to be experienced by the parents for many years (perhaps throughout their lives). He defines inner representations "as characterizations or thematic memories of the deceased, and the emotional states connected with these characterizations and memories." Parents can interact with their inner representations of the child through such means as:

- *Memory:* bringing the child to mind often
- *A sense of presence:* the feeling that the child is still there with them in some way
- *Hallucinations:* the experience of seeing or hearing the child
- *Incorporation* of the characteristics or virtues of the child into their own personalities (e.g. rescuing lost animals as the child had often done)

The available findings suggest that staying in contact with the inner representation of the dead child makes it easier for the survivors to keep their worldviews intact. The sorrow and sense of loss are still there, but the feeling that something of the child still lives with or within them seems to reduce doubts about their worldviews.

We must make two important points about the inner representation of the dead child as observed by Klass and some others:

1. These symbolic interactions with the deceased are not signs of pathology—for example, it is not "crazy" to sense the child's presence or even to catch fleeting glimpses of the child. These experiences often accompany normal grief. (There are limits, of course; a person who becomes absorbed in fantasies of the deceased and cannot attend to the realities and obligations of daily life is in need of help.)
2. The positive value of continuing the relationship with the dead child seems to contradict griefwork expectations. It may be wise to refrain from either pressuring bereaved parents to detach themselves from their memories or insisting that they incessantly recall the child to mind. Individual differences should be respected.

Some mothers have not only come through the grief of perinatal death, but also become stronger persons as a result. In her study, Talbot (1998–1999) found that the hardiness of some mothers:

> seems to have been forged in the fire of agonizing grief—grief which has been consciously confronted and transformed into the gift of compassion…. They have lit a pathway to survival and personal growth: By identifying and incorporating a loved one's best characteristics, it is possible to find ways to honor the past while building a future. By understanding what has been learned from loss and grief, it is possible to reach out and help make the world a better place for self and others. (1998–1999, p. 184)

The Future of the Marital Relationship after the Death of a Child

The loss of a child creates stress and strain for the family unit as a whole. A careful review of the literature (Oliver, in press) has identified strong and common effects on the marital relationship, including the following:

- The death of a child can have serious repercussions for the bereaved couple's sexuality. Often sexual intimacy diminishes both in quality and frequency, sometimes disappearing altogether. Nevertheless, many couples report an increased need for physical contact and comfort and achieve a high degree of intimacy through hugging and holding each other.
- The parents often report feeling more irritable and more likely to direct anger at each other. This can become particularly destructive when one parent blames the other, either for the death or for past actions related to the lost child.
- Communication tends to break down for bereaved couples. It is fairly common for each person to withdraw into grief and therefore away from the other. Not only is communication reduced, but there may also be "emotional numbing or a shutdown of self-disclosure or emotional exchange via denial or intellectualization of feelings" (Oliver, in press). This is the pattern sometimes known as the *conspiracy of silence*.

- Despite these and other problems, most couples do not divorce after the death of a child or even seriously consider the possibility. However, the the research on this topic is beset with methodological difficulties.
- Available research indicates that the death of a child is catastrophic for some, but not all, marital relationships. Oliver recommends that when we encounter couples who are experiencing serious difficulties in their relationship, we might explore the possibility that the death of a child—including an aborted or stillborn infant—might be the underlying source of the distress.

The Grief of Grandparents

Grandparents and parents experience many of the same feelings of loss. In addition, grandparents also are likely to experience vicarious grief for the parents (Kastenbaum, 1987) as well as their own direct grief over the death of the child. It hurts them to realize how much their adult children are sorrowing for the death of the grandchild. Furthermore, it is even more unexpected for people to outlive their grandchildren Such an unexpected and "untimely" death can generate a worldview crisis similar to that of the parents.

White (1999) has found that the death of a grandchild causes extreme anguish, regardless of the child's age. All of the studies she reviewed found "Reactions of profound sadness, shock, disbelief, numbness, and physical symptoms" (1999, p. 156) Most of the bereaved grandparents had a strong need to talk about their grandchildren. This need could be frustrated if the family responded with withdrawal and silence, or if communication patterns between the grandparents and their adult children had previously been inadequate.

Some grandparents felt helpless because they could not protect their adult children from the pain of loss—similar, perhaps, to the frequent desire of parents to shield their young children from awareness of death and dying. Nevertheless, grandparents often provided valuable support to the bereaved parents just by being there with them, as well as by helping with chores and expenses. The overall message is clear: grandparents often are much affected by the death of a child and have a significant role to play in the family's response.

BEREAVEMENT IN LATER LIFE

We are vulnerable to bereavement at any age. We will now see that the later adult years carry an increased vulnerability but also a vitality and resilience that exceed what one might have expected.

Sorrow upon Sorrow, Loss upon Loss

Life satisfaction does not necessarily decline with age. Gerontologists have discredited the assumption that usefulness and the enjoyment of life end at a certain age. Nevertheless, it is also true that the longer a person lives and forms loving attachments, the more there is to lose. Loss may follow upon loss, taxing the individual's ability to cope. This is the concept of *bereavement overload* (Kastenbaum, 1969). A long-lived person is more likely to have survived many people to whom he or she was deeply attached. Furthermore, personally significant losses other than death can lead to grief responses. Loss of physical abilities, employment, social respect, and familiar environments are all life changes that can trigger responses similar to those that occur when an interpersonal relationship is terminated by death. We accumulate these losses just by staying alive over an extended period of time.

What changes would be expect in people *of any age* who have been forced to cope with too many losses in too short a period of time? They might try to reconstitute their personal world by replacing the losses, or they might lose themselves in work or other engrossing activities. These alternatives, however, are often closed to elders. What now? The person may simply take these emotional blows "on the chin." I am referring here to the process of developing bodily symptoms when grief cannot be handled adequately by the psychological structure. The person becomes increasingly preoccupied with bodily functions, often is in a state of discomfort, seldom has free energy to invest in new activities or relationships.

Furthermore, the experience of multiple losses may lead to a sense of extreme caution. "I had better not care about anybody or anything else. Sooner or later I will lose these people and things as well. And I just cannot bear to lose and mourn again."

The whole constellation of "old behaviors," then, can develop from multiple, unbearable bereavement. Suicide attempts, both direct and indirect, also can be generated from such a psychological state. The individual may give up when stricken by a relatively minor ailment and allow the condition to worsen or reduce his or her activities so drastically that both body and mind are in poor tone to respond to any kind of stress. Such considerations suggest that bereavement in old age is a condition deserving careful and systematic attention.

Older people are vulnerable to deaths of many kinds—not only the death of a spouse, but also of siblings, adult children, grandchildren, and even parents. I have stood at the side of a 74-year-old man as tears ran down his cheeks because his 97-year-old father was dead. An outsider might rush to the conclusion that the death of a very old parent should not mean so much to a child also advanced in years. Consider, however, how long this relationship had to develop and flourish and what a blow it now was to go on without the father he had known for three quarters of a century. Parent-child bonds may continue strongly for many decades.

It is not only the death of a human member of the family that can prove devastating. On several occasions, I have discovered that an elderly patient with whom I was working first sank into a depressed, no-point-in-living state following the death of a pet. Weisman (1990–1991) has observed that it is particularly disturbing when the owner had consented to euthanasia for his or her terminally ill companion animal. "The person-animal bond, or better, the person-pet bond, is in my opinion as authentic as any other relationship characterized by mutuality and love" (1990–1991, p. 245). What might seem to be "the depression that comes with age" can turn out to be a grief reaction to the death of an animal companion as well as to the death of a human companion.

Resilient Coping

The overall picture, however, is more positive than has usually been assumed. negative. Many elderly men and women have proven themselves quite resilient when tested by loss. Older widows and widowers were found to cope with bereavement at least as well as younger adults in major studies reported by Stroebe and Stroebe (1993), and McCrae & Costa (1993). Most of the bereaved adults in both studies showed the ability to cope with their losses in a resourceful and functional manner. Older bereaved people, as a group, were no less resilient.

Older widowed people often have effective coping abilities that help them to get on with their lives even though they regard the death of a spouse as having been the most stressful event they have ever experienced. After months of high stress after the death, many are able to restore order and hope to their lives. An additional finding is of particular interest: Practical problems of day-by-day functioning are likely to be especially difficult for older bereaved people. Assistance with home repairs, financial transactions, transportation, and other "little things" can make the difference between living independently at home or being forced into a more dependent lifestyle.

An elderly bereaved person often has a wealth of experience and skills that can not only be applied to reintegrating his or her own life, but also to enriching the lives of others. Often this person needs only positive human companionship and a little help with some of the details of everyday life to continue as a resourceful and well integrated member of society.

Grief Responses to Traumatic and Stigmatized Deaths

The *way* in which a person has died can have a significant influence on the grievers' responses. Two kinds of death modalities are especially hard on the survivors. *Traumatic* deaths are those that suddenly and unexpectedly end a life in a violent manner. These usually take the form of murder, suicide, war, accident, or natural disaster. Those who attempted to rescue Oklahoma City bombing victims were themselves traumatized by find-

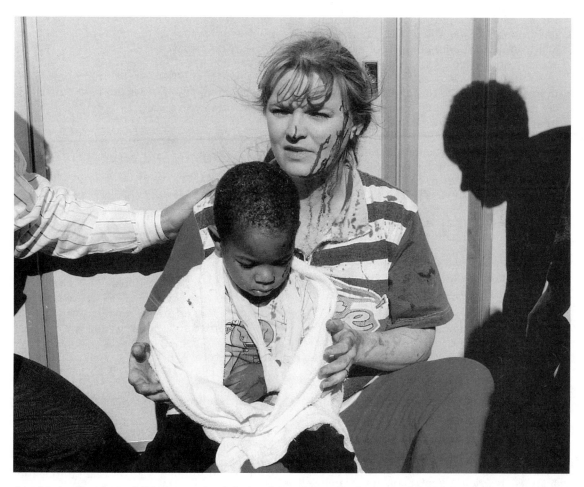

Comfort is offered to a child who survived the bombing of the Alfred E. Murrah Federal Building in Oklahoma City. Acts of violence not only take lives, but also place survivors at risk for post-traumatic stress disorder and other complicated grief reactions.

ing the shattered bodies of people who had been alive and healthy only a few minutes before the explosion. NATO troops who discovered the mass graves of civilians massacred in Kosovo were also exposed to a devastating emotional experience. All those who lost a loved one in the bombing or the massacre are likely to have grief experiences that are especially intense and complicated because of the traumatic nature of the deaths. *Stigmatized* deaths are those regarded by society as immoral, shameful, and discrediting. People whose terminal

illness is AIDS-related are more vulnerable to avoidance and criticism from society than people with most other types of terminal condition. Suicides also tend to be stigmatized forms of death that place additional burdens on the grievers.

Unfortunately, trauma sometimes is piled on trauma, for example, when a family member has been murdered. Sprang and McNeil (1995) identify the following sources of stress on family members who have already been devastated by the traumatic death:

- Family members are usually not in the communication loop—not kept well informed by police and court authorities, not consulted about their own feelings or given the opportunity to ask their own questions.
- If family members go to the courtroom, they are forced to relive the trauma repeatedly, from the perspective of both prosecution and defense.
- Defense attorneys often attack the character of the murder victim in order to deflect the blame from the accused. "Blaming the victim" can be extremely distressful to the family.
- Family members may see the accused killer for the first time and experience acute emotional upset.

The death of a drunken driver can have both traumatic and stigmatized responses in surviving family members and friends. Sprang and McNeil observe:

> Many survivor-victims (especially parents) may feel they have failed to protect their loved one from harm and may hold themselves responsible for not preventing the death. The result is increasing levels of hopelessness and helplessness that are exacerbated by the criminal justice system and by societal responses. (1995, p. 89)

To understand the grief experience, then, we must also understand personal and social responses to the particular way in which the individual died. A serious complication in the family's recovery from grief may be the impact of the death on their memory of the person who has died (Riches & Dawson, 1998). Intrusion by the media as well as the process of criminal investigation can further impair the family's abilities to construct a balanced and positive memory of the deceased person and integrate this memory into their ongoing lives.

ARE BEREAVED PEOPLE AT HIGHER RISK FOR DEATH?

There are many stories about people who die soon after the death of people who were important in their lives. Most often we hear about the widow or widower who seemed to die of grief not long after the spouse's death. The impressions we form on the basis of such reports can be misleading because of the built-in bias. For example, seldom do we tell each other about people who are doing just fine years after the death of a long-term spouse. The anecdotal reports raise important questions, but we must turn to large-scale studies for the answers.

Differential Mortality Risk: The Statistical Pattern

Most studies focus on the survivors of conjugal (spousal) bereavement. The findings for other types of bereavement are based upon fewer observations, yet seem to follow the same pattern. It is typical for studies to compare the mortality (death) rates of bereaved spouses with those of men and women of the same age whose marriages have not been terminated by death. *Mortality ratios* are calculated to represent any differences that might be found between populations of married and widowed people. It is understood, of course, that all groups will have mortality rates. When one population has the higher mortality ratio it is said to have *excessive mortality.*

What has been found? *Almost all studies have found excessive mortality rates for bereaved persons* (Stroebe & Stroebe, 1993). (The exceptions are a few studies with relatively small samples.) This pattern holds true in Europe and Japan as well as North America, and it was consistent throughout the twentieth century. (There are no adequate data to determine differential mortality in less-developed countries).

Who Is Most at Risk?

Gender and age are related to excessive mortality. Both widowers and widows are at higher risk than married men and women. The risk is even greater for widowers. The overall mortality rate is higher for males than females at every adult age level, and bereavement has the effect of further increasing the differential.

The relationship with age is not what one might have expected. Older adults have a higher mortality rate in general. However, bereavement does not introduce a disproportionately higher mortality risk for elderly adults. The tendency, in fact, is for younger adults to have a relatively higher excessive mortality rate after bereavement. The death of a spouse seems to produce a sudden rise in the mortality risk of young adults who otherwise are at relatively low risk of death.

Most at risk are young men whose wives have recently died. This risk is intensified if the death was sudden and unexpected. The bereavement-related deaths often occur within six months. These findings suggest that more attention should be given to the vulnerability of bereaved young men in the period of time immediately following the death. Lichtenberg (1990) offers his personal reflection on what a bereaved young man is likely to experience upon the sudden death of his wife. Lichtenberg survived and recovered—with the help of his friends—but remembers having felt "out of control: one moment I was torn apart, and the next moment I was calm. It was frightening to hurt, to be numb, to feel panic, and I worried that I would collapse" (1990, p. 86). We never want to forget that there is always a human story behind the statistics.

What are the Leading Causes of Death among the Bereaved?

There are two main findings to consider here. First, the leading causes of death among bereaved people are the same as those for the population in general: heart disease and cancer. Second, the chances of dying by sudden and violent means are greatly increased after bereavement.

Are these findings contradictory? Not really. Compare, for example, mortality from heart disease with mortality from suicide. Heart disease consistently has been the leading cause of death in the United States. Although suicide is also high on the list (seventh leading cause of death), the rate is much lower. The differential *rates* for heart disease and suicide are associated with marked differences in the *number of people* who die from these causes each year:

Cause	Rate	Number of Deaths
Heart Disease	289.5	720,058
Suicide	12.4	30,906

A 10 percent rise in the mortality rate for heart disease would signify that an additional 72,000

people had died from this cause in a year. A 100 percent rise in the suicide rate would signify that an additional 31,000 had died from this cause. Despite the 10-to-1 difference in this hypothetical example, the actual number of deaths from heart disease would remain much higher than the number from suicide. We need to understand the difference between rate and number of actual cases. With this understanding clear in our minds, we can now make sense of the increased mortality risks to which bereaved people are vulnerable.

The single greatest cause of excessive mortality among bereaved people is some form of heart disease, usually of a cardiovascular nature. These deaths often occur within a fairly short time of the bereavement. It has been relatively easy to establish the association between recent bereavement and increased risk of death from heart disease because we are dealing with large numbers. There is some evidence that liver cirrhosis, cancer, and infectious diseases also produce more deaths among bereaved people, but these patterns are more difficult to establish because of the lower incidence and other factors. For example, the many types of cancer may vary in their progression after the stress of bereavement and are also likely to take more time before reaching a terminal phase.

The most striking changes, however, occur with violent deaths, especially suicide. Stroebe & Stroebe conclude from their review of the literature that "enormously high suicide rates during the first week strongly suggest bereavement as the cause: the excesses found in one study were 66-fold for men and 9.6-fold for women" (1993, p. 187). As we have already seen, the total number of people who commit suicide after bereavement remains relatively small in comparison with the number who die of heart disease. Suicide, however, shows the greatest increase among all causes of death.

Most bereaved people come through their stress and sorrow in a resilient manner and are able to get on with their lives. Some people continue to struggle and may be in need of knowledgeable and caring assistance. And some become especially vulnerable to their own life-and-death crisis, whether by heart disease or suicidal ideation. People who care about other people will be sensitive to the heightened risks that may affect a person who has lost a loved one by death.

Hidden and Disenfranchised Grief

Grief may be intensified and its resolution delayed when the bereaved are denied the opportunity to express their feelings. This is the basic concern that researchers and counselors have in mind when they discuss *hidden* or *disenfranchised* grief. We may speak of a person's grief as "hidden" when it is not recognized by others because the individual has attempted to keep either the loss or the feelings about the loss to himself or herself. For example, Gail, a teacher, did not believe that she had the right to express her grief in the presence of her students:

> I knew I was heading towards a class in an hour's time. I knew that even within an hour I would not have myself pulled together enough to face the class. I mean, if you went and sat in front of a class and cried for forty minutes they would riot, because they haven't got the rapport with what is happening with you at the moment. (Rowling, 1995, p. 323)

Many other people also feel it inappropriate or forbidden to share their feelings of loss and sorrow with others. The grief may be hidden because the individual is not considered "entitled" to these feelings. In such a case, it can be said that the grief is "disenfranchised."

I have observed many examples of hidden and disenfranchised grief among nurses and other caregivers. For example, staff members of a long-term care facility may become very much attached to the people in their care. An aged woman with no living relatives may be "adopted" by a nurse who has lost her own grandparents. The caregiver may experience grief when this resident dies. However, our society does not generally acknowledge the "right" of a caregiver to grieve and mourn. The health care system in particular has long been intolerant of professionals who become "too involved" with their patients and "too upset" at their deaths. This tendency is still strong, although the emergence of the hospice movement and peer support groups is providing an alternative approach in

some settings. A bereaved nurse who is not accorded the right to grieve and mourn has to find some other way to deal with the stress. In a geriatric hospital, my colleagues and I noticed that staff members who had been emotionally close to recently deceased patients were more likely to be involved in single-car accidents and to experience a variety of illnesses requiring "sick days." These negative outcomes were sharply reduced after the staff organized peer support groups and gave each other permission to love and mourn their patients.

AIDS has brought many additional examples of disenfranchised grief. The lover-companion of a person with AIDS may not be considered "family" and therefore may be denied the right to mourn. In fact, lovers in general have often been excluded from supportive interactions because their relationship to the deceased person was not that of spouse, parent, child, or sibling. Social attitudes do change, however, and there is increasing recognition that lovers have both the need and the right to mourn. Unfortunately, though, professional support for nurses and other caregivers who work with AIDS patients is still not adequate (Demmer, in press).

Hidden and disenfranchised grief take many other forms. We have already noted that parents of stillborn babies often have been forced to keep their grief to themselves. The sorrow of losing a companion animal has also been excluded from serious consideration by society in many instances. Fortunately, there is growing awareness that authentic grief can occur in both instances and deserves society's recognition and compassion.

Lavin brings one of the most neglected forms of hidden grief to our attention in discussing the situation of the bereaved person who is developmentally disabled:

> If they have been sheltered all their lives, they may face the death of a loved one unprepared. Often parents shield their normal children from death and are reluctant to include them in the rites of mourning, keeping them away from wakes and funerals. There is a greater tendency for the parents of the developmentally disabled to continue the shielding process longer. Thus the disabled…may be denied access to mourning

rituals…and therefore are not exposed to role models who show them how to cope effectively with loss (1989, p. 231).

In both private homes and institutions, developmentally disabled people tend to be deprived of the opportunity to learn how to express and cope with their grief. Unfortunately, society may also persist in its assumption that the developmentally disabled are incapable of experiencing the loss, sorrow, and stress of bereavement. Adequate comfort and support may not be forthcoming because, in society's eyes, the grief does not exist. In an opening quotation, we read the words of a mother whose developmentally disabled child had died (Milo, 1997). The mother's grief was real and intense, even though other people might have assumed that this death could not have been so important.

You are likely to encounter other types of hidden and disenfranchised grief as you go through life—in others or in yourself. Awareness that a person is attempting to cope with unexpressed sorrow and loss is the first step to sharing this burden and opening the way for recovery.

LIMITED SUPPORT FOR THE BEREAVED

A widower is reducing his colleagues' anxieties when he goes right back to work and gives no indication that he expects special concern. "I am OK," he is saying in effect, "I am not mourning." A widow releases others from the more obvious forms of obligation by refraining from displays of mourning. "She's a strong woman," her friends say with admiration. A bereaved person among us tends to be more socially acceptable if signs of mourning are set aside. But the absence of mourning behaviors too easily gives the illusion that the person is "over" the grief reaction. This may be one of the reasons that some bereaved people have fears of going crazy. All of the anxiety and confusion, the depths of feeling, seem to be on the inside. The rest of the world continues to move along in its usual way. With little social recognition or tolerance for grieving, the individual can be made to feel as though his or her responses were abnormal or pathological.

American Society's Discomfort with Grief and Mourning

One test of how well a culture's death system is functioning can be made by examining the support it provides for the bereaved. There are some signs that American society does not pass this test, although there are also signs of improvement through peer support groups and death education. The men in the Harvard Bereavement Study did little to show the world that they were suffering the impact of a spouse's death. This seems to be in keeping with a mass, efficiency-oriented society. Mourning gets in the way. It may not seem to serve any real purpose. Pressures have been increasing against the expression of loss in many forms. There are still places in the United States where people will stop what they are doing when a funeral procession goes by, pedestrians standing in respectful silence and motorists waiting patiently, whether or not they know the identity of the deceased. But the funeral procession is a target of efficiency practitioners in many metropolitan areas. Abolition or restriction of this practice has been urged because it slows traffic. Similarly, there are pressures against the use of land for cemeteries. In some parts of the United States it is now almost impossible to open new cemeteries, and existing cemeteries have been criticized as wasteful and out of step with the times.

Memorialization of the dead and support for the bereaved have fallen relatively low on the list of priorities of the American death system. People still gather around for the funeral—often with reluctance—and for a short period of ritual and visiting. After that, however, the bereaved are frequently left alone. How long do colleagues sympathize with somebody who has suffered a significant loss? How long are relatives and neighbors prepared to be sensitive and supportive? I have noticed an increasing impatience with grief. Mourners are supposed to shape up after a short time and let others get on with their lives. In this cultural context, it is not surprising to come across a doctoral dissertation (DiMeo, 1978) featuring a "prescribed degrieving intervention method (DIM)" that requires but a single treatment session! DIM, indeed! Quicker is cheaper, better, more cost effective. But are we

The procession of mourners demonstrates not only individual grief, but also the resolve of society to go on with life after a death.

really prepared to line up for "degriefing" when overcome by profound sorrow and loss?

Time for Grief—
But Not Much Time

The potential conflict between the individual's need and society's demands can express itself in the practical question: "How much time should a person be allowed to grieve before returning to work?" We live in a society that emphasizes time rather relentlessly. The invention of the clock made it possible to measure time precisely and divide it into units of standard length. The Catholic Church was quick to use the clock to reinforce the discipline of monastery life. The belfry clock symbolized the subordination of the individual to higher authority. The subsequent rise of industrialization and science resulted in the further refinement of time and the heightened

general emphasis on schedules and deadlines (O'Malley, 1990). Soon we had "efficiency experts" who measured workers' effectiveness in carrying out a specified task and then tried to find ways to increase productivity per unit of time. Charlie Chaplin's experience with the wonderful new feeding machine in his classic film *Modern Times* illustrates the depersonalizing effects of industrialized time. An often bitter and sometimes violent succession of labor-management confrontations was required before the workday and workweek were reduced to their present dimensions. We still are influenced by our heritage of conflict regarding "company time" and "personal time."

What does all of this have to do with death? Sociologist Lois Pratt (1981) studied "grief by negotiation" in 40 large companies and has also compiled information from more than 600 other companies. She found that management had once granted bereavement leave as a matter of judgment and discretion. The new trend, however, is to specify bereavement leave as part of the formal agreements between management and labor. This means that the amount of time off a person is allowed for bereavement depends largely on the monetary value computed for this time. Pratt reports, "Although bereavement leave is a minor cost item in the overall benefits structure, it is handled in the same way as all benefits—within a cost framework" (1981, p. 322).

And what happens within this "cost framework" when there is a death in the family? The grieving survivor has distinctive personal feelings about the loss and may also have distinctive responsibilities to perform in the immediate period after the death. These personal matters, however, do not figure into the union-management agreement. What does count is the monetary equivalent of the time to which the survivor is entitled. And so we now have an answer to our question: *it is acceptable to grieve for three days after the death of specified people.* The standard policy is for leave to begin after the death, not while the dying person is still alive. "Sorry Dad—I'll be back when you're dead." Some contracts have become very specific about the arrangements. For example, if the death occurs on a Saturday, be back to work on Tuesday. It may be a better plan for the death to occur on Tuesday; then the survivor is not expected back until the next Monday. Our personal reaction is anything but brief and standardized, so a wedge is driven between the public recognition of bereavement and the private experience of grief.

Perhaps even more crucial is the question of whom an employee is entitled to mourn. A person who was very important to us might not be on the list of those for whom a full three-day leave is granted. We then may join the ranks of those with hidden or disenfranchised grief. There are signs that bereavement leave provisions are becoming a little more flexible to take into account the changing configuration of interpersonal relationships in our society. The family leave and medical care bill signed into law in 1996 is another step in the right direction, although mourning is still "processed" through the bureaucracy. More recent is an encouraging trend to provide counseling and more flexible

support to bereaved employees—though this is still the exception.

Perhaps our impatience with grief is one of the reasons that so much attention is given to the question of how long grief is supposed to endure. It is one of the questions most frequently raised by the public and bruited about by professionals. The sense of chronic time urgency that characterizes the type A personality also seems to characterize much of American society in general. We are reluctant to pause for death, and thinking about the dead is regarded as a waste of time.

American society's withdrawal of support from the bereaved represents a break from most historical traditions. Some religious and ethnic groups maintain a sense of closeness, of reconfirming bonds with each other. This may even include a legitimized relationship with the dead (as in Hmong society). The survivors may have prayers to say, offerings to make, vigils to keep. Within such a context, there is time and opportunity for personal grief to find expression in a socially approved form. The newly dead person can remain important during a critical period of psychological adjustment to the loss. The bereaved need not pretend that the funeral marks the end of the relationship with the parent, spouse, sibling, child, or friend. It is possible to have thoughts and feelings about the deceased, even to sense the presence vividly, without violating social norms. In this sense, societies that have functioned with less technological sophistication often have embodied more insights into the psychological needs of the bereaved. As a society, Americans may be uncomfortable with the seeming irrationality or inefficiency of grief. If so, this says rather more about dominant values in the United States than about the realities of core human experience.

MEANINGFUL HELP FOR BEREAVED PEOPLE

Society is coming to realize that we can help each other through our times of grief. One person who has contributed much to this encouraging development is Phyllis Silverman, founder of the Widow-to-Widow Program. Silverman's *Omega* interview (Kastenbaum, 1997) reveals many of the conceptual and practical issues that had to be resolved in establishing this pioneering peer support program.

Widow-to-Widow: The Phyllis Silverman Interview

There were no peer support programs to deal with bereavement, grief, and mourning when Silverman was completing her doctoral studies at Harvard. It was thought that grief was a kind of illness that had to run its course. Did Silverman accept this medical model?

> When we talk of grief as illness, we make it sound like a foreign or alien object that has invaded our bodies and which we must in some way expunge, as, for example, a wound that heals after the scab falls off, or a cold that must run its course. With the "proper treatment" we can make it go away. With this model we maintain a sense of ourselves as machines.... We get no sense of context, of the complexity of an experience, and of its fullness.

Silverman observed grief to be a central fact of human existence, not simply an illness from which we hope to recover.

> Grief shapes our experiences and who we are.... We can't get through life without having such experiences all the time. We grow, mature, meet people, leave people. People, living or dead, are part of who and what we are.... We don't "get over" people. We live in a web of relationships. We are still connected to the dead.... Because my father died, I haven't stopped being his daughter. When someone important dies we are changed by this loss. Our lives will never be the same.... The self we knew with that other person is gone. We need to reorganize, find a place for this relationship, and develop other selves.

Silverman does not agree with one of the major assumptions of griefwork theory, namely, that we must detach ourselves from the deceased in order to get on with our lives. She does agree, however, that grieving is work, and very hard work at that. In fact, one of her first research findings was that grief did not simply fade away after a brief period of crisis. Public health specialists at the time were endorsing a crisis theory of mental health and illness. With skillful professional intervention, the crisis should be resolved within about two weeks (well in keeping with our society's expectations for a "quick fix" to grief and anything else that ails us).

When I first offered this view to the widowed women I was working with—they laughed at me! They said that if you had your act together in two years—so that your head felt screwed on, so you could look ahead—you were lucky! The more I talked with the widowed, the more I realized that our models of grief were not correct.

Silverman eventually came up with a different model and with a different approach to helping bereaved people. This model includes the following principles:

- *Grief does not have a final outcome.* Bereavement leads to a series of changes over many years. "People grow, gain new perspective on who they are, and learn how to deal more resourcefully with their own feelings and with other people."
- *Grief can most usefully be regarded as a life transition.* Although bereavement does produce a crisis and grief does have significant physiological aspects, it is basically a human experience that alters one's relationship to self and others. Life does go on, but it goes on somewhat differently.
- *People can help each other.* One does not necessarily have to turn to professional assistance, although this may be indicated in some circumstances. Peer support—such as widows comforting each other—can be highly effective. Furthermore, when people with similar problems help each other, they do not thereby become "patients" who are dependent on the medical system. Support should also come from family members. "A network of social support is needed, and this support should include family members. There are usually several mourners in the death of a spouse, and they need each other to share their feelings about the deceased, to remember together, and to support each other as they acknowledge their pain and loss. They need friends to help with the concrete tasks of living and managing their family from the time before the funeral to the establishment of a lifestyle appropriate to their new situation."

Silverman introduced the Widow-to-Widow Program at a time when neither professional grief counselors nor other peer support groups had yet appeared. The program was very successful and was soon replicated throughout much of the nation. A variety of other peer support groups have since emerged, e.g., The Compassionate Friends who help parents who have lost a child through death (Klass, 1993). Silverman thinks of peer support as "the first line of defense. Most of us get through major crises in our lives with help from our friends." When people with similar problems help each other, all discover that they are not alone and all are in a position to learn valuable coping skills from each other.

Although many people seem to have found comfort in peer support groups of various types, there are hazards here as well. Julie Wambach (1983) also conducted a series of participant-observer contacts with self-help bereavement groups. She observed a rigid and constrictive philosophy that assumed widows should go through a sequence of stages of mourning in a prescribed time period. This rigid timetable and the concept of stages had no adequate basis in fact. Many widows felt pressured by the timetable and rigid expectations. Discrimination against the older widows was also observed. As Wambach notes, there are probably many important differences in the nature and functioning of self-help bereavement groups, so a reasonable degree of caution is recommended. Even the best of ideas can go wrong.

Helpful and Unhelpful Responses to a Bereaved Person

Not everything that we communicate to bereaved people is helpful. A study (Range et al., 1992) obtained ratings (from "most helpful to "least helpful" on a five-point scale) for a number of statements often made to bereaved people. The statements rated most and least helpful are shown in Table 11-3.

As you can see, the most appreciated statements were those that expressed the individual's commitment to being there for them. (The first two statements were by far the most favorably rated.) Asking specific questions or reminding them of specific sources of distress (e.g., "It was

TABLE 11-3

Five Most and Least Helpful Statements to Bereaved People

Most Helpful	Least Helpful
"I'm here if you need somebody to talk to."	"Didn't the funeral home do a good job?"
"If there is anything I can do, please let me know."	"Did you know this was going to happen?"
"Put your faith in God."	"Was he/she in much pain?"
"Tell me how you are feeling."	"It's okay to be angry at God."
"He/she will always be alive in your memories."	"It was so sudden!"

Source: Range et al., (1992): 25–32.

so sudden!") were comments that bereaved people felt they could do without. We should not generalize too much from one study, but it does suggest that we should have our own thoughts and feelings in order before we volunteer such statements. There is one question in particular that perhaps we should ask ourselves: "Is my message intended to comfort the bereaved person or control my own anxiety?"

Professional Help

Professional help has become more widely available in recent years. A number of counselors now have special training and experience with grieving people. When the response to bereavement is especially painful, debilitating, or prolonged, it is clear that sensitive professional intervention can be useful. One source of information is the Association for Death Education and Counseling: 638 Prospect Avenue, Hartford, CT 06105–4298; (203) 586–7503; fax: (203) 586–7550.

The importance of *timely* emotional support is underscored by the results of the Harvard Bereavement Study. Parkes and Weiss (1983) identify the need for improved sensitivity in breaking the news when death occurs unexpectedly and for being available to the bereaved person both immediately and for an extended time period. A suicide attempt and other extreme responses are sometimes real possibilities. Therefore Parkes and Weiss suggest:

> A contract for ending therapy should be drawn up and agreed to. From the very beginning, the patient should be aware that the aim of therapy is the achievement of autonomy.... Inevitably, the dependent patient will have a hard time after therapy has ended and may need brief help from another therapist at this time. It may sound strange to suggest that one should use psychotherapy to treat the end of psychotherapy but a short-term intervention of this kind may well help someone get through the severe grief that can follow termination of a therapy on which he or she has become heavily dependent. (1983, p. 256)

Timely emotional support can sometimes be offered at a much earlier point, when a person realizes that a loved one is terminally ill. It is not unusual to experience "anticipatory grief" while the friend or family member is still alive. There may be an impulse to devote much attention and feeling to the person while he or she is still with us, but at the same time an impulse to begin the process of distancing ourselves and becoming accustomed to life without our companion. Sensitive friends and caregivers can help the individual balance the conflicting emotional states and attitudes that are likely to arise during grief in advance of the loss.

Many useful publications are available for your further reading on recovery from grief, with or without professional assistance. These include books by Conner (1996), Klass, Silverman, & Nickman, (1996), Selder et al. (1997), and Worden (1991). Some helpful videos are identified in the appendix.

SUMMARY

A person important to us dies. This loss is known as *bereavement*. We experience a shifting mix of feelings including anxiety, anger, and confusion. This condition is known as *grief*. We express our bereavement and loss to other in ways that are culturally patterned. This is known as *mourning*. In this chapter, we have seen that grief does not necessarily run its course in a year or any other fixed period of time. Instead, each indi-

vidual and family has its own pattern of response and recovery that depends much on the nature of the death and the survivors' own general patterns of coping with stress and loss. Grief is more than an emotional state: it also is accompanied by the body's response to stress, especially in the neuroendocrine system. The health and even the survival of the survivors can be endangered by a severe or prolonged stress reaction.

There are marked cultural differences in the way people have learned to respond to a death, and these differences are represented in the diverse U.S. population as well as in other societies, as we have seen through numerous examples. In attempting to understand how people cope with loss, many counselors have turned to Freud's griefwork theory, which emphasizes the long and arduous process toward accepting the reality of the death and liberating oneself from the emotional pull of the deceased. More recent counselors and researchers suggest that it is not necessary to cast off the lost loved one; instead one can reconstruct the relationship and keep it going in a revised and more adaptive way. We have also seen that people differ considerably in the ways in which they recover—or fail to recover—from bereavement. Gender differences and the way in which the person died (e.g., suddenly, or with time to prepare for the loss) are among the important influencing factors, as is the nature of the relationship between the deceased person and the survivor.

Particular attention was given to grief and recovery when the deceased person is a child or spouse, as well as bereavement among grandparents and other elderly people. The limited support given to bereaved people in the United States was a subject of concern, and suggestions were offered for providing support to the bereaved people in our own lives.

REFERENCES

Adamolekun, K. (in press). Bereavement salutations among the Yorubas of Western Nigeria. *Omega, Journal of Death and Dying*.

Averill, J. R., & Nunley, E. P. (1993). Grief as an emotion and as a disease: A social-constructionist perspective. In M. S. Stroebe, W. Stroebe, & R. O. Hansson (Eds.), *Handbook of bereavement* (pp. 77–90). London & New York: Cambridge University Press.

Berger, A. S. (1995). Quoth the raven: Bereavement and the paranormal. *Omega, Journal of Death and Dying, 31,* 1–10.

Berlinsky, I., & Biller, E. (1982). *Parental death and psychological development.* Lexington, MA: Lexington Books.

Bliatout, B. T. (1993). Hmong death customs: Traditional and acculturated. In D. P. Irish, K. F. Lundquist, & V. J. Nelsen (Eds.), *Ethnic variations in dying, death, and grief.* (pp. 79–100). Washington, DC: Taylor & Francis.

Bowlby, J. (1969) *Attachment.* New York: Basic Books.

Bowlby, J. (1973) *Separation.* New York: Basic Books.

Bowlby, J. (1980) *Loss.* New York: Basic Books.

Bowling, A., & Windsor, J. (1995). Death after widow(er)hood: An analysis of mortality rates up to 13 years after bereavement. *Omega, Journal of Death and Dying, 31,* 35–50.

Bozeman, J. C. (1999). A journey through grief: An analysis of an adult child's grief in the loss of a mother. *Illness, crisis, and loss, 7,* 91–99.

Colp, R., Jr., (1975). The evolution of Charles Darwin's thoughts about death. *Journal of Thanatology, 3,* 191–206.

Conner, P. (1996). *Letting go: The grief experience.* Carrolton, GA: AUM Productions.

Cordell, A. S., & Thomas, N. (1997). Perinatal loss: intensity and duration of emotional recovery. *Omega, Journal of Death and Dying, 35,* 297–308.

De Frain, J., Martens, L., Stork, J., & Stork, W. (1990–1991). The psychological effects of a still-birth on surviving family members. *Omega, Journal of Death and Dying, 22,* 81–108.

Demmer, C. (in press). Death-related experience and professional support among nursing staff in AIDS care facilities. *Omega, Journal of Death and Dying.*

Despaulder, L. A., & Strickland, A. L. (1996). *The last dance.* Mountain View, CA: Mayfield.

DiMeo, V. V. (1978). Mourning and melancholia: A prescribed degriefing intervention method (DIM) for the reduction of depression and/or belated grief. Unpublished doctoral dissertation, United States International University, San Diego, CA.

Engel, G. L. (1963). A unified theory of health and disease. In D. Ingele (Ed.), *Life and disease* (pp. 7–24). New York: Basic Books, Inc.

Freud, S. (1959). Mourning and melancholia. *Collected papers,* (Vol. 4). New York: Basic Books, Inc. (Original work published 1919)

Furman, E. F. (1974). *A child's parent dies.* New Haven: Yale University Press.

Glick, L. O., Weiss, R. S., & Parkes, C. M. (1974). *The first year of bereavement.* New York: John Wiley & Sons.

Gorer, G. D. (1977). *Grief and mourning.* New York: Arno Press.

Guyer, B., Martin, J. A., MacDorman, M. F., Anderson, R. N., & Strobino, D. M. (1997). Annual summary of vital statistics—1996. *Pediatrics, 100,* 905–918.

Kastenbaum, R. (1969). Death and bereavement in later life. In A. H. Kutscher (Ed.), *Death and bereavement* (pp. 27–54). Springfield, IL: Charles C. Thomas.

Kastenbaum, R. (1974). Fertility and the fear of death. *Journal of Social Issues, 30* 63–78.

Kastenbaum, R. (1987). Vicarious grief: An intergenerational phenomenon? *Death Studies, 11,* 447–454.

Kastenbaum, R. (1993–1994). Phyllis R. Silverman: An *Omega* interview. *Omega, Journal of Death and Dying 28:* 251–260.

Kavanaugh, K. (1999) Recurrent perinatal loss in a low-income, African-American parent: A case study. *Omega, Journal of Death and Dying, 39,* 133–148.

Kim, K., & Jacobs, S. (1993). Neuroendocrine changes following bereavement. In M. S. Stroebe, W. Stroebe, & R. O. Hansson (Eds), *Handbook of bereavement* (pp. 143–159). London & New York: Cambridge University Press.

Klass, D. (1988). *Parental grief. Solace and resolution.* New York: Springer.

Klass, D. (1992–1993). The inner representation of the dead child and the worldviews of bereaved parents. *Omega, Journal of Death and Dying, 26,* 255–273.

Klass, D. (1993). Compassionate Friends. In R. Kastenbaum & B. K. Kastenbaum (Eds.), *Encyclopedia of death* (p. 56). Phoenix: Oryx

Klass, D., Silverman, P. R., & Nickman, S. L. (Eds.) (1996). *Continuing bonds: New understandings of grief.* Bristol, PA: Taylor & Francis.

Knapp, R. J. (1986). *Beyond endurance.* New York: Schocken.

Laudenslager, M. L., Boccia, M. L., & Reite, M. L. (1993). Consequences of loss in nonhuman primates: Individual differences. In M. S. Stroebe, W. Stroebe, & R. G. Hansson (Eds.) *Handbook of Bereavement* (pp. 129–142). Cambridge: Cambridge University Press.

Lavin, C. (1989). Disenfranchised grief and the developmentally disabled. In K. J. Doka (Ed.), *Disenfranchised grief.* (pp. 229–238. Lexington, MA: Lexington Books.

Levy, L. H., Derby, J. F., & Martinkowski, K. S. (1992). The question of who participates in bereavement research and the Bereavement Risk Index. *Omega, Journal of Death and Dying, 25,* 225–238.

Lichtenberg, P. A. (1990). Remembering Becky. *Omega, Journal of Death and Dying, 21,* 83–89.

Lieberman, M. (1996). *Doors close, doors open.* New York: C. P. Putnam's Sons.

Lindemann, E. (1944). The symptomatology and management of acute grief. *American Journal of Psychiatry, 101,* 141–148.

Lindstrom, T. C. (1995). Experiencing the presence of the dead: Discrepancies in "the sensing experiences" and their psychological concomitants. *Omega, Journal of Death and Dying, 31,* 11–22.

Lopata, H. Z. (1993). The support system of American urban widows. In M. S., Stroebe, W. Stroebe & R. O.

Hansen (Eds.), *Handbook of bereavement* (pp. 381–396). Cambridge & New York: Cambridge University Press.

Lund, D. A., & Caserta, M. S. (1997–1998). Future directions in adult bereavement research. *Omega, Journal of Death and Dying, 36,* 287–304.

McCrae, R. R., & Costa, P. T., Jr. (1993). Psychological resilience among widowed men and women: A 10-year follow-up of a national sample. In M. S. Stroebe, W. Stroebe, & R. O. Hansson (Eds.), *Handbook of bereavement* (pp. 196–207). Cambridge: Cambridge University Press.

Milo, E. M. (1997). Maternal responses to the life and death of a child with a developmental disability. *Death Studies, 21,* 443–476.

Moos, N. L. (1995). An integrative model of grief. *Death Studies, 19,* 337–364.

Nichols, I. A. (1989). Perinatal death. In K. J. Doka (Ed.), *Disenfranchised grief* (pp. 117–126) Lexington, MA: Lexington Books.

Oliver, L. (in press). Effects of a child's death on the marital relationship: A review. *Omega, Journal of Dying and Death.*

O'Malley, M. (1990). *Keeping Watch.* New York: Viking.

Parkes, C. M. (1972). *Bereavement.* New York: International Universities Press.

Parkes, C. M., & Weiss, R. S. (1983). *Recovery from bereavement.* New York: Basic Books.

Peppers, L. G. & Knapp, R. J. (1980). *Motherhood & mourning: Perinatal death.* New York, N.Y.: Praeger.

Pratt, L. (1981). Business temporal norms and bereavement behavior. *American Sociological Review, 46,* 317–333.

Rando, T. A. (1989). *Anticipatory grief.* In R. Kastenbaum & B. K. Kastenbaum (Eds.), *Encyclopedia of death* (pp. 12–15). Phoenix: Oryx,

Rando, T. A. (1992–1993). The increasing prevalence of complicated mourning: The onslaught is just beginning. *Omega, Journal of Death and Dying, 26,* 43–60.

Range, L. M., Walston, A., & Polles, P. M. (1992). Helpful and unhelpful comments after suicide, homicide, accident, or natural death. *Omega, Journal of Death and Dying, 25,* 25–32.

Riches, G., & Dawson, P. (1998). Spoiled memories: Problems of grief resolution in families bereaved through murder. *Mortality, 3,* 143–160.

Rosenblatt, P. C. (1983). *Bitter, bitter tears.* Minneapolis: University of Minnesota Press.

Rowling, L. (1995). The disenfranchising grief of teachers. *Omega, Journal of Death and Dying, 31,* 317–330.

Sanders, C. M. (1982–1983). Effects of sudden vs. chronic illness and death on bereavement outcome. *Omega, Journal of Death and Dying, 13,* 227–242.

Selder, F., Kachoyeanos, M., Baisch, M. J., Gissler, M., Santos, S. R. (Eds.), (1997). *Enduring grief: True stories of personal loss.* Philadelphia, PA: The Charles Press.

Sprang, G., & McNeil, J. (1995). *The Many Faces of Bereavement.* New York: Brunner Maazel.

Stroebe, M. S. (1992–1993). Coping with bereavement: A review of the grief work hypothesis. *Omega, Journal of Death and Dying, 26,* 19–42.

Stroebe, M. S., & Stroebe, W. (1993). The mortality of bereavement: A review. In M. S. Stroebe, W. Stroebe, & R. O. Hansson (Eds.), *Handbook of bereavement* (pp. 175–195).

Talbot, K. (1998–1999). Mothers now childless: Personal transformation after the death of an only child. *Omega, Journal of Death and Dying, 38,* 167–186.

Umberson, D., & Henderson, K. (1992). The social construction of death in the Gulf War. *Omega, Journal of Death and Dying, 25,* 1–16.

Walker, A. (1988). *To hell with dying.* San Diego: Harcourt Brace Jovanovich.

Wambach, I. A. (1983). Timetables for grief and mourning with and without support groups. Unpublished doctoral dissertation, Arizona State University.

Weinfield, I. I. (1990). An expanded perinatal bereavement support committee. *Death Studies, 4,* 241–252.

Weisman, A. D. (1990–1991). Bereavement and companion animals. *Omega, Journal of Death and Dying, 22,* 241–248.

White, D. L. (1999). Grandparent participation in times of family bereavement. In B. de Vries (Ed), *End of life issues* (pp. 145–166). New York: Springer.

Woodward, C. (1999: July 10). Grim words were ready for Nixon speech had moon landing gone bad. Associated Press dispatch.

Worden, W. (1991). *Grief counseling and grief therapy: A handbook for the mental health practitioner.* (Rev. ed.). New York: Springer.

GLOSSARY

Anticipatory Grief: Anxiety and sorrow experienced prior to an expected death.

Attachment Behavior: Originally: the communications and actions by which a mother and her young seek to preserve their proximity and security; now: the same in relation to any individuals.

Bereavement: The status of having lost a family member, friend, colleague, or other significant person through death.

Disenfranchised Grief: A response to a death in which the individual is not regarded as having the right to grieve and must keep the sorrow hidden.

Dissociative Flight: An extreme avoidant or denial response to a death.

Grief: The complex emotional, mental, social, and physical response to the death of a loved one.

Griefwork Theory: The process of gradually accepting the reality of the loss and liberating oneself from attachment to the deceased (Freud).

Intrapsychic: Within the mind.

Mourning: The expression of the sorrow of loss and grief in a manner understood and approved by the culture.

Spontaneous Memorialization: Voluntary public response to the death of a person by violence; characterized by expression of personal feelings and bringing mementos to the site of the death.

Stigmatized Grief: The response to a death that has occurred in a manner considered immoral or shameful.

Traumatic Grief: The response to a death that has occurred in a sudden and violent manner.

The funeral of Lady Diana, Princess of Wales: Public ritual accompanied intense personal response.

chapter 12

THE FUNERAL PROCESS

I have no weddings or baptisms in the funeral home and the folks that pay me have maybe lost sight of the obvious connections between the life and the death of us.
—Thomas Lynch, 1997

Above all, we give thanks for the life of a woman I am so proud to be able call my sister: the unique, the complex, the extraordinary and irreplaceable Diana, whose beauty, both internal and external, will never be extinguished from our minds.
—Earl Charles Spencer, in Walter, 1999

Pre-prepared funeral tributes. Solve funeral eulogy problems for ONLY $15. These funeral tributes come in sets of three all of which are about one minute long. They are especially written to enable you to mix and match them....
Send us your credit card details.
—A website, 1999

The funeral director of Milford, Michigan, was reflecting on fundamental changes in ways of life throughout the twentieth century. Most people were born at home and died at home.

There were households in which, just as babies were being birthed, grandparents were aging upstairs with chicken soup and doctors' home visits until, alas, they died and were taken downstairs to the same room the babies were christened in to get what was then called "laid out." Between the births and deaths were the courtships—sparkings and spoonings between boys and girls just barely out of their teens, overseen by a maiden aunt.... The smitten young people would sit on a "love seat"—large enough to look into each other's eyes and hold hands, small enough to prevent them from getting horizontal. (Lynch, 1997, p. 35)

As time went on, though, more and more of life's activities took place outside the home, although professional establishments that prepare the dead for final disposition became known as "funeral homes." Lynch's observations make it clear that we cannot understand how a society cares for its dead without also understanding how that society lives. More specifically, death in the

United States seems to have become increasingly estranged from intimate family life.

The funeral and memorial ceremonies for Princess Diana were the focus of public attention not only in Great Britain but also throughout much of the world. The sudden death of a member of the royal family would have been occasion enough for such attention, but she had become dear to the hearts of many people. Her brother's eulogy was elegant and graceful, as sampled in an opening quotation. But Earl Charles Spencer also used the occasion to criticize what he believed to be the rigidity and oppression of the royal family. Speaking of her sons, William and Harry, Spencer pledged that:

> We, your blood family, will do all we can to continue the imaginative and loving way in which you were steering these two exceptional young men so that their souls are not simply immersed by duty and tradition but can sing openly as you planned. We fully respect the heritage into which they have both been born, and will always respect and encourage them in their royal role. But we, like you, recognize the need for them to experience as many different aspects of life as possible to arm them spiritually and emotionally for the years ahead.

His message was clear, especially to the British public that had already soured on the behavior of its royal family. The eulogy was both praised and damned—praised because it voiced a truth that resonated with Diana's life, and damned because it brought a harsh note of conflict and division into a funeral service.

Not everybody feels up to the challenge of speaking at a funeral. Some of us may find ourselves caught between our wish to do the right thing and our inexperience in writing and public speaking. Purchasing "pre-prepared funeral tributes" is perhaps just a convenience that can help some of us to deal with a difficult situation. Perhaps, though, it is another step along the path to surrendering the most profound and personal events in our lives to specialists. Should I purchase a eulogy for my daughter from a computer bank prepared by people who didn't even know her? Would you call upon the words of a person who never met your mother or father as you spoke at their funerals? Ever more frequently, we

must make decisions about our own participation in funeral and memorial observances, and each decision either affirms or weakens our sense of meaningful involvement. It has also become increasingly important, therefore, to enhance our understanding of the funeral process.

WHAT DO FUNERALS MEAN TO US?

A funeral is an event that occurs at a particular occasion at a particular place. We take final leave of one of our companions, "pay our respects," and then get on with our lives again. But why go to a funeral? What good does that do anybody? In fact, why have funerals at all? Some people see the funeral as an outdated practice, soon to fade away as we move deeper into the new millennium. Perhaps we can replace elaborate, expensive, and inconvenient funeral services with the click-click of the computer keyboard as we visit the dear departed at their cyberspace addresses. But perhaps not. Perhaps there is something so fundamental in the human response to death that we need the physicality of the funeral.

I believe the funeral to be part of a deeper and more complex process in which we both separate ourselves from the dead and try to establish a new relationship with them. This chapter, therefore, examines not only the funeral as such, but also the total process through which society responds to the death of one of its members. We will look at both what is happening today and the cultural traditions from which our own needs, beliefs, and practices have emerged.

Public response to the murder of Habib Amirali Kabani, a Houston shopkeeper, demonstrates that our responses to a death are not limited to established patterns and rituals. Bouquets of carnations, asters, and roses appeared on the sidewalk at the entrance to the store. A stack of flyers announced a memorial service and the establishment of a fund for the family. Through notes taped to the store window, neighbors and patrons expressed their identification with this man and their anger, guilt, sorrow, and desire for revenge (Haney, Leimer, & Lowery, 1997). Even in the rush and fragmentation of society today, people still respond to especially disturbing deaths in a spontaneous way as concerned individuals. We

An angel presides over a grave in Richmond, Virginia's Hollywood Cemetery. Rich and powerful families once demonstrated status by building impressive funerary structures.

will return later in this chapter to *spontaneous memorialization* as an emerging response capability in the American death system.

Sociologist Tony Walter (1992) had the long centuries of British history to draw upon in his study of cemeteries and funerals. He could visit country churchyards in which the first graves were dug 500 years ago. Most impressive to the eye, however, are the elaborate monuments constructed in public cemeteries to honor—to aggrandize, one might say—those who lived and died as respectable citizens during the reign of good Queen Victoria. Walter asks us to confront the possibility that today we are long past the time when investing in the dead was a major value and source of satisfaction for society:

> It is one thing today to have a simple Georgian headstone or a well-constructed table tomb gently weathering in a country churchyard. It is something else to have a municipal cemetery stuffed with tottering Victorian sentimentality in which the once so affected heirs have long since lost interest. (1992, p. 106)

Reaching much further back into history, we read of David's sense of responsibility both to his father and his son *after their deaths:*

> David went and took the bones of Saul and the bones of his son Jonathan from the men of Jabesh-gilead, who had stolen them from the public square of Beth-shan. And they buried the bones of Saul and his son Jonathan in the land of Benjamin in Zela, in the tomb of Kish his father. (2 Sam. 21:12, 14)

King David's enemies valued these remain as negotiable symbols. Those who possessed these bones also possessed power. Politics aside, David was a son who would be in torment until he did the right thing by his father. A great many other people, before and after King David, have felt the same way: a proper funeral and secure disposition of the body are essential for the family's peace of mind.

These are only a few examples, however, of the considerations that come to the surface when we inquire into the meaning of the funeral process.

Let us make this inquiry more personal: what are *your* thoughts and feelings about the funeral process? Please answer the questions presented for your consideration in Box 12-1.

Respondents to these questions tend to sort themselves out into two major types: *rationalist* and *romantic*. A thoroughgoing rationalist would agree that funerals are an expensive waste of time at which people tend to get too emotional. Cemeteries should be phased out so the land can be used more productively; cremation is the ticket. It is sensible to recycle one's better organs after one no longer has use for them—but forget that morbid open-casket stuff and the hysteria it can induce! Recognize yourself? By contrast, a romanticist would agree that funerals are a comfort to the next of kin and are not all that expensive when one considers their meaning to the survivors. Funerals are decisive and memorable events, certainly not a waste of time. Furthermore, people should show more, not less, emotion at funerals, and not begrudge the dead a peaceful place to rest their bones. Recognize yourself?

Not all of the questions bear on the rationalist/romantic attitude split, however. We will return to these questions after we have acquainted ourselves with some of the major facets of the funeral process.

FROM DEAD BODY TO LIVING MEMORY: A PROCESS APPROACH

How do we transform our relationship to a living person into our acknowledgment of this person's death, and a lasting memory that is integrated into our ongoing lives? This process has many dimensions, ranging from the legal, technical, and financial to the personal and the symbolic. Sometimes the survivors succeed in converting what has become a dead body into a living memory. Sometimes the process fails, and both the immediate survivors and society at large must shoulder a burden of unresolved feelings and unanswered questions.

Common Elements of the Funeral Process

Although specific customs differ tremendously, certain basic elements often can be found.

Premortem Preparations

When a person is expected to die, we tend to be "on the alert." What is going to happen when? What should we do? The law recognizes that actions taken in contemplation of death are unique. Gifts made under the shadow of death, for example, are often taxed more severely. The Internal Revenue Service is dead set against allowing dying people to give money away to their loved ones, thereby escaping taxation. Perhaps today's reading for dying people and their families should be financial advisories such as *Death, Deeds, and Descendants* (Clignet, 1992).

Premortem preparations may be initiated by the dying person (e.g., specific instructions for cremation or burial, disposal of personal property, and so on) as well as by family, colleagues, and health care professionals. A family member may start to contact family and friends so that they can make plans to visit the dying person or at least attend the funeral. Colleagues may have a different type of preparation to make, such as replacing the coworker who will not be coming back to the job. The physician may be interested in removing an organ for transplant or in conducting an autopsy to determine the precise cause of death, and therefore must decide how best to obtain permission. A mortician may have already been consulted and may have carried out preliminary arrangements to see that the wishes of the family are respected. It may seem as though others are simply waiting and holding their breath as a person approaches death, but often there is considerable activity in preparation for dealing with the event when it does occur.

Immediate Postdeath Activities

A death becomes official when it is certified by a physician. Certificates vary slightly from state to state but, as seen in Figure 12-1, always require information on time, place, and cause of death. One immediate postdeath activity, then, is to convert the person into a statistic or, more accurately, to complete the recordkeeping that started with the certificate of birth. Another immediate action is to contact next of kin if they are not already on the scene. It is common for the body to be cleaned and wrapped in a shroud (these days, usually a plastic sheet). If the death occurred in a hospital, the body is either kept in the same room

---

BOX 12-1

THE FUNERAL PROCESS: A SELF-EXAMINATION OF ATTITUDES, FEELINGS, AND KNOWLEDGE

---

1. Funerals are a waste of time.

   Agree _____   Tend to agree _____
   Tend to disagree _____   Disagree _____

2. Bodies should be donated for scientific use.

   Agree _____   Tend to agree _____
   Tend to disagree _____   Disagree _____

3. Funerals are a comfort to the next of kin.

   Agree _____   Tend to agree _____
   Tend to disagree _____   Disagree _____

4. People often are too emotional at funerals.

   Agree _____   Tend to agree _____
   Tend to disagree _____   Disagree _____

5. The death of a family member should be published in the newspaper.

   Agree _____   Tend to agree _____
   Tend to disagree _____   Disagree _____

6. All things considered, most funerals are not excessively costly.

   Agree _____   Tend to agree _____
   Tend to disagree _____   Disagree _____

7. People often do not show enough emotion at funerals.

   Agree _____   Tend to agree _____
   Tend to disagree _____   Disagree _____

8. The size, length, and expense of a funeral should depend on the importance of the deceased person.

   Agree _____   Tend to agree _____
   Tend to disagree _____   Disagree _____

9. Allowing for some exceptions, cemeteries waste valuable space and should be diverted to other uses.

   Agree _____   Tend to agree _____
   Tend to disagree _____   Disagree _____

10. It would be preferable to be cremated.

    Agree _____   Tend to agree _____
    Tend to disagree _____   Disagree _____

11. It would be preferable to be buried in a cemetery.

    Agree _____   Tend to agree _____
    Tend to disagree _____   Disagree _____

12. A funeral director should be required to give a summary of laws stating what is and what is not required before the bereaved purchase a funeral.

    Agree _____   Tend to agree _____
    Tend to disagree _____   Disagree _____

13. The average cost of a funeral in the United States is between $ _____ and $ _____.

14. Embalming the body is required:

    Always _____
    Under certain specified circumstances _____
    Never _____

15. An open casket funeral can be held after body organs are donated:

    Always _____   Usually _____
    Seldom _____   Never _____

16. My idea of the perfect funeral process is the following:

    _____

    _____

    _____

17. For me the best or most useful aspects of a funeral are:

    _____

    _____

    _____

18. For me the worst or most distressing aspects of a funeral are:

    _____

    _____

    _____

    _____

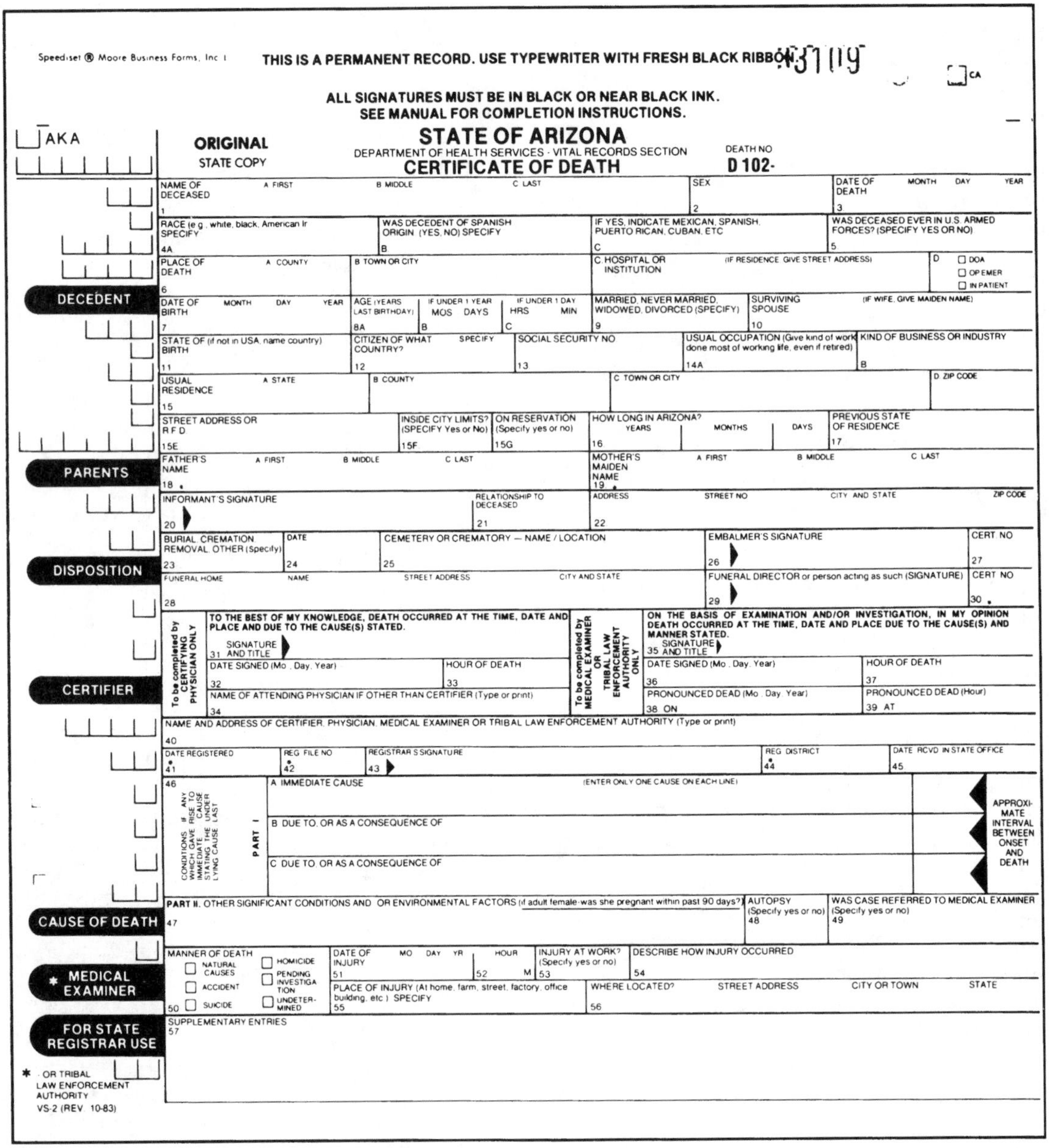

Speediset ® Moore Business Forms, Inc.

THIS IS A PERMANENT RECORD. USE TYPEWRITER WITH FRESH BLACK RIBBON.

ALL SIGNATURES MUST BE IN BLACK OR NEAR BLACK INK.
SEE MANUAL FOR COMPLETION INSTRUCTIONS.

AKA

ORIGINAL
STATE COPY

STATE OF ARIZONA
DEPARTMENT OF HEALTH SERVICES · VITAL RECORDS SECTION
CERTIFICATE OF DEATH

DEATH NO
D 102-

DECEDENT

1 NAME OF DECEASED — A FIRST, B MIDDLE, C LAST
2 SEX
3 DATE OF DEATH — MONTH, DAY, YEAR
4A RACE (e.g. white, black, American Ir) SPECIFY
B WAS DECEDENT OF SPANISH ORIGIN (YES, NO) SPECIFY
C IF YES, INDICATE MEXICAN, SPANISH, PUERTO RICAN, CUBAN, ETC
5 WAS DECEASED EVER IN U.S. ARMED FORCES? (SPECIFY YES OR NO)
6 PLACE OF DEATH — A COUNTY, B TOWN OR CITY, C HOSPITAL OR INSTITUTION (IF RESIDENCE GIVE STREET ADDRESS), D ☐ DOA ☐ OP EMER ☐ IN PATIENT
7 DATE OF BIRTH — MONTH, DAY, YEAR
8A AGE (YEARS LAST BIRTHDAY); B IF UNDER 1 YEAR MOS DAYS; C IF UNDER 1 DAY HRS MIN
9 MARRIED, NEVER MARRIED, WIDOWED, DIVORCED (SPECIFY)
10 SURVIVING SPOUSE (IF WIFE, GIVE MAIDEN NAME)
11 STATE OF BIRTH (if not in USA, name country)
12 CITIZEN OF WHAT COUNTRY? SPECIFY
13 SOCIAL SECURITY NO
14A USUAL OCCUPATION (Give kind of work done most of working life, even if retired)
B KIND OF BUSINESS OR INDUSTRY
15 USUAL RESIDENCE — A STATE, B COUNTY, C TOWN OR CITY, D ZIP CODE
15E STREET ADDRESS OR RFD
15F INSIDE CITY LIMITS? (SPECIFY Yes or No)
15G ON RESERVATION (Specify yes or no)
16 HOW LONG IN ARIZONA? YEARS, MONTHS, DAYS
17 PREVIOUS STATE OF RESIDENCE

PARENTS

18 FATHER'S NAME — A FIRST, B MIDDLE, C LAST
19 MOTHER'S MAIDEN NAME — A FIRST, B MIDDLE, C LAST
20 INFORMANT'S SIGNATURE
21 RELATIONSHIP TO DECEASED
22 ADDRESS — STREET NO, CITY AND STATE, ZIP CODE

DISPOSITION

23 BURIAL, CREMATION, REMOVAL, OTHER (Specify)
24 DATE
25 CEMETERY OR CREMATORY — NAME / LOCATION
26 EMBALMER'S SIGNATURE
27 CERT NO
28 FUNERAL HOME — NAME, STREET ADDRESS, CITY AND STATE
29 FUNERAL DIRECTOR or person acting as such (SIGNATURE)
30 CERT NO

CERTIFIER

To be completed by CERTIFYING PHYSICIAN ONLY
TO THE BEST OF MY KNOWLEDGE, DEATH OCCURRED AT THE TIME, DATE AND PLACE AND DUE TO THE CAUSE(S) STATED.
31 SIGNATURE AND TITLE
32 DATE SIGNED (Mo., Day, Year)
33 HOUR OF DEATH
34 NAME OF ATTENDING PHYSICIAN IF OTHER THAN CERTIFIER (Type or print)

To be completed by MEDICAL EXAMINER OR TRIBAL LAW ENFORCEMENT AUTHORITY ONLY
ON THE BASIS OF EXAMINATION AND/OR INVESTIGATION, IN MY OPINION DEATH OCCURRED AT THE TIME, DATE AND PLACE DUE TO THE CAUSE(S) AND MANNER STATED.
35 SIGNATURE AND TITLE
36 DATE SIGNED (Mo., Day, Year)
37 HOUR OF DEATH
38 PRONOUNCED DEAD (Mo., Day, Year) ON
39 PRONOUNCED DEAD (Hour) AT

40 NAME AND ADDRESS OF CERTIFIER, PHYSICIAN, MEDICAL EXAMINER OR TRIBAL LAW ENFORCEMENT AUTHORITY (Type or print)
41 DATE REGISTERED
42 REG. FILE NO
43 REGISTRAR'S SIGNATURE
44 REG. DISTRICT
45 DATE RCVD IN STATE OFFICE

CAUSE OF DEATH

46 PART I — CONDITIONS, IF ANY, WHICH GAVE RISE TO IMMEDIATE CAUSE STATING THE UNDERLYING CAUSE LAST
A IMMEDIATE CAUSE (ENTER ONLY ONE CAUSE ON EACH LINE)
B DUE TO, OR AS A CONSEQUENCE OF
C DUE TO, OR AS A CONSEQUENCE OF
APPROXIMATE INTERVAL BETWEEN ONSET AND DEATH
47 PART II. OTHER SIGNIFICANT CONDITIONS AND OR ENVIRONMENTAL FACTORS (if adult female - was she pregnant within past 90 days?)
48 AUTOPSY (Specify yes or no)
49 WAS CASE REFERRED TO MEDICAL EXAMINER (Specify yes or no)

* MEDICAL EXAMINER

50 MANNER OF DEATH — ☐ NATURAL CAUSES ☐ ACCIDENT ☐ SUICIDE ☐ HOMICIDE ☐ PENDING INVESTIGATION ☐ UNDETERMINED
51 DATE OF INJURY — MO, DAY, YR
52 HOUR M
53 INJURY AT WORK? (Specify yes or no)
54 DESCRIBE HOW INJURY OCCURRED
55 PLACE OF INJURY (At home, farm, street, factory, office building, etc.) SPECIFY
56 WHERE LOCATED? STREET ADDRESS, CITY OR TOWN, STATE

FOR STATE REGISTRAR USE

57 SUPPLEMENTARY ENTRIES

* OR TRIBAL LAW ENFORCEMENT AUTHORITY
VS-2 (REV. 10-83)

FIGURE 12-1
Death certificate in use in Arizona.

or transferred to some available nearby room pending the arrival of the next of kin. If a hospital is pressed for space, the decision may be made to remove the body to the morgue after a short time.

Preparations for Burial or Cremation

The interval between death and the final disposal of the body is important in its own right.

Often there are both practical and symbolic or psychological reasons for placing a "space of time" between death and final disposition. One of the most common reasons is to allow time for distant friends and relatives to gather for the funeral. Some deaths also raise questions that require action in the public interest. Was this death caused by negligence, suicide, murder? Was the deceased the victim of a disease that poses a hazard to the general population? When such questions exist, it is usually the medical examiner (or coroner) who must decide whether or not a full investigation is needed. A particular death, then, can initiate a sequence of investigative and public health actions. If the case is particularly difficult or controversial, the services of a medical specialist known as a *death investigator* may be sought.

For an example of the challenges that may confront a death investigator, please see Box 12-2.

An autopsy may be ordered by the medical examiner (under usual circumstances, the autopsy is an optional procedure that requires consent of the next of kin). When special public health problems exist, a person whose death has certain characteristics may become the focus of investigation. This happened when swine flu and Legionnaire's disease became problems in the 1970s, for example. Learning whether or not a particular condition has been associated with a particular death can provide important information for protecting others.

Burial or cremation may also have to await the clarification of financial arrangements. Did the deceased have an insurance policy with funeral benefits? Precisely who is prepared to spend how much for the funeral? Financial and legal matters and the family's need to arrive at a consensus may require a certain amount of time before final arrangements can be made. Problems can arise in less bureaucratic societies as well. Was there sorcery at work in this death? And, if so, was it a personal enemy within the tribe who must confess and make amends, or was it caused by another tribe as part of a traditional animosity? Again and again, circumstances may arise that require resolution before the proper final arrangements can be made.

The time interval also allows many symbolic and psychological needs to be met. Among some ethnic and religious groups, the survivors have specific tasks to perform after death. These tasks help the survivors to express their affection for the deceased and to demonstrate their ability to support each other during a period of loss or crisis. Carrying out these responsibilities is also felt to be an act of piety. If someone neglected to prepare special foods or create special objects to be placed in the grave, he or she would lose esteem in the group. The symbolic meaning is often more important than the length of the interval. The Cheyenne, for example, buried their dead quickly so that the ghosts would swiftly depart. By contrast, many societies took the trouble to mummify their dead as a way of keeping them as part of the community, calling upon their symbolic powers, or enhancing their chances for a brilliant afterlife.

The process of preparing the body varies greatly from society to society. For example, embalming is far from universal and was seldom practiced in the United States until thousands of soldiers died far from home during the Civil War. Embalming by a mortician is now a widespread practice in the United States, although it is not required by law unless the body is to be transported out of state or for some other clearly specified reason. Embalming can help to serve emotional and symbolic needs. For example, each year Arizona ships more than 3,000 bodies back to the hometowns of people who had left to spend their retirement in Arizona. "Postmortem emigration" also occurs in other Sunbelt states so that a body may be brought to a family plot in the hometown cemetery.

In some societies, attempts to embellish as well as preserve the body have taken considerable time, effort, and art. The ancient Egyptians' creation of mummies (*see Box 12-3*) is perhaps the most famous example, but it is by no means the only one. Some rich and powerful people in various Western nations have also demanded and received extensive postmortem treatment before burial. The wife of Louis XVI's minister "ordered her body to be preserved in alcohol, like an embryo" so that her widowed spouse could spend the rest of his life gazing at her beautiful face (Aries, 1981, p. 386). Distinguished social philosopher Jeremy Bentham, principal founder of the University of London, still has a place on the faculty although he died in 1832. He is represented

---

BOX 12-2
A DEATH INVESTIGATOR'S CHALLENGE: WAS THIS REALLY A SUICIDE?

The following is excerpted from the author's interview with Bruce L. Danto, M.D. (Omega, 1994–1995).

Would you give us an example of the kind of situation in which a death investigator's services might be called upon?

Perhaps most common is the case in which the cause or mode of death is equivocal. Relatives may want to prove that a suicide is a murder because at stake is a considerable inheritance from an insurance contract which prohibits suicide. Relatives may want a death studied because they don't like the members of the family who are survivors of the deceased. Insurance investigators may suspect fraud. A police department may feel that an intradepartmental investigation of a death is insufficient. Or the bereaved family members may simply feel that they cannot get over the death until they are certain that the cause and circumstances have been firmly established.

Here is an example. A 20-year-old soldier was found dead in his vehicle in a federal park area. His rifle was between his legs. He was declared a suicide after an autopsy was conducted in the Army camp. It was twenty years later that the case came to my attention because a former military policeman had a guilty conscience. He had been called to the scene of that death and for years was bothered by the facts that photographs of the death scene had been taken after the dead body had been removed to the hospital. He felt that those photographs were staged.... Now both he and the soldier's sister wanted to learn the truth, if possible.

All that was at hand was the autopsy report and the death photographs.... It became apparent that the wounds in the chest were not entrance wounds. There were two wounds, one of which was small and elliptical due to the forceful expulsion of the bullet's metal jacket from the body. This finding was suspicious to me because the autopsy described the entrance wound as being in the chest.... How could a person take a 30/30 caliber deer rifle and shoot himself in the back in a small automobile when the deceased himself was 6'5" tall? Photographs of the car's interior showed a bullet scar in the driver's door. It would be impossible to trace the path of the bullet that exited the chest to find out how it ended up on the closing rim of the door near the handle, assuming that the entrance wound was really on the chest. Finally, he kept his rifle on post as was required, but there was no sign-out slip. This means that the weapon somehow materialized in this man's hands without proper authority...

This is only part of the investigative work that this case required. The soldier's state of mind prior to his death and the status of his interpersonal relationships also had to be understood, and the body itself exhumed for study. When the death investigator had completed his work, it appeared that the soldier had not committed suicide but, rather, had been a homicide victim. This revised interpretation did not bring the young man back to life, but it did confirm the sister's belief that he had not committed suicide. Many years of doubt and anxiety might have been spared, and a killer might have been apprehended if more time had been given for a thorough investigation of this death before burial.

---

by his embalmed corpse and is said to have attended selected faculty meetings for many years after his death. (This may, in fact, be preferable to attending faculty meetings *before* one's death!) Millions have stood in line to see Lenin's carefully preserved body, and the physical remains of other political or symbolic leaders around the world have also been prepared for display. And when the last detachment of smartly marching soldiers abandoned Lenin's tomb, it was a clear message that the Communist Party was no longer in control.

Types of Burial

So familiar is the practice of embalming a deceased person, placing that person horizontally in

---

BOX 12-3
THE SACRED ART OF MUMMIFICATION: HOW AND WHY?

How were mummies made in ancient Egypt?

- The family selected the grade and price level of mummification, choosing from several wooden models. Royal mummification was, of course, of the highest quality whatever the expense. It was a first-class mummification, as described below.
- The internal organs were removed—the brain first, caught on an iron hook and fished out through the (slit) nostrils. The abdominal organs were then removed through an incision.
- In royal mummifications, the heart was replaced by the carved replica of a scarab (a dung beetle), symbolizing the perpetual cycle of life into death and death into life. The internal organs were transferred to canopic jars (stone vessels).
- The body cavity was thoroughly rinsed with palm wine.
- The face and body might have been reshaped to restore blemishes and disfigurations that occurred during the final illness or the mummification procedure. This could have included reshaping the breasts to provide a more natural appearance for a woman.
- Spices and many other aromatic substances were placed inside the body, which was then sewn up.
- The body was then covered by "divine salts" to foster drying and preservation. The standard period of time for the drying phase was forty days, followed by another thirty days for final preparations.
- The salted and dried body was washed and wrapped in linen strips that were undercoated with gum. Features such as eyes and eyebrows were drawn in ink on the linen to recreate the face.

- The mummy of a powerful person was placed in a tapered coffin, and the coffin itself was lodged within a sarcophagus (stone chamber) which was sealed into a tomb.
- It should be emphasized that this was mummification on the grand scale. The procedure was simplified and less expensive measures were used for people who lacked regal or other high-power status.

But why?

- The practical aim was to preserve the body by emptying it of its fluids and the parts most subject to rapid decay, producing a dehydrated but otherwise faithful—almost lifelike—version of the deceased person. When conducted by skillful embalmers and not desecrated by tomb-robbers, the results could be very impressive. There are pharaohs who look as though they are ready to reclaim their thrones more than three thousand years after they drew their last breath. The high art of mummification was itself achieved only after many years of trial and error, with frequent failures.
- The more crucial aim was to guide a spirit that departed from the body at death—the *ba*—back to its former physical home where its companion spirit—the *ka*—awaited its nightly visits. The preserved body made it easier for the winged *ba* to locate its companion spirit, *ka*. Some archeologists believe that the great pyramids were constructed not only to honor the sacred dead and protect their bodies, but also as a sort of astral communications center that provided a stronger signal for the communion of the spirits.

Principle sources: Ikram and Dodson (1998); Harris & Weeks (1973).

---

a coffin, and placing that coffin horizontally in a cemetery gravesite that we might consider this a natural and universal tradition. Not so. Both practical circumstances and belief systems have generated a variety of approaches. For example, many tribal societies throughout the world believe that the nature of one's afterlife is critically affected by the way in which that person's corpse is managed. One of the most common practices has been to place the body in a fetal position before burial (or burning, if that is the society's choice). The body is usually then wrapped or bound so that it will maintain this position, and then placed on its side. Is this position intended to resemble sleep and keep the spirit comfortable until it is ready to depart as a ghost who feels well served by his or her community? Some anthropologists think so; we really don't know. If you are Freudian-minded, you might also speculate on the frequent use of the fetal position as a possible attempt to return the deceased to the womb to be reborn. In some societies, people have been buried in a seated position, or even upside down. Sometimes members of a tribal society have clearly expressed their reasons, as when Solomon Islanders around the turn of the twentieth century reported that they bound their dead in seated positions, good and tight, so they wouldn't come back to terrify or annoy them.

Cremation seems to have been with us as along as ground burial. Some cultures have regarded assignment to the flames as a form of purification that helped to free the soul for its new form of existence. The Vikings, for example, built a spectacular long boat to set afire with the corpse of their king aboard. Cremation was not a realistic option for people who lived where trees were scarce. Sea burial has long been practiced on sailing vessels as a matter of practicality, but often enhanced by ritual that provided structure and meaning. Sky burial—placing a corpse on a high and open space where it can be consumed down to the bones by vultures or other carrion birds—was standard practice in Tibet and elsewhere. Some cultures had multiple ways of dealing with the dead. In former days, for example, Adaman Islanders buried those who died very young or very old in a shallow hole, but those who perished in their prime received the prestigious treatment of having their bodies placed on a tree platform. Dead strangers were cut into pieces and consumed by fire without ceremony because their ghosts immediately left for their homeland and therefore posed no local danger.

Can we possibly see our own practices through the eyes of other people? If so, we might wonder

Many cultures have devoted skills and resources to the care of the dead and their progress into the afterworld. The dynastic Egyptians, however, brought the art of mummification to its highest level.

why a corpse must be horizontal and why it is not buried with useful personal items. However, we might nod with approval at the headstone, interpreting this as a sensible way of keeping the beloved dead where they belong.

The Funeral Service

The funeral service itself is usually the centerpiece of the entire process. Two major purposes are achieved by the funeral service: final placement of the remains and society's public recognition that one of its members has made the transition from life to death. There are many variations of funeral services, both in American society and in other cultures. Perhaps the most familiar form is the church funeral service, in which respects are paid to the deceased in a church or funeral home, then mourners gather at the cemetery to hear eulogies and witness the casket being placed in the grave. Most often the arrangements for the service are carried out by the funeral director—ordering flowers, providing the hearse and possibly other vehicles, and so on. A member of the clergy usually presides over the commemorative services. In "small town America," the clergyperson often knew the family well; this seems to be somewhat less common today.

These basic functions can be influenced and distorted by intrusive events. Various factions of the family, for example, may collide because of longstanding grievances and hidden resentments. The ensuing tension can distract from the central purpose of the funeral services. A very elaborate funeral can also attract so much attention to itself that it is difficult to keep a focus on the deceased. A lack of consensus among the mourners can also be a source of distraction. One common example is the decision to have either an open or closed casket. These two choices are of almost equal popularity, which virtually guarantees that some visitors will be displeased with whatever choice is made. And even those who prefer an open casket may disagree on the way it has been accomplished. Should Louise's visage be restored to a semblance of the robust person she once had been or presented with the lines of exhaustion that developed during her last illness? Should Harry be displayed in his favorite old sloppy clothes or in an elegant dark suit that he would literally never have been caught dead in? For a variety of reasons, mourners can be distracted or disturbed by details of the funeral service. Nevertheless, the underlying purposes remain: to make a final disposition of the body and to use this occasion as a way of acknowledging that a life has passed from among us.

Memorializing the Deceased

Most societies attempt to fix the deceased in memory. In the United States, a death notice is often (but not always) published in a local newspaper. An obituary may also appear, especially if requested by the family. The newspaper often charges a fee to print an obituary unless the individual is considered especially "newsworthy." There is also a trend toward drastically restricting the number of obituaries published in newspapers serving large urban areas because of space and economical pressures. Does such a response

weaken the ability of our death system to meet the need of survivors? Do people feel abandoned and perhaps abused because the deaths of their loved ones are not acknowledged in the state's major newspaper? We do not know the answers to these questions, but it is obvious that traditional acknowledgments and responses to death are vulnerable to general social trends.

Traditional burial is almost always accompanied by a grave marker, whether simple or elaborate. This identified site provides the opportunity for survivors to return and pay homage to the deceased. Survivors often experience severe stress when war or natural catastrophe make it impossible to know precisely which grave is that of a relative or dear friend. Tens of thousands of unidentified soldiers lie buried in foreign lands, their graves usually marked by simple crosses. Many American families visited World War I burial grounds such as Flanders Field so they could at least be close to the place where their loved ones were probably interred. Survivors often experience the need to know precisely where the body has been placed and to have some type of appropriate marking. In our own time, families have experienced emotional pain for years because a member is still listed as "missing in action" in Vietnam. The increasing use of DNA testing may assist in the identification of people who have died in war or catastrophe and thereby ease some of the survivors' grief.

As we noted earlier, King David was not the last person to feel the need to recover the body and memorialize the spirit of a close family member. Whether it takes the form of lighting a candle on the deceased's birthday, saying prayers, or making sacrifices or gifts in the name of the deceased, memorialization appears to be one of humankind's deepest needs when separated from a loved one by death.

Getting On with Life

The funeral process is devoted to both completing society's obligations to the deceased and supporting the survivors in their grief. The "life-must-go-on" motif often takes the form of a festive occasion. Family, neighbors, and best friends gather to eat, drink, and share lively conversation. In former generations, the food was usually prepared by family members, representing a gift in the service of life. It was a mark of pride to offer fine ethnic delicacies in abundance, along with the beverages most favored by the guests. The prevailing mood was much different from the previous phases of the funeral process. The guests were now expected to enjoy themselves, to be vital and frisky. There might be dancing and, as the feasting proceeded, even some romancing.

This type of festivity started to give way as society became more impersonal, mobile, and technologically oriented, and as efforts were made to banish death from public awareness. A cup of coffee with a few family members and friends has sometimes replaced the elaborate proceedings of earlier generations. Although the size and splendor of the postfuneral gathering may differ greatly, the underlying function is the same—to help people redirect their attention to the continuation and renewal of life. This is why conversation may seem unnaturally lively and why people may seem to eat, drink, and laugh too much considering the recent death of an intimate. If you happen to walk in while a risqué story is being told, it is easy to be offended and think that insensitivity and disrespect are afoot. Often, however, lively and lusty behaviors after a funeral represent a partial release from tension and the compelling need to show each other that life can and should go on—"Harry (or Louise) would have wanted it that way!"

MAKING DEATH "LEGAL"

Society's claim on an individual is demonstrated clearly at the points of entry and of exit. Births and deaths have been recorded at the neighborhood church since medieval times. Demands of the faith required that each soul be entered into the books and therefore subject to the expectations of God and the state. A written notice was also required as the soul was released to join its maker—proof that the clergyman was carefully watching over his flock. These records were consulted if questions arose about kinship rights and obligations. Now, centuries later, the surviving records continue to be of social value. Historians seeking to understand the effects of a harsh winter in rural England in the seventeenth century or migration patterns in northern Italy

100 years later are almost certain to consult entries preserved at the local parish.

The certificates of birth and death (*see Figure 12-1*) today serve similar functions in a more secular society. The newborn and the deceased are affirmed as citizens beginning or ending their active roles in society. Church records now provide supplementary rather than official documentation. Despite all of the changes that have occurred through the years, governing authorities still insist on "keeping the book" on the individual. This may seem a peculiar insistence—that we must not only be alive but have proof of birth, that we must not only be deceased but have proof of death! It represents, however, the Western world's view of the social contract. I recently had the opportunity to empathize with a women who had the task of persuading the Social Security Administration that she is still alive, despite their "proof" of her death. (The SSA agreed with her opinion that she was still alive—and proved it by giving her another stack of forms to complete.) Society presumes that none of us belongs entirely to himself or herself but that all are subject to these "legalizations" both coming and going.

We will now examine in more detail some of the major features of making death legal as part of the contemporary funeral process.

Establishing the Facts of Death

A death is real, but it is not official until certified. Today it is usually a physician who is called upon to perform this task. The physician must establish the principal facts of the death and initiate an investigation if serious questions arise. *Cause* of death often requires that the physician identify several contributing factors. Some examples follow:

- "Cardiovascular accident, secondary to hypertension"
- "Pneumonia, secondary to lung cancer"
- "Hemorrhage, secondary to cancer of the larynx"
- "Septicemia, secondary to extensive third degree burns"

The actual situation may be even more complicated than the death certificate can express. A woman in her eighties suffers from heart and urinary tract disorders in addition to a loss of bone mass and resiliency (osteoporosis). One day while she is simply ascending a staircase, the brittle bones give way. She falls. Both hips are broken. Her already impaired cardiovascular system is subjected to further stress. Internal bleeding proves hard to control. Confined to bed and fitted with a catheter, she develops an infection that further saps her strength. Medical and nursing management become very difficult because treatments that might improve one condition can worsen another. Her lungs soon fill with fluid, and she dies. But what is *the* cause? Or what is the precise relationship among the many interacting factors that led to death? The physician may or may not be able to give a definite answer but often can specify the two or three major contributing causes.

The death certificate has its limits as a source of research data, Even so, the information it does provide can be quite useful. For example, the information about this elderly woman adds to a growing body of data that emphasizes the need for better understanding and clinical and environmental management to prevent falls.

Occasionally people dare to ask about the accuracy and reliability of the "cause of death" entries. The answers can be a little unsettling. A number of physicians have been exploring this question in the pages of the *Journal of the American Medical Association*. Two recent contributions (Hanzlick, 1993; Kaplan & Hanzlick, 1993) have found that relatively few death certificates specify the underlying cause. Many death certificates also omitted other information that would be needed to understand the circumstances of the individual's death. It is hard to escape the inference that some physicians are completing death certificates in a somewhat off-handed manner, losing sight of the service they could be providing to other physicians, researchers, and the public.

The cause of death is often the most salient item of information required on the certificate, but the other entries are also of potential significance. Who is the next of kin? Was the death related to occupational hazard or stress? Has there been an unusually high rate of death from the same cause in this geographical area in the past few years? Questions such as these can have many implications for the well-being of surviving individuals.

The Medical Examiner and the Autopsy

The legalization of death at times requires the intervention of the coroner or medical examiner. Funeral arrangements are suspended until the investigation is completed or the coroner decides that it is unnecessary. This additional procedure can inconvenience and distress the survivors, but it can also serve important purposes. It is possible, for example, that the death may have been caused by a condition that poses a continuing danger to the populace. What has become known as "Legionnaire's disease" was not well understood when it was first encountered in 1976. Public health authorities had no way of knowing whether this life-threatening affliction had resulted from some unusual combination of circumstances or whether it represented a new threat of major proportions. A decade later, autopsies again became vital sources of information as another essentially unknown condition began to claim its victims: AIDS. In both instances, public health authorities had to determine whether they were dealing with a limited or an extensive and uncontrolled threat to life. Physicians would have been remiss if they had certified the deaths in a routine manner, as would public health authorities if they had not immediately examined both living and deceased victims. Certain diseases trigger automatic reports to the coroner's office when discovered by a physician, either in a living patient or during an autopsy. In the Southwestern states, for example, physicians must report cases suggestive of plague. Such cases are very rare, almost always involving contact with disease-bearing fleas on dead or dying wild animals. Nevertheless, history has taught us to beware of any possible outbreak. The health care system's quick response to the emergence of a new type of life-threatening virus carried by rodents (hantavirus) was facilitated by the contributions of medical examiners.

Inquests are also ordered when there is reason to suspect that the death was the outcome of negligence or error. Was this patient given the wrong medication? Had this prisoner been held too long in an unheated jail cell? Did nursing home personnel fail to provide adequate nourishment to a "difficult" resident? It is obvious from all of these examples that the interests of society can be served on occasion by requiring an investigation after death.

The examination itself can vary in scope and effort. In some instances, it may be sufficient to look for one or two telltale signs (e.g., the trace of certain substances in the lungs or intestines, the presence or absence of cerebral hemorrhage). In other instances, a more comprehensive examination may be required (as illustrated by Box 12-2). Dissection and examination of the body may be considered necessary, along with a variety of laboratory tests, including bacteriological and toxicological.

Sometimes it is necessary to *exhume* a corpse for a further investigation of the cause of death. Removing a corpse from its burial site is a serious matter that requires careful thought and good judgment. Courts may order exhumation to obtain bullets, hair fragments, or other physical evidence that could bear on the cause of death in criminal cases, including malpractice. Corpses are also sometimes exhumed by accident, such as when a graveyard is disturbed by flood or construction activities.

The *autopsy,* or postmortem examination, often is conducted for other reasons as well. There may be no suspicion of foul play or negligence and no serious question about cause of death. Nevertheless, either the family or the medical facility may decide that there is something to be gained by an autopsy. Had this person lived for many years with a certain physical problem that had been suspected but never demonstrated? Was the slowly deteriorating mental condition of that person accompanied by brain changes such as might be caused by Alzheimer's disease? Answering questions such as these, case by case, can build up useful knowledge and develop implications for future research and treatment. Autopsies have also been considered for many years a source of valuable learning experiences for medical personnel, and in this way they contribute indirectly to improved health care.

Autopsies cannot be performed without permission from the next of kin or a person who has been given power of attorney. Usually further regulations surround the permission process to ensure that undue pressure is not placed on the family. In my experience, the decision whether or not to grant autopsy permission often depends on situational factors—the state of mind of the next of kin, for example, and that person's relationship to the deceased and to the physician. The request for autopsy permission can be difficult for all parties. The physician may hesitate to make this request so soon after the death, and the next of kin may have conflicting thoughts and fluctuating feelings. Effective communication and mutual trust are very important.

Body, Property, and the Law

Knowledge of current laws and statutes is important if the survivors are to avoid unnecessary conflicts, delays, and litigation. Attention must be given to insurance provisions and options and to the probate laws that regulate the inheritance of estates. Both insurance provisions and probate laws are subject to change, especially in these days of rapid change in the health care system. For example, Prudential, an insurance company, has an option that enables people to draw upon their benefits during the terminal phase of their lives instead of keeping it all as a death benefit for the survivors. Other insurance companies have been coming up with similar plans. It is useful to keep up-to-date with the available options and regulations. The advantages and limitations of drawing up a will and/or establishing a trust fund should be understood, and these documents should be supplemented by a letter of instructions that is readily available in time of need. There is reason to be cautious, though, when encountering promotional materials promising that their trust fund will solve all of one's problems.

Organ donation has emerged in recent years as an important option. After some years of dispute and uncertainty, "anatomical gifts" now have a firm legal foundation. The clearest way to exercise this option is for individuals to sign a simple legal instrument that offers any part of or all of their body for medical humanitarian purposes upon death. The provisions of the Uniform Anatomical Gift Act are satisfied by a brief statement of intention, signed by the individual and cosigned by two witnesses. Typically, such donor cards provide the following choice:

I give _____ any needed organ or parts

I give _____ only the following organs or parts _____

Your physician or a local hospital can provide an approved legal anatomical donor card; some states also include this form as part of the driver's license.

Unfortunately, a person's willingness to donate organs does not always lead to the intended outcome. Those responsible for the body upon death may not know that a donor card has been completed, or family members may oppose the anatomical gift (in which case the hospital or other medical organization is likely to forego the gift to avoid legal complications). Mixups and miscommunications within the medical network have thwarted the donor's purpose. Even when all else seems conducive to the organ donation, the tissues themselves may not meet the standards for transplanation—for example, when circumstances have made it impossible to procure the organs in a timely manner. There is growing conflict regarding priorities for organ donor recipients. Who should be next on the list for that much-needed tissue or organ—the person who is in most urgent need, or the person who lives in our city or state? Unfortunately, organ donation has entered the political sphere and become subject to adversarial proceedings. It would be refreshing if our society could set aside its talent for sharp-edged competition and find a more appropriate way to distribute these unique gifts of life.

Even greater difficulties have arisen for those who have attempted to exercise the option of *cryonic suspension*. This controversial procedure differs from all other forms of body disposal in one critical respect: the "deceased-to-be" intends to use his or her own body again! The hope encouraged by cryonicists is that bodies preserved at low temperatures (not quite freezing) can later be restored to life and treated successfully when cures are developed for the previously fatal illness. It has been recently estimated (Kastenbaum, 1994) that the bodies of about fifty people have been placed in cryonic chambers. No known attempts at restoration have yet been made. The current trend is toward preserving only the head. This procedure—yes, I think it's weird, too!—saves space and money. It also requires adding another major assumption: that the rest of the body can be reconstituted and then be given its memory and control headquarters, the head.

From the legal standpoint, cryonic suspension is a form of body disposal or burial. From the cryonicist's standpoint, these are people who exist somewhere in the borderlands between life and death. Whatever the ultimate truth might prove to be, cryonic interment is certainly a distinctive alternative—especially as compared with cremation!

Frequently, however, the expressed written wishes of people who have requested cryonic internment have not been honored at the critical moment. Discomfort, disbelief, and hostility on the part of the medical establishment have taken precedence over the patient's wishes, no matter how clearly expressed. The first human known to have been placed in cryonic suspension was Dr. William H. Bedford. In January 1967, his body was perfused with dimethylsulfide (DMSO) and packed in dry ice, then transferred to long-term storage in a chamber filled with liquid nitrogen. I know from my own research at the time when cryonic suspension was introduced that the most common response of public and health care professionals alike was disapproval shading into anger. Furthermore, legal aspects of cryonic suspension have not been established as clearly as have those of the more familiar alternatives for body disposal. The very concept of cryonic suspension arouses anxious hostility. At present American society is much more receptive to organ gifts than to the cryonic option. Some of the ethical questions associated with cryonics were identified in Chapter 6.

WHAT DOES THE FUNERAL PROCESS ACCOMPLISH?

The funeral process would not have become so important to so many societies unless it served significant needs and values. Some of the meanings have already been noted. This section considers a broader range of funeral observations and memorializations that will reveal even more about death system dynamics and the values at stake.

When Great People Die

Every life and therefore every death, should perhaps be considered of equal importance. In practice, however, societies consider some people more important than others. The loss of a great person often triggers a massive response. The question "Who does this society consider really important?" can be answered by observing the funeral process. But it can be observed from another perspective as well: *Given that a great person has died, what is it that society feels it must accomplish through the funeral and memorialization process?* Following are a few examples that illustrate the dynamics and principles involved.

The Silent Army of Ch'in Shih-huang-ti

Ch'in Shih-huang-ti was one of the most powerful monarchs who ever appeared in either the East or the West. He unified the peoples of an enormous and diversified region into nationhood and stimulated the development of a vigorous and distinctive culture. It was Ch'in, as the first emperor of China, who built the Great Wall more than two centuries before the birth of Christ.

In 1974 Ch'in's tomb was discovered. It is one of the most incredible archeological finds of all time. The tomb is encased within a large mound whose location was selected through the ancient Chinese practice of *feng-shui,* an occult art intended to deter evil spirits from disturbing either the deceased or the living. To call the site a tomb is an understatement—it answers better to the name of "palace." There are a variety of funerary buildings, each with a specific purpose; additionally, a set of double walls once protected the complex and the housing for guards and attendants. Ch'in's tomb was built near the graves of earlier rulers and was clearly designed to surpass them all.

Several huge underground chambers have been excavated. The first is a rectangle of approximately 700 by 200 feet. It is divided into eleven parallel corridors, the entire structure skillfully constructed with a combination of rammed earth, bricks, and timber crossbeams. In this pit, excavators found an entire army! Arthur Cotterell describes the scene:

The chambers are arranged in the battle order of an infantry regiment, which faces eastwards. Altogether it is estimated that there are 3,210 terra-cotta foot soldiers. They do not wear helmets; only Ch'in officers have these. But most of the infantry soldiers wear armour. These armoured men are divided into forty files; they stand four abreast in the nine wide corridors, and form two files in each of the narrow ones. The head of the regiment in the eastern gallery comprises a vanguard of unarmoured bowmen and crossmen, nearly 200 sharpshooters, drawn up in three north-south ranks. Their clothing is light cotton because they are fast moving, long-range fighters—the ancient equivalent of artillery. They would have fired their arrows from a distance, keeping away from hand-to-hand engagements, once contact was made with the enemy. The three ranks would have taken turns at firing, so as to keep a continuous stream of arrows. The majority carried crossbows with a 200-metre [650-foot] shooting range.

Between these sharpshooters and the armoured infantry are six chariots and three unarmoured infantry squads. Each chariot is pulled by four terra-cotta horses and manned by a charioteer and one or two soldiers. The guards would have wielded long flexible lances, possibly bamboos measuring as much as six metres [20 feet], in order to stop enemy soldiers from cutting off the heads of the horses. (1981, pp. 22–23)

The artistic craftsmanship devoted to the creation of this subterranean army and the enormous economic resources poured into the enterprise are truly staggering. And yet we may wonder "Why?" What purpose was served by such a vast expenditure of labor and resources?

I propose a set of interlocking answers to this question based upon historical materials, although we must always recognize the difficulties in trying to understand motivation from such a distance. Ch'in's motivation may well have included the following components:

- To support his claims as the greatest of all monarchs
- To impress the deities and ensure his place among the immortals

- To confound his enemies and secure a continuation of his royal succession

Ch'in made history, but he also made enemies. He placed enormous strains on the economy through his military adventures. He was also extreme in the administration of what he judged to be justice. Scholars who displeased him were buried alive. Any who disobeyed or displeased him were in danger of losing their lives. Revolution was prevented only by Ch'in's might and vigilance. Construction of a monumental tomb was one way, then, to display his ability to defend his regime even from the grave. The terra-cotta army originally was provided with real weapons, although enemies later were able to make off with them.

Ch'in continued to brandish his power as long as he could and for the same purposes that had guided his life. Like many another ruler, the first emperor of China craved immortality and sought every opportunity to gain this advantage for himself in both life and death. The fantastic tomb at Mount Li represents a continuation and culmination of his self-aggrandizing lifestyle. Just as he literally required that his subjects sing his praises throughout his life, so he established a mute army to protect his afterlife from both earthly and spiritual foes. Despite the effort and expense, however, the endeavor failed. A fierce peasant revolution soon toppled the regime, and it is only in our own time that China has been able to recover detailed knowledge about its first emperor.

Death Makes a Hero

Dynamics of a very different sort produced one of the most elaborate funeral processes of the nineteenth century when England's prince consort died unexpectedly after a short illness at the age of 42. Because Prince Albert of Saxe Coburg-Gotha was married to the illustrious Queen Victoria, we might have expected some pomp and circumstance. What actually happened, however, far exceeded the demands of a respectful tribute: a national cult developed around the late prince consort.

Some of the evidence remains available for inspection today. Simply examine the monuments and portraits throughout the British Isles—Balmoral, Aberdeen, Edinburgh, Nottinghamshire, South Kensington, Whippingham, Frogmore, Manchester, and so on. Among the physical tributes in London alone are a memorial chapel in Windsor Castle and the Albert Memorial, which itself is only part of the impressive Victoria and Albert Museum. Existing parks and facilities were renamed in his memory. Alfred Lord Tennyson wrote one of his most famous poems to honor him (*Idylls of the King*). The late prince consort quickly became the most popular image and topic in the land and also something of an industry. Many small statues and other items were manufactured and sold as memorabilia. One could purchase Prince Albert belt clasps, lamps, pencil cases, and stationery. Eventually his handsome likeness would be put on packages and cans of tobacco.

Albert's widow, the queen of England, demonstrated a worshipful attitude toward her late husband and did not allow people to speak of him in the past tense. His private rooms at three favorite residences were preserved just as they had been during his life. A nobleman who visited the queen observed:

> She talked upon all sorts of subjects as usual and referred to the sayings and doings of the Prince as if he was in the next room. It was difficult to believe that he was not, but in his own room where she received me everything was set out on his table and the pen and his blotting-book, his handkerchief on the sofa, his watch going, fresh flowers in the glass, etc., etc., as I had always been accustomed to see them, and as if he might come in at any moment. (Darby & Smith, 1983, p. 4)

The observant Lord Clarendon noted an implicit contradiction in the arrangements. On the one hand, there were the fresh clothes, jug of hot water, and clean towels laid out for the use of the prince, yet a tinted photograph of his corpse hung by the side of his bed. Obviously, the queen was having difficulty in reconciling her conflicting needs to acknowledge reality and to preserve the illusion that her beloved was still with her.

Queen Victoria of England gave her name to an entire age. She remained in mourning long after the death of her beloved husband, Prince Albert, and maintained his rooms as though he were about to return any day. One of her most comforting companions also is seen here: Sharp, who had a natural gift for looking mournful.

What purposes were achieved by the funeral and memorialization process for Prince Albert? I suggest the following:

1. *The elaborate memorialization process served the function of symbolically incorporating Albert into the British Empire.* In effect, he became an En-glishman after his death. This was both a gesture of support for their highly esteemed queen and a way of grafting Albert's attributes onto the national self-image. His noble figure would always stand at alert attention or gracefully sit astride a beautiful horse. The alternative was to lose for the national con-

sciousness one of the more picturesque and talented men of the day, whose qualities were not generally appreciated until a death that was felt to be both unexpected and premature. The memorialization also served as a sort of postmortem compensation for their cool attitude toward Albert (a foreigner) while he was alive. The need to incorporate and preserve what were now seen as his heroic attributes, however, was probably more powerful than the gesture of reconciliation.

2. *Albert's death provided an excellent opportunity to express current sentiment and belief.* Victorian England welcomed this opportunity to affirm values and attitudes that had been developing through the years. This was a period in which manifestations of mourning had become increasingly elaborate. There was implicit competition to see who could express bereavement most impressively. This was accomplished through dark clothing ("widow's weeds"), withdrawal from customary social activities and responsibilities, and idealization and memorialization of the deceased (as evidenced, for example, in the architectural tributes that were erected in cemeteries).

Linked with these customs were affirmations of belief in the certainty and blessings of immortal life. Queen Victoria and Prince Albert appeared to share the prevailing faith. The Victorians' own public self-image emphasized faith and propriety, although skeptics in the society were abundant enough and wondered what other motives were being served or disguised by ostentatious mourning. It was the Victorian age, after all, that provided Sigmund Freud and other pioneering psychoanalysts with the raw material for their exploration of hidden motives and thwarted impulses (Gay, 1984). Albert's death, then, provided a most attractive occasion for expressing private fears, doubts, and hopes in public guise.

The postmortem cult of the prince consort would not have developed had not the spirit of the times been so conducive. Albert could easily be seen as an ideal representation of almost every quality his generation would have liked to claim for its own. A further point should be noted: once the man was dead, his memory could be elaborated upon and fixed for posterity without the danger of competition from his ongoing life. It is often easier to admire dead heroes. They are less likely to turn around and do something that would force us to alter our judgment.

Many more examples could be given of elaborate funeral and memorialization processes for illustrious people. We would find both common and distinctive purposes underlying the practices. A common feature, for example, is the slow, stately tempo favored for the funeral procession itself and for the arrangements in general. This provides more time for the realization of the death and its meanings to sink in. By contrast, the final arrangements for a person not especially valued by society are likely to be simple and routine. It is not surprising that some people who have felt deprived in life have yearned for a dignified or even a spectacular funeral by way of compensation. Within the same society, then, we may find a few people who receive lavish attention in the funerary process while others anxiously hope and pray that their death will be given the basic respect due a human being.

The twentieth century also provided us with vivid examples of the lengths to which a society will go to memorialize one of its members—and of the political and emotional power that can remain associated with the corpse for many years. None of these examples is more compelling or instructive than the public afterlife of Vladimir Ilyich Ulyanov.

From Revolutionary to Relic

I'm standing beside Lenin. The man himself. Can it be true he died ten years ago? I really feel like I'm looking at a man sleeping. You find yourself walking on tiptoe so as not to wake him. In preserving the body of its historic leader the USSR has achieved the seemingly impossible. The embalming of Lenin is the most perfect example I've ever seen of the art—better even than the mummies of ancient Egypt. Don't the Russian scientists say Vladimir Ilich's body may be preserved for all eternity, without ever suffering the ravages of time? (An American visitor, quoted by Zbarsky & Hutchinson, 1997, p. 91)

Russian physicians and scientists gained new respect for the ancient Egyptians when they were ordered to preserve the body of Nicolai Lenin and did not completely succeed. Soldiers guard the tomb of Lenin whose postmortem political status has suffered a decline.

The basic facts about Lenin's life and death are well known. He was the architect of a failed revolution in Czarist Russia in 1905, left the country, but continued to plan and organize his resources for another try. In 1917 Russia was in crisis as the government proved unable either to conduct its war efforts successfully or meet the needs of the people at home. Nicholas II was overthrown. The leadership of the nation was in doubt as a provisional government was quickly thrown together but did not seem very promising. It was at this moment in history that a mysterious sealed train entered Russia from neutral Switzerland. Lenin was its most important passenger. Within a short time, his effective and ruthless leadership brought the Bolshevik Party to power—and the Soviet Union was thereby created. It would later be discovered that Germany, Russia's enemy in the Great War (World War I), had financed and facilitated this venture to knock Russia out of the war. Lenin had become the founding father of a new nation, and the communist experiment had been given its first major opportunity.

Seven years later, Lenin was dead. Wounded by an assassination attempt in 1918 and then partially debilitated by one or more strokes, he became more of a symbol than an active leader during the last year or so of his life. Lenin's death did not bring much personal sorrow. He was consistently described as an ice-cold person completely devoted to his plans and willing to do whatever was necessary to see them through, whatever the consequences to other people. However, his death did create a national crisis through the premature loss of the founding father and the savage infighting among those who hoped to take his place (the genocidal Josef Stalin coming out the winner, and the Russian people thereby the losers).

The newly formed Soviet Union, still in a perilous condition, could not afford to lose its father figure. The decision to embalm Lenin was not at all unusual under the circumstances. Ordinary embalming was not sufficient for the purpose, though. What if Lenin's corpse could be preserved indefinitely in a lifelike condition? And what if this corpse could be placed in a grand mausoleum that would dominate Red Square, the spiritual heart of the nation? And what if people could visit and see for themselves that their founding father, their peerless leader, was still with them?

The irony here should not be overlooked. The Soviet Union conceived by Lenin and his successors had no use for religion, for the ornate grandeur of the recently terminated Tsarist regime, or for "the cult of personality." The preservation of Lenin's body was all for the people, the workers. Nevertheless, a shrine was created for Lenin, who was henceforth to be revered as a de facto patron saint. One mausoleum after another was built until the permanent shrine was completed. The irony perhaps reached its peak when a statue dedicated to the heroic Russian worker was torn down in Red Square to make room for the new mausoleum.

Meanwhile, the task of preserving Lenin's body for the ages had not gone so well. The technique used immediately after his death was not effective. Ilya Zbarsky (1997), the last surviving member of the family that took over the maintenance of Lenin's corpse, reports that the first efforts were primitive, leading to serious deterioration of the body. The face and hands still looked presentable, though, and were regularly touched up with an ointment to prevent drying and cracking. The body was in such bad condition that serious thought was given to burial—but this would have been a national scandal, the admission that Soviet science had failed. Zbarsky describes the innovative techniques they had to come up with to preserve the already deteriorated body (interesting reading for those who are so inclined). The restoration process included cosmetic repair of the face and substitution of false eyes for real ones to prevent the sockets from further shrinking.

How has Lenin fared as a relic? Very well, and not so well. Millions of people have visited his tomb, which became one of the most visible symbols of both Russia and Communism. Furthermore, it is clear that through several decades, a visit to Lenin's tomb was emotionally significant to many Russians. But the Soviet Union has ceased to exist. Statues of Lenin have been pulled down in countries that once were subservient to Moscow. More Russians are in favor of burying Lenin's body than in continuing his exalted place in the mausoleum. Rumors are regularly heard that Lenin's mummified corpse will be stolen some night and buried before the police can react (or perhaps even with police involvement). This would be seen as a blow to the Communist Party, which is still an active force.

Strange, strange, strange—but then, not so strange after all. Many so-called "primitive" societies have not only venerated but also used their powerful dead. The skulls of past chiefs may be consulted for advice, for example. What we see in the memorial process for Lenin is an instructive reminder that modern society still has a core of "primitive" belief and feeling. This emotional core was strong enough to entice a materialistic antireligious regime into preserving and enshrining a corpse with so much determination that it might possibly have earned grudging praise from the ancient Egyptians.

Balancing the Claims of the Living and the Dead

Another major function of the funeral and memorialization process is to achieve a balance between the competing rights or claims of the living and those of the dead. This may sound like a strange idea. We often hear it said that funerals are for the living. In truth, however, the need to honor the claims of the dead is also a common and well-entrenched component of most death systems. It is expressed most clearly in funeral processes rooted in long-standing cultural traditions. Some of these traditions have been assaulted and eroded by changing social conditions. Nevertheless, even today the need to balance the claims of the dead and the living can be discovered if we look beneath the surface. First consider how this process expresses itself in three traditional contexts: rural Greece, the Kotas of southern India, and Orthodox Judaism.

In the Shadow of Mount Olympus

Potamia is a village in Northern Greece not far from Mount Olympus. The 600 people who live there remain in close physical and symbolic contact with the dead. The small cemetery is crowded with twenty or more grave markers that memorialize villagers who have died in the past few years. Anthropologist Alexander Tsiaras describes his entry into a building in the corner of the cemetery:

> Although I knew what I would find inside, I was still not fully prepared for the sight that confronted me when I opened the door. Beyond a small floorspace a ladder led down to a dark, musty-smelling area filled with the bones of many generations of villagers. Near the top of the huge pile the remains of each person were bound up separately in a white cloth. Toward the bottom of the pile the bones—skulls, pelvises, ribs, the long bones of countless arms, and legs—lay in tangled disarray, having lost all trace of belonging to distinct individuals with the disintegration of the cloth wrappings. Stacked in one corner of the building were metal boxes and small suitcases with names, dates, and photographs identifying the people whose bones lay securely within. (1982, pp. 10–11)

By local custom, bodies remain in the graveyard for five years and then are removed to the bone house. During this temporary burial, the survivors have ample time to visit their lost loved ones. The survivors' feelings often become expressed with great intensity as the time nears to exhume and transfer the body. Tsiaras recorded a mother's lament:

> Eleni, Eleni, you died far from home with no one near you. I've shouted and cried for five years, Eleni, my unlucky one, but you haven't heard me. I don't have the courage to shout any more. Eleni, Eleni, my lost soul. You were a young

plant, but they didn't let you blossom. You've been here for five years. Soon you'll leave. Then where will I go? What will I do? Five years ago I put a beautiful bird into the ground, a beautiful partridge. But now what will I take out? What will I find? (1982, p. 15)

In contrast to many cemeteries in the United States, the little graveyard in Potamia is often filled with mourners, usually women. They come not only to express their sorrows through song, speech, and prayer but also to tend the graves. Candles are kept burning at the foot of each grave, and the grounds are tended with scrupulous care. When the gravetending activities have been completed for the day, the women sit and talk to their dead and to each other. The conversation may center on death, and one mourner may seek to comfort another. But the conversation may also include other events and concerns. An important aspect of the village's communal life is mediated through their role as survivors of the dead. For the women especially, the graveyard provides an opportunity to express their *ponos* (the pain of grief). The men find a variety of outlets, but the women are usually expected to be at home and to keep their feelings to themselves. "A woman performs the necessary rites of passage and cares for the graves of the dead 'in order to get everything out of her system'" (1982, p. 144).

The Greek women attempt through their graveside laments and rituals to achieve a balance between the dead and the living. The custom of temporary burial has an important role in this process. The deceased person can still be treated as an individual and as a member of the community, somebody who retains the right of love, respect, and comfort. In effect, the deceased suffers a second and final death when the grave is destroyed and the physical remains are deposited with the bones of the anonymous dead. It is easier to cope with the symbolic claims of the dead when a definite time limit has been set—in this case a rather generous five-year period. Although the memory of the deceased will continue to be honored, removal of the remains to the bone house represents the reemergence of the life-oriented needs of the survivors.

The village cemetery can be a place for comforting socialization as people gather to look after family graves.

The survivors are *obliged* to tend the graves and carry out other responsibilities to the deceased. As Tsiaras points out, this process involves a symbolic interaction and continuation between the living and the dead. *The dead have the right to expect it, just as those who are now among the living can expect their survivors to honor their postmortem rights when the time comes.* In Potamia and in many other communities where traditional value systems remain in place, the obligations of the living to the dead are clear, specific, and well known.

Kotas and Orthodox Jews

Peoples as different as the Kotas of Southern India and Orthodox Jews dispersed throughout the world continue to carry out extensive rituals to ensure that both the dead and the living receive their due. Their observations differ greatly in detail. The Kotas, who cremate their dead,

believe that death is contaminating and all who come into contact with death are defiled. Through the rituals of two funerals, the Green Funeral and the Dry Funeral, the spirit of the deceased is assisted in departing to the "Motherland" and the survivors are thereby cleansed so that they might resume their normal life within the society. Since the concept of an afterlife is not clear to most Kotas, the adherence to ritual is seen more as a cleansing process for the survivors, than for the attainment of existence in another world for the deceased. (Goldberg, 1981–1982, p. 119)

Orthodox Jews obey strict laws and rituals that exclude embalming and cremation and require that funeral arrangements be simple and standard no matter what the family's financial status. An important feature of the response to a death is the special status given to the time between death and burial. This period is known as *Aninut*—a time in which time stands still (Schindler, 1996). During *Aninut*, the grieving survivors are exempted from all social and religious obligations other than arranging for the funeral. It is a time to be devoted to honoring the dead and reflecting on the loss that one has suffered. *Aninut* therefore helps the survivors to begin the long process of recovery from grief by providing a little time to focus on the death in their own private ways, without other distractions. The Burial *Kaddish* prayer affirms faith in God; *shiva*, the seven days of mourning, unites the family in grief.

Interestingly, the ritual action of washing your hands before sitting at *shiva* has its parallel in the more elaborate purification rites of the Kotas. The Kota, the Orthodox Jew, the rural Greek villager, and many others with long ethnic traditions must fulfill obligations to the dead. When these obligations have at last been faithfully performed, however, it is time for the living to again turn their full attention to life.

MEMORIES OF OUR PEOPLE: CEMETERIES IN THE UNITED STATES

At first a nation of farmers who visited small-town artisans and shops, the United States quickly became a coast-to-coast industrial power with humming factories, crowded cities, opportunistic ventures in every direction, and a large and mobile population. The history of cemeteries has faithfully moved in concert with our changing ways of life. In Colonial times, most of the dead were buried in a church graveyard. This practice continued into the early years of the republic. As the population increased, however, these early burial grounds often proved inadequate. The dead as well as the living were becoming crowded. Furthermore, cemetery upkeep was too often neglected, resulting in conditions that were not only unpleasant for the visitor but also dangerous to public health.

The New Haven Burying Ground is a surviving example of the response to this emerging need. The city established a cemetery in 1639, in what is now the center of New Haven (Plunkett, 1999). Graves were dug by friends and relatives, who placed them wherever it seemed suitable or convenient and also marked and tended them as they saw fit. Just twenty years later, there was already concern that the burial ground had become too crowded, but nothing was done about it. The poorly tended and helter-skelter burial ground had the virtue of being adjacent to a church, but it was otherwise becoming an increasing eyesore in the growing community. The closely packed gravesites did not speak well for dignity and respect. Moreover, the seasonal death toll from diseases such as malaria and tuberculosis further strained the resources of the graveyard. People with some awareness of public health concerns worried about the possibility that the burial ground itself might be a source of infection.

In 1796 the community finally responded with the establishment of the New Haven Burying Ground (also known as the Grove Street Cemetery). Care was taken to select land that was accessible and yet would not block further community development. Furthermore, each grave lot became the property of a purchasing family—here was one of the first cemeteries in which "the family plot" became established. Future generations could return to view their family plot and to consider whether they would also end up there. The New Burial Ground was added under similar regulations a few years later. Unfortunately, though, even cemeteries planned with personal and social dignity and public health in mind are vulnerable to conflict and change. Some citizens advocated and some opposed new church constructions that would create problems for the again-overcrowded burying ground. Many grave sites were neglected. Animals and vandals invaded at night, the former digging up graves and the latter desecrating memorial stones and littering. The people of New Haven again rallied and protected their cemetery. This basic story has been repeated in many cemeteries as communities cope with the challenges of urban change and the consequences of neglect.

Major changes in cemeteries occurred throughout the nineteenth century. One of the most important was the introduction of "memorial parks," also sometimes known as "landscapes of memory" (Linden-Ward, 1989). The first of these was Mount Auburn Cemetery (Cambridge, Massachusetts), whose spacious and inviting grounds quickly became the inspiration for similar developments throughout the nation. The Park Lawn–type establishment had its origins in the sensitivity of community leaders who believed that a visit to the dead should bring us into comforting touch with nature. The other major development was the establishment of national cemeteries to honor those who had fallen in war. Lincoln's Gettysburg Address on November 11, 1863, was given to dedicate the first national cemetery. By the end of the Civil War, there were fourteen national cemeteries for both Union and Confederate dead. The National Cemetery System today tends to the graves of more than two million veterans in more than a hundred sites throughout the country. In history's odd way of doing things, the United States became that much more of a nation when the dead of the Blue and the dead of the Gray were placed to rest in the same meadows.

The Neighborhood Cemetery

Pockets of traditional symbolic interaction with the dead still exist in American cities. While interviewing older people in small industrial cities, I often heard reference to the neighborhood cemetery. Although the cemetery may have been surrounded by deteriorating industrial buildings, it remained the focal point of continuity. One octogenarian, for example, said:

I know I should get out of this neighborhood. Hell, it isn't even a neighborhood anymore, not like the old days. But how can I sell this house? It's where my mother and father lived and died. And who'd look after them?…Oh, sure, I'm out there every Sunday at least to keep things as nice as I can. It's not their fault what's happened to this neighborhood. Me and a few others still meet there, we keep up the graves. And it's not just my parents. Just about everybody else is there, too, I mean, six feet under. I keep them company. They keep me company.

This man, by the way, was not at all of morbid disposition. He had an active and well-integrated lifestyle but drew some of his strength and self-esteem from the knowledge that he was continuing to fulfill his obligations to the dead.

Many other examples of continued bonding or symbolic transactions between the living and the dead can be associated with the funeral and memorialization process. Even in bustling, urban America survivors often select images, materials, and objects connected with the deceased to keep the beloved alive somehow, as part of themselves. Salient or treasured aspects of the deceased's personality become part of the survivor's lifestyle; therefore the memorialization process continues well beyond the funeral itself.

Ethnic Cemeteries in the United States

The shores of the United States have attracted millions of people who sought to make new lives for themselves and their children. Others were brought here involuntarily, wrenched from their homelands and sold into slavery. Still other people lived freely in forests and plains until they encountered the aggressive newcomers who would eventually transform a wilderness into a powerful industry-driven nation. Memories of this incredible variety of people remain with us in many forms. Poet Stephen Vincent Benet (1942) reflects on this heritage:

I have fallen in love with American names,
The sharp names that never get fat,
The snakeskin-titles of mining-claims,
The plumed war-bonnet of Medicine Hat,
Tucson and Deadwood and Lost Mule Flat….
I will remember Carquinez Straits,
Little French Lick and Lundy's Lane,
The Yankee ships and the Yankee dates
And the bullet-towns of Calamity Jane.
I will remember Skunktown Plain….
I shall not rest quiet in Montparnasse.
I shall not lie easy at Winchelsea.
You may bury my body in Sussex grass,
You may bury my tongue at Champmedy.
I shall not be there. I shall rise and pass.
Bury my heart at Wounded Knee.

The land also remembers. Ethnic cemeteries, often overlooked by society at large, still affirm that "our people" lived their own distinctive lives here and contributed to the nation's history. Following are a few examples of cemeteries whose responsibility is to preserve not physical remains, but memories and symbols of those who have gone before us.

1. *African American section, the Common Burying Ground, Newport, Rhode Island.* This colonial cemetery dates from 1650. More than 8,000 people were buried here until it became an historical site. Only a few years ago, a visitor realized that this was probably the only remaining burial site of African Americans in colonial New England. Ann Tashjian and her husband, Dickran Tashjian (1989), photographed and transcribed the gravestones and researched the history. Many of the gravemarkers describe the deceased as "servant," which is thought to have been a euphemism for "slave" (a term considered too harsh, even though accurate, in New England households of the time). Some of the gravestones are elaborate in design and execution, suggesting that the deceased had been held in high regard by the white families they served.

Do the gravestones or burial sites show any trace of the cultures and belief systems that the African Americans left behind when they were brought to the American colonies? None. Whatever beliefs and practices these people may have continued to cherish from their own tradition, upon their deaths the dominant white American culture of the time prevailed. If you visit this cemetery, make your way to the northern edge and you will see those African American gravemarkers that have survived the vicissitudes of time. You will see that they are similar to the other gravemarkers of the same time periods. Cherubs, for example, were popular adornments, and these appear on white and African American gravemarkers alike.

The cemetery itself, then, tells us something about the subordinate place of African Americans in colonial New England; in death as in life, their own culture was denied expression. The Tashjians found that a Free African Union Society, active in the Eighteenth century, had encouraged Afro Americans "to assume a dignified public appearance [at funerals] to protect the integrity of private grief" (1989, p. 192). Along with other evidence, this suggests that the occasion of death was seen as

having potential for racial tension, with the dominant white society seeking to maintain its control over the funeral services and burial. The longing to be free, so often expressed in gospel songs, takes on added significance here. In death an African American would become free of servitude, but the public memory of his or her existence would still be under the control of the dominant society.

2. *Navajo and Mormon companions, Ramah Cemetery, Ramah, New Mexico.* Members of The Church of the Latter-day Saints (often referred to as Mormons) started a community in Ramah, New Mexico, in 1876. The Ramah people of the Navajo nation had previously taken up residence in this area. The same graveyard serves families of both cultures, although their beliefs and practices differ markedly. The cemetery was established by the Mormons on a knoll surrounded by farm and ranch land. There are no large memorial statues, and the ground is covered by the native grasses and weeds.

The Navajo section includes seventy-one graves that could be positively identified. A few recent graves have commercially manufactured gravestones, and a few others are decorated with artificial flowers, but most are undecorated. "There is no indication of any attempt to bury family members side by side or close together. All the graves are approximately the same distance apart and are laid out in what is basically a straight line. The headstone or other marker and the grave are placed so that the main side of the marker and the head of the deceased point toward the West, and the deceased would face East if sitting or standing" (Cunningham, 1989, p. 204).

This description tells only part of the story, however. Beneath the earth, the Navajo culture expresses itself through valued objects placed with the dead. Turquoise jewelry is thought to have special powers, attributed both to the gemstones themselves and to the spirituality transmitted by the artists. In burying this jewelry with the deceased, the family both speeds its spirit on its journey to the afterlife and confuses and thwarts any *ch'iidii* (evil ghosts) that might covet these powerful objects.

The Mormon section (209 graves) has numerous markers, some of them homemade by family members. These markers display a large variety of style and materials, in contrast with the simple metal markers that identify the Navajo graves. The Mormon markers include examples of folk art revival, such as red sandstone carvings and "an actual picture of the deceased as a part of their design and contemporary sand-blasted stones which allow very intricate and exact representations of floral motifs and even recognizable representations of Mormon temples at Mesa, Arizona, and Salt Lake City, Utah" (1989, p. 204). The Mormon graves also differ from the Navajo in their spatial arrangement: they are usually grouped according to family relationships, including some joint stones for husband and wife. The memorial stones also provide more information about the deceased.

The Navajo and Mormon dead in New Mexico appear to be more companionable than the African Americans and colonial whites in Newport. The cemetery itself blends easily into its surroundings, the "landscaping" for both Navajo and Mormon left up to nature. The family-oriented Mormons preserved this orientation in the arrangement of graves and markers but did not impose their beliefs and practices upon their Native American neighbors nor object to the jewelry burials. For their part, some Navajos have chosen to become Mormon—or "semi-Mormon"—and have expressed the thought that the worst of the evil spirits have departed from the burial grounds because of the Mormons' presence.

Ironically, perhaps, the Mormons feel that this cemetery meets their needs because it pays respect to the dead in an appropriate manner, while the traditional Navajos find it satisfactory as a place that keeps the dead (and the dangerous ghosts they attract) away from the living. Navajo and Mormon appear to have respected and learned from each other in life and to have shared the land in a manner acceptable to both. And now, in death, they can lie under the same ground without requiring one faith to bow to the wishes of the other.

3. *Mexican Americans in San Antonio's San Fernando Cemetery.* The standardization of American life extends to many urban cemeteries: this one does not look much different from that one. Lynn Gosnell and Suzanne Gott describe some of the activity at a cemetery that has retained its special character:

> Throughout the year, but especially during religious and secular holidays, including Halloween, All Souls' Day, Christmas, Valentine's Day, Easter, Mother's Day, and Father's Day, the visitor to San Fernando takes part in an energetic practice of grave decoration and visual display. During these days, cars and trucks jam the narrow traffic lanes which provide access to each block of this ninety-three acre cemetery. Relatives crowd the burial grounds, bringing with them gardening tools, flowers, and other decorative materials.... Some people busily tend to a gravesite, while others take time to chat and remark on a particularly well-decorated grave site. Still others stand quietly, singly or in groups, near the grave of a loved one. Grave decorating days within San Fernando Cemetery are therefore marked by a lively social interaction between the living and a heightened interaction between families and their deceased loved ones. (1989, p. 218)

The visitors are Mexican Americans who follow Roman Catholic beliefs and practices. How important is this cemetery to them? Each family could continue to remember and honor its own dead privately, but having a cemetery to share with other people who hold similar beliefs and values adds several major dimensions to the memorial process. The dead have their special place, which the living can visit (just like one living person might visit another). Furthermore, when one arrives at the gravesite, there are things to do for the loved ones (again, reminiscent of what one living family member might do for another). No less important is the vista: "We are not the only people to have lost a loved one. It is the human condition. We are, all of us, together in our respect for the dead and our celebration of life." Finally, after the trip, the decorating, the interaction, the family returns home and is able to separate, for a while, from the dead. Some outsiders might be puzzled or even annoyed by all this activity at a cemetery—have they never felt isolated by a loss, and never carried a death around with them, unable to set it down even for a moment?

These are but three examples of ethnic cemeteries in the United States today. Can you find examples in your own area? And can you read the stories they tell?

THE PLACE OF THE DEAD IN SOCIETY: YESTERDAY AND TODAY

Society today places a strong emphasis on curing illness and preventing death. By contrast, most death systems in the past gave more emphasis to relationships with the dead. Following is a brief comparison of the place of the dead in the past, which will prepare us to consider the meaning and impact of what seemed to be a distinctly un-American phenomenon: The Vietnam Veterans Memorial.

When Are the Dead Important to the Living?

1. *The dead are more secure in past-oriented societies.* They maintain a role in the symbolic continuity of people with shared language and cultural values who have lived in the same place for many generations, perhaps even for centuries. If the past is known, valued, and seen as relevant to daily life, the dead are likely to be respected. For example, the Penang Gang people of central Borneo give new names or titles to their family members when they die. This practice represents their continuing affection for deceased people they loved and also provides them with powerful words (the death-names) that can be called upon in vows and curses (Brosius, 1995–1996). By contrast, in future-oriented societies the past is often seen as something to be transcended and improved upon. Technological knowledge, ever-changing, is more valued than the wisdom and values of the dead past, and the dead themselves are seldom considered relevant to everyday life.

2. *Geographical detachment from the dead will cause distress to the living, especially in past-oriented societies.* Vietnamese families who were relocated by the American military during "pacification" efforts expressed great anguish in having to depart from the land where the spirits of their remote and recent ancestors held sway. Native Americans were subject to the same kind of stress and loss for many years, and there are still active cases in which tribes are being pressured to move from their sacred ancestral lands. When we have all become ancestors, our decendents may feel even less concern for the dead because fewer people will have formed deep, long-term attachments to particular places (Scheidt, 1993).

3. *The dead will be remembered and "used" more often in societies in which children are highly valued as continuing the family soul over the gap created by death.* Research suggests that young Americans today do not generally regard children as important for this purpose (Kastenbaum, 1974). Each individual (and each generation) is seen as having its own moment in the sun, free to pursue its own pleasures and values but not linked inexorably, as was often the case in the past.

4. *Longer life expectancy and low vested power of the elderly tend to make the dead less important.* In earlier times, many people died at an age we would now consider premature. Such deaths often are especially painful and disruptive to the survivors. The incomplete lives are therefore more likely to be carried forth in memory, propelled by their unfinishedness. Today more people live to an advanced age, and the survivors do not have a sense of incompleteness that must be compensated by memorialization. Furthermore, in today's youth oriented world, older people do not as often control property and wealth and therefore are less powerful and less in need of being honored or placated. Older people also seem to be losing some of the special status once enjoyed when they were thought of as close to the gods and ancestral spirits.

5. *A society lacking unifying and transcending themes will assimilate the funeral and memorialization process into its utilitarian motives.* The rural Greek villagers, the Kota, and the Orthodox

Jews each in their own way, persist in treating the dead in a manner intended to bestow honor and respect as well as eventually to free the survivor for renewal of life. The time, expense, and inconvenience of this process do not discourage them, nor do the misunderstanding, ridicule, and hostility that they might on occasion receive from others.

When a society does not have strong shared values of a unifying and transcending type, the funeral process loses its special status. The cost of the funeral may become the most salient concern. If the living no longer attach importance to the dead, the funeral might as well be as inexpensive as possible. Similarly, not too much time should be "wasted" on funeral rituals. (Even in the slower-paced, rural South, I have heard mourners complain that a funeral "dragged on too long. One flower girl wasn't enough! They had to have three, and all of them took their own sweet time!") *For the dead to be useful, they have to be functional, just like everybody else, and earn their place.* If public recognition of the dead continues to diminish, donating organs may be one of the few ways in which the dead can remain a part of society.

6. *Societies that live close to nature need the assistance of the dead to promote fertility and regeneration.* The Merian of Madagascar, for example, make sure that the female element (the body) has thoroughly decomposed so that the male element (the bleached bones) can emerge purified and ensure that both the people and their harvests will be fertile (Bloch, 1982). The decomposition process is thought to be dangerous, but it is also very important. A Merina cannot shrink from the reality of decay as people tend to do at Western funeral services, because it is from decay that the miracle of regeneration is wrought. Bloch sees one of the major functions of the Merina funeral process as transforming death into life. The dead are very important because it is literally from their breath and bones that the species regenerates itself.

American Memory and the Vietnam Veterans Memorial

With the rise of technology and industrialization, the dead have been losing status. There are signs, however, that many people have been longing to reintegrate the dead into their lives if society is ready to support this need. Perhaps the most striking example is the way in which the people of the United States have taken the Vietnam Veterans Memorial to their hearts. What would persuade a nation so often described as "death-denying" to become so moved by a memorial to a war that we wanted to forget as quickly as possible? And why would so many people not only make a pilgrimage to the memorial, but also bring objects of personal and symbolic meaning to leave there?

The illuminating story of the Vietnam Veterans Memorial is well told by Kristin Ann Hass (1998). She recounts the fierce objections to Maya Lin's design for the memorial wall. It was too abstract, too intellectual. The black stone suggested mourning rather than heroism. The divided response to the design clearly revealed the nation's divided response to the war itself: had we won a noble victory, or had the war been a human disaster, a senseless killing field? One of the decisive factors in the decision to create the memorial was the support given by many veterans of the conflict, who felt that making war should be not celebrated but that the names of their buddies deserved to be honored and remembered.

The innovative design of the memorial wall proved to be ideally suited for its purpose. Everything about the wall invites reflection and personal involvement. The reflection is literal as well as symbolic: visitors see themselves mirrored by the wall at the same time that they read the names. We all become part of the wall and its memories, if only for the moment. Furthermore, how the names are *not* arranged makes its own point. The conventional and the arbitrary were set aside when it was decided not to present the names in alphabetical order. Rank, military unit, and home state were also ignored. Instead, with unassailable logic, the names are placed in order of death. It would be difficult to devise a more compelling way to make it clear that men and women died as individuals and should be remembered as such.

The Vietnam Veterans Memorial has made such a deep impression on so many people because the record of deaths reminds us of the personal lives of those whose names are on the wall.

The Vietnam Memorial Wall initially faced a wall of criticism, but since has been recognized as a compelling remembrance of the men and women who did not return from the war.

It has made such a deep impression because it makes public the private grief of so many people. And it has made such a deep impression because it encourages reflection and healing of the nation after a painful and divisive chapter in our history—one that bears some comparison with the Civil War in that regard. That so many people continue to bring something of their own to leave at the wall also suggests that this memorial still has much work to do.

> The things left at the Wall make a lot of noise. They constitute a remarkable conversation. It is a conversation about the shape of the nation, the status of the citizen, and the problem of patriotism. It is a conversation about the impossibility of loss, the deaths of sons, and the births of granddaughters.... It is impassioned and unfin-

ished, and it gives us a tremendous opportunity to witness the process of ordinary Americans struggling to make meanings of, to make sense of, the Vietnam War and all of its difficult and complicated legacies.

child's painting	red panties	Zippo lighter
eagle feather	cornhusk	cookie
stuffed dog	poem	key chain
tissue with lipstick	(1998, pp. 123–124)	

Remembering those who died during the Vietnam War has contributed much to the national consciousness about deaths in general. Hass observes that the AIDS quilt and a number of other large-scale remembrances of death have followed in the wake of the wall. In other words, as a nation we are once again finding a way to integrate those we have lost into our ongoing lives. This can only make us stronger. Another important example of our renewed appreciation for the symbolic relationship between the dead and the living is illustrated by the Vermillion Accord and the actions that have since followed.

An Ethical Position on the Treatment of Human Remains: The Vermillion Accord

The central problem here has been well expressed by Glen W. Davidson:

"Do you know where *your* ancestors are?" This question, on a South Dakota pickup truck's bumper sticker, captures the essence of contemporary controversies over human remains. A day seldom goes by without the media informing us about people in this world who are offended, scandalized, or manipulated through the use of human remains…the vivid images of faithful Iranians trying to touch the body of Ayatollah Ruhollah Khomeini and the bearers losing control of the bier; of the French wrestling with the desecration of a Jewish cemetery by vandals who disinterred an elderly man's body and impaled it on an umbrella; of the unending anguish of MIA family and friends over the absence of a body from conflict in Vietnam; of armed Mohawk Indians holding Canadian soldiers to a standoff over the issue of a municipality expanding a golf course onto a native cemetery; of Philippine foreign policy shaped by the quarrel over the final resting place of Ferdinand Marcos; and the legal battles over the ethics and legality of medical researchers using discarded body tissues without the knowledge of the donor—all examples, by no means exhaustive, of the daily struggle of human beings to enact in every death the values of their society. According to a myth of identity common to many peoples, not to know where the ancestors are is to violate the most basic value of life that results in being confined to a realm of chaos, drift, or hell. (1990, p. 491)

Strong protests by Native Americans over the desecration of gravesites and the appropriation of human remains and sacred artifacts provided much of the stimulus for the First Intercongress on the Disposition of the Dead. Sponsored by the World Archeological Congress in August 1989, this unusual meeting brought representatives of native peoples around the world together with scientists and others who have a special interest in the topic. One of the outcomes of this conference was a statement that became known as The Vermillion Accord (the meetings having been held in Vermillion, South Dakota).

The main points of the accord:

- Universal respect shall be given to the mortal remains of the dead.
- Disposition of human remains will be made in accordance with the wishes of the dead themselves whenever this is known or can be reasonably inferred.
- The wishes of the local community will be respected "whenever possible, reasonable, and lawful."
- The scientific value of studying human remains will be respected whenever such value can be demonstrated to exist.
- Negotiations with an attitude of mutual respect shall be conducted to accommodate both the legitimate concerns of communities for the proper disposition of their ancestors and the legitimate concerns of science and education. (Day, 1990)

Arizona's celebrated Heard Museum had anticipated the accord by several years when it voluntary returned to Native American tribes some of the most valuable artifacts it had received from private collectors. The museum directors explained that these sacred objects would have been used by the Native American community as a whole; for them to have been hidden away by collectors was equivalent to theft. Some other museum have since done the same. The Vermillion Accord of itself does not immediately correct all grievances and assure that mutual respect will prevail from now on. It does, however, establish both a goal and an affirmation of a principle that can help to heal society in general.

"You Were the Best Dog Ever": The Pet Cemetery

I have turned over the rocky ground of Massachusetts and the dry sands of Arizona to bury several very important cats. When the previous dog of the family died quietly in his basket-bed, none of us could regard Toby's body as only the corpse of an animal. Millions of other people have had close attachments to their pets—or to animals they have worked with: the horse who drew the milkman's wagon, the dog who guided its visually impaired owner, and so on. Attachment does not automatically end at death, whether the loss be that of another human or of an animal companion.

The pet cemetery is one instructive example of the way in which some people attempt to cope with the death of an animal companion. The modern version of the pet cemetery seems to have started in France around the turn of the twentieth century. Not only dogs and cats, but also horses, monkeys, rabbits, birds (and a lioness) have been buried there. Perhaps the most famous "resident" is Rin-Tin-Tin, once the reigning animal star of Hollywood. However, the impulse to honor the memory of an animal companion through a funeral and burial process has been expressed throughout history. There are examples among the ancient Greeks and in the early years of our own nation. In the United States, 145 pet cemeteries are affiliated with the International Association of Pet Cemeteries, an organization that attempts to set professional standards and provide public information. It is estimated that perhaps another 250 have not affiliated themselves.

Pet cemeteries in the United States express some of the same mixed and changing attitudes toward death that characterize our society in general. For an example, consider Pet Rest Memorial Mortuary and Cemetery. Located just up the road from Arizona State University (Tempe), Pet Rest provided the opportunity for a study by Vivian Spiegelman and me (1990). At the time of our visits, Pet Rest resembled many another small cemetery, a fenced-in, park-like space with a variety of grave markers. Some graves were decorated with plastic flowers; some markers include a photographic or sculptured representation of the deceased. Ceramic cats played inside a white picket fence at one gravesite. But we also noticed that the burial ground was not well cared for. Some monuments had already fallen into the weedy grass, and there was a general impression of neglect. What had happened?

Pet Rest had become a "dead cemetery,"—no more burials were allowed, and nobody had accepted the responsibility for maintenance. If there is a villain to this piece, it is the pressure of urban development. The continuing influx of people into Arizona, the change from an agricultural to a residential community, the transformation of a small college into one of the nation's largest universities—these are among the factors that contributed to the decline and eventual destruction of Pet Rest. The land had become too valuable now to be "wasted" on dead animals. City officials were also uncomfortable with having death on display while attempting to "upscale" commercial properties in the area. Meanwhile, those who cared enough for their pets to purchase a "final resting place" were both distressed about the present circumstances and fearful about the future. In this sense, Pet Rest was proving vulnerable to pressures of economic and social change that also affect many "regular" cemeteries across the nation. Other pet cemeteries have been forced to relocate the physical remains when the land was literally sold from over them, and there are reports that in some instances the remains were simply carted away and dumped. And now, just a few years after our study, Pet Rest no longer exists, its "eternal memory" on the way to being replaced by a nationally franchised restaurant.

Those who see the pet cemetery as a meaningful way of remembering animal companions may have to confront some painful economic and political realities. However, many other people have found it consoling to conduct their own memorial services upon the death of a pet, and to satisfy themselves with photographs in the family album—and, perhaps, a trip to the local animal shelter to save a life that might otherwise be lost. (We came home with Honey, the current dog in residence, and Ezra, a bonus cat as well, not to mention a subsequent trio of kittens from an animal rescue service).

Pet cemeteries have invited parody and mockery on occasion. And people have sometimes behaved oddly after the death of a four-footed (or feathered) friend. Nevertheless, those who understand and value the bonds of affection that can form between one creature and another may judge that "too much" love is not the worst thing that might be said of a person.

CURRENT DEVELOPMENTS: A FUNERAL DIRECTOR'S PERSPECTIVE

As we have already seen, funeral and memorialization practices are very much part of the world of the living and, therefore, subject to change. An interview with Tom Carrick, one of the most respected funeral directors in the Southwest, proved helpful in identifying some of the major challenges and developments.

- *The impact of AIDS?* "Everybody in the funeral industry over-reacted at first. Now we realize that we can do our part in dealing with AIDS and cannot behave in a discriminatory manner. We do give more attention to personal safety. Precautions are used in handling all cases now because one can never be certain about AIDS. For example, we wear gloves every time we touch a cadaver. Instead of smocks, we now use rubber aprons and complete protective clothing, including eye wear. All "sharps" go into specified and controlled waste containers. Essentially, funeral personnel are doing the same things that health care providers and other people who provide personal services are doing—being more careful."

- *Have there been changes in the way that funeral directors do business over the past few years?* "Enormous changes. Laws have changed and regulations have increased. For example, we are now mandated to provide full price disclosures to the public. Written consents are required for embalming. Employees must be given time off for continuing education sessions. Fair employment practices have increased access by women who are entering this field in larger numbers than ever before. These changes provide benefits to the public. Sometimes, though, a funeral director will feel resentful at being *made* to do these things. But health care professionals and many others must also accommodate themselves to laws and regulations that are intended to benefit the public."

- *Have these regulations affected your cost of operations?* Yes, considerably so. Every funeral home has had to remodel to provide access for handicapped individuals and to meet other health and safety standards. For examples, chemicals must be stored in sealed compartments with security locks so that people do not become exposed to any risk from them. Most of these changes are worthwhile, but they are costly. We feel a little oppressed sometimes not by legitimate requirements, but by the confusing and overlapping levels of regulatory authority that can take much of our time and energy away from direct service to the public."

- *You mentioned that more women have become funeral directors in recent years. How has this change been received and perceived?* "The public has had a favorable response. Many client families feel more comfortable in dealing with women. Frequently it is a widow who is making the arrangements. She may perceive a woman funeral director as more understanding and sympathetic. In the past there was a reluctance to hire women and only a few women were qualified. Part of this reluctance came from the enormous amount of lifting that is involved. But now women work in construction; women drive trucks; women work successfully in many occupations that were thought to be for men only. It's not that the conditions of work have changed so much—it's the attitudes that have changed about what women can and should do. Funeral directing is a very conservative business that tends to be slow in adapting to change. In metropolitan areas we see more rapid change than in rural areas."

- *What does a person have to know to become a funeral director?* "A person needs to become proficient in anatomy, chemistry, restorative art, pathology, business, accounting, and some law. These subjects are included in the licensure exams. Once a person is licensed, it is important to keep up with new developments through continued education, for example, handling situations in which contagious diseases might be involved. Unfortunately, there has been a tendency for continued education sessions to be oriented toward marketing and sales, rather than consumer services. Our field could benefit by increasing the quantity and quality of continued education—and, fortunately, the trend is in this direction."

- *Can you take us through the typical or most common funeral?* "The funeral itself will typically begin with a musical prelude, followed by an opening prayer. About half the people we deal with are 'churched.' This leaves the other half in need of a presiding clergyperson, so we frequently recommend one. Some families give a high priority to the choice of a particular clergyperson. Others say, 'I don't care who you get for my Mom's funeral. I want it brief!' This illustrates the larger differences in how families approach funeral planning. Some are concerned about every detail; some couldn't care less.

    "After the opening prayer there are often introductory remarks by a person who represents the family. In recent years there has been more participation by family and friends. In particular, more teens are stepping up to contribute to the memorialization. Any number of family and friends may give scripture readings, recite poetry, eulogize the deceased, or play music, either live or recorded. Words of comfort are usually offered by the clergyperson, but others may also express themselves in their own words."

- *What is the usual time-length of a funeral these days?* "The typical funeral lasts between twenty and forty minutes. This duration has been consistent over the years. The public seems to prefer brief services. I don't really know why this is the case. Perhaps this would be a good topic to investigate."

- *And what about the question of open or closed casket?* "Most people still prefer the casket open for a portion of the time. Today it is most common for the deceased to wear their own clothing. It is usually a suit, shirt, and tie for man, a dress for a woman. There are regional differences, however. Yesterday we had a funeral in which the man wore a western shirt and jeans. This might seem unusual in New York City, but not here [Arizona] or in Aspen. If somebody never wore a suit or necktie, why should they be forced to change their habits now? If a lady was always seen in a pink dress, they're probably going to bury her in a pink dress, and get pink flowers…"

- *How much is the typical funeral likely to cost?* "The national average is between $6,000 and $8,000 for a complete traditional funeral. This includes both mortuary and cemetery expenses, such as the burial plot, flowers, clergy, musicians, and limousine. The cost differs somewhat from one place to another. It tends to be higher in the eastern than in the western states."

- *How common is cremation?* "It's now close to 50 percent in Arizona. Cremation is much more likely to be chosen in Sunbelt areas where people have relocated late in their lives and are away from their roots. It's perceived as too expensive to have two funeral services, one here and one in the place of their origin. We are a more mobile society these days, so more people find themselves in this situation. Solely from the standpoints of economy and simplicity, it is easier to cremate and have the ashes sent to Iowa.

    "About half of those who choose cremation also choose earth burial. This may be a significant development because less space is needed for urn burial as compared with an adult grave. For those who are concerned about the availability or cost of cemetery space, cremation followed by earth burial could contribute to the solution. Churches are now starting to add *columbaria*. These are walls—either inside or outside—that contain niches for the placement of ashes (or, *cremains*, as these are often called)."

- *What is your experience with preplanning funerals?* "This has become a big issue. Preplanning is strongly encouraged both by industry and consumer groups. It can be very useful to the family in avoiding the need to make numerous major decisions at the time of death. Disagreements can arise within the family that add tension and conflict to the loss and sorrow. Preplanning can be done either with or without prepayment. The advantage of prepaying is that it locks in the price. If this is not a concern, then the family still can benefit by preplanning."

- *There are different opinions about the appropriateness of including children in the funeral process. How do you see this?* "I'm all for it. Death is part of life. Children should be exposed to it as often as it occurs. Parents may be poorly prepared to educate our kids about death and dying, but the best way to do that is to attend funerals when opportunity presents itself. We shouldn't be running and hiding from death. The ideal funeral should be an uplifting experience, reinforcing all the values this person stood for, and why we loved this person and are here today."

- *From the practical standpoint, in your role as a funeral director what is your worst case scenario about what might go wrong?* "I worry most about breakdown of equipment. What if the hearse breaks down, or the air conditioning fails in the summer months either in the building or the limousine? Actually, we had a breakdown Saturday. There were forty cars in line when the alternator went out. The hearse stopped in the middle of the road. We radio-dispatched, a replacement vehicle was sent, and we caught up fifteen minutes later. The potential for family upset is high when something like this happens, but this family took it in course.

"In some 30,000 funerals only one stands out as a total embarrassment to me personally. I call it 'The Funeral from Hell.' Every conceivable thing went wrong—from equipment failures right down to the cemetery digging the wrong grave! Mom's name was even on the headstone, but they dug 25 feet away on a 115-degree day. To make it even worse, the death was a sudden and tragic one. Oh, yes, and the sound system at the church picked that day to quit working; actually, it exploded! A key family member was late, one limo didn't show up, and another broke down. There was a mix-up with the flowers as well. Fortunately, this was the memorable exception and I don't feel the need to have another funeral memorable in this way, ever!"

- *Looking back over thirty years as a funeral director, what stands out as most important to you personally?* "I've walked in the shoes they're walking in, and I think people appreciate that. I identify with their loss, so it is natural for me to offer all the time they need and all the understanding I can bring to the situation. I remind myself each time that I am a total stranger who has been invited into a family's life at a time of loss and sorrow. My challenge is to put them at ease. This is not easy: 'How can I relax—my mother just died!' I derive my satisfaction from helping people through these stressful situations.

"I would like the readers of this book to know that we, as a society in general, need to understand how much death is part of life. As parents and teachers we don't do a particularly good job of it. We are still a death-denying society. We don't talk about funerals unless we just came from one!"

IMPROVING THE FUNERAL PROCESS

This chapter began with the question "Why have funerals?" You were offered a set of questions to help you identify your personal attitudes and knowledge base. Now we have explored some major aspects of the funeral process together and, along the way, found answers to the questions of fact. You are now in a position to review your own attitudes toward the funeral process in general as well as your own personal involvement. Perhaps you will select for yourself one of the extreme positions: that funerals are either an expensive and morbid waste of time and money, or that funerals should constitute the central juncture of private and public interactions. A position somewhere between these extremes would hold that the funeral process does serve important human needs, but that the process could be improved. Many of the purposes underlying funeral processes have already been noted. Perhaps the most basic need of all is to help the survivors achieve the emotional realization that one of their fellow mortals has in fact died and that they must find a way to go on in this person's absence. Nevertheless, many are convinced that the traditional commercial funeral process does not always meet these needs adequately and that alternatives should be explored.

Alternative Funerals

The usual suggested alternative is for a swift, simple, and inexpensive form of body disposal rather than a more elaborate, public process. Even "churched" people with conservative religious orientations sometimes feel that funerals are too expensive and elaborate (Bergen & Williams, 1982). These small-town, Midwestern Protestants, however, also believe that the funeral and memorialization process provides an important source of support for the survivors. They prefer an alternative type of funeral in which there is less formal ritual and more opportunity for the entire congregation to participate actively and comfort the bereaved. Active participation in some aspect of the funeral process is likely to be of value to the survivors. An increasing number of funeral directors welcome greater participation by the families and are receptive to requests for special elements in the funeral process.

The death awareness movement has improved the ability of both the survivors and funeral director to respond to the specific situation rather than to rely upon a standardized ritual and service. The nature and the scope of funeral arrangements can be designed through the collaboration of the survivors and the funeral director. At times the dying person is also willing and able to specify important details. In answering the open-ended questions at the beginning of this chapter, you may have come up with some valuable ideas for alternative funeral arrangements. An attitudinal climate is now developing in which it is becoming easier to consider alternatives. This requires more open communication among the survivors and between the survivors and the funeral director than what has often taken place.

Although the specific ceremonies may change and become more diversified, it is likely that most funeral services will continue to have a ritualistic quality. Margaret Mead has defined ritual as the "ability of the known form to reinvoke past emotion, to bind the individual to his own past experience, and to bring the members of the group together in a shared experience…[giving] people access to intensity of feelings at times when responsiveness is muted" (1976, p. 903). Facing death is certainly one of those situations that challenge our individual integrity and group feeling and that therefore seem to issue a call for ritual. But in our own times, it is not always easy to tolerate rituals. Mead continues, "Contemporary American celebrations suffer from our objections to anything we can classify as ritualistic, repetitive, or even familiar."

Today many observers believe that our society needs ritual more than ever before. We are faced with so many changes in our lives and have such a difficult time in relating ourselves simultaneously to past, present, and future that rituals can serve the vital function of confirming our bonds with people and symbols beyond the moment.

Those who prefer a simple and inexpensive funeral are likely to find support and assistance through *memorial societies*. These are nonprofit organizations that help people to arrange basic, dignified, and economical funerals and memorial gatherings. The type of funeral process cultivated by memorial societies could be characterized as "down to earth" and has appealed to many people who have other priorities for their limited financial resources and/or disapprove of elaborate funeral observations. (For up to date information on local memorial societies, write to: Continental Association of Funeral and Memorial Societies, Inc., 1828 L Street, N.W., Suite 1100, Washington, DC 20036 or Memorial Society Association of Canada, Box 96, Station A, Weston, Ontario M9N 3M6, Canada.)

Spontaneous Memorialization in Response to Violent Death

We return now to an alternative type of response to a death that was described briefly at the beginning of this chapter. It is markedly different from both the traditional funeral and memorialization process in American society and the other alternatives that have emerged in recent years.

Spontaneous memorialization has been defined as a public response to deaths that are violent and unanticipated (Haney, Leimer, & Lowery, 1997). This response develops when people who are not supposed to be at risk for death are killed in vicious and senseless ways. Not all violent deaths elicit this response: the public must feel a sense of connection or identification with the victim. Spontaneous memorialization does not and cannot replace traditional funeral rituals. Instead, it emerges as an adjunct ritual that extends the opportunity for mourning to individuals not conventionally included in traditional rites and calls attention to the social and cultural threat raised by these deaths.

Precisely what is the spontaneous memorialization process? It usually takes place at the site of the death or at some other place associated with the deceased. It differs in this respect from traditional services, which take place at a funeral home, church, or cemetery. Each individual makes a personal decision about participating: no one is automatically included or excluded. People who did not know the deceased person may be touched by the death and decide to participate. As Haney et al. put it: "Spontaneous memorialization extends the boundaries of who is allowed or expected to participate in the mourning process." There is no formal organization of the response to the death, at least at first. People respond out of their shock, sorrow, or anger, and together they find a way of expressing their feelings. There are also no set time limits. "Spontaneous memorialization ebbs and flows as individual mourners make their pilgrimages and contribute their offerings, either immediately after the death or during the weeks or months that follow. Individual mourners may visit the site once or return again and again, either alone or accompanied by others."

Mementos are left at the site of the death. These may include a wide variety of objects— flowers, teddy bears, bibles, even beer cans. A few of the objects that have been left at the Vietnam Memorial Wall have already been mentioned; the total, ever-expanding list goes on and on. What is common to these diverse mementoes is that each has symbolic meaning to the individual mourner and has some connection to the victim's life. Haney et al. add that "these ritual objects may reflect emotions, such as anger or vulnerability, which may be felt but typically are not displayed in traditional American death rituals." The mourners often raise funds to assist survivors of the victim, and may also become advocates for improved public safety measures.

Spontaneous memorialization is focused on the feelings of many individuals toward the person who has been a victim of violence. It is also a response to the increasing tide of violence that threatens society's values and sense of security. Here we see individuals coming together of their own volition to create a memorialization process that demonstrates community solidarity and concern in the face of deaths that should not have happened. Violent deaths shatter our expectations that people should be able to enjoy a long life before succumbing to "natural causes." Society's death system has not proven capable of

preventing violent deaths, and often cannot even *explain* them very well. The emergence of spontaneous memorialization, however, reveals that in opening our hearts to victims of violent death and their survivors, we are affirming values that are at the core of our existence as a society.

SUMMARY

The funeral is part of a deeper and more complex process in which we both separate ourselves from the dead and try to establish a new relationship with them, which we can carry forward in our lives. We have examined the meaning of the funeral process in many places and times, including our own. It has become clear that the way a society cares for its dead tells us much about the beliefs and lifestyles of that society in general. You were invited to reflect on your own attitudes, feelings, and knowledge about the funeral process, considering whether you are more a rationalist or a romantic.

Much attention was given to the process of transforming a dead body to a living memory. We identified basic elements of the funeral process, such as establishing the facts of death, the autopsy, the death investigator, legal issues, organ donation, premortem preparations, immediate postdeath activities, preparations for burial or cremation, the types of options that have been used, the funeral service itself, and the longer process of memorializing the deceased. Along the way, we gave particular attention to the sacred art of mummification as brought to a high level by the ancient Egyptians. We gained further insight through the case histories of three influential people whose deaths were the occasion for extraordinary memorialization: Ch'in shih-huang-ti, the first emperor of China, Prince Albert, husband of Queen Victoria, and Lenin, founder of the Soviet Union.

Another major function of the funeral and memorialization process is to achieve a balance between the competing claims of the living and the dead. We learned how the dead have been regarded within three traditional contexts: rural Greece, the Kotas of southern India, and orthodox Judaism. Next we came back home to see how cemeteries in the United States have been shaping memories from colonial times to the present, and how the nature and upkeep of these cemeteries have been closely related to powerful events such as the Civil War, and socio-technological change. We also visited several ethnic cemeteries to see how the challenges of diverse people living together are reflected in the way their deaths are memorialized. We wondered under what circumstances the dead are most important to the living and learned that the dead are more secure in past-oriented societies (and under several other conditions that were identified).

The Vietnam Veterans Memorial was seen to be a compelling new development that has helped to heal a divided nation, long given to avoiding death but urgently needing a way of remembering those who died so young and so far away. We also learned of increased sensitivity and sense of responsibility for the disposition of human remains, as made salient through The Vermillion Accord. Memorialization of our animal companions was considered through a visit to Pest Rest Memorial Mortuary and Cemetery (itself a recent casualty to urban development). Our curiosity about the current status of funeral practice led us to an interview with a funeral director, who provided frank and engaging answers to many of our questions. We then reminded ourselves that a variety of alternative funeral and memorialization possibilities exists, including the ever more common phenomenon of public spontaneous response to a particularly disturbing death or deaths.

REFERENCES

Aries, P. (1986). *The hour of our death.* New York: Knopf.

Benet, S. V. (1942). American names. In *Poetry of Stephen Vincent Benet* (pp. 367–368). New York: Farrar & Rinehart.

Bergen, M. B., & Williams, R. R. (1982). Alternative funerals: An exploratory study. *Omega, Journal of Death and Dying, 12,* 71–78.

Bloch, M. (1982). Death, women, and power. In M. Bloch & J. Parry (Eds.), *Death and the regeneration of life.* Cambridge: Cambridge University Press, pp. 1–44.

Brosius, J. P. (1995–1996). Father dead, mother dead: Bereavement and fictive death in Penan Gang society. *Omega, Journal of Death and Dying, 32,* 197–226.

Clignet, R. (1992). *Death, deeds, and descendants.* Hawthorne, NY: Aldine de Gruyter.

Cotterell, A. (1981). *The first emperor of China.* New York: Holt, Rinehart & Winston.

Cunningham, K. (1989). Navajo, Mormon, Zuni graves: Navajo, Mormon, Zuni ways. In R. E. Meyer (Ed.), *Cemeteries and gravemarkers* (pp. 197–216). Ann Arbor: University of Michigan Research Press.

Darby, E., & Smith, N. (1983). *The cult of the prince consort.* New Haven: Yale University Press.

Davidson, G. W. (1990). Human remains: Contemporary issues. *Death Studies, 14,* 491–502.

Day, M. H. (1990). The vermillion accord. *Death Studies, 14,* 641.

De Uriarte, R. (1996: August 25). Huge volume of obituaries forces limits. *The Arizona Republic.*

Gay, P. (1984). *Education of the senses.* New York: Oxford University Press.

Goldberg, H. S. (1981–1982). Funeral and bereavement rituals of Kota Indians and Orthodox Jews. *Omega, Journal of Death and Dying, 12,* 117–128.

Gosnell, L., & Gott, S. (1989). San Fernando Cemetery: Decorations of loss in a Mexican-American community. In R. E. Meyer (Ed.), *Cemeteries and gravemarkers* (pp. 217–236). Ann Arbor: University of Michigan Research Press.

Haney, C. A., Leimer, C., & Lowery, J. (1997). Spontaneous memorialization: Violent death and emerging mourning ritual. *Omega, Journal of Death and Dying, 35,* 159–172.

Hanzlick, R. (1993). Improving accuracy of death certificates. *Journal of the American Medical Association, 269,* 2850.

Harris, J. E., Weeks, K. R. (1973). *X-raying the pharaohs.* New York: Charles Scribner's Sons.

Hass, K. A. (1998). *Carried to the wall.* Berkeley: University of California Press.

Ikram, S., & Dodson, A. (1998). *The mummy in ancient Egypt.* London: Thames & Hudson Ltd.

Kaplan, J., & Hanzlick, R. (1993). Improving the accuracy of death certificates. *Journal of the American Medical Association, 270,* 1426.

Kastenbaum, R. (1974). Fertility and the fear of death. *Journal of Social Issues, 30,* 63–78.

Kastenbaum, R. (1994). R. C. W. Ettinger: An *Omega* interview. *Omega, Journal of Death and Dying, 30,* 159–172.

Kastenbaum, R. (1994–1995). Bruce L. Danto, M. D.: An *Omega* interview. *Omega, Journal of Death and Dying, 30,* 79–104.

Linden-Ward, B. (1989) Silent city on a hill: Landscapes of memory and Boston's Mount Auburn Cemetery. Columbus: Ohio State University Press.

Lynch, T. (1997). *The undertaking: Life studies from the dismal trade* (1st ed.). New York: W.W. Norton.

Mead, M. (1972). Towards a human science. *Science, 191,* 903–909.

Plunkett, T. (1999). The New Haven burying ground. A brief history and discussion of the Grove Street Cemetery. http://archnet.uconn.edu/archnet/topical/historic/grovestreet.html.

Rodman, G. B. (1996). *Elvis after Elvis*. Florence, KY: Routledge.

Rowles, G. (1984). Private communication.

Scheidt, R. J. (1993). Place and personality in adult development. In R. Kastenbaum (Ed.), *The Encyclopedia of adult development* (pp. 370–376.) Phoenix: Oryx.

Schindler, R. (1996). Mourning and bereavement among Jewish religious families: A time for reflection and recovery. *Omega, Journal of Death and Dying, 33,* 121–130.

Spiegelman, V., & Kastenbaum, R. (1990). Pet Rest Cemetery: Is eternity running out of time? *Omega, Journal of Death and Dying, 21,* 1–13.

Tashjian, A., & Tashjian, D. (1989). The Afro-American section of Newport, Rhode Island's common burying ground. In R. E. Meyer (Ed.), *Cemeteries and gravemarkers* (pp. 163–196). Ann Arbor: University of Michigan Research Press.

Tsiarias, A. (1982). *The Death rituals of rural Greece.* Princeton: Princeton University Press.

Walter, T. (1992). *Funerals and how to improve them.* North Pomfret, VT: Hodder & Stoughton.

Walter, T. (1999). (Ed.) *The mourning for Diana.* New York: New York University Press.

Zbarsky, I., & Hutchinson, S. (1997). *Lenin's embalmers.* London: The Harvill Press.

GLOSSARY

Aninut: The interval between death and burial in which "time stands still" and family members are given the opportunity to grieve in private (Jewish).

Autopsy: Medical examination performed on a corpse.

Cemetery: A place set aside for burial of the dead.

Ch'iidii: Evil ghosts who rob graves (Navajo).

Cremation: Reduction of a corpse to ashes in a burning chamber.

Death Certificate: Required legal form completed or verified by a physician, including basic information on the deceased person and cause(s) of death.

Cryonic Suspension: Preserving a (certified dead) person at a near-freezing temperature with the intention of subsequent revival, treatment, and restoration to healthy life.

Death Investigator: Physician who examines autopsy findings and other evidence when there are questions about circumstances and cause of death.

Embalming: A procedure that retards physical deterioration of a corpse; includes introduction of a preservative fluid.

Eulogy: Words said or written to respect and praise a deceased person.

Exhumation: Also known as "disinterment," the removal of a corpse from its place of burial.

Funeral: The rituals, observances, and procedures that accompany the burial or other disposition of the body of a deceased person.

Kaddish: Prayer on behalf of a deceased person (Jewish).

Obituary: A (usually brief) published report that provides information on a person's life after his or her death.

Organ Donation: Providing heart, kidney, cornea or other tissues available for the benefit of another person. Some types of organ donations can be made by living donors; others are available only from people who have been certified as dead.

Ponos: The pain of grief (Greek).

Postmortem: After death.

Premortem: Before death.

Spontaneous Memorialization: Voluntary public response to the death of a person by violence; characterized by expression of personal feelings and bringing mementos to the site of the death.

Vermillion Accord: A position statement on the ethical principles that should govern our treatment of human remains (based on a conference in Vermillion, South Dakota).

Young lovers who died before they could experience the fulfillment of their union might find themselves in the Elysian Fields for an eternity of pleasure, or so a Roman poet suggested.

chapter 13

DO WE SURVIVE DEATH?

That cadavers of the dead, borne by I know not what spirit, leave their tombs to wander among the living, terrorizing them and annihilating them, then return to their tombs which open by themselves before them, is a fact that would be difficult to accept if in our age numerous examples didn't prove it and if accounts did not abound.
—William of Newburgh (twelfth century), quoted by Schmitt, 1998, pp. 61–62.

I found myself looking down on myself, and the doctors and nurses around me. I could hear everything they were saying, and I wanted to tell them not to feel so bad, that I couldn't stand the pain anymore and I liked it where I was. I was somewhere it was so beautiful and peaceful that I wanted to stay there forever. I did not actually see anyone I knew, or anything in particular. There was a bright, but soft light, and I felt the most comforting sense of peace. I don't think I really knew the meaning of the word before. Suddenly I thought, "B (my husband) can't possibly bring up M alone. I had better go back. And that is the last thing I remember. I am absolutely positive that I decided to come back. Since that time I have no fear of dying.
—From the Near-Death Experiences Report (NDER) archives of Ian Stevenson, M. D.

As Lord Krishna said to his disciple:
Who thinks that he can be a slayer,
Who thinks that he is slain,
Both these lack knowledge:
He slays not, is not slain.
Never is he born nor dies;
Never did he come to be, nor will he
ever come to be again:
Unborn, eternal, everlasting be…
As a man casts off his worn-out clothes
And takes on new clothes,

So does the embodied soul cast off his worn-out bodies
And enter others new
—K. Kramer, *The Sacred Art of Dying,* 1988, p. 32

Behold, I show you a mystery; We shall not all sleep, but we shall all be changed, In a moment, in the twinkling of an eye...for the trumpet shall sound, and the dead shall be raised incorruptible, and we shall be changed.... So when this corruptible shall have put on incorruption, and this mortal shall have put on immortality, then shall be brought to pass the saying that is written, Death is swallowed up in victory, O death, where is thy sting? O grave, where is thy victory?
—I Corinthians, 15

Life in paradise meant leisure and loving in a natural setting. Men and women were naked. Generally paired, they spent their time relaxing in the grass, bathing and swimming, or simply strolling about.... Troops of young men meet in sport with gentle maidens, and Love never lets his warfare cease. There are all on whom Death swooped because of love....
—C. McDaniel & B. Lang, *Heaven, a History, 1988,* p. 125

There is life after death.

No, there isn't.

It would be a very good thing if there were an afterlife.

No, it wouldn't.

It would be so comforting if we could communicate with those who have crossed to the other side.

Comforting? It would be terrifying!

The prospect of the survival of death has stimulated faith, hope, and curiosity, but also dread, violence, and skepticism through the centuries. Before examining the current status of this topic, we will prepare ourselves with a selective historical review. This will take us to the question of whether or not survival is something that has to be proved. We will then consider several types of possible evidence for survival, beginning with near-death experiences, which have been the focus of interest for the past three decades. Next we will see how two phenomena from antiquity—

ghosts and reincarnation—are faring today. Finally we will return to the question of whether or not survival (and what kind of survival) would be a good thing, concluding with a consideration of the links between survival beliefs and death by suicide or other forms of killing.

CONCEPT OF SURVIVAL IN HISTORICAL PERSPECTIVE

The opening quotations introduce us to a diversity of ideas and experiences. An educated man of the twelfth century was reluctant to believe that there were dangerous ghosts roaming the English countryside, but he judged that the evidence was too overwhelming to ignore or deny. Historians and anthropologists tell us that dangerous ghosts have been making people nervous throughout the world since ancient times. For example, the Romani (more commonly known as "gypsies") have long feared that the *mulo* (the living dead) might take revenge against those who mistreated them in life (Crowe, 1996). There is also a special kind of evil spirit, the *marime*, that inhabits even the amiable dead, so corpses must not be touched. It is dangerous even to mention the name of the dead. The British and the Romani had plenty of company in these beliefs. A widespread conviction held that the dead mingle with the living, and often in ways that are not exactly comforting.

By contrast, the near-death experience (NDE) presents itself as immediate and vivid reality to the individual. The death that it suggests does not belong to somebody else's wandering spirit: it is one's own adventure, a private experience. One might try to describe this episode to others, but only the experiencing individual knows the NDE from the inside. Although NDERs (near-death experience reports) are not new, it is only in recent years that they have received widespread attention.

The third quotation comes to us from the Hindu tradition, in which birth as well as death are seen as illusions. The spirit or soul is always in process. There is no death that one must survive. It is in our nature to be "everlasting," even though we may not have a conscious memory of who we were in previous incarnations. The Buddhist tradition offers a somewhat different vision of reincarnation. The self is not a fixed entity that perishes at death and returns to life in another physical form. What we in Western cultures usually think of as the self is fluid, ever-changing. The self cannot die, because the self never exists as a fixed entity. On the other hand, we are always dying and undergoing rebirth through the course of our lives. This process continues after "death." What survives is the pattern of consciousness that has been shaped through many previous births, lives, and deaths.

The passage from I Corinthians—among the most influential words in the history of Western culture—presents still another view of human survival. This message has been subjected to several interpretations over the years. For example, does this transformation occur for all or only some people? Does it occur on a person-by-person basis or for all eligible humans in one ultimate "twinkling?" There is an obvious attitudinal difference between the New Testament vision and those associated with NDERs and the Hindu

and Buddhist traditions. Death had been the enemy, the relentless adversary against which no human strength or strategy could prevail. Now death has been defeated, its sting made harmless, and consigned to is own grave ("swallowed up in victory"). This electrifying message from the early years of Christianity differs from the experience of "the most comforting sense of peace" in NDERs. In the latter there is no sense of a victory over a formidable enemy, no mocking of death. One might make a speculative case for the NDE as proof that death has indeed had its sting deactivated, but there is little or nothing of the Corinthian attitude in NDERs.

People come to these differing interpretations of survival by different routes. NDEs often make a very strong impression on an individual: how can we *not* believe our own perceptions and feelings? By contrast, reincarnation has come through the centuries as a guiding vision of life to many Hindus and Buddhists. NDEs persuade on the basis of personal experience; reincarnation doctrine persuades on the basis of its intrinsic appeal and cultural heritage. Eternal life as victory over death also has intrinsic appeal, supported by the persuasive power of a strong religious and cultural heritage. A direct experience of triumph over death has not been salient in mainstream Christian belief. Those on the conservative side of the Christian spectrum sometimes judge that the NDE is a distraction and perhaps even an illusion, that detracts from the core message of the faith.

The final quotation above takes us directly to heaven—or at least one version of heaven. If there is survival—then what? An appealing answer was in the Roman air about a century before the birth and death of Jesus. The poet Tibullus pictured the afterlife as a paradise garden where lovers would enjoy each other's company forevermore. Tibullus asserted that in times gone by (the so-called "Golden Age"), people enjoyed free and uninhibited lovemaking. This pleasure was no longer available in the "modern" world, but it still awaited those who died young and in love. The paradise garden vision, with its naked lovers strolling and rolling in the grass, was revived in poetry and art many years later as humanism emerged from the middle ages. However, just around the corner of time from Tibullus were the life and death of Jesus and the church doctrines authored by Paul. The garden paradise and the much more melancholy afterlife scenarios held by the Jewish faith were soon to be overshadowed by the Christian vision. As we will see, questions remain about not only the survival of death, but also the form in which this survival occurs.

Does Survival Have to Be Proved?

The beliefs and customs that have come down to us across the millennia suggest that most people in most societies took survival as a fact. It was not uncommon to bury the dead with tools and implements they would find useful in the next life. Even more common was the assumption that the dead continued their interest in the living, either as guides and advisors or as malevolent, vengeful spirits. When impressive civilizations arose, ideas about the afterlife became elaborated and woven into theology, philosophy, poetry, song, and drama. For example, both the Egyptians and the Greeks of antiquity believed that the soul of the deceased journeyed to a kind of underworld. The poet Virgil even suggested a specific location for Hades (a predecessor of the Christian Hell): the entrance can be found near the volcanic Mount Vesuvius, where pent-up vapors and mysterious sounds issue from the mysterious realm below.

Survival beliefs varied in their details. Often the next life was seen to be perilous or otherwise undesirable, with such welcome exceptions as Tibullus' vision of a paradise garden. As we reach historical times, we discover at least a few skeptics or dissenters. A remarkable example was Titus Lucretius Carus, a Roman poet who was a contemporary of Virgil. Lucretius (54 B.C.) made the argument that "nothing can be produced from nothing," and, further, that "a thing... never returns to nothing, but all things after disruption go back into the first bodies of matter." Nature continually shapes, destroys, and reshapes her basic materials. Although no complete annihilation takes place, no imperishable soul is immune from the general principle of transformation. Granting some important exceptions, however, the ancient world seemed to hold a strong consensus favoring some type of survival.

Major systems of religious thought and practice arose later in both the East and the West. Beliefs in survival became important elements in Buddhist, Hindu, Islamic, and Christian thought. Standing on the verge of the Christian message was the rather complex and contradictory set of beliefs held within Judaism. McDannell and Lang (1988) have identified three currents within Jewish survival belief:

1. *Yahweh is the god of life—and this life is all that we have.* We should therefore live for this one life in this one world that God has given to us. This belief has been attributed to the Sadducee sect, most of whom were in the upper class of society and therefore in a superior position to enjoy life and exercise power. It was the Sadducees' contention that the Holy Scriptures offer no promise of an afterlife. One can experience the presence of God in everyday life, so there is no need to ask for more.

2. *The faithful among the dead will arise to participate in a new and improved society.* This concept, associated with the Pharisees, shared the Sadducees' primary interest in life on earth. Bad things happen to good people, however, and there are many obstacles to worshipping and living as one would choose to do. This dilemma would be resolved when "the dry bones of a conquered Israel would rise up and claim their place on a renewed earth" (1988, p. 21). Only the right kind of person would live again, however, and the main point of this return was to create a more perfect society on earth.

3. *There is a spiritual, rather than a physical, after life in which the individual soul contemplates God.* This concept, associated with the Essenes, shifted the emphasis from materialistic life on earth to a more liberated and purified existence on another plane. The Essenes were not political activists hoping to restore the independence of Israel, but people of a philosophical disposition who had their eyes turned toward the prospect of spiritual immortality.

The Essene conception was the most recent of the three belief systems to emerge within the Judaic tradition and had some features that were already pointing toward the Christian interpretation.

These new religious systems eventually gained dominance over the many local cults and over such fading theocracies as the pantheon of gods on Mount Olympus. Survival beliefs started to change their character within the new systems. There was now a stronger emphasis on the afterlife as a reward for goodness and punishment for sloth and evil. Believers were motivated to develop certain virtues and obey certain rules in order to enhance their chances of a favorable afterlife. There were bitter disputes about the specifics of the afterlife and its relationship to life on earth. Nevertheless, relatively few people denied the existence of a divine purpose and power or the survival of death.

The rise of independent thought and the achievements of the scientific method started to "rock the boat" of faith in the eighteenth century, and the turbulence continues today. Many thoughtful people struggled to reconcile science and religion, while others felt that they had to choose between progress and salvation. Nineteenth-century thinkers often felt impelled to write about immortality or survival, especially in the wake of Darwin's research. This trend continued into the early years of the present century. Some writers attacked religious beliefs in the name of science, while others performed the opposite service for religion. Strenuous efforts defended belief in an afterlife on the basis of scientific concepts and evidence.

Interest in the science-vs.-religion controversy on survival eventually subsided among scholars and influential thinkers. Many people came to their own conclusions and had less interest in the debate. The questions have not gone away, however, and historical events have given the issue new momentum from time to time. The suffering and death generated by World War II made its impact on a new generation of thinkers, from whom the existentialism movement developed (Kastenbaum, 1993b). Death had once again become a philosophical problem, this time in association with the problem of evil as demonstrated by the brutality of person against person. "Does even God care anymore?" became a related question that led to "Death of God" theology (Rubenstein, 1992).

Genocide, massacre, persistent vegetative states, the AIDS epidemic, the hospice movement, the Living Will, and physician-assisted suicide are among other developments that have altered the context within which the survival question is considered. We are confronting new kinds of life-and-death decisions, such as the response to people who are in a persistent vegetative state, the birth of a child with severe defects, and the demand for euthanasia or assisted suicide. These situations are stimulating some people to look at the survival question again. In fact, one emerging phenomenon, NDE has itself become a popular source of information suggestive of survival. A heightening of interest in "past lives" has done the same for evidence that might support reincarnation.

Basically, survival of death is a question for some people and an answer for others. These differences have persisted to the moment of death. Adam Smith, the famed economist, quipped to his friends, "I believe we must adjourn this meeting to some other place." Poet John Milton said farewell with the words, "Death is the great key that opens the palace of eternity." Others have died with their doubts and questions still intact. A tough-minded New England farmer, in his ninetieth year and within a day of his death, shared his thoughts with me. "Everybody I know's dead has stayed dead. Stubborn damn bunch, they get something in their mind!" Asked about his plans, he replied, "I'll rise at roseydamn dawn with wings on my ass or I'll just— (laughs-coughs)—I'll go on rotting like I been rotting. Ask me tomorrow!"

There are still other reasons to give careful consideration to this topic: If there is survival, what form does it take? How has the idea of survival been used and abused? What should the prospects of cessation or survival mean to us? Is survival the most or the least desirable possibility? And—perhaps the most practical question— how do our attitudes and beliefs regarding survival influence the ways in which we live and die?

What do you think of all of this? Please complete the self-quiz in Box 13-1. This will give you the opportunity to bring some of your own attitudes and beliefs to the surface and to compare them with what others have reported.

BOX 13-1
SURVIVAL OF DEATH? A SELF-QUIZ

1. I believe in some form of life after death.

   ____ Yes   ____ No

2. I have the following degree of confidence that my answer is correct.

   ____ Completely sure   ____ Very sure
   ____ Somewhat sure   ____ Not sure at all

3. If you *believe* in some form of afterlife, describe on a separate sheet of paper precisely how you picture or understand the nature of life after death. If you *do not believe* in life after death, describe what you think it would be like if it were true.

4. Suppose that you really wanted to persuade somebody that there is *no* life after death. What evidence, experiences, or line of reasoning would you use? Be as specific as possible and put your heart into it, as though you wanted very much to convince a person that there is no afterlife and had to call upon the strongest objections to this belief.

5. Suppose now that you wanted to persuade somebody that there *is* life after death. What evidence, experiences, or line of reasoning would you use? Again, be specific and put your best efforts into it.

6. You have already stated your own ideas and beliefs. What kind of experience, evidence, or logic could persuade you to change your mind? It does not matter if you consider the contrary evidence or experience to be very unlikely. What might lead you to change your mind if it did happen or were true?

7. Suppose that you actually have changed your mind. You have discovered that your present belief is mistaken. What difference would it make in your life? In what ways and to what extent would your life be different if you had to accept the opposite of your present belief about life after death?

8. What influence has your actual belief or disbelief had upon the way you live? What decisions has it influenced, and in what way?

9. What do you think would be the best thing about life after death (whether or not you are a believer)?

10. What would be the worst thing about life after death?

11. How did you come to your present belief or disbelief about life after death?

12. What would you tell a child who asks what happens when a person dies?

Place your answers in an imaginary sealed envelope for consideration after the clinical and research dimensions of the survival question have been examined in this chapter.

NEAR-DEATH EXPERIENCES: NEW EVIDENCE FOR SURVIVAL?

Renewed attention was given to the survival question with the publication of a book entitled *Life After Life* in 1975. Physician and philosopher Raymond A. Moody, Jr. listened to the experiences of men and women who had recovered after coming close to death. Some of these people had suffered cardiac arrest; all had been in serious peril. Moody's report and discussion of these NDERs became a surprise best seller. Almost im-

mediately additional NDERs appeared from many sources. Some people had had such experiences years before but were reluctant to speak about them until Moody's book brought the phenomenon into the open. The same was true for some physicians and other allied health workers who had encountered occasional NDERs in their practice and now felt more comfortable about sharing them.

Moody selected fifty cases from his collection for analysis. Some of these people were said to have been pronounced dead by a physician; all

FIGURE 13.1
A person's spirit floats over her body in an out-of-body experience.

appeared to have been close to the end. Moody found fifteen elements that occurred frequently (but not necessarily all elements occurred in each interview). The NDER account quoted at the beginning of this chapter is a typical example. Following is one from Moody's collection:

I was hospitalized for a severe kidney condition, and I was in a coma for approximately a week.... During this period when I was unconscious, I felt as though I were lifted right up, just as though I didn't have a physical body at all. A brilliant white light appeared to me. The light was so bright that I could not see through it, but going into its presence was so calming and so wonderful. There is just no experience on earth like it. In the presence of the light, the thoughts or words came into my mind: "Do you want to die?" And I replied that I didn't know since I knew nothing

about death. Then the white light said, "Come over this line and you will learn." I felt that I knew where the line was in front of me, although I could not actually see it. As I went across the line, the most wonderful feelings came over me—feelings of peace, tranquillity, a vanishing of all worries." (1975, p. 56)

This report illustrates some of the major features of a primary NDE. Instead of panic or despair, there is a sense of serenity and well-being. The sensation of being "lifted right up" is also one of the most striking characteristics. Known popularly as the "out-of-body experience," this state has a more technical name as well: the *autoscopic experience*. Rising and floating are also common experiences reported, as well as a sense of journey, a going toward something. A "brilliant white light" may be discovered as the journey continues.

BOX 13-2
COMPONENTS OF A NEAR-DEATH EXPERIENCE

- I felt as though I were dead.

- I felt at peace; a pleasant experience; no suffering.

- I was separated from my body. I entered a dark region.

- I heard a voice...I encountered a kind of presence.

- I could see this spiritual being...I spoke with the spirit.

- I reviewed my whole life.

- I saw lights ahead of me...lights all around me...

- I actually entered into the light.

- I saw the most beautiful colors.

Source: Based upon Greyson's (1989) revision of Ring's *NDE Scale.*

Furthermore, there is often a turning-point encounter. The individual reports feeling as though he or she had a choice about death at this time. Moody comments:

> The most common feelings reported in the first few moments following death are a desperate desire to get back into the body and an intense regret over one's demise. However, once the dying person reaches a certain depth in his experience, he does not want to come back, and he may even resist the return to the body. This is especially the case for those who have gotten so far as to encounter the being of light... As one man put it most emphatically, "I never wanted to leave the presence of this being." (1975, p. 11)

It later became clear that NDEs have been known for many centuries (Zaleski, 1987). Other researchers also found an abundance of NDEs (Ring, 1989). Obviously the type of experience confided to Moody was not limited to the survivors who had happened to come his way.

The question now arose: How is this remarkable experience to be explained? It is here that we enter the realm of continuing controversy. *Does the NDER constitute proof for survival of death?*

Evidence Favoring the NDE As Proof of Survival

Moody has stated repeatedly that the reports he collected do not provide evidence for survival.

"In my opinion anyone who claims that near death experiences prove or give scientific evidence of an afterlife is only betraying his ignorance of what terms like evidence or proof mean" (Moody, 1980). He reaffirmed this position recently, adding, "I am a complete skeptic regarding the possibility that science as we know it or any sort of conventionally established methodological procedures will be able to get evidence of life after death or to come to some sort of rational determination of this question" (Kastenbaum, 1995a, p. 95). The argument in favor of NDERs as proof of survival seems to be proceeding without the support of the person who first brought this phenomenon to general attention.

What has been learned from systematic research? Psychologist Kenneth Ring took the lead in establishing research procedures for the study of NDEs (1980; 1989). He developed a scale to assess the depth of intensity of an NDE and therefore made it possible to study the phenomenon in more adequate detail. The components of this scale are summarized in Box 13-2. A very intense NDE would include all of these components, some of which are also rated according to their vividness or depth.

Ring found that age, sex, economic status, and the type of near-death experience (e.g., automobile accident, surgery, etc.) did not seem to make a difference. NDEs occur in many types of situations and among many kinds of people. Ring estimates that an NDE occurs in about one of every three cases studied. Although this means that two of every three people who have survived a brush with death did *not* report an NDE, the number of those now on record is in the thousands. How many have had NDEs without coming to the attention of researchers? "It seems reasonable to assume that there must be many millions who have and, because of modern cardiopulmonary resuscitation measures, many more who will" (Ring, 1989, p. 194).

According to Ring's studies, NDEs seem to have had a powerful effect on many survivors. Subsequent studies have confirmed this finding. After a brush with death, people often have a renewed sense of purpose in life. Daily life also becomes more precious to them. And what about the fear of death? Many survivors report that they have become much less concerned about dying and death; there was something very comforting and reassuring about their close encounter. These changes in perception and attitude were seldom found among people who had near-death episodes without near-death experiences. The differences were greatest between people who had deep or intense NDEs and those who reported no NDE at all. People who could recall intense NDEs were much more likely to think of these as spiritual experiences that had changed their lives, whether or not religion had played an important role for them before these experiences. It appears, then, that the renewed purpose, appreciation of life, and sense of spirituality are closely associated with the experience rather than simply with the fact of a life-threatening encounter.

The Sabom Study: Independent Verification of NDE Phenomena

We come now to a study that stands by itself—and that seems to be becoming increasingly lonely as the years go by, for lack of company. Cardiologist Michael B. Sabom (1982) was among the earliest contributors to NDE research. His findings for the most part are consistent with those of Ring and other researchers.

What gives the work of Sabom and his colleagues particular distinction is the effort to compare the survivors' subjective reports with the information available in hospital records and re-

trievable from staff members. Could a person in the midst of an NDE make observations that could not have been—*should* not have been—possible if trapped within a horizontal, impaired, and endangered body? Sabom knew that people who have not been adequately anesthetized occasionally show a memory for events that happened during their surgery. Could the NDE be the same sort of occurrence? He thought not. The NDER bears "no resemblance to the nightmarish experiences reported by inadequately anesthetized patients. Visual details of an operation are not later retrievable by hypnosis from the subconscious minds of patients who had been anesthetized, although spoken words can sometimes be recalled" (1982, p. 80).

Sabom was able to establish a positive correspondence between what a few patients "saw" and what did in fact take place during a life-and-death medical procedure. In a preliminary study, he learned what kinds of educated guesses people tend to make about cardiopulmonary resuscitation (CPR) so that he would not credit a survivor with a specific and accurate description unless it was well justified by the evidence. The key information came from six survivors who had recalled specific details of their near-death crises. In each of these cases, the individual recalled having seen one or more specific events and developments that could not have been obtained through guesswork or prior knowledge of CPR. In other words, there was independent evidence that some individuals who reported an NDE did in fact gain information consistent with out-of-body status.

Sabom did not rush to the conclusion that his findings proved survival of death. Nevertheless, he believed that the autoscopic phenomenon may be authentic, that some type of split between mind and body can occur during points of crisis, and that during this altered state a person can make accurate observations of immediate reality and enter into the mystical state of being often reported for NDEs..

Eliminating Other Explanations

Other researchers favored simpler explanations for the NDE, explanations that did not require the assumption that a person had returned from the dead. Glen Gabbard and Stuart Twemlow (1984) were among the first to make a strong case against the competing theories.

1. NDEs are not caused by nor are they necessarily symptoms of mental illness. Very few people who reported NDEs showed signs of psychopathology.
2. NDEs are not related to level of education. Therefore, it cannot be said that the NDE is either something that is "imagined" by people with little formal education or "created" by people with perhaps too much education.
3. There is no evidence that NDEs occur mostly among people who previously had been fascinated by mystic or other unusual phenomena.
4. The NDE does not have much similarity to dreams. In comparing their NDERs with studies of normal dreams, Gabbard and Twenlow observed more differences than similarities. Therefore, it cannot be said that the survivors "dreamed" their experiences, if we are to use the term "dream" in its usual sense.

These findings suggest that NDEs cannot be easily explained as a dream state, or as a function of easily known factors such as education or mental illness. However, the poor showing of these alternative interpretations does not necessarily prove the survival hypothesis. There are other alternative hypotheses still to consider, as well as some problems with the data and logic of the survival interpretation.

Some Problems with NDE Findings

Scientific findings are no better than the methods and analytic procedures from which they come. Bruce Greyson (1999), one of the most distinguished researchers in this field, has identified significant flaws and limitations in most of the available studies. He notes that there is no standard way of determining whether a particular report qualifies as an NDE. Researchers use various procedures and seldom make it clear just what standard they are applying. It is difficult to draw conclusions when we cannot be sure that people have been talking about and studying the same phenomenon. Greyson finds that some researchers

…have defined the near-death experience as virtually any conscious experience an individual can recall following a close brush with death…But studies employing such a definition have included experiences that are typical of organic hallucinations and quite atypical of what is customarily thought of as a near-death experience. The definition of NDEs as encompassing *all* perceptions of *all* persons in a near-death state is clearly at odds with the common usage of the term, in which only a minority of persons who come close to death actually have an NDE (1999, p. 9)

In defense of NDE researchers, it should be said that (1) subjective experience is difficult to categorize and analyze under any conditions, and (2) it is especially difficult here because our definitions of death have become so ambiguous and unsettled (*see Chapter 2*).

Can interviews and questionnaires prove that NDE survivors have actually survived death? Consider one of the more ambitious studies. Melvin Morse and his colleagues interviewed 100 adults who had reported NDEs, as well as 50 people in each of five comparison groups. Data for all of the participants included lifestyle, religious and spiritual profiles, medical and psychiatric history, a family bonding scale, and a set of eight psychometric-type measures. In *Transformed by the Light* (1992), Morse claims that he has provided a scientifically established explanation as well as evidence for survival of death.

However, there are problems:

- Most of the book consists of NDERs very much like those familiar for almost two decades. Not only is there nothing new about in these reports, but many do not even come from the study: the author has just selected some of his favorite anecdotes.
- The author imposes his views on the respondents. Two examples: "In honesty, Dr. Morse, I don't think the experience has changed me at all" (1992, p. 3). Donna had just finished telling of the night she had almost died. The interviewer-author did not accept her statement. Why? "Although no one had conducted a study to examine the actual transformations that occur, *I was certain from my own experiences that every person who has an NDE is transformed in*

some way" (1992, p. 6) (italics added). After further questioning, Donna brought out additional details of her life since the NDE. "So it looks like your near-death experience *has* changed things for you." *Researchers do not reject data that disappoint them and substitute their own feelings of certainty. If he had already drawn firm conclusions "although no one had conducted a study," why bother to do this study?*

Here is another example: "I had a patient who was born with a severe brain disorder that causes the brain to die slowly. The parents had a very difficult time understanding why their child was dying. They tended to blame themselves with irrational guilt since the true cause of this horrible disorder is not known. The mother had used cocaine early in the pregnancy and was convinced that her drug use was the cause. The father, on the other hand, thought that the brain disorder was caused by bad genes that he had passed on.

"In the midst of all this, the mother began to talk about a vision she had had before the baby was born. She was awakened in the middle of the night by a lady in white who said, 'Your baby was not meant to be and must come back with me now.'

"I tried to get them both to accept that as the explanation for their child's fatal illness. What better explanation could there be, I asked, than that this baby was not meant to be?

"Rather than accept this spiritual vision, the parents became more bitter and angry" (1992, pp. 211–212).

This researcher was not collecting data for a rigorous test of theory but was demanding that his respondents agree with him.

- Few data are actually reported from the study itself, and conclusions are reached that are not supported by the data. For example, "The significance of these results is that visions of light or near-death experiences result in lowered death anxiety." In fact, nothing in the design of this study justifies claiming a cause-and-effect relationship among any of the elements.
- The author explains the NDE as an event that occurs in the right temporal lobe of the brain at the time of death. It is said to involve the activation of a "second brain" that transcends

bodily death, as well as changes in the individual's electromagnetic field. The effect is achieved through an experience of light that can be described as "the glow of God." *All of this is presented as proven fact. No proof is given in this book or in the citation of scientific references.* It is a fascinating speculative theory that the author presents as though proven fact.

Unfortunately, "studies" of this kind may find ready acceptance among those who are predisposed to agree with the conclusions, while also tending to cast doubt over the whole field of NDE inquiry.

Evidence and Logic against the Near-Death Experience As Proof of Survival

Following are a number of logical and empirical objections to interpreting NDEs as evidence for survival:

1. As previously mentioned, some people who return from a close encounter with death do not have experiences of the primary NDE. They recall nothing at all or only vague and dreamlike fragments. If death is universal, how could the NDE be otherwise if it is truly a visit to the other side?

2. Some survivors return with nightmarish experiences that neither increase their spirituality nor decrease their fear of death. Atwater (1992) reports that these cases are more frequent than previously thought, and can be compared with visions of Hell. I have collected both positive and negative reports myself (*see Box 13-3*).

3. The primary, or Moody-type, NDE occurs sometimes in situations in which the individual is in no bodily peril of death. The out-of-body component of the NDE has also been reported frequently as a specific phenomenon, for example, in parapsychological experiments in which there is no life-threatening situation. Gabbard & Twemlow (1991) conclude that "the state of *mind* of the near-death subject is far more important than the state of the *body*" (1991, p. 46). NDEs may be triggered by the belief that one is close to death or some other impending catastrophe.

BOX 13-3
SOME FRIGHTENING NEAR-DEATH EXPERIENCES*

- "There were so many pews on each side, and each pew was filled with people wearing black robes with hoods. I couldn't see their faces but if I turned my eyes I could see the inside of the hoods were lined with red...I stood there wondering where I was and what I was doing there, when a door opened to the right of the altar and out came the devil.... I saw that what he was pouring from the jug was fire, and I screamed, dropped the goblet, and started to run" (Irwin and Bramwell, 1988, p. 42).

- "I was thrilled to meet this person or was it an angel and then all at once I saw that she or it was truly horrible. Where the eyes were sup-

posed to be were slits and kind of blue-green flames flickered through them, through the eye-places. I can still see this demon, this whatever-it-was. With my eyes wide open, I can still see it" (1988).

- "She told me to go back. I didn't want to. I said I was so happy being where I was, not that I knew where I was. I thought she was being mean to make me go back into that bloody wrecked body. I could feel myself shaking and crying. I didn't feel good any more" (1988).

*Told to the author by survivors of motor vehicle accidents.

---

4. Careful research of medical records shows that many people who report NDEs actually had not come close to death. The most thorough study found only about half of the NDE reporters had survived a life-threatening illness or injury. Nevertheless, they believed that they had been dead or very near death even if they had not been in serious danger. Some patients had decided for themselves that they had been "dead" or "clinically dead." Others misinterpreted what they had been told by doctors or nurses. The researchers comment that "having had the NDE itself may have led some people to believe retrospectively that their condition must have been worse than it otherwise seemed" (Stevenson, Cook, & McClean–Rice, 1989–1990, p. 52).

5. The fact that many kinds of people report NDEs in many kinds of situations has weakened such alternative explanations as mental illness or a strong predisposition toward fantasy. However, there are also findings that do suggest relationships between the specific circumstances and the specific nature of the NDE. People who had been in severe pain were more likely than others to experience a

sense of distance from their bodies. Gabbard & Twemlow (1984) note that, "In hypnotic pain experiments, it is a common suggestion to dissociate the painful part from the body so that it is treated as 'not self'. Furthermore, patients who had been under anesthesia were especially likely to see brilliant lights and hear unusual sounds. These effects occur with many people who have been anesthetized, whether or not their conditions were life-threatening. Results such as these indicate that the overall picture is not that simple.

6. We hear NDEs only from the survivors. There is no evidence that what happens when a person really dies "and stays dead" has any relationship to the experiences reported by those who have recovered from a life-threatening episode. In fact, it is difficult to imagine how there could ever be such evidence; the very fact that a person has recovered disqualifies their report of "permanent death." There is always an observing self that categorizes the observed self as inert or dead. This split consciousness may result in the opinion that "I was dead," but there was always another "I" lively and perceptive enough to make that judgment.

Mystical, depersonalization, and hyperalertness responses to crisis

Several explanations have been offered as alternatives to the conclusion that NDE survivors have actually returned from the dead. These explanations do not deny the experiences as such, nor the emotional significance and meanings that might be drawn from them. The alternative explanations, however, do attempt to provide interpretations that are plausible and that remain within the framework of basic clinical and research knowledge.

What are these alternative explanations? Psychiatrist Russell Noyes, Jr. and his colleagues conducted a series of studies with people who survived a variety of life threatening crises. He and his colleagues found a set of common features in these reports. Three major factors emerged from the statistical analyses: mystical, depersonalization, and hyperalertness.

The *mystical* dimension of experiences close to death includes the feeling of great understanding, sharp and vivid images, revival of memories, the sense of harmony, unity, joy, and revelation. There may also be visions and strange bodily sensations. The *depersonalization* dimension includes loss of emotion, the sense of the self being detached both from the body and the world, an altered sense of time objects appearing small and far away, strange sounds, and the body having been altered in some weird way. The *hyperalertness* dimension includes the feeling that vision and hearing have become sharper, thoughts either more vivid or more dull, and speeded up or blurred. One has an overall feeling of being mechanical in both thoughts and movements.

Hyperalertness and depersonalization are interpreted as part of the same neural mechanism whose function it is to help the human organism react to dangerous circumstances. Noyes suggests that this is an adaptive mechanism that combines opposing reaction tendencies, "the one serving to intensify alertness and the other to dampen potentially disorganizing emotion" (Noyes, 1979, p. 78). When this mechanism is working properly, a person is able to cope exceptionally well (coolly, calmly, objectively) in the midst of a crisis. Noyes writes:

On a psychological level depersonalization may be interpreted as a defense against the threat of death. Not only did people in the studies...find themselves calm in otherwise frightening situations but they also felt detached from what was happening.... *The depersonalized state is one that mimics death*[italics added]. In it a person experiences himself as empty, lifeless, and unfamiliar. In a sense he creates psychologically the very situation that environmental circumstances threaten to impose. In so doing he escapes death, for what has already happened cannot happen again; he cannot die, because he is already dead. (1979, p. 79)

This is a cogent and powerful explanation because it is in contact with NDE data and with the broader realm of psychobiological dynamics.

The dimension of mystical consciousness is seen by Noyes as being somewhat apart from the depersonalization-hyperalertness mechanism. This feature occurs most often with people who are dying from physical disease. Noyes suggests that the physiological changes associated with terminal illness may induce altered states of consciousness in which experiences of a mystical type are more likely to appear.

When Do People *Not* Have NDEs? An Alternative Explanation

I have suggested a related possible explanation with two components (Kastenbaum, 1995a). First, you might expect that those who are closest to death—in the most perilous physical condition—should be the most likely to have intense NDEs. The available evidence, however, finds just the opposite (Greyson, 1989). Survivors who had been very close to death reported fewer experiences of any kind than those who had been less jeopardized. This weakens the assumed connection between NDEs and death. It also highlights a question that has been somewhat neglected: Precisely when does an NDE occur? There is no firm answer. Quite possibly the NDE is a memory created on the way back. In other words, it is not necessarily what the person experiences at the peak of the crisis but rather represents an attempt to make sense of the profound and confusing events that have transpired. The greatly impaired physical function close to the point of death does not allow much in the way of either perception or thought. On the way back, however, some people may be able to integrate their extraordinary but chaotic experiences through a memory story whose content and texture are drawn from the psychobiological response itself as well as from individual and cultural factors.

A second component of the NDE might arise from the specific nature of the life-threatening condition. It is true that several studies have failed to find a relationship between the nature of the death threat and the production of an NDE. Such a relationship is more likely to be observed, however, if you attend to the individual's role in the crisis. A driver faced with an impending collision is much more likely to make an emergency maneuver than to split off into an autoscopic experience. In general, we engage in instrumental actions—we do something—when the circumstances permit. This is a survival mechanism: action to avoid catastrophe. The NDE is more likely to occur when the jeopardized person has no instrumental action available. In such a situation, the NDE serves a quieting, energy-conserving function. The sense of serenity implies the activation of self-produced brain opiates (endorphins). This altered state enables body functions to continue at a basic level with minimum expenditure of energy and is represented at the psychic level by comforting imagery. The imagery becomes more coherent as the individual recovers, although in retrospect it is attributed to an earlier phase of the crisis.

Are NDEs hallucinations?

Still another explanation has been offered by psychologist Ronald K. Siegel. He regards NDEs as having an hallucinatory character, based on his research on the neuropsychology of drug effects (Siegel, 1992). The specific content of hallucinations is influenced by the individual's expectations and the nature of the physical and psychological environment. When facing death— or believing that one is facing death, one may experience the activation of memories that have been stored in the brain for many years…going back even to prenatal existence:

The feelings of peace and quiet may be related to the original state of intrauterine existence when there is complete biological equilibrium with the environment. The experience of moving down a dark tunnel may be associated with the clinical stage of delivery in which the cervix is open and there is a gradual propulsion through the birth canal…the dying or near-death experience triggers a flashback or retrieval of an equally dramatic and emotional memory of the birth experience.… To the extent that this reasoning is correct, the experience of dying and rebirth in the afterlife may be a special case of state-dependent recall of birth itself. (Siegel, 1980, p. 920).

Why the hallucinations in the first place? Siegel notes that the sensory world of a terminally ill person may be drastically reduced. This lack of external stimulation encourages the release or escape of stored memories. These memories re-enter conscious awareness as though they were perceptions. The result is the experiential state known as *hallucination.*

NDEs as Exercises in Religious Imagination?

Carol Zaleski, an expert in religious studies, examines what she calls *Otherworld Journeys* that have been reported from ancient times to the present. Following is one of her examples:

Four days ago, I died and was taken by two angels to the height of heaven. And it was just as though I rose above not only this squalid earth, but even the sun and moon, the clouds and stars. Then I went through a gate that was brighter than normal daylight, into a place where the entire floor shone like gold and silver. The light was indescribable, and I can't tell you how vast it was. (1987, p. 58)

This quotation is from a deeply religious man by the name of Salvius who had been left for dead one evening on a funeral bier. He was said to have revived and, inspired by his vision, he became a bishop. Zaleski's perceptive review of "otherworldy journeys" offers some interesting comments along with the wealth of examples. She concludes that "a fundamental kinship" exists between these visions (or NDEs) and the imaginative powers that we use in everyday life:

We are all, in a sense, otherworld travelers. Otherworld visions are products of the same imaginative power that is active in our ordinary ways of visualizing death; our tendency to portray ideas in concrete, embodied, and dramatic forms; the capacity of our inner states to transfigure our perception of outer landscapes; our need to internalize the cultural map of the physical universe, and our drive to experience that universe as a moral and spiritual cosmos in which we belong and have a purpose…we are able to grant the validity of near-death testimony as one way in which the religious imagination mediates the search for ultimate truth. (1987, p. 205)

Similarly, Grosso discerns a connection between myths of voyage and the near-death experience. Using one of his own dreams as a starting point, he recalls that "I found myself dragging a coffin up a hill. But the form of the coffin…also suggested a boat" (1991, p. 52). Pursuing this dream and its associations led Grosso to a study of journey and death imagery. He suggests that both powerful dreams and the typical NDE liberate the person from a limited and routinized view of life. The person is then free to discover (or rediscover) another realm. Return from an NDE is similar in this respect to awakening reluctantly from a splendid dream: "Near-death travelers return to the ordinary world under protest, feeling at once cursed, haunted, and driven by memories of their brief brushes with paradise" (1991, p. 58).

The NDER As a Healing and Illuminating Metaphor

Zaleski, Grosso, and several other researchers have seen NDERs as productions of minds that find themselves in extraordinary situations. The NDE is a kind of mental construction that attempts to explain and make the best of the situation. The experience may include a sense of going someplace one has never been before, proceeding from the known to the marvelously unknown.

Recent and ongoing studies are taking this approach in new directions. Allan Kellehear (1996) finds that the pattern of response expressed in NDERs has much in common with response patterns for a variety of other crisis situations. What the NDE presents to us, then, is a vivid example of the human mind—actually our entire psycho-socio-biological selves—attempting to cope with unusual and threatening events. These events might have either a direct or a symbolic relationship with death. For example, people who believe that all they have worked and hoped for in their lives is being destroyed may experience symbolic death imagery even though they are not in an actual life-or-death situation. What we think of as the NDE is one example of a larger class of experiences in which we try to reorganize ourselves in threatening situations. We often emerge from these situations stronger and wiser—but there is also the possibility that we may come out of these episodes damaged or even shattered. In this view, the NDE tells us something about the way we try to come through an episode that can be either disastrous or illuminating.

The NDER can be viewed as a narrative text that itself contributes to healing and illuminating an individual who feels caught in a make-or-break situation. A profoundly unsettling and chaotic immediate experience is transformed into a text through which the individual finds meaning and can therefore go ahead with his or her life as an integrated person after an episode of discontinuity and threatened disintegration (Kastenbaum, 1996). A key to the analysis of NDERs is the concept of an *enabling metaphor* that I have recently introduced into the study of unusual personal narratives. Discovery of the enabling metaphor in a personal narrative makes it possible to understand perceptions, images, and feelings that previously appeared obscure, incoherent, and inconsistent. It is a "Rosetta Stone" through which we can translate sequences of unusual, even bizarre, events such as those found in many NDERs. The images and impressions themselves are difficult to catch in our usual categories of meaning—often people characterize their NDEs as basically "indescribable." If an individual can come up with a metaphor that encompasses the entire experience, however, it becomes possible to create a somewhat coherent and meaningful narrative out of the many vivid impressions.

The metaphor of an out-of-body journey serves this purpose well in NDERs. Wilson (1996) has examined this guiding metaphor in fifty NDERs. She finds that the guiding metaphor of an out-of-body journey plays a significant role in the individual's ability to come out of the episode with the conviction that the order and meaning in the universe go beyond the limits of one's own conscious existence. It is this sense of order—often characterized specifically as "peace and harmony"—that may provide an enduring sense of comfort with life and death after a NDE. A person has crossed the threshold of everyday experience, gone through a strange and compelling episode, and returned to a well-defined state of being, perhaps rather improved for having had the experience.

What Are We Learning from Near-Death Experience Reports?

The NDE clearly is of interest as a remarkable human experience. But were the survivors really dead? Do such reports provide evidence for survival of death? These questions remain controversial. In my judgment, the case for the NDE as proof of survival has too many logical and empirical flaws to accept, despite the fact that some worthwhile research has been done. But what are we to make of Sabom's six survivors with demonstrably specific and accurate recollections? If this finding could be replicated in careful studies, we might have to revise our thinking, although the prospect has dimmed as years continue to pass without such follow-up research.

Recent case studies reported by Kelley, Greyson, and Stevenson (in press) are encouraging to those who believe that NDERs can possibly provide evidence for survival:

There are three features that we believe suggest the possibility of survival, especially when they all occur in the same experience. These features are: enhanced mental processes at a time when physiological functioning is seriously impaired; the experience of being out of the body and viewing events going on around it as from a position above; and the awareness of remote events not accessible to the person's ordinary senses.

This interpretation has significant logical and methodological problems to overcome, but it does at the very least suggest that there may be more to the NDE than current theories and research can adequately explain.

Another interesting new approach also focuses on altered states of consciousness. Whinnery (1997) compares the loss of consciousness that occurs with acceleration during fighter aircraft operation (or ground-based centrifuge simulation) with NDE reports. The "G-LOC problem," as it is known, continues to present a challenge to fighter aviation medicine. Pilots who black out under acceleration stress are in danger for their lives. Whinnery concludes that:

The major characteristics of G-LOC experiences that are shared in common with NDEs include tunnel vision and bright lights, floating sensations, automatic movement, autoscopy, out-of-body experiences, not wanting to be disturbed, paralysis, vivid dreamlets of beautiful places, pleasurable sensations, psychological alterations of euphoria and dissociation, inclusion of friends and family, inclusion of prior memories and thoughts, the experience being very memorable (when it can be remembered), confabulation, and a strong urge to understand the experience. (1997, p. 245)

Clearly, then, there is much in common between typical NDE reports and the reports given by pilots who have undergone G-LOC. These similarities do not prove anything, but they certainly encourage further exploration of both experiential states and the physiological conditions that influence them so strongly.

Near-death reports also offer the opportunity for a greater understanding of the role of subjective experience in contemporary life and the effect of media and other social forces on the ways in which we interpret our own states of being (Kastenbaum, 1998a; 1998b). From early childhood onward, we are strenuously influenced by society not only to behave, but also to think and feel in conformity with expectations. Mass media bombard us with an unrelenting profusion of images and messages that encourage us to fit into the mold. Near-death experiences, whatever else they might be, are assertions of our own individual inner lives—and perhaps also of something universal in human nature that is not entirely overridden by societal pressures.

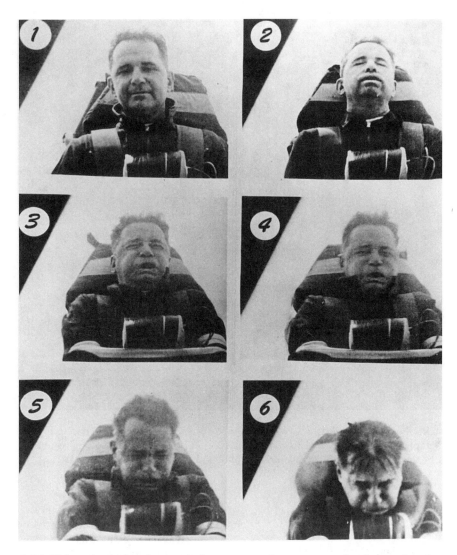

G-LOCK is a physical and mental phenomenon that occurs under the acceleration stress that is being experienced here by a pilot in a centrifugal chamber. It has been suggested that near-death reports have much in common with this experience.

THE DEAD AS EVIDENCE FOR SURVIVAL

People have searched for proofs of survival for many centuries, long before the health sciences enabled people to survive close calls with death and thereby increased the frequency of NDEs.

Often what has been taken as proof are encounters with spirits of the dead. If the living and the dead can communicate with each other, there must be some form of afterlife. A big "*if,*" but one that has enticed and convinced many people. We will consider several types of reported encounters, starting with the deathbed escort.

Spirit photography flourished a century ago. Ghosts and angels appeared in many photographs proving survival of death beyond a doubt. (Well, not exactly. Experts revealed how the fakery was achieved, and some photographers confessed to their tricks.)

Deathbed Escorts: Safe Conduct to the Other World

Mythology and folklore provide many examples of a guide who escorts the living across the border to death. This guide often takes a form very similar to the "gentle comforter" personification of death discussed in an earlier chapter.

One of the most famous in recent times is "gray lady" who started to appear to dying patients in a London hospital many years ago. When a modern physician decided to examine this legend, he discovered that new instances were still being reported. Dying patients insisted that the gray lady visited them often and even filled their water jugs. The reports were always of a gray uniform, but the staff nurses actually wore blue. These patients did not know that gray was the color of the nurses' uniforms when the hospital was new. For other examples, consult Sir William Barrett's (often criticized, but interesting to read) *Death-bed Visions* (1926/1986).

An adventuresome research team examined the deathbed escort phenomenon in both the United States and India. Karlis Osis and his colleagues (Osis, 1961; Osis & Haraldsson, 1977) collected observations from more than 2,000 physicians and nurses. Their major findings follow:

1. Patients at times were observed to be interacting with a visitor or apparition that others could not see. These patients were clear of mind and in possession of their mental faculties, not drugged, confused, or delusional.

2. The visitations usually came to people who were known to be dying, but there were also instances in which the deathbed escort appeared to a person who was not thought to be gravely ill—and that person did pass away shortly afterward.

3. The visitations were not always welcome. It sometimes appeared that the escort had to convince the patient that the time was near.

4. The escorts were varied. Some people saw the apparition of one of their parents; others believed they were interacting with an angel or messenger of God.

5. Occasionally something happened that the physicians or nurses themselves could witness:

> In the room where he was lying, there was a staircase leading to the second floor. Suddenly he exclaimed "See, the angels are coming down the stairs. The glass has fallen and broken." All of us in the room looked toward the staircase where a drinking glass had been placed on one of the steps. As we looked, we saw the glass break into a thousand pieces without any apparent cause. It did not fall; it simply exploded. The angels, of course, we did not see. A happy and peaceful expression came over the patient's face and the next moment he expired. Even after his death the serene, peaceful expression remained on his face. (Osis & Haraldsson, 1977, p. 42)

The deathbed visions had similar features in the United States and India, despite substantial cultural differences. The visions could be distinguished easily from ordinary hallucinations, and many patients had received no sedation.

Do these reports provide evidence for survival? The data were retrospective, therefore memory-dependent, and could not be independently verified. Furthermore, it is possible that many, if not all, of the deathbed visitors were wish-fulfilling fantasies, deriving from the special needs of the dying person and perhaps released by physiological changes such as decreased oxygen uptake in the brain. The escorts may well have been created by the dying person's own unconscious and projected into the outer world. One part of the dying person's self would therefore be able to communicate with another part through the hallucination, thereby overcoming the internal bar-riers within the personality. Although reports of deathbed visions can be collected when the effort is made, they are still rather unusual. I have witnessed perhaps a dozen incidents in which a person near death seemed to be interacting with a companion that we could not see, and I have been told of others. However, but there is no basis for holding that all or even most people near death have such experiences. Perhaps deathbed escorts are highly selective in their visitations, but perhaps they exist in the mind of the dying person and nowhere else.

Guardian Angels

Angels might seem to be completely out of place in the computerized, time-shifting, fax-sending, genetic recombinatorial world of the late twentieth century. Perhaps that is just why these messengers of heaven, the angels, have reclaimed attention in the past few years. A person who is lonely, alienated, stressed, anxious, bereaved, disappointed, or confused may welcome the comfort and assurances offered by a guardian angel, somebody who is looking out for us in a changing, impersonal, and troubled world.

But what is the connection with death and survival? Historically, angels have often played the role of *psychopomps* (Kastenbaum, 1993a), spiritual beings dispatched by the gods to escort the soul of the dying person safely to the next life. The angel as deathbed escort has figured in religious traditions that preceded the Christian era and is still to be discovered in other traditions today. The "beings of light" encountered in some NDEs might seem to qualify as guardian angels, as also indicated by the enduring sense of well-being that people have reported years after the experience. I have been told of angels who were once relatives or close friends and visited to provide comfort and assurance.

What are we to make of angels? Following are some alternatives:

- *Send the angels packing:* We could find "all this angel business" ridiculous—without foundation other than in superstition and wishful thinking.
- *Embrace the angels as true companions.* They are real because some people are certain they have met angels and because certain writings also assert their existence.

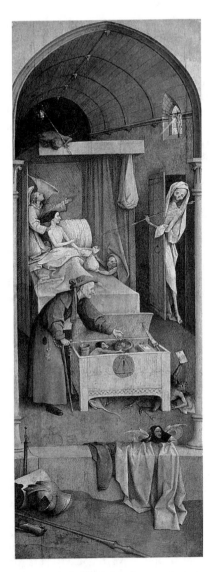

Heaven or hell? Salvation or damnation? This was a momentous issue often to be settled on the deathbed as angels and demons fought for possession of the soul.

- *Welcome the angels as personifications that allow us to engage in a valuable form of self-talk.* They exist as symbolic constructions through which deep human needs can be expressed and, possibly, spiritual solutions discovered.

These alternative interpretations have differential consequences. For example, a brusque rejection implies that experiences of angels are hallucinatory and, therefore, pathological. A life-endangered person who has such experiences might therefore be considered no longer of sound mind. I do not encourage this interpretation, nor is it consistent with the observations of researchers such as Siegel (1992), who are specialists in the neurophysiology of hallucinations. Like NDEs, "experiences with angels" *are* experiences and should arouse open-minded interest rather than hasty condemnation.

To accept angels as "real" in the same sense as nurses and shortstops, however, could lead to unfortunate results. One may become engrossed in belief systems and rituals that are exercises in uncontrolled fantasy and thereby lose opportunities to cope more effectively with the intellectual, emotional, social, and spiritual challenges of death. For an informative "pro-angel" discussion that respects the reader's intelligence, one might consult Sophy Burnham's *A Book of Angels* (1990). This book offers an informative survey of angels as part of cultural traditions from the remote past to the present.

Perhaps angels will always be with us because they represent something within us that transcends the demands and limits of everyday life. In times of crisis—including, but not limited, to terminal illness and grief—we might find it valuable to open ourselves to images and avenues of self-communication that are often neglected when life runs a smooth course. Whether or not angels (including the evil devil) exist in any other sense, they do seem to wait "in the wings" of our mental theater, awaiting their cues when the action becomes tense and the outcome uncertain.

Communicating with the Dead? The Medium and the Channeler

Today there are *channelers* through whom the dead speak—or so believers think. This is not new stuff. In the past, practitioners went by a different name, however. The *medium* was a person considered to have an unusual sensitivity to communications from the deceased. Interest in *spiritism* ran high from the middle of the nineteenth century onward, faded away, then rebounded in recent years with a new vocabulary. These alleged communications with the dead were taken as proof of survival by many people.

When Spiritism Was in Flower

Bogus mediums have been exposed repeatedly. Unprincipled charlatans have often preyed upon the sorrows and hopes of the bereaved and the uncritical innocence of the curious. After repeated exposures (for example, by celebrated illusionist Harry Houdini), many eventually confessed to their deceptions. Nevertheless a core of ardent believers in spiritual contact with the dead remained undeterred, while others wrote off the entire spiritism enterprise as a class exercise in which people who wanted to believe in the miraculous found their willing suppliers.

Interest in alleged communication with the dead was stimulated by the emergence of science and technology in the second half of the nineteenth century and aroused again after many families suffered bereavement during World War I. The doctrine of an afterlife seemed in jeopardy. Some people fought against the inroads of science with the weapons of emotion and scripture. Others decided to bend science's methods to their own use. In 1882, people of both types joined in the establishment of the British Society of Psychical Research (SPR). The scholars and scientists who founded this group included some of the most respected people of their time.

They tried almost every method that came to mind. A Census of Hallucinations (one of the first major public surveys) was taken. Personal observations suggestive of communications with the deceased were critically examined, and most were discarded. This left a core of incidents that they believed deserved to be taken more seriously. F. W. H. Myers presented many of these in his monumental two-volume work, *Human Personality and Its Survival of Bodily Death* (1903/1975). A "spirit photography" approach also became

popular for a while—how could we not believe in spirits of the departed if we could see them with our own eyes? These productions were also quickly discredited by professional photographers and astute observers who discovered how easy it was to produce pictures of deceased people and disembodied forms. Seeing was not necessarily believing after all.

Of more promise were *automatic writing* and *trance reception*. Automatic writing was a *dissociative state* in which a person wrote rapidly—sometimes amazingly so—while seeming to be unaware of this activity. The thoughts seemed to write themselves down as messages from some other person, whether living or deceased. Automatic writing provided a written text that could be examined at leisure and checked against external data. Trance phenomena then appeared; Today the experiences would be called an altered state of consciousness. In the trance state, individuals become receptive to thoughts and personalities that appeared alien to themselves. Trance states could be witnessed and monitored.

Strategies were devised to detect fraud and self-deceit. The "sensitive" or "medium" became the focus of survival research. The life of more than one impressive medium was made miserable by the controls and invasions of privacy demanded by skeptical investigators. And many a medium was in fact exposed as fraudulent—sometimes merely by having a light turned on at the wrong (or right) time. Few of these mediums passed through investigations unscathed, and even these cases have remained controversial.

The burden of proof remains very much on those who would call upon the medium for evidence of survival. Few *séances* have been conducted and reported under conditions exacting enough to be evidential, and fewer still produced survivalistic communications. One can choose to hold fast to a few reports that have not been "debunked," or one can choose to emphasize the preponderance of fraudulent and inadequate reports.

Channeling and Past-Life Regression

The central question "Is there survival of death?" was not decisively answered by those who observed mediums in action. The change of terminology from *medium* to *channeler* has not altered the situation in any significant respect. Few channeling interactions have been conducted and reported in a manner that could be taken as evidential. Two of the most obvious reasons are that (1) scientific evidence is seldom the primary goal of channeling sessions, and (2) it is not easy to establish a situation that is favorable to both the (supposed) channeling process and its scientific evaluation. However, we do have examples in which what was taken to be highly persuasive evidence proved to be anything but.

Perhaps the most famous case of channeling in recent times was the story of Bridey Murphy. Under hypnosis, a twentieth-century American woman named Ruth Simmons recounted her experiences as "Bridey Murphy," who was said to have been born in Ireland in 1768 and to have died there in 1864. The books reporting this account (Bernstein, 1950; Bernstein, 1985) became best-sellers and laid the foundations for the current interest in so-called past-life regression. Unfortunately this good story was later found to be a concoction from a variety of experiences Simmons had had in this life. The experiences emerged during the hypnotic sessions as hidden memories that were organized into coherent narratives. The most authentic-sounding memories of Ireland had slipped into her mind from her childhood visit to the World's Fair in St. Louis, where an Irish village had been recreated. A great many reports of past lives have surfaced since Bridey Murphy came and went, and the same doubts and limitations remain. "My past life" seems to function as an enabling metaphor that opens the door to memory fragments and fantasies that come together as reports of an actual set of meaningful experiences.

Ghosts

It is not easy to take ghosts seriously today— even if we substitute the more respectable-sounding term, *apparitions*. Ghosts have been for so long the stuff of campfire stories, parodies, and late-night movies that they might now seem to be the least promising source of evidence for survival. But they deserve a little better than that. For one thing, ghosts have had a long and re-

spectable place in culture, religion, and drama. Many societies have accepted ghosts as quasi-citizens. Everyday life without the possibility of interaction with departed spirits just wouldn't have been the same in these societies. We could not hope to understand the beliefs and practices of villagers in the Delhi region of India if we did not also understand the power of ghosts and the need to take great care in dealing with them. The villagers are cautious in their dealings with one another, because an aggrieved neighbor could become quite a troublesome ghost (Freed & Freed, 1993). Ghosts have a formidable social reality in many cultures.

For another thing, as we enter a new millennium in an urban society, everyday people still report encountering everyday-type ghosts. These are not at all like the stereotypes associated with haunted houses. They are an entire family downstairs in the rented house, making breakfast for themselves, the aroma of freshly brewed coffee rising to the visitor's bedroom. The ghost is an old man who sits quietly reading a newspaper at the same hour every evening. The ghost is a cat who visits so often that he is considered a part of the family (even by the dog) and whose habits have become as familiar to them as their own. The quite down-to-earth and sensible woman who told me about the ghost cat had not at first thought it was even worth mentioning because "it was just part of our life; it was just there when it wanted to be." Myers (1903/1975) was more impressed with such innocuous ghosts than with the more elaborate reports he collected of formidable apparitions with their mysterious purposes and profound messages. Who would have invented such useless ghosts, and why? Apparitions that did *not* fit into cultural belief systems and did not seem to have any particular agenda or message seemed more credible to Myers than those featured in ghost stories.

Nevertheless, it is the consequential spirit who has attracted the most attention and who has most often been taken as proof of survival. Perhaps most common is the ghost who visits to provide comfort during a time of crisis. For example:

My mother died in June. One Sunday morning early, we had a terrible thunderstorm. My husband was working away at the time, and as I have always been very nervous of storms, I went downstairs, taking the baby with me, and my eldest daughter also came down with me. She could see how I was shaking with fright. Suddenly I felt a very slight pressure on my shoulders, and heard my Mother's voice say, "don't be afraid Winnie dear, nothing will harm you." I immediately stopped shaking, and felt quite calm, and my daughter noticed the change in me, and said, "What's happened, Mum, you don't look frightened any more." (Green & McCreery, 1989, p. 201)

Another popular ghost-figure is the one who comes to warn us of danger: there is a problem with the electrical system in the new house; the bridge is unsafe to cross, and so on. How should a person respond to episodes in which one seems to have been comforted or warned by a ghost? Most people who have related such experiences to me were not quite sure just what had happened. Was that really a ghost? Are there really such things as ghosts? They had no way of knowing for certain. On the other hand, it was nice to be comforted, and there was no harm in taking the warning seriously enough to check it out.

As we might expect, ghosts have not fared well in research—the tighter and more controlled the situation, the less inviting for spirit visitors. In the heyday of spiritism, some mediums regularly produced apparitions at their séances—and were often enough discovered to have created these ectoplasmic beings from materials such as a quickly inflated goat's bladder. Still, there is something cheerful about thinking that there might be a form of survival that enables friendly spirits to visit now and again.

Unfortunately, as noted in the quotation that opened this chapter, ghosts sometimes do go bad—very bad! Fear of the dead is closely related to fear of angry or evil ghosts. This gives us a connection between two facets of the death system: how a society respects and cares for the dead, and how it tries to go on with life after a living person has become a memory. Some of us might speak of "griefwork," but others might speak instead of trying to placate the discontented dead. Plainly, it is not always comforting to believe in an afterlife—

not when it is stressful enough to motivate spirits to do mean and vicious things, and not when one is on the receiving end of such mischief.

The Ghost Dance: A Peaceful Vision Becomes a Tragedy

Beliefs have consequences, whether grounded in fact or not. Freed and Freed (1993), for example, have shown how ghost beliefs have interfered with the adoption of hygienic measures and health care interventions that could have saved lives. There is not much one can do if ghosts are to blame for illness and death except to engage in rituals that might or might not work. Consider an example from U.S. history in which a belief in ghosts and survival had tragic consequences for the living.

By the 1880s, life had changed radically for the Native American peoples who had once called this land their own. The whites were in control practically everywhere. Some of the tribes living in the Great Plains had continued to fight for their independence and just recently been defeated. Hard times indeed. Meanwhile, Jack Wilson was growing up. He was an orphan from the Paiute people who had been raised by a white family on their Nevada ranch. It was thought that he was the son of Tavibo, a Paiute who had prophesied that the whites would not long enjoy their dominance. They would be literally swallowed up by the earth—and all of the dead Native Americans would return to life as part of the great celebration.

Jack Wilson was chopping wood one day when he heard a great noise, headed off to find the source, and then fainted away. When he regained normal consciousness, he remembered having experienced a spiritual vision—similar in some respects to later near-death experience reports. Wovoka (the new name he had taken) had been to heaven, met his mother and other deceased people, and conversed with God (Hittman, 1990). He now had a mission: to persuade his people to live a righteous life in the eyes of God. His people must not drink whiskey. They must not fight. They must love one another and live in peace with the whites. Wovoka, like Tavibo before him, encouraged his followers to

The Lakota Sioux (shown here in 1892) and other Native American tribes performed exhausting dance rituals hoping to invoke their ancestors to rescue them from invaders, who had taken over their lands and driven them to the very edge of survival.

continue their traditional circle dance while singing religious songs. This was a way of affirming their community bonds and also of dedicating themselves to God and the right life. By most accounts there was nothing warlike about this ceremony.

Nevertheless, as Wovoka's influence and message spread throughout the western states, a militant spirit did arise around some campfires (Mooney, 1996). The earlier prophecy about the destruction of the whites and the raising of the dead became associated with the new movement. Some of the tribes recently defeated in combat with the United States Army came to believe that the dead could protect them, and the ghost dance was created in the depths of their desperation. Fasting and dancing to the point of trance and exhaustion brought the warriors into contact with the powerful spirits of the dead,

who were also longing for liberation. From these rituals came the idea of a sacred article of clothing that could protect the warriors from the white man's bullets. They would be safe in their ghost shirts if attacked by soldiers. With rituals, courage, and perseverance, they would overcome. Accordingly, they did not give as much attention to defensive precautions as they would have without such special protection. They were in no position to defend themselves when attacked in their encampment at Wounded Knee—an attack that was more slaughter than military operation. Belief in ghosts and their powers contributed to the massacre, though the savagery of the attack upon women and children became the shame of the army when the facts became known.

These are but a few examples that can be drawn from history. The belief that spirits of the dead survive and can have crucial influence on our lives has led some people to misplace their trust and to neglect opportunities for protecting and enhancing their own lives.

Reincarnation

The ancient belief in reincarnation has come back to life in recent years in Europe, Australia, and North America, having remained influential in Asia and Africa through the centuries. Although Hindu and Buddhist versions of the reincarnation doctrine are the most widely known, a great many other religions of more limited domain have featured this idea. Judeo-Christian religious authorities generally have opposed reincarnation beliefs—but with only partial success. The idea of living more than one life seems to thrive even when it does not fit well into a particular religious dogma. Many in the U.S. today who believe in reincarnation were raised in the Christian tradition but became attracted to the concept of life as a continuing journey from one embodiment to another. The popularity of this belief was stimulated by so-called past-life regressions (recall Bridey Murphy) and then again by heightened interest in the survival of death as near-death experience reports made the rounds. Reincarnation beliefs have a long heritage, and are cherished by many people in many lands.

Is there any evidence for reincarnation that would be persuasive to people who are not easy to persuade? One researcher stands out for his many years of careful investigation. Ian Stevenson, a distinguished professor of psychiatry, has been studying what he calls phenomena "suggestive of reincarnation." His *Twenty Cases Suggestive of Reincarnation* (1974) did much to establish the credibility of reincarnation research, and he has since produced many other books and articles on the subject.

A hallmark of Stevenson's approach is intensive case-by-case analysis. Readers are left to draw their own conclusions. This method combines the art of the researcher with that of the detective. Stevenson's work is lucid, systematic, and detailed. His series of case histories is a model of its kind. Readers, therefore, have no easy way out. We can refuse to examine evidence suggestive of reincarnation because the idea itself appears incredible. If we do examine the evidence,

however, it becomes difficult to make a quick and decisive judgment.

Stevenson characterizes the typical case as one that starts early in childhood, usually between ages 2 and 4.

The child often begins talking about this previous life as soon as he gains any ability to speak, and sometimes before his capacity for verbal expression matches his need to communicate. Some children make only three or four different statements about a previous life, but others may be credited with 60 or 70 separate items pertaining to different details in the life remembered.... In most cases the volume and clarity of the child's statements increase until at the age of between five and six he usually starts to forget the memories; or, if he does not forget them, he begins to talk about them less. Spontaneous remarks about the previous life have usually ceased by the time the child has reached the age of eight and often before. Unexpected behavior...nearly always accompanies the statements the child makes about the previous life he claims to remember, or occurs contemporary with them. This behavior is unusual for a child of the subject's family, but concordant with what he says concerning the previous life, and in most instances it is found to correspond with what other informants say concerning the behavior of the deceased person about whom the subject has been talking, if such a person is traced. (Stevenson, 1974, p. 324)

Stevenson recognizes that findings are always subject to more than one interpretation. As noted in the opening quotation, he has been compiling photographic and other documentary evidence whenever possible. Even so, and with all of his precautions, it is all but impossible to rule out the possibility of coincidence or that a child may have acquired information in some other manner and used it to construct a previous identity. In an *Omega* interview, I asked Stevenson about the difficulties involved in his research.

The effort to exclude the normal transmission of information exists also in cases in which the two families are completely unknown to each other and perhaps live many miles apart. I have often had to content myself with saying that normal communication was improbable; only rarely can I say it was impossible. For example, in a case in Delhi the two families concerned did not live far apart, but an immense gulf of wealth, education, and religion made it unlikely that they could ever have met; and they said they had not. Yet we learned that both families had bought vegetables at the same market. Could the subject's family have overheard someone in the market talking about the murder of which the subject spoke? I cannot be sure that this did not happen, although it seems unlikely. (Kastebaum, 1993, p. 169)

Stevenson now has investigated a large number "cases suggestive of reincarnation" from Burma, India, Sri Lanka, Turkey, Lebanon, and Native Americans. Smaller sets of cases have come from Brazil, Nigeria, Finland, Thailand, the United Kingdom, and the United States. Cases seem to come to attention more readily in cultures that favor belief in reincarnation. Whether belief somehow generates the experiences, or whether the experiences simply are easier to share within a sympathetic cultural milieu is difficult to determine. The specific elements in each case would have to be explained in any event.

Recently Stevenson published a mammoth collection of case studies accompanied by medical records and photographs that bear on the validity of children's statements about a past life. He selected cases that had all of the following characteristics:

1. The child described the way he or she died in a past life.
2. The child has a birthmark or birth defect consistent with that form of death (e.g., two bullet wounds in the chest; a knife wound on the neck).
3. An investigator identifies a deceased person whose life and death match the past life story given by the child.
4. Medical records documenting the specific cause of death and condition of the body are obtained.
5. There is a very close match between the fatal wounds suffered by the deceased person and the marks or defects found on the child at birth.

Stevenson offers these physical evidence match-ups as the best available evidence "suggestive of reincarnation." Readers who wish to examine these cases in depth to draw their own conclusions should consult *Reincarnation and Biology: A contribution to the Biology of Birth Marks and Birth Defects.* (1997a), a two-volume set of more than 2,000 pages with many photographs. A summary and discussion of these findings are found in *Where Reincarnation and Biology Intersect* (1997b). Now that Stevenson's remarkable contributions are available for study, one might well hesitate to draw conclusions about reincarnation until reading this material with the care that the author took in collecting, analyzing, and presenting the cases.

Two of the many questions that might be asked about Stevenson's study are worth mentioning here. First, why were so many of the reported past lives ended by sudden and violent death? The number of murders and other violent deaths in Stevenson's sample goes well beyond general expectations. Second, how could anybody be reincarnated unless everybody is reincarnated? The test of universality was applied earlier in this chapter to NDEs, which were found clearly lacking in this respect. It might be argued that everybody does become reincarnated but that only a few achieve conscious awareness. This explanation would be difficult, perhaps impossible, to put to the test.

There is an even more radical possibility: death may not be the same for everybody. Of all possibilities considered in this chapter, the prospect of pluralistic death might well be the most extreme. It could be the possibility that would most challenge our basic assumptions about the nature of life and the universe. There is survival after death, or there is not survival—or so it is generally believed. The rational mind may find either of these alternatives more acceptable than the possibility that death might be different at different times to different people in different situations. Nevertheless, as I have suggested elsewhere, this bizarre-seeming idea appears consistent with some basic precepts of the philosophy of science (Kastenbaum, 1995b). The idea that death might be relative to life and context opens the possibility that there might be both survival and nonsurvival!

SHOULD WE SURVIVE DEATH?

"Should we survive death?" may seem to be a peculiar question. The quest for prolongation of life is among the most ancient of human themes. We find it expressed in the *Epic of Gilgamesh,* which has come down to us from the Sumerian people who lived more than 3,000 years before the Christian era. The elaborate Tibetan and Egyptian rituals governing our relationship to the next life are perhaps the best known of their kind, but anthropologists have discovered and historians have reconstructed other examples as well. Most of the world's great religions have generated images of an afterlife that are often powerful enough to influence the everyday functioning of individuals and society. Furthermore, scientific endeavor often has been motivated by the hope of achieving victory over death, whether we scan as far back as the medieval alchemist or examine the current scene in medical research.

And yet not everybody takes comfort in the survival doctrine. The person who fears an eternity of torture and damnation is one obvious exception, yet this is not the only basis for questioning the desirability of an afterlife. Consider these comments from college students regarding item 3 in the self-quiz that started this chapter. These respondents believe in life after death and attempted to describe it:

- I really can't answer that question. That's funny, isn't it? Here I am, a good Christian and I believe in heaven and all that, but I can't get what it's all about clear in my mind. I think my problem is in the idea of a literal heaven, a Sunday school fairytale. I can't really accept that anymore, but I don't have anything to replace it.

- You tell me! I imagine eternity as a state of perfection. No more worries, no more problems. Best of all, no more deadlines and exams! But then what? All I can imagine is God and all the rest of us posing forever for our portrait with this transcendental smile on our faces. I'd go crazy! I need to worry and rush around and fight against time or I'm not really myself. It will be beautiful and peaceful. More beautiful and peaceful than anything we can know on earth. Maybe the closest would be a long and relaxed Sunday afternoon. What makes a Sunday afternoon so great, though, is that it comes after one hectic week and before another. I don't know how I would do if there was only Sunday afternoon. This is probably a dumb way to think about heaven, but it's the best I can do.

Perhaps there is more appeal in the type of afterlife envisioned by many tribal peoples: it was much like the familiar here-and-now life, with such understandable activities as hunting, fishing, preparing and enjoying feasts, outsmarting adversaries, demonstrating valor, and so forth. Such conceptions of the afterlife involve not only continuing activity but also change, risk, and danger.

The intellectual and the mystic may have ways of envisioning a Christian afterlife that is neither literal nor dull. Some believers, however, are uncomfortable with a heaven that seems just too heavenly and therefore remote from their own lives and thoughts.

A more radical orientation can also be taken toward the desirability of survival. There are two main components here: (1) we do not deserve survival, and (2) the prospect of survival encourages the worst side of human nature.

The first component can be supported by all of the cruelty, stupidity, greed, and pettiness found in the lives of individuals and societies through the centuries. Make your own list. How many examples of genocide will you include? How many examples of fortunes being made by inflicting suffering on others? How many examples of wanton destruction, of royal whim or bureaucratic arrogance? History and literature (not to mention the daily news) provide more examples than we can use. Whatever items we may choose for our list, the conclusion might be the same: *Homo sapiens* has by no means earned the right to survival beyond the grave. We have yet to prove on a consistent basis that we can use the lives given to us with wisdom and good-heartedness. We might also count against ourselves the ways in which we often waste time and, therefore, life. Should eternal life be granted to those who have demonstrated so little ability to use the hours and days of earthly life? If much of our discretionary time is merely filled or killed, what claim dare we make on immortality?

The second component is no more complimentary to the human race. One of the arguments here is that the prospect of eternal life has been used repeatedly to manipulate believers in the service of power and greed and, at times, raging fanaticism. The toll in lives and brutalization is high enough if we count only violence within and between religious establishments. The guarantee of immortal blessing for those who die while slaughtering designated enemies has led to some of history's most ferocious battles. The toll rises when we consider all of the other manifestations of intolerance that can draw strength from belief in a life everlasting. The moral case against survival, then, is that we might be forced to become better people and learn to make more constructive use of our time on earth if we did not have the prospect of an afterlife as either an all-dominating or fail-safe goal.

A thorough consideration of Eastern thought and practice would add still other dimensions. The way of the Buddha, for example, differs greatly from the Christian conception of life-death-afterlife (Truitner & Truitner, 1993). "Death," in effect, disappears for those who can attain a heightened spiritual development in which birth and beginnings, cravings and ambitions also dissolve. The character of the Buddhist survival doctrine is also distinctive in its implications for both individual and social action. Militant violence against others, for example, does not flow readily from this tradition.

Nevertheless, arguments can still be advanced against the desirability of this survival doctrine. Consider a single example: The Buddhist philosophy encourages inwardness, the cultivation of the inner self. The turning inward, however, with its cosmic agenda, can lead to neglect of pressing concerns on the worldly plane. A holy person pursuing the ultimate spiritual development may contribute inadvertently to the persistence of poverty, suffering, and inequality that could have been modified by vigorous action in the world. In this sense, a doctrine pointed toward spiritual transcendence of life and death might work against the improvement of conditions on earth. Neither Buddhists nor Christians necessarily ignore the everyday human condition. There have always been activists who envision their own mission as both individual and social-humanitarian. Nevertheless, the question can be raised: does a dominating vision of the afterlife divert and obstruct attention from flesh-and-blood realities here and now?

BUT WHAT KIND OF SURVIVAL?

Suppose that there is survival after death. I can imagine a roomful of people who are in agreement with this statement—yet each might have a very different conception of the afterlife. Following is what they might tell us:

- "Survival? Yes, as a burst of pure energy. The person dies, and at the last moment of life there is a discharge of electromagnetic radiation. Does this death flash continue in some form, and does it encode and preserve the individual's identity? Perhaps. This we do not know yet. But the burst of electromagnetic radiation can be documented."

- "Have you seen a ghost? Most apparitions, or ghosts if you will, seem rather lost and slow witted, not like the real people they once were, more like shadows or representations. What sometimes happens after death is that a temporary trace of the person remains in the locale. You might call this a force field. When you encounter this 'person-shaped' force field, you have encountered something that exists in nature. But it does not exist for long, and it is not the survived person, but his or her energy traces, and these will soon fade."

- "Fading, that is just what happens, but not in the way that you have proposed. When people die, they move from the realm of light to the realm of darkness. There is survival here, in this underworld, but it is a sad survival, a slow fading away to blank, characterless beings who lose all that made them passionate and knowing individuals. The Greeks called them shades. Poor lost souls, poor wandering creatures in a cosmic nightmare."

- "These quaint ideas miss the real point. There is true immortality—but not for everybody.

Like much else in life, survival of death is *conditional*. What is it conditional on? This surpasses our understanding at present—but it might well be that people who develop great spiritual strength will not perish along with their bodies. The soul does not possess immortality; rather it may have the potential for immortality. And so the lives of many of us may end when we think they do, at physical death, but the lives of some people may continue because they have become real in a different way."

- "Survival? How can you avoid it? We are born but to die, and die but to be reborn. Not only those of us who are at the moment human beings, but all living things (and perhaps 'inanimate' things as well) go through cycle after cycle of existence. There are so many beginnings and so many ends; but for most of us, no Beginning and no End."

- "We live. We die. We are judged. We are damned or we are granted salvation through the mercy of the Lord. The righteous dwell forever with the Lord; those who live in ignorance or defiance will know the fires of hell."

- "Human life is—or should be—a progression toward enlightenment, toward spiritual development. This does not have much to do with the external forms of religion, but rather with each person's journey from ignorance to understanding, from concern with individuality and materiality to becoming part of a more universal consciousness. The passage from life to death is but one transition in this long journey, and what the person brings to death—and takes from death—depends upon his or her level of spiritual development at that point."

- "Leaving this life produces an altered state of consciousness. In this sense, somebody survives, but this is not quite the same somebody we have been all along. There are many examples of altered states as part of our life experiences, so death may be simply the most impressive and transfiguring of these changes."

- "What crazy people! The juice of the silly-berry has made you see things as they are not and fail to see things as they are. A person dies, of course. This always happens. And then that person just goes on with his life or with her

life. This always happens, too. The next life is much like this one. There are pleasures. There are troubles. One can say the wrong thing or touch the wrong person and get oneself killed again, too. What else is a person to do in the next life but those things this person has always known and has always tried to do? These strange stories I hear from you—well, I do not like them very much, but maybe I will like them better if you have saved some of that powerful silly-berry juice for me!"

All of the views paraphrased above have been expressed at various times. The concept of the next life being essentially a continuation of the present life has been held by many tribal peoples over the centuries. By contrast, the "death flash" theory is a recent proposal based upon experiments on electromagnetic radiation in living tissues (Slawinski, 1987), and the "trace field" theory seems to have been first proposed by Myers (1903/ 1975). "Conditional immortality" was suggested by one of the few twentieth century philosophers who took the question of survival as a serious intellectual issue (Hocking, 1957). A specialist in the study of altered states suggests that death results in—what else?—an altered state (Tart, 1990).

What attitude should we take toward these competing views? All speak of survival in some form, yet the forms differ markedly from one another. We can decide not to trouble ourselves with the less familiar or more disturbing concepts and stick with whatever ideas we brought with us to the beginning of this chapter. Or we can pause for at least a moment to acknowledge that humankind has imagined more than one kind of survival and may have still other versions to discover. Even (or especially) those concepts that most trouble us might be valuable in what they suggest about the nature of minds that dare to think beyond the limits of everyday experience.

YOUR THOUGHTS ON SURVIVAL: A REVIEW

Your thoughts on survival of death were invited at the beginning of this chapter. Now compare your responses with those of health professionals and other college students. Following are some of the findings:

1. Most health care professionals and college students who have answered these questions do believe in some form of life after death (ranging from 71 percent to 87 percent in various samples). However, a Gallup Poll (1991) finds that reincarnation as a specific form of survival is affirmed by only 23 percent of its general adult respondents.

2. Almost half (48 percent) of the believers across the samples report themselves "completely sure." About one believer in seven (14 percent) is "not sure at all."

3. Although belief in survival is somewhat more frequent and confident among females and among the older health care professionals, believers outnumber nonbelievers for both sexes at all ages studied.

4. The New Testament and accepted tradition are most often cited as sources that would be used to convince others of survival. The next most common answer is that we need faith in God and immortality to make it through the tribulations of life.

5. Some believers (from 28 percent to 45 percent) were unable or unwilling to indicate how they would try to persuade a believer to the opposite conclusion (item 4). The most commonly used approach by both believers and nonbelievers is that the body does stop functioning, the mind depends on the body, and the dead do not actually come back to us.

6. Believers seldom were able or willing to specify any possible evidence, event, or experience that might lead them to change their opinion about survival, whereas almost all nonbelievers could think of something (a general "scientific breakthrough," for example, or "a powerful personal experience, like really having a dead person I know very well come back to me in some kind of vision and say things that made me realize I wasn't making it up myself"). Highly confident believers were even less likely to imagine anything that could lead them to change their minds.

7. Both believers and nonbelievers showed a great deal of variability about the way that their views of survival may be affecting their lives. Believers tended to say that they drew strength from the prospect of survival but did not often specify examples.

8. Beliefs were formed early in childhood, according to almost all respondents, but the nonbelievers were more likely to have reconsidered this topic in recent years.

9. What to tell a child proved to be most difficult for those who were not very sure of their position on survival, whether believers or nonbelievers. Nonbelievers more frequently expressed some conflict or uncertainty in what to say, but wavering believers also had their difficulties. Responding to a child's questions can test our own belief system. (Review *Chapter 10* for suggestions on discussing death with children.)

This overview of the way other people have responded to questions about survival suggests that believers are less open to possible negative evidence than nonbelievers are to positive evidence.

But what of national data? Surveys indicate that about seven of ten people in the United States believe in an afterlife (Klenow & Bolin, 1989–1990). Those in the 18–29 age range are somewhat less likely to believe in an afterlife when compared with those in the 30–59 range. Although it is often assumed that belief in afterlife is especially common among old people, surveys find that those over 60 are actually a little less likely to hold this belief when compared with middle-aged people. Another interesting finding is that African Americans have a lower incidence of belief in an afterlife (about 55 percent)) than whites (about 71 percent). Believers are slightly more common among women than men (72 percent to 67 percent). Strong beliefs in afterlife are expressed most often by Protestants (86 percent). Most Catholics (74 percent) also report confidence in their beliefs, but relatively few Jews (8 percent) indicate that they have firm beliefs in an afterlife.

Statistics such as these have some value as a way of monitoring the beliefs of the American public. However, the questions associated with survival of death cannot really be settled by survey results nor by insisting more loudly than the other person that our views are the only views that matter.

THE SUICIDE-SURVIVAL CONNECTION

Throughout this book, we have been following the theme of "death on demand" as it has been expressing itself throughout our death system. We have seen, for example, that the idea of a "Living Will" caught on surprisingly well—as an idea—but that a year later most people still had not executed such a document. And we have also seen how this option has recently become an element in the bureaucratic machinery of our health care system—with results yet to be determined. Additionally, we have seen that the concept of suicide has become blurred to some extent by the emergence of physician-assisted deaths. As previously noted, these deaths can be interpreted as assisted suicide, but also as euthanasia—and as murder.

The terms that we select can make a difference. For example, health care professionals might be more responsive to requests for "deliverance" or "euthanasia" than for "assisted suicide," and more responsive to "assisted suicide" than to "murder." Nevertheless, an underlying thought is common regardless of the terminology: shorten this life (or hasten this death). The belief in and desire for immortality takes us in the opposite direction: never death…always life. Now let us import these contrasting ideas into the same picture. Is there not a similarity implied? Those who would end their lives precipitously and those who envision immortality are agreed in their dissatisfaction with simply living until they die. One person may be unable to bear the thought of facing another day of suffering or disappointment, the other may be unable to bear the thought of facing another day that takes him or her that much closer to death. "I can't go on!" and "I can't go on unless I know there will always be a going on!" are states of being with something rather basic in common. It is the aversion to living as best as one can

within the limited span of days available to all mortals.

Exposing oneself to death and assuring the bliss of eternal life have been closely linked at times. When Christianity was a new sect, many tried to emulate Jesus through martyrdom at the hands of the Roman authorities. A thousand years later, both Islamic and Christian warriors sought deaths that would earn them entry into their respective realms of eternal bliss. The idea that people who die an heroic death will make it to Heaven (or Valhalla) more swiftly or surely has been a motif in many cultures.

Today we are experiencing an ever-shifting mixture of both ancient and contemporary themes. It may be useful to open our eyes to the new configurations of suicide/survival ideation and behavior. Greyson (1992–1993) has provided one example of what might be learned through research. He finds that people who report near-death experiences subsequently have stronger antisuicide attitudes. One might have expected the opposite. The NDEs are often so liberating, so pleasant—shouldn't this make death more attractive? Well, yes, it does for many people. However, an NDE seems to inspire a greater appreciation for life. Most NDE survivors believe in an afterlife but are staunch in their rejection of the idea of foreshortening this life in order to reach the next life more rapidly.

And what about those who believe that there simply is no death? This is by far the most common response we find in an ongoing study of people who identify themselves with the "New Age" movement. As one respondent put it, death "is just changing clothes." What remains to be learned is whether or not suicide will be seen as an action that is unimportant, therefore not to be prevented or mourned. Some respondents have already expressed the view that what seems to be a premature and tragic death is nothing to be upset about because (1) death really isn't anything, and (2) if it happened that way, why that's the way it was supposed to be. What do you think?

We have known for some time what Hamlet thinks. In that most famous of monologues, he begins with the question: "To be or not to be?" For a moment it looks as though death, not-being, will be his answer.

and by a sleep to say we end
The heart-ache and the thousand natural shocks
That flesh is heir to, 'tis a consummation
Devoutly to be wish'd. To die, to sleep…(III: 1)

Hamlet would not continue to suffer the "natural shocks that flesh is heir to." Understandable, of course. But notice how that subtle mind proceeds to deceive himself, or to attempt deception: "tis a consummation devoutly to be wish'd." But is death really a consummation? If he copes differently with his ordeal, Hamlet and Ophelia might yet have each other—now there would be a consummation! The imagery of sexual fulfillment is substituted for the reality of death, making it easier to edge his way toward the grave. He continues to blur the reality of death by again reassuring himself: "To die, to sleep." That's all death is…sleep…and who's afraid of sleep? So, he's going to pack it in then, right? Not so fast!

To sleep: perchance to dream: ay, there's the rub;
For in that sleep of death what dreams may come
When we have shuffled off this mortal coil,
Must give us pause….

Hamlet pauses. In a moment he arrives at the image of bloody suicide: "When he himself might his quietus make with a bare bodkin." But there is that one troubling reason to stay his hand:

…the dread of something after death,
the undiscover'd country from whose bourn
No traveller returns, puzzles the will
And makes us rather bear those ills we have
Than fly to others that we know not of.

Every day there are people who confront their own "to be or not to be" dilemmas. Each person, each dilemma is unique. Nevertheless, all involve assumptions about life, death, and afterlife. Perhaps we can be wiser companions in these situations if we have explored our own undiscovered countries deeply enough to offer them a life-giving pause.

SUMMARY

Most people in most societies throughout the centuries have believed in some form of survival.

Several of these belief systems were described. Only since the rise of science and technology have there been substantial widespread doubt and question. Much of this chapter, therefore, was concerned with evidence. You were asked to put your own ideas and beliefs on the line in a self-quiz. We then looked into near-death experiences in some detail because these reports have often been taken as proof of survival. The basic near-death experience was described (summarized in Box 13-2) and we noted that many who have had this kind of experience reported that their lives had changed—for the better—as a result. The NDE material offered as proof of survival was reviewed and critiqued. We also considered several theories that attempt to explain the NDE, including the spiritual/survival explanation and also alternatives that interpret the NDE as (1) a split-off psychological reaction to stress, (2) a quieting, energy conserving function when we can do nothing to extricate ourselves from a life-threatening situation, (3) an hallucination produced by psychophysiological changes, (4) an exercise in religious imagination, (5) a healing and illuminating metaphor, and (6) a stress response that parallels the G-LOC experience of pilots subjected to extreme acceleration pressure.

Next we examined another source of possible evidence for survival: the dead themselves or their spirit representatives. This discussion included deathbed escorts or visions, guardian angels, contacts made through mediums and channelers and my personal favorite, ghosts. The tragic consequences of belief in the reality and power of ghosts was illustrated by the Ghost Dance, through which some Native American peoples hoped to invoke the protection of their ancestors and raise them from the dead, but instead exposed themselves to massacre. Reincarnation, although usually associated with Asian and African belief systems, has gained a large following in the United States and other western nations in recent years. Ian Stevenson's careful and prolific research into "evidence suggestive of reincarnation" was the center of our attention.

Before concluding, we forced ourselves to consider the question of whether we, *should* survive death. This was followed by perhaps an even more unsettling question: what kind of survival?

We then reviewed your thoughts on the survival question and took note of the subtle but significant links between survival beliefs and suicide. Quite enough for one chapter?

REFERENCES

Atwater, P. M. H. (1992). Is there a Hell? Surprising observations about the near-death experience. *Journal of Near-Death Studies, 10,* 149–160.

Barrett, W. (1926/1986). *Death-bed visions.* Northampton: Aquarian.

Berstein, W. (1965). *The search for Bridey Murphy.* Garden City, NY: Doubleday.

Blackmore, S. (1993). *Dying to live.* Buffalo: Prometheus.

Burnham, S. (1990). *A Book of angels.* New York: Ballentine.

Crowe, D. M. (1996). *A history of the Gypsies of Eastern Europe and Russia.* New York: St. Martin's Griffin.

Freed, R. S., & Freed, S. A. (1993). *Ghosts: Life and death in North India.* New York: American Museum of Natural History, Anthropological Papers, Number 72.

Gabbard, G. O., & Twemlow, S. W. (1984). *With the eyes of the mind.* New York: Praeger.

Gabbard, G. O., & Twemlow, S. W. (1991). Do "near-death experiences" occur only near-death? *Journal of Near-Death Studies, 10,* 41–48.

Gallup, G. (1991). Gallup Poll: *Fear of Dying.*

Green, C. & McCreery, C. (1989). *Apparitions.* Oxford: Institute of Psychophysical Research.

Greyson, B. (1989) The Near-Death Experience Scale. In R. Kastenbaum & B. K. Kastenbaum, (Eds.), *The Encyclopedia of death.* Phoenix: Oryx, pp. 192–193.

Greyson, B. (1992–1993). Near-death experiences and antisuicidal attitudes. *Omega, Journal of Death and Dying, 26,* 81–90.

Greyson, B. (1999). Defining near-death experiences. *Mortality, 4,* 7–20.

Grosso, M. (1991). The myth of the near-death journey. *Journal of Near-Death Studies, 10,* 49–60.

Hittman, M. (1990). *Wovoka and the ghost dance.* Lincoln: University of Nebraska Press.

Hocking, W. E. (1957). *The meaning of immortality in human experience.* New York: Harper.

Holden, J. M., & Joesten, L. (1990). Near-death veridicality research in the hospital setting: problems and promise. *Journal of Near-Death Studies, 9,* 45–54.

Irwin, H. J., & Bramwell, A. B. (1988). The devil in heaven: A near-death experience with both positive and negative facets. *Journal of Near-Death Experiences, 7,* 38–43.

Kastenbaum, R. (1993). Psychopomp. In R. Kastenbaum & B. K. Kastenbaum, (Eds.), *The Encyclopedia of Death.* New York: Avon, p. 211.

Kastenbaum, R.(1993a). Reconstructing death in postmodern society. *Omega, Journal of Death and Dying, 27,* 75–90.

Kastenbaum, R. (1993b) Ian Stevenson: An *Omega* interview. *Omega, Journal of Death and Dying, 28,* 165–182.

Kastenbaum, R. (1995a). Raymond A. Moody, Jr.: An *Omega* interview. *Omega, Journal of Death and Dying, 31,* 87–98.

Kastenbaum, R. (1995b). *Is there life after death?* London: Prion.

Kastenbaum, R. (1996). Near-death reports: Evidence for survival of death? In L. W. Bailey & J. Yates (Eds.), *The near-death experience reader.* (pp. 245–264) New York: Routledge.

Kastenbaum, R. (1998a). Near-death reports: Evidence for survival of death? In L. W. Bailey & J. Yates (Eds.), *The near-death experience reader.* (pp. 245–264) New York: Routledge.

Kastenbaum, R. (1998b). Temporarily dead. *Readings, 13,* 16–21

Kellehear, A. (1996). *Experiences near death.* New York: Oxford University Press.

Kelly, E. W., Greyston, B., & Stevenson, I. (in press). Can experiences near death furnish evidence of life after death? *Omega, Journal of Death and Dying.*

Klenow, D. J., & Bolin, C. (1989–1990). Belief in an afterlife: A national survey. *Omega, Journal of Death and Dying, 20,* 63–74.

Kramer, K. (1988). *The sacred art of dying.* Mahwah, NY: Paulist Press.

Lucretius (Titus Lucretius Carus). *On the nature of things.* (Original work 54 B.C.)

McDannel, C., & Lang, B. (1988). *Heaven: A history.* New Haven: Yale University Press.

Moody, R. A., Jr. (1975). *Life after life.* Atlanta: Mockingbird Books.

Moody, R. A., Jr. (1980). Commentary on "The reality of death experiences: A personal perspective" by Ernest Rodin. *Journal of Nervous and Mental Disease, 168,* 265.

Moody, R. A., Jr., (1988). *The light beyond.* New York: Bantam.

Mooney, J. (1996). *The ghost dance.* North Dighton, MA: JG Press, Inc.

Morse, M. (1990). *Closer to the light.* New York: Villard.

Morse, M. (1992). *Transformed by the light.* New York: Villard.

Myers, F. W. H. (1975). *Human personality and its survival of bodily death.* (vol. 1–2). New York: Arno Press. (Original work published 1903).

Noyes, R., Jr. (1979). Near-death experiences: Their interpretation. In R. Kastenbaum (Ed.), *Between life and death.* New York: Springer, pp. 73–88.

Osis, K. (1961). *Deathbed observations by physicians and nurses.* New York: The Parapsychology Foundation.

Osis, K., & Haraldsson, E. (1977). *At the hour of death.* New York: Avon.

Ring, K. (1980). *Life at death.* New York: Coward, McCann & Geoghegan.

Ring, K. (1989). Near-death experiences. In R. Kastenbaum & B. K. Kastenbaum (eds.), *The encyclopedia of death.* Phoenix: Oryx, pp. 193–196.

Rubenstein, R. (1992). *After Auschwitz.* (2nd ed.). New York: Stein & Day.

Ring, K. (1992). *The Omega Project.* New York: William Morrow.

Ring, K., & Lawrence, M. (1993). Further evidence for veridical perception during near-death experiences. *Journal of Near-Death Studies, 11,* 223–230.

Sabom, M. B. (1982). *Recollections of death.* New York: Simon & Schuster.

Schmitt, J. C. (1998). *Ghosts in the middle ages.* Chicago: University of Chicago Press.

Siegel, R. K. (1980). The psychology of life after death. *American Psychologist, 35,* 911–931.

Siegel, R. K. (1992). *Fire in the brain.* New York: Dutton.

Slawinski, J. (1987). Electrometic radiation and the afterlife. *Journal of Near-Death Studies, 6,* 79–94.

Stevenson, I. (1974). *Twenty cases suggestive of reincarnation.* (Rev. ed.). Charlottesville, VA: University Press of Virginia.

Stevenson, I. (1997a). *Reincarnation and biology. A contribution to the etiology of birthmarks and birth defects.* (Vol. 1-2). Westport, CT: Praeger.

Stevenson, I. (1997b). *Where reincarnation and biology intersect.* Westport, CT: Praeger.

Stevenson, I., Cook, C. W., & McClean-Rice, N. (1989–1990). Are persons reporting "near-death experiences" really near death? A study of medical records. *Omega, Journal of Death and Dying, 20,* 45–54.

Stevenson, I., & Greyson, B. (1996). Near-death experiences: Relevance to the question of survival after death. In L. W. Bailey & J. Yates (Eds.), *The near-death experience reader.* New Haven: Yale University Press, pp. 199–206.

Tart, C. (1990). Who survives? Implications of modern consciousness research. In G. Doore (Ed.), *What survives?* Los Angeles: Jeremy P. Tarcher, pp. 138–152.

Truitner, K., & Truitner, N. (1993). Death and dying in Buddhism. In D. P. Irish, K. F. Lundquist, & V. J. Nelsen (Eds.), *Ethnic variations in dying, death, and grief,* (pp. 125–136). Washington, DC: Taylor & Francis.

Whinnery, J. E. (1997). Psychophysiologic correlates of unconsciousness and near-death experiences. *Journal of Near-Death Studies, 15,* 231–258.

Wilson, M. (1996) *A study of enabling metaphors in near-death experience reports.* Tempe, AZ: Arizona State University. Unpublished Masters thesis.

Zaleski, C. (1987). *Otherworld journeys.* New York: Oxford University Press.

GLOSSARY

Autoscopic Experience: Perceiving one's own body as though from above, a facet of the out-of-body experience.

Channeler: A person with the reputed power to communicate with the past lives of himself, herself, or others.

Depersonalization: A sense of emotional distance from one's own body and self.

Endorphins: The most thoroughly studied of a class of substances produced by the brain, with effects on mood and awareness.

G-LOC: An altered state of consciousness with many similarities to near-death experiences but produced by the stress of extreme acceleration in fighter planes or ground simulations.

Holographic Memory: A vivid mental state in which one does not simply recall but actually seems to be experiencing past situations.

Hyperalertness: A state of heightened attention, usually to danger signals.

Immortality: The persistence of spirit, soul, or personality after death. Not all afterlife beliefs hold that people survive death on a permanent basis; therefore not all survival has immortal status.

Medium: A person with the reputed power of receiving messages from the dead.

Metaphor: Something that represents something else. The *enabling metaphor* represents a large and complex set of events or experiences.

Near-death Experience (NDE): Images, perceptions, and feelings recalled by some people after a life-threatening episode. The near-death experience report (NDER) is the account of such experiences.

Psychometric-type measures: Questionnaires and tests whose responses can be quantified.

Reincarnation: The return of the spirit or soul in another physical form after death.

Rosetta Stone: An ancient tablet whose inscription, when decoded, made it possible to understand a forgotten language.

Seance: Literally, a sitting. The name given to sessions with a medium.

Yahweh: A name given to God in the Old Testament.

Connecticut nurse Jane Boggini provides food, care, and encouragement to a boy in Angola. She is a member of Doctors Without Borders, a recipient of the 1999 Nobel Peace Prize.

chapter 14

HOW CAN WE HELP?

The promise of death education and counseling

In the weeks that followed Josh's (19-month old) sudden death, Toby (2 ½ years old) began to imitate all Joshua's mannerisms, including his baby-talk. It was as though, in a desperate attempt to make everything better for the grown-ups, he had decided to "be" his dead brother, a notion I find particularly heart-wrenching.
—R. W. Weinbach, quoted by Iserson, 1999, p. 136

With little peeks over his shoulder as his mother was rolled out the door, Tristen told me when he becomes president, he's going to make a law that no one's mother will have to be carried out in a plastic bag. I told him it was a good law to make.
—Laura R. Smith, 1996, p. 16

Before he got sick, the most physical contact we would have was a warm handshake. A real blessing during that last month in the hospital was that we both felt more free to display affection.... I would kiss him on the forehead. I massaged his feet with lotion. I could tell he liked it. So did I.
—A man reflecting on caring for his dying father, quoted by Chethik, in press

On a medical floor, with perhaps two-thirds of the patients suffering eventually fatal diseases, I say to a nurse, "What's happening?" and she replies, walking on down the hall. "Same ol' same ol'." Nothing new, nothing exciting. On in an Intensive Care Unit in the same hospital, "What's going on?" The resident replies, with a little shrug of her shoulders, "People are living, people are dying." Again, no surprises, nothing new. The routine goes on.
—Daniel F. Chambliss, 1996, p. 119

Prayer, I guess, is my way of "checking in" with God whenever I feel the need or desire to do so.
—A hospice volunteer (S. Schneider & R. Kastenbaum, 1993, p. 477)

Feeling helpless to help is one of the most demoralizing experiences we can encounter when a person close to us is dying or grieving. Fortunately, however, many people have demonstrated that it is possible to help each other in such circumstances. There are now certified grief counselors, as well as teachers, nurses, social workers, and other service providers who have developed skills in comforting and guiding people who are attempting to cope with dying, death, and loss. But many of us can be helpful even though we may not have a professional level of education and experience, as this chapter will show.

The parents of young Toby and even younger Josh recognized that the surviving child's reversion to baby talk was a meaningful and intentional action. Somebody else might dismiss Toby's behavior as silly and not connect it with Josh's death—or even punish the boy for being so childish. Fortunately, Toby's parents took a different approach:

> It was very important then to let Toby know that we loved him for being himself, and that he did not have to "become" Josh to gain our approval. So we never admonished him for taking the role of Josh, but we did remind him often that we loved him very much. (Iserson, 1999, p. 136)

A certified death educator and counselor in Oregon helped 10-year-old Tristen and his 8-year-old brother, Clayton, through the end phase of their young mother's terminal illness. During their sixth visit together in the hospital room, she started to discuss with the brothers the various times in people's lives when they have to say goodbye to places, things, and each other.

> Tristen crawled up right in front of me and looked me in the eyes. "In case you didn't notice. I don't want to talk about this." His look was steady. I was so proud of him for speaking up. "Thank you, Tristen. I'm really glad you told me and I respect your need not to talk about this right now." I patted his shoulder and we went on to play with something else. (Smith, 1996, pp. 13–14)

"I cried all the way home and into the night," Smith reports, but she also felt the sense of love that the dying woman, her fiancee, and her children had shared with each other. She knew that the road ahead for the children, although very difficult, would be that much easier because of loving memories.

It was not a death educator, but an adult son who spent many hours by his father's bedside as the older man died of kidney failure. The son experienced a sense of closeness and closure. Journalist Neil Chethik (in press) interviewed men to learn how they dealt with the deaths of their fathers. In general, he found that sons who spent time caring for the father before the death or talking with him directly about the death reported that such actions helped them in their grieving process afterward. Communication and sharing did much both to comfort the dying father and to help the sons go on with their lives.

The implicit rules that govern the communications and behaviors of health care personnel protect them from emotional wounds. It would be too painful and too disorganizing to face up to the profound human realities that confront them every day. The transition from life to death is transformed from the momentous and mysterious to the ordinary (Chambliss, 1996). Not only the individual nurse or physician, but also the entire system of beliefs and procedures reduces the humanity of the dying person to the routine—unless there happens to be something special and exciting about the case. The doctors and nurses may suffer greatly when this protective system breaks down—or when a staff member has not been sufficiently socialized into the system.

By contrast, doctors, nurses, and community volunteers who choose to work with hospice programs usually are able to focus more on the whole person, rather than only the terminal illness. They also usually have less need to protect themselves from the impact of dying and death. Their work does not become a "failure" when the person dies, nor do their own death anxieties explode. We found (Schneider & Kastenbaum, 1991; 1993) that most hospice staff members and volunteers call upon personal prayer—a communication between themselves and God—to give them the strength to go on. One volunteer was speaking for many others when she told us, "I feel it is a privilege to be with a person at this vulnerable and sacred time of their lives." No respondents described themselves as discovering prayer or becoming religious as a result of their

Hospice volunteers report that they draw personal strength from prayer, though they do not impose their own religious beliefs and practices on patients and families.

experiences with dying people; it was the other way around. People who had already found prayer to be a source of strength continued to call upon this source as they encountered the challenges of hospice work. They did not ask for divine intervention or miracles in their prayers, nor did they impose these prayers on patients and families. Praying was a way of staying in touch with themselves and their deepest beliefs.

We have alternatives, then. These include trivialization and avoidance of the dying person; crippling episodes of personal anxiety; and integrating dying, death, and grief into the fabric of our lives. Understanding and developing positive alternatives to avoidance and anxiety is one of the prime challenges faced by death educators and counselors.

DEATH EDUCATORS AND COUNSELORS: THE "BORDER PATROL"

Most people who serve as death educators and counselors draw upon personal experiences as well as academic and professional education. Death educators and counselors do not necessarily agree on all issues, but most understand that the boundary between the land of the living and the land of the dead is as subtle as the next breath we take.

Some people still have difficulty in understanding how death can be studied or taught. Others are fearful that strangers under the guise of educators and counselors will invade the sanctity of their innermost beliefs and attempt to force some kind of unwelcome change upon them. Questions may also be raised by researchers, educators, and counselors in other fields. Is there a solid basis for this field, or does death education purvey only untested assumptions and fantasies? What do people derive from death education and counseling? And what *should* people derive?

We begin our exploration with a brief historical introduction, then examine the current scene in death education and counseling, and conclude with some observations about future prospects and challenges.

DEATH EDUCATION IN HISTORICAL PERSPECTIVE

The term "death education" itself and the field to which it refers did not become a recognizable part of our society until the 1960s, as noted in Chapter 3. In the broader sense, however, we have never been without some form of instruction and guidance.

From Ancient Times

Ancient documents from Tibet and dynastic Egypt offer detailed accounts of what becomes of the soul after death and what preparations can be made ahead of time to improve one's chances for a safe passage. These documents have become known in the Western world as "books of the dead." Their emphasis is heavily weighted toward funeral and memorial practices and the fate of the soul after death. For example, it helps if one knows the names of the underworld demons and deities and the challenges they will put to the spirits of the deceased. It is crucial to be well prepared. In dynastic Egypt, for example, forty-two gods sit in judgment as the newly dead person confesses his or her faults and misdeeds. The

dead person's soul is then measured against a feather: paradise is ahead if the scale balances perfectly. The outcome if the soul fails to pass this test is something we really would not want to know. Ancient death education, then, often had much to do with one's preparation for the ordeal of judgment after taking that last breath.

By contrast, much of contemporary death education focuses on people attempting to cope with death in the midst of life—the hospice nurse, the grieving family member, the individual who has just learned that he or she has a life-threatening disease. It might seem a little odd to us that some cultures would emphasize education for the dead and the mourners. Ancient Egyptians or Tibetans, however, might have difficulty with *our* priorities and preoccupations: for example, the mass of regulations that surround eligibility and reimbursement for hospice care could appear as formidable to them as the priestly injunctions for funeral rituals or postmortem behavior in the underworld seem to us.

Down through the centuries, many religious leaders, philosophers, and creative artists have offered a variety of images and ideas about our relationship to death. One of the most basic and common themes has been the fleeting nature of life. Job (13:12) laments: "Man that is born of a woman is of few days, and full of trouble. He cometh forth like a flower, and is cut down: he fleeth also as a shadow, and continueth not." The Old Testament repeatedly compares human life with the grass that withers and is blown away by the whirlwind. The evanescence of life is linked with the limits of human knowledge and power. Do we suppose ourselves to be lordly beings? Proverbs (27:1) quickly deflates us: "Boast not thyself of tomorrow; for thou knowest not what a day may bring forth." If we cannot even be sure of having a tomorrow, how can we claim knowledge and power?

It is not only the Judeo-Christian tradition that has attempted to bring awareness of our mortality to the fore. The collection of stories known as *The Arabian Nights* is best known for the celebration of sensuality, but death is also given eloquent attention. The following passage demonstrates how awareness of our mortality might provide the basis for a mature philosophy of life:

O sons of men,
Turn quickly and you will see death
Behind your shoulder.
Adam saw him,
Nimrod saw him
Who wound his horn in the forest,
The masters of Persia saw him.
Alexander, who wrestled with the world
And threw the world,
Turned quickly and saw death
Behind his shoulder....
O sons of men,
When you give yourselves to the sweet trap of life
Leave one limb free for God.
The fear of death is the beginning of wisdom
And the fair things you do
Shall blow and smell like flowers
On the red and fiery day.
(Mathers, 1974, pp. 300–301)

Notice the similarities as well as the differences between the perspectives offered by the *Old Testament* and *The Arabian Nights*. Both emphasize the brevity of human life and the possibility of sudden death at any time. Both suggest that for these very reasons it would be foolish to allow ourselves to be carried away by our own triumphs and ambitions. Both contrast the power of God with the powerlessness of mortals. But the emotional tone is not at all the same. The troubled, fleeting shadow portrayed in the *Old Testament* seems to find neither pleasure nor solace. By contrast, the readers of Scheherazade's tales of one thousand and one nights are expected to give themselves to "the sweet trap of life." What are we to do, then? Should we spend our lives lamenting and "eating worms" before the worms eat us? Or should we enjoy the sweet trap while we can, knowing full well that our pleasures and triumphs will not endure because *we* will not endure?

It is worth keeping this divergence in mind. Death education and counseling today carry forward the awareness that death is a central fact of life. Once we have the basic facts in mind, however, we still have a choice of what attitudes to take toward these facts, what lessons to draw from them. At one extreme, we might crawl into a box and wait for the end; at the other, we might attempt to live in a feverish quest for thrills. Perhaps "the fear of death is the beginning of wis-

dom," but it is only the beginning. We still have the challenge of developing a coherent and meaningful life based upon our awareness that "all flesh is as grass."

The *New Testament* introduced a radically different perspective: "Whoso eateth my flesh, and drinketh my blood, hath eternal life; and I will raise him up at the last day" (John 6:54). "And this is the promise that he hath promised us, even eternal life" (John 3:15). "And the sea gave up the dead which were in it; and death and hell delivered up the dead which were in them: and they were judged every man according to their works. And death and hell were cast into the lake of fire" (Revelation 20:13–14).

In centuries to come, Christians would differ among themselves on many death-related issues (e.g., is it faith, good works, or predestination that ensure triumph over death?). Right from the start, however, it was clear that at the core of Christianity was its bold contention that man had been redeemed from death through Jesus.

The Christian "death education lesson" differed markedly from those of the *Old Testament* and the *Arabian Nights*. We do not have to go through life in sorrow and lament, nor surrender to the "sweet trap" with the bittersweet knowledge that it will soon snap shut upon us. Instead, we should feel joyful about the life to come after this brief and unsatisfactory sojourn on earth is completed. This rousing lesson did not escape change through time, however. As the Christian faith grew larger and its membership became more diverse, other themes became increasingly significant. Three related themes remain influential today, although all have been challenged within as well as outside the Christian orbit:

1. Death is punishment for all humans because of Adam and Eve's disobedience in seeking forbidden knowledge (original sin doctrine).
2. Death is a test that will separate the worthy from the unworthy: the final exam of all final exams.
3. Life on earth is just something we must endure; its pleasures are insubstantial, if not deceptive. Death, therefore, is a blessed release.

Not all Christians subscribe to these views. However, they have the cumulative weight of centuries behind them and are still influential today. Death educators and counselors would have to be exceedingly naive to ignore this powerful and complex heritage. For example, the fact that the Christian tradition includes images of death both as punishment and as blessing should alert us to the many possible implications. "I am eager to fulfill myself through death" can be a compelling wish that competes with the equally compelling fear, "What if I am judged to have lived a sinful and unworthy life?" To take another example: a born-again minister paid an unexpected and unrequested visit to a woman hospitalized with a terminal illness. He burst into her room with these words: "God knows what a sinner you are! Prepare yourself for the moment of judgment!" The astonished woman quietly replied, "God and I have never given each other any trouble." Undeterred, he made repeated attempts to bully the exhausted woman into confessing her sins and placing her life into his hands. Upon learning of this incident, the official hospital chaplain was even more distressed than the woman who had fallen victim to this brutal "educational" or "counseling" intervention. Unfortunately, there is a potential for harming people at vulnerable points in their lives by attempting to impose one's own beliefs upon them. Responsible death educators and counselors hold a variety of religious beliefs themselves, but they also are aware and respectful of the traditions that influence their students and clients.

Those with a sense of history have the further realization that traditional ways of communicating about death might not be entirely appropriate or effective in today's world. These traditions developed in societies that differed from ours in many ways. In medieval times, for example, most people lived in small, agrarian communities. They had little education, little contact with people outside their own circle. The concepts of having "inalienable" human rights, holding one's own political and religious opinions, and being free to pursue unlimited personal interests and ambitions were unknown. People lived in a low-technology society that was fairly stable from generation to generation and that offered little protection against the forces of nature and the disasters encountered in everyday life. When darkness fell at night, few would venture out of doors where both real and fantasy terrors lurked. Little faith could be placed

in the wrong-headed "medical" treatments of the time, which frequently caused as much suffering as the diseases themselves. Many newborn babies failed to survive into adulthood. Infections associated with childbirth, wounds, and injuries often proved fatal to adults, and epidemics periodically decimated the population.

Some of the most vivid and forceful traditions reached their peak and faded away before our own era. The dance of death, for example, was a compelling image introduced by poets, artists, and performers in the thirteenth century, if not earlier. The living and the dead were portrayed as engaging in a slow and solemn dance together. The *danse macabre* theme often depicted Death as a skeletal figure who laid claim to all mortal souls, whether low or high born (Kastenbaum, 1993b). "We all look the same to Death: kings, bishops or peasants, we are all mortal beings" was part of the core message. And a powerful message this was—bearing in mind that society was highly stratified at the time, with a few "high and mighty" people lording it over the masses. The zing of this message gradually decreased as the ruling classes became destabilized by social and technological changes that continue into our own time. Nevertheless, some twentieth-century artists still found powerful uses for dance-of-death imagery, and millions of viewers have watched Woody Allen trip the light fantastic with a shrouded companion in the final moments of his movie *Love and Death*.

Another significant tradition arose in the fifteenth century: Christian guidebooks for priests and others who might be in the position to help people in their last days and hours of life (Kastenbaum, 1993a). This has become known to historians as the *Ars moriendi* tradition—literally, the art of dying well. These guidebooks differ in many ways from the writings on dying and death that have appeared in our own time. For example, most of the guidebooks limited themselves to describing rituals that should be performed as part of the deathbed scene. Two themes already mentioned—death as punishment and as a test of the soul's worthiness—tended to dominate. People were never more at risk than at the moment of death. The priest tried to help the dying person resist the assaults and temptations of the demons who hoped to consign the soul to the flames of hell. As we will see later, there might be a subtle link between the priestly soul saver and at least one image of the modern death educator/counselor.

Despite these differences, however, the *Ars moriendi* guidebooks were motivated by some beliefs and concerns that have reappeared in our own death awareness movement. These include: (1) the view that *how* a person dies is significant; therefore (2) some deaths are better than others; so (3) a "good death" is a real achievement, and (4) it flows more readily from a life that has been lived in the recognition of mortality, with (5) the support of caring people who have also prepared themselves properly for the encounter with death.

The capstone of the *Ars moriendi* tradition was reached in 1651 with the publication of Jeremy Taylor's *Rules and Exercises of Holy Dying*. The Reverend Mr. Taylor recommended that we all give ourselves a daily "refresher course" on life and death. Today we might describe this kind of exercise as a life review. Taylor, however, would not have us wait until we are well up in years and reluctantly aware that this final act of life is not long in coming:

> For, if we make but one general account, and never reckon till we die…we shall only reckon by great sums, and remember nothing but clamorous and crying sins, and never consider concerning particulars, or forget very many…. But if we observe all the little passages of our life…see every day sins increase so fast, and virtues grow up so slow…we may see our evil and amend it…. *As therefore every night we must make our bed the memorial of our grave, so let our evening thoughts be an image of the day of judgment.* (1651/1977, pp. 48–49)

Death education and counseling had to begin anew after centuries of avoidance. What is the nature of death education and counseling today? We begin with death education.

DEATH EDUCATION AND COUNSELING: THE CURRENT SCENE

We can gain a quick view of the changed scene by becoming familiar with an organization known as Association for Death Education and Counseling (ADEC). This nonprofit organization was incorporated in 1976 with the purpose of improving the quality of death education and death-related counseling (Leviton, 1993). In pursuing these goals, ADEC has introduced national training workshops and certification procedures for death educators and counselors.

If you attend one of ADEC's national conferences, you will probably be impressed with the combination of maturity and receptivity to new knowledge. What you will not see is the person who has read one book and attended one workshop and is ready to impose his or her ignorance upon the world. The "pop death" people have pretty much come and gone.

Fortunately, the most valuable elements of the early death awareness movement have continued to flourish. The typical participant is a person who is well aware of his or her own death-related feelings and has had direct experience in one or more areas of real-life concern (e.g., supporting families after the death of a child, counseling people who have tested positive for the AIDS virus, training hospice volunteers, etc). You will probably find this person to be compassionate, realistic, welcoming of newcomers, and blessed with a resilient sense of humor. For weird people who are committed to bizarre projects, we will have to look elsewhere.

Some people may still put themselves forward as death educators or counselors without possessing either the personal or experiential qualifications. The minister who burst into the dying woman's hospital room was motivated by his personal agenda, not by the expressed needs of a person he had never met. The teacher who does not even know that journals such as *Omega* and *Death Studies* exist will be lecturing from assumptions and limited personal observations that often are at variance with the facts. (Please see *Appendix* for useful journal, book, and organizational sources.) There are still places where unqualified people can function in the role of death educators or counselors, but with increasing professional and public sophistication, these opportunities are diminishing. Every year more educators and counselors qualify themselves for certification by ADEC.

What we should expect from death education and death educators is a question that has not yet been fully resolved. Perhaps there will never be a definitive answer because people come to this topic with a variety of needs and expectations.

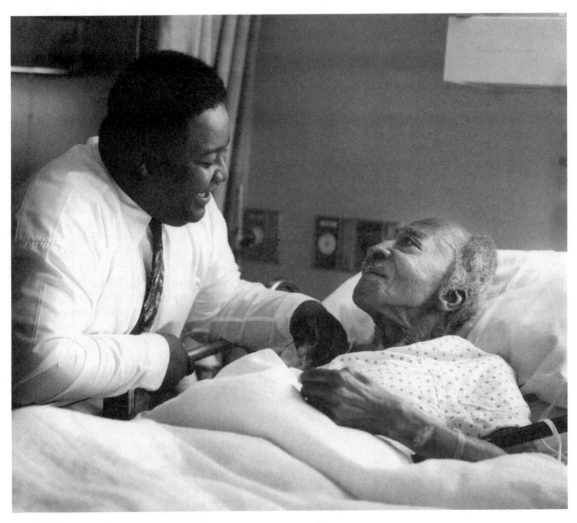

A caring relationship is often the best medicine for a terminally ill person.

Students in my classes, for example, often enroll with the purpose of adding to their competencies as nurses, paramedics, social workers, counselors, or psychologists. Others have had personal experiences, such as the death of a parent or the serious illness of a spouse, that give the topic special urgency. Others are keenly interested in working with the dying or the bereaved; still others have become curious about some particular facet of death (e.g., funerals, near-death experiences, etc.). All of these expectations can be addressed in a death education course, but it is difficult to give them all equal attention. Although the classroom situation is flexible enough to permit a mix of thought and feeling, structure and openness, it may not be able to meet all students' needs.

Clinical skills are probably developed best in clinical situations. Classroom examples can be helpful, but case experience and supervision are also needed. "Deep learning"—an experience that is emotional as well as intellectual—can be achieved at times in the classroom, but this more often requires a series of in-depth and intimate discussions that are not always possible within academic constraints. It is useful, then, for all participants to recognize what can and should be accomplished in a particular course, conference, or workshop and what must be achieved in other settings.

Richard A. Kalish (1980–1981) observes that the death educator came along at a time when two of society's most important traditional roles had undergone significant change. According to Kalish's analysis, the priest was once the dominant person who mediated our relationship to death ("priest" is used here in the generic sense). The physician gained increasing importance, however, as society shifted its orientation from hopes of a better life after death to a longer and healthier life on earth. The death educator entered the scene, then, when society was no longer as enthusiastic about accepting an afterlife as a substitute for a long and fulfilling life on earth— but also at a time when society had judged that the physician did not have the "magic," either. This situation led Kalish to portray death educators as "deacons who will never become priests." The priest and the physician both possess a kind of vested power and authority not shared by the death educator (who may, however, also *be* a priest or physician!). Death educators or "deacons" can come into conflict with priests and physicians by venturing onto their turfs in ways considered unwelcome or competitive. Death educators can also seem to be promising too much and thereby set themselves up for failure: "Death educators and counselors are treading sacred ground, and must be expected to be attacked for their errors, their vanities, any signs of greed or lust or need of power" (1980–1981, p. 83).

Kalish's point that death educators and counselors must be aware of their role relationships with other professionals is well taken, as is the caution that they should refrain from creating unrealistic expectations on the part of students or clients. Furthermore, skill in teaching or learning about death does not fully equip a person for therapeutic interventions outside the classroom. Social pressures may also encourage death educators to deliver a "comforting product rather than a searching encounter." The result of sugarcoated superficialities in the name of death education can be an *illusion of understanding and con-*

trol. Death is not just one more fact of life to be placed alongside another. However, once a course number has been assigned and all academic niceties have been observed, there may be the unearned assumption that "we covered death today" (Kastenbaum, 1977).

Effective death educators come from a variety of established fields, such as psychology, psychiatry, medical ethics, nursing, sociology, and the ministry. It is valuable to have a solid grounding in one or more substantive fields as well as particular competency in death-related topics.

The Expanding Scope of Death Education

The scope of death education is gradually expanding to include a greater variety of people who are responsible for human services. This steady and successful expansion suggests that the programs are effective in meeting needs. For example, Air Force mortuary officers report that death education has provided valuable guidance, assistance, and emotional support for their difficult task of informing and working with bereaved families (Rosenbaum and Ballard, 1990). There is, however, a significant exception to the continued growth of death education. A survey of 423 public schools found that there is still relatively little death education being offered in the entire range from prekindergarten through the twelfth grade (Wass, Miller, & Thornton, 1990). Only about one school in ten reported having any kind of death education program. The possibility of providing occasional death education at the "teachable moment" by discussing recent death-related events is seldom utilized. It is possible that many teachers do not feel secure in opening discussions on such emotion-laden topics as the death of a teacher or student. Survey results show that the teachers are being offered very few opportunities to develop their own expertise in this area. Suicide prevention/intervention programs are no longer quite as rare, though, with about one in every four schools reporting some kind of effort in this area. The authors suggest that "public attitudes toward death may not have changed as dramatically as we would like, and the 'death avoidance' previously observed by social scientists may still be prevalent today" (1990, p. 262).

Another way to evaluate the effects of death education programs is to explore their possible effect not only on the direct participants but on other people as well. Some evidence indicates that "ripple effects" do occur. One study found that a three-week university symposium not only had positive value for the student and faculty participants, but also affected the thoughts and feelings of other people on the campus who had not taken the course themselves (Cook, et al., 1984–1985). They were stimulated by what they had heard about the symposium and engaged in more conversations about death-related matters. It is likely that ripple effects occur in many other death education situations as well. For example, I have had several contacts with adults who had been unable to share their concerns about death until the subject was brought up in their children's classrooms. In another recent instance, I spoke about sudden death situations to an introductory class in human communication. One of the students had survived an automobile accident in which a friend had been killed. The driver was now this student's roommate and had never said a word about the accident and the death. The communication student decided it was time to do something about this situation, and over the next few days he and his roommate talked—and wept—about the tragedy. Later he reported, "We both have grown up a lot, I think—and _____ doesn't have those screaming nightmares anymore." My experience is probably typical of those of many other death educators whose students report that their friends and family express curiosity and use the course as an occasion to bring up their own thoughts and feelings. There are probably some disturbing incidents as well, when an enthusiastic student runs up against a friend or family member who is appalled at the idea of discussing death.

Durlak reviewed studies on the effects of death education. He observes:

> Not everyone is afraid of or uncomfortable with death, and thus not every participant should be expected to show reduced negative feelings about death after a death education program. Even if all participants are highly anxious about death, one particular program might work more effectively for some than others. (1994, p. 256)

As Durlak also notes, death education programs are complex interventions that offer information, modeling, support, and persuasive communications. We should also expect their effects to be complex and to vary with the personality and experience of the students. It would be simplistic to maintain that death education courses have the basic function of reducing death anxiety. As we have seen (*Chapter 1*), little solid information is available on what constitutes the "right" level of death anxiety. Furthermore, most people express only a moderate level of death anxiety most of the time, if the most commonly used assessment techniques are to be believed. In addition, the term *death anxiety* is often used in a vague way. Precisely what are we trying to reduce? Furthermore, anxiety is a valuable signal: it tells us that something is disturbing our peace of mind. Perhaps we should respond to death anxiety as a clue and see where it leads us, rather than moving swiftly to dull or displace the symptom. In some circumstances, the reduction of death anxiety could be an appropriate, and perhaps even an urgent, goal of educational efforts. However, I do not think it would be wise to conceive of death education primarily as an instrument for reducing death anxiety.

Death education is not a standardized product that can be prescribed and administered in precise dosages. It is a complex process that depends much upon the interacting personalities of instructor and students and upon much else as well—for example, the scholarly and professional qualifications of all participants, the specific purpose of the course, the amount of time that can be devoted to this enterprise. Furthermore a more intense situation arises when death suddenly intrudes into the lives of students or instructors. It is during these challenging times that we all learn a good deal more about ourselves and have the opportunity to put what we think we know and believe into practice.

COUNSELING AND THE COUNSELORS

Not everybody has the sense of personal security and confidence to provide services to terminally ill or grieving people. Some health care professionals continue to avoid human contact with dying people and their families as much as possible. Sherman's (1996) study of nurses is the latest to find that people who report higher levels of personal death anxiety are less willing to work with dying people—especially those with many symptoms to manage. However, Sherman also found that the willingness to work with terminally ill people can be influenced either positively or negatively by the quality of social support available from other health care providers. It is difficult to open oneself to the emotional challenges of interacting with a dying person if one feels alone and abandoned by colleagues for doing so.

Although our emphasis here is on counseling and psychotherapy, we will also look at the experiences of other people who provide direct services to terminally ill patients, their families, the grieving, or the suicidal. These include the many nurses, social workers, clergy, and hospice volunteers who sometimes enter into close personal relationships with people who are confronting death. Counseling, like education, can occur under informal circumstances or as part of a systematic program. The boundary between counseling and education can also be crossed easily from either side. A classroom discussion, for example, may become transformed into an advice-sharing session to help a student decide whether or not to continue his or her practice of avoiding funerals. Similarly, a priest who is counseling the spouse of a dying person may be able to reduce anxiety by providing specific information about church beliefs and practices. In exploring counseling and the counselors, then, we are not entirely forgetting death education.

Characteristics of Professionals in the Death System

It is an article of faith that people who would help others must also be well aware of their own personalities and in control of their own conflicts. This requirement seems applicable to all caregivers who accept responsibility in death-related situations, whether they are ministers or social workers, psychiatrists or hospice volunteers. It is useful, then, to examine the death concerns of mental health professionals as Morrison, Vanderwyst, Cocozza, & Dowling, (1981–1982) have done. They found that professionals representing five different fields were neither more nor less

anxious than people in a comparison population. However, those who had never been married and those with a serious medical illness expressed higher levels of death concern. It may be reassuring to learn that mental health specialists are as "normal" as everybody else in their self-reported death attitudes. However, the unexpected finding that never-married mental health professionals express a higher level of death concern merits further investigation. Perhaps more attention should be given to the interaction between a caregiver's personal life and his or her orientation toward death—and perhaps the Morrison study should be repeated to learn whether any changes have taken place in the last few years.

Another approach has been taken by Neimeyer and colleagues (1983), who asked medical residents in pediatrics to provide autobiographical information and to complete the Death Threat Index, a more sophisticated instrument than the usual death anxiety scale. Additionally, the residents were asked to respond to a pair of case history vignettes. They were to imagine themselves as being the attending physician in each case and to make several ratings. Further information was obtained when a group of more advanced medical residents was asked to rate each of the study participants on his or her actual effectiveness in helping patients and their families cope with death. Here, then, is one of the few studies that not only obtains in-depth information on the respondents, but also attempts to compare self-reports with information from an external source. The researchers found that, yes, there was a relationship between personal feelings and style of interacting with dying patients. The medical residents who felt most strongly threatened by death were also those who most often used avoidance strategies when caring for a dying patient. These were the young physicians who busied themselves in reviewing charts and finding other things to do instead of meeting their patients' needs for personal contact, information, guidance, and emotional support. We might well expect similar findings among other health care specialists when personal death anxiety leads to the avoidance of meaningful interactions with patients and their families.

The most extensive study of caregivers' responses to working with dying people was conducted by Mary L. S. Vachon (1987), who herself had extensive experience as a helping person. She interviewed about 600 professional caregivers from hospitals, palliative care facilities, chronic care institutions, and voluntary agencies. The caregivers included Australians and Europeans as well as Canadians and Americans. As might be expected, most of the caregivers were women, and most of the men in her sample were physicians. Vachon placed the problem in the broad perspective of occupational stress. What was the basic source of stress for physicians, nurses, and others who care for dying patients? And how did they cope with this stress?

Her answer might be surprising—especially to those who have not worked in a health care setting. The findings are crisply expressed in one of her chapter titles: "Dying Patients Are Not the Real Problem." The caregivers reported that they were most stressed by their work environment and occupational roles, not by their direct work with dying patients and their families. They had many specific stresses to report, such as poor communication within the health care facility, conflicts between one unit and another, lack of continuity as employees came and went, and so on. Many of the specific stresses were continuous or recurring and showed themselves through inadequate patterns of communication. As Vachon noted, it is possible that underlying death anxiety contributed to the stress and communication difficulties, but the overall evidence points to the significance of environmental variables.

Vachon's findings ring true. Tense, anxious, frustrated, and exhausted caregivers have difficulty bringing their best selves to dying patients and their families. For example, we do not have to assume that a nurse who withdraws from a dying person is motivated by her own excessive death anxieties. It is perhaps even more likely that she is caught in a role conflict (between technical expert and humane caregiver), a time bind, and an ambiguous situation created by poor interstaff communications. And those professional caregivers who do have intense death-related fears are not likely to find much opportunity to reduce or resolve them on the job. This makes it tempting for them to "go with the flow" and perpetuate a brisk, distant, noninteractive strategy of making it through the day—in other words, reducing the profound to the ordinary and the routine, as we have already seen.

Whatever improves communication among caregivers is likely to reduce frustration and anxiety. Delving into a caregiver's personal anxieties may not always be the most useful place to begin. Instead, we might help him or her to be more helpful with terminally ill people and their families by preventing or reducing the systematic stresses encountered in the workplace. Growing research literature identifies specific sources of stress (e.g., Riordan and Salzer, 1992). It has also been found that burnout and staff turnover are relatively low among hospice nurses (Turnipseed, 1987) suggesting that some of the principles and practices of a well functioning hospice might be applied to other health care settings as well.

Careful selection, effective training, and a supportive work environment should be given high priority whether we are dealing with professional or volunteer caregivers in death-related situations. Caregivers themselves often are well aware of their lack of preparation for communicating with terminally ill people and their families. McGrath, Yates, Clinton, & Hart (1999), for example, found that communication problems were a major source of stress for nurses who work with dying patients and their families. The nurses were strongly motivated to help but often felt "very uncomfortable and distressed as I really didn't know how to answer these questions." Their perceived failures in communicating with dying people stayed with them as a continuing source of stress, "But never did I talk to them about their feelings about death or dying. I wanted to, I knew I should, but I couldn't. I felt lost for words" (McGrath et al., 1999, p. 24).

Fortunately, it is possible to improve our skills and thereby also reduce our anxieties in communicating with people in difficult situations. Attention can be given to body language as well as verbal communication. People preparing for careers in nursing, medicine, social work, and other human service fields have often found it useful to take courses and workshops to improve their communication skills.

Counseling and Psychotherapy

People do not necessarily need counseling or psychotherapy when death enters their lives. Sometimes the needed strength can be drawn from love, friendship, a familiar environment, and one's own beliefs, values, and coping resources. Financial security and competent nursing and medical care are also likely to help see the person through. Before considering counseling or therapy, then, it is usually wise to assess the total situation. Perhaps what this man needs is a more effective pain management regime; perhaps what this woman needs is the opportunity to spend some time with the sister or brother she has not seen for years. Counseling and therapy are options that may be worth considering, but not to the neglect of the many other factors that might provide comfort and peace of mind.

Many counselors believe that one of the most important goals is to help their clients to summon up their own inner strengths. A sense of helplessness can reduce an individual's ability to cope with illness, not only physically but also psychologically. A counselor can help to restore self-confidence, relaxation, and a renewed sense of still being a valuable and lovable person. This more positive psychological state is thought to have a favorable effect on bodily response, for example, through improved cardiovascular circulation or more vigorous functioning of the immune system. The success of a healing-oriented approach depends as much upon the caregiver's personality as on his or her "technique." It is difficult to imagine a nervous, time-conscious, and hard-driving personality achieving the same results as a firm, but patient and gentle individual. Those who provide counseling or psychotherapy in death-related situations are wise to select an approach that is in harmony with their own personalities as well as one that is well grounded in the knowledge of human nature.

Two very different examples support this point. At one extreme is what might be termed the *healing care approach,* as represented by an entire team of therapists who have worked with severely impaired and terminally ill geriatric patients (Kastenbaum, et al., 1981). Therapeutic touch, singing together, and interpreting each other's dreams and fantasies are among the untraditional modalities used in addition to dialogue. Conveniences such as carefully scheduled sessions and a formal setting are put aside. The therapists make themselves available when needed at any hour of the day or night. Not all caregivers would find this approach acceptable or possible, but it may be the treatment of choice when a person is at risk of dying alone and in despair.

Quite different is the behavior modification approach (Sobel, 1981). Some behavioral principles were used by the healing care therapists, and have been incorporated into a variety of other approaches. However, when the overall approach is behavior modification, there is more of a "rational" as contrasted with an emotion-intensive framework. One does not have to be an exceptionally intuitive person to conduct successful behavior modification. In fact, spontaneity at the wrong time might interfere with the treatment plan. The behavior modification approach may be taken not only with the dying patients themselves, but also with the professional and personal support network. For example, a systematic desensitization technique might help reduce some of the anxieties of the dying person's spouse and thereby also reduce the anxiety in their interactions.

There is no definitive list of counseling and therapeutic approaches that can be effective in death-related situations, nor is there compelling evidence to demonstrate that one approach is generally superior to another. Furthermore, there is no reason to suppose that all dying people require such interventions. Counseling and therapy do have a place, however, in the total spectrum of services that should be available. For people grieving over the death of loved ones, peer support groups are often very helpful (Lieberman, 1996). People who have already made strides toward recovery from grief seem to know when a newly bereaved person needs words of comfort, approval for anger, a hug—or companionable silence.

HOW WE ALL CAN HELP

We all can help by realizing that *prosocial action* is well within our capabilities. Even though we live in a world in which self-interest and competition are salient, we are a species that has repeatedly demonstrated concern and compassion for others. As a matter of fact, some of our other fellow creatures have also shown this ability.

You may have read about this incident in the newspapers and seen it for yourself on television news on August 16, 1996. A 3-year-old had fallen into the outdoor gorilla exhibit at the Brookfield Zoo in Illinois. He landed eighteen feet down in the rock-studded pit, injured, unable to move, and probably unconscious. A gorilla, Binti Jua, saw what had happened. She rushed over to the

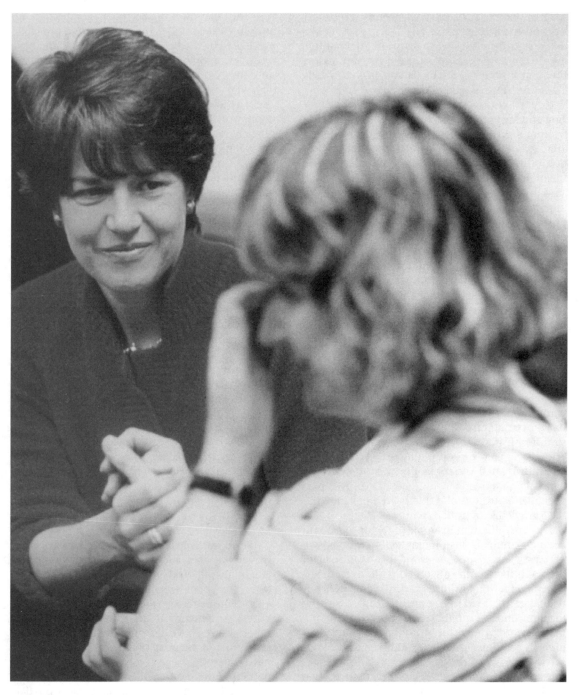

Sometimes it is a good friend, sometimes it is a professional counselor who enables people to rediscover their own strengths in life and death situations.

injured boy with Koola, her own 16-month-old daughter, clinging to her back. The gorilla gently took the boy in her arms and brought him to a gate, where he could be rescued easily. The boy survived his injuries. It turns out that Binti had been raised by humans, but it is possible that, as a good mother, she would have saved the little boy's life anyway.

Binti Jua's *prosocial* action is a useful reminder that murder, suicide, loss, and indifference do not tell the entire story. An aging Sigmund Freud came to the conclusion that our journey through life spins around our relationship to opposing instincts: *Eros,* the drive toward experience, stimulation, and love; and *Thanatos,* the drive toward self-destruction and death. According to Freud, the only hope for survival of the human race as well as a rewarding life for individuals is to moderate the force of Thanatos with the caring and joy of Eros (Freud, 1915; 1917). Later, Abraham Maslow (1954; 1968) made the cogent counterargument that we do not always have to transform instinctual dangers and conflicts into positive feelings, but that the healthy and creative side of our personalities comes directly from healthy and creative experiences. Either way, there is a caring and loving side to human nature that can be called upon when we face peril and loss—as well as in our everyday interactions. Developing our own caring impulses should be a major priority for individual and society. And when we need a refresher course, perhaps we can call upon that outstanding death educator and counselor: Binti Jua!

One way in which we can help, then, is to recognize our potential for helping and not feel obliged to leave everything to "experts." The experts will usually tell you that there is no substitute for the comforting presence of a family member or intimate friend. Another way in which we can help is to become more competent in communicating with each other about sudden, unexpected deaths. Communication is especially difficult because nobody really wants to break the bad news and nobody wants to hear it. There is no magic way to convert a tragedy into a positive situation. However, some approaches are better than others in helping people start the long and difficult process of acknowledging and coping with unexpected loss. An excellent resource is Kenneth Iserson's book *Grave Words: Notifying Survivors about Sudden, Unexpected Deaths* (1999). It provides useful suggestions, not only to his fellow physicians, but to all of us who might find ourselves in the situation of telling—or listening to—bad news. For example, we can learn how to recognize and deal with the explosive anger that a person may express upon learning of the unexpected death. Iserson provides guidelines for telephone notification as well as direct conversation in a variety of circumstances. He emphasizes the importance of clear and accurate communication to avoid adding confusion to grief:

> Although to some it may seem cruel and to others obvious, notifiers must use one of the "D" words when informing survivors about a death. "D" words include: "Died," "Death," and "Dead." For many reasons, including their own discomfort, many notifiers prefer to use euphemisms instead. The more common ones use such phrases as "passed away," "passed on," "left us," "checked out," "fatally injured," "gone," "deceased," or "expired." But it is better if you use a "D" word. (Iserson, 1999, p. 43)

Iserson also offers a detailed guide to ways we can continue to be helpful during and after the funeral or memorial service. He reminds us, for example, how useful it can be to run errands, arrange child-care schedules, arrange for housekeeping chores to be done, do grocery shopping or yard work, care for pets, and so forth. Here and elsewhere, Iserson provides abundant examples of things that all of us can do when the lives of people we care about are disrupted by sudden and unexpected death.

Another way we can help is to improve our awareness of the total family response to death. We respond to dying, grief, and loss as individuals, but also as members of family constellations that often have their own style of coping with stress. Elliott J. Rosen's *Families Facing Death* (1998) focuses not on the sudden death, but on the sometimes lengthy period of time in which family life is under stress in the anticipation of death. His observations include some facts that have not been generally appreciated, for example, the early onset of family stress:

A family actually begins to address the prospect of loss with the very first symptoms of disease. As incredible as this may seem, when any member of a family is stricken with illness, even the mildest of physical ailments, the family automatically begins a process of adaptation to preserve threatened homeostasis.... If little Mary Smith gets the sniffles, her parents may become overly solicitous, aware of every twitch of the youngster's nose. Mary may want to crawl into Mommy's lap, a behavior she had more or less abandoned, and Mommy will readily comply. (Rosen, 1998, p. 76)

Families sense the threat quickly and do what they can—for as long as they can—to keep things seeming and feeling "normal." The more aware we are of such family dynamics, the more likely we are to provide intelligent and effective support.

These are but a few of the ways in which we—all of us—can help each other.

SUMMARY

Often there is a feeling of helplessness when people close to us are dying or grieving. We think that perhaps we should just stand back and leave it all to the experts. This chapter proposes that there is much all of us can do, whether as professional care providers, family members, friends, colleagues, or neighbors. Learning how to communicate effectively—both verbally and nonverbally—is a key.

We saw that death education and counseling have their roots in ancient times. In the past, the emphasis often was on guiding people safely from one life to the next. Much of the emphasis today is on individuals and families facing death or living with grief. Common to both past and current philosophies is the belief that death is a central fact of life and deserves our most serious and enlightened attention. We cannot simply repeat the approaches taken in the past, however, because conditions of life in ancient and medieval times differ so much from our own. Nevertheless, attention to the Arabian perspective on mortality and the Christian *Ars moriendi* guidebooks reminds us that we are not the first to face life-and-death issues.

The modern death awareness movement in the United States established itself during the 1970s with such developments as the founding of the Association for Death Education and Counseling. Effective death educators come from a variety of fields, including anthropology, psychology, psychiatry, medical ethics, nursing, social work, sociology, and the ministry. The scope of death education continues to expand, now reaching more people who are preparing for professional caregiving careers. Nevertheless, many human service providers (teachers, in particular) still complete their studies without preparation for helping the dying, grieving, or suicidal people they will encounter from time to time. Professional caregivers often experience intense stress as they struggle not only to communicate with patients and families, but also to cope with difficult work environments. It has become clear that improved communication among caregivers is needed to reduce their frustration and anxiety. People do not necessarily need counseling or psychotherapy when death enters their lives. Often the needed strength can be drawn from love, friendship, a familiar environment, and one's own beliefs, values, and coping resources. Financial security and competent nursing and medical care are also important.

We all can help each other when facing death-related stress and loss. Specific examples were given regarding communication in unexpected, sudden death situations and understanding family responses to life-threatening illness. Expert care providers often play a significant role, but there is no substitute for compassion and companionship from one person to another.

REFERENCES

Aries, P. (1981). *At the hour of our death*. New York: Knopp.

Chambliss, D. F. (1996), *Beyond caring*. Chicago: University of Chicago Press.

Chethik, N. (in press). *Fatherloss*. New York: Hyperion.

Cook, A. S., Olgenbnuns, K. A., & Lagoni, I. (1984–1985). The "ripple effect" of a university sponsored death and dying symposium. *Omega, Journal of Death and Dying, 15,* 185–190.

Durlak, J. A. (1994). Changing death attitudes through death education. In R. A. Neimeyer (Ed.), *Death anxiety handbook* (pp. 243–262). Washington, DC: Taylor & Francis.

Freud, S. (1915). Thoughts for the times on war and death. In *Collected works of Sigmund Freud* (Vol. 4, pp. 288–317).

Freud, S. (1917). Mourning and melancholia. In *Collected works of Sigmund Freud,* (Vol. 4, pp. 152–172).

Iserson, K. V. (1999). *Grave words. Notifying survivors about sudden, unexpected deaths.* Tucson: Galen.

Kalish, R. A. (1980–1981). Death educator as deacon. *Omega, Journal of Death and Dying, 11,* 75–85.

Kastenbaum, R. (1977). We covered death today. *Death Education, 1,* 85–92.

Kastenbaum, R. (1993a). Ars Moriendi. In R. Kastenbaum & B. Kastenbaum (Eds.), *Encyclopedia of death* (pp. 17–19). New York: Avon.

Kastenbaum, R. (1993b). Dance of death. In R. Kastenbaum & B. Kastenbaum (Eds.), *Encyclopedia of death* (pp. 67–70). New York: Avon.

Kastenbaum, R., Barber, T. X., Wilson, S. G., Ryder, B. L., & Hathaway, L. B. (1981). *Old, sick and helpless: Where therapy begins.* Cambridge, MA: Ballinger.

Kastenbaum, R., & Schneider, S. (1991). Does ADEC have a prayer? A survey report. *The Forum Newsletter, 16* (5), 1,12–13.

Kincade, J. E. (1982–1983). Attitudes of physicians, house-estaff, and nurses on care for the terminally ill. *Omega, Journal of Death and Dying, 13,* 333–344.

Leviton, D. (1993). Association for Death Education and Counseling. In R. Kastenbaum & B. Kastenbaum (Eds.), *Encyclopedia of death* (p. 19). New York: Avon.

Lieberman, M. (1996). *Doors close, doors open.* New York: Grosset/Putnam.

Maslow, A. H. (1954). *Motivation and personality.* New York: Harper & Row.

Maslow, A. H. (1968). *Toward a psychology of being.* New York: Van Nostrand Reinhold.

Mathers, E. P. (1974). (Translator). *The book of the thousand nights and one night.* (Vol. 2). New York: St. Martin's.

McGrath, P., Yates, P., Clinton, M., & Hart, G. (1999). "What should I say?" Qualitative findings on dilemmas in palliative care nursing. *The Hospice Journal, 14,* 17–34.

Morrison, J. K., Vanderwyst, D. Cocozza, J., & Dowling, S. (1981–1982). Death concerns among mental health workers. *Omega, Journal of Death and Dying, 12,* 179–190.

Neimeyer, C. J., Behnke, M., & Reiss, J. (1983). Constructs and coping: Physicians' responses to patient death. *Death Education, 7,* 245–266.

Riordan, R. J. & Saltzer, S. K. (1992). Burnout prevention among health care providers working with the terminally ill: A literature review. *Omega, Journal of Death and Dying, 25,* 17–24.

Rosen, E. (1998). *Families facing death.* (Rev. ed.). San Francisco: Jossey-Bass.

Rosenbaum, S. D., & Ballard, J. A. (1990). Educating Air Force mortuary officers. *Death Studies, 14,* 135–146.

Schneider, S., & Kastenbaum, R. (1993). Patterns and meanings of prayer in hospice caregivers: An exploratory study. *Death Studies, 17,* 471–485.

Sherman, D. W. (1996). Nurses' willingness to care for AIDS patients. *Image, Journal of Nursing Scholarship, 28,* 205–214.

Smith, L. R. (1996). Gillian's journey. *The Forum Newsletter (American Association for Death Education and Counseling), 22,* 1, 14–16.

Sobel, H. (Ed.) (1981). *Behavior therapy in terminal care.* Cambridge, MA: Ballinger.

Taylor, J. (1977). *The rules and exercises of holy dying.* New York: Arno. (Original work published 1651)

Turnipseed, D. J., Jr. (1987). Burnout among hospice nurses: An empirical assessment. *Hospice Journal, 3,* 105–119.

Vachon, M. L. S. (1987). *Occupational stress in the care of the critically ill, the dying, and the bereaved.* Washington: Hemisphere.

Wass, H., Miller, M. D., & Thornton, G. (1990). Death education and grief/suicide intervention in the public schools. *Death Studies, 14,* 253–268.

GLOSSARY

Ars Moriendi: The art of dying well. First presented in illustrated books of the fifteenth century.

Artificial Hydration: Providing fluids through an intravenous tube. ("Artificial nutrition" can also be provided in this way.)

Danse Macabre: A visual image of personified Death leading people to their graves in a slow, dignified dance (first appearing in thirteenth century).

Death Threat Index: A self-report measure of some aspects of death anxiety.

Prosocial: Thoughts, feelings, and actions motivated by the intention to help others.

The celebration of life can not only continue, but also take on special meaning when "the days draw down to a precious few."

chapter 15

GOOD LIFE, GOOD DEATH?

Trying to Make Sense of It All

As I walked into Dad's room I was struck by how small he looked. Above him an oscilloscope traced the electrical activity of his heart, and chrome IV poles framed the head of his bed. The IV in his left arm was attached to a bottle of saline, and a plastic bag of antibiotic solution was piggy-backed into the tubing at his wrist. Another IV, this one a large-bore catheter that entered the subclavian vein just below the midportion of his right collarbone, was attached to a three-way stopcock valve. Through it saline was flowing at a to-keep-open rate; also attached to the stopcock was a manometer that provided measurement of central venous pressure, a guide to his volume status. The third channel led to a dopamine drip with its own infusion pump that was standing by, just in case that medication was needed to raise his blood pressure. Oxygen tubing ran from his nose. A call button was pinned to his pillow. A urine bottle hung at his bedrail. On his bedside table was a cafeteria tray with his untouched breakfast, a pitcher of water, and a menu of the next day's meals.

    "Hi, Dad," I managed to say. "How are you doing?"
—Ira Byock, M. D., 1997, p. 15

"The party is still going on. I don't want to go."
—Billie S., a woman receiving hospice home care

LUSAKA, Zambia—AIDS, not war, has turned Africa into a "killing field" and will wipe out enough adults to create 13 million orphans in the next 18 months, the United Nations children's agency said Wednesday. Such cataclysmic statements at the 11th international AIDS in Africa conference were aimed at prodding African governments—which spend more on defense than on health—to act against the scourge of the continent.
—Angus Shaw, September 16, 1999

I don't know if that computer play station deal is the best or the worse thing we ever bought for our kids. They're at the computer or, I should say, in the computer practically all the time, seems that way. Two worlds in our house and I don't know if I want to know which world they like best.
—Sharon T., mother of two boys

We have moved together through a territory both familiar and unfamiliar. The territory encompassed by this book is familiar because much of what we have surveyed has its setting in our own society. And it is familiar because we have looked at human interactions, children developing their ideas about the world, adults encountering challenge, the facts behind the headlines, and, perhaps most significantly, the workings of our own minds. All of these familiar landmarks took on unfamiliar aspects, however. The human interactions included comforting or discomforting responses to dying people and to grief when a relationship ended in death. Our visit to the world of childhood revealed curiosities and anxieties about death that adults usually assume are not of concern to the young. The headlines often opened the way to discovering the extent of suicide, homicide, and other destructive patterns within our society. Our minds revealed something of their struggle to acknowledge the reality of risk and death while at the same time trying to protect us against a keen awareness of mortality. Furthermore, we repeatedly found a diversity of ideas and opinions on core issues, including the nature and meaning of death.

What does it all add up to? How should we think about death in all of its forms? Death sometimes makes itself known to us as a thought that curls around the edges of our minds for a moment before it disappears again. Sometimes it is the invisible blow we feel when we see the marks of mortality in the appearance of a person we love. And sometimes it is the bodies trapped in the crushed automobile or scattered at the scene of a mass murder. These aspects of death (along with so many others) are hard to bring together within a simple and pleasingly rational framework. It is in our nature, however, to try to make

sense of our experiences. Each of us will continue to integrate our thoughts and feelings about death in our own way.

This chapter explores several issues that you might find worth considering as you review your own perspective. A unifying theme is proposed in the form of a question: *good life, good death?* Many people have come to believe that a "good life" prepares the way for a "good death." This has long been a component of religious beliefs as expressed, for example, by Jeremy Taylor (1665/1970) in his *The Rules and Exercises of Holy Dying.* Some have drawn the lesson that we should live each day as though it is our last. Buddhist philosophy emphasizes a continuous flow in which life and death move together in everything we do (Gyatso, 1985). A good death is intrinsically related to a good life because what we call "life" and what we call "death" have always been companions. Variations on this theme have developed in recent years. For example, Avery D. Weisman, a pioneering psychotherapist and researcher with terminally ill people, introduced the influential concept of an *appropriate death,* that is, the death people would choose for themselves if they really had a choice (Weisman, 1972). A "good" death, then, might be very different from one person to another, the key factor being the "fit" between a person's unique life and the way that his or her life comes to an end. Others focus on the importance of having lived a full and rewarding life. People who can accept their lives are more likely to experience a "good death." Partisans of this view include Erikson (1950) in his theory of lifespan development, and Tomer and Eliason (1996) in their regret theory of death anxiety.

That a good life leads to a good death is an appealing concept. At this point, however, let's keep it in mind as a possibility to be explored, rather than a demonstrated fact. We will be in a better position to reflect on it as this chapter and book come to a close. First we will read a case history that can open the door to our inquiry.

A FATHER DIES; A MISSION BEGINS

Ira Byock, M.D. is president of the American Academy of Hospice and Palliative Medicine and a leading advocate for improved care of terminally ill people. It was early in his medical career that his father was struck with a fatal illness. Byock was stunned, moved, and instructed by this experience. Consider just a few aspects of his experience:

- *He saw his father connected to a life support system.* Byock describes this scene in the opening quotation. And what a disturbing scene it was. As a physician, Byock recognized and understood the function of all of the equipment connected to the small-looking man in the bed. As a son, he felt disoriented by the devices that surrounded his father and established a barrier between them. How do you relate to a person who has become a component of a life support system; what do you say? "'Hi, Dad,' I managed to say. 'How are you doing?'" Here is a situation that has confronted an increasing number of people in recent years. From the standpoint of the family member, this situation presents daunting barriers to communication. One could hardly feel more awkward and unnatural. We know less from the standpoint of the person who is the centerpiece of the life support system. Often consciousness and responsiveness are impaired, but sometimes the person can hear and understand what is being said. A scene such as this would be difficult to describe as "good death" by either the patient or the family member.

But wait—the purpose of life support systems is to, well, support life! As it turned out, Byock's father recovered from this particular life-threatening episode with the assistance of these devices and competent nursing care. This made it possible for the family to have more time together with the father still an active participant. It might have been anything but a "good death" if he had died during this episode, but as it happened, persistent medical and nursing care gave him a little more time to live. Situations such as these caution us against sweeping and simplistic conclusions about the relationship between life support systems and the "good death."

- *His father's death occurred later, peacefully, at home.* "He appeared suddenly to be relaxed, as if the work, whatever it had been, was over. He was peaceful, no longer sweating, and his breathing was easy and deep, though irregular. Mom stood touching his foot, and Anita and I sat on each side of the bed touching his arms, as he drew his last breath and left. For the next hour we continued our vigil: hugging one another, crying intermittently, grieving openly and together" (1997, p. 24). Even without analyzing the concept of the "good death" in any detail, it is obvious that this final scene was much more positive than the in-hospital life support situation. Sy Byock seemed to experience the moment of death as a relief and release. There was no way of knowing whether or not he had any awareness of the situation, but if he did, it would have been the loving presence of his family. A sense of unity and completion was experienced by the family itself, much different from the alienating hospital situation. The same person and the same family, then, had two very different experiences, one at the brink of death and one at the actual final moment.

- *A death changes a life.* Byock was intensely involved with his father and other family members during his father's final illness. The death was expected. Indeed, Byock may have been the first to recognize the early symptoms as indications of a fatal condition. Even with all of this knowledge and expectation, however, he was stunned by the death. It was so difficult to accept the fact that he would never see his father again. Furthermore, this personally significant loss broke through all that Byock had learned as a physician about managing terminal illness. He realized that the health care system was at war with death and, therefore, with dying people. Physicians and their emergency response teams engaged in dramatic attempts to prolong or restore life, such as by heart resuscitation. These were futile exercises. The patients die anyway. Please excuse my quoting again; Byock's observations here speak so strongly to my own experiences as a psychologist in geriatric care facilities:

> If death on the wards was macabre, in the ER it was ghastly. In the hands of the medical system, even passings that should have been peaceful turned gruesome. Nursing homes, for example, routinely sent patients only moments away from death to the hospital by ambulance, lights and sirens blazing. By transferring the almost-dead to the emergency room, nursing homes could claim a mortality rate of nearly zero, while providing evidence to families, and any interested attorneys, that "everything possible" had been done. This bizarre scenario extended not only to sudden deaths but also to people who were unconscious, in the final moments of dying, and expected to die. Even though the medical people knew that death had arrived and any efforts would be futile, the system and their training compelled them to attempt CPR before they could pronounce someone officially dead. (1997, p. 27)

Byock is a physician who, touched by his father's death and appalled by the mismanagement of dying people in the health care system, has contributed much to medical education and the improvement of terminal care. He transformed himself from a well-trained insider into a change agent dedicated to awakening the establishment to the need for more humane and effective care. Byock does not spell out his idea of "good death" as such, but his observations clearly identify one major negative and one major positive: Futile medical procedures perpetuate the health care system's unwillingness to face the reality of dying and death and can even constitute a kind of assault on the patient, in which respect and dignity lose out. The opportunity for family and patient to have time together in familiar surroundings can encourage meaningful communication and the affirmation and demonstration of loving relationships. Whatever else "good death" might be, it is more likely to occur within a supportive interpersonal framework and without medical interventions that are both futile and alienating. We will continue to work with the concept of "good death" as we move along.

A Shift in the Meaning of Life and Death?

"Dying well" is perhaps a more accurate term than "good death" because the emphasis is usually on what occurs while the person is still living. Nevertheless, our interpretations of death are likely to influence our attitudes toward end-of-life experiences. A person who regards death as destination and fulfillment may have a different set of expectations and priorities than does a person who regards death as end or outcome. Five alternative interpretations were considered in *Chapter 3*. These were all structural or cognitive models. Each proposed its own version of the nature of death. We can refresh our memory with the help of Table 15-1.

We observed that each of these interpretations has its distinctive implications for how we might think about life and how we might prepare ourselves for death. We have also looked at our *feelings* about death, especially in *Chapter 2*, when we focused on anxiety, denial, and acceptance. Now we want to look again at our death-related thoughts and feelings because it is possible that some shifts are taking place as we move through the twenty-first century. One of these developments is associated with the emergence of a cybernetic society and will be considered a little later. Here we consider the words of Billie S., the hospice patient who sighed, "The party is still going on. I don't want to go." She is not the only person who feels this way. It appears that a long life has become more attractive for many people. This has something to do with the fact that more people are living longer. By itself, though, a long life has not always been welcome. Throughout world history, many people have feared growing old because of possible infirmity, suffering, and abandonment. Death has often been regarded as a release.

TABLE 15-1

Meanings That Have Been Given to Death

- Death is an enfeebled form of life.
- Death is a continuation of life.
- Death is perpetual development.
- Death is waiting.
- Death is cycling and recycling.

This attitude has not been restricted to elderly people, however; infirmity, suffering, and indignity can occur at any age. Suicide has been one way of acting on the feeling that life can be cured only by death. Another path to the release of death has been systematic degradation of health and heightened risk-taking, such as by the abuse of alcohol and other drugs. Less obvious is the quiet withdrawal from life. Activities that once were attractive may now seem either out of reach or only further sources of distress. Some seek, but others avoid close relationships as a way of edging closer to escape from life. If we read history at ground level—the lives of everyday people—we encounter repeatedly the scourges of poverty, famine, illness, bereavement, oppression, and war. Life was hard and dangerous. Many people had to ask themselves, "Why go on?" even as they struggled to go on.

Lullabies, those charming and comforting songs we sing to sleeping babies, actually have their origins in misery so deep and pervasive that the desire to live was strenuously challenged by the temptation to get it all over with. Kalle Achte (1989) tells us:

> Lullabies originated during the centuries that most people lived in agricultural communities, did hard work, and battled against the forces of nature. Famine was an ever-present threat, and epidemics killed many people, especially young children.... A woman's life was especially difficult at that time. Some mothers may have felt that death offered the only release from a joyless life and continuous labor. The mother's own depression and frustration may have been crucial factors in the origins of lullabies with death themes. Perhaps overworked and depressed mothers transferred their own death wishes to the child. (1989, pp. 177–178)

An example of a death-themed lullaby:

> Today Vanyushka will die
> the funeral will be held tomorrow
> we shall bury Vanya
> and toll the big bell (1989, p. 177)

Achte also tells us that death-ridden lullabies became much less common as the conditions of life improved for many people—and that's our very point here. Life has been looking better to people fortunate enough to receive such benefits as abundant food and improved health care, and such perks as the automobile and the VCR. Accordingly, there is more competition for attitudes toward death that were forged during periods of history when for most people life was hard, dangerous, and brief.

These models differ markedly from each other and could be regarded as representing a variety of ways in which to respond to the sorrows and stresses of life. For example, we might contrast the ancient "death is an enfeebled form of life" with the radical new Christian doctrine that "death is waiting" (for a spiritually enhanced afterlife). Believers in both models of death shared the same difficult life conditions. Their expectations and behaviors might have differed significantly, however. A person who maintained the older belief might regard death as not so dramatically different from life. One gets worn down from aging and hard times, and so drifts from one shade of enfeebled life to another. There is not that much to fear from death, because one has already lost so much, and there is not much to expect from death, because the decline continues to continue. By contrast, the Christian vision of death offered a transformation. The miseries and uncertainties of life could be exchanged for the blessings of heaven. Death therefore could seem a lot more appealing than the frustrations, disappointments, sorrows, and suffering of life. This positive outlook, however, was shadowed by the fear of damnation and punishment. Perhaps a stressful life would be followed by an even more stressful experience after death. The stakes were high for Christians: salvation or damnation.

Today fewer people think of death as either a terrifying punishment or a release from a burdensome life. Those with a more positive attitude include many elderly men and women who are active, vigorous, and strongly engaged with life. Attitude studies find that many elderly people are well satisfied with their lives. A retired public health officer, for example, told me, "I am finally discovering who I am after all these years, and having the time of my life. The absolute time of my life!"

We would not want to exaggerate the differences between the past and the present in attitudes toward life and death. Many people treasured life and did all they could to survive in difficult circumstances. There were also people then as well as now who "had it made" and were more interested in having a pleasant life continue than in entering a promised land after death. Nevertheless, there seems to be a subtle shift in recent years. People may hold traditional beliefs about the nature and meaning of death and yet not give these beliefs quite so central a position. Another way of saying this is that death may be becoming less *salient* in everyday life. We may still have our own individual mixes of anxiety, denial, and acceptance, and yet feel less intensely about death as either an overpowering catastrophe or a transcendent blessing.

Perhaps you recall the *regret theory* of death anxiety (*see Chapter 1*). This theory suggests that people who consider themselves to have full and satisfying lives are less anxious about death because they have already lived well. This is a plausible concept and has some supportive observations. Nevertheless, this view might be incomplete. I have known many people who have been well weathered by life. They have had their share of losses, sorrows, and disappointments. But—regret? Not really. Willa T., a woman in her mid-80s, nearly blind for the past several years, offers her understanding of life in response to an open-ended interview question.

You can't change the past. All the bad stuff was part of all the good stuff. You can't really pick and choose. All in all, I've had more in life than I had any right to expect. But, listen, I want more. More life. I don't want to hear about "them pearly gates." I don't want to see them pearly gates any time soon. It's not that I have any problem with death. I don't. Do you understand? It's that I'm used to living and I haven't used up living. Poor Razzi was the same way. She died last night, you know, or early in the morning. I am not afraid of that happening to me, but, oh, it would be a shame, wouldn't it, to have to leave when there's so much more in front of you every day!

Within this perspective, Death is not an awesome figure, terrifying or beatific. Instead, Death is more the spoilsport who turns out the lights and says "The party's over" before we are ready to go. At present there has been little or no research into this subtle shift from strong attitudes—positive or negative—to the feeling that life is so rewarding and meaningful that it should just go on and on. What have you noticed—and what do you make of it?

HORRENDOUS DEATH

Today millions of people continue to suffer deprivation, lack of opportunity, oppression, and high vulnerability to violence. There are places in the world—including the United States—in which poverty is widespread, hunger frequent, and health care inadequate. Furthermore, certain societal practices destroy lives, sometimes in direct and brutal ways, sometimes in less direct but nevertheless efficient ways. Death educators, counselors, and researchers usually focus their attention on individuals and families who are attempting to cope with terminal illness, grief, or suicidality. A few thanatologists, though, have been urging more attention to the deaths that some people impose on others, especially in cruel and degrading ways. Prominent among these advocates is the distinguished public health educator Dan Leviton, who introduced the seminal concept of *horrendous death*. Following is an interview with Leviton.

1. *Precisely what is a horrendous death—how does it differ from other deaths?*

   Horrendous death (HD) is the label given to deaths that are caused by people, usually affecting large populations, and often torturous, violent, and preventable. HD sometimes is motivated by the intention to kill others. Examples are death resulting from war, terrorism, homicide, genocide, and intentioned racism (e.g., lynching) as well as environmental assault. But HD may also result from accidents, drug misuse, suicide, environmental degradation, hunger, poverty, and indirect effects of racism. Another characteristic of HD is that it is premature. Most of us wish to die peacefully in our sleep in old age with minimal suffering. It is the rare person who envisions dying of HD. Exceptions are those who have had a close call with HD, or who have had loved ones or close friends die this way. Most of us are unable to think of our children, grandchildren and mates dying this way. In this sense HD is always premature, "unnatural," and a surprise. The usual response of survivors is "I can't believe it." As a death educator since the late 1960s I am familiar with the concept of denial of death, but I never realized its depth until embarking on this Quixotian project to prevent HD. Nor did I realize how such denial prevents us from acting in our own interest simply because so few of us think about dying a HD—until it happens.

2. *An example or two of specific deaths that were horrendous?*

Read any newspaper or watch CNN. Look at Kosovo; Littleton, Colorado; or perhaps your own neighborhood—one doesn't have to look far. Many books describe and document these horrors (e.g., Fullilove et al., 1998; Gilligan, 1996; Lifton, 1986; McCall, 1994; Rummel, 1990, 1991a, 1991b). Here are some news reports collected when I was researching material for two books on this subject (Leviton, 1991a; Leviton, 1991b).

- Poison gas attack kills hundreds—more than 100 Kurds, men, women, and children killed. —*Washington Post,* March 24, 1985.
- Constant war takes toll on survivors.... Thirty-five percent of newly delivered babies are born physically deformed or emotionally retarded because their mothers "couldn't take it [war] anymore and turned to tranquilizers such as Valium during pregnancy." —*Fort Myers News-Press,* July 22, 1985.
- The production and testing of nuclear weapons since 1945 has resulted in more than 1,680,000 embryonic, fetal and infant deaths.... The global victims of fallout from nuclear testing are estimated to be almost 16 million. —*Breakthrough,* a publication of global Associates, Fall 1975/Winter 1986.
- The International Committee of the Red Cross estimates that about 30,000 children starved to death in Angola in 1982, and no one noticed. —*Washington Post,* September 2, 1984.
- In a grisly protest against "inhuman" living conditions, inmates in two state prisons in Belo Horizonte [200 miles from Rio De Janeiro] have methodically selected and slain five of their number in the last two months.... At dawn Wednes-

day, the lottery claimed its fifth victim, as Roberto Carlos de Oliveira, 19, was strangled with a rag and pummeled to death by six prisoners.... Startled from his sleep, de Oliveira pleaded with his assailants, "For the love of God, don't kill me," according to one inmate's testimony. "Here, God's name doesn't count," one of the attackers was reported to have responded. —*Washington Post,* May 25, 1985.

Can you think of yourself or the person most beloved to you—or, for that matter, your companion animal—burning to death as a result of a flame thrower, that almost universal military weapon, or burning to death in an explosion from a terrorist's bomb? These are characteristic forms of HD, and they happen to real people.

3. *What led or motivated you to come up with this concept?*

By training I am a health educator who specializes in thanatology and gerontology. Thus, I am interested in improving individual and community health and well-being. Anything that reduces unnecessary mortality, morbidity, and suffering is in my purview.

I read Herman Feifel's classic, *The Meaning of Death* (1959). His thesis was that our attitudes toward death—especially denial—affect individual and community behavior. He saw death in much the same way as Freud saw our repression of the sexual drive, that is, as a powerful factor affecting human behavior. My variation of Feifel's insight and that of other early leaders in thanatology was that the denial of death affected not only society but individual and global health and well-being.

A second motivating factor was the common sense observation that many deaths are caused by people. As a husband and father I vowed to do what I could to ensure that my kids and wife did not die a HD. It is deadly not to act. I know that if anyone can die a HD anywhere, my family can die similarly. So my actions, while altruistic, are also self-serving. They have survival value.

Another motivation was the realization that we do have research-based social policies that could prevent the various forms of HD—but are not implemented. They deal with underlying root causes and outcomes and include early warning and surveillance systems. *Where are these policies?* They languish on the shelves of the United Nations and World Health Organization, the Stockholm International Peace Research Institute, the Children's Defense League, the Sierra Club, and a variety of national and international think tanks, governmental, and nongovernmental agencies. What a waste!

So I set about to develop a process that would integrate themes of thanatology and public health in order to implement existing social policies that could prevent HD. A second goal was to try to galvanize others to address this issue, the most important and profound of our time.

4. *Do you see any encouraging signs that individuals and societies are becoming aware of horrendous death and taking steps to prevent it?*

I am encouraged by the sense that the public is organizing and reacting to the unhealthy, chaotic state of the world. On the other hand we are too slow to act to prevent the catastrophes that might be associated with HD. As a global society, and certainly in the U.S., we are not good at *prevention of catastrophes*. We, meaning government, usually act after the fact, that is, in terms of intervention, rehabilitation, and rebuilding. HD does not allow us this luxury.

Your question alludes to one of the most important of our time. Is personal experience with HD a prerequisite to action? Is experience the only way we learn? If so, then my view of the future is indeed pessimistic, for it suggests that we need a calamity such as a thermonuclear-bio-chemical-germ accident, act of terrorism, or war to galvanize us for national or global action. Do our loved ones have to die or do we have to be directly threatened before acting? I would hope not.

Here is an example of what could be done if we are able to help people recognize HD as a threat before it becomes a clear and immediate personal issue. One model of action would be a Manhattan-type project similar to that which produced the atomic bomb during World War II (Rhodes, 1986). At that time, the finest scientific minds were mobilized for the task. Cost was no object. The HD version would not pro-

duce a bomb. Instead the representatives of power in many domains (banking, finance, industry, media, philanthropy, religion, medicine, public health, and so forth) would examine existing policy to improve the quality of global health and well-being. Recommendations from leaders in many fields of endeavor could be effective where other approaches have yet to succeed. Robert McNamara, former U.S. Secretary of Defense, has proposed a similar idea (McNamara, 1995).

A Manhattan-type project would probably be the most efficient means to achieve our goal, but there are other approaches that also should be explored because we cannot wait for a Manhattan project. For example, universities with their diverse expertise should make a significant contribution. Furthermore, the function and utility of the academy might be clarified and seen as more meaningful in the eyes of the public through integrated education, service, and research to protect the well-being of present and future generations.

Another approach is our advocacy work. For example, since 1972 I have directed the Adult Health and Development Program at the University of Maryland (see our web page at http://www.inform.umd.edu/HLHP/AHDP). We train students and volunteers to work on a one-to-one basis with institutionalized or noninstitutionalized older adults to improve the latter's health and well-being. One of the goals is to "contribute to world peace and global cooperation by integrating a variety of individuals into a mutually supportive and purposeful group" (Leviton, 1995; Leviton, Kennedy, Woodruff & Like, 1998). Thanks to a variety of grants we have trained representatives from about 40 universities and colleges (including one in Beijing, China) to have their own Adult Health and Development Program.

5. *Is there anything that one person—such as the person reading this book—can do?*

You bet! Here is a partial list, but every reader can add to it.

- Run for office with quality of health and prevention of HD as a priority.
- Demand the same of political candidates. I mean really demand! We need to take a proactive approach.

Earthquakes are among the most destructive of natural disasters. Unfortunately, the death toll sometimes has been increased by builders interested in raising profits by cutting back on construction quality, as demonstrated by the disasters in Taiwan and Turkey.

- Discover information from sources outside the mainstream media. They are owned and operated by wealthy corporations whose priorities and motives may not be entirely oriented toward public health and well-being. Learn of political power and economics. My personal preferences are scientific journals and magazines such as *The Nation, Z,* and *World Watch.*
- Speak out. Don't be afraid to make politically incorrect statements.
- Ask questions.
- Share your concerns with others.

(End of interview)

Soon after completion of this interview, two similar events occurred, with similar results. Earthquakes in Turkey and Taiwan killed many people and left many others homeless. And out-rage was expressed soon after these catastrophes: faulty construction of homes and other buildings had contributed much to the number of casualties. Builders had used cheap materials and slipshod methods. I hesitated to mention Turkey and Taiwan by name because the same thing has happened in many other places as well, not excluding the United States.

As Leviton also implies, horrendous death may be the outcome of something as commonplace as economic priorities: for example, making more money more easily comes before safe housing. This suggests that possibilities for horrendous death exist in many situations, perhaps whenever protection of life seems to conflict with personal motives, corporate profit, or governmental power. An opening quotation reported international concern about the astonishingly high AIDS-related death rate in Africa. It was charged that the nations involved spent more on the military than they did on a health crisis that was decimating their population. Again, giving priority to weapons rather than health care has not been limited to any one nation or region. It seems so easy to pursue one's routine interests—money and power being high on the list—and so difficult to realize that such a pattern of action places many people at risk for horrendous death.

Perhaps we should give more attention as well to force of habit and inertia. An industry or a nation that has always done things in a certain way is likely to continue doing so even when there are unfortunate consequences. International concern for human rights, environmental protection, and public health and safety has gathered strength only in recent years, long after many societal units established their own ways of doing things. Apart from everything else, it may be regarded as just plain "inconvenient" to consider the life-and-death implications of practices that have always seemed suitable for doing business as usual.

Two central issues await further attention: (1) Does thanatology have any business concerning itself with death on the larger scale as distinguished from individual and family situations? (2) How can people be helped to appreciate the reality of other people—those who are not flesh-and-blood companions in their own lives?

The answer to the first question remains in doubt at present. Some death educators and other thanatologists believe we should focus our attention on helping the dying, the grieving, and the suicidal. Supporting this view is the judgment that few thanatologists are qualified by training to make significant changes in social policy and practice. It is also feared that entry into the arena of horrendous death (including events such as those discussed in *Chapter Eight*) might take away from the more traditional concerns related to dying and death. Others believe that we would be ignoring too important a reality by ignoring large-scale phenomena such as horrendous death. How can we be so concerned about an individual here and a family there and not also be concerned about social forces that result in premature and sometimes barbaric forms of death for many other people? Advocates of a broader thanatology also recognize that few death educators, counselors, and therapists have back-

grounds that favor large-scale social action. On the other hand, nothing will be accomplished unless the effort is made, and the educational dimension of an effective social movement may be well within the competency of death educators. People in both camps would be interested in learning what you think about this choice: focus our attention on dying, grief, and suicide, or look also at larger-scale social phenomena that affect the questions of who dies, when, and how?

The Golden Rule Revisited

The subject would be closed if we decided against including the kinds of phenomena Leviton describes as horrendous death. Let us suppose, though, that we do include the objective of preventing deaths that result from human indifference or malice. Leviton has proposed a course of political action. Another approach also deserves consideration. Few guides to life are more familiar than what has sometimes been called the Golden Rule: *Do unto others as you would have them do unto you.* This simple guide has often proven difficult to follow even for those who accept it in principle. Perhaps you have come across a copy of this notorious sign that has found its way into some offices: *The beatings will continue until morale improves.* Beatings, threats, and demands that we should be "nice" to each other have not proven spectacularly successful. Rational demonstrations that we are all better off if we respect and cooperate with each other have also had only occasional success.

World culture has long been faced with a discordant pair of propositions. One is the *should,* as in "We should treat each other with respect and compassion." The other is the *observational,* as in "Every day I see self-interest, malice, and indifference in human interactions." This tension between ideals and reality courses through the spiritual teachings of world religions, critical decision making on the national and international level, and our own day-by-day interactions. This tension has its many twists and turns. For example, at this writing peacekeeping forces in Kosovo and East Timor have already had to use lethal weapons to prevent violence. In the domestic sphere, this kind of irony was not lost on the mother who saw her young son hit another child. "Don't hit!" she commanded, as she slapped her son. A moment later, she was flushed with embarrassment. "Oh, my God—what have I done!" It can be difficult for the most well-meaning person to pursue the ideal of the Golden Rule when confronted with stress, complexity, and conflict.

Horrendous death can be regarded as the extreme case. Sometimes our failure to "do unto others" results in hurt feelings, strained relationships, missed opportunities, and the like. Sometimes a buildup of anger, distrust, or simply indifference to others becomes the bomb whose fuse is ignited by circumstances. If we can be impressed only by massive numbers, perhaps we should remind ourselves of the eleven million Russian peasants who were systematically killed—by their own countrymen—either through starvation or murder *(see Chapter 8)*. More than six million Jews, many of them loyal German citizens, were victims of the Nazis' "final solution." Both the Russian (Conquest, 1986) and the Nazi (Friedlander, 1995; Goldhagen, 1996) catastrophes had their origins in the most dangerous of all territories: the human mind. "Peasants" and "Jews" were not like us. They were subhuman and therefore meant to be exploited, ignored, or destroyed in accordance with our own plans and aspirations.

It is typical of horrendous death practices that those responsible for the killing feel they did nothing wrong (at least at the time and for some time thereafter). So powerful is this sense of emotional insulation from the killing that people may refuse to believe what happened even in the face of overwhelming evidence (e.g., Lifton, 1986; Lipstadt, 1994).

Lessons to be learned from so much suffering and death demand our utmost attention. What lesson stands out most clearly? *The golden rule is flagrantly disregarded and horrendous death becomes a more imminent prospect when we do not feel a basic bond with other people.* The study of human development and its psychopathology reveals that we cannot take such a bonding process for granted. Infants and children who are deprived of loving parents or parent surrogates often show an inability to form intimate relationships with others. Children growing up in dysfunctional families often have mixed experiences of affection, neglect, and cruelty that interfere with their ability to create and maintain close relationships. Whatever contributes to a loving and supportive home environment, then, in all likelihood also contributes to the development of human feeling and empathy.

Another level of social influence can inhibit the development of emotional bonds with others. The division of the human race into *Us and Them* has been a common mind-set throughout history. This mind-set does not involve a fundamental inability to respect people and form rewarding relationships. People who are regarded as belonging to the in-group may be respected, cherished, and protected. There is little sense of human bonding, though, for those who are regarded as outsiders. The "rules of engagement" may be so different that outsiders are taken to be fair prey (as in slavery or crime) and to have no claim to human rights.

Often a tradition passed along from generation to generation emphasizes how superior, moral, and entitled We are, and how inferior, untrustworthy, and illegitimate They are. People who are compassionate, helpful, and loyal to each other may consider it their right—or duty—to keep Them in their place or even, when sufficiently provoked, to wipe Them off the face of the earth. Read or listen to the experiences of people who were either the perpetrators or the victims of mass violence. You are likely to encounter again and again the dehumanization of the victim. "They are not at all like us—they are stupid beasts, unworthy creatures, vermin to be destroyed." Furthermore, belief in a radical difference between Us and Them has often been inculcated as a way of avoiding the moral misgivings and horror that one would otherwise feel in inflicting suffering and death.

It is much easier to treat others as less than human if we do not actually know them. We are no longer as free to act upon images, assumptions, and stereotypes when we see for ourselves that they are, like us, real and unique persons. "Do unto others…" too often has an escape clause. We may feel that we should do right by others if they are not really Other. And Other may include a large proportion of the human race: people who speak a different language, come in a different color or gender, or simply live in the wrong side of town or even just across the symbolic turf border within the same neighborhood. Can group esteem exist without putting down other groups? Can we develop the willingness and ability to feel ourselves a part of the total human community? Positive answers to these questions would go a long way toward avoiding distrust and contempt that have prepared the way for inflicting horrendous death, by either direct action or callous indifference.

Positive signs already exist. Some people have learned from racial discrimination, the Holocaust, and other twentieth-century disasters. Furthermore, the far reaches of the world are now within personal range for people who interact through e-mail and the Internet. Many industries and corporations involve multicultural partnerships; many campuses are enriched by students and faculty of the most varied backgrounds. Travel has also developed friendships that cross over national, racial, and ethnic lines. Disasters in Bosnia, Kosovo, Turkey, Taiwan, and East Timor, for example, all had personal meanings to some of my students who, in turn, helped the rest of us to put a human face on the tragedies. Whatever enhances communication and personalization should help to develop human bonds that provide some protection against horrendous death.

One powerful trend, however, has the potential for weakening our sense of deep connection with others. It can also blur our awareness of the difference between real and virtual life—and, therefore, between real death and its electronic counterfeit. We must pay another brief visit to the compelling satellite world of so-called "virtual reality."

Are We Live or on Tape? The Life-and-Death Challenges of Virtual Reality

Face-to-face encounters almost completely dominated human interactions until technological innovations offered supplements, enhancements, and replacements. Photography not only altered our sense of identity, but also transformed our relationship to the past, especially to loved ones who now could still be with us, just as they were earlier. The tiny framed oval photograph of grandmother and the portrait showing the entire family as it once was became among the most cherished of possessions. Photographs provided a powerful new way for the dead to speak to the living. This point is well made in the movie *Dead Poets Society*. A teacher (Robin Williams) directs his students to study a photograph of an earlier generation of students. The intense aliveness of this vanished generation becomes a unique lesson to the present generation of students. The dead were once young and full of life, just like the students of today. The lesson here: seize the day! In this and in many other ways, photographs have added an enduring visual context within which today's lives and deaths gain resonance.

The telephone had its own distinctive transformational effect. The human voice, with all its subtle tones and inflections, now could transcend distance. The pangs of separation and absence—so closely associated with bereavement—could be relieved by the sound of a familiar, reassuring voice. And so the process has continued, with every significant new form of communication having its effects on our symbolic relationship with both life and death. Sound recording not only revolutionized the place of music in society, but also rescued conversations and speeches from being carried away in the ever flowing river of time. "Are we live or on tape?" became a question with philosophical as well as practical implications. Does it really matter whether the voice we hear is that of a person who is speaking to us in "real time" (another new concept)? The voice and message are the same when taped—even if the speaker is deceased. The ear processes the sound in the same way (given an accurate recording) whether the message comes live or on tape, from the living or from the dead.

Another important dimension has been the remarkable new ability to shift time. Those who were born into the age of electronics might take time-shifting for granted as they program the VCR to record a show for later viewing. Nevertheless, time-shifting is among the features that most distinguish the present day from the human past. The role of time in human life was nailed by Persian poet Omar Khayyam in the eleventh century:

The Moving Finger writes; and, having writ,
Moves on: nor all your Piety nor Wit
Shall lure it back to cancel half a Line,
Nor all your Tears wash out a Word of it
(Khayyam, 1990, p. 42)

Time rules. Operating through time, life does not give us a second chance. Errors cannot be corrected; failures cannot be repaired. No matter how clever or religious we might be, time takes its own course and, with that course, all that we hold dear, including life itself. How should we come to terms with death, given this view of time? Some people attempted to prove Khayyam wrong by delving into alchemy or magic to prolong youth and life. The quest for perpetual youth was a desperate and occasionally inspired effort to bend time to human desire (Kastenbaum, 1995). Others decided to burn their candles brightly and live as intensely as they could within a shortened frame of time. Still others sought to distract themselves from the disappearing sands of time by drink or other means. Time was not fragmented into stopwatch or nanosecond measures, but was regarded as the long, slow, unopposable wave that swept away kingdoms as inexorably as it did an individual's youth and life.

Time's rule has now been challenged. We can convert immediate experience to the time-insensitive format of digital encoding. Essentially, time becomes number (or the electronic equivalent of number). Life remains perishable in the stream of time, but episodes within life can be stored "for later viewing at our convenience."

What are the implications of these changes on our views of life and death? Perhaps you can recall from earlier chapters how difficult it is for children to develop and for adults to face the basic facts of death. The popularity of the idea that death is a kind of sleep reveals our reluctance to recognize it on its own terms. We are often grateful for any opportunity to escape the recognition of mortality even (or especially) when in jeopardy. Technology's very good tricks of recording and time-shifting can play right into our preference for keeping death out of awareness. Every time we take advantage of a time-eluding technology, we might be making it that much easier to blur the difference between "virtual" and "real reality."

Consider a person who has had limited primary social interaction during infancy and childhood. Place a computer in front of that person, providing access to a vast universe of images and symbols. Give that person the opportunity to manipulate the images and symbols. Allow that person the power of trashing and deleting whatever

does not please. Add the attraction of game playing. And to this game playing, add a personal impulse that has been stimulated by mass media society since childhood: the pleasures to be found not only in victory but also in destruction.

Some of the most popular computer-mediated games are variations on the shooting galleries long popular in carnivals and fairs. With the embellishments of vivid graphics, one can zap the alien invaders or blast away at other life form images. The most technologically updated aliens are the latest stand-ins for Others: people who are not like us and therefore suitable as targets for our rage, pride, and entertainment. Competing to see who can run up the highest score of targets destroyed in a computer game is an activity that comes painfully close to representing our society's aggressive edge. That the group of people most attracted to such computer games also produces the most real-life killers is a connection as difficult to overlook as it is to interpret with any degree of confidence.

Do one more "favor" for this computer-linked person. Give him or her the opportunity to interact through innumerable "chat rooms," (which are not rooms at all but electronic artifacts). The people with whom this person interacts may or may not be the people they represent themselves to be. More significantly, it is possible to carry on this attenuated form of interaction to the neglect of real-life relationships, which are notoriously complex, shifting, and sometimes "messy." Furthermore, the real people in our lives are not always available when we need them, but computer-mediated interactions are always available, just a mouse-click away. Real-life relationships also have a way of making demands on us when we would rather not be bothered. One might often prefer the company of cybernetic-generated or -mediated spirits to that of flesh-and-blood mortals.

The crucial point, of course, is that the images and icons displayed on our monitors are not flesh-and-blood mortals. No heart stops beating when with the touch of a finger, we trash or discard. Is it possible that our computer-bred, computer-linked person will fail to appreciate the crucial difference between the real death of real people and the pseudolethality that flourishes in virtual reality? At present we have no solid information on the effect of the computer lifestyle on our orientation toward life and death. Perhaps there is little basis for concern. But perhaps the many hours spent linked to computers rather than engaged in direct interactions will make it even easier for us to evade the realization that death is a central fact of real life.

And perhaps it will become even easier to make decisions that endanger the lives of people we have never met, through a few keystrokes. There is less reluctance to harm people who are not known individually and whose suffering and death will not be seen. The sixty million (not a misprint) peasants who starved to death during China's catastrophic farm reform movement were not family, friends, or neighbors of the country's leaders. The planners and leaders did not have to see the effects of decisions they made at a distance. When bombs were first dropped on a civilian population (Guernica, Spain), there was a reaction of widespread shock and outrage. Aerial assault on civilian populations persisted and intensified, however, in part because those who unleashed their bombs with the push of a button or the slide of a lever could not see the faces and mangled bodies below. The action involved in pushing a button (or clicking a mouse) can produce the effect of playing a game, sending a communication, or destroying lives.

The law-abiding, peacefully occupied person who is engrossed in computer-mediated interactions might also have rich and deep connections with other real-life people. Perhaps most people are also able to switch back to human reality when they turn off the computer. The various forms taken by virtual reality might prove to be enhancements to the understanding and appreciation of life and not much of a threat. On the other hand, the concerns expressed here might prove to be all too well founded. We just don't know yet whether coming generations will have a firm grasp of both virtual reality and the kind of reality experienced by mortal beings.

"THE GOOD DEATH": FANTASY OR REALITY?

What can we say now about the relationship between a life and its death? Does having lived a "good life" contribute to ending with a "good death?" And what about the reverse? Can the way a person dies alter the meaning and quality of that person's entire life? "Good death" has been kept in quotation marks throughout this chapter to keep us alert to the fact that there are many opinions to choose from, including views that dismiss the whole idea of a good death. Here we will dispense with the quotation marks and get right to the central issues. We will also continue to speak of the good death, the term that has come into general usage, even though what we are really concerned with here is the way in which a life comes to its end. Some of the most important observations and ideas can be summarized in the following propositions, which you are invited to evaluate based on your own experience and judgment. In doing so, you will notice that some of the propositions seem to be at odds with one another, and that the propositions are difficult to compare because they draw upon different realms of observation, evidence, and belief. And so—to the challenge!

Proposition 1: We can agree that some forms of death are terrible even if we cannot always agree on what constitutes a good death. People should be spared such terrible deaths. Terrible deaths are dominated by suffering. There is physical pain to the point of agony. There may also be extreme mental pain, such as when a mother sees her child being killed while she herself is dying. Torture and humiliation, which were often part of horrendous death in the twentieth century, aimed to destroy people spiritually as well as physically.

Perhaps the basic definition of a terrible death is this: it is the death that most people most desperately want to avoid, for themselves and for their loved ones. Because suffering is universal, it is not unreasonable to assume that people everywhere fear a death marked by extreme physical, mental, and spiritual suffering. Although a proposition could hardly be more obvious, there is a complication to consider. Some people have believed that suffering is a valuable experience: we *should* suffer because this either helps to pay for our sins or promotes our spiritual growth. This belief can be held to a lesser or greater degree. In the past, the extreme position has been used to argue against providing pain relief to women in labor; in our time, pain relief may be withheld from terminally ill people for similar reasons. However, terminally ill people today rarely see any inherent value in suffering. It is an unfortunate situation when a care provider and a dying patient have very different ideas about the value of suffering.

Proposition 2: A good death should enact the highest values held by society. Both individuals and society benefit from such a death. An individual is seen as accomplishing something of exceptional merit. Society is strengthened by having one of its members demonstrate allegiance to its values with his or her last breath. Furthermore, each person's death is important as a possible test of both individual character and society's strength. This emphasis on how a person faces death contrasts sharply with the "failed machine" model that has often been implicit in medical management. The community and its health care professionals cannot turn away from a dying person if there is something important that all believe should be accomplished as life gives way to death.

But *what* precisely is to be accomplished at the end of life? The answer to this question varies. One of the most dramatic models is heroic death. The person is to die bravely. Kamikaze pilots and Sioux warriors were among the many men who accepted combat missions in which their deaths were almost assured. In Norse mythology, the Vikings who died as battlefield heroes were rewarded with an afterlife in Valhalla. Both women and men are included among the martyrs—people who chose death rather than renounce their religious faith. The type of suicide that Durkheim described as altruistic *(see Chapter 7)* may also belong here. Heroic death usually involves an element of choice: loyalty to one's people or God takes precedence over staying alive.

Heroic deaths seem always to have been exceptional and, therefore, especially admired and remembered. Not everybody has the opportunity or the ability to end his or her life in a way that dramatically affirms core social values. Many more people, however, have been able to demonstrate their social conscience by facing death with resolute allegiance to the values they cherish. For example, some cultural traditions hold that one should bear suffering in silence. I have known people who did not speak of their pain nor seek comfort and relief during their final illness. They were determined to live up to what was expected of them by tradition.

Others have acted in accordance with cultural expectations such as going off to a particular place or even assuming a particular physical position when death is near. Some traditions also expect dying people to offer memorable last words. A striking example is that of the *jisei* (farewell verse) written by Japanese Zen Buddhist monks and Haiku poets. Although the tradition has varied over the centuries, it was often considered best to be sitting upright at the moment of death, using one's last words to offer a poem to those gathered around. In contrast to religious traditions in which last words are supposed to be pious, the *jisei* often is playful and surprising.

If we embrace Proposition 2, then, we should expect to discover a great many variations—as many ideas about the good death as there are societal values. One of the most striking variations is oppositional death. People who have become bitter or disillusioned may use their last words and energies in attacking society's values. For example, a hospice chaplain spoke to me soon after having left the bedside of a dying woman who had rejected him and cursed God. He was shaken by this encounter, but already starting to make sense of it.

> She couldn't have said anything that would have upset me more, and she knew it. Life had been a kind of poison to her for a long time, since her son, then her husband died. I think this was her getting the poison out and her using the strongest word she knew—that would be God. [A strange kind of prayer?] That's exactly what it was. A strange kind of prayer. I will go back to her—and she will take my hand.

It is likely that societal expectations influence the way we deal with the end of our lives even if we are not attempting to achieve a particular kind of death. Most experienced caregivers have learned to suspend their own expectations and attend instead to the cultural values most cherished by terminally ill people and their families.

Proposition 3: The good death is one in which our most significant personal relationships are affirmed. These relationships may also embody societal and religious values, but it is their personal meanings that are especially cherished. Our studies of deathbed scenes, actual (Kastenbaum, 1994; Kastenbaum, 2000) and imagined (Kastenbaum

& Normand, 1990), find that relationships are usually the uppermost concern. People most often desire the companionship of those who have shared their lives through the years. This does not mean that dying people want to have all of the people in their lives with them constantly. Sometimes it is enough to be with a person a time or two in order to achieve a sense of closure in the relationship. In some circumstances, the dying person may feel more comfortable with only indirect interactions with certain people because of certain tensions or concerns. Even when interpersonal contact is minimal or indirect, however, the quality of the interaction may help to affirm the value of the relationship. That one smile or handclasp might be enough to let others know that they have been appreciated.

Effective palliative care has done much to provide opportunities for continuing and affirming relationships near life's end. The relief of pain without the dulling of consciousness has helped people to have many quality interactions that otherwise would not have occurred. Being able to spend more time at home has also enhanced the opportunity for natural interactions.

The good death as one in which our most meaningful personal relationships are affirmed has many implications for the way in which we shape our lives. People whose interpersonal relationships have been prevailingly antagonistic, conflictual, or distant are less likely to have loving companions at their side near the end of life. Furthermore, nurses and other service providers may also find it difficult to establish caring relationships with people who have cultivated an abusive attitude toward others throughout their lives. Personal characteristics that earn the respect and affection of others throughout the years often contribute to a warm and supportive interpersonal network at the end of life.

Proposition 4: The good death is one in which there is a transfiguring personal experience. As death approaches, one feels a profound sense of beauty, love, or understanding. The moment of death is also the peak experience of life. This construction of the good death has been with us in many forms throughout the centuries. The Moody-type near-death experience *(see Chapter 13)* has brought renewed attention to this mystical state of being. The final pages of Tolstoy's *The Death of Ivan Ilych (see Chapter 1)* provide a dramatic literary example, but we also find some real-life people who seem to have powerful and distinctive experiences near the end of their lives (Kastenbaum, 1994). Perhaps a subtle remote influence on the current interest in a transfiguring moment of death is the medieval fascination with deathbed conversions and miracles (Aries, 1981).

Several frames of mind can be associated with the good death as a transfiguring experience:

- *A sense of adventure:* "Life has been a series of adventures—why not death as well?"
- *A sense of mystical awareness:* "I just know there is more to life than the everyday, so the moment of death may open these mysteries to me."
- *A sense of escaping from a disappointing life:* "This transfiguring moment will make up for the hurts and sorrows I have experienced in life."
- *A need to avoid the stressful realities of dying and separation:* "I will get myself to think only of the beauty and wonder of dying, not the physical side of it, and not the interpersonal issues."

Some people, at the end of their lives, seem to have a distinctive and powerful experience that we cannot share. Others apparently slip away as though into a deeper sleep, and we may choose to interpret this also as the outer manifestation of a transfiguring state of being. Do *most* people die with an exalted experience? That is quite a different question, and the answer is likely to depend on whether we rely primarily upon faith and hope or on what can be learned through direct observation.

Proposition 4 remains a powerful model of the good death, but one that at times serves to distract us from the "ordinary" challenges faced by dying people and their families. There has been a tendency to scrub dying and death clean before these anxiety-arousing topics can be acknowledged. "Healthy dying" (Kastenbaum, 1979) is a theme that attempts to sugarcoat the actual stress and loss experienced by most terminally ill people. The model of the good death as transfigured life is sometimes put into the service of a strenuous effort to avoid dealing with disturbing realities. The idea of the good death as a peak experience might be compelling enough that it does not need an assist from denial.

Proposition 5: The good death is one in which people continue to be themselves as long as possible, preferably to the very end. This view is close to Weisman's (1972) concept of an appropriate death: the death a person would choose for him- or herself. It is not identical, though, because some people would prefer to take a different turning at the end of their lives (e.g., a heroic or transfiguring death).

Most of the terminally ill people in the National Hospice Demonstration Study *(see Chapter 5)* who were asked about the last three days of their lives expressed a preference for a familiar routine: a day like any other, at home, with the people who meant the most to them. In a more recent study, elderly Israelis also emphasized the value they placed on continuity (Leichtentritt & Rettig, in press). This value encompassed the funeral and memorial process as well. One respondent expressed his thoughts in this way:

My funeral should correspond with whom I am…[with] the way I lived my life. My family knows I do not want them to sit Shiva over me…. I do not wish people to mourn after me in this way—it is not who I am.

Another respondent had a different emphasis:

I am willing to suffer a lot. I am willing to tolerate pain, but I am NOT willing to tolerate a disrespectful process…. I have seen funerals in my life that were disrespectful—that is exactly what I do not wish for…. When I said that I wish for a respectful process…it does not end the moment I close my eyes.

Many people seem comfortable with the idea of ending their lives much as they have lived. This model of the good death is usually consistent with the model that emphasizes affirming one's closest interpersonal relationships. Again, the hospice movement has proved valuable in helping many people to continue being themselves through the final phase of life.

FROM GOOD LIFE TO GOOD DEATH: A PERSONAL STATEMENT

Obviously we cannot simply choose or create a model of the good death and take it home until needed. Circumstances not completely under our control are likely to affect the conditions of our death. Furthermore, we might hesitate to shape our lives around the end of our days; a case can be made for enjoying each day as it comes and not burying ourselves prematurely. Perhaps there is a way to integrate a realization of death with our ongoing lives, doing justice to both. And perhaps no two of us would do this in quite the same way.

Here, then, is one person's way of doing it—or, rather, trying to do it, because intention does not always rule events or even one's own feelings. Here is what I try to do, based in unequal parts on what I have learned, what I don't know, and what I feel. This statement is offered only as an example that might be useful to you as you review your own approach.

- I hope to achieve an ongoing balance between awareness of risk and danger and a free and open attitude toward life. I do not want to put myself or others in jeopardy by engaging overmuch in denial or related defensive strategies *(see Chapter 1)*. This awareness of possible threat to life encompasses physical, environmental, and man-made sources of danger. Yet I do not intend to crawl into a hole and pull the hole down with me. Like most other people who have been active in death-related studies, I enjoy life a lot and intend to keep doing so.
- I realize that I have a very limited ability to influence the large forces and events that in turn influence how long people live and how they die. Nevertheless, I also notice how surprisingly many opportunities there are to do something in a positive direction. Sometimes this is as simple as listening a little more intently or offering an alternative way to deal with a situation, perhaps just by demonstrating that alternative in my own behavior.
- I doubt that my death or anything associated with my death will be able to make up for the mistakes and shortcomings of my life. This means that I do not rely on a ninth inning rally, although that would be exciting. Instead, I feel that I have to try for a good "at bat" in every opportunity that comes along. That may or may not influence the final score, but nevertheless it seems to be the best way to play the game within the decided limits of my ability.

- The Buddhist and Hindu perceptions of what we call life and what we call death as a coexisting flow makes a lot of sense to me. No—not to the point that I dismiss the idea of death as the end of life as I have come to know it. But I do recognize at least some of the little births and little deaths that accompany us throughout life and from which we might be wise enough to learn.

- I know something of grief and loss, so I have some sensitivity to these feelings as they mark the faces, words, and lives of others as well. I try to be aware—at the right time, when it most counts—that the person with whom I am interacting may still be struggling with the pain of loss while trying to move on with life.

- I appreciate life the more. As a youth, I went along pretty much assuming that life was both within and all about me and therefore could be taken for granted. Studies of dying and death, as well as personal experiences, have taught me to treasure life in all of its forms. Yes, that does include the gigantic wolf spider that dropped down beside me one evening and decided I was OK while at the same time I was deciding he (she?) was OK. Life in the trouble-making twinkle in an aged person's eyes. Life in the open-eyed wonder of a young child. Life in the here-right-now intensity of an athlete. Life in the who-cares-where-we-are engrossment of lovers. I can understand, I think, why encounters with death have soured some people on life. But it happens that death has given me—and I think many other thanatologists—an ever fresh appreciation for life.

SUMMARY

This chapter has given us an opportunity to reflect on some (certainly not all) of the issues we have been encountering throughout the book. We were particulary interested in the meaning of the good death and how this might relate to the ways in which we live.

A physician's response to the terminal illness of his father reminded us of how much both medical management and family support influence the outcome. Ira Byock, M.D., touched by his father's death and appalled by the mismanagement of dying people in the health care system, became an effective force for the improvement of terminal care. Eliminating futile medical procedures and providing opportunity for family and patient to have time together in natural surroundings can be seen as basic preparation for a good death.

We then noticed that the traditional meanings given to death now face a new competitor or, more accurately, a newly strengthened competitor. More people today are enjoying long, healthy, and materially enhanced lives. Death is therefore less tempting as a release from the stresses and sorrows of life (once a major factor in the lullabies sung to babies). We also noted that "not wanting to leave the party" is a trend that stands the regret theory of death anxiety on its head. According to regret theory, people who feel that they have led satisfying lives are less anxious about death. However, more people may now regret (rather than fear) death just because life seems so pleasant that it should go on and on.

Horrendous death was discussed as the extreme opposite of the good death. An interview with Dan Leviton, an expert on horrendous death, brought to light further information on the many ways in which people have either inflicted suffering, humiliation, and death on others, or have achieved the same result through indifference and neglect. Leviton offered suggestions for preventing horrendous death, and we also revisited the Golden Rule as a guide to protecting lives. The harm done by perpetuating the Us-versus-Them distinction was given special consideration.

An influential new sociotechnological development also commanded our attention. Computer-generated and -mediated imagery provides what amounts to an alternative universe of experience and interaction. We wondered about the possible impact of virtual reality on our conceptions of life and death and, therefore, on the meaning of a "good death." Photography, sound recording, and time-shifting technology have also contributed to a sense of mastery over the transience of the moment and the inexorable flow of time. Will people who are born with two umbilical cords—one connected to their mother, the other to a computer—have full appreciation for real life and real death? Questions such as these were raised here in the hope of stimulating closer observation and thought.

Sociologists (Hart, Sainsbury, & Short) consider the good death to be a social construction—why doesn't that surprise us! The sociological view also holds that ideas of the good death of make us conform to social values. We respect this view but see the situation as being more complicated. Five propositions about the good death are identified: (1) We can agree that some deaths are terrible even if we cannot always agree on what constitutes a good death. The terrible death is dominated by suffering. (2) The good death should enact the highest values held by society. Here the heroic and the oppositional death were given particular attention. (3) The good death is one in which our most significant personal relationships are affirmed. (4) The good death is one in which there is a transfiguring personal experience. (5) The good death is one in which people continue to be themselves as long as possible, preferably to the very end.

In conclusion, I offered a personal statement about the good life and the good death.

REFERENCES

Achte, K. (1989). Lullabies of death. In R. Kastenbaum & B. K. Kastenbaum (Eds.), *Encyclopedia of death* (pp. 176–178). Phoenix: Arno.

Aries, P. (1981). *At the hour of our death.* New York: Knopf.

Byock, I. (1997). *Dying well.* New York: Riverhead Books.

Conquest, R. (1986). *The harvest of sorrow.* New York: Oxford University Press.

Erikson, E. H. (1950). *Childhood and society.* New York: W. W. Norton.

Feifel, H. (Ed.) (1959). *The meaning of death.* New York: McGraw-Hill.

Friedlander, H. (1995). *The origins of Nazi genocide: From euthanasia to the final solution.* Chapel Hill, NC: London. The University of North Carolina Press.

Fullilove, M. T., Heon, V., Jiminez, W., Parsons, C., Green, L. L., & Fullilove, R. E. (1998). Injury and anomie: Effects of violence on an inner-city community. *American Journal of Public Health, 88,* 924–927.

Gilligan, J. (1996). *Violence: Our deadly epidemic and its causes.* New York: Putnam.

Goldhagen, D. J. (1996). *Hitler's willing executioners.* New York: Alfred A. Knopf.

Gyatso, Tenzin, the 14th Dali Lama (1985). *Kindness, clarity, and insight.* Trans. J. Hopkins. Ithaca: Snow Lions Publications.

Hart, B., Sainsbury, P., & Short, S. (1998). Whose dying? A sociological critique of the "good death." *Mortality, 3,* 65–78.

Hoffman, Y. (1986). *Japanese death poems.* Rutland, VT & Tokyo: Charles E. Tuttle.

Kastenbaum, R. (1979). "Healthy dying": A paradoxical quest continues. *Journal of Social Issues, 35,* 185–206.

Kastenbaum, R. (1994). Is there an ideal deathbed scene? In I. B. Corless, B. B. Germino, & M. Pittman (Eds.). *Dying, death, and bereavement* (pp. 109–122). Boston: Jones & Bartlett.

Kastenbaum, R. (1995). *Dorian, graying: Is youth the only thing worth having?* New York: Baywood.

Kastenbaum, R. (2000). *The psychology of death.* (3rd ed.). New York: Springer.

Kastenbaum, R., & Normand, C. (1990). Deathbed scenes as imagined by the young and experienced by the old. *Death Studies, 14,* 201–218.

Khayyam, O. (1990). *The Rubaiyat of Omar Khayyam.* Trans. E. FitzGerald.

Leichtentritt, R. D., & Rettig, K. D. (in press). The good death: Reaching an inductive understanding. *Omega, Journal of Death and Dying.*

Leviton, D. (Ed.), (1991a). *Horrendous death and health: Toward action.* New York: Hemisphere.

Leviton, D. (Ed.), (1991b). *Horrendous death, health, and well-being.* New York: Hemisphere.

Leviton, D. (1995). Horrendous death: Linking thanatology and public health. In J. Kauffman (Ed.), *Awareness of mortality* (pp. 185–213). Amityville, NY: Baywood Publishing Company.

Leviton, D., Kennedy, J., Woodruff, R., & Like, K. (1998). *ADHP manual for staffers.* (3rd ed.). College Park, MD: University of Maryland.

Lifton, R. J. (1986). *The Nazi doctors: Medical killing and the psychology of genocide.* New York: Basic Books.

Lipstadt, D. (1994). *Denying the Holocaust.* New York: Plume.

McCall, N. (1994*). Makes me want to holler: A young black man in America.* New York: Random House.

McNamara, R. S. (1995). *In retrospect: The tragedy and lessons of Vietnam.* New York: Times Books.

Rhodes, R. (1986). *The making of the atomic bomb.* New York: Simon & Schuster.

Rummel, R. J. (1990). *Lethal politics: Soviet genocide and mass murder since 1917.* New Brunswick: Transaction Publishers.

Rummel, R. J. (1991a). *China's bloody century: Genocide and mass murder since 1900.* New Brunswick: Transaction Publishers.

Rummel, R. J. (1991b). *Democide: Nazi genocide and mass murder.* New Brunswick: Transaction Publishers.

Shaw, A. (1999, Sept 16). Experts fear AIDS turning Africa into "killing field." *Associated Press* dispatch.

Taylor, J. (1665/1970). *The rules and exercises of holy dying.* New York: Arno.

Tomer, A., & Eliason, G. (1996). Toward a comprehensive model of death anxiety. *Death Studies, 20,* 343–366.

Weisman, A. D. (1972). *On dying and denying: A psychiatric study of terminality.* New York: Behavioral Publications.

GLOSSARY

Appropriate Death: The way a person would choose to have his or her life come to an end.

Genocide: Killing people because of their nationality, religion, race, or any other group characteristic.

Horrendous Death: A premature and unexpected death caused by other people. Often violent and painful.

Quixotian: A brave but misguided and futile attempt to do something great (see *Don Quixote*).

APPENDIX: SELECTED LEARNING RESOURCES

Guide

A. National Organizations
B. Scholarly and Professional Journals
C. Selected Videos
D. Internet Resources

Resources with focus on children are italicized

A. National Organizations

Academy of Hospice Physicians
P.O. Box 14288
Gainesville, FL 32604-2288
(352) 377-8900

AIDS ORGANIZATIONS

AIDS National Interfaith Network
1400 Eye St. NW, Rm 1220
Washington, DC 20005
(212) 239-0700

AIDS Resource Foundation for Children
182 Roseville Avenue
Newark, NJ 07107
(201) 483-4250

American Institute of Teen AIDS Prevention
(817) 237-0230

Centers for Disease Control AIDS Clearinghouse
P.O. Box 6003
Rockville, MD 20849-6003
(800) 458-5231

Family AIDS Network
1601 North Kent St., Suite 1003
Arlington, VA 22209
(703) 243-8726

National Association of People with AIDS
1413 K St. NW
Washington, DC 21005
(202) 898-0414

National Minority AIDS Council
1913 13 St. NW
Washington, DC 20009
(202) 483-6222

National Native American AIDS Prevention Center
134 Linden St.
Oakland, CA 94607
(510) 444-2051

National Women's Health Network
514 10th St. NW #40
Washington, DC 22004
(202) 347-1140

Alcor Life Extension Foundation (cryonics)
7895 E. Acoma Drive, #110
Scottsdale, AZ 85260-6916
(480) 922-9013

AMEND (Aiding Mothers and Fathers Experiencing Newborn Death)
4324 Berrywick Terrace
St. Louis, MO 63128
(314) 487-7582

American Association of Suicidology
4201 Connecticut Avenue NW, Suite 310
Washington, DC 20008
(202) 237-2280

American Cancer Society
1599 Clifton Road NE
Atlanta, GA 30329
(404) 320-3333

American Cemetery Association
1895 Preston White Drive, Suite 220
Reston, VA 20191
(800) 645-7700

American Cryonics Society
P.O. Box 1509
Cupertino, CA 95015
(800) 523-2001

American Heart Association
7272 Greenville Ave.
Dallas, TX 75231
(214) 373-6300

American Hospice Foundation
1130 Connecticut Ave., NW, Suite 700
Washington, DC 20036-4101
(202) 223-0208

American Sudden Infant Death Syndrome Institute
6065 Roswell Road
Atlanta, GA 30328
(800) 847-7437

Association for Death Education and Counseling
638 Prospect Ave.
Hartford, CT 06105-4250
(860) 586-7503

Cancer Information Service
National Cancer Institute
Building 31, Room 1OA24
9000 Rockville Pike
Bethesda, MD 20892
(800) 4-CANCER

Candlelighters Childhood Cancer Foundation
7910 Woodmont Ave., Suite 460
Bethesda, MD 20814
(800) 366-2223

Center for Crime Victims and Survivors, Inc.
P.O. Box 6201
Clearwater, FL 34618
(813) 535-1114

Center for Loss and Life Transition
3735 Broken Bow Road
Fort Collins, CO 80526
(800) 922-6051

Center to Improve Care of the Dying
1001 22nd St., Suite 802
Washington, DC 20037
(202) 467-2222

Children's Hospice International
1101 King St., Suite 131
Alexandria, VA 22314
(800) 242-CHILD

Choice in Dying
200 Varick St.
New York, NY 10014
(800) 989-9455

Compassionate Friends, Inc.
P.O. Box 3696
Oak Brook, IL 60522
(212) 366-5500
(708) 990-0010

Concerns of Police Survivors (COPS)
P.O. Box 3199
South Highway 5
Camdenton, MO 65020
(800) 784-COPS

Cremation Association of North America
401 North Michigan Ave.
Chicago, IL 60611
(312) 644-6610

Crisis Prevention Institute, Inc.
3315-K North 124th St.
Brookfield, WI 53005
(800) 558-8976

Dougy Center (for bereaved children)
P.O. Box 86582
Portland, OR 97286
(503) 775-5683

Hemlock Society
P.O. Box 101810
Denver, CO 80250
(800) 247-7421

Hospice Association of America
519 C St. NE
Washington, DC 20002
(202) 546-4759

Hospice Foundation of America
2001 S St. NW, Suite 300
Washington, DC 20009
(202) 638-5419

Hospice Nurses Association
5512 North Umberland St.
Pittsburgh, PA 15217
(412) 687-3231

International Association of Pet Cemeteries
5055 Route 11
Ellenburg Depot, NY 12935
(518) 594-3000

Last Acts
The Robert Wood Johnson Foundation
P.O. Box 2316
Princeton, NJ 08542
(609) 452-8701

Leukemia Society of America
600 East 3rd Ave.
New York, NY 10016
(212) 573-8484

Living Bank (organ donation)
P.O. Box 6725
Houston, TX 77265
(800) 528-2971

Make-A-Wish Foundation of America
100 West Clarendon, Suite 2200
Phoenix, AZ 85013
(800) 722-9474

Mothers Against Drunk Driving (MADD)
511 East John Carpenter Freeway, Suite 700
Irving, TX 75062
(800) 438-MADD

National Association of Military Widows
4023 25th Road, North
Arlington, VA 22207
(703) 527-4565

National Center for Death Education
Mount Ida College
777 Dedham St.
Newton, MA 02159
(617) 928-4649

National Coalition to Stop Handgun Violence
100 Maryland Ave., NE
Washington, DC 20002
(202) 544-7190

National Funeral Directors Association
11121 West Oklahoma Ave.
Milwaukee, WI 53202
(414) 541-2500

National Hospice Organization
1901 North Moore St., Suite 901
Arlington, VA 22209
(703) 243-5900

National Institute for Jewish Hospice
8723 Alden Drive, Suite 652
Los Angeles, CA 90048
(213) 467-7423

National Organization for Victims Assistance
1757 Park Road NW
Washington, DC 20010
(202) 232-6682

National SIDS Resource Center
8201 Greensboro Drive, Suite 600
McLean, VA 22102
(703) 821-8955

Oncology Nursing Society
501 Holiday Drive
Pittsburgh,PA 15220-2749
(412) 921-7373

Parents of Murdered Children, Inc.
Unit B-41
100 East Eighth St.
Cincinnati, OH 45202
(513) 721-5683

Project on Death in America
Soros Open Society Institute
888 Seventh Ave.
New York, NY 10106
(212) 887-0150

SHARE Pregnancy and Infant Loss Support, Inc.
National SHARE Office
Saint Joseph Health Center
300 First Capitol Drive
St. Charles, MO 63301
(800) 821-6819

Starlight Foundation International
12424 Wilshire Boulevard, Suite 150
Los Angeles, CA 90025
(310) 207-5558

Sunshine Foundation
2001 Bridge St.
Philadelphia, PA 19124
(800) 767-1976

United Network for Organ Sharing
1100 Boulders Parkway
Richmond, VA 23225
(800) 243-6667

B. Scholarly and Professional Journals

American Journal of Hospice Care
Prime National Publishing
470 Boston Post Road
Weston, MA 02193

Crisis, International Journal of Suicide and Crisis Studies
Hogrefe & Huber, Publishers
14 Bruce Park Ave.
Toronto, Ontario M4P 2S3
Canada

Death Studies
Taylor & Francis, Ltd.
1101 Vermont Ave. NW, Suite 200
Washington, DC 20005

Hospice Journal
Haworth Press
10 Alice St.
Binghamton, NY 13904

Illness, Crisis and Loss
The Charles Press
P.O. Box 15715
Philadelphia, PA 19103

Journal of Palliative Care
Centre for Bioethics
110 Pine St.
Montreal, Quebec H2W 1R7
Canada

Journal of Personal and Interpersonal Loss
Taylor & Francis, Ltd.
1101 Vermont Ave NW Suite 200
Washington, DC 20005

Mortality
Carfax Publishing, Taylor & Francis Ltd.
Customer Service Department
47 Runway Road, Suite G
Levittown, PA 19057-4700

Omega, Journal of Death and Dying
Baywood Publishing Company
26 Austin Ave.
Amityville, NY 11701

Suicide and Life-Threatening Behavior
Guilford Press
72 Spring St.
New York, NY 10012
Columbia, SC 29208

C. Selected Videos

A Personal Understanding of Death. An Introduction to Death and Dying.
This series of ten half-hour video documentaries presents case histories, the personal stories of people directly involved in dying, death, and grief, as well as illuminating commentary. Program titles:

1. What is Death?
2. The Dying Person
3. Facing Mortality
4. The Deathbed
5. Fear of Death and Dying.
6. Sudden Death
7. A Child's View of Death
8. Grief and Bereavement
9. Death Rituals
10. The Good Death

Death, Society, and Human Experience is the textbook resource for this series. Robert Kastenbaum served as consultant. Faculty and student manuals are also available: Annenberg/CPB Multimedia Collection. P.O. Box 2345, South Burlington, VT 05407-2345

AIDS & Your World
Teenagers and young adults discuss their reactions and what they learned when AIDS entered their lives. 24 minutes. Fanlight Productions.

A Cradle Song
Provides information on Sudden Infant Death Syndrome and parental responses to the loss. 32 minutes. Fanlight Productions.

A Fate Worse Than Death
Follows several families who must decide whether to withdraw life support from a loved one in a coma or vegetative state. 50 minutes. Fanlight Productions.

A Friend Called Lyle
Profiles a 39-year-old woman who is dying of breast cancer. 30 minutes. Milestone Media, Inc.

A View to Kill: Witnessing an Execution
Linda Kelley, president of Parents of Murdered Children, witnessed the execution of a man responsible for killing two of her children. The program raises questions about the psychology and ethics of retribution and encourages public discussion. 52 minutes. Films for the Humanities and Sciences.

AIDS in Rural America
Documentary that reveals the effects of AIDS in small-town America. Presents the stories of several people whose lives have been touched by the epidemic and the community's continued denial of this reality. 28 minutes. Filmmakers Library.

Children Die, Too

Explores grief responses to the death of a child, with suggestions for helping family members cope with this tragedy. 26 minutes. Films for the Humanities and Sciences.

Death and Dying: The Physician's Perspective

Explores the ways in which physicians talk about death and make decisions about intervention and communication with patient and family. 29 minutes. Fanlight Productions.

Death on My Terms—Right or Privilege

Individuals and groups discuss arguments for and against physician-assisted suicide. 57 minutes Terra Nova Films.

Dying Wish

Explores the ways in which families and caregivers attempt to make end-of-life decisions. 52 minutes. Films for the Humanities and Sciences.

Final Rest

Shows how staff of a funeral home perform their functions. (Realistic and informative, but may not be suitable for some audiences). 25 minutes. Filmmakers Library.

Juveniles and the Death Penalty

A *48 Hours* program that visits death row inmates who committed murder before they were 18. Interviews with surviving family members, prosecutors, and defense attorneys. 58 minutes. Films for the Humanities and Sciences.

The Kevorkian File

Presents excerpts of videotaped conversations between Dr. Kevorkian and several of his patients, along with discussions by family members and health care professionals. 55 minutes. Terra Nova Films.

Letting Go: A Hospice Journey

Shows how hospice care can help children and adults through documentary exploration of three terminally ill people and their families and discussions with hospice team members. 90 minutes. Films for the Humanities and Sciences.

Living Fully Until Death

Interviews with three people facing death through Lou Gehrig's Disease, luekemia, and lung cancer, all of whom have found ways of keeping control of their lives. 28 minutes. Fanlight Productions.

Medicine at the Crossroads: Life Support

Attitudes toward health care near the end of life are compared in Sun City, Arizona; Benares, India; and rural Ireland. 55 minutes. Terra Nova Films.

Not a Simple Story/Out in Silence

Two videos on a single cassette, both exploring AIDS in the Asian Pacific American community, including both heterosexual and homosexual men and women. 37 minutes. Filmmakers Library

Rude Awakenings: Spiritual Support in the Time of AIDS

Explores issues of spirituality from the points of view of people with AIDS and clergy of various faiths. Fanlight Productions.

So Violent a Nation

Bill Moyers is host of this examination of the effect of violence on life in the United States. Episodes include a hospital emergency room, a police officer on a dangerous beat, and interviews. 60 minutes. Films for the Humanities and Sciences.

Suicide: The Teenager's Perspective

Offers advice on identifying and preventing suicidality in teenagers; shows how a Texas community banded together after an outbreak of teen suicides. 25 minutes. Films for the Humanities and Sciences.

Survivors

A fact-based drama exploring the impact of AIDS on an African American family. Deals with the harsh realities of isolation experienced by AIDS victims who are outside the gay community. 48 minutes. Filmmakers Library.

The Right to Decide

Explains the Patient Self-Determination Act and includes patient-physician interviews. 43 minutes. Fanlight Productions.

There Was a Child

Explores the impact of losing a pregnancy or the birth of a stillborn child on three mothers and a father. 32 minutes. Fanlight Productions.

D. Selected Internet Sources

Caution: Internet resources are subject to deletions, additions, and other changes.

General Sites with Multiple Hotlinks

Bereavement Resources
www.funeral.net/info/brvres

GriefNet
www.rivendell.org

Mental Health Net
www.cmhc.com/

Yahoo's Death Page
www.yahoo.com/Society_and_Culture/Death/

WEBSTER
www.katsden.com/death/index.html

Funerals and Memorializations

Funeral and Memorial Societies of America
www.ubiweb.c.champlain.edu/famsa.directory.htm

Internet Cremation Society
www.cremation.org

Pet Grief Support Page
www.petloss.com

World Wide Cemetery
www.interlog.com/cemetery

Death Education Opportunities

Cultural Diversity
www.excepc.com/dboals/diversit.html

DeathNet
www.rights.org/deathnet/open.html

Interactive Bereavement Courses
www.bereavement.org/index.html

Sociology Online Library
www.fisk.edu/vl/Sociology/Overview.html

Humor

The Bones
www.thebones.com

Professional and Caregiver Resources

American Association of Suicidology
www.cyberpsych.org

Last Acts
www.lastacts.org

Association for Death Education and Counseling
www.adec.org

Kairos Support for HIV/AIDS Caregivers
the-park.com/kairos/

National Center for Posttraumatic Disorder
www.dartmouth.edu/dms/pts/dindex.html

Suicide Information & Education
www.siec.ca

Project on Death in America
www.soros.org/death.html

Trauma
www.ozemail.com.av/dwillsb/trauma.htm

INDEX